French Lyric Diction

French Lyric Diction

A Singer's Guide

Jason Nedecky

Oxford University Press is a department of the University of Oxford. It furthers
the University's objective of excellence in research, scholarship, and education
by publishing worldwide. Oxford is a registered trade mark of Oxford University
Press in the UK and certain other countries.

Published in the United States of America by Oxford University Press
198 Madison Avenue, New York, NY 10016, United States of America.

© Oxford University Press 2023

All rights reserved. No part of this publication may be reproduced, stored in
a retrieval system, or transmitted, in any form or by any means, without the
prior permission in writing of Oxford University Press, or as expressly permitted
by law, by license, or under terms agreed with the appropriate reproduction
rights organization. Inquiries concerning reproduction outside the scope of the
above should be sent to the Rights Department, Oxford University Press, at the
address above.

You must not circulate this work in any other form
and you must impose this same condition on any acquirer.

CIP data is on file at the Library of Congress
ISBN 978-0-19-757384-6 (pbk.)
ISBN 978-0-19-757383-9 (hbk.)

DOI: 10.1093/oso/9780197573839.001.0001

Paperback printed by Marquis Book Printing, Canada
Hardback printed by Bridgeport National Bindery, Inc., United States of America

Contents

Acknowledgements	ix
Preface	xi

PART ONE   Singing in French

Introduction	3
Characteristics of the French Language	3
Le style soutenu	4
1. The International Phonetic Alphabet in French	5
French Phonemes	5
Other Symbols	7
2. French Vowel Sounds	11
The Vowel Diagram	11
Primary Cardinal Vowels	12
Mixed Vowels	14
Mute *e*: The French Schwa	15
Vocalic Aperture	20
Nasal Vowels	22
Vocalic Length	24
Semiconsonants	25
3. French Consonant Sounds	29
Articulation of French Consonants	29
Plosives	30
Fricatives	31

vi | CONTENTS

	Nasal Consonants	32
	Lateral *l*	32
	The French *r*	33
	Mute *h* and Aspirated *h*	37
	Borrowed Affricates in French	40
	Pronunciation of Consonants: Voiced, Unvoiced, or Silent?	40
	La détente de la consonne—Consonant Release	44
4.	The 'Consonant-Vowel Flow' of the French Phrase	45
	French Syllabification	45
	Le groupe phonétique—The Phonetic Group	48
	L'enchaînement consonantique—Consonant Linking	49
	L'élision vocalique—Vocalic Elision	51
	Hiatus	51
	The Phonetic Group in French Recitative	52
	Methods for Transcription in French	53
5.	*Liaison*	55
	Liaison from an Historical Perspective	55
	Liaisons obligatoires—Required *Liaisons*	56
	Liaisons facultatives—Optional *Liaisons*	56
	Liaisons interdites—Forbidden *Liaisons*	57
	Spelling and Pronunciation in *Liaison*	63
	Making Decisions about *Liaison*	69
	Liaison in Exceptional Cases	72
	The Use of *Liaison* in Common Vocabulary	78
6.	Mute *e* in French Poetry and Vocal Music	93
	The Role of Mute *e*	93
	Treatment of Mute *e* in the Score	94
7.	Special Pronunciation Considerations	107
	L'accent d'insistance—French Emphatic Stress	107
	L'harmonisation vocalique—Vocalic Harmonization	109
	La gémination consonantique—Consonant Lengthening	111
	Words with Variable Pronunciations	114
	Numbers	120

PART TWO   French Pronunciation A–Z

	Preamble to Part Two	127
	A Comprehensive Pronunciation Guide to French Orthography	128

CONTENTS | vii

PART THREE   Pronunciation Dictionaries

Preamble to Part Three   245
Pronunciation Dictionary of Proper Nouns   246
Pronunciation Dictionary of Borrowed Italian Musical Terms   307

Bibliography   309
Index   313

Acknowledgements

This book would not have been possible without the support of my colleagues and friends. I am indebted to Nathalie Paulin, who carefully proofread the manuscript for accuracy and content. Likewise, I must heartily thank Françoise Sutton, Drs. Louis Chalon & Danielle Deheselle, and especially François Le Roux for their expert recommendations on the pronunciation of proper nouns.

I would like to acknowledge Rosemarie Landry, who has always shown me generosity and collegiality, and Anne Constantin, whose friendship has been a source of much inspiration both musically and personally. I am very grateful to Mark Wilson, who first introduced me to the world of French vocal music and its interpreters. I would be remiss not to recognize the late Nico Castel, who instilled in me a passion for language in singing many years ago.

The excellent New York City team at Oxford University Press deserve particular mention: Executive Editor Norm Hirschy, Senior Editor Michelle Chen, Editorial Assistant Sean Decker, and Copyeditor Timothy DeWerff—as do Egle Zigaite and Phillippa Clubbs in the U.K., and Ellora Sengupta in India.

Sincere thanks to my brother for his assistance in designing the cover art, and to my parents for their encouragement from the start. This book is dedicated to my wife, Eve Rachel, and to our three children.

—Jason Nedecky
April, 2023

Preface

A comment heard all too often in the world of singing is, 'French is my worst language!' This book may be a helpful resource in the English-speaking musician's pursuit of a better understanding of French lyric diction. It consists of three parts. A concise, yet comprehensive description of the French language as it is sung in opera and *mélodie* of the nineteenth and twentieth centuries is the focus of Part One. Naturally, operetta and sacred repertoire (i.e., oratorio, cantatas) set to French text are included by extension in this account. Particular attention is given to pronunciation in a refined esthetic, where tradition and artistic expressivity play important roles. Musical examples from the repertoire illustrate all topics. The French language itself (i.e., grammar and vocabulary) is not specifically treated.

Part Two consists of a detailed French pronunciation guide. It gives an alphabetical account of the pronunciation norms of French orthography. The reader may refer to this guide for information on any French spelling.

Two pronunciation dictionaries make up Part Three. Transcriptions for over 10 000 proper nouns are given in the first dictionary. Included are the names of people, places, and things relating to French vocal repertoire and the wider French-speaking world. The book ends with a short guide to the pronunciation of some of the most common Italian musical terms as they are normally used in a modern French setting. Part Three is not intended to be studied page by page. Rather, it may be used to look up pronunciations of names and terms.

In the context of a classroom diction course, Part One will be the most beneficial. The musical examples and phrases of text from the repertoire found in the first part, as well as the French model words in italics given in Part Two, make for good in-class practice. The instructor may wish to supplement this with additional worksheets, assignments, and the like.

PART ONE

Singing in French

Introduction

Diction is, so to speak, the esthetic of articulation. It is the overriding concern, the supreme control that orders, balances, embellishes the several mechanisms of elocution. [. . .] Like his voice, the very words [the singer] pronounces must be imbued, saturated, with the thought he wishes to convey. His brain and his heart must bestow upon [. . .] the sound, enough thought, enough psychic virtue, that this sound so subtly produced will move, exalt, desolate, enrapture or intoxicate by the combined effect of the music and the word.

HAHN, *Du chant*

Reynaldo Hahn (1874–1947) stated his strong opinions on lyric diction in a series of public lectures, which were given in Paris in 1913 and 1914 and published shortly after as *Du chant*. For Hahn, diction is much more than clear enunciation and careful pronunciation. It is the primary vehicle for artistic expression, giving life to words. In a sense, 'good diction' may be considered an art unto itself.

Characteristics of the French Language

The pursuit of 'good diction' in French singing begins with the study of the defining features of the language.

- There are sixteen French vowel sounds—eight primary cardinal vowels, three mixed vowels, four nasal vowels, and the schwa—as well as three semiconsonants.
- The prevalent 'mute *e*' takes the form of a schwa with lip-rounding.
- Each syllable contains only one vowel sound.
- There are no contour diphthongs in French.
- Word stress occurs on the final syllable (not including word-final mute *e*). There is no secondary word stress in French.
- Word stresses are superseded by a primary phrasal stress on the final syllable of the French phrase (not including word-final mute *e*).
- The language moves in a 'consonant-vowel flow': a syllable begins with a short consonant sound, and gives way to a sustained monophthong (i.e., 'pure', single vowel sound).

French Lyric Diction. Jason Nedecky, Oxford University Press. © Oxford University Press 2023.
DOI: 10.1093/oso/9780197573839.003.0001

4 | FRENCH LYRIC DICTION

- Three special linguistic features help maintain the consonant-vowel flow: consonant linking, vocalic elision, and *liaison.*
- Written French is 'unphonetic': several letters often spell a single sound, silent letters are common, and one spelling may equate to multiple possible pronunciations.

Le style soutenu

The term *style soutenu* can be roughly translated as 'elevated tone' or 'formal register', and may refer both to the French written language, as well as its delivery. Although *style soutenu* is not specifically attributed to any one place, it most closely resembles the language customarily spoken in a formal setting by educated Parisians. The standard pronunciation heard in French vocal music is widely regarded as a form of *style soutenu*. The origins of this pronunciation for the stage can also be traced to the traditions of the Comédie-Française.[†]

Style soutenu vs. Everyday Speech

Those who have studied French will notice significant differences between *parler courant*, or everyday speech, and the *style soutenu* of French vocal music. The main ones are:

- For many singers (especially outside of France), uvular *r* is still not used in French opera and *mélodie*; it was traditionally reserved for *chanson* (popular song), cabaret singing, spoken dialogue, and sometimes operetta.
- *Liaison* is much more frequent in sung French.
- Mute *e* is usually pronounced in sung French, set in the score as its own syllable.
- Nasalized *o* is typically more closed in sung French.
- A glottal stop /ʔ/ before vowel sounds is generally avoided in French vocal music.
- Only specifically formed vowel sounds are sung.

An Evolving Language

A few changes in pronunciation that have emerged in France over the course of the last century bear mentioning here. Even though many of them are now firmly established in speech, they are generally considered unacceptable in vocal music.

- The vowel /œ̃/ has merged with the vowel /ɛ̃/; they are now both pronounced as a very open, central, nasalized vowel.
- 'Dark' /ɑ/ has disappeared.
- Word-final /ɛ/ often closes to /e/.
- Unstressed open /ɔ/ often closes somewhat.
- Word-final closed vowels, as well as the consonants /l/ and /ʀ/ often devoice.[‡]

[†] The Comédie-Française is the French national theatre established in Paris by Louis XIV in 1680.

[‡] Devoicing of /i/, /y/, /u/, and /e/ at the end of phrases is extremely common in everyday speech. Curiously, the devoiced vowels are typically followed by the unvoiced palatal fricative /ç/, which may be of variable length: *Mais oui !* [mɛ wiç] (oh yes!), *bien entendu* [bjɛ̃ nãtãdyç] (naturally), etc. Uvular *r* and the phoneme /l/ are also usually devoiced in spoken French when either one occurs between a plosive or fricative and dropped word-final mute *e*, as in *people* [pœpl̥] (people), *maigre* [mɛgʀ̥] (thin), *souffle* [sufl̥] (breeze), etc. This is addressed further in Chapter 3.

The International Phonetic Alphabet in French

The International Phonetic Alphabet (IPA) is a system of phonetic notation based on the Latin alphabet. One IPA symbol is allocated to each 'phoneme', or speech segment. Devised by the International Phonetic Association as a standardized representation of the sounds of spoken language, IPA is regularly employed by linguists, phoneticians, speech pathologists and therapists, foreign language teachers, lexicographers, translators, actors, and singers. It has become widely used in vocal music over the last several decades. Descriptions of the notations shown in this book are provided in the pages that follow.

French Phonemes

The phonemic inventory of the French language is outlined in the two tables that follow. A model word in French is provided for each phoneme, along with a near-equivalent foreign word example, in English whenever possible.

Vowel and Semiconsonant Phonemes

Phonetic Symbol	French Example	Approximation
Primary Cardinal Vowels		
/i/	_il_ (he)	h_e_
/e/	_été_ (summer)	h_a_lo (first part of diphthong)
/ɛ/	_belle_ (beautiful)	b_e_ll
/a/	_chat_ (cat)	sh_y_ (first part of diphthong)

French Lyric Diction. Jason Nedecky, Oxford University Press. © Oxford University Press 2023.
DOI: 10.1093/oso/9780197573839.003.0002

/ɑ/	*âme* (soul)	f<u>a</u>ther
/ɔ/	*b<u>o</u>tte* (boot)	b<u>u</u>t (with added lip-rounding)
/o/	*be<u>au</u>* (handsome/nice)	g<u>o</u> (first part of diphthong)
/u/	*n<u>ou</u>s* (we)	n<u>oo</u>se

Mixed Vowels

/y/	*t<u>u</u>* (you)	*<u>ü</u>ber* (German)
/ø/	*bl<u>eu</u>* (blue)	*sch<u>ö</u>n* (German)
/œ/	*s<u>œu</u>r* (sister)	*H<u>ö</u>lle* (German)

Schwa

/ə/	*g<u>e</u>nou* (knee)	—

Nasal Vowels

/ɛ̃/	*m<u>ain</u>* (hand)	—
/ɑ̃/	*t<u>em</u>ps* (time)	—
/õ/	*n<u>on</u>* (no)	—
/œ̃/	*br<u>un</u>* (brown)	—

Semiconsonants

/j/	*d<u>i</u>eu* (god)	<u>y</u>ou
/w/	*<u>ou</u>i* (yes)	<u>w</u>e
/ɥ/	*l<u>u</u>i* (him)	—

Consonant Phonemes

Phonetic Symbol	French Example	Approximation
Plosives		
/p/	*<u>p</u>auvre* (poor)	*<u>p</u>overo* (Italian)
/b/	*<u>b</u>alle* (ball)	<u>b</u>all
/t/	*<u>t</u>éléphone* (telephone)	*<u>t</u>elefono* (Italian)
/d/	*<u>d</u>ix* (ten)	*<u>d</u>immi* (Italian)
/k/	*<u>c</u>alme* (calm)	*<u>c</u>alma* (Italian)
/g/	*<u>g</u>arçon* (boy)	<u>g</u>uard
Fricatives		
/f/	*<u>f</u>aux* (false)	<u>f</u>alse
/v/	*<u>v</u>al* (valley)	<u>v</u>alley
/ʃ/	*<u>ch</u>er* (dear)	<u>sh</u>are
/ʒ/	*<u>j</u>our* (day)	plea<u>s</u>ure
/s/	*<u>s</u>ous* (under)	<u>s</u>ew
/z/	*<u>z</u>éro* (zero)	<u>z</u>ero
/ʁ/	*<u>r</u>ouge* (red)	*<u>r</u>ot* (spoken German)

Nasals

/m/	_mère_ (mother)	_m_other
/n/	_nez_ (nose)	_n_ero (Italian)
/ɲ/	_gagner_ (to win/earn)	o_gni_ (Italian)
/ŋ/[†]	_camping_ (camping)	camp_ing_

Lateral

/l/	_lit_ (bed)	_l_eaf

Tap and Trills

/ɾ/	_paradis_ (paradise)	ve_r_y (historic Received Pronunciation)
/r/ and /rr/	_terreur_ (terror)	_r_ed (historic Received Pronunciation)
/ʀ/	_rouge (red)_	_r_ot (spoken German)

Affricates[†]

/ts/	_tsar_ (czar)	hi_ts_
/dz/	_Zeus_	li_ds_
/tʃ/	_match_ (game)	ma_tch_
/dʒ/	_djinn_ (genie)	_g_enie

Other Symbols

Greater precision in transcription is possible with the use of special IPA characters called diacritics. These small indications are added above, below, or beside phonemes in order to provide more detail about pronunciation. Phonetic notation using diacritics is often called 'narrow transcription', while a simpler notation of phonemes alone is called 'broad transcription'. The latter is generally more familiar to singers. Narrow transcriptions are shown in this book when they might lend more specificity to phonemic description.

Diacritics and Additional IPA Phonemes

Symbol	Name	Description	Example
/ /	phonemic transcription	beginning and end of notation of (a) character(s)	/ʒ/
[ ]	phonetic transcription[‡]	beginning and end of notated pronunciation	_je suis_ [ʒə sɥi] (I am)
ː	vocalic lengthening	the vowel is quite long	_peur_ [pœːɾ] (fear)

† In French, these phonemes are technically considered to be borrowed from other languages.

‡ The use of transcription delimiters varies greatly. In this book, slashes / / are used around single phonetic characters or small groups of them in isolation, while square brackets [ ] are used to show notation of words or phrases.

8 | FRENCH LYRIC DICTION

ˑ	vocalic half-lengthening	the vowel is somewhat long	*chaîne* [ʃɛˑnə] (channel)
ˈ ˌ	syllabic stress†	stress on the following syllable	*télédiffuser* [teledifyˈze] (to broadcast on tv)
.	syllabic break	indicates barrier between syllables	*diversification* [di.vɛr.si.fi.ka.sjõ]
ʲ	palatalized	the consonant is articulated on the hard palate	*qui* [kʲi] (who)
ʷ	labialized	the consonant is articulated with lip-rounding	*chaud* [ʃʷo] (hot)
ᵊ	*détente*	the consonant is clearly released	*Mab* [mabᵊ]
ʰ	aspirated	the plosive is followed by a small release of air	calm [kʰɑm]
˺	inaudible release	consonant release is not heard	hot dog [hɑt˺ dɑg˺]
̪	dentalized	the consonant is articulated at the top teeth	*tendre* [t̪ã:d̪rə] (tender)
̝	raised	the vowel is more closed	*thé* [te̝] (tea)
̞	lowered	the vowel is more open	*homme* [o̞mə] (man)
̹	more rounded	the vowel has greater rounding of the lips	*le* [lə̹] (the)
̱	retracted	the consonant is articulated further back	*rouler* [ṟule] (to roll)
̥	devoiced	pronunciation without vibration of the vocal cords	*aigle* [ɛgl̥] (eagle)
/χ/	devoiced uvular *r*	alternative notation for /ʁ̥/	*maître* [mɛtχ] (master)
/ʔ/	glottal stop	stroke at the glottis before an initial vowel	the end [ði ʔɛnd]

† Secondary word stress, as in 'proˌnunciˈation', is not found in French.

The following is a short list of markings other than IPA characters that are used in this book.

Extra Markings

Marking	Name	Description	Example
‿	linked consonant	indicates the use of consonant linking and *liaison*	*nous‿avons* (we have)
|	no linking	indicates consonant linking or *liaison* is not made	*et | elle* (and she)
-	silent letter	indicates a letter is not pronounced	*tôt̶* (early)

In order to provide context, IPA phonemes from several other languages—especially English—are used in this book.

Foreign Phonemes

Phonetic Symbol	Example
/æ/	c<u>a</u>t
/ɪ/	k<u>i</u>d; *m<u>i</u>t* (German)
/ʊ/	p<u>u</u>t; *<u>u</u>nd* (German)
/ʏ/	*k<u>ü</u>ssen* (German)
/ʌ/	<u>u</u>p
/h/	<u>h</u>er
/ɫ/	hee<u>l</u>
/ɹ/	<u>r</u>ed
/θ/	<u>th</u>ree
/ð/	<u>th</u>e
/ç/	*i<u>ch</u>* (German)
/x/	*a<u>ch</u>* (German); *nava<u>j</u>a* (Spanish)

Items of Note

In this text, two additional icons are used:

⚠ for unexpected cases and exceptions to pronunciation rules in French singing.

⧖ for outdated aspects of pronunciation, which were once the norm in French singing, but now seem rarely to be observed.

2

French Vowel Sounds

Vowel sounds are very specifically formed in French. They require greater muscular involvement in general than English vowel sounds. Practice is required in order to master the tongue, jaw, and lip positions that are essential to authentic French vowel sounds.

There are sixteen vowel sounds in French—more than in English, Italian, or German. In French, there are no contour diphthongs (i.e., two vowel sounds that share a single syllable). The French vowel sounds are composed of eight primary cardinal vowels, three mixed vowels, four nasal vowels, and a neutral vowel called schwa.

The Vowel Diagram

The French vowel sounds are shown on the following page in a vowel diagram. This representation was designed by British phonetician Daniel Jones (1881–1967). Its shape approximates the oral cavity, where the opening of the mouth is at the left. The terms 'front' and 'back' refer to where the tongue is at its highest point in the mouth. The terms 'closed'[†] and 'open' refer to the space between the tongue and the roof of the mouth. The closer the tongue is to the roof of the mouth, the more closed the vowel is. Phonemes to the left of the dots are called 'unrounded' vowels. Lip-rounding is not a feature of those vowels.

---

† Technically, the correct linguistic term is 'close vowel'; however, in the world of singing, 'closed vowel' is more common. The latter is used in this book.

French Lyric Diction. Jason Nedecky, Oxford University Press. © Oxford University Press 2023.
DOI: 10.1093/oso/9780197573839.003.0003

Phonemes to the right of the dots are 'rounded' vowels, meaning the lips protrude. The more closed the rounded vowel is, the more protruded the lips are.

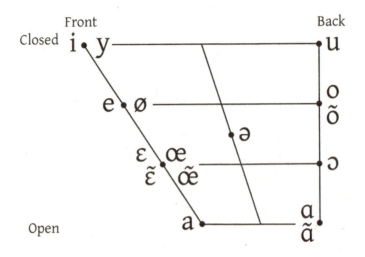

Primary Cardinal Vowels

Cardinal vowels are specifically defined vocalic positions, of which the first eight are the most common in all languages. All eight of these 'primary cardinal vowels' are found in French. The following is a description of these phonemes, given in counter-clockwise order in which they are found on the vowel diagram.[†] For each phoneme, the most regular French spellings are shown with model words.

/i/

i î ï y

Remarks

'French *i*' is the most closed front vowel. It is unrounded. Unlike German or English, there is no open /ɪ/ variant in standard French. Model words: /i/ in *il* (he), *île* (island), *naïf* (naive), *lys* (lily).

/e/

-ai e é -er -ez

Remarks

'Closed *e*' is unrounded. It is considerably more closed than in English or Italian, and must never form part of a contour diphthong. For these reasons, it is like the German variant. A narrow transcription of this vowel can be expressed with the

---

[†] Recommendations for vowel modifications in singing are not included in descriptions of the French vowel phonemes.

notation /ẹ/. Model words: /e/ in *j'ai* (I have), *pied* (foot), *et* (and), *été* (summer), *chanter* (to sing), *vous chantez* (you sing).

/ɛ/
ai ay e è ê ë ei -et ey

Remarks

'Open *e*' is unrounded. It has many spellings in French. It is essentially the same vowel sound as in English, but must never open too much, or 'spread'. Model words: /ɛ/ in *aile* (wing), *vrai* (true), *Souzay*, *les* (the), *belle* (beautiful), *esprit* (spirit), *lèvres* (lips), *rêve* (dream), *Noël* (Christmas), *neige* (snow), *bouquet*, *poney* (pony).

/a/
a

Remarks

'Bright *a*', or *a antérieur* (front *a*), is by far the most common of the two variants of French *a*. It is unrounded. In order to distinguish it from /ɑ/, it is helpful to keep this vowel quite bright (forward and closed)—approaching English /æ/. A narrow transcription of this vowel can be expressed with the notation/ạ/. Model words: /a/ in *chat* (cat), *Manon*.

/ɑ/
â a

Remarks

'Dark *a*', or *a postérieur* (back *a*), is unrounded. It occurs much less frequently in French than its brighter counterpart. In a stressed syllable, this vowel is long before any consonant sound. Over-darkening of this vowel sounds artificial. Although it is often no longer heard in modern standard spoken French, this vowel is still sung in lyric diction. Model words: /ɑ/ in *âme* (soul), *las* (tired), *base*, *passé* (past).

/ɔ/
au o

Remarks

'Open *o*' is rounded. It is much more open than in English, Italian, or German, especially in a stressed syllable. English speakers may find the correct position for this vowel by introducing lip-rounding to the English /ʌ/. For example, 'up!' [ʌp] with the same tongue position plus lip-rounding becomes « *hop!* » [ɔp]. A narrow transcription of this vowel can be expressed with the notation/ọ/. Model words: /ɔ/ in *Fauré*, *botte* (boot).

14 | FRENCH LYRIC DICTION

/o/
au eau o -o ô

Remarks

'Closed *o*' in French is much more closed and rounded than in English or Italian, and must never form part of a contour diphthong. For these reasons, it is like the German variant. A narrow transcription of this vowel can be expressed with the notation /o̞/. Model words: /o/ in *au̲be* (dawn), *bea̲u* (handsome/nice), *no̲s* (our), *po̲t, ro̲se* (rose/pink), *écho̲* (echo), *drô̲le* (funny).

/u/
ou

Remarks

'French *ou*' is the most closed back vowel. It is much more closed and rounded than in English. Unlike German or English, there is no open /ʊ/ variant in standard French. A narrow transcription of this vowel can be expressed with the notation /u̞/. Model words: /u/ in *no̲us* (we), *Go̲unod*.

Mixed Vowels

A mixed vowel is a combination of the tongue position of a front vowel with the lip-rounding of a back vowel. Mixed vowels are found in French and German. In French, there are three mixed vowel sounds, shown in the following tables with their most regular spellings. Descriptions and model words are given for each one.

/y/
u û

tongue		lips
/i/	+	/u/

Remarks

'French *u*' is the most closed front vowel, and is very rounded. The German open /ʏ/ mixed vowel does not exist in standard French. Model words: /y/ in *tu̲* (you), *flû̲te*.

/ø/
eu œu

tongue		lips
/e/	+	/o/

/œ/

eu œu

tongue		**lips**
/ɛ/	+	/ɔ/

Remarks

'French *eu*' (also as *œu*) may be either closed and rounded /ø/, or open and rounded /œ/. Explanation is provided later in this chapter in the section on vocalic aperture. The same vowel sounds are found in German. Model words: closed /ø/ in *bleu* (blue), *berceuse* (lullaby), *europe*, *vœu* (wish); open /œ/ in *peur* (fear), *sœur* (sister).

Mute *e*: The French Schwa

Schwa is the term for a neutral, unstressed vowel sound. It is represented by the /ə/ symbol.† In French, it is sometimes referred to as *chva* [ʃva]. The actual phonetic value for this vowel can vary greatly between languages, and even within a language. Unlike the schwa sounds of German and English, which are represented by the same symbol, the French schwa is rounded. A narrow transcription of the French schwa can be expressed with the notation /ə̹/.

Known as *e muet*, or 'mute *e*', its aperture is between that of /ø/ and /œ/. The following culinary term contains a progression of these vocalic apertures, from closed and more rounded, to open and less rounded:

queue	***de***	***bœuf***	(oxtail)
ø	ə	œ	
closed	⟵⟶	open	
more rounded		less rounded	

Clarifying the Term 'Mute *e*'

The term 'mute' is unfortunately rather misleading. It does not mean that the letter *e* is necessarily silent. In French vocal music, mute *e* is in fact most often pronounced as a schwa with lip-rounding, as described above. Other terms

† Sometimes /œ/ is used to express mute *e* in transcription, perhaps in an effort to ensure that non-native singers interpret the schwa symbol with lip-rounding. On the condition that the lips are rounded, the /ə/ symbol is a better representation, since /ə/ and /œ/ constitute two separate vowels. Mute *e* is less open than /œ/. Mute *e* cannot be lengthened, but /œ/ often is. By definition, mute *e* cannot be stressed, while /œ/ can be stressed. Compare the vowel sounds of the words *que* [kə] (that/which), and *cœur* [kœːɾ] (heart), or those of the polysyllabic words *donne* [dɔnə] (gives), and *donneur* [dɔnœːɾ] (giver). The difference between /ə/ and /œ/ is unmistakable.

are sometimes encountered for this unique vowel sound, including *e instable* (unstable *e*), *e inaccentué* or *e atone* (unstressed *e*), and *e caduc* (deciduous *e*). That last term is quite instructive: like leaves on a tree, *e caduc* in spoken French holds firm at times, and is shed at others. In modern spoken French, a complex set of criteria determines which *e* is pronounced, and which is dropped. Of course, native speakers comply in their everyday speech without giving it any thought.† In vocal repertoire, it is quite simple: one should assume that whenever mute *e* is assigned a note value and pitch, it is meant to be sung as a rounded schwa. In most cases, mute *e* is notated as a vowel in its own syllable.

The Spelling of Mute *e*

The pages that follow give an account of all the possible spellings of mute *e*.

The letter *e* is mute *e* as the last letter and only vowel of a syllable. This spelling is by far the most common occurrence of mute *e*.

G. Fauré : *Mai* (Hugo)

Le sen-tier qui fi - nit   où__ le che-min com - men - ce,
/ə/   /ə/ /ə/   /ə/
(The path that ends where the road begins)

The spelling *-es* exists as the plural form of words with mute *e*.

H. Duparc : *Phidylé* (Leconte de Lisle)

Aux pen - tes des sour-ces mous-su - es,
         /ə/   /ə/   /ə/
(On the slopes of mossy springs)

The spelling *-es* is found in verb endings, most notably in the second-person singular, and in *nous sommes* (we are), *vous êtes* (you are), and *vous faites* (you make/do).

---

† Mute *e* is usually dropped in everyday speech when it is word-final—e.g., *homme* [ɔm] (man)—or when it is between consonant sounds—e.g., *appeler* [aple] (to call). The main exceptions, where /ə/ is normally retained in spoken French, occur when mute *e* comes after a consonant cluster and is followed by another consonant—e.g., *brebis* [bʀəbi] (ewe), *chambre d'hôte* [ʃɑ̃bʀə doːt] (bed and breakfast)—and when mute *e* is followed by a consonant plus a semiconsonant—e.g., *auguste roi* [ɔgystə ʀwa] (noble king), *celui* [səlɥi] (this one), *vous veniez* [vu vənje] (you were coming). This is only a basic sketch. Many subtle variations are possible. (Note that uvular *r* is indicated as /ʀ/ in sections of this book pertaining especially to spoken French.)

G. Bizet: ***Carmen***—*Habanera* (Meilhac, Halévy)

Si tu ne m'ai - mes pas,
/ə/
(If you do not love me)

A. Caplet: ***Trois fables de Jean de la Fontaine***—*Le corbeau et le renard* (De La Fontaine)

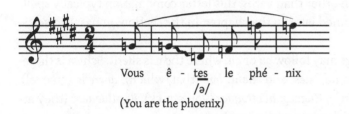

Vous ê - tes le phé - nix
/ə/
(You are the phoenix)

The spelling *-es* is found at the end of proper nouns, as in *Charles, Georges, Gilles, Jules, Bruxelles* (Brussels), *Londres* (London), *Nîmes, Versailles*, etc.

N. Boulanger: *Versailles* (Samain)

Ô Ver - sail - les,
/ə/
(O Versailles)

The spelling *e* before double *-ss-* is found in the prefixes of a few words, such as *dessous* (below), *dessus* (above), and *ressentir* (to feel). In this spelling, the first *s* is printed before the hyphen, in the syllable with mute *e*.

M. Ravel: ***Don Quichotte à Dulcinée***—*Chanson romanesque* (Morand)

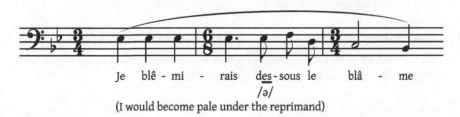

Je blê - mi - rais des - sous le blâ - me
/ə/
(I would become pale under the reprimand)

The spelling **-ent** is found the third-person plural verb ending.

R. Hahn: ***Études latines***—*Tyndaris* (Leconte de Lisle)

(They love the Latin Muses)

NOTE: In parts of speech other than verbs, this letter combination typically spells /ã/. This is explained later in the chapter, in the section on nasal vowels.

Any of the above spellings may follow *gu* or *qu*, where the *u* is silent. Schwa is therefore also encountered as **ue**, **-ues**, and **-uent**: *que* (that/which), *querelle* (quarrel), *longue* (long), *longues* (long), *Hugues, tu attaques* (you attack), *ils attaquent* (they attack), *tu vogues* (you sail), *ils voguent* (they sail), etc.

A. Roussel: ***Deux poèmes chinois*** (Opus 47)—*Favorite abandonnée* (Roché)

(To make this long night)

G. Fauré: ***Cinq mélodies de Venise***—*Mandoline* (Verlaine)

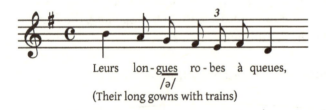

(Their long gowns with trains)

NOTE: When mute *e* spelled as *-es* or *-ent* is set to its own note(s) in the score, and is followed by a word beginning in a vowel sound, *liaison* is usually made after /ə/ from the *-s* or *-t*, as explained in Chapter 5.

G. Fauré : *Mai* (Hugo)

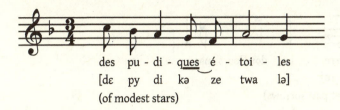

des pu - di - ques é - toi - les
[dɛ py di kə ze twa lə]
(of modest stars)

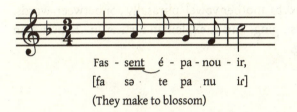

Fas - sent é - pa - nou - ir,
[fa sə te pa nu iʀ]
(They make to blossom)

There is one case in which the French schwa is not spelled with the letter *e*. It is the spelling *ai* in the *fais-* combination, which almost always begins a conjugation of the verb *faire* (to make/do).

H. Berlioz : *Les nuits d'été*—*Villanelle* (Gautier)

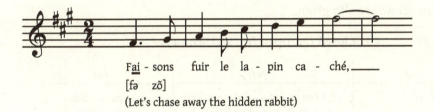

Fai - sons fuir le la - pin ca - ché,
[fə zɔ̃]
(Let's chase away the hidden rabbit)

When Not to Sing Mute *e*

As previously stated, mute *e* is meant to be sung in vocal music when it is assigned a note value and pitch. If mute *e* occurs back-to-back with another vowel, however, it is usually not set on its own in the score. When it isn't set, it should not be sung. The vowel must instead be elided completely. This can occur within a word, most commonly in the future and conditional verb tenses. The following two musical examples feature verbs in the future tense.

G. Bizet : *Carmen*—*Acte III* (Meilhac, Halévy)

et nous joue - rons la bel - le,
[ʒu ʀɔ̃]
(and we'll gamble for the beautiful girl)

H. Duparc: *Chanson triste* (Lahor)

(I will forget past sorrows)

Mute *e* also frequently occurs next to another vowel 'phrasally', or between words. In this case too, it is dropped in singing. This is explained further in Chapter 4, in the section on consonant linking.

Vocalic Aperture

The degree to which a vowel is open or closed constitutes its vocalic aperture. In French, some spellings correspond to fixed vocalic apertures. Others can be realized both as open and closed vowel sounds, with the correct aperture discernable in most cases by the position of the spelling within a word.

Three tables follow, showing sets of open and closed French vowel sounds in the most common of spellings and word positions. In the case of the first set, the spellings for schwa are also given.

Closed /e/, Open /ɛ/, and Schwa /ə/

/e/	/ɛ/	/ə/
é	ai at the end of a word, or before pronounced or silent letter(s)	e as the last letter of a syllable
e before final silent consonant(s) other than *s* or *t*	ay ey ei -et è ê ë	-es as verb ending or plural of mute e
-ai verb ending	e before a pronounced consonant in the same syllable	-ent verb ending
the word *et* (and)		*fais-* stem of the verb *faire* (to do)
	ces, des, les, mes, ses, tes, est (these, the, my, his/her/one's/its, your, is)	

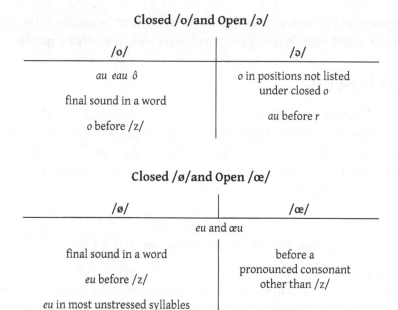

'In-between' Apertures

The guidelines for vocalic aperture shown above reflect an established system in standard French pronunciation. Nevertheless, the actual vowel sounds pronounced by native French speakers tend to stray somewhat from 'the rules'. This should not be a cause for concern; indeed, such is the case with any language, including English. In truth, there exists a continuous gradation of aperture between the points labelled 'open' and 'closed'.

There are many reasons why the vowel sounds exhibited by native French speakers seem to differ from the recommendations. In everyday speech, for example, there is a tendency for some vowel sounds to close slightly. In many cases, this is due to the position of the vowel in relation to the sounds around it. This topic is addressed in part in Chapter 7, in the section on vocalic harmonization.

In general, a good rule of thumb in French is that an unstressed open/closed vowel is typically **slightly less** open/closed than a stressed one. Since word stress in French predictably occurs on the final syllable, this means that the unstressed syllables before it are the ones where aperture is liable to fluctuate. Consider the word *monotone* [mɔnɔtɔnə] (monotonous), for example. According to the guidelines, all three syllables should contain a matching open /ɔ/. Even in careful pronunciation, however, the first two syllables very often do not sound as open as the final syllable. This is perfectly normal, since those first two instances of *o* are unstressed, and tend therefore to veer slightly from an open aperture.

Singers are occasionally asked for a vowel that is between open and closed. The word in question almost always fits the described scenario, where the vowel is in an unstressed syllable. An added diacritic marking on that phoneme could help to express more clearly the true characteristics of the intended sound.

22 | French Lyric Diction

To know the system of pronunciation based on orthography is the best bet. From there, slight modifications are usually easily implemented if need be.

Nasal Vowels

Vowel nasalization is a rather unique feature of French. It does not occur in English, Italian, or German. There are four French nasal vowels. The basic phonemes without nasality also exist in French. The IPA diacritic ˜ indicates a vowel is nasalized. The most regular spellings of the four French nasal vowels follow, with descriptions and model words for each one.

$$/\tilde{\varepsilon}/$$
aim ain ein im in ym yn -en after *é, i, y*

Remarks

'Nasalized open *e*' is unrounded. It has several spellings. An alternative transcription of /æ̃/ is perhaps a more accurate representation, although the monophthong /æ/ does not exist in French, (which makes it appear slightly odd). Nevertheless, many singers find the notation /æ̃/ very helpful in finding the right vowel. Despite a shift of the vowel sound in modern spoken French, this is still the standard pronunciation for lyric diction. Note that the spellings *-éen*, *-ien*, and *-yen* end in /ɛ̃/ (and not /ɑ̃/). Model words: /ɛ̃/ in *faim* (hungry), *main* (hand), *plein* (full), *simple*, *fin* (end), *Olympia, larynx, européen* (European), *bien* (well), *citoyen* (citizen).

$$/\tilde{\alpha}/$$
am an em en

Remarks

'Nasalized dark *a*' is unrounded, and is spelled with the letter *e* or the letter *a*. Both spellings are pronounced the same way, which can be illustrated with the correct pronunciation of the word *enfant* [ɑ̃fɑ̃] (child). Model words: /ɑ̃/ in *champ* (field), *enfant, temps* (time).

$$/\tilde{o}/$$
om on

Remarks

'Nasalized *o*' is always spelled with the letter *o*. Most dictionaries show /ɔ̃/ for this vowel, as this is considered the standard spoken version. In French vocal music, it is customarily pronounced more closed and more rounded. Native English speakers often confuse this vowel with /ɑ̃/. They are different vowel sounds, which can be illustrated with the correct pronunciation of the word *chanson* [ʃɑ̃sõ] (song). Model words: /õ/ in *nom* (name), *non* (no).

$$/\tilde{\text{œ}}/$$
um un

Remarks

'Nasalized *o-e*' is rounded, and is always spelled with the letter *u*. To form this vowel accurately, begin with /ɛ/, add lip-rounding to form /œ/, then nasalize it. Despite a shift of the vowel sound in modern spoken French, this is still the standard pronunciation for lyric diction. Model words: /œ̃/ in *parfum* (perfume), *brun* (brown).

Memorize this phrase of familiar French words in order to recall the four nasal vowel sounds:

    « un   bon   vin   blanc »   (a good white wine)
    /œ̃/   /õ/   /ɛ̃/   /ã/

Introduce slight nasality into these vowels. The jaw and lips should never 'close off' the sound, nor should the soft palate fall too far down. A little goes a very long way.

When to Nasalize a Vowel

Nasalization occurs when a vowel precedes an *m* or *n* that is either word-final, or is followed by a different consonant. When an *m* or *n* is doubled, or is followed by a vowel, there is no nasalization of the preceding vowel.

⚠️   The notable exception to this is in the spellings *emm-*, *en-*, and *enn-*, where the nasal vowel /ã/ and the consonant /m/ or /n/ are almost always both pronounced before a vowel, as in *emmener* [ãməne] (to take), *enivré* [ãnivre] (intoxicated), and *ennui* [ãnɥi] (boredom). This exception does not apply to the word *ennemi* [ɛnəmi] (enemy).

Denasalization of vowels occurs systematically with certain masculine adjectives in *liaison*. This is treated in detail in Chapter 5.

Inadvertent Articulation of Interpolated Nasal Consonants

The *m* or *n* of a nasal vowel serves the purely orthographic function of 'spelling' nasality. It is not to be pronounced. Except in *liaison*, even the slightest articulation of the consonant is incorrect. It's an easy rule to learn in theory, but difficult to put into practice. The unwanted interpolated phoneme is especially prevalent when the nasal vowel is followed by a plosive consonant. A nasal vowel before /t/ or /d/ can cause the inadvertent introduction of /n/—*entendre* (to hear). A nasal vowel before /k/ or /g/ can cause the inadvertent introduction of /ŋ/—*encore, en garde!* (again, watch out!). A nasal vowel before /p/ or /b/ can cause the inadvertent introduction of /m/—*une ombre implacable* (a relentless shadow). (This error occurs independently from the *n/m* nasal spelling—*un peu* (a little) could produce an unwanted /m/ despite the spelling of the nasal vowel with *n*, just as *no̱m de famille* (surname) might yield an unwanted /n/, not /m/.)

The problem has to do with timing the consonant articulation. The only way to avoid this mispronunciation is to ensure that the tongue does not anticipate the plosive consonant in the next syllable. The nasal vowel should be unaltered in its formation, until the following plosive is articulated quickly and efficiently.

Vocalic Length

As in other languages, an important feature of authentic French speech is the variable duration of vowel sounds. Although each syllable in the score is typically assigned its specific note value, it is nevertheless important to consider the language as it is spoken, independent of any musical setting. This helps to inform the shaping of text in the sung phrase. Moreover, when it comes to cases where note values are not as fixed, understanding the system of vocalic length is vital. This is particularly relevant in recitative, and of course in dialogue, where there are no such indications.

In spoken French, there is a regular system for determining vocalic length of individual words. In general, vowel sounds in unstressed syllables are all considered to be short, while some vowel sounds are typically lengthened when they occur in certain contexts within a stressed syllable. For example, the /o/ of *rosé* [ʀoze] (rosy) is quite short; however, the same /o/ of *rose* [ʀo:zə] (rose/pink) can take about twice as long to say. The chart which follows outlines this system. (See Chapter 4 for information on the way in which individual word stress behaves in the French phrase.)

Vocalic Length in French

All unstressed vowel sounds are **short**	*ciseaux* [sizo] scissors, *étang* [etã] (pond), *rêvant* [ʀɛvã] (dreaming), *façon* [fasõ] (way), *château* [ʃato] (castle), *total* [tɔtal], *oser* [oze] (to dare), *journée* [ʒuʀne] (daytime), *bureau* [byʀo] (office), *euro* [øʀo], *heureux* [œʀø] (happy), *linceul* [lɛ̃sœl] (shroud), *enfin* [ãfɛ̃] (at last), *honteux* [õtø] (shameful), *lundi* [lœ̃di] (Monday), *demain* [dəmɛ̃] (tomorrow)
Word-final stressed vowel sounds are **short**	*vieilli* [vjɛji] (aged), *il a chanté* [ʃãte] (he sang), *il chanterait* [ʃãtəʀɛ] (he would sing), *il chantera* [ʃãtəʀa] (he will sing), *lilas* [lila] (lilac), *corbeau* [kɔʀbo] (crow), *hibou* [ibu] (owl), *barbu* [baʀby] (bearded), *aveu* [avø] (confession), *matin* [matɛ̃] (morning), *océan* [ɔseã] (ocean), *coton* [kɔtõ] (cotton), *chacun* [ʃakœ̃] (each one), *belle* [bɛlə] (beautiful)
Stressed /ɑ/ /o/ /ø/ /ɛ̃/ /ã/ /õ/ /œ̃/ are **long** before any pronounced consonant or group of consonants	*câble* [kɑ:blə] (cable), *aube* [o:bə] (dawn), *affreuse* [afʀø:zə] (ghastly), *prince* [pʀɛ̃:sə], *danse* [dã:sə] (dance), *onde* [õ:də] (wave), *humble* [œ̃:blə]

FRENCH VOWEL SOUNDS | 25

Stressed /i/ /ɛ/[†] /a/ /ɔ/ /u/ /y/ /œ/ are **long** before any of these consonants: /ʀ/ /z/ /ʒ/ /v/ /vʀ/	_surprise_ [syʀpʀi:zə], _rêve_ [ʀɛ:və] (dream), _étage_ [eta:ʒə] (storey), _horloge_ [ɔʀlɔ:ʒə] (clock), _jour_ [ʒu:ʀ] (day), _refuge_ [ʀəfy:ʒə], _œuvre_ [œ:vʀə] (work)
Stressed /i/ /ɛ/ /a/ /ɔ/ /u/ /y/ /œ/ are **short** before all other pronounced consonants:	_police_ [pɔlisə], _avec_ [avɛk] (with), _animal_ [animal], _homme_ [ɔmə] (man), _groupe_ [gʀupə] (group), _flûte_ [flytə] (flute), _œuf_ [œf] (egg)

Note that /e/ and /ə/ are always short.

Vocalic Half-Lengthening[‡]

Most French speakers also slightly lengthen vowels in stressed syllables before voiced plosives or voiced plosive clusters with _l_ or _r_, and word-final mute _e_—that is, in the following endings: _-be, -ble, -bre, -de, -dre, -gue, -gle,_ and _-gre_. This half-lengthening can be shown with /ˑ/, as in _tube_ [tyˑbə], _table_ [taˑblə], _libre_ [liˑbʀə] (free), _rude_ [ʀyˑdə], _foudre_ [fuˑdʀə] (lightning), _vague_ [vaˑgə] (wave), _aveugle_ [avœˑglə] (blind), and _tigre_ [tiˑgʀə] (tiger). The practice of half-lengthening is further extended in the case of /ɛ/ to the endings _-gne, -le, -me, -ne,_ and for most speakers, in any word with the spellings _ê_ and _aî_: _daigne_ [dɛˑɲə] (worthy), _zèle_ [zɛˑlə] (zeal), _j'aime_ [ʒɛˑmə] (I like/love), _reine_ [ʀɛˑnə] (queen), _frêle_ [fʀɛˑlə] (frail), _maître_ [mɛˑtʀə] (master).

The following three words demonstrate a progression from shortest to longest /œ/ vowel:

> _un œuf_ [œf] (an egg)
> _un meuble_ [mœˑblə] (a piece of furniture)
> _une heure_ [œ:ʀə] (an hour)

Semiconsonants

Semiconsonants are found in English, Italian, German, and French. A semiconsonant may be thought of as a compressed vowel that 'glides' into the main vowel sound of the syllable. This syllabic sharing of semiconsonant and main vowel is called _synérèse,_ or 'syneresis'. A semiconsonant is normally encountered before a vowel sound in a word; however, the French /j/ can also be found after a vowel.

---

† ⧗ In recordings of French vocal music, it is very common to hear lengthened, stressed /ɛ:/ 'morph' as it approaches the consonant of the following syllable, in what sounds very much like a diphthong. Many, if not most great French singers well into the mid-twentieth century exhibit this tendency, whereby /ɛ:/ closes to /e/ or /j/ by the end of the syllable. Although quite fashionable at one time, this habit now sounds dated, and is no longer actively encouraged.

‡ For the sake of clarity, vocalic half-lengthening is not shown in the examples provided in this book; nevertheless, the practice is both systematic and widespread, and therefore can be freely incorporated where appropriate.

The most regular spellings of the three French semiconsonants follow, with descriptions and model words for each one.

/j/
i ï y -il -ill-

Remarks

The 'yod' or '*j* glide' is also found in English, Italian, and (with slight variation) in German. In French, it occurs before a vowel other than schwa in the first three spellings shown above. It can also occur after a vowel sound, in the *-il* and *-ill-* spellings. This post-vocalic semiconsonant is somewhat unique to French. Not all words that have these spellings are pronounced with /j/, though. Three common words that end with *-ille* as /ilə/ are *mille* (thousand), *ville* (city), and *tranquille* (peaceful). Model words: /j/ in *di̲eu* (god), *aïe̲ux* (ancestors), *les ye̲ux* (eyes); /aj/ in *déta̲il* (detail), *méda̲ille* (medal); /ɛj/ in *sole̲il* (sun), *abe̲ille* (bee); /ij/ in *fami̲lle* (family); /œj/ in *de̲uil* (mourning), *orgue̲il* (pride), *fe̲uille* (leaf/sheet), *cue̲illir* (to pluck); /uj/ in *fen̲ouil* (fennel), *gren̲ouille* (frog).

/w/
ou o before *i, y*

Remarks

The '*w* glide' is also found in English and Italian. In French, it is most often encountered as *ou* before a vowel other than schwa. Three other key spellings are *oi* as /wa/, *oin* as /wɛ̃/, and *oy* before another vowel as /waj/. Model words: /w/ in *o̲ui* (yes); /wa/ in *r̲oi* (king); /wɛ̃/ in *l̲oin* (far); /waj/in *r̲oyal*.

/ɥ/
u

Remarks

The 'French *u* glide' does not exist in English, Italian, or German. It occurs in French before a vowel other than schwa, and is frequently encountered before /i/. English speakers often incorrectly realize this semiconsonant as /w/. It requires a more 'slender' position, with the tongue high and forward. Model words: /ɥ/ in *l̲ui* (him), *p̲uissant* (powerful).

Diérèse—Dieresis

When two vowel spellings share a syllable, the first is normally a semiconsonant. In one case, however, each is pronounced in its own syllable, as back-to-back monophthongs. This is known as *diérèse* or 'dieresis', and regularly occurs in the following progression:

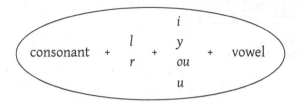

oublier [u.bli.e] (to forget)†
éblouir [e.blu.iʀ] (to dazzle)
cruel [kʀy.ɛl] (cruel)

G. Fauré: *Le papillon et la fleur* (Hugo)

⚠ The exception to this rule is the progression of consonant + *lui* or *rui*, where instead of the monophthong /y/, the semiconsonant /ɥ/ is retained, as in *bruit* [bʀɥi] (noise), *fruit* [fʀɥi] (fruit), and *pluie* [plɥi] (rain).

Dieresis vs. Syneresis in the Score

A word that contains syneresis is sometimes encountered in the music as dieresis. In such a case, the lyrical setting elicits a certain 'drawing out' of the semiconsonant, whereby an extra syllable is acquired. When back-to-back vowels are given separate notes, and are divided with a hyphen, the vowel before the hyphen should be sung as a monophthong /i/, /u/, or /y/, instead of the 'compressed' /j/, /w/, or /ɥ/ semiconsonant sound. The musical examples that follow are of two Debussy settings of the same text, in which he treats the syllables of the word *persuader* (to convince) differently.

---

† In the progression of consonant + *li* or *ri* + vowel, many speakers interpolate /j/ before the second main vowel sound. This is also widely accepted in singing. The first example above could therefore also be [u.bli.je].

C. Debussy: *En sourdine* (1882) (Verlaine)

Lais-sons-nous   per - sua - der
                  [pɛr sɥa de]

(Let us be won over)

C. Debussy: **Fêtes galantes, série I**—*En sourdine* (1891) (Verlaine)

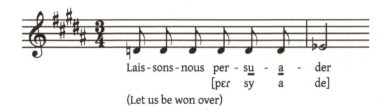

Lais-sons-nous per - su - a - der
               [pɛr sy a de]

(Let us be won over)

Some words with syneresis cannot be set as dieresis. *Puis* (then) is an example of one such word. It can only be set as [pɥi], and will never be encountered as « *pu-is* » [py.i]. Since syllabification is notated in the score, the singer does not normally have to make decisions about such divisions.

3

French Consonant Sounds

In singing, French consonant sounds must be articulated efficiently and with precision. They should not disturb the *legato* line of sustained vowel sounds. It could therefore be argued that, in a broad sense, all French consonants may be thought of as intervocalic. Temptation to prolong, or dwell on consonant sounds for expressive reasons—an approach often encouraged in English and German—should generally be avoided in French. These topics will be treated in detail in this chapter.

Articulation of French Consonants

Each consonant sound is classified phonetically based on three criteria: whether it is voiced or unvoiced, where it is articulated, and how it is articulated. Thus, a 'voiced dental plosive' is the classification for the regular sound of French letter *d*.

French Lyric Diction. Jason Nedecky, Oxford University Press. © Oxford University Press 2023.
DOI: 10.1093/oso/9780197573839.003.0004

Below is a cross-section of the vocal tract with labels indicating the points of consonant articulation.

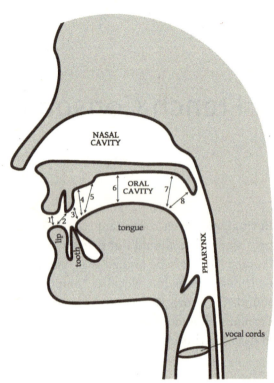

Place of Articulation

1. bilabial
2. labio-dental
3. dental
4. alveolar
5. post-alveolar
6. palatal
7. velar
8. uvular

Plosives

Plosive consonants are produced by a stoppage of the airflow, followed immediately by its release. The articulations, phonetic representations, and most regular spellings of the French plosive consonant phonemes are shown in the following table.

bilabial		dental		velar	
unvoiced	voiced	unvoiced	voiced	unvoiced	voiced
/p/	/b/	/t/	/d/	/k/	/g/
p	*b*	*t*	*d*	*c q*	*g*

Remarks

/b/   is essentially the same as in English.

/p/   is not aspirated, which means it is followed by very little or no puff of air. This is different from the aspirated English and German variant (which can be expressed in narrow transcription with the notation /p^h/).

FRENCH CONSONANT SOUNDS | 31

/t/ is dental, meaning it is articulated with the tip of the tongue on the back of the top front teeth. A narrow transcription of this dentalized consonant can be expressed with the notation /t̪/. It is also not aspirated. This is different from the English and German variant (which can be expressed in narrow transcription with the notation /tʰ/).

/d/ is dental. A narrow transcription of this dentalized consonant can be expressed with the notation /d̪/.

NOTE: In an effort to avoid the so-called wet English *t* and *d* pronunciations, singers often overcompensate in French by articulating the dental plosives /t/ and /d/ so lightly that they disappear. They must be clear and audible. The place of articulation for the English *th* spelling (unvoiced /θ/ and voiced /ð/) is only slightly further forward than that of the French dental plosives, and is therefore a good point of reference.

/k/ is not aspirated. This is different from the English and German variant (which can be expressed in narrow transcription with the notation/kʰ/).

/g/ is essentially the same as in English.

NOTE: The place of articulation of /k/ and /g/ shifts in French, according to the position within a word. A closed front vowel either before, and especially after, one of these plosives causes its articulation to be more forward. When the most front and closed vowel /i/ follows one of these plosives, it can be articulated as far forward as the hard palate, as in q̲ui (who) and G̲uy. The palatalized variants of these plosives can be expressed in narrow transcription with the notations /kʲ/ and /gʲ/.

Fricatives

Fricative consonants are produced by friction of the airflow through a narrow opening. The articulations, phonetic representations, and most regular spellings of the French fricative consonant phonemes are shown in the following table.

labio-dental		alveolar		post-alveolar	
unvoiced	voiced	unvoiced	voiced	unvoiced	voiced
/f/	/v/	/s/	/z/	/ʃ/	/ʒ/
f ph	*v*	*c s*	*s z*	*ch*	*g j*

Remarks

Fricatives in French are essentially the same as their English counterparts. In addition to the phonemes shown above, uvular /ʁ/ is also a fricative. It is the norm for *r*

32 | FRENCH LYRIC DICTION

in spoken French, and as of recently, is also heard in French vocal music. Further explanation is provided later in this chapter, in the section on French *r*.

Careful consideration of the articulation of /ʃ/ and /ʒ/ reveals that, as in English, these phonemes usually involve lip-rounding. In French, they may have slightly more lip-rounding, or 'labialization', than in English, especially when next to a rounded vowel, as in *chaud* (hot) and *joue* (cheek). These labialized consonant sounds can be expressed in narrow transcription with the notations /ʃʷ/ and /ʒʷ/.

Nasal Consonants

Nasal consonants are produced with a blockage of the airflow in the mouth, and its release through the nose. The articulations, phonetic representations, and most regular spellings of the French nasal consonant phonemes are shown in the following table.

bilabial	dental	palatal	velar
/m/	/n/	/ɲ/	/ŋ/
m	*n*	*gn*	*ng*

Remarks

/m/   is essentially the same as in English.

/n/   is normally articulated slightly further forward than in English, on the teeth. A narrow transcription of this dentalized consonant can be expressed with the notation /n̪/.

/ɲ/   is somewhat like a compression of /nj/ into one phoneme, but with the tip of the tongue on the back of the bottom teeth. This phoneme is not found in English or German, but is found in Italian.

/ŋ/   is used in borrowed foreign words, notably for English nouns ending in *-ing*. It has the same articulation as in English.

Lateral *l*

The lateral consonant *l* is produced with the release of the airflow by the sides of the raised tongue. Its articulation, phonetic representation, and spelling are shown in the following table.

dental
voiced
/l/
l

Remarks

/l/   is quite far forward in French, on the teeth. A narrow transcription of this dentalized consonant can be expressed with the notation /l̪/. The velarized, or 'dark' /ł/ of English words such as 'heel' [hił] is to be avoided altogether, as is the practice in everyday spoken French of devoicing l—*peuple* [pœpl̥] (people), as mentioned in the Introduction.

The French *r*

There are two articulations of *r* used in French vocal music: a front, or apical variant, and a back, or uvular variant. These two variants are very distinctive in position and resulting sound. (It should go without saying, perhaps, that the English 'burred *r*'—represented by the IPA symbol /ɹ/—must always be avoided in French.)

Apical (Front) Articulation of *r*

The apical variant is articulated with the front part, or 'blade' of the tongue, as either flipped /ɾ/ or rolled /r/. Flipped /ɾ/ consists of only one touch (tap) of the tongue at the alveolar ridge, while rolled /r/ requires a vibration (trill) of the tongue with a stream of air at the alveolar ridge. The apical variant is always voiced. Until recently, apical *r* had always been the norm in French vocal music. It is now considered to be the more conservative of the two variants.

Uvular (Back) Articulation of *r*

The uvular variant is articulated with the back part, or 'dorsum' of the tongue, as either fricative /ʁ/ or trilled /ʀ/. Fricative /ʁ/ is produced with a narrow stream of air between the back of the tongue and the uvula. Trilled /ʀ/ is articulated by the stream of air causing the uvula to vibrate (trill) against the back of the tongue. These uvular articulations sound quite similar. Fricative /ʁ/ is much more widespread in spoken French than a fully trilled /ʀ/. The trilled form sounds somewhat more robust. (Think of the characteristic articulation of *r* in Édith Piaf's singing.) Uvular *r* can regularly devoice in French, especially in the fricative form.

A Long History of the Two Variants

Uvular *r* is an important feature of modern spoken French. It is also heard in other European languages, including spoken German. Historians are unsure as to how and why uvular *r* came to be a part of French speech. It was first observed in the spoken language in about the mid-seventeenth century, mainly in Paris, and at court. It remained a secondary pronunciation to the apical variant for a very long time. The proper articulation of apical *r* is described in the

Act II pronunciation lesson of the infamous 1670 play with music, *Le bourgeois gentilhomme* by Molière (1622–1673):

> The *r* [is pronounced] by bringing the tip of the tongue up to the roof of the mouth so that, being brushed with force by the air going out, it continually gives way then returns to the same place, making a sort of trembling.
>
> MOLIÈRE, *Le bourgeois gentilhomme*

For at least two hundred years, the uvular *r*—also known as *r grasseyé*—is very often regarded as an inferior, weakened form of apical rolled *r*. In the first edition of the *Dictionnaire de L'Académie Française* (1694), the verb « *grasseyer* » is defined as « *parler gras* », which can mean 'to speak in a thick way', or 'fleshy pronunciation', or even 'crude pronunciation'. The entry goes on to say that this refers to a mispronunciation of certain consonants, especially *r*.

It is said that in the late eighteenth century, still only about a quarter of Parisians spoke with uvular *r*. By the late nineteenth century, however, it had become the most commonly heard variant in speech in the capital city.[†] In 1907, the phonetician Paul Passy (1859–1940) reported that uvular *r* had become prevalent in Paris; however, he goes on to say:

> In the country, even within twelve miles of Paris, and in the small towns, **r** is almost exclusively used, though the use of **ʀ** is rapidly spreading. On the whole **r** is probably still used by the majority of French people.
>
> PASSY, *Sounds of the French Language*

In the subsequent decades of the twentieth century, uvular *r* spread quickly throughout the rest of France, and to most other French-speaking regions. Today, it is an important feature of standard French that is ubiquitous in the spoken language.

Tastes for Articulation of *r* in French Singing

The co-existence of apical *r* and uvular *r* causes a great deal of controversy in the modern world of French singing. Until very recently, uvular *r* in opera and *mélodie* had all but been rejected. In 1896, Sigurd Fredrik Euren (1858–1926) wrote in his study on the pronunciation of French *r*:

> It has been said, and is still said, that singers and actors prefer the apical *r*, because they find it more resonant, and more harmonious. That must be true for singers, because it is evident that the apical *r*, being a sound which is formed in the front

---

† This is explained by Euren, *Étude sur l'R français*, 3.

part of the mouth, lends a clearer characteristic to singing that is also, so to speak, more unobstructed.

EUREN, *Étude sur l'R français*

In the Passy text of 1907, the sentiment is the same:

But singers, public speakers, and actors still prefer [apical *r*] because it is a more sonorous and pleasant sound than ʀ, and less tiring to the throat.

PASSY, *Sounds of the French Language*

For at least the first three quarters of the twentieth century, apical *r* continued to be taught as the norm for French vocal music, while uvular *r* was reserved for spoken dialogue, *chanson* (popular song), cabaret singing, and sometimes operetta. Reynaldo Hahn wrote about this in the 1940s:

One has never heard a single great singer use the uvular *r* in singing serious, solemn, dramatic, delicate, poetical or sentimental music.

HAHN, *Thèmes variés*

Even though uvular *r* was routinely employed in the speech of French artists of the last century, it is very evident in recordings that, almost without exception, they still overwhelmingly favoured the apical *r* in their singing. The sung apical *r* in French is nearly the same flipped /ɾ/ and rolled /r/ as in sung Italian, German, and historical English. French singers normally articulate apical *r* with the blade of the tongue slightly further back, nearing the post-alveolar position. They often also realize it with labialization (lip-rounding). These slight modifications lend a distinctive 'covered' quality to the consonant sound, which is apparent (to varying degrees) on innumerable recorded examples. These details may be considered subtle aspects of authentic pronunciation of the French apical *r*, which can be expressed in narrow transcription with the notation /r̠ʷ/.

It was only in the last two or three decades of the twentieth century that the taste in France finally shifted in favour of *grasseyement* in singing. Uvular *r* is now completely commonplace in opera and *mélodie*—especially in *mélodie* of the twentieth century, most notably in settings of contemporary poetry. Sometimes repertoire from the nineteenth century and earlier is given special treatment, whereby the preservation of apical *r* is seen to lend a more historically informed flavour to a piece.

Why Choose Either Variant of *r*?

The reasons most often given in favour of uvular *r* are that it is more natural (i.e., closer to speech), less foreign-sounding, less affected, and not as dated. While all this is true, it is also important to realize that the composers, poets/librettists, and original performers of all but the most recently composed French repertoire would not have expected the use of uvular *r*. The choice to sing it would therefore be somewhat of a departure from the original. Such a modernization comes with a cost. As outlined in the Euren quotation above, there are linguistic and vocal advantages of the front articulation of apical *r* over the back articulation of uvular *r*.

There is another problem in singing uvular *r* that is worth mentioning. As is the case with the consonant *l*, the consonant *r* tends to devoice in spoken French in many positions. This is true of uvular *r* when it is realized both as the trilled /ʀ/, and especially as the fricative /ʁ/. (Note that the latter can also be transcribed with the phoneme /χ/.)[†] Devoicing is especially prevalent after a plosive or fricative and before word-final mute *e*, as in *ombre* [õ:bʀ̥] (shadow), *propre* [pʀɔpʀ̥] (own/clean), *tendre* [tã:dʀ̥] (tender), *être* [ɛtʀ̥] (to be), *maigre* [mɛgʀ̥] (thing) *sucre* [sykʀ̥] (sugar), *givre* [ʒi:vʀ̥] (frost), *chiffre* [ʃifʀ̥] (number). It may also occur in other positions, especially before an unvoiced consonant within a word. The devoiced uvular *r* can sound quite unattractive in singing, especially when it is prolonged. It is therefore very often 're-voiced' when employed in French vocal music. This artificial re-voicing of uvular *r* is not easy—even for native French singers—and can sound cumbersome and contrived.

Outside of France, apical *r* is still very often heard in performance, and taught in singing. For staged works, it is ultimately the decision of the conductor, diction coach, and sometimes the director, as to which *r* is preferred. Nowadays, it is expected that singers master both variants.

Pronunciations of French r

Phonetic Symbol	Variant	Name	Description	Devoiced Form
/ɾ/	apical	flipped *r*	alveolar tap	—
/r/		rolled *r*	alveolar trill	—
/ʁ/	uvular	*r grasseyé*	uvular fricative	/ʁ̥/ or /χ/
/ʀ/			uvular trill	/ʀ̥/

To 'Flip' or to 'Roll'?

When singing with the apical *r*, there is a great deal of freedom to choose between flipped /ɾ/ and rolled /r/. Theoretically, a single flip is considered sufficient in

---

† For the sake of simplicity, this book uses /ʀ/ as a 'catch-all' notation of uvular *r* in any of its variants. It should be assumed that when it is encountered in this book, /ʀ/ may stand for any of the fricative/trilled, voiced/devoiced variants.

French. This is in keeping with typical French consonant articulation that is not drawn out. Unlike Italian, there is no hard-and-fast rule in French stating that an intervocalic *r* must be flipped. Notwithstanding, rolled /r/ is not normally recommended for a single *r* between vowels.

G. Fauré: *Chanson d'amour* (Silvestre)

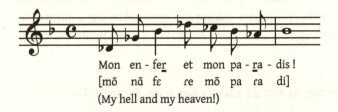

Mon en - fer et mon pa - ra - dis!
[mɔ̃ nã fɛ ɾe mɔ̃ pa ɾa di]
(My hell and my heaven!)

There are plenty of occasions for a good rolled /r/ in French singing. In fact, it is normally possible wherever heightened expressivity is intended. The section on lengthening of doubled consonants in Chapter 7 proposes other opportunities to roll *r*.

G. Fauré: *La rançon* (Baudelaire)

Pa - raî - tra le ter - ri - ble jour,
[tɛr ri blə]
(The terrible day shall appear)

Apical *r* is lost very easily when it is word-final, or when it is immediately followed by another consonant. Care must be taken to sing it very clearly and deliberately in these cases. A short rolled /r/ can help. Careful release of a flipped /ɾ/ is also possible, as described later in this chapter, in the section on consonant release. The denser the musical setting, the quicker the passage of text, and the larger the hall, the more important this becomes in order for the *r* to 'speak' clearly.

Mute *h* and Aspirated *h*

Unlike English and German, a single letter *h* in French is not pronounced as the unvoiced glottal fricative /h/. Instead, it is silent. When *h* is the first letter of a word, that word begins with the following vowel sound. There are two types of initial letter *h* in French: *h muet*, or 'mute *h*', and *h aspiré*, or 'aspirated *h*'. **In both cases, they are silent.** Mute *h* is typically encountered in words of Latin origin, and is by

38 | French Lyric Diction

far the more common of the two. Aspirated *h* is often traced to words of Germanic origin, and in many common interjections. Whether an initial *h* is mute or aspirated has a great impact on pronunciation. A final consonant sound may be linked to a word beginning in mute *h* by use of consonant linking, vocalic elision, or *liaison*. (These terms are explained in Chapters 4 and 5.) Such connections are forbidden to a word beginning in aspirated *h*. For example, in *l'honneur* (the honour), *une͜ horloge* (a clock), and *un grand͜ homme* (a great man), linking to the mute *h* is made in each case; however, in *la | harpe* (the harp), such a linking is prevented by the aspirated *h*.

Look up initial *h* words in a good dictionary. Aspirated *h* is normally indicated by one of these symbols: * † ' ' '

A Short List of Common Words and Names with Aspirated *h*

ha !	*hanche*	*hautaine*	*hideux*	*houblon*
habanera	*handicap*	*hautbois*	*hiérarchie*	*houblonner*
hâbler	*hangar*	*haute-contre*	*hiérarchique*	*houe*
Habsbourg	*hanneton*	*hauteur*	*hiératique*	*houille*
hache	*Hanovre*	*Havane (La)*	*hiéroglyphe*	*houp !*
hacher	*Hanséatiques*	*Haye (La)*	*hilaire*	*houri*
hachette	*haquet*	*hé !*	*hip !*	*hourque*
Hachette	*haranguer*	*hein ?*	*hisse !*	*hourra !*
Hadès	*harasser*	*Heine*	*hisser*	*housser*
hadji	*harcèlement*	*hem !*	*ho !*	*houx*
hagard	*harceler*	*hemlock*	*Hobart*	*huard*
Hague (La)	*harceleur*	*hennir*	*hoche*	*Huascar*
Hahn	*harceleuse*	*hennissant*	*hocher*	*hublot*
haie	*hardi*	*hennissement*	*hochet*	*huche*
haillon	*haricot*	*hep !*	*hockey*	*hucher*
Haïm	*haricoter*	*héraut*	*holà !*	*huchet*
haine	*harnacher*	*hérisser*	*hollandais*	*hue !*
haineuse	*harnais*	*hérisson*	*Holst*	*Huguenots (Les)*
haineux	*harnois*	*héron*	*homard*	*Hugues*
haïr	*harpe*	*héros*	*hongrois*	*huit*
hâler	*harpon*	*herse*	*honte*	*hulotte*
haleter	*hasard*	*hêtre*	*honteuse*	*hululation*
Halles (Les)	*hâte*	*Hétu*	*honteux*	*hululer*
halot	*hâter*	*heu ?*	*hop !*	*hum!*
halte !	*hauban*	*heurtement*	*hoquet*	*humer*
Haltière (De La)	*hausse*	*heurter*	*hoqueter*	*Huns*
Hambourg	*hausser*	*hi !*	*hormis*	*hurler*
hamburger	*haussier*	*hibou*	*hors*	*hussard*
hameau	*haut*	*hic*	*hotte*	*hussite*
Hamelle	*hautain*	*hideuse*	*hou !*	*hutte*

Special Cases

The word *héros* (hero/heroes) has aspirated *h* in both the masculine singular and plural forms, so linking to it is not possible.

J.-P. Rameau: ***Hippolyte et Aricie***—*Acte III* (Pellegrin)

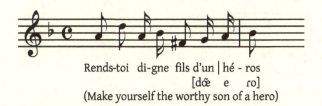

Rends-toi di-gne fils d'un | hé - ros
[dœ̃ e ʀo]
(Make yourself the worthy son of a hero)

Curiously however, all other derivatives of this word instead have mute *h*, as in *l'héroïne* (the heroine), *l'héroïque* (the heroic), *l'héroïsme* (heroism), etc. Another tricky word is *hélas* (alas). It has mute *h*, and so *liaison* to it is permitted.

G. Fauré: ***Poème d'un jour***—*Adieu* (Grandmougin)

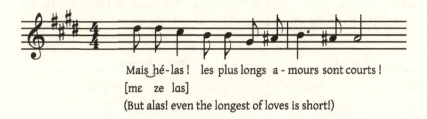

Mais hé-las! les plus longs a - mours sont courts!
[mɛ ze lɑs]
(But alas! even the longest of loves is short!)

Sometimes, however, tradition dictates that *liaison* to *hélas* should be left out, as in the following musical example. In this case, *hélas* is an interjection that is best kept apart from the text around it, as reinforced by the punctuation.

G. Bizet: ***Carmen***—*Je dis que rien ne m'épouvante* (Meilhac, Halévy)

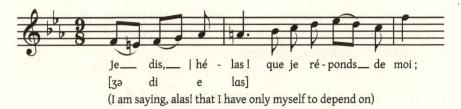

Je__ dis,__ | hé - las! que je ré - ponds__ de moi;
[ʒə di e lɑs]
(I am saying, alas! that I have only myself to depend on)

Articulating *h* in Rare Instances

In exclamations and violent sentiments, aspirated *h* is sometimes lightly pronounced as /h/ in French, thereby 'breaking the rule' that *h* is always silent. This is possible in vocal repertoire. It is heard more in opera than in *mélodie*. Some common examples of articulated h are h̲olà! (hey!), h̲alte! (stop!), je te h̲ais! (I hate you), c'est une h̲onte (it's a shame), oh̲o!, ah̲a!

C. Gounod: *Faust*—Acte IV (Barbier, Carré)

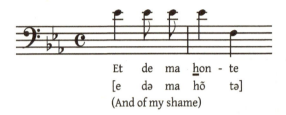

Et   de   ma   hon - te
[e   də   ma   hõ   tə]
(And of my shame)

Borrowed Affricates in French

An affricate is a combination of a plosive plus a fricative. Unlike English, Italian, and German, affricates do not naturally occur in French. There are, however, four such phonemes that are regularly borrowed in the French language.[†] The articulations, phonetic representations, and most regular spellings of these borrowed affricates are shown in the following table.

	alveolar		post-alveolar	
	unvoiced	voiced	unvoiced	voiced
	/ts/	/dz/	/tʃ/	/dʒ/
	ts	z zz	tch	dj

Remarks

The phonemes /tʃ/ and /dʒ/, as well as the rarer /ts/ and /dz/, are approximated in French, as in *ma̲t̲ch* (game), *d̲j̲inn* (genie), *t̲s̲ar* (czar), and *Z̲eus*. In polysyllabic words, the two sounds of each affricate are technically divided in accordance with the rules of French syllabification, as outlined in Chapter 4: *luncher* [lœ̃t.ʃe] (to lunch), *budget* [byd.ʒɛ] (budget), *mezzo* [mɛd.zo], *grazioso* [ɡrat.sjo.zo]. Native French speakers naturally pronounce such words with slightly less 'compression' of the two phonemes. In singing, the same can be done.

Pronunciation of Consonants: Voiced, Unvoiced, or Silent?

The pronunciation of a consonant letter can vary greatly in French, depending mainly on its position within a word. The following tables provide a summary of

---

† The letter *x* in French is realized either as a single phoneme, or as two phonemes: /ks/ or /gz/. These double-phoneme realizations of *x* are also often considered affricates.

the most regular phonetic values for the spellings of single consonants and digraphs (two consonant letters pronounced as a single sound). A more detailed account, including exceptions to these generalizations, and plenty of model words, is found in Part Two.

Pronunciation Overview of French Consonants

Spelling	Pronunciation	Description
b	/b/	usually
c	/k/	'hard' before *a, o, u,* or a consonant; usually 'hard' as last letter
	/s/	'soft' before *e, i, y*
	~~c~~	silent as last letter after nasal vowel
ç	/s/	always
d	/d/	usually
	~~d~~	usually silent as last letter
	/t/	in *liaison*
f	/f/	usually
g	/g/	'hard' before *a, o, u,* or a consonant other than *n*
	/ʒ/	'soft' before *e, i, y*
	~~g~~	usually silent as last letter after another consonant
h	~~h~~	always silent
j	/ʒ/	always
k	/k/	always
l	/l/	usually
	~~l~~	sometimes silent as last letter
	/j/	sometimes after *i* or when doubled after *i*
m	/m/	usually
	~	often nasalizes preceding vowel
n	/n/	usually
	~	often nasalizes preceding vowel
p	/p/	usually
	~~p~~	usually silent as last letter
q	/k/	always
r	/ɾ/ or /ʀ/	usually
	~~r~~	silent in *-er, -ier* endings (all verbs, some nouns)
s	/z/	intervocalic and in *liaison*
	/s/	most other cases, including after nasalizing *m* or *n*
	~~s~~	sometimes silent as last letter; nearly always silent following another silent letter
t	/t/	usually
	/s/	sometimes before *i*
	~~t~~	usually silent as last letter
v	/v/	always

w	/v/	usually
	/w/	sometimes
x	/ks/	usually, except:
	/gz/	in *ex-* before a vowel
	/z/	in *liaison*
	/s/	in a few words
	x̶	usually silent as last letter
z	/z/	usually
	z̶	usually silent as last letter

Pronunciation of French Digraphs

Spelling	Pronunciation	Description
ch	/ʃ/	usually 'soft'
	/k/	'hard' before a consonant
gn	/ɲ/	nearly always
ng	/ŋ/	in borrowed spellings
ph	/f/	always
ss	/s/	always
th	/t/	always

Silent Consonants

Spelling and pronunciation in French are complicated by a profusion of silent letters. Although French pronunciation has evolved a great deal from its Latin roots, the French system of orthography has not kept pace. The abundance of silent consonants in the language is proof of this. Consonants frequently remain in the spelling of words, even though those letters often have not been pronounced for centuries.[†]

Pronounced Word-Final Consonants

c f l r

These letters are usually pronounced at the end of a word. The word 'C<u>A</u>R<u>E</u>F<u>U</u>L!' is a good way to remember them.

---

† In earlier poetry, additional silent consonants are frequently encountered. The ***Deux épigrammes de Clément Marot*** of Ravel, and the later Debussy settings of François Villon and Charles d'Orléans are good examples. Such words are typically sung with modern pronunciation, (i.e., the superfluous consonant letters are silent), despite the antique spellings that appear in the score.

FRENCH CONSONANT SOUNDS | 43

Silent Word-Final Consonants
d p s t x z
These letters are usually not pronounced at the end of a word. The little phrase 'TA**X**I**S** **D**O **ZIP**!' is a good way to remember them.

-er -ier
These word-final spellings feature closed /e/ plus silent -r in all verbs, as well as some nouns and names—notably those ending in -cher and -ger.

Silent Word-Final Nasalized Spellings
m n
Spellings with nasalizing *m* and *n* at the end of a word are silent. (Borrowed words and names often behave differently.) The spelling may simply be word-final, or it may involve other silent consonants, as in:

-mb(s), -mp(s), -mpt(s), -m(s), -nc(s), -nct(s), -nd(s), -ng(s), -ngt(s), -n(s), -nt(s)

In these spellings, the consonants are all silent, and the vowel before is always nasalized.

Always Silent
h
The letter *h* is reliably silent in French.

Pronouncing Consonants before Word-Final Mute *e*
It is important to remember that a consonant letter is pronounced when it is followed by a vowel within a word, even if that consonant is normally silent at the end of a word. This is particularly relevant in the many instances where a consonant occurs before word-final mute *e*:

> *plomb* [plõ] (lead) vs. *colombe* [kɔlõːbə] (dove)
> *franc* [fɾã] (frank) vs. *la France* [fɾãːsə]
> *il est grand* [gɾã] (he is tall) vs. *elle est grande* [gɾãːdə] (she is tall)
> *un rang* [ɾã] (a row) vs. *on range* [ɾãːʒə] (one tidies)
> *outil* [uti] (tool) vs. *utile* [ytilə] (useful)
> *nom* [nõ] (name) vs. *gnome* [gnoːmə] (gnome)
> *balcon* [balkõ] (balcony) vs. *icône* [ikoːnə] (icon)
> *loup* [lu] (wolf) vs. *loupe* [lupə] (magnifying glass)
> *le berger* [bɛɾʒe] (the shepherd) vs. *la bergère* [bɛɾʒɛːɾə] (the shepherdess)
> *un vers* [vɛːɾ] (a verse) vs. *il verse* [vɛɾsə] (he pours)
> *le vent* [vã] (the wind) vs. *il vente* [vãːtə] (it's windy)
> *flux* [fly] (flow/stream) vs. *luxe* [lyksə] (luxury)
> *vous attrapez* [atɾape] (you catch) vs. *une trapèze* [tɾapɛːzə] (a trapeze)

La détente de la consonne—Consonant Release

A significant difference between French and English is the way in which final consonants are articulated. In everyday spoken English, final consonants—especially plosives—are often barely heard at all at the end of syllables. Consider, for example, how *t* and *g* sound in a typical North American pronunciation of 'hot dog' [hɑt̚ dɑg̚]. Naturally, in English singing, fully articulated consonants are expected. In French, consonant articulation goes one step further. A noticeable voicing—like a brief schwa—is made after a final consonant sound. It occurs regularly after both voiced and unvoiced consonants. That same borrowed word in French is *hot-dog* [ɔtᵊ dɔgᵊ] in careful pronunciation. This follow-through of the final consonant sound is known as *la détente de la consonne* (relaxation of the consonant), and can be expressed in narrow transcription with the notation /ᵊ/, as shown above. 'Consonant release' is particularly important to an authentic articulation of any consonant sound ending a syllable, especially when word-final.

C. Gounod : ***Roméo et Juliette***—*Mab! la reine des mensonges* (Barbier, Carré)

Mab!   la rei - ne des — men - son - ges
[mabᵊ]
(Mab! the queen of lies)

Consonant release also helps with intelligibility. As stated earlier in this chapter, this is especially true for flipped /ɾ/. When it is word-final, or occurs before another consonant, flipped /ɾ/ benefits greatly from a clear and intentional release. Without it, the consonant easily gets lost in these contexts.

F. Poulenc : *Main dominée par le cœur* (Éluard)

Main do - mi - née par le cœur —   Cœur do - mi - né par le lion —
[paɾᵊ lə kœɾᵊ   kœɾᵊ dɔ mi ne paɾᵊ lə ljɔ̃]
(Hand ruled by the heart   Heart ruled by the lion)

4

The 'Consonant-Vowel Flow' of the French Phrase

As previously stated, one of the main tenets of French pronunciation is that in every syllable, a short consonant sound gives way to a pure, sustained monophthong. This practice is often labelled as the 'consonant-vowel flow'. Much has been written about it, and for good reason. Understanding the concept begins with an analysis of French syllabification. The conventions for syllabic division in French are very straightforward. They are less complicated than, for example, those of English or German.

French Syllabification

The English word 'out-ra-geous' and the French equivalent, « *ou-tra-geux* » exhibit several differences at the syllabic level. The *tr* combination in the French example is not split up. It is printed—and articulated—as a unit which begins the second syllable. All three syllables in the French example are 'free syllables', meaning they end in vowel sounds. Naturally, there are no diphthongs in the French example. In the English word, two of the three syllables are 'checked syllables', meaning they end in consonant sounds, and two syllables feature diphthongs. These seemingly small details point to systemic differences in pronunciation between the two languages.

Orthographic Syllabification: Division of French Words as Spelled

In the score, individual words are normally divided into syllables with hyphens. For singers, the most important information to be gleaned from the division of syllables on any page of the score concerns the pronunciation of the letter *e*. When another

French Lyric Diction. Jason Nedecky, Oxford University Press. © Oxford University Press 2023.
DOI: 10.1093/oso/9780197573839.003.0005

letter follows *e* in the same syllable, be it silent or pronounced, the vowel sound is normally either /ɛ/ or /e/; however, as outlined in Chapter 2 in the spellings for mute *e*, when *e* is the last letter and only vowel of a syllable, it is almost without exception mute *e*. Consider the word *venez* (come). Printed in the score as « *ve-nez* », the first *e* is pronounced /ə/. In the second syllable, *e* is followed by a silent *z*, and is therefore closed /e/. Because there are so many French spellings that involve the letter *e*, knowing this simple guideline can prevent a great number of mispronunciations. For example, the words *besoin* (need) and *chevelure* (hair) are pronounced [bə̞zwɛ̃] and [ʃə̞vəly:ʀə], not [bɛ̞zwɛ̃] and [ʃɛ̞vəly:ʀə]; the names *Debussy* and *Benoît* are pronounced [də̞bysi] and [bə̞nwa], not [dɛ̞bysi] and [bɛ̞nwa]; the name *Degas* is pronounced [də̞ga], not [de̞ga]!

Phonetic Syllabification: Division of French Words as Sung

The way in which syllables are hyphenated in the score can be slightly misleading when it comes to timing consonant articulation in singing. Doubled consonants, and groups of consonants within a word, are split up over two syllables on the page. Ideally, however, a doubled consonant should be articulated at the beginning of the second of those two syllables, and it should not be given any extra length. The word *belle* (beautiful), for example, is printed as « *bel-le* », but is pronounced [bɛ.lə]. Similarly, a word containing multiple consonants, such as *esprit* (spirit), is printed as « *es-prit* ». Although the *s* belongs to the first syllable, it must never cause the preceding vowel to be truncated. Instead, it is as though the *s* were connected to the second syllable: [ɛ→spʀi]. Thus, even checked syllables should be realized in singing rather like free syllables. This is especially different from singing in English, Italian, or German.

Pierre Bernac (1899–1979) writes about the importance of long, pure vowels, and the danger of over-singing consonants:

> A fundamental rule can be set down: '*In French, more so than in any other language, to obtain a proper line, a proper legato, one must fill the entire duration of each note with the vowel sound.*' In other words: in French, one has to carry the vowel sound *unaltered* right through the whole duration of the musical sound, *without anticipating at all the following consonant.* It is the only possible procedure to get both the music of the words and the music itself. [. . .] It is strictly forbidden in French to sing on the consonants (except, of course, for a very special effect).
>
> BERNAC, *Interpretation of French Song*

The following table shows French syllabification. Syllabic divisions as spelled and as sung are both described.

French Syllabification

Orthographic Division (on the page)	Phonetic Division (as sung)	Descriptions
de-vi-ner (to guess)	[də→vi→ne]	An intervocalic consonant begins the next syllable orthographically and phonetically.
tou-cher (to touch)	[tu→ʃe]	The digraphs ch, gn, ph, and th begin the next syllable orthographically and phonetically.
ga-gner (to win/earn)	[ga→ɲe]	
pro-phè-te (prophet)	[prɔ→fɛ.tə]	
pa-thé-ti-que (moving)	[pa→te.ti.kə]	
é-clair (flash)	[e→klɛːɾ]	A two-letter group of consonant + l or r begins the next syllable orthographically and phonetically.
gi-vre (frost)	[ʒiː→vɾə]	
ar-bre (tree)	[a→ɾbɾə]	Two or more consonants are divided orthographically over syllables. (The letter s is somewhat unstable in its position before/after the hyphen.) Two-letter groups of digraphs, or consonant + l or r are always printed together. Any consonant that appears before the hyphen should be articulated as late as possible.
mar-cher (to walk)	[ma→ɾʃe]	
ath-lè-te (athlete)	[a→tlɛ.tə]	
es-pion (spy)	[ɛ→spjõ]	
ob-sti-né or obs-ti-né (stubborn)	[ɔ→psti.ne]	
don-ner (to give)	[dɔ→ne]	Doubled consonants are divided between the syllables orthographically, but are pronounced as a single phoneme in the second syllable.
tran-quil-le (peaceful)	[trã.ki→lə]	
fil-le (girl/daughter)	[fi→jə]	
ac-cès (access)	[a→ksɛ]	In words with cc and gg followed by e, é, è, ê, i, œ, or y, each of the two consonants receives its own articulation—the first of which, printed before the hyphen, should be articulated as late as possible.
sug-gé-rer (to suggest)	[sy→gʒe.ɾe]	
ex-i-le (exile)	[ɛ→gzi.lə]	Hyphenation involving intervocalic x and y is avoided in written French. It is however prevalent in vocal music, where syllables are always divided. The orthographic rules are somewhat loose: x and y tend to be printed before the hyphen in the score, although they are also sometimes seen after it (usually to avoid a syllable containing a single, isolated vowel letter). When x constitutes a single sound, it is articulated in the second syllable. When it comprises two consonant sounds, the first should be articulated as late as possible. For the y spelling, /j/ belongs to the second syllable, regardless of the syllabic division on the page.
soix-ante (sixty)	[swa→sãː.tə]	
fuy-ez (flee)	[fɥi→je]	
voy-a-geur (traveller)	[vwa→ja.ʒœːɾ]	
es-say-er (to try)	[e.sɛ→je]	
lu-xe (luxury)	[ly→ksə]	
fi-xé (fixed)	[fi→kse]	
ay-ant or a-yant (having)	[ɛ→jã]	
ba-ya-dè-re (Bayadere)	[ba→ja.dɛː.ɾə]	
pa-ys (country)	[pɛ→i]	

48 | FRENCH LYRIC DICTION

Le groupe phonétique—The Phonetic Group

The French phrase sounds more like a series of syllables than a sequence of words. As previously stated, each syllable in the phrase moves from consonant sound to vowel sound, regardless of the spaces that separate the words on the page. This can make aural comprehension of the French language difficult for non-native speakers.

The term given to this cohesive series of syllables is *le groupe phonétique*, or the 'phonetic group'. Comprising words closely linked by meaning and grammar, the phonetic group is a syntactical unit. It may consist of a mere two or three words, or may extend to several words. A sentence may contain one or more phonetic groups.

Word Stress and Primary Phrasal Stress

L'accent d'intensité, or French 'word stress', is extremely predictable. Without exception, the stress of each and every polysyllabic word is on the final syllable, not counting word-final mute *e*. There is no secondary stress in French. Consider the English word 'pro͵nunci'ation', which contains both a primary and a secondary stress (as indicated), in contrast with the French equivalent « *prononcia'tion* », with a single word stress on the final syllable. Because this system of word stress is so consistent in French, dictionaries do not even indicate it. In other languages, word stress is much more varied—and also much more important—than in French. In fact, in a French phrase, individual word stresses tend to fall away, and are instead superseded by *l'accent tonique*, or the 'primary phrasal stress', occurring on the final syllable of the entire phonetic group, (not including word-final mute *e*).[†]

There are three basic ways in which the primary phrasal stress is realized in French. The speaker may 'lean' on, and slightly delay, the initial consonant of the stressed syllable. The speaker may also lengthen the vowel of the stressed syllable, particularly in cases where that vowel is already naturally prone to lengthening. (See the section on vocalic length in Chapter 2.) Finally, there may be a sudden rise or fall in the pitch of the speaker's voice on the accented syllable.[‡] Any one, two, or even all three of these tactics are possible for the primary phrasal stress. What is generally not observed in French is a 'punching' of the stressed syllable, by means of sudden force or increased volume. That is much more typical of English speech.

The boundaries of a phonetic group are somewhat free, and are determined in large part by the speaker. It is the delivery of the primary phrasal stress on the

---

† Chapter 7 provides information on another type of stress within the French phonetic group, called *l'accent d'insistance*.

‡ A detailed analysis of intonation in spoken French, albeit important for singers, lies outside the scope of this book. When it comes to roles with dialogue, a basic understanding of this topic is required.

final syllable of the phonetic group which delineates its end. This linguistic practice is a rather unique feature of French prosody. In vocal music, it affords artistic freedom for both the composer's setting and, to some extent, the singer's interpretation of it.

Examining the Phonetic Group

Consider the following sentence: *Sans aucun doute il a chanté sa première mélodie à l'école de musique.* (Undoubtedly he sang his first art song at music school.) For most speakers, there are three phonetic groups: « *sans aucun doute* », « *il a chanté sa première mélodie* », and « *à l'école de musique* ». The word stresses on the final syllables of *aucun, chanté, première,* and *école* are minimized when they are assembled into the sentence.[†] Instead, primary phrasal stresses occur only on the syllables « *-dou-* » of *doute,* « *-di-* » of *mélodie,* and « *-si-* » of *musique*:

Sans aucun <u>dou</u>te il a chanté sa première mé<u>lo</u>die à l'école de mu<u>si</u>que.

In an elevated tone, the consonant-vowel flow of the phonetic group that governs the progression of syllables is maintained by three linguistic phenomena: *enchaînement consonantique* or 'consonant linking', *élision vocalique* or 'vocalic elision', and *liaison*. (They are treated in detail in the following sections and in the next chapter.) The sentence above features all three: consonant linking from « *doute* » to « *il* », wherein the mute *e* is elided, and from « *il* » to « *a* », vocalic elision in « *l'école* », and *liaison* from « *sans* » to « *aucun* ». There is one unavoidable instance of back-to-back vowel sounds, called *hiatus* (also treated in this chapter) over the barrier between the last two phonetic groups, from « *mélodie* » to « *à* ».

Sans‿aucun <u>dou</u>te il‿a chanté sa première mé<u>lo</u>die à l'école de mu<u>si</u>que.

L'enchaînement consonantique— Consonant Linking

Within the phonetic group, when a word begins in a vowel sound, the final consonant sound of the previous word is linked to it. This important linguistic feature is called *l'enchaînement consonantique* or 'consonant linking'. The same

---

† Although individual word stress tends to be minimized within the phonetic group, it is often still observed to some degree, especially in words with lengthened vowels. This is very often the case when French poetry is read aloud. For example, in the sentence above, the /ɛ/ of *première* could be realized as half-long /ɛ·/, particularly if the phrase were declaimed in a deliberate way.

linking occurs from the final consonant sound in a word to the initial mute *h* of the next word.

F. Poulenc: *Bleuet* (Apollinaire)

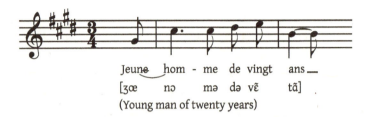

(Young man of twenty years)

Dropping Word-Final Mute *e* in Consonant Linking

Consonant linking frequently occurs over a mute *e* at the end of a word, thereby causing a complete dropping of the /ə/ syllable. This is the case in the musical example above with mute *h*, as well as in the following two musical examples.

G. Fauré: *Clair de lune* (Verlaine)

(Your soul is a chosen landscape)

F. Poulenc: *Le travail du peintre—Juan Gris* (Éluard)

(A single whole for ever and ever)

Consonant linking over a mute *e* between words is often reflected in notation (especially in older editions), in that syllabification is given with 'extra' hyphenation.

This is the case in the following musical example, where « *hou-le in-cli-ne* », is printed; (« *houle in-cline* » would also have been correct).

G. Fauré: *Les berceaux* (Sully Prudhomme)

L'élision vocalique—Vocalic Elision

The grammatical phenomenon known as *l'élision vocalique* or 'vocalic elision' refers to the dropping of final *a*, *i*, and mute *e* of monosyllabic words. Its purpose is to prevent back-to-back vowel sounds. The consonant sound of the monosyllabic word is linked to the initial vowel sound of the next word. The only words that take vocalic elision are *ce, de, je, la, le, me, te, se, ne, que*, and *si* (the latter to *il* and *ils* only). The dropped vowel is indicated in the score by an apostrophe, and so, unlike consonant linking, it is not left up to the singer to decide:

je + ai → j'ai (I have)   *tu la + aimes → tu l'aimes* (you like/love her)

que + on → qu'on (that/which one)   *si + il y a → s'il y a* (if there is)

Hiatus

The relatively rare case in which a consonant sound does not occur between syllables is known as *hiatus* [jatys]. In English, the same word is used. Here, two or more vowel sounds occur back-to-back in adjacent syllables. These vowel sounds are 'bridged' as smoothly as possible, without pauses, gaps, or glottal stops.

F. Poulenc: ***Parisiana**—Vous n'écrivez plus?* (Jacob)

In speech, when the same vowel sound is repeated, the voice 'pulses' slightly with each repetition, as in the awkward yet descriptive sentence often cited in French textbooks: *Papa a à aller à Arnes.* (Dad has to go to Arnes.)

Hiatus is also possible within a word. This is quite often enountered as dieresis, as described in Chapter 2. In the following musical example, a silent *h* separates the vowel sounds of adjacent syllables.

E. Chausson: *La caravane* (Gautier)

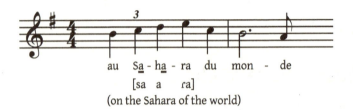

Several common words are spelled with intervocalic *h*, as in *dehors* [dəɔːr] (outside).† Hiatus within a word is also seen with a *tréma* ¨ (dieresis diacritic) over *i* or *e* as the second of two vowels,‡ as in *Noël* (Christmas) and *maïs* (corn), and when the vowel *e* is marked with *accent aigu* ´ (acute accent) or *accent grave* ` (grave accent) as in *goélette* (schooner), and *poète* (poet). The two vowels are sung back-to-back, each as a monophthong.

Hiatus is seen as rather unfavourable in French. In fact, the *t euphonique* or 'euphonic *t*' is employed specifically to separate the vowel sounds of subject and verb, as in « *a-t-il des amis ?* » ('does he have friends?'). Traditionally, hiatus is rigorously avoided in French poetry because it is considered displeasing to the ear.

The Phonetic Group in French Recitative

Recitative in French repertoire differs greatly from the Italian tradition. The natural cadence of Italian speech, often treated to rapid-fire delivery in recitative, is altogether foreign to French opera or oratorio of any period. In fact, there is no real equivalent of a French *recitativo secco*. Instead of true *parlando* style, recitative in French repertoire is typically set as *arioso* form of one kind or another. This

---

† Hiatus involving mute *e* followed by another vowel is only possible with the letter *h*, wherein mute *e* is never dropped. Both /ə/ and the vowel after *h* are pronounced back-to-back as separate syllables. This may occur within a word, as in *dehors* [dəɔːr] (outside), or phrasally with initial aspirated *h*, as in *le héros* [lə eʀo] (the hero).

‡ *Tréma* ¨ is also seen in rare instances over the vowels *u* and *y*. In general, apart from a few German names and ancient names ending in a vowel + *-üs*, the spelling *ü* in French follows a 'hard' *g* /g/ only, and is pronounced /y/. The spelling *ÿ*, also seen in a few names, generally follows the same pronunciation rules as the spelling *ï*.

so-called *récitatif mesuré*, or 'measured recitative', is ubiquitous in French repertoire from the seventeenth to the twentieth centuries—be it Lully, Rameau, Gluck, Berlioz, Gounod, Saint-Saëns, Massenet, Debussy, Poulenc, and any point along the way. The commonalities through the ages are that the stressed syllables of phonetic groups are set to the strong beat(s) of the measure, and metres often shift every few bars (especially in earlier works) in order to catch these stressed syllables, which are typically assigned the longest note values. The vocal line is normally accompanied by entire sections of the orchestra, or even the full orchestra.

C. Gounod : *Roméo et Juliette*—*Que fais-tu, blanche tourterelle* (Barbier, Carré)

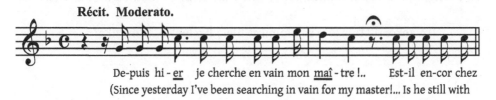

From the point of view of diction, singers should bear in mind that in this measured French recitative, note values can be sung roughly as printed. Above all, one should not be in a great a hurry with the text. It should be sung. The underlying rhythmic pulse, while certainly supple and flexible, cannot be altogether abandoned for a completely 'free' delivery. Unlike *recitativo secco* of Italian opera, the conductor will not be sitting out scenes of French recitative!

Methods for Transcription in French

There are a several possibilities for the phonetic representation of French text. The use of spaces between every syllable is one method. Although it is not often seen, this system does rather neatly highlight the consonant-vowel flow from syllable to syllable. The transcription of each syllable begins in a consonant phoneme, and ends in a vowel phoneme. The sentence given earlier in this chapter—*Sans aucun doute il a chanté sa première mélodie à l'école de musique.*—would be represented syllabically as:

[sɑ̃ zo kœ̃ du ti la ʃɑ̃ te sa prə mjɛ rə me lɔ di a le kɔ lə də my zi kə]

54 | FRENCH LYRIC DICTION

Use of the syllabic barrier dot is another method of transcription that is quite regularly encountered. The dot is typically shown in order to separate the syllables within a word, while spaces are used between the words. The consonant-vowel flow of syllables is maintained in transcription. The final consonant sound of a word is placed at the start of the next word when that word begins in a vowel sound:

[sã zo.kœ̃ du ti la ʃã.te sa prə.mjɛ.rə me.lɔ.di a le.kɔ.lə də my.zi.kə]

Finally, it is also possible to group together the syllables within a word, with spaces shown between the words. Again, final consonants are shown after the space before word-initial vowel sounds. This is the transcription method used in this book:

[sã zokœ̃ du ti la ʃãte sa prəmjɛrə melɔdi a lekɔlə də myzikə]

Liaison

5

Liaison refers to the linking of two words by pronouncing a normally silent consonant at the end of the first word before an initial vowel sound of the second word. *Liaison* is an extremely important and rather unique linguistic phenomenon in French that is not practised in English, Italian, or German. In addition to consonant linking and vocalic elision, it plays an integral role in maintaining the consonant-vowel flow. The term *liaison* itself means connection, or linking. It is usually borrowed and used freely in English.

Liaison from an Historical Perspective

Much has been written about how *liaison* was employed over the centuries. Simply put, frequent *liaison* was at one time considered a provincial way of speaking. As the French language evolved to drop many final consonants, those who were well educated avoided making *liaison* in their speech, so as to disassociate themselves from rural folk who could not keep up with the times. By the mid-nineteenth century, however, the prevailing attitude toward *liaison* had reversed. The use of frequent *liaison* by the urban upper class had become proof of their education. People of letters could demonstrate their awareness of proper spelling by linking silent consonants to initial vowels, thus signalling their background and upbringing to all those who heard them speak. Although French speakers today use *liaison* quite sparingly in everyday speech, the tendency is still to make frequent *liaison* in more formal settings, especially in poetry and, by extension, in vocal music.

The best way for singers to approach the topic of *liaison* is to become familiar with which connections are required, optional, and forbidden.

French Lyric Diction. Jason Nedecky, Oxford University Press. © Oxford University Press 2023.
DOI: 10.1093/oso/9780197573839.003.0006

56 | FRENCH LYRIC DICTION

Liaisons obligatoires—Required *Liaisons*

Liaisons that are required in all levels of modern speech, and in singing, are described in the scenarios that follow.

Liaison is made from an article or an adjective to a word it describes or modifies: *un ami* (a friend), *les amis* (the friends), *mon ami* (my friend), *aucun ami* (no friend), *ces amis* (these friends), *quels amis* (which friends), *bons amis* (good friends).

Liaison is made between subjects, pronouns, objects, and verbs that are directly related to each other grammatically: *on est* (one is), *est-on ?* (is one?), *on les écoute* (one listens to them), *nous en avons besoin* (we need it), *allez-y !* (go ahead!), *apportez-les-y* (bring them there), *c'est important* (that's important).

Liaison is made from a monosyllabic preposition or adverb to the following word: *dès hier* (as of yesterday), *en hiver* (in winter), *chez elle* (at her place), *moins agréable* (less pleasant), *sans un bruit* (without a sound), *quant à* (as for), *très agile* (very agile).

Liaisons facultatives—Optional *Liaisons*

Pronunciation deemed suitable for the stage was at one time within the purview of the Comédie-Française. For centuries, the practices of this venerable institution were considered the gold standard. In general, the recommendation for *liaison* was to make it wherever possible, in order to avoid hiatus. In fact, in classical poetry, **any** potential *liaison* within a verse[†] was technically considered permissible! To some extent, this concept is carried on in French vocal music. Where a *liaison* is considered optional, there is a good chance that it may be used in singing. It is most often expected that optional *liaisons* be made from the so-called *consonnes flexionnelles*, or 'inflecting consonants'. These are the consonant letters used to show verb conjugation and the plural form. Other less obvious optional *liaisons* are also possible.

Optional *liaisons* are heard frequently in singing, but less in speech. They may occur as described in the scenarios that follow.

Liaison can be made from a noun or an adjective in the plural form to the following word: *les femmes aiment* (women like), *gâteaux au chocolat* (chocolate cakes), *les enfants heureux* (happy children), *les invités ont dit* (the guests said), *fleurs à vendre* (flowers for sale), *les mêmes étudiants* (the same

---

† The term 'verse' as used in this book refers to a line of poetry, not an entire stanza.

students), *jeunes‿et beaux* (young and beautiful), *belles‿amies* (beautiful friends), *agréables‿à voir* (pleasing to see).

Liaison can be made from the pronouns *nous* (we/us) and *vous* (you) to most parts of speech: *pour nous‿à faire* (for us to do), *êtes-vous‿en avance?* (are you early?), *nous‿y sommes* (we're there), *vous‿aussi* (you as well).

Liaison can be made from a verb—including conjugated forms, participles, auxiliary verbs, **and** infinitives—to most parts of speech: *il vient‿avec nous* (he is coming with us), *il était‿aimé* (he was loved), *tu aimes‿entendre* (you like to hear), *mélodies chantés‿en plein air* (songs sung outdoors), *songer‿à* (to dream about).

Liaison can be made from most conjunctions to the following word: *mais‿alors* (but then), *quand‿il veut* (when he wants).

Liaison can be made from many polysyllabic prepositions to the following word: *depuis‿hier* (since yesterday), *pendant‿un mois* (for one month), *après‿un an* (after a year).

Liaison can be made from many polysyllabic adverbs to the following word, especially those ending in *-ment*: *follement‿aimé* (madly loved).

Liaison can be made from most negations to the following word: *pas‿un mot* (not a word), *ce n'est point‿assez* (it is not enough), *ne va jamais‿au jardin!* (never go into the garden!).

In 'The Use of *Liaison* in Common Vocabulary' section at the end of this chapter, further detail about optional *liaisons* is provided.

Liaisons interdites—Forbidden *Liaisons*

There are several instances where *liaison* is not made, even in *style soutenu*. *Liaisons* which are forbidden in all levels of modern speech and in singing are described in the scenarios that follow.

Liaison cannot be made **from** a noun in the singular form, or a proper noun.[†]

E. Chausson: **Poème de l'amour et de la mer**—Le temps des lilas (Bouchor)

Le prin - temps | est triste
[pʁɛ̃   tɑ̃   ɛ]
(Spring is sad)

[†] The rather long list of exceptions where *liaison* may be permitted from a noun in the singular form can be found later in this chapter, in the section '*Liaison* in Exceptional Cases'.

Debussy : ***Pelléas et Mélisande***—Acte V (Maeterlinck)

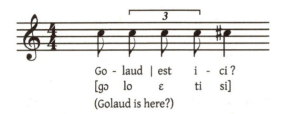

Liaison cannot be made **to** aspirated *h*.

É. Satie : *Omnibus automobile* (Hyspa)

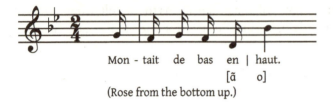

Liaison cannot be made **to** the word *oui* (yes).

J. Offenbach : ***La vie parisienne***—Acte III (Meilhac, Halévy)

Liaison cannot be made **from** the word *et* (and).

C. Debussy : ***Pelléas et Mélisande***—Acte I (Maeterlinck)

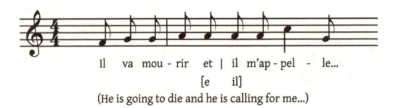

Liaison cannot be made over a breath, a printed rest, or a comma that divides separate clauses.

A. Thomas: ***Mignon**—Oui, je veux par le monde* (Barbier, Carré)

Je te fais mes a-dieux, | Et j'ouvre en-fin mon ai - le
[a djø   e]
(I bid you farewell, And I spread my wings at last)

⚠ *Liaison* is permitted when syllables are divided over several bars, as often encountered in opera. In addition to the following musical example, Juliette's Waltz from Gounod's ***Roméo et Juliette*** (« je te garde dans mon‿âme ») and Olympia's Aria from Offenbach's ***Les Contes d'Hoffmann*** (« les‿oiseaux dans la charmille ») are other well-known instances.

G. Donizetti: ***La fille du régiment**—Ah ! mes amis quel jour de fête !* (Bayard, De Saint-Georges)

Pour mon â - me Quel __ des - tin ! __
[mõ   na   mə]
(For my soul, what a fate!)

Liaison cannot be made **from** final *-rd*, *-rs*, or *-rt*. Instead, consonant linking is made from the *r*.

E. Chausson: *Le charme* (Silvestre)

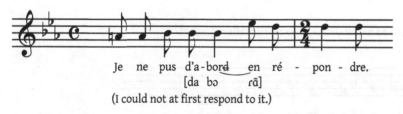

Je ne pus d'a-bord en ré - pon - dre.
[da bɔ   rã]
(I could not at first respond to it.)

C. Saint-Saëns: *La Cloche* (Hugo)

Tu dors en ce mo - ment
[dɔ   rã]
(You sleep at this time)

A. Roussel: ***Quatre poèmes***—*Nuit d'automne* (De Régnier)

⚠ In inversion of verbs ending in *-rd* and *-rt*, *liaison* is made in singing with /t/.

M. Ravel: ***Chansons madécasses***—*Nahandove* (De Parny)

⚠ When word-final *-s* indicates the plural form, *liaison* is made in singing with /z/. Since plural *-rs* occurs frequently, this is an especially important exception.

C. Debussy: ***Fêtes galantes, série I***—*En sourdine* (Verlaine)

C. Gounod: ***Roméo et Juliette***—*Acte III* (Barbier, Carré)

Liaison cannot be made **from** the first part of a compound noun in the plural form.

O. Messiaen: ***Chants de terre et de ciel***—*Arc-en-ciel d'innocence* (Messiaen)

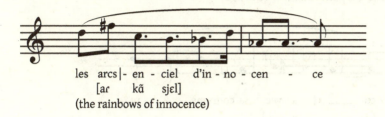

les arcs|- en - ciel d'in - no - cen - ce
[aɾ   kɑ̃   sjɛl]
(the rainbows of innocence)

Liaison cannot be made **from** the word *eux* (they/them).

G. Fauré: *C'est la paix!* (Debladis)

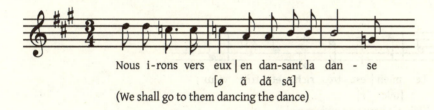

Nous i-rons vers eux | en dan-sant la dan - se
[ø   ɑ̃   dɑ̃ sɑ̃]
(We shall go to them dancing the dance)

Liaison cannot be made **from** pronouns (other than personal pronouns). The most notable are:

> *chacun* (each one)
> *ceux, celles* (those)
> *lequel, laquelle, lesquel(le)s, auxquel(le)s, desquel(les)* (which, to which, of which)
> *quelqu'un* (someone)
> *quelques-un(e)s, quelques autres* (some people)
> *le mien, les mien(ne)s, le tien, les tien(ne)s, le sien, les sien(ne)s, les nôtres, les vôtres, les leurs* (mine, yours, his/hers/one's/its, ours, theirs)
> *l'un, les un(e)s* (the one, the ones)
> *certain, certains* (a certain person, some people)
> *plusieurs* (several of them)
> *d'aucuns* (some)

NOTE: Some of the words on the above list also exist as other parts of speech (adjectives, etc.). It is when they function as pronouns that *liaison* is not made, where they are most often encountered at the beginning of a phonetic group.

E. Chabrier: *Villanelle des petits canards* (Gérard)

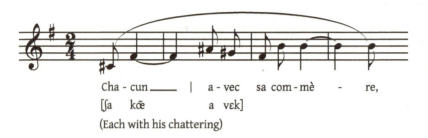

Cha - cun | a - vec sa com - mè - re,
[ʃa kœ̃ a vɛk]
(Each with his chattering)

G. Bizet: **Carmen**—Trio: *Mêlons! coupons!* (Meilhac, Halévy)

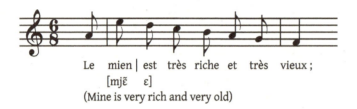

Le mien | est très riche et très vieux;
[mjɛ̃ ɛ]
(Mine is very rich and very old)

There are also many 'one-off' words—often prepositions—from which *liaison* is not made, including *alors* (so/then), *demain* (tomorrow), *enfin* (finally), *loin* (far away), and *sinon* (otherwise). These isolated cases are described in 'The Use of *Liaison* in Common Vocabulary' section at the end of this chapter. The following musical example includes one such word. Note the short rest, which is a signal some composers routinely give in order to reinforce the desire for *liaison* not to be made.

F. Poulenc: **Banalités**—*Fagnes de Wallonie* (Apollinaire)

si - non | u - ne chan - son é - nig - ma - ti - que
[si nɔ̃ y nə]
(other than an enigmatic song)

Spelling and Pronunciation in *Liaison*

The silent consonants that regularly become pronounced in *liaison* are n, r, t, z, d, s, and x.† For the first four consonants, the matter is quite simple. The articulations are: word-final nasalizing -n as /n/, -r as /ɾ/, -t as /t/, and -z as /z/.

The pronunciations of -d, -s, and -x shift in *liaison*:

$$d \rightarrow /t/ \quad s \rightarrow /z/ \quad x \rightarrow /z/$$

F. Poulenc: ***Miroirs brûlants**—Tu vois le feu* (Éluard)

quand il joue, quand il rit
[kã til ʒu kã til ri]
(when he plays, when he laughs)

L. Delibes: *Les filles de Cadix* (De Musset)

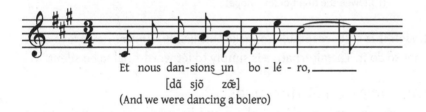

Et nous dan-sions un bo - lé - ro,
[dã sjõ zœ̃]
(And we were dancing a bolero)

R. Hahn: *Si mes vers avaient des ailes* (Hugo)

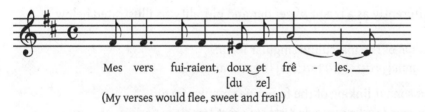

Mes vers fui-raient, doux et frê - les,
[du ze]
(My verses would flee, sweet and frail)

⌛ One other pronunciation shift in *liaison* is the rather rare articulation of word-final -g as /k/. Frequently cited as examples in French pronunciation textbooks of the past are the expressions « *un joug insupportable* » or

---

† In addition to these regular occurrences of *liaison*, there are a few others that crop up: the letter *c* is pronounced as /k/ in *liaison* in a few compound words and expressions, e.g., *franc arbitre* (free will), the letter *g* can be pronounced as /k/ in *liaison* (treated in this section), and the letter *p* is pronounced as /p/ in *liaison* from the words *beaucoup* (much/a lot) and *trop* (too/too much) only.

« un joug odieux » (an unbearable yoke), which notably appear in the Old Testament of the Bible, as well as « un sang impur » (an impure blood), known from the French national anthem, *La Marseillaise*. There is some rare occasion to make this particular *liaison* in the repertoire.

G. Meyerbeer : **Les Huguenots**—Acte IV (Scribe, Deschamps)

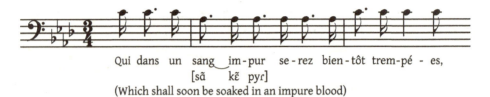

Qui dans un sang im-pur se-rez bien-tôt trem-pé - es,
[sã kɛ̃ pyr]
(Which shall soon be soaked in an impure blood)

Other examples of possible *liaison* from -g are rare, but do exist.

J. Massenet : **Poème du souvenir**—*Un souffle de parfums s'élève* (Silvestre)

Sui-vait le vol_____ d'un long es - poir ;_____
[lõ kɛs pwar]
(Followed the flight of long hope)

Although it is still acceptable to make this *liaison*, singers nowadays often opt not to do it. The alternative is simply to let word-final -g be silent.

Slight Pronunciation Differences

In *style soutenu*, the use of consonant linking and *liaison* sometimes help distinguish very similar phrases. Pronunciation variations, though minute, can provide clarity and context. Consider the adjective *grand* (big/great), which is pronounced slightly differently as a result of gender and plurality, as illustrated below.

Liaison of the masculine singular form:
un grand artiste [grã tartistə] (a great artist)

Consonant linking of the feminine singular form:
une grande artiste [grã dartistə] (a great female artist)

Liaison of the masculine plural form:
de grands artistes [grã zartistə] (great artists)

Liaison of the feminine plural form:
de grandes artistes [grãdə zartistə] (great female artists)

Alteration of Masculine Adjectives Ending in *-er* and *-ier* in *Liaison*

A systematic change in pronunciation occurs in adjectives ending in *-er* /e/ and *-ier* /je/, whereby the vowel opens, and *liaison* is made from *-r*, as /ɛːr/ and /jɛːr/.[†]
The pronunciation of these words in *liaison* is therefore the same as their feminine counterparts—*léger* (light) becomes just like *légère*, *premier* (first) becomes just like *première*.

M. Ravel: ***L'heure espagnole***—*Scène III* (Franc-Nohain)

This change occurs **only** in adjectives in the masculine singular form, which is almost exclusively encountered in the words *léger*, (light), *premier* (first), and *dernier* (last). It is **not** to be applied with *liaison* in any other *-er* or *-ier* endings, including verbs in the infinitive, in which the vowel must remain closed /e/.

H. Duparc: *L'invitation au voyage* (Baudelaire)

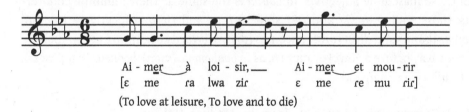

Denasalization of Masculine Adjectives in *Liaison*

A word-final *-n* is always pronounced in *liaison* as /n/ after a nasalized vowel, as demonstrated in the following musical examples.

C. Debussy: ***Trois ballades de François Villon***—*Ballade de Villon à s'amye* (Villon)

---

† Uvular *r* functions the same way as apical *r* in consonant linking and *liaison*.

C. Gounod: **Faust**—*Acte II* (Barbier, Carré)

(More than a faithful friend)

C. Gounod: **Roméo et Juliette**—*Je veux vivre* (Barbier, Carré)

(remain in my soul)

There are, however, a few cases where denasalization occurs in *liaison* with word-final -n. Most masculine adjectives in the singular form that end in /ɛ̃/ and /jɛ̃/ systematically lose their nasality. This is true for the spellings *-ain* and *-ien*, as well as the *-yen* and *-ein* endings—the latter two limited almost exclusively to the words *moyen* (means/middle) and *plein* (full). The adjectives *bon* (good) and *divin* (divine) also lose nasality, and there is a vocalic shift. The pronunciation for all of these masculine adjectives in *liaison* is the same as their feminine counterparts: those ending in /ɛ̃/ and /jɛ̃/ shift to /ɛn/ and /jɛn/ respectively, *bon* [bõ] becomes [bɔn],† and *divin* [divɛ̃] becomes [divin]. (Words beginning in *bon-* behave the same way before a vowel or mute h, as in *bonhomme* (man), *bonheur* (happiness), and *bonifier* (to enhance).)

G. Bizet: **Carmen**—*Près des remparts de Séville* (Meilhac, Halévy)

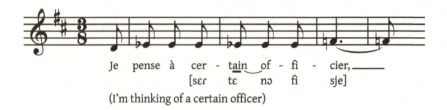

(I'm thinking of a certain officer)

---

† ⧖ At one time, many French singers also denasalized the possessive adjectives *mon* (my), *ton* (your), and *son* (his/her/one's/its) in *liaison*, as in *mon amour* [mɔ namuʁ] (my love). This now sounds quite dated.

F. Poulenc: *Les mamelles de Tirésias*—Acte II (Apollinaire)

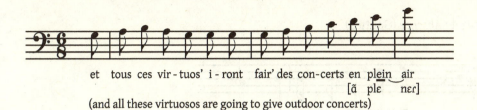

et tous ces vir-tuos' i-ront fair' des con-certs en plein air
[ã plɛ nɛɾ]
(and all these virtuosos are going to give outdoor concerts)

J. Massenet: *Ce que disent les cloches* (De La Vingtrie)

Comme un an-cien a-veu.
[ã sjɛ na vø]
(Like a past confession.)

C. Gounod: *Faust*—Acte III (Barbier, Carré)

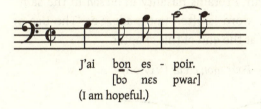

J'ai bon es-poir.
[bɔ nɛs pwaɾ]
(I am hopeful.)

H. Berlioz: *L'enfance du Christ*—Deuxième Partie (Berlioz)

Le di-vin en-fant a-do-rè - rent.
[di vi nã fã]
(They adored the divine infant.)

Nasality is retained in *liaison* in the words *bien* (well/good) and *rien* (nothing), which are encountered frequently (albeit not as adjectives).

G. Bizet : *Absence* (Gautier)

re-viens, ma bien - ai - mé - e ;
  [bjɛ̃   nɛ   me   ə]
(come back, my beloved)

C. Debussy : ***Chansons de Bilitis***—*La Flûte de Pan* (Louÿs)

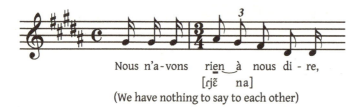

Nous n'a-vons   rien à nous di - re,
           [rjɛ̃   na]
(We have nothing to say to each other)

The word *combien* (how much/how many) retains nasality in *liaison* in the same way as *bien*; however, *liaison* from this word is often not made. See 'The Use of *Liaison* in Common Vocabulary' section at the end of this chapter.

Rhené-Baton : ***Dans un coin de violettes***—*Pour mon cœur* (Vivien)

Sa - che com-bien est   grand   ce bien - fait
       [kɔ̃ bjɛ̃ nɛ]
(Know how great this blessing is)

Masculine adjectives which are subject to denasalization in the singular form are pronounced 'normally' in the plural form: that is, they retain nasality, and *liaison* can be made with /z/.

C. Saint-Saëns : ***Cinq poèmes de Ronsard***—*À Saint-Blaise* (De Ronsard)

Et leur don - ne bons é - poux :
              [bɔ̃   ze pu]
(And give them good spouses)

C. Chaminade: *Colette* (Barbier)

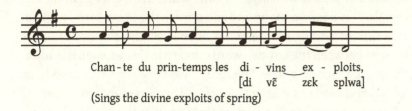

(Sings the divine exploits of spring)

Making Decisions about *Liaison*

The Importance of Syntax

There are several criteria by which an optional *liaison* may be considered. Above all, the grammar and syntax of a phrase must be explored carefully. Words belonging to one phonetic group are most often quite easily linked together. *Liaison* between words belonging to separate phonetic groups, however, can be problematic. In the following musical example, *liaison* would not be a good choice from « nous », because the subsequent verb « est » does not agree. It is in the third-person singular, and corresponds instead to « la jeunesse ».

J. Massenet: *Rien ne passe!* (Monrousseau)

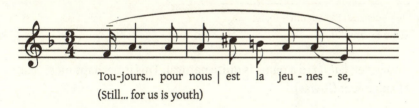

(Still... for us is youth)

A case like the one above leaves little room for debate. Of course, it takes some knowledge of French grammar in order to spot it. Ideally, the singer should be familiar with how to identify inverted syntax like this in order to make good decisions about *liaison*.

Liaison Can Affect Meaning

Another important consideration is whether *liaison* could have an impact on how text is understood by the listener. The singer must bear in mind that the audience often does not have the benefit of seeing the printed text. Could a misunderstanding therefore be created because of an added consonant? For example, *trop‿au lit* (in bed too much) with *liaison* is easily confused with *trop poli* (too polite). Similarly, *liaison* can change the very meaning of a phrase. There are two such examples cited regularly in French pronunciation textbooks. The first is: *un marchand de draps anglais*. The phrase with *liaison* means 'a merchant of English sheets', wherein « *draps‿anglais* » is bound as noun and adjective in the plural form. Without *liaison*, the phrase means 'an English merchant of sheets'. The absence of *liaison* creates some distance between the last two words, and so in this version, the adjective describes the person, not his goods. The second example regularly cited is: *un savant aveugle*. If *liaison* is made as « *savant‿aveugle* », the phrase means 'a learned blind person', wherein « *savant* » is an adjective that modifies the noun « *aveugle* ». On the other hand, since *liaison* is not permitted from a noun in the singular form, the parts of speech are understood to be reversed when *liaison* is omitted. Thus, « *savant* » is heard as the noun, and « *aveugle* » functions as the adjective. In the rendering without *liaison*, the phrase means 'a blind scholar'.

Liaison to Names

Many singers opt not to make *liaison* to proper nouns that begin in vowel sounds. In the following well-known musical example, *liaison* from the verb could suggest the name « *Zescamillo* ».

G. Bizet : **Carmen**—Duo : *Je suis Escamillo* (Meilhac, Halévy)

Je suis —— | Es - ca - mil - lo, ——
(I am Escamillo)

In other cases, however, *liaison* to a name is quite natural. This is perhaps most true from *c'est* (it is) and *c'était* (it was).

G. Fauré : **Cinq mélodies de Venise**—*Mandoline* (Verlaine)

C'est Tir - cis —— et c'est —— A - min - te,
[sɛ   ta mɛ̃   tə]
(There's Tircis and there's Aminte)

Liaison Should Suit the Text and the Speaker

Liaison that introduces a potentially awkward repetition of a consonant sound is often avoided. This is the case in the following musical example, where /z/ is repeated.

H. Duparc: *Chanson triste* (Lahor)

Dans tes yeux|a-lors je boi-rai Tant de bai-sers|et de ten-dres-ses
(From your eyes then shall I drink so many kisses and so much tenderness)

The indications not to make *liaison* in the well-known passage above do not constitute strictly forbidden cases. In fact, it is sometimes heard with one or both of them, such that all syllables of the verses are kept intact, and that the word *baisers* is understood in the plural form. If *liaison* with a repeated consonant sound is to be made, the singer must be careful not to overdo it.

There are several other rather nuanced criteria by which *liaison* may be judged. Consider whether *liaison* suits the sentiment, mood, and tone of the text. In general, optional *liaisons* can readily be made in phrases with exalted, grand, refined language. Versified poetry also tends to accept *liaison* more easily than prose. In a conversational tone, with simpler language of an unsophisticated nature, fewer *liaisons* are typically suggested. Most often, this includes the texts of folksong and *chansons* (popular song). Social status and level of education of the speaker are important considerations when it comes to optional *liaison*. This applies to *mélodie*, but of course, it is in opera where it is most noticeable. The way in which the text is delivered should be in keeping with the character. It is fitting that a *comtesse* should speak with more *liaison* than her *soubrette*; a military *général* might employ more *liaison* than a *brigadier*. In the following musical example, a simple rural household is the setting, where an exasperated provincial girl tries desperately to settle a screaming infant. No *liaison* here from the verb.

F. Poulenc: ***Cinq poèmes de Max Jacob***—Berceuse (Jacob)

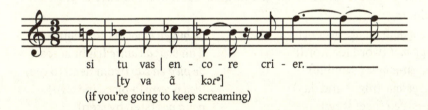

si tu vas | en - co - re cri - er.
[ty va ɑ̃ kɔʁə]
(if you're going to keep screaming)

Liaison Should Suit the Music

It is important to consider carefully the sound of *liaison* in the musical phrase. Does the extra consonant aid or hinder *legato*? Of course, the setting of the vocal line must also be examined. In general, small intervals, with smooth voice leading, and gentle rhythmic motion accept *liaisons* well, while *liaisons* in large leaps, and rhythmically active passages can easily sound cumbersome. Of course, this varies on a case-by-case basis.

72 | FRENCH LYRIC DICTION

Differences of Opinion on *Liaison*

Georges Le Roy (1885–1965), Comédie-Française actor and Conservatoire pedagogue, states:

> Apart from the prescribed rules, and even in their application, *liaison* is a question of euphony and of taste.
>
> LE ROY, *Grammaire de diction*

Indeed, so often a decision about *liaison* comes down to 'what sounds right', and *le bon goût* (good taste), which are admittedly extremely difficult to quantify. In fact, optional *liaison* can be cause for great debate among experts. In the opera world, it is not out of the ordinary for conductors, directors, coaches, language advisors, and repetiteurs to engage in heated discussion in rehearsal with a singer regarding the merits of making or not making a particular *liaison*! Printed resources seem to agree on the subject in broad terms; however, conflicting information abounds regarding which specific words and parts of speech can or cannot accept *liaison*, and under what circumstances.

Skilled interpreters can often make a phrase come across rather well with or without optional *liaisons*. (When there is hesitation about a particular case, singers sometimes make an 'either/or' marking such as ⌴ between the words in the score!) One tip on the matter is that, in general, no *liaison* should ever be oversung. Provided that it is articulated delicately, a subtly made optional *liaison* can, in many instances, win over even the most dubious critic.

Liaison in Exceptional Cases

Exceptions Where *Liaison* May Be Permitted from a Noun in the Singular Form

⚠ *Liaison* is made from a noun in the singular form in some fixed expressions, including:

accent aigu (acute accent)
mot à mot (word for word)
croc-en-jambe (stumble)
nuit et jour (night and day)
pot-au-feu (beef stew)
en temps et lieu (in due course)
de point en point (point by point)
de temps en temps (from time to time)
de temps à autre (from time to time)
de bas en haut (from the bottom up)
de haut en bas (from top to bottom)
de fond en comble (thoroughly)

de but en blanc (point blank)
d'un bout à l'autre (right across)
de pied en cap (from head to toe)
pied à terre (a place in town)
pas à pas (step by step)
vis-à-vis (facing/opposite)
pot au lait (milk jug)
pot aux roses (a dark secret)
pot au noir (the doldrums)
le pont aux ânes (old chestnut)
le tout ensemble (all together)
du tout au tout (completely)

R. Hahn: *Paysage* (Theuriet)

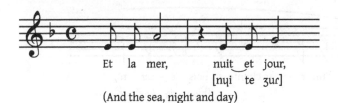

(And the sea, night and day)

⚠   *Liaison* is also occasionally made with /z/ from a small list of nouns in the singular form in order to maintain *legato* where an especially unpleasant hiatus would otherwise occur. They are: *voix*, *bois*, *fois*, and *temps*. Two musical examples of each follow.

Voix (voice)

C. Saint-Saëns: **Samson et Dalila**—*Ce Dieu que votre voix implore* (Lemaire)

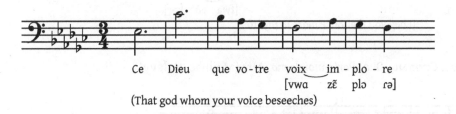

(That god whom your voice beseeches)

J. Massenet: **Manon**—*Obéissons quand leur voix appelle* (Meilhac, Gille)

(Let us obey when their voice calls)

Bois (wood)

J.-B. Lully: **Amadis**—*Bois épais* (Quinault)

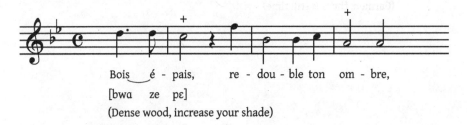

(Dense wood, increase your shade)

G. Fauré: *Nell* (Leconte de Lisle)

Plus __ d'un ra-mier chante au bois é - car - té,
[bwɑ ze kaɾ te]
(More than one dove is singing in the isolated wood)

Fois (time)

D.-F.-E. Auber: ***Le domino noir***—Duo: *Parlez! quel destin est le nôtre?* (Scribe)

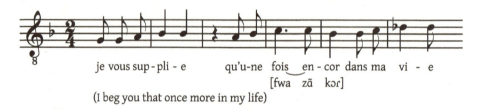

je vous sup - pli - e   qu'u-ne fois en-cor dans ma vi - e
[fwɑ zɑ̃ kɔɾ]
(I beg you that once more in my life)

G. Bizet: ***Carmen***—Duo: *Parle-moi de ma mère* (Meilhac, Halévy)

U - ne fois à Sé - vil - le
[fwɑ zɑ]
(Once in Seville)

Temps (time)

G. Bizet: ***Carmen***—Duo final: *C'est toi! C'est moi!* (Meilhac, Halévy)

Car - men, __ il est temps en - co - re
[tɑ̃ zɑ̃ kɔ ɾə]
(Carmen, there is still time)

J. Massenet: ***Werther**—Ô nature pleine de grâce* (Blau, Milliet, Hartmann)

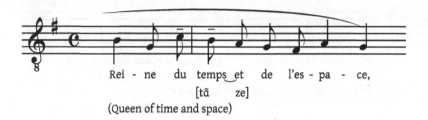

(Queen of time and space)

NOTE: Liaison is not made from the word *temps* when it functions as the subject of the phrase.

C. Debussy: ***Trois chansons de France**—Rondel* (D'Orléans)

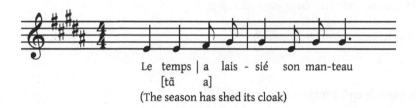

(The season has shed its cloak)

⚠ Two additional nouns that link with /t/ may be added to this list, with caution: *enfant* and *nuit*. It seems that the use of *liaison* from these words is not as prevalent as it once was; nevertheless, it is still possible, especially before an adjective. Four musical examples for each follow.

Enfant (child)

W. A. Mozart: *Dans un bois solitaire* (Houdar de la Motte)

(a child was sleeping there in the shade)

F. Halévy: ***La juive**—Si la rigueur et la vengeance* (Scribe)

(Let us open our arms to the lost child!)

J. Massenet : ***Hérodiade***—*Il est doux, il est bon* (Milliet, Grémont)

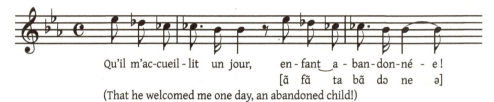

Qu'il m'ac-cueil-lit un jour, en-fant a-ban-don-né - e !
[ã fã ta bã dɔ ne ə]
(That he welcomed me one day, an abandoned child!)

F. Poulenc : ***Chansons gaillardes***—*Sérénade* (anon.)

Et quand cet En-fant est cha-grin,
[sɛ tã fã tɛ]
(And when this Child is saddened)

Nuit (night)

C. W. Gluck : ***Iphigénie en Tauride***—*Acte I* (Guillard)

des-cend dans la nuit in-fer-na - le,
[nɥi tɛ̃ fɛr na lə]
(comes down on that infernal night)

H. Berlioz : ***La damnation de Faust***—*Voici des roses* (Berlioz, De Nerval, Gandonnière)

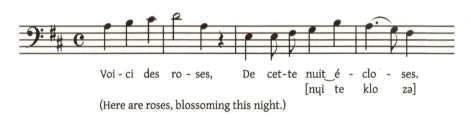

Voi-ci des ro-ses, De cet-te nuit é - clo - ses.
[nɥi te klo zə]
(Here are roses, blossoming this night.)

G. Bizet : ***Les pêcheurs de perles***—*Je crois entendre encore* (Carré, Cormon)

Ô nuit en-chan-te-res - se
[nɥi tã ʃã tə rɛ sə]
(O enchanting night)

G. Fauré : *La chanson du pêcheur* (Gautier)

Sur moi la nuit im - men - se
[nɥi tim mã sə]
(Upon me the immense night)

Obscure *Liaisons*

In some cases, *liaison* that would not typically be heard in speech may be relatively common in a lyric setting. In his treatise on pronunciation, written over a century ago, linguist Philippe Martinon (1859–1917) muses:

> It is also not impossible that poetry should one day become the Conservatory or the Museum of *liaisons*; it would preserve them as it preserves so many other antiquated things.
>
> MARTINON, *Comment on prononce*

Much of the *liaison* 'rule breaking' of the exceptions for nouns can be attributed to the strong tendency in vocal music to avoid hiatus. The propensity to keep words belonging to a phonetic group phonologically intact is another compelling factor. Here, employing *liaison* provides a means to an end. An infinite number of unexpected *liaisons* could therefore theoretically be added to the above list of fixed expressions and special cases. Understanding this concept helps demystify improbable *liaisons* that are from time to time encountered in the repertoire, such as the infamous line « *l'archet aux doigts* » of Mallarmé, which is (or was) regularly interpreted with *liaison* in the Debussy setting.

C. Debussy : *Apparition* (Mallarmé)

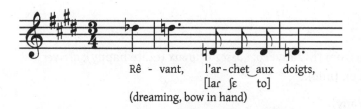

Rê - vant, l'ar - chet aux doigts,
[laʁ ʃɛ to]
(dreaming, bow in hand)

Although « *archet* » is a noun in the singular form, a strong case for *liaison* can be made. 'Bow in hand' in this line constitutes a phonetic group, and functions as an expression similar to the fixed ones already mentioned. There are many recordings of this *mélodie* where the *liaison* in question is made.

The Use of *Liaison* in Common Vocabulary

The following is an alphabetical list of words encountered in the repertoire. For each word, information is provided about how *liaison* is typically handled from a grammatical point of view in vocal music. Examples are provided to lend clarity and context. Articles, nouns in the plural form, verbs, adjectives, and monosyllabic prepositions and adverbs (where *liaison* is normally expected in singing), as well as nouns in the singular form, and the non-personal pronouns cited on page 61 (where *liaison* is forbidden), are not generally included, unless specific mention is of particular benefit. *Liaisons* that should not be made **to** words with initial vowel sounds are also given; if no mention is made, it can be assumed that *liaison* to an initial vowel is acceptable under normal circumstances.

— A —

d'Abord (at first/for a start)
Liaison is forbidden from this word as an adverb or an interjection, as it ends in *-rd*: *d'abord | il ratisse ses étroites allées de sable* (first he rakes his narrow paths of sand).

Ailleurs, d'Ailleurs (elsewhere, by the way)
Liaison is forbidden from these adverbs, as they end in *-rs*: *cherchons ailleurs | une couronne* (let us search for a crown elsewhere); *c'est d'ailleurs | une bonne question* (moreover it's a good question).

Alors (so/then)
Liaison is forbidden from this adverb, as it ends in *-rs*: *que dirai-je alors | au Seigneur ?* (what shall I say then to the Lord?).

Après (after)
Liaison is readily made from this word as a preposition: *après‿un rêve* (after a dream).
Liaison is not usually made from this word as an adverb: *et après | elle est partie* (and after she left).

Assez (enough)
Liaison is readily made from this adverb: *assez‿heureux* (quite happy); *arriver assez‿à temps* (to arrive on time).

Aucun (none/not one/any)
Liaison is readily made from this word as an adjective: *aucun‿homme en ce lieu* (no man in this place).

Auparavant (formerly)
Liaison is forbidden from this adverb: *il était auparavant | heureux* (he was happy before).

LIAISON | 79

Aussitôt (immediately)
Liaison is readily made from this adverb to a past participle, and in the expression
aussitôt après (immediately after): *aussitôt annoncé* (immediately announced).
Liaison from this adverb is otherwise not usually made: *aussitôt | ici*
(immediately here).

Autant (as much as)
Liaison can be made from this adverb to a verb in the infinitive, and to *il(s)/elle(s)*:
autant il aime celui-ci, autant il déteste l'autre (he likes this one as much as he hates
the other one); *sans pour autant aller à ça* (without going as far as that).
Liaison from this adverb is otherwise not usually made: *autant | y aller* (might as
well go there).

les Autres, d'Autres (the others, others)
Liaison is not usually made from these words as indefinite pronouns: *les autres | ont
eu tort* (the others were wrong); *d'autres | ont été belles* (others were beautiful).
NOTE: This guideline is sometimes relaxed in singing; *liaison* is
        occasionally made.

Autrefois (in times past)
Liaison can be made from this adverb to an adjective: *autrefois élégant* (at one time
elegant).
Liaison from this adverb is otherwise not usually made: *autrefois | un roi de Thulé*
(once a king of Thule).
NOTE: This guideline is sometimes relaxed in singing; *liaison* is
        occasionally made.

Avant (before), ***Devant*** (in front of)
Liaison is readily made from these words as prepositions: *avant une heure* (before
1 o'clock); *devant un mur* (in front of a wall).
Liaison is not usually made from these words to *et* or *ou*: *avant | ou après* (before
or after); *devant | et derrière* (in front and behind).
Liaison is not usually made from these words as adverbs: *mais avant | il faut étudier*
(but before that we must study); *devant | est un jardin* (facing is a garden).

— B —

Beaucoup (much/a lot)
Liaison is readily made from this adverb: *beaucoup aimé* (much loved).

80 | French Lyric Diction

Bien (well/good)
Liaison is readily made from this word as an adverb; nasality is retained: *je suis bien heureuse* (I am very happy); *la bien-aimée* (the beloved one).
Liaison is not usually made from this word as a noun and/or to *et* or *ou*: *du bien | en foule* (loads of fun), *tu vas bien | ou non ?* (are you well or not ?); *du bien | et du mal à la fois* (good and bad all at once). See also earlier in this chapter in the section 'Spelling and Pronunciation in *Liaison*'.

Bientôt (soon)
Liaison is not usually made from this adverb, except in the expression *bientôt après* (soon after): *bientôt | elle arrivera* (soon she'll arrive).

Bon (good)
Liaison is readily made from this word as an adjective (but not as a noun); denasalization occurs: *va, mon bon ami* (go, my good friend). See also earlier in this chapter in the section 'Spelling and Pronunciation in *Liaison*'.

$$- C -$$

Cependant (however/yet)
Liaison can be made from this adverb to an adjective or a past participle: *et cependant elle est si calme maintenant* (and yet she/it is so calm now); *cependant effrayé* (frightened however); *cependant acheté* (bought however).
Liaison is not usually made from this adverb when it stands on its own in the phrase: *cependant, | en leur douce ivresse* (however, in their sweet intoxication).

Certes (of course)
Liaison is forbidden from this adverb: *certes | il faut bien dire* (of course it must be said).

Chez (at the home/place of)
Liaison is readily made from this preposition; however, it is not usually made to a proper noun: *chez elle* (at her place); *chez | Alain* (at Alan's place).

Combien (how many/how much)
Liaison is not usually made from this adverb, except to an adjective or to conjugations of the verbs *être* (to be) and *avoir* (to have); nasality is retained: *combien | en a-t-il ?* (how much of it does he have?); *combien est-ce que ça coûte ?* (how much does that cost?); *combien avez-vous ?* (how many do you have?). See also earlier in this chapter in the section 'Spelling and Pronunciation in *Liaison*'.

Comment (how)
Liaison is readily made from this adverb: *comment allez-vous ?* (how are you?); *et comment il se nomme ?* (and what is his name?).

— D —

Debout (standing/upright)
Liaison is forbidden from this adverb: *calme et debout | encore* (calm and still standing).

Dehors (outside)
Liaison is forbidden from this adverb, as it ends in *-rs*: *dehors | il faisait beau* (it was nice out).

Demain (tomorrow)
Liaison is forbidden from this adverb: *dès demain | il faut choisir* (as of tomorrow it must be decided).

Depuis (since)
Liaison is readily made from this word as a preposition: *depuis‿hier* (since yesterday).
Liaison is not usually made from this word as an adverb: *elle l'a depuis | admis* (she has since admitted it).

Désormais (henceforth)
Liaison can be made from this adverb, in particular to an adjective: *désormais‿impossible* (from now on impossible).
Liaison from this adverb is otherwise not usually made: *je ne suis plus désormais | ici que la pauvre petite victime* (from now on I can only be a poor little victim).

Dessous, Dessus (below, above)
Liaison is readily made from these words as prepositions: *dessous‿un prunier blanc* (underneath a white plum tree).
Liaison is not usually made from these words as adverbs: *mais dessous | il cachait autre chose* (but underneath he was hiding something else); *ne vous faites donc plus là-dessus | aucun souci* (so don't you worry about it any more).

Devant *see* **Avant**

Divin (divine)
Liaison is readily made from this adjective; denazalisation occurs: *le divin‿enfant* (the divine enfant). See also earlier in this chapter in the section 'Spelling and Pronunciation in *Liaison*'.

Donc (well/so/then)
This word is always pronounced with /k/ as a conjunction or an adverb before an initial vowel in the following word: *qui donc‿est cette femme ?* (who is this woman then?); *donc‿il faut s'en aller* (so one must go away). See also Chapter 7: 'Words with Variable Pronunciations', which includes scenarios where the final *-c* is silent.

82 | FRENCH LYRIC DICTION

Dont (of which/whom)
Liaison is readily made from this relative pronoun: *dont un amoureux rossignol* (which an amorous nightingale).

Dorénavant (from now on)
Liaison is forbidden from this adverb: *il faut dorénavant | être à l'heure* (one must be on time from now on).

Droit (straight)
Liaison is readily made from this word as an adverb (but not as a noun): *aller droit au cœur* (to go straight to the heart).

— E —

Elles *see* **Ils**

En (in/some/of them)
Liaison is readily made from this word as a preposition, a pronoun, and an adverb, except in an imperative clause in inversion of the verb: *en allant* (in going); *en effet* (in fact); *j'en achète* (I am buying some); *parlons-en | ensemble* (let's talk about it together).
Liaison is readily made to this word in all cases, except from a noun in the singular or plural form: *donnons-en* (let's give some); *servez-vous-en* (use it); *qu'est-ce que les gens | en pensent ?* (what do people think of that?).

Enfin (finally)
Liaison is forbidden from this adverb: *il nous arrache enfin | au trépas* (it snatches us at last from death).

Envers (towards)
Liaison is forbidden from this preposition, as it ends in *-rs*: *envers | et contre tout* (against all odds).

Environ (about)
Liaison is forbidden from this adverb: *environ | un an* (about a year).

Et, Ou (and, or)
Liaison is forbidden from the conjunction *et*: *et | encore elle* (and also her).
Liaison can be made to these conjunctions, and is often heard in singing: *masques et bergamasques* (masks and Bergamo masks); *et les narcisses et les roses* (the daffodils and the roses); *femme aux bras doux et frais* (woman with sweet fresh arms); *garçons ou filles* (boys or girls); *œuvres charmantes ou belles* (charming or beautiful works).
Liaison is often avoided to these conjunctions after inversion of the verb: *aimons-nous | et dormons* (let us love and sleep); *suivez-nous | ou non* (follow us or not).

Liaison is also often avoided to these conjunctions when several things are described or listed, and when clauses have different subjects (particularly where a break between phonetic groups occurs): *guerrier fameux* | *et fort bon gentilhomme* (famous warrior and very fine gentleman); *le temps des lilas* | *et le temps des roses* (the time for lilacs and the time for roses); *tu m'appelais* | *et j'ai quitté la terre* (you called to me and I left the earth); *ne me touchez pas,* | *ou je me jette à l'eau* (don't touch me, or I'll throw myself into the water); *l'effort de deux hommes* | *ou trois* (the efforts of two or three men).

Eux (they/them)
Liaison is forbidden from this personal pronoun: *eux* | *aussi* (them too).
Liaison can be made to this personal pronoun: *ce sont‿eux!* (it's them!); *en passant devant‿eux* (in passing before them). See also **Vers**.

Exprès (intentionally)
Liaison is forbidden from this adverb: *elle s'est exprès* | *adressée à lui* (she intentionally spoke to him).

— F —

Fort (strong/strongly/very)
Liaison can be made from this word as an adverb to an adjective or an adverb, and in expressions: *fort‿aimable* (very friendly); *fort‿aimablement* (very pleasantly); *je serais fort‿aise de partir avec vous* (I'd be most happy to leave with you).
Liaison is not usually made from this word as an adjective: *un fort* | *excès de vitesse* (a large excess of speed).

— H —

Hélas (alas)
Liaison can be made to this word, which begins with mute *h*, especially when it functions as an adverb in the phrase, and/or when it follows the word *mais*: *mais‿hélas! les plus longs amours sont courts!* (but alas! even the longest of loves is short!); *mais‿hélas près de la fontaine* (but unfortunately by the fountain).
Liaison is not usually made to this word as an interjection: *je dis,* | *hélas!* *que je réponds de moi* (I say, alas! that I have only myself to depend on); *chacun,* | *hélas! porte ici-bas* (each one, alas! carries here below). See also Chapter 3: 'Mute *h* and Aspirated *h*'.
NOTE: This word is always pronounced with final /s/.

Hors, Hormis (out of/apart from, except for)
Liaison is forbidden from these prepositions: *hors* | *un seul* (apart from one alone); *adieu à tous, hormis* | *à vous* (farewell to all, except to you).

84 | FRENCH LYRIC DICTION

Liaison is never made to these prepositions, as they begin in aspirated *h*:
en bondissant | hors du toril! (leaping out of the bullpen!); *mais | hormis cela*
(but apart from that).

— I —

Ils, Elles (they/them)
Liaison is readily made from these words in simple cases of personal pronoun to
verb: *ils_ont* (they have); *elles_aiment* (they like).
Liaison can be made from these personal pronouns in inversion of the verb to
the words *y* or *en* only: *peuvent-ils_y aller?* (can they go there?); *doivent-elles_en
parler?* (should they talk about it?); *ont-elles | un chat?* (do they have a cat?); *sont-
ils | intelligents?* (are they intelligent?); *vont-elles | écouter?* (will they listen?).
NOTE: This guideline is sometimes relaxed in singing; *liaison* is occasionally
        made from these personal pronouns to past participles and verbs in
        the infinitive: *où sont-elles_allées?* (where did they go?); *vont-ils_aimer?*
        (will they love?); *pouvaient-elles_entendre?* (were they able to hear?).
Liaison from the word *elles* is otherwise not usually made: *elles | à Paris?* (them
in Paris?); *elles | aussi?* (them also?); *elles | ou vous?* (them, or you?); *une lettre à
elles | adressée* (a letter addressed to them).
Liaison is readily made to these personal pronouns in all cases, except from a
noun in the singular or plural form: *parlent-elles* (do they speak);
autant d'airs | ils ont chantés! (so many arias they have sung!).

— J —

Jadis (in times past)
NOTE: This adverb is always pronounced with final /s/, including before a
        vowel: *un soldat qui jadis a déserté* (a soldier who long ago deserted).

Jamais (never/ever)
Liaison is readily made from this adverb: *il n'est jamais_attendu* (it is never
unexpected); *que votre cœur à jamais_oublie ce rêve* (may your heart forever forget
this dream).

— L —

Les (they/one/of it)
Liaison is readily made from this word in most simple cases of article to noun:
les_oiseaux (the birds).
Liaison can be made from this word as a direct object pronoun in an imperative
clause in inversion of the verb to the word *y* only: *menez-les-y* (lead them there);

donnez-les | *aux enfants* (give them to the children); *comptons-les* | *encore une fois* (let's count them once again); *chantes-les* | *avec énergie* (sing them with energy); *écoutez-les* | *en solitaire* (listen to them alone).

NOTE: This guideline is sometimes relaxed in singing; *liaison* is occasionally made to words other than *y*: *prenez-les̬avec vous* (take them with you).

Loin (far away)

Liaison is forbidden from this adverb: *le jour est loin* | *encore* (the day is still far off).

Longtemps (a long time)

Liaison can be made from this adverb, in particular to an adjective, to another adverb, and to the words *à* or *en*: *longtemps̬amoureux de lui* (in love with him for a long time); *longtemps̬encore* (still a long time); *si longtemps̬à chercher ma ceinture perdue* (such a long time looking for my lost belt); *longtemps̬en France* (a long time in France).

— M —

Maintenant (now)

Liaison can be made from this adverb, in particular to an adjective or a past participle: *je suis maintenant̬heureux de vous dire* (I am now pleased to tell you). *Liaison* from this adverb is otherwise not usually made, in particular when it stands on its own: *et maintenant* | *à l'autre* (and now to the other one).

Mais (but)

Liaison is readily made from this conjunction, often over a comma: *mais̬ici* (but here); *mais̬à travers la foule* (but through the crowd); *mais̬il me plaît* (but he pleases me); *mais̬ hélas!* (but, alas!).

— N —

Néanmoins (nevertheless)

Liaison can be made from this adverb, in particular to an adjective or a past participle: *néanmoins̬utile* (useful nevertheless); *néanmoins̬ignoré* (nevertheless unknown).

Liaison from this adverb is otherwise not usually made, in particular when it stands on its own in the phrase: *néanmoins* | *on est d'accord* (nevertheless we are in agreement).

86 | FRENCH LYRIC DICTION

Non (no/not)
Liaison is forbidden from this adverb: *vous, ma Mère, et non | une autre* (you, my Mother, and not another).

NOTE: When it is part of a compound word, or as a hyphenated prefix, *liaison* can be made, and denasalization occurs: *non‿activité* (inactivity).

Nous, Vous (we/(to) us, you/(to) you)
Liaison is readily made from these personal pronouns in most cases, including all forms of inversion of the verb: *nous‿avons* (we have); *vous‿êtes* (you are); *allez-vous‿en* (go away); *préparez-vous‿y* (get ready for it); *hâtons-nous‿à l'ouvrage!* (let us hasten to work!); *révélez-Vous‿à moi* (reveal Yourself to me); *d'où vous êtes-vous‿enfuie?* (where did you flee to?); *avez-vous‿oublié le soleil?* (have you forgotten the sun?); *pouvons-nous‿arrêter?* (may we stop?); *comment chantez-vous‿ainsi?* (how do you sing like that?).

Liaison is not usually made from these personal pronouns when they are emphasized and/or stand alone in the phrase: *nous | et vous* (us and you); *vous | ici?* (you here?); *nous | au tombeau* (we to the tomb); *lui et vous | attaqués!* (him and you attacked!).

NOTE: This guideline is sometimes relaxed in singing; *liaison* is occasionally made.

— O —

On (one)
Liaison is readily made from this word in most simple cases of personal pronoun to verb: *on‿est venu* (one came).

Liaison can be made from this personal pronoun in inversion of the verb to the words *y* or *en* only: *peut-on‿y aller?* (can we go there?); *doit-on‿en parler?* (should we talk about it?); *qu'a-t-on | apporté* (what did one bring?); *a-t-on | un livre?* (does one have a book?); *est-on | heureux?* (are you happy?); *veut-on | écouter?* (do you want to listen?).

NOTE: This guideline is sometimes relaxed in singing; *liaison* is occasionally made.

Liaison is readily made to this word, except from a noun in the singular or plural form: *peut-on voir ce miracle?* (can one see this miracle?); *que de batailles | on a gagnés!* (how many battles have been won!).

Ou   see **Et**

Où (where)
Liaison can be made to this adverb: *mais‿où donc est-elle?* (but where is she then?); *je vais‿où m'appelle l'amour de ma belle* (I go where the love of my sweetheart calls).

Liaison is sometimes avoided when this adverb stands at the beginning of a phonetic group (often dependant on the interpretation of the phrase): *mais je sais | où elle est* (but I know where she/it is).

Oui (and)
Liaison is forbidden to this adverb: *il a dit | oui* (he said yes).

— P —

Parfois (sometimes)
Liaison can be made from this adverb, in particular to an adjective:
parfois‿agréable (sometimes pleasant).
Liaison from this adverb is otherwise not usually made: *parfois | en été* (sometimes in the summer).

Partout (everywhere)
Liaison can be made from this adverb, in particular to an adjective, a past participle, or in an adverbial phrase: *partout‿accueillant* (welcoming everywhere); *partout‿adoré* (loved everywhere); *partout‿ailleurs* (everywhere else).
Liaison is not usually made from this adverb when it stands on its own in the phrase: *partout | on est admiré* (one is admired everywhere).

Pendant (during)
Liaison is readily made from this preposition: *de vous garder au moins pendant‿une heure* (to keep you for at least an hour).

Plus See Chapter 7: 'Words with Variable Pronunciations'.

Plutôt (rather)
Liaison can be made from this adverb to an adjective, a past participle, in an adverbial phrase, and to the words *à* or *en*: *plutôt‿aimable* (rather friendly); *plutôt‿avancé* (rather advanced); *la colère plutôt‿encor que la démence* (anger even more than madness); *plutôt‿à droite* (rather to the right); *ou plutôt‿en même temps* (or rather at the same time).
Liaison from this adverb is otherwise not usually made: *ou plutôt | après l'avoir fait* (or rather after having done it).
NOTE: Although *liaison* is possible from *plutôt* to the word *à*, it is not usually made to *au(x)*, so that the awkward succession of [toto] is avoided: *demandez plutôt | aux étoiles* (sooner ask of the stars).

Pourtant (yet)
Liaison can be made from this adverb, in particular to an adjective: *pourtant‿aimable* (yet likeable).
Liaison from this adverb is otherwise not usually made: *il est pourtant | un crime* (though it is a crime).

88 | FRENCH LYRIC DICTION

Puis (then)
Liaison is readily made from this adverb, even over a comma: *puis il revient* (then it returns); *puis, il s'est enfui* (then, he fled).

— Q —

Quand (when)
Liaison is readily made as /t/ from this word, both as a conjunction and as an adverb: *quand on va* (when one goes); *quand est-ce qu'il arrive ?* (when does he arrive?).

Quant à (as for)
Liaison is always made in this expression (and its other two forms—*quant au*, and *quant aux*): *quant à toi, beau soldat* (as for you, handsome soldier).

Quelquefois (sometimes)
Liaison can be made from this adverb, in particular to an adjective:
quelquefois émouvant (sometimes moving).
Liaison from this adverb is otherwise not usually made: *je l'ai quelquefois | observée* (I sometimes observed her).
NOTE: This guideline is sometimes relaxed in singing; *liaison* is occasionally made.

— R —

Rien (nothing)
Liaison is readily made from this indefinite pronoun; nasality is retained. It is especially common to adverbs, verbs in the infinitive, past participles, and to the words *autre, à, à la/au(x), y,* or *en*: *elles ne font rien ensemble* (they aren't doing anything together); *ne rien entendre* (to hear nothing); *tu n'as rien appris* (you have learned nothing); *il n'y a rien autre à faire* (there is nothing else to do); *nous n'avons rien à nous dire* (we have nothing to say to each other); *je ne pouvais rien y faire* (I couldn't do anything about it); *sans rien en dire* (without saying anything).
Liaison is not usually made from this word as a noun, or to *et* or *ou*: *un rien | effraie l'enfant* (the slightest thing frightens the child); *il n'y a rien | et elle se plaint* (it's nothing and she is complaining). See also earlier in this chapter in the section 'Spelling and Pronunciation in *Liaison*'.

LIAISON | 89

— S —

Salut (hail/greetings)
Liaison can be made from this word as a noun or a verb in the imperative, in particular to the word à: *Salut à la France !* (Hail to France!); *Salut au juge d'Israël !* (Hail to the judge of Israel!).

⧖　　　At one time, *liaison* from *salut* was made much more frequently in singing. This can be heard on many older recordings.

Liaison is not usually made from this word as an interjection: *Salut, | ô gai printemps !* (Greetings, o merry springtime!).

Selon (according to)
Liaison is forbidden from this preposition: *mais selon | un baptême* (but in accordance with a baptism).

Sinon (otherwise)
Liaison is forbidden from this conjunction: *sinon | une chanson énigmatique* (other than an enigmatic song). See also earlier in this chapter in the section '*Liaisons interdites*—Forbidden *Liaisons*'.

Sitôt (as soon as)
Liaison can be made from this adverb, in particular to a past participle: *sitôt achevé* (as soon as it's completed).
Liaison from this adverb is otherwise not usually made: *sitôt | ensemble, ils se parlent* (as soon as they're together, they talk).

Soit   See Chapter 7: 'Words with Variable Pronunciations'.

Soudain (suddenly)
Liaison can be made from this word as an adjective; denasalization occurs: *un accident soudain et inattendu* (a sudden and unexpected accident).
Liaison is forbidden from this word as an adverb: *soudain | en traits de flamme* (suddenly in shafts of flame).

Souvent (often)
Liaison is readily made from this adverb, in particular to an adjective or a past participle: *souvent inexpérimenté* (often inexperienced); *souvent assis* (often seated); *mais souvent on m'accuse* (but often I am accused).

Suivant (following)
Liaison is readily made from this word as a preposition: *suivant un rythme doux* (following a gentle rhythm).

90 | FRENCH LYRIC DICTION

Surtout (especially)
Liaison can be made from this adverb, in particular to an adjective, a past participle, and to the words *à* or *en*: *surtout intéressant* (particularly interesting); *je l'ai surtout appris* (I learned it in particular); *surtout en vue de la fête* (especially in preparation for the party); *surtout à cause de la situation* (largely due to the situation).

— T —

Tant (as much/so much)
Liaison is readily made from this adverb in most cases: *toi que j'ai tant aimé* (you whom I love so much).
Liaison is not usually made from this word as a noun: *il gagne tant | à l'heure* (he earns so much per hour).

Tantôt (shortly/earlier/sometimes)
Liaison is possible from this adverb, in particular to the words *à* or *en*: *tantôt à Paris* (earlier in Paris); *tantôt en France* (earlier in France).
Liaison from this adverb is otherwise not usually made: *tantôt | un monsieur*, *tantôt | une madame* (sometimes a gentleman, sometimes a lady).
NOTE: Although *liaison* is possible from *tantôt* to the word *à*, it is not usually made to *au(x)*, so that the awkward succession of [toto] is avoided: *tantôt | au contraire* (sometimes on the contrary).

Tard (late)
Liaison is forbidden from this adverb, as it ends in *-rd*: *tu viens trop tard | en ce jour de malheur* (you come too late on this unhappy day).

Tôt (early/sooner)
Liaison is not usually made from this word, except in the expression *tôt ou tard* (sooner or later): *l'amant qui te charmera, tôt ou tard te trompera* (the lover who shall charm you will sooner or later deceive you); *il est arrivé tôt | aujourd'hui* (he arrived early today).

Toujours (always/still)
Liaison is made from this adverb when it directly modifies the following adjective, adverb, or past participle, as well as in the expression *toujours est-il que* (the fact remains that): *toujours heureux* (always happy); *toujours ainsi* (always thus), *il a toujours aimé l'opéra* (he has always loved opera).
Liaison from this adverb is otherwise not usually made: *toujours | à l'aube* (still at dawn); *toujours | un grand malheur* (always a great misfortune). See also Chapter 7: 'Words with Variable Pronunciations'.

LIAISON | 91

⧗ At one time, *liaison* from *toujours* was made much more frequently in singing, even when the following word is not directly modified by *toujours*. This can be heard on many older recordings.

Tous   See Chapter 7: 'Words with Variable Pronunciations'.

Tout, Toutes (all/everything)
Liaison is readily made from these words as adjectives, adverbs, or pronouns: *pendant tout_un an* (for an entire year); *j'étais tout_ému* (I was entirely moved); *elles étaient toutes_émues* (they were entirely moved); *entre nous, tout_est fini* (between us, everything is over); *il le fait tout_autrement* (he's doing it completely differently).
Liaison is also made from the word *tout* as a noun in some well-known expressions: *le tout_ensemble* (all together).
Liaison is otherwise not usually made from *tout* as a noun when preceded by the article *le*, or as a direct object (after which a break between phonetic groups is likely):   *le tout | est plus grand que la partie* (the whole is bigger than the part); *il fait tout | au même temps* (he does everything at the same time).

Toutefois (notwithstanding/however)
Liaison can be made from this adverb, in particular to an adjective or a past participle: *toutefois_impossible* (nevertheless impossible); *toutefois_approuvé* (approved however).
Liaison from this adverb is otherwise not usually made, particularly when it stands on its own in the phrase: *toutefois | il est possible* (notwithstanding it is possible).

à Travers (through/across)
Liaison is forbidden from this prepositional phrase, as it ends in *-rs*:   *à travers | un immense espoir* (through an immense hope).

Trop (too/too much)
Liaison is readily made from this adverb, and the vowel normally opens: *chacune ici a déjà trop_à faire* (each woman here already has too much to do); *je tiens trop_à mon nouvel emploi* (my new work means a lot to me); *pour avoir été trop_aimé* (for having loved too much). See Chapter 7: 'Words with Variable Pronunciations'.
Liaison is not usually made from this word as a noun: *il y en a trop | ici* (there are too many here).

92 | French Lyric Diction

— V —

Vers (toward/around)

Liaison is forbidden from this preposition, as it ends in -*rs*: *conduit-moi vers* | *elle* (lead me toward her).

NOTE: *Liaison* is occasionally made from this preposition in the phrase *vers eux* (toward them), but this is fairly rare, and by no means obligatory.

Volontiers (gladly)

Liaison is forbidden from this adverb: *il prendrait volontiers* | *un verre* (he would gladly have a drink).

Vous *see* ***Nous***

6

Mute *e* in French Poetry and Vocal Music

The Role of Mute *e*

Mute *e* is most often realized as a pronounced vowel sound in French vocal music, and factors prominently in the syllabic count of each verse of poetry. It constitutes the vowel sound of nearly a quarter of all syllables in a lyric setting. When French poetry is read aloud or sung in vocal music, one is keenly aware of the prevalence of this sound.

In vocal music, mute *e* helps to sustain the mellifluous succession of vowels from syllable to syllable, between which consonant divisions occur as brief, intervocalic events. This is evident in the following musical example. If the text of this passage were delivered in everyday speech, the mute *e* could be dropped in most or even all cases.

C. Debussy : *Pelléas et Mélisande—Acte II* (Maeterlinck)

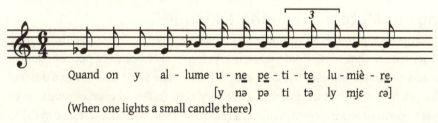

(When one lights a small candle there)

On Poetic Metre and Rhyme

In most languages, the subtle variation in syllabic duration and strength creates an inherent prosodic rhythm. A short, recurring rhythmic pattern of syllabic stress in poetry is called a 'foot'. Analysis of English poetry begins with scansion of the verses, whereby the feet are identified. They are labelled as iambic, trochaic, etc. In poetry in the French language, however, there is an absence of such patterns, because a single primary phrasal stress exists on the final syllable of each phrase. As such, it is often said that the French language is essentially arrhythmic.

With the absence of rhythm, the form of French poetry is governed chiefly by the number of verses in the poem and syllables in each verse, as well as the rhyme scheme. French poets adhere strictly to the all-important syllabic count. For example, no line of French *alexandrin* (alexandrine) is made up of more or fewer than its designated twelve syllables. In fact, intentional misspelling of words—such as *avec* (with) and *encore* (again), as « *avecque* » with mute *e* added, and « *encor* » with mute *e* removed—is accepted poetic licence, helping to satisfy the syllabic count of each verse. Mute *e* is tallied in this count in all positions, except when verse-final, or, in some poetry, at the *césure* (cesura: a break in the verse, often at the halfway point).

The importance of rhyme in French poetry cannot be overstated. The poet Théodore de Banville (1823–1891) famously said of it:

> Rhyme is the only balance in poetry and it is the whole of poetry.
>
> DE BANVILLE, *Petite traité de poésie*

An integral component of French rhyme is the way in which mute *e* is handled. A verse that ends in a word without mute *e* as the last letter is known as *rime masculine*, or 'masculine rhyme', whereas one with a verse-final mute *e* is known as *rime féminine*, or 'feminine rhyme'. Rhyme scheme—*rimes plates* (rhyming couplets: AABB), *rimes croisées* (alternate rhyme: ABAB), *rimes embrassées* (enclosed rhyme: ABBA), etc.—is determined not only by the repetition of vowel and consonant sounds, but also by these patterns of gendered verse endings.

Treatment of Mute *e* in the Score

Settings of Mute *e* in Feminine Rhyme

French composers pay special attention to feminine rhyme. The conventions most often observed are that verse-final mute *e* is set on a weaker beat, as a note of equal or shorter value than the stressed syllable, most often on the same pitch or as a descent from the pitch of the stressed syllable, either by step (often in *appoggiatura*), or by leap. This treatment lends a certain musical release of tension of the stressed syllable.

C. Gounod : **Faust**—*Ah ! je ris de me voir si belle* (Barbier, Carré)

Comme u - ne de-moi-selle, Il me trou-ve-rait bel - le,
(Like a lady, he would find me so beauitful)

G. Fauré: *Dans les ruines d'une abbaye* (Hugo)

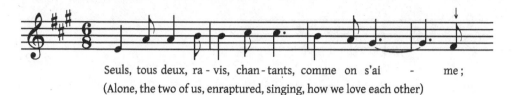

Seuls, tous deux, ra‑vis, chan‑tants, comme on s'ai ‑ me;
(Alone, the two of us, enraptured, singing, how we love each other)

Singing Mute *e* After a Vowel in Feminine Rhyme

Mute *e* is normally elided when it is back-to-back with another vowel. In feminine rhyme consisting of a free syllable, however, verse-final mute *e* is very often set on its own in the score. Stated more plainly: a mute *e* directly following another vowel at the end of a phrase is most often meant to be sung. This is usually clearly indicated in the score, where mute *e* is allocated its own syllable. Verse-final mute *e* can be set after a vowel sound in the combinations /iə/, /eə/, /uə/, /yə/, and occasionally /waə/. A hyphen typically divides the two syllables.

C. Gounod: **Faust**—*Avant de quitter ces lieux* (Barbier, Carré)

je __ con ‑ fi ‑ e.
[ʒə kõ fi   ə]
(I entrust)

C. Saint-Saëns: *Dans les coins bleus* (Sainte-Beuve)

Ô bien ‑ ai ‑ mé ‑ e,
[bjɛ̃ nɛ me ə]
(O beloved one)

C. Gounod: **Roméo et Juliette**—*Ah! lève-toi, soleil!* (Barbier, Carré)

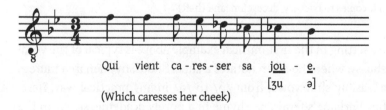

Qui vient ca ‑ res ‑ ser sa jou ‑ e.
                              [ʒu ə]
(Which caresses her cheek)

J. Massenet : ***Cendrillon***—Acte II (Cain)

(The Unknown Woman!...)

G. Fauré : ***La bonne chanson***—*Donc, ce sera par un clair jour d'été* (Verlaine)

(partner in my joy)

Occasionally, mute *e* in feminine rhyme is 'acknowledged' by the composer in the notation, but realistically, cannot be sung. The following well-known musical examples illustrate this scenario.

C. Debussy : ***Mandoline*** (Verlaine)

(And their soft blue shadows)

G. Bizet : ***Carmen***—*Quintette : Nous avons en tête une affaire* (Meilhac, Halévy)

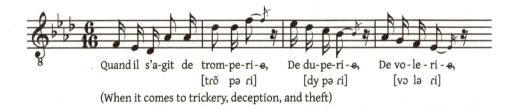

(When it comes to trickery, deception, and theft)

The odd little mute *e* setting in the first musical example above is typical of the vocal writing of early Debussy, where he often notates a superfluous, hyphenated mute *e*. The singer cannot feasibly shift vowel from /ø/ to /ə/ in any practical way. Here, the notation satisfies Verlaine's feminine rhyme in a purely academic sense. In the second musical example, Bizet also recognizes the mute *e* at the end of each word, set in this case with ties to grace notes. At the tempo of this quintet, however, there isn't the time to sing /iə/. These words are never interpreted with schwa in performance.

One will have surely noticed the rather creative ways in which mute *e* is notated in these two musical examples. Explanations for these notations and others follow.

The 'Special Slur' in Feminine Rhyme

The notation of a slur from the note assigned the syllable with primary phrasal stress to the last note of the phrase with verse-final mute *e* is widespread in the music of composers such as Massenet, Debussy, Hahn, and Poulenc, among others.[†] This marking—which we shall dub the 'special slur' in feminine rhyme—reflects an idiomatic phrasing-off at the end of a verse.

Very often, the slurred descent is a step.

É. Lalo: ***Le roi d'Ys****—Vainement, ma bien-aimée* (Blau)

Puis-qu'on ne peut flé - chir ces ja - lou - ses gar - dien - nes,
(Since these protective keepers cannot be swayed)

J. Massenet: ***Manon****—Adieu, notre petite table* (Meilhac, Gille)

Oh! oui,_____ c'est lui que j'ai - me!
(Oh! yes, it is he whom I love!)

L. Delibes: ***Lakmé****—Où va la jeune Indoue* (Gondinet, Gille)

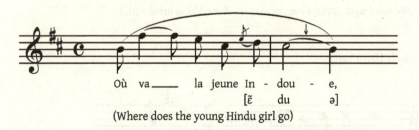

Où va_____ la jeune In - dou - e,
  [ɛ̃   du   ə]
(Where does the young Hindu girl go)

---

† Some composers, including Saint-Saëns, Chausson, and Fauré, do not typically mark this special slur. Nevertheless, the same musical treatment of verse-final mute *e* is evident in their settings.

C. Debussy: *Apparition* (Mallarmé)

Que mê-me sans re-gret et sans dé-boi-re lais - se
(That even without regret or disappointment leaves)

The special slur in feminine rhyme is also found in downward leaps.

C. Gounod: **Faust**—*Faites-lui mes aveux* (Barbier, Carré)

Ré-vé-lez à son â - me   Le se-cret de ma flam - me,
(Reveal to her soul the secret of my ardour)

J. Massenet: **Manon**—*Adieu, notre petite table* (Meilhac, Gille)

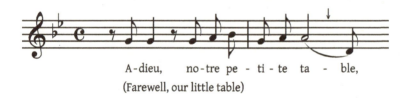
A-dieu,   no-tre pe-ti-te ta - ble,
(Farewell, our little table)

J. Massenet: **Werther**—*Va! laisse couler mes larmes* (Blau, Milliet, Hartmann)

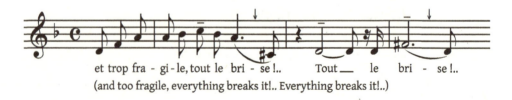
et trop fra-gi-le, tout le bri - se!..   Tout le bri - se!..
(and too fragile, everything breaks it!.. Everything breaks it!..)

R. Hahn: *À Chloris* (De Viau)

Tout ce qu'on dit___ de l'am-broi-si - e
(All that is said about ambrosia)

F. Poulenc: ***Les mamelles de Tirésias***—*Non Monsieur mon mari* (Apollinaire)

(I am a feminist I am a feminist)

The leap downward to mute *e* is sometimes surprisingly large. The following musical examples are a few of the many to be found in the repertoire.

H. Duparc: *L'invitation au voyage* (Baudelaire)

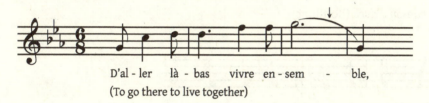
(To go there to live together)

L. Delibes: ***Lakmé***—*Duo: Sous le dôme épais* (Gondinet, Gille)

(I tremble, I tremble with fear!)

J. Massenet: ***Werther***—*Pourquoi me réveiller, ô souffle du printemps?* (Blau, Milliet, Hartmann)

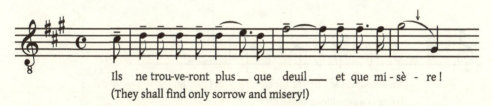
(They shall find only sorrow and misery!)

C. Debussy: ***Chansons de Bilitis***—*La chevelure* (Louÿs)

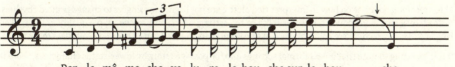
(By the same tresses, mouth upon mouth)

Tied Mute *e*

In the mid-nineteenth century, many composers began to experiment with setting text in a manner that more closely resembles everyday speech. The note of a stressed syllable is quite often tied to a very short note with mute *e*. This has already been seen in the early Debussy and Bizet musical examples on page 96, wherein there should be no attempt to sing the schwa. Notwithstanding, a tied mute *e* is typically sung as a short vowel in most instances. The main note of the stressed syllable is often stretched **ever so slightly**, so that the note with the mute *e* is introduced a **fraction** later than indicated. Singers often release the note with the mute *e* **slightly** early.† This interpretation intensifies the 'strong-weak' feel, whereby the primary phrasal stress gives way to mute *e*.

G. Bizet: *Chanson d'avril* (Bouilhet)

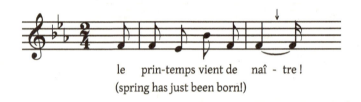

le prin-temps vient de naî - tre !
(spring has just been born!)

The tied mute *e* notation is intended to rid the vocal line of affectation. It allows for a more natural, less pretentious delivery. A prime example of it is to be found throughout the score of **Carmen**. While Bizet treats the text of the rather dignified roles with the conventional setting for verse-final mute *e*, he employs the tied mute *e* method where a more vulgar, rugged character is inferred. This includes the music of the heroine herself.‡

G. Bizet: **Carmen**—*L'amour est un oiseau rebelle* (Meilhac, Halévy)

L'a - mour est un oi - seau re - bel - le
(Love is a rebellious bird)

† These recommendations on how to interpret tied mute *e* are not licence for singers to change printed rhythms. Instead, they aim to introduce subtle flexibility to the setting, which mimics the supple quality of the spoken language. These practices are commonplace in fine French singing, and can be heard on countless recordings.

‡ It is interesting to note that in less formal settings and/or passages sung by lower-status characters, there is often a strong correlation between an increase in the number of dropped mute *e* in the score, and a decrease in the expectation for optional *liaison* to be made.

This particular notation is observed in the music of many composers, in both opera and *mélodie*.

C. Debussy: ***Ariettes oubliées**—Green* (Verlaine)

Tou - te so - nore en - co - re
(Still fully ringing)

R. Hahn: ***Chansons grises**—L'heure exquise* (Verlaine)

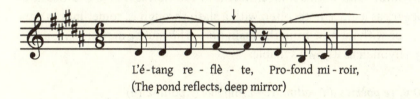

L'é-tang re - flè - te, Pro-fond mi - roir,
(The pond reflects, deep mirror)

Post-Romantic Settings of Mute *e*

By the turn of the twentieth century, some composers push the boundaries even further, often eliminating most or all settings of mute *e* as a syllable carrying any appreciable value. No longer is verse-final mute *e* the only focus of such cuts. Any mute *e* dropped in everyday speech may also be omitted from the musical setting, even though it ought to be counted as a syllable. For composers like Ravel and Poulenc, this practice is often freely carried into the vocal line. Such disregard for the traditions that had for so long defined French lyric writing was initially met with great opposition by critics of a conventional bent. This more 'spoken' approach to text-setting gained acceptance in vocal music over time, and eventually became quite standard. In settings of free verse and prose poetry from the period, it is routine.

In order to convey this speech-like feel in the score, several clever notations are adopted for mute *e*. In the musical examples on the following pages, the resulting final consonant release is marked with the /ə/ symbol.

Ties are used frequently. The syllable with mute *e* is no longer separated by a hyphen, but is printed together with the rest of the word. Often two short note values tied together stand in place of where a single note would suffice. The two tied notes should not be sung as equal values. The vowel of the main syllable should instead account for nearly all of the combined value of the tied notes, with a consonant release timed at the very last moment. This notation is a sort of vestige of the once-sounded mute *e*.

M. Ravel: ***Histoires naturelles***—*Le paon* (Renard)

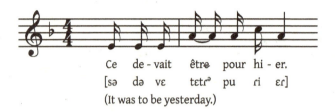

Ce de - vait être pour hi - er.
[sə də vɛ tɛtrᵊ pu ɾi ɛɾ]
(It was to be yesterday.)

Another common notation is for the note with mute *e* to be printed smaller in the score. The rhythmic value of this smaller note is in addition to that of the measure. It usually appears as a grace note, often with a slash through it, sometimes in parentheses, with or without a tie from the main note. The mute *e* may or may not be divided with a hyphen as its own syllable.

F. Poulenc: ***Quatre poèmes d'Apollinaire***—*L'Anguille* (Apollinaire)

sans faire de chi - chi
[sã fɛɾᵊ də ʃi ʃi]
(without making a fuss)

D. Milhaud: ***Les soirées de Pétrograde***—*La Martiale* (Chalupt)

Par les gor - ges sans rou - te.
[rutᵊ]
(By canyons without a road)

L. Delafosse: ***Quintette de fleurs***—*Deux bluets, deux roses, deux lis* (De Montesquiou)

Voi - ci mes fiè - vres. Les blu-ets vont aux fronts pâ - lis.
[fjɛvrᵊ]
(These are my fevers. Cornflowers go to pale foreheads.)

Occasionally, the syllable containing a verse-final mute *e* is printed on its own, but under a rest instead of a note. A tie from the main note is also usually employed in this notation.

R. Hahn: *Sur l'eau* (Sully Prudhomme)

(Or of a rock that sheds a tear every hour)

There are also examples of the text itself being altered. Especially common is the use of an apostrophe in place of a mute *e* spelling.

F. Poulenc: ***La voix humaine*** (Cocteau)

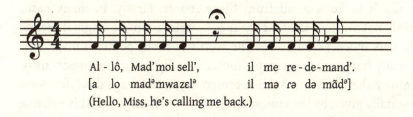

(Hello, Miss, he's calling me back.)

Parentheses are sometimes added around mute *e*, as ' (e) '. In the following musical example, mute *e* is elided, and *liaison* is not made from -s. Instead, consonant linking is made from the *t* which precedes the mute *e* ending in the feminine plural form.

F. Poulenc: ***Cinq poèmes de Paul Éluard*** —*Il la prend dans ses bras* (Éluard)

(Brilliant rays glimpsed for a moment)

Interpreting Mute *e* Tastefully

As presented in this chapter, there are many treatments for the notation of mute *e* in French vocal music. All of these conventions aim to capture the light, unstressed quality of the vowel sound in one way or another. It cannot be overstated that great care must be taken in singing mute *e*, so that those same characteristics are reflected in the interpretation. When the vowel is sung, it should never be accented or drawn out unnaturally.

A Note on Editions

It is recommended that the French edition of any work be consulted whenever possible. (This is likely to come as little surprise.) In most cases, there will be only one French edition of a published work. The most prominent French music publishing houses are longstanding institutions, where it is not uncommon for a family firm to pass the *fonds* of material down through several generations. Over the decades, one firm may sell to another. The acquired plates are very often used by the new owners. Indeed, we encounter even now in the twenty-first century such venerable names as Choudens, Heugel, Enoch, Durand, Salabert, Eschig, Leduc, Lemoine, etc.—either independently operated, or under the umbrella of some parent company. Impressions from the original plates are very often still in use, as digitized files.

There is much to be learned from these scores. Firstly, in many cases (though certainly not always), the text tends to be printed in the original French language only. It is much easier to see the words without poetic translations, which are typically italicized in a myopic font. Secondly, and more importantly, markings relating to key elements such as tempo, style, and stage direction were most often originally given by the composer in the French language. It is a shame that these indications are frequently tampered with in later, foreign renderings. Perhaps the most egregious departure from the intentions of the composer to be found in the non-French vocal edition is the omission of small, yet significant markings in the score. The most blatant of such omissions is the removal of the 'special slur' in feminine rhyme. It has all but disappeared from modern, non-French scores and anthologies. One must draw the conclusion that editors view it to be redundant, (since the marking is not an indication of a complete phrase, or of a slur in a melismatic setting of a single syllable over multiple notes, or of a tie between two notes on the same pitch). Of course, this little symbol—idiomatic for so many composers—captures a nuance in the phrasing of the language that is uniquely French. The indication is all but superfluous, and it is a shame to see it disappear.[†]

---

† It is possible that the removal of the 'special slur' indication in printed scores contributed to the decline in the use of *portamento*—« *port de voix* »—in French vocal music. Although stylistic practice is outside the scope of this book, it is well worth noting that the vocal connections made in the descending interval between the stressed syllable and verse-final mute *e* are a clear and unmistakable feature of great French singing of the past.

Composers maintained close professional relationships with their publishers. The editions of their works as they knew them are still relevant. This is not to say that these original French editions are all free from error—far from it, sometimes! They do, however, impart valuable information, and are well worth the trouble to acquire.

7

Special Pronunciation Considerations

There is no better way to discover the nuances of a sung language than to listen carefully to its leading interpreters of the past and present. In terms of French vocal music, the first three topics described in this chapter are perhaps the most significant of such special considerations. With tasteful application, these techniques can improve textual clarity, and augment a singer's interpretative palette. At the end of the chapter, two other challenging topics are treated: individual words that are pronounced differently depending on context, and guidelines for the pronunciation of French numbers.

L'accent d'insistance—French Emphatic Stress

As described in Chapter 4, individual word stresses (*accents d'intensité*) give way to a single primary phrasal stress (*l'accent tonique*) at the end of the phonetic group (*le groupe phonétique*). Another type of stress is also possible in French, when the speaker wishes to highlight a certain word or words within the phonetic group. It is known as *l'accent d'insistance* or 'emphatic stress'. In the important word, a syllable other than the final one may be accentuated. That is to say, a 'wrong' syllable is intentionally stressed! What would sound like a mispronunciation in another language is instead simply perceived by the French ear as strong emotion. This concept of stress that can shift is quite unique to the French language. It is also a special part of French singing that cannot be practised in any way in English, Italian, or German vocal music.

Theoretically, any syllable of a word apart from one with mute *e* may acquire emphatic stress. In most cases, it falls on the first syllable beginning in a consonant. That is very often the initial syllable of the word (or the only syllable of

French Lyric Diction. Jason Nedecky, Oxford University Press. © Oxford University Press 2023.
DOI: 10.1093/oso/9780197573839.003.0008

a monosyllabic word). The speaker accents that consonant. When a vowel sound begins a word, the stress may be on the second syllable, where the first consonant is to be found. Alternatively, the speaker may place an accent on the initial vowel itself, which may even feature a glottal stop. More than one emphatic stress is entirely possible in a single phonetic group. The voice usually rises suddenly in pitch on the emphasized syllable, causing it to stand out in the sentence:

> *Il est toujours très en retard !* (He is always very late!)
> *Je n'ai carrément aucune idée !* (I have absolutely no idea!)
> *Pas mercredi, mais jeudi !* (Not Wednesday, but Thursday!)
> *C'est épouvantable !* (That's dreadful!)

Using Emphatic Stress in French Vocal Music

Emphatic stress is prepared on the syllable preceding it. The singer often makes a little *crescendo* on that syllable, as a lead-up to the main event. A slight lift from it is also quite common. Then, on the stressed syllable itself, a certain placing of the initial consonant is made, in a very deliberate way. For consonants that can be sustained, more time is allocated to them than what is otherwise normal in French. For plosive consonants, which cannot be sustained, or when the singer wishes to stress an initial vowel sound, a small accent is made after a brief stop of the sound.[†] In other words, the emphatic stress in French singing is realized in much the same manner as a doubled consonant in Italian or German. (It cannot be denied that here, we see a rule broken!) This approach can be heard by fine interpreters of the repertoire. Like spoken French, it may be applied in opera and *mélodie* wherever the text and setting permit, as to the taste of the experienced performer.

Emphatic Stress as a Tool for Expression

It is sometimes said that it is very difficult to make French text understood by the audience. Without a doubt, the arrhythmic nature of the language coupled with the consonant-vowel flow phenomenon can unfortunately lead to a delivery that is bland, monotonous, devoid of relief, practically robotic. When employed tastefully, the emphatic stress provides an attractive solution. A well-informed interpreter of the French repertoire uses emphatic stress not only to improve overall intelligibility of the text, but also to lend to the performance an expressivity that may be multifaceted and highly personalized.

---

† It is even possible to pronounce the consonant of a *liaison*, then to make a lift directly **after** it! A fine example of this phenomenon, which is sometimes referred to as *liaison indirecte* (indirect *liaison*), is in Apollinaire's *Sanglots*, set by Poulenc as the last song of **Banalités**: « *Qui vinrent de très loin et sont un* [sõt | oẽ] *sur nos fronts* » (Who came from very far away and are one under our brows).

Emphatic Stress in the Score

Composers have capitalized on the expressive nature of emphatic stress by 'writing it in' to their music. The contour of the vocal line—especially the use of dotted figures in upbeats—is a clear indication of the composer's intentions.

A. Thomas: **Hamlet**—*Ô vin, dissipe la tristesse* (Barbier, Carré, after Shakespeare)

Et le ri - re mo - queur!
(And the mocking laughter!)

Often, a musical accent of some description is included over the note in question. Massenet's ubiquitous *traits* (*tenuto* markings) are a prime example.

J. Massenet: **Manon**—*Obéissons quand leur voix appelle* (Meilhac, Gille)

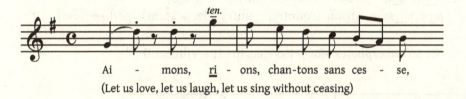

Ai - mons, ri - ons, chan-tons sans ces - se,
(Let us love, let us laugh, let us sing without ceasing)

L'harmonisation vocalique—Vocalic Harmonization

A very controversial topic in French singing is *l'harmonisation vocalique*, or 'vocalic harmonization'. This refers to the modification of the aperture of the unstressed, pretonic vowel sound in order to match that of the following vowel in the stressed syllable. It is extremely common in everyday speech, but becomes increasingly rare the more elevated the tone of the language. In the formal esthetic of most French vocal music, it is traditionally avoided altogether. Since it is, however, considered normal in spoken French, the singer may opt to employ vocalic harmonization with caution in text of a conversational or informal tone—especially in quickly notated passages—and of course, in dialogue.

Harmonization in Polysyllabic Words

By far the most frequent instances of vocalic harmonization occur when unstressed, pretonic /ɛ/ in a free syllable (i.e., one that ends in a vowel) is followed in the stressed syllable by one of the closed vowels /i/, /y/, or especially /e/. It is encountered most often in the spelling *ai*. It is also possible in the spellings *ei* and sometimes *ê*, as well as the spellings *ay* and *ey* when followed directly by another vowel. In these cases, pretonic /ɛ/ closes to align itself with the aperture of the vowel in the next syllable. There are a few words that regularly take vocalic harmonization, even in an elevated tone. The most notable are *aimer* (to like/love)—and in particular, *baiser* (kiss/to kiss)—and their derivatives. In the few cases where the spelling *ay* is divided into two syllables, vocalic harmonization is also very common, notably in the words *abbaye* (abbey), and *pays* (country), and their derivatives.

The following examples demonstrate where vocalic harmonization can be made.

> *abb<u>a</u>ye* (abbey) [abɛi] → [abei]
> *a<u>i</u>gu* (acute) [ɛgy] → [egy]
> *a<u>i</u>mer, a<u>i</u>mez, a<u>i</u>mé(es), bien-a<u>i</u>mé(e)* (to love/like, love/like, loved/liked, beloved) [ɛme] → [eme]
> *ass<u>e</u>yez-vous* (sit down) [asɛje] → [aseje]
> *b<u>a</u>iser, b<u>a</u>isers, b<u>a</u>isez, b<u>a</u>isé(es)* (to kiss, kiss, kisses, kissed) [bɛze] → [beze]
> *b<u>ê</u>tise* (mistake/naughtiness) [bɛtiːzə] → [betiːzə]
> *ess<u>a</u>yer* (to try) [esɛje] → [eseje]
> *l<u>a</u>isser, l<u>a</u>issez, l<u>a</u>issé(es)* (to let, let) [lɛse] → [lese]
> *n<u>e</u>iger, n<u>e</u>igé* (to snow, snowed) [nɛʒe] → [neʒe]
> *p<u>a</u>ys, p<u>a</u>ysage, p<u>a</u>ysan* (country, countryside, peasant) [pɛi] → [pei]

F. Poulenc : ***Métamorphoses**—Reine des mouettes* (De Vilmorin)

Ro - se d'a<u>i</u>-mer   le ba<u>i</u> - ser qui cha-gri - ne
        [de me]   [be ze]
(Blushing from loving the kiss which troubles you)

Harmonizing the Monosyllable

There is a long tradition for the stage whereby the six common monosyllables ending in *-es* are delivered with open /ɛ/, despite the fact that they are pronounced with closed /e/ in the everyday speech of most French speakers. Even pronunciation textbooks not specific to lyric diction regularly acknowledge this, with special mention often given to the topic. Here are two such explanations from Pierre Fouché (1891–1967) and Philippe Martinon (1859–1917):

> In the theatre, the monosyllables *ces, des, les, mes, ses, tes* are pronounced with /ɛ/.
> FOUCHÉ, *Traité de prononciation*

> In truth, many actors, teachers, orators, endeavour still to articulate *lès hommes* […] it is correct at most in singing, which has its own requirements.
> MARTINON, *Comment on prononce*

In French opera and *mélodie*, open /ɛ/ is the norm for the vowel in these monosyllables. It is the notation given throughout this book. The singer must never allow the vowel in these words to become **too** open; (in fact, a narrow transcription could be shown with the notation /ɛ̝/). That being said, some singers opt to make vocalic harmonization in these monosyllables, as well as in the word *est* (is). The closure of the vowel happens in the same way as described above, and is especially heard where the text must be sung at a quick tempo.

F. Poulenc: ***Calligrammes**—Aussi bien que les cigales* (Apollinaire)

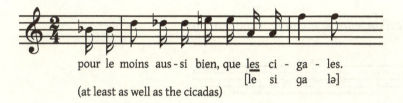

pour le moins aus - si bien, que les ci - ga - les.
                                    [le si   ga   lə]
(at least as well as the cicadas)

It is important to bear in mind that vocalic harmonization is always to be considered with discretion. The shifts in vowel sounds described in this section are by no means obligatory.

La gémination consonantique— Consonant Lengthening

In Italian and German, the lengthening of doubled consonants is an important aspect of lyric diction. In French singing, however, consonant sounds are short, and give way to pure, sustained monophthongs in every syllable. As a rule, one should not linger on French consonants, even if they are doubled in the spelling of a word. The /p/ of *opéra* (opera) and *opposé* (opposed), for example, is articulated in the same manner, despite the difference in spelling.

    La gémination consonantique, or 'consonant lengthening', is very rare in French. Apart from the lengthening which can occur as a function of emphatic stress (as explained above), there are a few important exceptions to the rule.

Lengthening of Doubled Consonants in Prefixes
The most obvious example in which lengthening is permissible is in the spellings *ill-*, *imm-*, *inn-*, and *irr-* at the beginning of words. Here, the singer may phonate longer on these voiced consonants.[†]

[†] Most French pronunciation textbooks cite further possibilities of consonant doubling in careful pronunciation—Bernac mentions it briefly (*Interpretation*, 21)—for example: gra<u>mm</u>aire (grammar), sy<u>ll</u>abe (syllable), and even with plosives, such as a<u>bb</u>aye (abbey), a<u>dd</u>ition, etc. In general, although certainly not out of the question in an elevated tone, this practice isn't actively encouraged in vocal music.

112 | FRENCH LYRIC DICTION

M. Ravel: ***Don Quichotte à Dulcinée***—Chanson à boire (Morand)

(To hell with the bastard, illustrious Lady)

G. Fauré: ***Poème d'un jour***—Rencontre (Grandmougin)

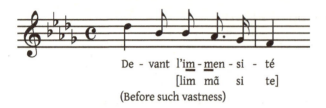

(Before such vastness)

H. Berlioz: ***Les Troyens***—Acte III (Berlioz)

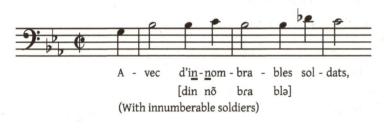

(With innumberable soldiers)

⚠ The word *innocent* and its derivatives are not subject to this special doubling. Articulation with a 'single' /n/ is normal.

F. Poulenc: ***Le travail du peintre***—Jacques Villon (Éluard)

(Irreparable life)

Lengthening (Rolling) the -rr- Spelling

In addition to instances of heightened expressivity, and the *irr-* prefix, another case where *r* may be rolled[†] at the singer's discretion is in the *-rr-* spelling of certain verbs. A rolled *r* helps to differentiate closely related verb tenses in a small number of *-ir* verbs, most notably in *courir* (to run) and *mourir* (to die). This can also occur in careful speech.

il mourait [il muɾɛ] (he was dying)
il mourrait [il murrɛ] (he would die)
vous courez [vu kuɾe] (you run)
vous courrez [vu kurre] (you will run), etc.

E. Chausson : *Les papillons* (Gautier)

et j'y mour - rais.
[mur rɛ]
(and I would die there)

NOTE: Although /r/ indicates a rolled *r*, the transcription /rr/ is customary for the rolled *-rr-* spelling, as in the musical example above.

Lengthening of Consonants That Are Doubled Phrasally

In the relatively rare case where a word ends in a consonant sound that is immediately repeated at the start of the next word, that consonant sound may be lengthened. This helps to ensure that the text is understood. The practice is limited in French singing to consonant phonemes that can be sustained.

M. Ravel : ***Cinq mélodies populaires grecques**—Le réveil de la mariée* (Calvocoressi)

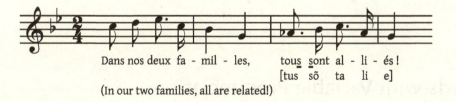

Dans nos deux fa - mil - les, tous sont al - li - és !
                                [tus sɔ̃ ta   li   e]
(In our two families, all are related!)

---

† When uvular *r* is sung, it may also be lengthened in each of the cases described.

The most common example of phrasal lengthening is when the pronoun *il* (he/it) is followed by the direct object *le, la,* or *l'* (him/her/it). Consider the following two musical examples, wherein the second has lengthened /ll/.

L. Cherubini : *Médée*—Acte I (Hoffman)

s'il a pu la quit - ter pour moi,
[si la pu]
(if he could leave her for me)

E. Chausson : *Le colibri* (Leconte de Lisle)

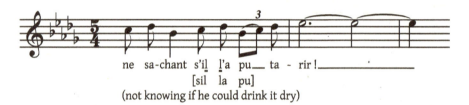

ne sa-chant s'il l'a pu ta - rir!
[sil la pu]
(not knowing if he could drink it dry)

Traditional Lengthening

One final mention must be given to the pronunciation of the male title role in Debussy's opera *Pelléas et Mélisande*. This name has always traditionally been sung as [pɛllea:s] with lengthened /ll/.

C. Debussy : ***Pelléas et Mélisande***—Acte I (Maeterlinck)

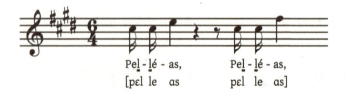

Pel - lé - as,   Pel - lé - as,
[pɛl le as   pɛl le as]

Words with Variable Pronunciations

The pronunciation of many words can vary in French, depending on where they occur in the sentence, and how they are used.[†] The following such

---

† See also Chapter 5: 'The Use of *Liaison* in Common Vocabulary' for further description of many of the words in this section.

SPECIAL PRONUNCIATION CONSIDERATIONS | 115

words bear special mention. Many of them are encountered regularly in the repertoire.

Bœuf(s); Œuf(s) (bull/bulls; egg/eggs) are pronounced [bœf] and [œf] in the singular form, [bø] and [ø] in the plural form.

F. Poulenc: ***Cinq poèmes de Max Jacob***—*Souric et Mouric* (Jacob)

un bœuf pour faire é - ta - lon.
[bœf]
(a bull to use as a stud)

C. Debussy: ***L'enfant prodigue***—*L'année en vain chasse l'année* (Guinand)

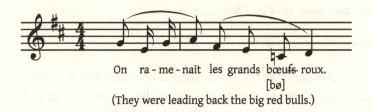

On ra - me - nait les grands bœufs roux.
[bø]
(They were leading back the big red bulls.)

F. Poulenc: ***Le travail du peintre***—*Pablo Picasso* (Éluard)

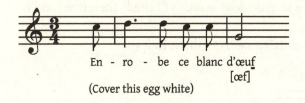

En - ro - be ce blanc d'œuf
[œf]
(Cover this egg white)

M. Ravel: ***L'enfant et les sortilèges***—*Part I* (Colette)

Por - te tous ses œufs au mar - ché !
[ø]
(Carries all her eggs to market!)

Christ is pronounced [krist], but in ***Jésus-Christ*** (Jesus Christ), the pronunciation is [kri].

F. Poulenc : ***Quatre poèmes de Max Jacob***—*Poète et ténor* (Jacob)

le Christ est mon bien
[krist]
(Christ is my beloved)

C. Debussy : *Noël des enfants qui n'ont plus de maisons* (Debussy)

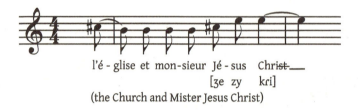

l'é - glise et mon - sieur Jé - sus Christ
[ʒe zy kri]
(the Church and Mister Jesus Christ)

Donc (well/so/then) is a notoriously tricky word when it comes to the pronunciation of the final -*c*. In modern spoken French, it is normally pronounced as /k/. Traditionally, in vocal music, the word is pronounced [dõ] before a consonant, and at the end of a phrase. It is pronounced [dõk] at the beginning of a clause, before an initial vowel, and when particular emphasis is required, for example, in 'proposition/consequence' structures, such as « *je pense, donc je suis !* » ('I think, therefore I am!').

G. Bizet : ***Carmen***—*Duo final : C'est toi ! C'est moi !* (Meilhac, Halévy)

frap - pe moi donc,
[dõ]
(strike me then)

R. Hahn : ***Les feuilles blessées***—*Donc, vous allez fleurir encor* (Moréas)

Donc, vous al - lez fleu - rir en - cor,
[dõk]
(So, you shall blossom again)

Os (bone/bones) is pronounced [ɔs] in the singular form, and [o] in the plural form.

C. Gounod: ***Roméo et Juliette***—*Mab! la reine des mensonges* (Barbier, Carré)

F. Poulenc: ***Poèmes de Ronsard***—*Je n'ai plus que les os* (De Ronsard)

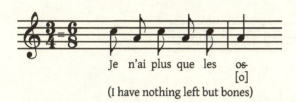

Plus (more/in addition/plus) is normally pronounced [ply]. It is pronounced [plyz] in *liaison* when the word is used as an adverb. It is pronounced [plys] as a noun (especially at the end of the phrase), and when it means 'in addition' or ' + '.

G. Bizet: ***Carmen***—*Duo final: C'est toi! C'est moi!* (Meilhac, Halévy)

C. Debussy: ***Pelléas et Mélisande***—*Acte II* (Maeterlinck)

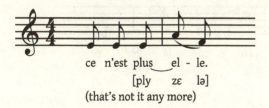

F. Poulenc: *La voix humaine* (Cocteau)

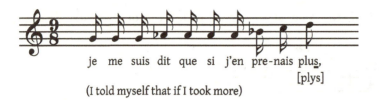

je me suis dit que si j'en pre-nais plus,
                                                  [plys]
(I told myself that if I took more)

Soit (so be it/very well/be) is pronounced [swat] in *liaison* and when the word stands on its own, otherwise it is pronounced [swa].

G. Bizet: *Carmen*—Acte II: Duo (Meilhac, Halévy)

Eh   bien!   soit!   a - dieu!
                      [swat]
(Well then! so be it! Farewell!)

C. Debussy: *Ariettes oubliées*—Green (Verlaine)

Et qu'à vos yeux si beaux___ l'hum-ble pré-sent soit doux.
                                                                 [swa]
(And to your beautiful eyes, may the humble gift seem sweet.)

Toujours (always/still) is normally pronounced [tuʒur]. *Liaison* as [tuʒurz] may be made when it directly modifies the following word.

H. Berlioz: *La damnation de Faust*—Autrefois un roi de Thulé (Berlioz, De Nerval, Gandonnière)

Tou - jours   u - ne   lar - me   lé - gè - re
[tu ʒu   ry   nə]
(Always a slight tear)

F. Poulenc: *Le bestiaire—Le dauphin* (Apollinaire)

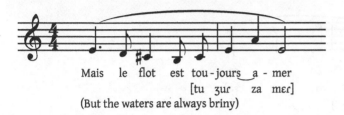

(But the waters are always briny)

Tous (all/everybody) is pronounced [tu] as an adjective, and [tus] as a pronoun. When it occurs as a masculine adjective in the plural form, it can be pronounced [tuz] in *liaison*, as in the expression « *à tous_égards* » (in all respects).

G. Fauré: *Ici-bas* (Sully Prudhomme)

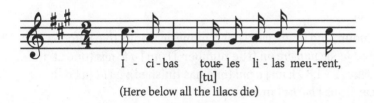

(Here below all the lilacs die)

G. Bizet: *Carmen—Acte III: Final* (Meilhac, Halévy)

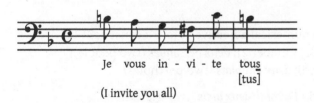

(I invite you all)

Trop (too/too much) is pronounced [tro]. In *liaison*, the vowel often opens slightly, as [trɔp].

C. Debussy: *Pelléas et Mélisande—Acte II* (Maeterlinck)

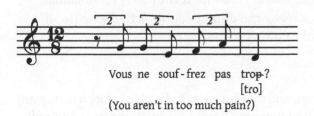

(You aren't in too much pain?)

G. Charpentier: *Louise*—*Depuis le jour* (Charpentier, Saint-Pol-Roux)

Trop heu - reu - se...
[trɔ pœ ʀø zə]
(Too happy...)

Numbers

In French, the pronunciation of final consonants of numbers is quite irregular. A list of some guidelines follows.

1 ○ Un/Une

[œ̃], [ynə] alone, as a noun, and as an article or a numerical adjective before a consonant or aspirated *h*: *le numéro un* (the number 1); *un | à la fois* (one at a time); *un | et un font deux* (1 + 1 = 2); *un | a fini* (one has finished); *un lit* (a bed); *un | haricot* (a/one bean); *une | hache* (an axe).

[œ̃n], [yn] as an article or a numerical adjective in *liaison*: *un‿arbre* (a/one tree); *une‿école* (a/one school).

2 ○ Deux

[dø] alone, as a noun, and as a numerical adjective before a consonant or aspirated *h*: *le numéro deux* (the number 2); *deux personnes* (two people); *deux | ont fini* (two have finished); *deux | hublots* (two portholes).

[døz] as a numerical adjective in *liaison*: *deux‿amis* (two friends).

Optional *liaison* can be made from *deux* in some expressions, such as *deux‿ou trois* (2 or 3); *deux‿à deux* (2 by 2); *de deux‿en deux* (by twos); *de deux‿à trois, de deux‿à quatre*, etc. (from 2 to 3, from 2 to 4, etc.); and in equations: *deux‿et deux font quatre* (2 + 2 = 4).

NOTE: In the Fauré setting of *Au bord de l'eau* with text by Sully Prudhomme, liaison is often made: *s'asseoir tous deux‿au bord du flot qui passe* (to sit together on the bank of a flowing stream).

3 ○ Trois

[tʀwa] or [tʀwɑ] alone, as a noun, and as a numerical adjective before a consonant or aspirated *h*: *le numéro trois* (the number 3); *trois | ont fini* (three have finished); *trois voitures* (three cars); *trois | harpes* (three harps).

[tʀwaz] or [trwɑz] as a numerical adjective in *liaison*:   *trois aigles* (three eagles).

Optional *liaison* can be made from *trois* in some expressions, such as *trois ou quatre* (3 or 4); *trois à trois* (3 by 3); *de trois en trois* (by threes); *de trois à quatre, de trois à cinq*, etc. (from 3 to 4, from 3 to 5, etc.); and in equations: *trois et deux font cinq* (3 + 2 = 5).

5 ○ *Cinq*

[sɛ̃] as a numerical adjective before a consonant or aspirated *h*:   *cinq portes* (five doors); *cinq hameaux* (five hamlets).

[sɛ̃k] in all other cases: *le numéro cinq* (the number 5); *cinq ont fini* (five have finished); *cinq os* (five bones).

6, 10 ○ *Six, Dix*

[sis] and [dis] alone, as nouns, and in 6/8 metre: *le numéro six* (the number 6); *dix ont fini* (ten have finished); *Louis Six* (Louis VI); *six-huit* [sisɥit] (6/8 metre).

[si] and [di] as numerical adjectives before a consonant or aspirated *h*:   *six filles* (six girls); *dix garçons* (ten boys); *six hérissons* (six hedgehogs).

[siz] and [diz] as numerical adjectives in *liaison*, and in the numbers 18 and 19: *six amis* (six friends); *dix hommes* (ten men); *dix-huit* (18); *dix-neuf* [diz nœf] (19).

7 ○ *Sept*

[sɛt] always, without exception: *le numéro sept* (the number 7).

8 ○ *Huit*

[ɥi] as a numerical adjective before a consonant or aspirated *h*:   *huit fenêtres* (eight windows); *huit homards* (eight lobsters); the same is true of *dix-huit* and *vingt-huit*:   *dix-huit chevaux* [dizɥi] (18 horses); *vingt-huit livres* [vɛ̃tɥi] (twenty-eight books).

[ɥit] in all other cases: *le numéro huit* (the number 8); *le numéro dix-huit* (the number 18); *le numéro vingt-huit* (the number 28); *huit ont fini* (eight have finished); *huit ans* (eight years).

Liaison is never made to this number, except in the composite numbers *dix-huit* (18) and *vingt-huit* (28):   *les | huit élèves* (the eight students).

9 ○ *Neuf*

[nœf] nearly always: *neuf anges* (nine angels).

[nœv] before the words *ans* (years), *autres* (others), *heures* (o'clock), *hommes* (men), and for some speakers, *enfants* (children) only.

122 | French Lyric Diction

10 ○ Dix *see Six, Dix*

11 ○ Onze

[õzə] nearly always: *le numéro onze* (the number 11).

Liaison is never made to this number, except in telling time: *il est‿onze heures* (it's 11 o'clock); *il était‿onze heures* (it was 11 o'clock); *les | onze maisons* (the 11 houses).

17 ○ Dix-sept

[dis sɛt] *dix‿sept* and [di sɛt] *dix-sept* are both correct.

18 ○ Dix-huit *see Huit and Six, Dix*

19 ○ Dix-neuf *see Six, Dix*

20–29 ○ Vingt

[vɛ̃] alone, as a noun, and as a numerical adjective before a consonant or aspirated *h*: *le numéro vingt* (the number 20); *vingt fois* (twenty times); *vingt | ont fini* (twenty have finished); *vingt | harpons* (twenty harpoons).

[vɛ̃t] as a numerical adjective in *liaison*, and in the numbers 21 to 29: *vingt‿animaux* (twenty animals); *vingt‿hirondelles* (twenty swallows); *vingt‿et-un* (21); *vingt-deux* (22); *vingt‿trois* (23); etc. (24 . . . 27); *vingt‿huit* (28); *vingt‿neuf* (29).

21 ○ Vingt-et-un *see Vingt and Un*

28 ○ Vingt-huit *see Vingt and Huit*

80 ○ Quatre-vingt(s)

The same rules for *vingt* are followed, except: [katʁəvɛ̃] in *quatre-vingt-un* (81) and *quatre-vingt-onze* (91).

[katʁəvɛ̃z] as an numerical adjective in *liaison*: *quatre-vingts‿autres* (eighty others); *quatre-vingts‿hommes* (eighty men).

100 ○ Cent(s)

[sɑ̃] alone, as a noun, as a numerical adjective before a consonant or aspirated *h*, and in *cent | un* (101), *cent | huit* (108), and *cent | onze* (111) and their derivatives: *le numéro cent* (the number 100); *cent | ont fini* (one hundred have finished); *cent personnes* (one hundred people); *la cent | huitième fois* (the hundred and eighth time).

[sɑ̃t] in *cent* and [sɑ̃z] in *cents* as numerical adjectives in *liaison:* *cent‿ouvriers* (a hundred workers); *trois cents‿ouvriers* (three hundred workers); *cent‿histoires* (a hundred stories); *trois cents‿histories* (three hundred stories).

Pronunciation of Numbers in Dates

The first of the month is the only date to use the ordinal number in French: *premier* (first). It is connected by *liaison* to the months that begin in vowels: *avril, août, octobre* (April, August, October). As a masculine adjective, *liaison* from *premier* is made with an opening of the vowel to /ɛ/, as in *le premier‿octobre* (October 1st)— a date which happens to be in a line sung by the *2ᵉ Commissaire* in Poulenc's **Dialogues des Carmélites**. In an elevated tone, optional *liaison* can be made from the number *deux* (2) as the second day in a month beginning with a vowel, as either *le deux‿avril*, or *le deux | avril* (April 2nd). In the case of all other dates, the official recommendation is always to pronounce numbers as if they were on their own, and without *liaison—le 3* [tʀwɑ], *le 5* [sɛ̃k], *le 6* [sis], *le 8* [ɥit], *le 10* [dis], *le 20* [vɛ̃], etc.; however, all of the possible pronunciation variants for these numbers as outlined above are regularly heard in dates in everyday speech.

PART TWO

French Pronunciation A–Z

Preamble to Part Two

> Official French orthography is needlessly complicated, often ambiguous,
> sometimes deceiving.
>
> GRAMMONT, *Traité pratique*

Linguist Maurice Grammont (1866–1946) is quite direct about the problematic nature of French spelling. Consider the word *oiseaux* (birds). It could be argued that
none of its seven letters yields the expected sound. (Its pronunciation is [wazo],
not [ɔisəayks]!) While this orthographical sleight-of-hand is admittedly a feature
shared with English, to a large extent, it is also true that in German, and certainly
in Italian, this is not the case. In those languages, the relationship of spelling to
pronunciation is much more immediate.

Format of Part Two

The guide that follows is an account of the pronunciation norms for the letter
combinations that spell the regular sounds of the French language in an elevated
tone. Entries are given in alphabetic order by spelling. For groups of letters, al-
phabetization is made by the first letter. Two or more accepted pronunciations
are given where they coexist. For every spelling, word examples in italics are
given, with English translations (unless the word is spelled identically in English,
or altered very slightly by the simple removal of an accent marking over a letter,
particularly in proper nouns). In some cases, the examples provided are of rather
uncommon words. They are included with an aim to represent the difficult
subtleties of the language. (Of course, in many cases, some of this vocabulary
is of a highly specialized nature, and not often encountered in the repertoire.)
Letter combinations in the feminine and plural forms, as well as pronunciations
particular to *liaison*, are indicated where most common, but are by no means
exhaustive. Further explanation is provided when required after each entry as
'NOTE(s)'.

The amendments proposed in the well-known French spelling reform of 1990
are not reflected in this guide. Although many of the revisions in that official doc-
ument simplify pronunciation matters, they are not the spellings to be found in

the scores of French vocal music, which naturally pre-date those updates by some considerable length of time in the overwhelming majority of cases.

For spellings that are regularly borrowed from other languages—particularly English, Italian, and German—standard pronunciation *à la française* is shown at the end of each entry as a special note. If the spelling is not found in French, but occurs frequently in borrowed words, it is allocated its own alphabetized listing. The English *emprunts* (loanword examples) are most often transcribed fully in the guide, while the transcriptions of borrowed proper nouns and Italian musical terms are to be found in Part Three of this book.

The symbol /:/ marks vowel sounds that are always lengthened. When a spelling is found in several contexts in which lengthening may or may not occur, /:/ is not marked, but should be incorporated where appropriate. Vocalic half-lengthening is not shown. In spellings where syneresis and dieresis are both possible, the former is given with /j/, /w/, and /ɥ/; of course, these spellings are often set in the score to their own syllables, instead containing /i/, /u/, and /y/ respectively. These topics are all explained in Chapter 2. Flipped /ɾ/ is shown, but rolled /r/ is of course also possible in certain contexts, as explained in Chapter 3. Likewise, uvular *r* in its several forms often replaces apical *r* in modern singing practice, and always replaces it in speech. The spellings of affricates for borrowed words are given in their 'compressed' notation (i.e., as /ʧ/). When they occur over syllabic barriers, they often separate somewhat (i.e., as /t.ʃ/).

Look up words in groups of letters; for example, the word cited above—*oiseaux* (birds)—consists of seven letters, but would only require three searches in this guide:

oi	→	/wa/
s	→	/z/
eaux	→	/o/

A Comprehensive Pronunciation Guide to French Orthography

— A ∘ [a] —

a, à /a/

in most cases—usually before a consonant (other than a single *m* or *n* unless it is followed by another vowel), or as the last letter of a word:

on a (one has), *à* (to/at), *Abimélech*, *accord* (chord), *adieu* (farewell), *aéroport* (airport), *afin que* (so that), *aguets* (vigilance), *ahuri* (stupefied), *ainsi* (thus), *Ajax*, *Akhtamar*, *alors* (so/then), *amour* (love), *Anacréon*, *anhéler* (to pant), *Aod*, *apaiser* (to calm down),

French Pronunciation A–Z | 129

aquarelles (watercolours), *Aragon*, *asile* (asylum), *atelier* (workshop), *avec* (with), *axe* (axis), *azure* (blue), *balle* (ball), *ça* (that), *Carmen*, *dame* (woman/lady), *Diane*, *dragon*, *égal* (equal), *s'épanouir* (to blossom), *flac!* (splash!), *garçon* (boy), *halte* (break/stop), *Hamelle*, *idéal* (ideal), *jamais* (never/ever), *Jane*, *Kamir*, *la* (the), *là* (there), *malgré* (despite), *manoir* (manor), *Manon*, *Narbonne*, *opaque*, *palme* (palm), *Phanuel*, *piano*, *Qatar*, *Rameau*, *rage*, *Salabert*, *Stéphano*, *tapage* (noisy disturbance), *Valentin*, *Wallonie*, *Xavier*, *yaourt* [ǀjauɾt] (yoghurt), *Zacharie*

/ɑ/
in traditional pronunciation, suitable for vocal music, in the following cases:

when bearing an *accent circonflexe* ˆ (circumflex)—*see â*

before /z/ in the spellings *as* and *az*:
Achaz, *base*, *Basile* (Basil), *braser* (to braze), *brasier* (inferno), *case* (box), *caucasien* (Caucasian), *Damase*, *Depraz*, *Dugazon*, *écraser* (to crush), *emphase* (emphasis), *extase* (ecstasy), *gaze* (gauze), *gazette*, *gazeux* (gaseous/fizzy), *gazier* (gas fitter), *gazon* (grass), *gymnase* (gymnasium), *jaser* (to gossip), *Jason*, *Pégase* (Pegasus), *phase*, *phrase* (phrase/sentence), *raser* (to shave), *topaze* (topaz), *vase*

when part of the word-final spelling -*as* where *s* is silent, and in the spelling -*ass*- in derivatives of those words:
amas (heap), *amasser* (to accumulate), *appas* (charms), *bas* (bottom/low), *basse* (bass), *cas* (case), *compas* (compass), *Degas*, *Ducasble*, *Dumas*, *glas* (tolling bell), *gras/grasse* (fat), *Judas*, *las/lasse* (tired), *lilas* (lilacs), *Lucas*, *Montparnasse*, *Nicolas*, *Parnasse* (Parnassus), *pas* (not/step), *passer* (to pass), *repas* (meal), *tas* (pile), *tasse* (cup), *Thomas*, *trépas* (death), *trépasser* (to pass away), *verglas* (ice)

⚠ /a/ in the word *bras* (arm), in the second-person singular -*as* verb ending, and as the plural form of final -*a*:   *tu as* (you have), *tu chanteras* (you will sing), *tu parlas* (you spoke), *opéras* (operas), *papas* (dads)

before /s/ in word-final -*as*, often in names:
as (ace), *atlas*, *Delmas*, *Dukas*, *hélas* (alas), *Moréas*, *Pelléas*, *Tirésias*

when a word ends in -*able*, -*abre*, or -*avre*:
il accable (he overwhelms), *il cabre* (he rears up), *cadavre* (corpse), *Calabre* (Calabria), *candélabre* (candelabra), *Cantabre*, *il délabre* (he ruins), *diable* (devil), *fable*, *Fabre*, *glabre* (clean-shaven), *havre*

(haven), *Le Havre*, *labre* (lip), *Labre*, *macabre*, *il navre* (he upsets), *sable* (sand), *sabre*, *Le Vélabre*, *zabre* (beetle), and for most speakers, in derivatives of those words: *diablesse* (she-devil), *diabolique* (diabolical), *sabler* (to sandblast)

⚠ /a/ in the words *cinabre* (vermillion), *érable* (maple), *étable* (stable), *palabre* (endless discussion), *stable, table*, and when the -*able* suffix means 'capable/worthy of': *aimable* (likeable), *capable*

when part of the suffixes -*asion*, -*assion*, -*ation*: *narration, occasion* (chance), *passion*

for most speakers in specific words and names:
a (the letter 'a'), *affres* (torments), *ah!, Anne, bah!* (well!), *baron, barre* (bar), *bêta* (idiot), *bramer* (to bell/wail), *cadre* (frame), *Calais, carriole* (cart), *carrosse* (carriage), *casser* (to break), *Chablis, Chabrier, charron* (wheelwright), *clamer* (to state), *classe* (class), *condamner* [kõdane] (to condemn), *crabe* (crab), *damner* [dane] (to damn), *entrelacs* [ãtrəla] (interlacing), *esclave* (slave), *espace* (space), *fa* (the note F), *flamme* (flame), *gagner* (to win/earn), *gare* (station), *gare à toi!/vous!* (watch out!), *gars* [ga] (lad), *Hahn, Jacob, Jacques, jadis* [ʒadis] (in times past), *Jeanne, k* (the letter 'k'), *la* (the note A), *lacs* [la] (snare), *ladre* (miser), *maçon* (mason), *manne* (manna), *marraine* (godmother), *marron* (chestnut), *miracle* (miracle), *oracle* (oracle), *parrain* (godfather), *racle* (scraper), *rafle* (raid), *rare* (rare), and derivatives of those words: *barrer* (to block/cross out), *barrière* (barrier), *classer* (to classify), *déclamer* (to declaim), *déclasser* (to downgrade), *enflammer* (to set on fire), *érafler* (to raid), *racler* (to scrape), *réclame* (advertisement)

NOTES for English loanwords:
Vowel sounds are usually approximated.
/ɛ/ is common in words with the closed *e* diphthong: *baby* [bɛbi], *Blake, Shakespeare*.
/a/ is common in words with /æ/: *mackintosh* [makintɔʃ].
/o/ in words such as *ball, hall* and the spelling *aw*: *basket-ball* [baskɛtboːl], *crawl* [kroːl] (front crawl), *music-hall* [myzikoːl] (music hall), *talkie-walkie* [toki woki] (walkie-talkie), *walkman* [wokman].
/ɔ/ in *yacht* [jɔt].

aa **/aa/**
in ancient and biblical names, where *aa* accounts for two syllables:
Aaron, Baal, Galaad (Galahad), *Phraatès* (Phraates)

FRENCH PRONUNCIATION A–Z | 131

/ɑ/

in a few cases:

Fervaal, *le Graal* (The Holy Grail), *kraal*

NOTES:

When the spelling *aa* is pronounced as a single *a* vowel, there
is a great deal of instability between /ɑ/ and /a/, especially in
monosyllabic names: *Haas, Maar, Maastricht, Staal*.
The language *afrikaans* (Afrikaans) is pronounced [afrikans] or
[afrikɑ̃:s].
Isaac can be pronounced either with a single or a repeated *a* vowel.

â

/ɑ/

nearly always:

âme (soul), *appât* (bait), *Bâle* (Basel), *bât* (packsaddle), *Cléopâtre*
(Cleopatra), *dégât* (damage), *Delâtre, gâteau* (cake), *hâle* (tanned),
idolâtre (idolizing), *lâche* (coward), *mât* (mast), *Neufchâtel, opiniâtre*
(obstinate), *pâle* (pale), *Pâques* (Easter), *pâtes* (pasta), *râpe* (grater),
surpâturage (overgrazing), *tâche* (task), *verdâtre* (greenish)

⚠ /a/ in the *passé simple* verb endings *-âmes* and *-âtes*, and in the
imperfect subjunctive verb ending *-ât*:   *nous coupâmes* (we cut),
vous coupâtes (you cut), *qu'il coupât* (that he cut)

æ

/e/

in words and names of Greek or Latin origin:

ægypan [eʒipɑ̃] (nymph), *Æschylus, cæcum* [sekɔm] (cecum),
et cætera [ɛt seteɾa], *Lætitia*

aë

/aɛ/

in most names:

Ezraël, Gaël, Ismaël, Israël, Jaëll, Jezraël, Laërte, Nathanaël, Raphaël, Vaëz

/ae/

in older spellings of names where *ë* is in a free syllable (i.e., ending
in *ë*, not a consonant), now usually spelled *aé*:

Gaëtan, Phaëton

NOTES:

/ae/ or /aɛ/ in the name *Micaëla*.
/a/ or /ɑ/ in a few names: *Maëstricht, Ruysdaël, De Staël*.
/ɛ/ in a few names: *De Maësen, Scaër*.

132 | FRENCH LYRIC DICTION

-aen, aën /ɑ̃/
in names:
Caen, Messiaen, Saint-Saëns

ah /a/
in most cases:
Abraham, ahuri (stupefied), *Allah, Cahors, dahlia, Déborah, Dinorah,*
fellah, Ispahan (Isfahan), *Lahor, Mahler, Manoah, Nahum, poussah*
(roly-poly), *Sahara, syrah*

/ɑ/
for many speakers in onomatopoeic interjections, and in the
traditional pronunciation of some words and names:
ah!, bah! (well!), *brahmane* (Brahmin), *Hahn, Kahn, ouah!* (wow!),
pouah! (yuck!), *Ptah*

⚠ /ah/ is the usual pronunciation in the name *Nahandove*, from
Ravel's **Chansons madécasses**, with text by Évariste de Parny.

ai, aî, aie /ɛ/
in most cases—usually before a consonant (other than *l*, or a
single *m* or *n* unless it is followed by another vowel):
aide (help), *aigle* (eagle), *ailes* (wings), *j'aime* (I like/love), *air* (air),
Aix, anglaise (English), *bai* (colour: bay), *Baudelaire, chaîne* (chain/
channel), *connaître* (to know), *faible* (weak), *fraîche* (fresh/cool),
gaine (sheath), *haine* (hatred), *Lemaître, maître* (master), *naître*
(to be born), *paiement* (payment), *paître* (to graze), *paraître* (to appear),
je souhaite (I wish), *traître* (traitor), *Verlaine, vraiment* (really)

in most cases at the end of a word or name:
que j'aie (that I have), *baie* (berry), *balai* (broom), *haie* (hedge),
La Monnaie, plaie (wound), *vrai* (true)

⚠ /e/ in first-person singular verb endings, and the words *gai* (gay)
and *quai* (wharf)—*see below for details, under /e/*

before (a) silent letter(s), especially in the spellings *aid, aient, aies,*
ais, ait, aît, aix:
que tu aies (that you have), *ils avaient* (they were having),
Beaumarchais, je chantais (I was singing), *il connaît* (he knows), *délais*
(delays), *faix* (burden), *Françaix, Gervais, laid* (ugly), *lait* (milk), *mai*
(May), *tu paies* (you pay), *paix* (peace), *plaies* (wounds), *portrait*
(portrait), *Taix, il volait* (he was flying/stealing)

Notes for *liaison*:
Where *liaison* is permitted in singing, it is made from these spellings with /t/ and /z/: *l'on m'avait averti* (I was warned), *les étoffes flottaient au vent* (the material floated in the wind), *je te fais un promet* (I'm making you a promise), *que tu aies un cœur sensible* (that you have a sensitive heart).

/e/
in first-person singular verb endings:
j'ai (I have), *j'aurai* (I will have), *je chantai* (I sang)
⚠ /ɛ/ in inversion of the verb in first-person singular:
quand pourrai-je [puʀɛːʒə] (when shall I be able to)

in the words *gai* (gay) and *quai* (wharf), regardless of gender or plurality:
gaie, gais, gaies, quais
Note:
In *gaîté/gaieté* (cheerfulness) and *gaîment/gaiement* (happily), /e/ is more usual, while /ɛ/ is heard in very careful pronunciation only.

in the traditional pronunciation of *je sais* (I know), and for many speakers also in *tu sais* (you know).
Note:
This pronunciation is still very much the norm in French vocal music.

in vocalic harmonization when one of the closed vowels /i/, /y/, and especially /e/ occurs in the next syllable:
aigu (acute), *aimer* (to like/love), *plaisir* (pleasure).
Note:
Vocalic harmonization is often avoided in careful pronunciation, including vocal music.

⚠ /ə/ before a vowel in the *fais-* stem of the verb *faire*, and the word *faisan* (pheasant) and derivatives: *nous faisons* (we are doing), *faisable* (feasible), *faisan* (phesant), *faisandé* (gamey), *faisander* (to hang meat), *faiseur* (maker), *bienfaisant* (beneficial), *malfaisant* (destructive), *satisfaisant* (satisfactory)

Notes for loanwords and foreign names:
/ɛ/ in English vocabulary: *cocktail* [kɔktɛl], *mail* [mɛl] (email).
/aj/ in German vocabulary, approximating the diphthong: *Kaiser* (emperor).

134 | FRENCH LYRIC DICTION

aï	*see* ï
-aid,	*see* **ai**
-aient, -aies	
-ail	/aj/

always:
ail (garlic), *bail* (lease), *corail* (coral), *détail* (detail), *émail* (enamel),
Raspail
NOTE:
/ɑːj/ in the traditional pronunciation of the word *rail* (rail/track).

-aill- /aj/

in most cases, especially in verbs:
Bailleul, Chailley, détailler (to give details), *émailler* (to enamel),
Pailleron, Tailleferre, travailler (to work), *je travaille* (I work),
tu travailles (you work)

/ɑj/

in traditional pronunciation, especially in nouns:
bataille (battle), *broussaille* (undergrowth), *Cornouailles* (Cornwall),
entrailles (innards), *Fontrailles, funérailles* (funeral), *graillon* (burnt
fat), *haillons* (rags), *limaille* (filings), *Maille, mangeaille* (pigswill),
muraille (wall), *De Noailles, ouailles* (flock), *paille* (straw), *quincaillerie*
(hardware store), *rocaille* (loose stones), *taille* (carving/shaving),
tenaille (pliers), *trouvaille* (discovery), *Versailles, victuailles*
[viktɥɑːjə] (provisions), *volaille* (poultry), *Xaintrailles*

⚠ /aj/ in several words: *caillot* (clot), *faille* (rift), *maillet* (mallet),
maillot (undershirt), *médaille* (medal), *taille* (waist size/height),
vaillant (courageous)

in the traditional pronunciation of a few verbs, especially when
there is a corresponding noun ending in *-aille*:
batailler (to battle), *brailler* (to yell out), *cailler* (to curdle),
chamailler (to squabble), *cisailler* (to shear), *criailler* (to shriek),
débrailler (to dishevel), *écailler* (to peel/chip), *écrivailler*
(to scribble), *ferrailler* (to clash), *mitrailler* (to pelt/bombard),
piailler (to chirp), *railler* (to deprecate), *rimailler* (to versify),
tailler (to carve/cut)

FRENCH PRONUNCIATION A–Z | 135

NOTES:

/ɑj/ in the traditional pronunciation of the spelling -âill-, found only in *bâiller* (to yawn) and derivatives: *bâillement* (yawn), *bâillonner* (to gag/silence), *entrebâillé* (half-open).

For all of the words above with the spellings -*ail* and -*aill*-, /aj/ with 'bright' *a* is more modern, and is generally the norm; 'dark' /ɑ/ is also suitable for vocal music.

aim, ain /ɛ̃/

at the end of a word, or before a consonant, which may be either silent or pronounced:

Alain (Alan), *bain* (bath), *crainte* (fear), *daim* (buck), *essaim* (swarm), *faim* (hunger), *Franc-Nohain*, *grain*, *humain* (human), *incertain* (uncertain), *Jourdain*, *lointain* (distant), *maintenant* (now), *nain* (dwarf), *onzain* (eleven-verse strophe), *pain* (bread), *quatrain*, *Romains* (Romans), *saint* (saint), *train*, *Urbain*, *Vulcain* (Vulcan), *Yvain* (Ywain), *zain*

NOTE:

The *aim* and *ain* spellings are not nasalized before a vowel.—*see* **ai**

NOTES for *liaison*:

⚠ Denasalization occurs in *liaison* as /ɛn/ from masculine adjectives in the singular form ending in the spelling -*ain*: *d'un certain âge* (of a certain age), *un vain espoir* (a vain hope), *vilain enfant* (naughty child).

-ais, *see* **ai**
-ait, aît,
-aix

am /ɑ̃/

before a different consonant, which may be either silent or pronounced:

Ambroise (Ambrose), *amphithéâtre* (amphitheatre), *ample*, *bambin* (toddler), *champ* (field), *Delambre*, *Étampes*, *framboise* (raspberry), *Guincamp*, *hampe* (shaft), *ïambe* (iamb), *jambe* (leg), *Lampsaque*, *Mozambique*, *noctambule* (night owl), *pamplemousse* (grapefruit), *Quincampoix*, *ramper* (to crawl), *Samson*, *tampon* (stamp), *vampire*, *Zambie* (Zambia)

NOTE:

The *am* spelling is not nasalized before a vowel.—*see* **a**

/am/

at the end of a few common borrowed words:
macadam (tarmac), *quidam* (any person), *tram* (streetcar)

⚠ /ã/ in the name *Adam*

NOTES:
The word *dam* is pronounced [dã] in the expression *au grand dam de* . . . (to the great displeasure of . . .), and [dam] as the interjection *dam !* (damnation!)

NOTES for nasalization of loanwords and foreign names:
/ã/ in some cases: *camping* [kãpiŋ], *Hambourg*, *shampooing* [ʃãpwɛ̃] (shampoo), *Samson*.
/am/ in other cases, especially at the end of a name: *Abraham*, *Amsterdam*, *Hamlet*, *Ozanam*, *Priam*, *Ramsès*.

amm

/am/

in most cases:
ammoniaque (ammonia), *calligramme* (calligram), *gamme* (musical scale/range), *gramme* (gram), *Grammont*, *Jammes*, *mammifère* (mammal), *programme*, *savamment* (learnedly), *télégramme* (telegram), *vaillamment* (valiantly)

an

/ã/

at the end of a word, or before a different consonant, which may be either silent or pronounced:
an (year), *anglais* (English), *bande* (strip/band), *charmant* (charming), *danser* (to dance), *élan* (momentum), *fantôme* (ghost), *grand* (big/tall), *hanches* (hips), *Ispahan* (Isfahan), *janvier* (January), *kangourou* (kangaroo), *lancer* (to throw), *manteau* (coat), *Nantes*, *océan* (ocean), *pantalon* (trousers), *quand* (when), *rang* (row), *santé* (health), *Talleyrand*, *Urgande*, *volcan* (volcano), *La Wantzenau*, *Xanthe* (Xanthus), *yatagan* (yataghan), *Zanzibar*

in borrowed words, usually from languages other than English, Italian, or German, including ancient and biblical names:
Florestan, *Jonathan*, *Nathan*, *ottoman*, *Pakistan*, *ramadan*, *sultan*, *Tristan*

NOTE:
The *an* spelling is not nasalized before a vowel or mute *h*.—*see a*

Notes for nasalization of loanwords and foreign names:
This spelling is highly unstable.

/ã/ in some cases, especially in names with adopted French spellings: *Bradamante, cantabile, dandy* [dãdi], *Dante, Michel-Ange* (Michelangelo), *Nilakantha, Sancho Pança, sandwich* [sãdwiʃ] or [sãdwiʃ], *Schola Cantorum, Transylvanie* (Transylvania), *yankee* [jãki].

/an/ in other cases, especially in German names: *Atlanta, barman* [baɾman] (bartender), *Dowland, fan* [fan], *Franz, Nahandove, Quantz*

/ã/ and /an/ are often both correct: *Antonia, Chianti, Manzanilla, Mercadante.*

⚠ Occasionally, the nasal vowel plus the nasal consonant is heard as /ãn/: *andante* [ã(n)dã(n)te].

ann   /an/
in most cases:
anneau (ring), *anniversaire* (birthday/anniversary), *Ayio Costanndino, banni* (exiled), *Cannes, Hoffmann, Nanny, en panne* (broken down), *Schumann, suranné* (outdated), *De Tavannes, Vanni-Marcoux, Zimmermann*

-ans   /ã/
in most cases:
céans (in this place), *Conflans, dans* (in), *Le Mans, D'Orléans, sans* (without)

/ã:s/
in a few names:
Exelmans, Huysmans, Lans

ao   /aɔ/
in most cases:
extraordinaire (extraordinary), *Sabaoth*

/ao/
at the end of a word, or before a silent letter:
cacao, chaos (chaos), *Hidraot*

⚠ /o/ in *curaçao* [kyɾaso]

aô   /o:/
in the river *Saône*

138 | FRENCH LYRIC DICTION

-aon	/ã/ in most cases: *faon* (fawn), *paon* (peacock), *taon* (horsefly) NOTE: The word *paon* in *Le jugement de Pâris* scene of Offenbach's **La belle Hélène** is deliberately mispronounced as [paõ] in order to create a rhyme with a comic effect. /aõ/ in most cases in ancient names: *Lycaon, Machaon, Phaon, Pharaon* (Pharaoh), *Saint-Julien-d'Arpaon*
-aonn-	/an/ in words deriving from *-aon*: *faonne* (female fawn), *paonne* (peahen), *paonneau* (peacock chick), *paonner* (to peacock/show off)
aou, aoû, *-aoul*	/u/ in most cases: *Aoustin, août* [u] or [ut] (August), *Le Faou, saoul* (drunk) /au/ in a few cases: *Alaouddin, caoutchouc* (rubber), *Chaource, Naouri, Raoux, yaourt* [jauɾt] (yoghurt) in derivatives of *août* (August): *aoûtat* (harvest mite), *aoûtement* (quick ripening in summer), *aoûter* (to ripen in August), *aoûtien* [ausjɛ̃] (August vacationer)—*see also -t for notes on* **août**.
⚠	/aul/ in the names *Raoul* and *Raoult*
-ap	*see -p*
as, -as, *-ass-*	*see a, -s*
-at	*see -t*

FRENCH PRONUNCIATION A–Z | 139

au /o/

in most cases:

aube (dawn), *Bauges, Caux, dauphin* (dolphin), *Flaubert, gauche* (left), *haut* (top/high), *Jaubert, Lausanne, mauve, naufrage* (shipwreck), *Paulin, rauque* (hoarse), *sauf* (except for), *taupe, Vauban*

⚠ /ɔ/ in *mauvais* (bad) and in *Paul* (but not *Paule* or *Pauline*)

NOTE:
/o/ opens to /ɔ/ for many speakers in an unstressed syllable, particularly at the beginning of a word, and in the prefix *auto-* (auto-/self-): *augmente* (augments), *auguste* (noble), *austère* (severe), *authentique* (authentic), *automate* (automaton), *automatique* (automatic), *auxiliaire* (auxiliary).

NOTES for loanwords and foreign names:
/o/ in many German names: *Austerlitz, Dachau, Faust, Lévi-Strauss.*
/aw/ in a few Italian names, and approximating the diphthong in many German names: *Aurispa, Fischer-Dieskau, Zwickau.*
/o/ and /aw/ are both heard in many German names, and some Italian names: *Claudio, Nicklausse, Stockhausen, Strauss.*

-aud, -ault, /o/
-aulx, -aut, always:
-aux *Archambault, aulx* (garlic), *aux* (at/to the), *Barrault, chaud* (hot), *Delvaux, Dusaulx, faux* (false), *Golaud, haut* (top/high), *héraut* (herald), *joyaux* (gems), *maux* (ills), *Milhaud, sursaut* (burst), *taux* (rate), *Thibault*

NOTES for *liaison*:
Where *liaison* is permitted, it is regularly made in singing from the spelling *-aux* with /z/, and from *-aut* with /t/: *je rêve aux‿amours défunts* (I dream of love lost), *faut‿il qu'en un jour* (must it be that in one day).

-aul- see l

aur /ɔɾ/

in most cases:
aurore (dawn), *dinosaure* (dinosaur), *Fauré, maure* (moor), *taure* (heifer)

ay /ɛ/

at the end of a word, or before a consonant, nearly always in names:
Chardonnay, Maynard, Orsay, Raymond, saynète (sketch/scene), *tokay* (Alsatian Tokay)

/ɛj/

in most cases before another vowel:
ayant/ayez/ayons (having/have), *balayer* (to sweep), *bégayement* (stammer), *crayon* (pencil), *déblayement* (removal), *essayer* (to try), *j'extrayais* (I was extracting), *étayage* (propping up), *frayeur* (fright), *layette* (baby clothes/table leaf), *payer* (to pay), *rayé* (crossed out/striped), *trayeuse* (milkmaid)

NOTES:
/ɛjj/ in verb tenses with the -*ayi*- spelling, distinguishing them from tenses pronounced /ɛj/ with the spelling -*ay*-: *vous balayions* [ba.lɛj.jõ] (you were sweeping), *nous essayions* [e.sɛj.jõ] (we were trying), *que vous payiez* [pɛj.je] (that you pay).
Most of these words have an alternative form with -*aie*- instead of -*aye*-. In these cases, the pronunciation /ɛ/ for the -*aie*- spelling is the norm, without the semiconsonant /j/ or the schwa /ə/: *je balaye* [balɛjə] vs. *je balaie* [balɛ] (I sweep), *on payera* [pɛjɐra] vs. *on paiera* [pɛra] (one will pay); *payement* [pɛjəmã] vs. *paiement* [pɛmã] (payment).

/ej/

in vocalic harmonization: *essayer* (to try), *payer* (to pay)
NOTE:
Vocalic harmonization is often avoided in careful pronunciation, including vocal music.

/ɛi/

in *abbaye* (abbey), *pays* (country), *paysage* (countryside), and *paysan* (peasant)
NOTE:
Vocalic harmonization is prevalent in these words, which are very often pronounced with /ei/, even in careful pronunciation.

/aj/

in some cases before a vowel:
bayadère (Bayadere), *bayer* (to gape at), *fayot* (bean/creep), *Lafayette, Mayas, Mayol, mayonnaise, papayer* (papaya tree)
NOTE:
/ajj/ in tenses of the verb *bayer* (to gape at) with the -*ayi*- spelling, distinguishing them from tenses pronounced /aj/ with the spelling -*ay*-: *nous bayions* [baj.jõ] (we were gaping at), *que vous bayiez* [baj.jez] (that you gape at).

FRENCH PRONUNCIATION A–Z | 141

Notes for loanwords and foreign names:
/ɛ/ is the norm in English vocabulary, encountered mainly in word-final -ay: *Broadway, Greenaway, tramway* [tɾamwɛ] (streetcar line).
/aj/ for borrowed German names, approximating the diphthong: *Haydn*.

-aye, -ayes   /ɛ/
in most names:
Deshayes, De La Fresnaye, La Haye, Hesbaye, Houssaye, De Laboulaye, Lahoussaye, De Lapommeraye, Puisaye, Saint-Germain-en-Laye, Vibraye

/ajə/
in a few cases:
Biscaye (Basque), *cipaye* (sepoy), *cobaye* (guinea pig), *Hendaye*

⚠ /ɛi/ in the word *abbaye* (abbey), subject to vocalic harmonization—*see* **ay** above

-az   *see* **-z**

— B ∘ [be] —

b   /b/
in most cases, including at the end of a word or name:
abeille (bee), *abhorrer* (to abhor), *arbre* (tree), *bain* (bath), *balle* (ball), *De Banville, bas* (bottom/low), *Béatrice, beau* (handsome/nice), *belle* (beautiful), *besoin* (need), *beugler* (to moo/low), *beurre* (butter), *bien* (well/good), *Bizet, blanc* (white), *bon* (good), *botte* (boot), *Boué, bouger* (to move), *brun* (brown), *buisson* (bush), *bulle* (bubble), *Bunsen, club* [klœb], *Debussy, éblouir* (to dazzle), *fable, Gabriel, hublot* (porthole), *Ibrahim, Jacob, Kléber, libre* (free), *Mab, Narbal, obéir* (to obey), *poubelle* (trash can), *Québec, robe* (dress), *sable* (sand), *trembler* (to tremble), *Urbain, vibrer* (to vibrate), *web* [|wɛb] (world-wide-web), *xénophobie* (xenophobia), *Yverdon-les-Bains, Zétulbé*

/p/
before /s/ or /t/:
abcès (abscess), *Absalon, Habsbourg* (Habsburg), *observer* (to observe), *obtenir* (to obtain), *subtil* (subtle)
⚠ /b/ in *subsistance* [sybzistã:sə] (subsistence/keeping), *subsistant* (remaining), *subsister* (to live on)
Note:
/p/ or /b/ in *subside* (grant/allowance) and derivatives: *subsidiaire* (subsidiary).

142 | FRENCH LYRIC DICTION

b

silent as the last letter of a word or name after a nasalizing *m*:
aplomb, *Cristophe Colomb* (Cristopher Columbus), *plomb* (lead metal)

⚠ /b/ in the nautical term *rhumb* [rɔ̃:b] (navigation by compass)

bb

/b/
always:
Les Abbadides (the Abbadids), *Abbas*, *abbaye* (abbey), *abbé* (abbot/
priest), *gibbeux* (hilly/humped), *gibbon*, *Lubbert*, *rabbin* (rabbi)

**-berg,
-bourg**

see **g**

— C o [se] —

c

/k/
'hard' before *a*, *â*, *o*, *ô*, *u*, or a consonant other than *h*:
acoustique (acoustic), *boucle* (buckle), *câble* (cable), *Caen*, *Cain*,
Calais, *calme* (calm), *causer* (to chat), *Claude*, *cœur* (heart), *contre*
(against), *coq* (rooster), *côté* (side), *Cotignac*, *couard* (coward), *cousin*,
Croiza, *cuisine* (kitchen), *Cupidon* (Cupid), *discours* (speech), *écureuil*
(squirrel), *Fourcaud*, *Goncourt*, *Hector*, *icône* (icon), *Jacmart*,
Kinémacolor, *lucratif* (profitable), *microbe*, *nocturne* (nocturnal), *oncle*
(uncle), *Pascal*, *Quincampoix*, *rococo*, *sacré* (sacred), *tact*, *Ucalégon*,
vacarme (din), *Wisconsin*, *xylocope* (carpenter bee), *Yolcos*, *zircon*

in many cases as the last letter of a word, especially in names:
arc (arc/arch/bow), *Balzac*, *Bernac*, *chic* (stylish), *duc* (duke), *Duparc*,
estoc (rapier), *flic* (cop), *grec* (Greek), *hic* (snag), *indic* (informant),
Karnac, *lac* (lake), *Lavignac*, *Marc*, *mec* (guy), *Noriac*, *onc* (never), *parc*
(park), *Polignac*, *Poulenc*, *public*, *roc* (rock), *Signac*, *tic-tac* [tik tak]
(tick-tock), *turc* (Turkish), *ubac* (north-facing), *De Vilbac*

in *liaison* from a few words, compound words, and expressions:
from *franc* (frank), as in *franc‿et quitte* (free and clear) and
franc‿arbitre (free will), from *croc*, as in *croc‿-en-jambe* (stumble)

/s/
'soft' before *e*, *é*, *è*, *ê*, *i*, *œ*, *y*, or *æ*:
ancêtre (ancestor), *ancien* (ancient/former), *Annecy*, *bicyclette*
(bicycle), *cæcum* [sekɔm] (cecum), *ce* (this), *Cécile* (Cecilia), *cèdre*
(cedar), *celle* (this one), *Cendrillon*, *ceux* (those), *cinéma* (movie
theatre), *Cinti-Damoreau*, *cœliaque* (celiac), *cygne* (swan), *Darcieux*,
espèce (species), *face*, *glacé* (icy), *harceler* (to harass), *Ignace*,

FRENCH PRONUNCIATION A–Z | 143

jacinthe (hyacinth), *kilocycle*, *linceul* (shroud), *Mercédès*, *Mycène*
(Mycenae), *noces* (wedding), *océan* (ocean), *Pacifique* (Pacific),
De Quincy, *rincer* (to rinse), *souci* (worry), *triceps*, *vice*, *Wenceslas*,
xanthophycées (yellow-green algae), *Yourcenar*, *zélatrice* (zelatrix)

-c-

sometimes silent as the last letter of a word or name:
accroc (snag/tear), *broc* (pitcher), *caoutchouc* (rubber), *clerc* (clerk),
croc (fang), *Domerc*, *escroc* (swindler), *estomac* (stomach), *franc*
(frank), *Leclerc*, *marc* (coffee grounds), *porc* (pork), *tabac* (tobacco)
NOTES:
In the Kleinzach aria of Offenbach's **Les Contes d'Hoffmann**,
estomac (stomach) and *tabac* (tobacco) are to be mispronounced
intentionally with /k/, creating verses that rhyme in /ak/.
Donc (well/so/then) is pronounced [dõk] or [dõ]. See Chapter 7:
'Words with Variable Pronunciations'.

in the word-final spelling -cs in *lacs* [lɑ] (snare/trap) and
entrelacs [ɑ̃trəlɑ] (interlacing), as well as in words with silent
word-final -c in the plural form:
clercs (clerks), *crocs* (fangs), *porcs* (pork)

⚠ /g/ in the following words:
second (second) and derivatives: *secondaire* (secondary); *eczéma*
(eczema), *zinc* [zɛ̃:g], and for some speakers in *anedcote*

NOTES for Italian loanwords and names:
/tʃ/ before *e* or *i*:   *dolce*, *Pulcinella*.
/tʃ/ or /ttʃ/ in the spelling *ci* before another vowel: *Ritter-Ciampi*.

ç /s/
always in this spelling of « *c cédille* » (c with cedilla):
il acquiesçait (he was acquiescing), *Besançon*, *ça* (that), *déçu*
(disappointed), *français* (French), *François* (Francis), *Lurçat*, *maçon*
(mason), *Néqueçaur*, *Plançon*, *suçoter* (to suck), *nous transperçons*
(we pierce), *tronçon* (section), *Valençay*

-cc- /k/
before *a*, *o*, *u*, or a consonant:
accabler (to overwhelm), *accompagner* (to accompany), *accroc*
(snag/tear), *accuser* (to accuse), *Boccace* (Boccaccio), *Ecclésiaste*
(Ecclesiastes), *Flaccus*, *occasion* (chance), *occlusion* (obstruction),
occuper (to fill/occupy), *Rébecca*, *succomber* (to succumb), *toccata*

144 | FRENCH LYRIC DICTION

/ks/
before *e, é, è, i,* or *y:*
accent, accélérer (to accelerate), *accès* (access), *accident, coccyx*
[kɔksis], *occident* (west), *succès* (success), *vaccin* (vaccine)

NOTES for Italian loanwords and names:
/tʃ/ before *e* or *i:*   *cappuccino, Puccini.*
/tʃj/ for the spelling *cci* before another vowel: *capriccio.*
/k(k)/ consonant lengthening of 'hard' double *-cc-* may or may
not be made in musical terms and names: *staccato.*

-cch-   **/k/**
always, most often in names:
Bacchus, ecchymose (hematoma), *Macchabées* (Maccabees),
saccharine (saccharin)

ch   **/ʃ/**
'soft' in most cases before a vowel:
anche (reed instrument), *Bachelet, bouche* (mouth), *cacher*
(to hide), *Chabrier, chanter* (to sing), *chat* (cat), *chaud* (hot), *chenille*
(caterpillar), *cher* (dear), *chez* (at the home/place of), *chien* (dog),
Chillon, chocolat (chocolate), *Choisnel, chou* (cabbage), *cochon* (pig),
chuinter (to hiss), *chut !* [ʃt] (sh!), *chute* (fall), *douche* (shower),
échelle (ladder), *Fouchécourt, gâchette* (trigger), *Hachette, inachevé*
(uncompleted), *juché* (perched), *Karachi, lâcher* (to let go), *mâchoire*
(jaw), *niche, perchoir* (perch), *quiche, ruche* (hive), *que tu saches* (that
you know), *triche* (cheating), *ulotriche* (frizzy-haired), *vache* (cow)

in many scholarly words, including the suffixes *-archie, -chique,*
-chisme, -chiste, -machie, and the prefix *archi-:*
anarchisme (anarchism), *architecte* (architect), *archives* (archives),
bachique (bacchanalian), *hiérarchie* (hierarchy), *monarchiste*
(monarchist), *tauromachie* (bullfighting)

in ancient names assimilated into French, and at the end of
French names:
Achille (Achilles), *Anchise* (Anchises), *Auch, Delpech, Foch, Marrakech*
(Marrakesh), *Psyché* (Psyche), *Quimerch, Rachel*

/k/
'hard' before another consonant:
Chloé, Chloris, Christ, chtonien (chthonic), *Kœchlin, synchroniser*
(to synchronize), *technique* (technique)

FRENCH PRONUNCIATION A–Z | 145

⚠ /ʃ/ in a few cases before another consonant: *chtarbé* (bonkers), *chva* (schwa)

in many names and scholarly words, often of Latin or Greek origin, including those beginning in *archa-* and *arché-*: *Achab, Achilléide* (the Achilleid), *archaïque* (archaic), *archéologie* (archeology), *Charon, chœur* (choir/chorus), *écho* (echo), *Franchomme, Michel-Ange* (Michelangelo), *orchestre* (orchestra), *orchidée* (orchid), *La Périchole*

at the end of biblical names and several words assimilated into French: *Abimélech, Baruch, cromlech* [krɔmlɛk], *Énoch, krach* [krak] (market crash), *Lamech, loch, Moloch, varech* (kelp)

⚠ silent ch in *almanach* [almana] (almanac)

NOTES:
/ʃ/ in *bronchite* (bronchitis) and derivatives: *bronchitique* (bronchitic).
/k/ in *bronchial* (bronchial) and derivatives, as well as the prefix *broncho-*: *bronchoscopie* (bronchoscopy).
/ʃ/ is the norm, but /k/ is also correct in *pachyderme* (pachyderm).

NOTES for loanwords and foreign names:
/tʃ/ in some English words: *coaching* [kotʃiŋ], *ranch* [rɑ̃:tʃ].
/ʃ/ in other cases: *Chaucer*.
/tʃ/ or /ʃ/ in a few cases, including Spanish and English vocabulary, especially English names beginning in *Ch-*: *challenge* [tʃalɛndʒ] or [ʃalɑ̃:ʒə], *chulos* [ʃylo] or [tʃulɔs], *Churchill, lunch* [lœntʃ] or [lœ̃:ʃ], *sandwich* [sɑ̃dwitʃ] or [sɑ̃dwiʃ]; *punch* (fist: punch) is pronounced [pœntʃ], *punch* (drink: punch) is pronounced [põ:ʃ].
/k/ in Italian vocabulary: *Chianti*.
/k/ in German vocabulary where /x/ is in the original language, and when /x/ or sometimes /ç/ is at the end of a word after a vowel, especially in names: *Bach, Eisenach, Munich, Offenbach, Pachelbel, Zurich*.
/ʃ/ in German vocabulary where /ç/ is in the original language, especially in names: *Altkirch, Liechtenstein, Richter*.

ck, cq, cqu /k/
always, often in names, including at the end of a word after a nasalizing *n*: *Ackermann, Annick, bifteck* (steak), *Clicquot, Darracq, Dufourcq, Franck, Gluck, grecque* (Greek), *hacker* [|akœ:r], *Jacques, jockey* [ʒɔkɛ], *Lecocq,*

146 | FRENCH LYRIC DICTION

> *Maeterlinck, nickel* [nikɛl] (spotless), *Nicklausse, Nuncq, pickpocket*
> [pikpɔkɛt], *rock* [rɔk], *en stock* (in stock), *stockage* (storage), *ticket*
> [tikɛ], *Van Dyck, Weckerlin*

⚠ silent ~~cq~~ at the end of a few names: *Clercq, Leclercq, Le Clercq*

-ct

/kt/
in some cases:
compact (dense/compact), *contact, correct, direct, impact, indirect,*
intact, tact, tract (leaflet)

~~ct~~
in other cases:
amict (amice), *aspect* (appearance), *instinct, respect, succinct* (brief),
suspect

NOTES:
Silent ~~ct~~ is the norm, but /kt/ is also correct in *circonspect*
(discreet), *distinct* (distinct/separate from), and *suspect*.
/kt/ is the norm, but silent ~~ct~~ is also correct in *exact*.
/kt/ is the norm, but /k/ is also correct in *verdict* and *district*.
Silent ~~ct~~ is the norm, but /k/ is possible in careful pronunciation
for *aspect, instict,* and *respect* before a vowel in the next word,
especially in expressions, such as *respect humain* [rɛspɛ kymɛ̃]
(human respect).

-ction

see -tion

-cts

see -ts

cueil,
cueill

/kœj/
always:
accueil (welcome), *Arcueil, cercueil* (coffin), *cueillaison* (harvesting/
picking time), *cueillette* (picking/collecting), *cueillir* (to pluck),
cueilloir [kœjwaːr] (fruit basket), *recueil* (collection/volume)

— D ○ [de] —

d

/d/
in most cases:
Admète (Admetus), *bourdonner* (to buzz), *cadrer* (to frame),
daim (buck), *dans* (in), *Daphné, Debussy, des* (some), *Détroyat,*

FRENCH PRONUNCIATION A–Z | 147 ·

deuil (mourning), *deux* (two), *diable* (devil), *diplôme* (diploma),
docile (compliant), *Don José, douanier* (customs officer),
doux (gentle/soft), *drôle* (funny), *duit* (dyke), *Dunkerque* (Dunkirk),
dur (harsh), *édifice* (building), *Feydeau, gredin* (rascal), *Houdain,*
D'Indy, jadis (in times past), *Kodaly, ludion* (Cartesian diver),
monde (world), *Nadir, odeur* (odour), *pardon, Quasimodo,*
rude (harsh), *soldat* (soldier), *Tauride, Ubalde, verdeur* (greenness),
Widor, xiphoïde (sword-shaped), *Yémaldin, Zaïde*

/t/
in a few cases before an unvoiced consonant:
adscrit [atskɾi] (assigned), *adsorber* [atsɔɾbe] (to adsorb)

-*d*

~~d~~

usually silent as the last letter of a word or name:
allemand (German), *Armand, Arnauld, on s'assied* (one sits), *badaud*
(gawker), *Bertrand, chaud* (hot), *elle coud* (she sews), *crapaud* (toad),
Cuénod, Edmond, froid (cold), *Gounod, grand* (big/tall), *Michaud, il*
moud (he mills), *muid, nid* (nest), *nœud* (knot), *pied* (foot), *quand*
(when), *Reynauld, Rimbaud, rond* (round), *Saint-Cloud, il sied* (it is
seemly), *on vend* (one sells)
NOTE:
Silent final *d* remains silent at the end of the first part of a
compound word before another consonant: *Grandjean, Piedcourt.*

/d/
as the last letter of a few words and especially names:
Alfred, bled (backwater), *Le Cid, David, éphod* (ephod), *Léopold, oued*
(wadi), *plaid* [plɛd], *raid* [ɾɛd], *sud* (south), *week-end* [|wikɛnd], *Yniold*

/t/
in *liaison*

NOTES for *liaison*:
Where *liaison* is permitted in singing, it is made with /t/,
especially from words ending in a nasal vowel plus -*d*: *quand‿on*
veut se faire adorer (when one wants to be adored), *il m'apprend‿à*
jouer (he teaches me to play), *la poule pond‿un œuf* (the chicken lays
an egg), *elle s'assied‿à son rouet* (she sits at her spinning wheel).
Liaison is very rare from verbs ending in -*oud* (i.e., only in a very
elevated tone): *elle coud‿et file* (she sews and spins).

148 | FRENCH LYRIC DICTION

Liaison is essentially forbidden from masculine adjectives ending in a non-nasal vowel plus word-final -d, notably *chaud* (hot), *froid* (cold), and *laid* (ugly), except perhaps if the adjective were to precede the noun it modifies (rare).

NOTES for loanwords and foreign names:
/d/ is the norm, including as the last letter of a word, or the end of a part of a compound word: *feld-maréchal* (field marshal), *feldspath* (feldspar), *lied, Madrid, Siegfried.*
/t/ is common before an unvoiced consonant in a few cases: *Bedford, Hondschoote, Hudson, Mandchourie, vodka* [vɔtka].

dd	/d/ always: *addition, Alaouddin, Bouddha, reddition* (surrender/rendering)
desc-, dess-	*see e*
dg, dj	/dʒ/ in borrowed vocabulary: *budget* [bydʒɛ] (budget), *Cambodge, Djamileh, djinn* [dʒin] (genie)
dh	/d/ always: *Adhémar, adhésif* (adhesive), *Dheune, jodhpurs* [ʒɔdpuːr] or [ʒɔdpyːr], *Prudhomme, Prudhon, rédhibitoire* (crippling), *Stendhal*
dj	*see dg*
-ds	*see -s*

— E ○ [ə] —

e	/ə/ when it is the last letter and only vowel of any syllable, or after silent ꜧ: *achever* (to finish), *Benoît, celui* (that one), *de* (of), *dehors* (outside), *fugue, genou* (knee), *haleter* (to pant), *image, je* (I), *Leconte de Lisle, longue* (long), *mener* (to lead), *ne ... pas* (not), *ordre* (order), *Pacifique* (Pacific), *provenance* (origin), *que* (that/which), *remords* (remorse), *Rodrigue, semaine* (week), *tenir* (to hold), *urne* (urn), *velours* (velvet), *il est venu* (he came), *xylème* (xylem), *yole* (skiff), *zèbre* (zebra)

FRENCH PRONUNCIATION A–Z | 149

as -*es* in the plural form of mute *e*:
amoureuses (in love), *apprises* (learned), *peuples* (peoples),
tables (tables)

as -*es* in the second-person singular verb ending:
tu quittes (you leave), *que tu eusses* (that you had)

as -*es* in *nous sommes* (we are), *vous êtes* (you are), *vous faites*
(you make/do), and in the *passé simple* verb tense:
nous eûmes (we had), *nous marchâmes* (we walked), *vous fûtes*
(you were), *vous chantâtes* (you sang)

NOTES for *liaison*:
Liaison is made in singing with /z/ from -*es* as mute *e* in the plural
form and in verb endings; when mute *e* is set in the score, this
liaison prevents hiatus: *et les belles_écouteuses* (and the beautiful
listeners), *des feuilles_et des branches* (leaves and branches),
tu m'aimes_et tu me suivras (you love me and you'll follow me),
nous sommes_à genoux (we are on our knees), *vous êtes_un*
vrai paladin (you are a true paladin).

as -*es* at the end of many names:
Bruxelles (Brussels), *Charles, Georges* (George), *Gilles, Jules, Londres*
(London), *Nîmes, Versailles*

as -*ent* in the third-person plural verb ending:
ils marchent (they walk), *ils marchèrent* (they walked)

NOTES for *liaison*:
Liaison is made in singing with /t/ from the -*ent* verb ending;
when mute *e* is set in the score, this *liaison* prevents hiatus:
cent hommes marchent_à sa suite (a hundred men walk in his wake).

in *dessous* (below) and *dessus* (above), and in words beginning in *ress-*:
ressentir (to feel), *ressort* (spring), *ressources* (resources)

⚠ /e/ in *ressusciter* (to rise from the dead), *ressayer* (to try again),
ressuyer (to dry out)

⚠ /e/ is is the norm in the traditional spelling of a small group of
words that are 'missing' *accent aigu* ´ (acute accent); many of the
words are now often spelled with *é*. /ə/ is only ever heard in a few
of these words in very careful pronunciation: *assener* (to strike),
besicles (old spectacles), *brechet* (keel), *gelinotte* (grouse), *placebo*,
senestre (sinister), *trompeter* (to trumpet).
In several names: *Breguet, Bremond, Clemenceau, Grevisse, Reber, Siebel*.
In the word *diesel* [djezɛl].

150 | FRENCH LYRIC DICTION

⚠ /ɛ/ is the norm for the first of two consecutive syllables with *e*;
/ə/ is only ever rarely retained in the first syllable for such
words in very careful pronunciation: *breveté* (patented),
genevois (Genevan), *grenelé* (granulated), *seneçon* (ragwort),
and the group of nouns (often specialty trades shops) ending
in *-eterie*: *bonneterie* (hosiery shop), *briqueterie* (brickworks),
buffleterie (leather work), *caqueterie* (clucking), *graineterie*
(seed shop), *marqueterie* (inlay work), *mousqueterie* (musketry),
paneterie (bread bakery), *papeterie* (stationery shop), *parqueterie*
(parquetry), *pelleterie* (furriery)

/ɛ/
before a pronounced consonant in the same syllable:
amen, belle (pretty), *cruel, Daniel, esclave* (slave), *Exbrayat, exemple*
(example), *fervent, Germain, Hector, Isabelle, jersey, kellnerine,
De Lerme, merle* (blackbird), *nerf* (nerve), *ouvert* (open), *Ravel,
spectacle* (show), *taverne* (inn), *univers* (universe), *veste* (jacket),
waters [|watɛːɾ] (toilets), *zeppelin*

⚠ /ə/ is the norm for most speakers, but /ɛ/ is also possible in
the spelling *-ell-* in a few names and words: *Angellier, dentellier*
(lacemaker), *interpeller* (to call out), *Montpellier, prunellier*
(sloe bush)

/e/
before a silent consonant other than *t* or *s*:
je m'assieds (I sit), *elle s'assied* (she sits), *Auger, chanter* (to sing),
clef (key), *Grovlez, Laisnez, vous mangez* (you eat), *pied* (foot),
Saint-Tropez, il sied (it is seemly), *Taittinger*

in words beginning in *eff-, ess-, desc-, dess-*, as well as in a few
words beginning in *ress-*:
effacer (to erase), *essuyer* (to wipe), *dessin* (drawing), *descendre*
(to go down), *ressusciter* (to rise from the dead), *ressayer* (to try
again), *ressuyer* (to dry out); as well as in *ecc-* and *ell-* which are
limited to the words *ecclésiastique* (ecclesiastical), *ellipse*, and
derivatives: *elliptique* (elliptic)
NOTES:
/ɛ/ is maintained in these prefixes only in very careful
pronunciation. The practice of *e* closing to /e/ before a doubled
consonant is often extended further in everyday speech. In a

FRENCH PRONUNCIATION A–Z | 151

polysyllabic word, unstressed *e* may close before double *-ff-*,
-ll-, *-mm-*, *-nn-*, *-tt-*, and especially *-ss-*, particularly in the first
syllable of a word: *beffroi* (belfry), *décennie* (decade), *excellent*,
flemmard (lazybones), *message, nettoyer* (to clean). Normally, this is
not observed in careful pronunciation, except in names.

⚠ /ə/ in *dessus* (above), *dessous* (below), and in some words beginning
in *ress-*: *ressentir* (to feel), *ressort* (spring), *ressources* (resources)

~~e~~

silent at the end of a syllable when back-to-back with another
vowel or mute *h*, either within a word, or phrasally:
votre âme (your soul), *je créerai* [kɾeɾe] (I will create), *dévouement*
(dedication), *douceâtre* (sickly-sweet), *Dulcinée* (Dulcinea), *féerie*
[feɾi] (fairyland), *jeune homme* (young man), *j'oublierai* (I will
forget), *on paiera* (one will pay), *soie* (silk), *il tuera* (he will kill)
NOTE:
Often set as mute *e* /ə/ after another vowel, especially when
verse-final after /e/, /i/, /u/, /y/, and occasionally /wa/:
chantée (sung), *joie* (joy), *joue* (cheek), *perdue* (lost), *vie* (life).

NOTES for loanwords and foreign names:
/ə/ in some weak syllables of English and German vocabulary
where schwa is also common in the original language. Final
syllables with schwa remain unstressed when borrowed in
French: *lieder, Covent Garden*.
/e/ in free syllables (i.e., ending in *e*) in Italian, Spanish, and
Latin vocabulary, as well as a few English words: *crescendo, deo,
Geminiani, pedigree* [pedigɾe], *Remendado, revolver* [ɾevɔlvɛːɾ] *señor*,
sombrero, torero.

é **/e/**
nearly always:
aîné (elder), *bébé* (baby), *j'ai chanté* (I sang), *désir* (wish), *ébène*
(ebony), *école* (school), *Édouard, éfaufiler* (unravel), *égal* (equal),
éhonté (brazen), *éjection* (ejection), *Élias, Émile, énorme* (enormous),
éon (eon), *épine* (thorn), *équipe* (team), *érable* (maple), *ésotérique*
(esoteric), *été* (summer), *évanoui* (unconscious), *faché* (angry), *gré*
(will), *héros* (hero), *idéal* (ideal), *Jérôme, kérosène* (kerosene), *léger*
(light), *Mélisande, numéro* (number), *opéra* (opera), *La Périchole*,
qualité (quality), *rosé* (rosy), *sérénade* (serenade), *thé* (tea),

université (university), *vélo* (bike), *wagnérien* (Wagnerian), *xénophobie* (xenophobia), *ypérite* (mustard gas), *zéro* (zero)

NOTE:

It is customary for the *accent aigu* ´ (acute accent) to be omitted from the upper-case *E* spelling: *Edouard, Emile*

⚠ /ɛ/ in inversion of the verb in first-person singular: *dussé-je* [dysɛːʒə] (would that I)

⚠ /ɛ/ in future and conditional verb tenses where *é* in the final syllable of the verb stem is followed in the next syllable with /ə/, such as *céder* (to cease), *célébrer* (to celebrate), *espérer* (to hope), *préférer* (to prefer), *protéger* (to protect): *je célébrerais* [selɛbrɑrɛ] (I would celebrate), *tu céderas* [sɛdərɑ] (you will cease), *vous me protégerez* [prɔtɛʒəre] (you will protect me)

⚠ /ɛ/ in some words where *é* is followed in the next syllable with /ə/; some of these words are now spelled with *è*. /e/ is sometimes retained in very careful pronunciation, especially when the schwa in the next syllable is pronounced quite deliberately: *abrégement* [abrɛʒəmɑ̃] (abbreviation), *afféterie* [afɛtəriə] (affection), *allégement* [alɛʒəmɑ̃] (reduction), *allégrement* [alɛgrəmɑ̃] (cheerfully), *céleri* [sɛləri] (celery), *crémerie* [krɛməriə] (creamery), *échelon* [ɛʃəlõ] (rung), *élever* [ɛləve] (to raise), *émeraude* [ɛməroːdə] (emerald), *événement* [evɛnəmɑ̃] (event), *féverole* [fɛvərɔlə] (field bean), *médecin* [mɛdəsɛ̃] (doctor), *Mézeray, réglementation* [rɛgləmɑ̃tasjõ] (set of rules), *Saint-Barthélemy, sécheresse* [sɛʃərɛsə] (dryness/drought), *Thévenard, Vézelay*

è, ê, ë

/ɛ/

in most cases:

Athanaël, bière (beer), *Carême* (Lent), *diadème* (diadem), *extrême* (extreme), *fièvre* (fever), *guêpe* (wasp), *Hyères, Israël, Jaurès, koinê/koinè* [kɔjnɛ] (Koine Greek), *lèvres* (lips), *Molière, Noël* (Christmas), *Oroès, Ploërmel, quête* (quest), *rêver* (to dream), *salpêtre* (salpetre), *tête* (head), *Uzès, vêtu* (dressed), *Wèbre, Xerxès* (Xerxes), *yèble* (elderwort), *zèle* (zeal)

/e/

in older spellings where *ë* is in a free syllable (i.e., ending in *ë*, not a consonant), now usually spelled *é*:

Chloë, Gaëtan, goëland (gull), *goëlette* (schooner), *goëmon* (seaweed), *Noëmie, Phaëton* (Phaeton) in the borrowed word *eurêka* [øɾeka] (eureka), and in vocalic harmonization of *ê* when one of the closed vowels /i/, /y/, or /e/ occurs in the next syllable:

bêtise (mistake/naughtiness), *fêter* (to celebrate), *têtu* (stubborn)
NOTE:
Vocalic harmonization is often avoided in careful pronunciation, including vocal music, particularly in the case of these spellings.

ea, eâ   /a/
after 'soft' *g*:
mangeable [mɑ̃ʒablə], *nous mangeâmes* (we ate), *qu'on rangeât* (that one tidied), *rougeâtre* (reddish)

after *j* in the name *Jeanne* (Jean) and derivatives: *Jeanneton, Jeannette, Jeannine*
NOTE:
/ɑ:/ in traditional pronunciation of the name *Jeanne*.

NOTES for English loanwords:
Vowel sounds are usually approximated.
/i/ in *cold-cream* [kold kɾim], *dealer* [dilœːɾ] (drug dealer), *Keats,* *leader* [lidœːɾ], *Shakespeare, speaker* [spikœːɾ] (announcer).
/ɛ/ in *break* [bɾɛk] (pause/station wagon), *steak* [stɛk].
/œ/ in *yearling* [ljœɾliŋ].

eai   /ɛ/
after 'soft' *g*, as the final sound in a word:
geai [ʒɛ] (jay-bird), *il changeait* (he was changing), *Langeais,* *je mangeais* (I was eating)

/e/
after 'soft' *g*, in the first-person *passé simple* verb tense:
je mangeai [mɑ̃ʒe] (I ate)

ean   /ɑ̃/
after 'soft' *g* and in the name *Jean*:
affligeant [afliʒɑ̃] (distressing), *changeant* (unpredictable), *dirigeant* (director), *mangeant* (eating), *obligeance* (kindness), *vengeance* (vengeance)

eau, -eaux	**/o/** always: *Anseaume, beau* (handsome/nice), *Beaumarchais, Bordeaux, château* (castle), *Cocteau, eaux* (waters), *gâteau* (cake), *Micheau, Rameau, ruisseaux* (streams), *Saint-Morceaux, veau* (veal), *Watteau*
ecc-	*see **e***
ee	**/i/** in many English loanwords: *green* [gɾin], *sleeping* [slipiŋ] (sleeping car), *spleen* [splin] (melancholy), *tweed* [twid], *week-end* [|wikɛnd], *yankee* [|jãki]
	/e/ in some borrowed vocabulary: *Beethoven, freesia* [fɾezja], *pedigree* [pedigɾe]
	/ɛ/ in other borrowed vocabulary, especially names: *Meyerbeer, Peer Gynt*
ée	**/e/** in the future and conditional verb tenses: *je créerai* [kɾeɾe] (I will create), *nous créerions* [kɾeɾjõ] (we would create)

ée continued:

always at the end of a syllable, especially when word-final:
année (year), *Coppée, Dulcinée* (Dulcinea), *féerie* [feɾi] (fairyland), *gréement* (rigging), *Médée* (Medea), *Orphée* (Orpheus), *Persée* (Perseus), *on suppléera* (one will replace), *vallée* (valley), *Zachée* (Zacchaeus)

NOTES:
In this spelling in French words, *e* is not /ə/ when a letter follows it in the same syllable (other than in the *-es* and *-ent* endings); the *é* and *e* instead form hiatus in two separate syllables: *Bethléem* (Bethlehem), *déesse* [deɛsə] (goddess), *européenne* (European), *néerlandais* (Dutch), *réel* (real), *réescompte* (rediscount), *surréel* (surreal).
Often set as /eə/ when verse-final: *ô bien-aimée* (o beloved).

| *éé* | **/ee/**
always, as the past participle of a verb stem ending in *é*:
ils ont agréé (they authorized), *j'ai créé* (I created) |

FRENCH PRONUNCIATION A–Z | 155

-éen /eɛ̃/
always:
européen, lycéen (high school student), *Phocéen* (resident of Marseille)
NOTE:
/eɛnə/ in the *-éenne* feminine ending: *européenne* (European),
lycéenne (high school student), *Phocéenne* (resident of Marseille).

eff- see *e*

-eh /ɛ/
in a few cases:
Djamileh, eh!, Taïpeh (Taipei)
NOTE:
Eh! is also often pronounced [e].

ei /ɛ/
in most cases—usually before a consonant (other than *l*, or a
single *m* or *n* unless it is followed by another vowel):
baleine (whale), *eider* [ɛdɛːɾ], *Fouleix, Madeleine, Meissonnier, neige*
(snow), *reine* (queen), *La Seine, seize* (sixteen), *treize* (thirteen),
verveine (verbena)
NOTES:
/ɛj/ in the word *eidétique* (eidetic).
/ɛ/ in the spelling *-eî-* , found only in the word *reître*
(reiter/thuggish soldier).

/e/
in vocalic harmonization:
il a neigé (it snowed), *veiller* (to watch over)
NOTE:
Vocalic harmonization is often avoided in careful pronunciation,
including vocal music.

NOTES for loanwords and foreign names:
/aj/ in most German vocabulary, approximating the
diphthong: *Éguisheim, Eichendorf, Freiberg, Kleinzach, leitmotiv.*
⚠ /ɛ/ has mostly disappeared for this spelling, notably in the French
border villages ending in *-heim*, which are pronounced /(h)ajm/,
and borrowed names ending in *-stein*, which are pronounced
/ʃtajn/ or /stajn/. The traditional pronunciation with /ɛ/ is
only occasionally still heard in a few cases: *Durkheim, Gérolstein,
Rubinstein.*

156 | FRENCH LYRIC DICTION

-eil, -eill- /ɛj/
always:
abeille (bee), *appareil* (device), *Arveiller*, *conseil* (advice), *Corneille*,
Creil, *Desbazeilles*, *Marseille*, *Mireille*, *orteil* (toe), *pareil* (the same as),
se réveiller (to wake up), *soleil* (sun), *sommeil* (slumber), *La Treil*,
Vaucorbeil, *vermeil* (vermillion), *vieille* (old)

eim, ein /ɛ̃/
at the end of a word, or before a consonant, which may be either
silent or pronounced:
ceinture (belt), *dessein* (intent), *Einvaux*, *enceinte* (pregnant),
frein (brake), *peindre* (to paint), *il peint* (he paints), *Reims*, *seing*
(signature), *teint* (complexion)
NOTE:
The *ein* spelling is not nasalized before a vowel.—*see* **ei**

NOTES for *liaison*:
⚠ Denasalization occurs in *liaison* as /ɛn/ from masculine adjectives
in the singular form ending in the spelling -*ein*, most notably in
the word *plein* (full):   *en plein͜ air* (outdoors).

ell-, -elle- *see* **e**

em /ã/
before a different consonant, which may be either silent or
pronounced:
Ansembourg, *assembler* (to assemble), *camembert* (Camembert
cheese), *embarquer* (to board), *embrasser* (to kiss), *embuer* (to shroud),
empire, *Gembloux*, *printemps* (spring), *remplacer* (to replace),
sembler (to seem), *tempête* (storm), *temps* (time), *Trempont*
NOTES:
The interjection *hem !* (ahem!/hmm!) is pronounced [|ɛm].
The *em* spelling is not nasalized before a vowel.—*see* **e**

NOTES for nasalization of loanwords and foreign names:
/ɛ̃/ in Latin vocabulary, ancient names, and a few other foreign
names, including some German names: *D'Aremberg*, *Nuremberg*,
sempervivum [sɛ̃pɛrvivɔm] (succulent), *Sempronius*, *Wurtemberg*.
/ã/ in only a few names: *Luxembourg*.
/ɛ̃/ or /ã/ in some cases: *Wissembourg*.
/ɛm/ at the end of a word, (especially of Latin origin) assimilated
into French, and in some foreign names: *Bethléem* (Bethlehem),
harem [aʀɛm], *idem* (ditto), *item*, *Kremlin*, *Lemberg*, *modem*, *Nemrod*,
requiem [ʀekɥijɛm], *semplice*, *tandem*, *tempo*, *totem*.

FRENCH PRONUNCIATION A–Z | 157

emm-   /ãm/
at the beginning of nearly all words, (but not in names):
emmagasinage (stocking up), *emmanchure* (armhole), *emménagement*
(moving in), *emmêler* (to tangle), *emmener* (to take), *emmerdeur*
(damn nuisance), *emmieller* (to drizzle with honey), *emmitoufler*
(to wrap up)
NOTE:
/ɛm/ or /ãm/ in *emmétrope* (emmetropic) and *emmétropie*
(emmetropia).

/ɛm/
at the beginning of names:
Emma, Emmanuel, Emmanuelle, Emmaüs
NOTES:
/e/ in an unstressed syllable is the norm in everyday speech.
The examples above with open /ɛ/ are for careful pronunciation,
suitable for vocal music.

-emm-   /ɛm/
in most cases:
dilemme (dilemma), *flemme* (laziness), *gemme* (gem), *Hellemmes,
Jemmy, lemme* (lemma), *Lemmens, Waremme*

/am/
in the word *femme* (woman)

in adverbs ending in the spelling *-emment*:
ardemment (passionately), *diligemment* (diligently), *évidemment*
(evidently), *excellemment* (excellently), *fréquemment* (frequently),
indifféremment (indiscriminately), *prudemment* (cautiously),
urgemment (urgently), *violemment* (violently)

en   /ã/
in most cases before a different consonant, which may be either
silent or pronounced:
cent (a hundred), *dent* (tooth), *enfant* (child), *ensemble* (together),
enthousiasme (enthusiasm), *entre* (between), *fendre* (to crack), *gens*
(people), *Givenchy, Henri, mensonge* (lie), *Senlis, tendre* (tender),
vent (wind)

at the end of a few French names, and the word *en* (in/some/of them):
Écouen, Rouen

Notes for *liaison*:
Liaison is made from the word *en* with /n/ after the nasal
vowel: *en‿été* (in the summer).

/ɑ̃n/
as a prefix before a vowel or mute *h*:
s'enamourer (to fall in love), *enharmonique* (enharmonic),
enivré (intoxicated).

⚠ /ɑ̃/ in a few words where *en-* is a prefix to the stem of a word
with aspirated *h*: *enhardir* [ɑ̃ardiːr] (to embolden), and *enharnacher*
[ɑ̃arnaʃe] (to harness)

/ɛ̃/
in a few words, mostly of scholarly origin:
appendice (appendix), *appendicite* (appendicitis), *agenda* (agenda),
centrum (central), *consensus*, *examen* (exam), *hendécasyllabe*
(11-syllable line), *hendiadys* [ɛ̃djadis], *mémento* (handbook/diary),
menthol, *mentor*, *placenta*, *référendum* (referendum), *rhododendron*

in words and French names beginning in *ben-* before a consonant, or
penta-:
bengali, *Benjamin*, *De Benserade*, *benzine*, *pentagonal*, *pentagone*
(pentagon), *pentatonique* (pentatonic)

in other French names:
*Agen, Dupuytren, Elven, Gensonné, Giren, Guichen, Lalbenque, Lesneven,
Magen, Mendès, Penthièvre, Pleyben, De Quélen, Rosporden, Rostrenen*

at the end of a word when preceded by *é, i, ï,* or *y*, and in
conjugations of the verbs *venir* (to come) and *tenir* (to hold) and
derivatives:
D'Ayen, bien (well/good), *Les Boïens* (the Boii), *chien* (dog), *il contient*
(it contains), *européen* (European), *moyen* (means/middle), *païen*
(pagan), *il tient* (he holds), *je viens* (I come)

/ɛn/
at the end of many scholarly words:
abdomen, amen, gluten, pollen, solen (razor clam), *spécimen* (specimen)

Notes for nasalization of loanwords and foreign names:
/ɛ̃/ is quite common: *Abencérages, Blehen, Gutenberg, Mencius.*
/ɑ̃/ in only a few names: *Hortensius, Marienbourg.*

/ən/ is possible in weak syllables of English and German names: *Birkenfeld, Covent Gar<u>den</u>, Liechtenstein.*
/ɛn/ in most cases, especially at the end of a word: *Baden, Britten, cadenza, crescendo, Carmen, Éden* (Eden)*, Gwendoline, Hymen, Offenbach, policemen* [pɔlismɛn]*, Remendado, suspense, week-end* [|wikɛnd].
Gentleman is pronounced [dʒɛntləman] or [(d)ʒɑ̃tləman]. In Satie's *La Diva de l'Empire*, with text by Bonneau and Blès, *gentlemen* is most often sung as [dʒɛntləmɛn] or [dʒɛntɛlmɛn].

⚠ Occasionally, the nasal vowel plus the nasal consonant is heard as /ɛ̃n/: *cadenza* [kadɛ̃(n)dʒa]*, senza* [sɛ̃(n)dʒa].

-enc   **/ɛ̃:k/**
nearly always in names:
Mézenc, Paulhenc, Poulenc, Thorrenc

enn-   **/ɑ̃n/**
nearly always at the beginning of a word, (but not in names):
enneigé (covered with snow)*, ennoblir* (to ennoble)*, ennoyage* (flooding)*, ennui* (boredom)*, ennuyer* (to bore)

/ɛn/
at the beginning of names and a few words:
ennéacorde (nine-stringed)*, ennéade* (ennead)*, ennéagonal* (nine-sided)*, ennéagone* (nonagon)*, D'Ennery, Ennius, Ennodius*
NOTE:
/e/ in an unstressed syllable is the norm in everyday speech. The examples above with open /ɛ/ are for careful pronunciation, suitable for vocal music.

⚠ /en/ in *ennemi* (enemy) in careful pronunciation, suitable for vocal music. In everyday speech, /ɛn/ is the norm, and is also frequently sung in vocal music.

-enn-   **/ɛn/**
in most cases:
antienne (refrain)*, biennal* (biennial)*, Derenne, Étienne, garenne* (wild rabbit)*, gnossienne, Hennevé, Jenny, penne* (quill)*, Rennes, la sienne* (his/hers/one's/its)*, Vienne*

in the *-enne* ending:
canadienne (Canadian), *Parisienne* (Parisian woman), *sicilienne*
(Sicilian)

in the words *nenni* (nay), and *hennir* (to neigh) and derivatives:
hennissement (whinny)

NOTE:
/e/ in an unstressed syllable is the norm in everyday speech.
All examples given above for *-enn-* with open /ɛ/ in unstressed
syllables are for careful pronunciation, suitable for vocal music.

⚠ /an/ in *couenne* [kwanə] (rind); *solennel* (solemn) and all
derivatives: *solennellement* (solemnly)

-ens

/ɑ̃/
in most cases:
Confolens, Doullens, encens (incense), *gens* (people), *je sens* (I feel/
smell), *suspens* (outstanding item)

/ɑ̃ːs/
in a few cases:
cens (ground rent), *contresens* (misinterpretation), *Dulaurens, Gens,
Lens, sens* (sense/senses)

/ɛ̃ːs/
in many names:
Choudens, Cluytens, Dens, Flourens, Rubens

/ɛ̃/
in a few names:
Les Éduens (the Aedui), *Eybens*

-ent

/ɑ̃/
in nouns, adjectives, adverbs, and names:
absent (absent), *accent, argent* (money), *Avent* (Advent), *bâtiment*
(building), *comment* (how), *Florent, lent* (slowly), *Nogent, Saint-
Laurent, souvent* (often), *urgent, Vincent*

/ə/
in the third-person plural verb ending:
ils marchent (they walk), *ils marchèrent* (they walked)

FRENCH PRONUNCIATION A–Z | 161

NOTES for *liaison*:
Liaison with /t/ is customary from the *-ent* verb ending; when mute *e* is set in the score, this *liaison* prevents hiatus: *cent hommes marchent à sa suite* (a hundred men walk in his wake).

eo, eô

/ɔ/
after 'soft' *g*:
flageolet [flaʒɔlɛ] (flageolet/tin whistle), *Geoffroy* (Geoffrey), *Georges* (George), *Georgette, rougeole* (measles)

/o/
always after 'soft' *g* in the spelling *-geot*:
bargeot [barʒo] (nutcase), *cageot* (crate), *Demugeot, pageot* (sea bream), *Peugeot, Sauvageot, Vougeot*

in *geôle* [ʒoːlə] (jail) and derivatives:
geôlier [ʒolje] (jailer), *Geôlier*

-eoi-

/wa/
after 'soft' *g*:
bougeoir [buʒwaːr] (candlestick), *bourgeois, Luxembourgeois* (Luxembourgish), *mangeoire* (feeder), *ils rougeoient* (they glow red), *villageoise* (villager)

in the verbs *asseoir* (to sit) and *seoir* (to befit) in the infinitive only

-eon, -eons

/õ/
after 'soft' *g*:
bourgeon [burʒo] (bud), *esturgeon* (sturgeon), *nous mangeons* (we eat), *pigeon, surgeon* (plant: sucker)

-er

/e/
in some cases, notably verbs in the infinitive, as well as nouns and names ending in the spellings *-cher* and *-ger*:
aider (to help), *Auger, bâiller* (to yawn), *baiser* (kiss/to kiss), *Bellanger, Berger, Bollinger, Boulanger, brouiller* (to scramble), *bûcher* (pyre), *chanter* (to sing), *Clésinger, clocher* (belfry), *conseiller* (to advise), *danser* (to dance), *écouter* (to listen), *Erlanger, étranger* (stranger), *fermer* (to close), *Foucher, goûter* (to taste), *Grancher, habiter* (to live), *Hillemacher, imposer* (to impose), *jeter* (to throw), *kilométrer* (to measure out in kilometres), *léger* (light), *louer* (to rent), *marcher* (to walk), *Messager, Metzinger, nager* (to swim),

oreiller (pillow), *Pol Roger, pousser* (to push), *quitter* (to leave),
rocher (rock), *Royer, sauter* (to jump), *Suger, super*
(verb: to pump/get blocked), *Taittinger, tourner* (to turn),
utiliser (to use), *verger* (orchard), *zoner* (to hang around)

NOTES for *liaison*:
Liaison is made in singing with /ɾ/ from verbs in the infinitive:
aimer‿à loisir (to love at leisure).

⚠ *Liaison* from masculine adjectives in the singular form ending in /e/
shift to /ɛɾ/ in *liaison*, most notably from the word *léger* (light):
un léger‿ennui (a mild boredom).

/ɛːɾ/
especially at the end of some nouns, and in many names:
amer (bitter), *Aser, Auber, Auer, Baguer, Bessemer, Bœgner, Brauner,
Busser, cancer, cher* (dear), *Cléomer, Courtomer, cuiller* (spoon),
Déméter, Diémer, Doumer, Éliézer, enfer (hell), *Esther, éther* (ether),
Euler, Fechner, fer (iron), *Fuller, Garner, Gesler, Glover, Guebwiller,
Haller, hiver* (winter), *Honegger, Huntziger, Ikelmer, Jupiter, Kléber,
Lanester, Launer, Lucifer, Mesquer, Metzler, Mocker, Murger, Necker,
Neuwiller, Niédermeyer, Œser, Perlemuter, Peutinger, Plouer,
Pont-Audemer, Prosper, Quimper, Reber, Reyer, Risler, Sander,
Singer-Polignac, super* (as adj. or adv.) *Sylvaner, Usher, Wiéner*

NOTES for loanwords and foreign names:
/ɛːɾ/ in some English and German vocabulary, either as the final
-er syllable which acquires stress in French, or in a
non-final syllable of very common names: *Brander, cocker* [kɔkɛːɾ]
(cocker spaniel), *Kreutzer, Mahler, Meyerbeer, poker* [pɔkɛːɾ],
revolver [ɾevɔlvɛːɾ], *Sacher, setter* [sɛtɛːɾ], *Vancouver, Wagner,
Weber, Werther*.
/œːɾ/ in the stressed final syllable of some other common English
nouns: *bootlegger* [butlɛgœːɾ], *dealer* [diloeːɾ] (drug dealer),
hacker [|akœːɾ], *hamburger* [|ãbœɾgœːɾ], *leader* [lidœːɾ], *scooter*
[skutœːɾ] (moped), *speaker* [spikœːɾ] (announcer), *steamer* [stimœːɾ].
/œːɾ/ and /ɛːɾ/ are both heard in a few English words ending in *-er*:
clipper [klipɛːɾ] or [klipœːɾ] (boat: clipper), *pull-over* [pylɔvɛːɾ] or
[pulɔvœːɾ] (sweater), *supporter* [sypɔɾtɛːɾ] or [sypɔɾtœːɾ].
/ɛːɾ/ in the word *boxer* as the breed of dog, /œːɾ/ as the men's
underwear.
Borrowed English vocabulary ending in /œːɾ/ is now often
spelled *-eur*.

FRENCH PRONUNCIATION A–Z | 163

-ers /e/
in some names, and in the plural form of words ending in /e/:
Angers, baisers (kisses), *Desnoyers, Desrochers, pensers* (thoughts),
rochers (rocks), *vergers* (orchards)

/ɛːr/
in some cases:
Arvers, Auvers, De Boufflers, divers (varied), *envers* (towards), *Nevers,
à travers* (through/across), *univers* (universe), *vers* (toward/around)

/ɛrs/
in a few cases:
Albers, cers (Cers wind), *Demers, Hers, Mamers, Roulers, Seghers*

es /ɛ/
in monosyllabic articles and possessive adjectives *ces, des, les, mes,
ses, tes* (these, the, my, his/her/one's/its, your)

in the word *est* (is)

Notes:
Although these monosyllables are typically pronounced with
/e/ in everyday speech, /ɛ/ has always been the norm for vocal
music. With this pronunciation, the vowel must not be **too** open.
/e/ is possible in vocalic harmonization when one of the closed
vowels /i/, /y/, and especially /e/ occurs in the next syllable: l̲es
bébés (the babies). This vocalic harmonization is normally avoided
in careful pronunciation, including vocal music.

/ə/
in the plural form of the mute -*es* ending:
amoureuses (in love), *apprises* (learned), *peuples* (peoples), *tables*
(tables)

in the second-person singular verb ending:
tu quittes (you leave), *que tu eusses* (that you had)

in *nous sommes* (we are), *vous êtes* (you are), *vous faites*
(you make/do), and in the *passé simple* verb tense:
nous êumes (we had), *nous marchâmes* (we walked), *vous fûtes*
(you were), *vous chantâtes* (you sang)

at the end of many names:
Arles, Arnes, Bordes, Bruges, Bruxelles (Brussels), *Charles, Chartres,
Chavannes, Cornouailles* (Cornwall), *Delibes, Fresnes, Georges* (George),

Gilles, Hugues, Jacques, Jules, Landes, Limoges, Londres (London),
Longines, Malesherbes, Nantes, Nîmes, De Noailles, Rennes, Versailles

NOTE:
Often -*es* is set as /ə/ after another vowel, especially when verse-final after /e/, /i/, /u/, /y/, and occasionally /wa/:   *aimées*
(loved), *tu dénoues* (you untie), *proies* (prey), *vendues* (sold),
fantaisies (visions/whims).

NOTES for *liaison*:
Liaison is made in singing with /z/ from the -*es* spelling in
monosyllabic articles. It is also made from mute *e* in the plural
form, and in verb endings; when mute *e* is set in the score, this
liaison prevents hiatus: *les adieux* (farewells), *et les belles écouteuses*
(and the beautiful listeners), *des feuilles et des branches* (leaves and
branches), *tu m'aimes et tu me suivras* (you love me and you'll follow
me), *nous sommes à genoux* (we are on our knees), *vous êtes un vrai
paladin* (you are a true paladin).

-*ès*	/ɛ/

at the end of many common words:
abcès (abscess), *accès* (access), *agrès* (gymnastic equipment),
après (after), *congrès* (congress/convention), *cyprès* (cypress),
décès (death), *dès* (from/starting at), *excès* (excess), *exprès*
(intentionally), *grès* (stoneware), *insuccès* (lack of success), *lès*
(near), *près* (near), *procès* (lawsuit), *profès* (professed: religious
initiate), *succès* (success), *très* (very)

/ɛs/
at the end of all other words, which tend to be scholarly:
aloès (aloe), *kermès* (mealybug), *palmarès* (prize list), *xérès* (sherry)

at the end of a name, almost without exception:
Agnès, Devriès, Mendès, Mercédès, Moralès

-*esl-*, -*esm-*	*see* -*esn-*

-*esn-*	/en/

in names, especially with the spellings *Chesn-, Fresn-, Quesn-, Mesnil*
and derivatives:
*Beaumesnil, Le Chesnay, Chesnoy, Dumesnil, Duquesnel, Fresnay,
Fresneau, Fresnel, Mesnil, Miromesnil, Quesnel, Quesnoy*

FRENCH PRONUNCIATION A–Z | 165

NOTE:
/ɛn/ is also possible in these names in careful pronunciation, suitable for vocal music.

/ɛn/
in a stressed syllable in names:
Beauchesne, Duchesne, Dufresne, Duquesne, Fresnes, Lechesne

/ɛsn/
in a few names:
Besnehard, Desnos, Lesneven.

NOTE:
Names with the spellings *-esl-* and *-esm-* generally behave in the same way.
/e/ (or /ɛ/ in careful pronunciation) in an unstressed syllable:
Meslier, Nesmy.
/ɛ/ in a stressed syllable: *Nesle, Pesmes.*
/ɛs/ in some names: *Esménard, Presley.*

ess-   *see **e***

-ess-   /ɛs/
in a stressed syllable:
Bresse, Gresse, Lespesses, promesse (promise), *tendresse* (tenderness), *vitesse* (speed)

in an unstressed syllable, in careful pronunciation:
lessive (detergent), *message, Messager, messieurs* (sirs), *Pessard, pressentiment* (premonition), *tesson* (shard), *tressaillir* (to tremble), *tresser* (to braid)
NOTE:
/e/ in an unstressed syllable is the norm in everyday speech.
The examples above with open /ɛ/ are in careful pronunciation, suitable for vocal music.

-et, -êt   /ɛ/
nearly always:
alphabet, Ansermet, apprêt (preparation/affectation), *benêt* (simple), *billet* (ticket/note), *bouquet, Bourget, Breguet, Caplet, Daudet, duvet* (down/quilt), *effet* (effect), *Euzet, filet* (net), *forêt* (forest), *guichet* (box office), *Gravollet, hoquet* (hiccup), *Huchet, inquiet* (worried), *intérêt* (interest), *Jolivet, jouet* (toy), *Latarjet, livret* (booklet), *Manet, Massenet, menuet* (minuet), *Monet, motet, muet* (mute), *mulet* (mule), *navet* (turnip), *Nicolet, objet* (object), *Odet, Paquet, prêt* (ready),

166 | FRENCH LYRIC DICTION

projet (project), *Radiguet, regret, Sauguet, sujet* (subject), *toupet*
(hairpiece), *Trenet, violet* (purple), *Vuarnet, Watelet, ysopet*

⚠ /ɛt/ in *net* (clear/distinct), and the names *Japhet* (Japheth) and *Têt*

⚠ /e/ as the conjunction *et* (and)

NOTES for loanwords and foreign names:
/ɛt/ for some Latin and English vocabulary: *Becket, et cætera*
[ɛt setɛɾa], *Hamlet, pickpocket* [pikpɔkɛt], *tacet* [tasɛt].
/ɛ/ in other cases: *cricket* [kɾikɛ], *ticket* [tikɛ], *Mahomet*.

-ët   *see -oët*

-ets, -êts   *see -et, -ts*

eu   /ø/

when it is the final sound in a word—either as the last letter, or
before (a) silent letter(s):
Arrieu, banlieue (suburb), *bleu* (blue), *Boïeldieu, cheveux* (hair),
dieu (god), *jeu* (game), *Lekeu, lieu* (place), *Mathieu* (Matthew),
De Montesquieu, monsieur (sir), *messieurs* (sirs), *peu* (little), *il pleut*
(it's raining), *Richelieu, Saint-Brieuc, tu veux* (you want), *Yseult*.

in a stressed syllable before /z/:
berceuse (lullaby), *Chartreuse, on creuse* (one digs), *dangereuse*
(dangerous), *Greuze, heureuses* (happy), *Meuse, Les Rocheuses*
(Rocky Mountains), *voluptueuse* (voluptuous)

in the stressed syllable of a few words before /d/, /k/, /m/, /t/,
/tɾ/, or /ʒ/:
émeute (riot), *Eudes, feutre* (felt), *Leuctres, leude* (vassal), *Maubeuge,*
meute (pack of animals), *neume, neutre* (neutral), *Pentateuque*
(Pentateuch), *Polyeucte, pleutre* (cowardly)

in the stressed syllable of a few isolated words before /g/ or /l/:
meule (millstone), *teugue* (forecastle), *veule* (spineless), *zeugme*
[zø:gmə] (zeugma)

in an unstressed syllable of a verb in the infinitive, which also
remains closed when conjugated:
ameuter [amøte] (to rouse), [il amø:tə] (he rouses), *beugler* [bøgle],
il beugle [bø:glə] (it bellows/lows)

in an unstressed syllable, often at the beginning of a word or name:
bleuet (cornflower), *Eugène, Eugénie, eunuque* (eunuch)
euphémisme (euphemism), *Euphrate* (Euphrates), *europe*,
Eurydice (Eurydice), *Eustache, Heugel, jeudi* (Thursday), *Leucade*
(Lefkada), *Meudon, meunier* (miller), *Neustrie* (Neustria), *neurologie*
(neurology), *Peugeot, peupliers* (poplars), *pneumonie* (pneumonia)

⚠ /œ/ in words with *-eur-* in an unstressed syllable: *De Beurnonville,*
Meursault, pleurnicher (to snivel)

⚠ /œ/ in an unstressed syllable of a word derived from one
containing stressed /œː/: *jeunesse* (youth), since the root word
jeune (young) has /œ/

Notes:
Many singers harmonize the word *heureux/heureuse* (happy)
as [øɾø], [øɾøːzə]. It derives from the archaic stem *heur* [œːɾ]
(good fortune), as in the words *bonheur* (happiness) and *malheur*
(misfortune). It is therefore advisable to keep the first syllable of
heureux/heureuse open.
/ø/ is recommended in the compound word *peut-être* (maybe);
/oe/ is also possible.

/œ/
in a stressed syllable before a pronounced consonant other than
those listed above, especially /z/:
aveugle (blind), *beurre* (butter), *couleur* (colour), *Deneuve, fleur*
(flower), *gueule* (mouth/mug), *jeune* (young), *Lesueur, Levasseur,*
meuble (furniture), *neuf* (nine), *peuple* (people), *peur* (fear), *Villeneuve*

/y/
in conjugations of the verb *avoir*, as the past participle *eu* (had),
and in the *passé simple* and imperfect subjunctive verb tenses:
j'/tu eus, il/elle/on eut, ils/elles eurent (I/you/he/she/one/it/they
had), *que j'eusse, que tu eusses, que nous eussions, que vous eussiez,*
qu'ils/elles eussent (that I/you/we/you/they had)

in a few cases after *g*, where *g* is 'softened' to /ʒ/ by *e*:
chargeure (cartridge), *égrugeure* (shavings), *gageure* (great feat),
mangeure (nibbling), *vergeure* (wire netting)

Notes for German names:
/œj/ in many cases, approximating the diphthong: *Freund, Kreuzberg.*
/ø/ in traditional pronunciation of some German names: *Bayreuth,*
Freud, Kreutzer.
/œj/ and /ø/ are both heard in some cases: *Neumann, Neustadt.*

168 | FRENCH LYRIC DICTION

eû	/y/ in conjugations of the verb *avoir* in the *passé simple* and imperfect subjunctive verb tenses: *nous eûmes, vous eûtes* (we/you had), *qu'il eût* (that he had)
	⚠ /ø/ in *jeûne* (fasting) and *jeûner* (to fast)
-euil, -euill-	/œj/ always: *deuil* (mourning), *écureuil* (squirrel), *Feuillantines, feuille* (leaf/sheet), *Feuillet, Lafeuillade, Neuilly, seuil* (doorway), *veuillez* (please), *Veuillot, Vieuille*
-eun, -eung	/œ̃/ in a few words and French names: *à jeun* (on an empty stomach), *Meung, Neung*
eus	*see eu*
-eut	*see -t*
-eux	/ø/ always: *aïeux* (ancestors), *amoureux* (in love), *chanceux* (lucky), *Des Grieux, deux* (two), *Dutilleux, eux* (they/them), *jeux* (games), *Lamoureux, Monteux, je peux* (I can), *queux* (tails), *tu veux* (you want)
ew	/ju/ in some English loanwords and names: *interview* [ɛ̃tɛɾvju], *interviewer* [ɛ̃tɛɾvjuve] (to interview), *interviewer* [ɛ̃tɛɾvjuvœːɾ] (interviewer), *New Delhi, New Jersey, Newton* /u/ in other English loanwords and names: *Andrew, Lewis, New York*
ex-, exc-, exs-	*see -x-, -xc-, -xs-*
ey	/ɛ/ at the end of a word, or before a consonant, nearly always in names:

Ceylan (Ceylon), *Durey, Feydeau, Grey, Heyrieux, Lapeyrette,*
Leguerney, Peyre, Pleyben, Reynaldo, Sousceyrac, Teyte, Varney

/ɛj/
before another vowel:
nous asseyons (we sit), *vous asseyez* (you sit), *r grasseyé* (uvular *r*),
mareyage (fish trade), *seyant* (proper)
NOTE:
/ɛjj/ in verb tenses with the *-eyi-* spelling, distinguishing them
from tenses pronounced /ɛj/ with the spelling *-ey-*: *nous asseyions*
[a.sɛj.jõ] (we were sitting), *que vous asseyiez* [a.sɛj.je] (that you sit).

/ej/
in vocalic harmonization:
asseyez-vous (sit down), *grasseyer* (to use a uvular pronunciation)
NOTE:
Vocalic harmonization is often avoided in careful pronunciation,
including vocal music.

NOTES for English loanwords and names:
/ɛ/ is the norm, encountered mainly in word-final *-ey*: *geyser*
[ʒɛzɛːr], *hockey* [ʃɔkɛ], *jockey* [ʒɔkɛ], *poney* [pɔnɛ] (pony).

-ez ## /e/
in most French words, notably as a second-person plural verb ending:
assez (enough), *vous chantez* (you sing), *chez* (at the home/place of),
vous danserez (you will dance), *lez* (near), *vous marcheriez*
(you would walk), *nez* (nose), *vous parliez* (you were talking),
rez-de-chaussée (ground floor)

at the end of some names:
Auguez, Cherbuliez, Deprez, Douarnenez, Dumouriez, Duprez, Grez,
Grovlez, Guez, Laisnez, Morez, Renwez, Saint-Tropez, Sciez, Séez

NOTES for *liaison*:
Liaison is regularly made in singing with /z/, notably from second-
person plural verb endings: *assez heureux* (quite happy), *chez elle*
(at her place), *chantez à Dieu* (sing to God), *vous irez au théâtre*
(you will go to the theatre).

/ɛːz/
in the word *fez* and some names:
Boulez, Deldevez, Potez, Suez, Thorez, Wallez

170 | FRENCH LYRIC DICTION

NOTES:
/ɛːz/ or /e/ in a few names: *Buchez, Duez, Forez, Mouchez.*
/ɛːz/ or /ɛs/ in many names from the south of France and
Spain: *Senez, Gomez, Rodriguez.*

-ëz

/ɛːz/
in a few names, after a vowel:
Cloëz, Legoëz

— F ○ [ɛf] —

f

/f/
in most cases:
Alfred, bifteck (steak), *café* (coffee), *Diaforus, enfermer* (to lock away),
façon (way), *faire* (to make/do), *Fantin-Latour, Fauré, faux* (false),
Favre, fenêtre (window), *Féraldy, feu* (fire), *feuille* (leaf/sheet), *Fidès,
fierté* (pride), *fin* (end), *Flaubert, fond* (bottom/background), *fouetter*
(to whip), *Fournier, Franck, Fugère, fuite* (leak), *girafe* (giraffe),
Honfleur, if (yew), *inférieur* (lower), *juif* (Jewish), *kéfir* (kefir), *Lacouf,
De Monfort, naufrage* (shipwreck), *Ouf, Piaf, qualifié* (skilled), *rafler*
(to clear our), *soif* (thirsty), *tarif* (price), *uniforme, veuf* (widower),
Wolf, xylofer, yttrifère (yttriferous), *zincifère* (zinciferous)

⚠ /v/ when the word *neuf* is followed by the words *ans* (nine years),
autres (nine others), *heures* (9 o'clock), *hommes* (nine men), and
for some speakers, *enfants* (nine children) only. See Chapter 7:
'Numbers'.

f̶
sometimes silent as the last letter of a word:
cerf (stag), *clef* (key), *nerf* (nerve), *chef d'œuvre* (masterpiece)

silent in compound names with *Clef-* and *Neuf-*:
Clefmont, Neufchâteau

NOTES:
Serf (peasant) is usually pronounced [sɛrf], but is occasionally
pronounced [sɛːr].
Bœuf(s) and *œuf(s)* (bull/bulls) and (egg/eggs) are pronounced
[bœf], [oef] in the singular form, and [bø], [ø] in the plural form.
See Chapter 7: 'Words with Variable Pronunciations'.

fais-

*see **ai***

ff /f/
always:
affoler (to panic), *Aïtoff*, *différent* (different), *effet* (effect),
Offenbach, *office* (agency/service), *Pitoëff*, *raffiné* (refined),
ça suffit (that's enough), *Suffren*, *Taffanel*, *Truffaut*

— G o [ʒe] —

g /g/
'hard' before *a, â, o, u,* or a consonant other than *n*:
aigre (sour), *bague* (ring), *Chagall*, *dague* (dagger), *église* (church),
Fargue, *gant* (glove), *garçon* (boy), *gars* [ga] (guy/guys), *gâteau*
(cake), *gauler* (to knock down), *Gluck*, *Golaud*, *gonflé* (inflated),
goutte (drip), *gros* (large), *guano*, *guérir* (to heal), *guerre* (war),
guinder (to hoist), *Guise*, *Guitry*, *Gunsbourg*, *Gustave*, *gueule*
(mouth/mug), *gueux* (pauper), *Hugo*, *Isbergues*, *jaguar*, *Kœnig*,
lugubre (mournful), *migrer* (to migrate), *nougat*, *ogre*, *purgatoire*
(purgatory), *Quérigut*, *regret*, *segment*, *tigre* (tiger), *Ugalde*, *vagabond*,
wagnérien (Wagnerian), *xylographie* (xylography), *Ygraine*, *Zuniga*

in some cases as the last letter of a word after a vowel or a
consonant other than *n*:
erg, *grog* [grɔg] (rum hot toddy), *zigzag*

NOTE:
/g/ in the spelling *-berg* of the borrowed English word *iceberg*
[ajsbɛrg] and many names: *Freiberg*, *Heidelberg*, *Lemberg*,
Schoenberg, *Wal-Berg*.
⚠ silent *g* in a few such names: *Furstemberg*, *Gutenberg*, *Nuremberg*,
Wurtemberg

/ʒ/
'soft' before *e, é, è, ê, i, î,* or *y*:
argent (money), *berger* (shepherd), *cage*, *danger*, *Égée* (Aegeus),
fange (mire), *Geneviève*, *il gèle* (it freezes), *gens* (people), *génial*
(brilliant), *gingembre* (ginger), *Girod*, *gîte* (vacation rental), *givre*
(frost), *gymnase* (gymnasium), *Hygie* (Hygieia), *ingénu* (naive), *jugé*
(judged), *kérogène* (kerogen), *lige* (liege), *magie* (magic), *nager*
(to swim), *oxygène* (oxygen), *phrygien* (Phrygian), *Quatrefages*,
Régine, *sage* (wise), *tige* (stem), *urgent*, *vierge* (virgin), *Walpurgis*,
xylophage (wood-boring insect), *Yssingeaux*, *zonage* (zoning)

172 | FRENCH LYRIC DICTION

~~g~~

usually silent as the last letter of a word, most often after another
silent consonant, or before another silent consonant at the end of
a word:
doigt [dwa] (finger), *long* (long), *vingt* [vɛ̃] (twenty)

silent in names ending in *-bourg*:
Bourg (in Western France), *Brandebourg* (Brandenburg), *Cobourg*
(Coburg), *Édimbourg* (Edinburgh), *Faubourg*, *Fribourg* (Freiburg im
Breisgau), *Gainsbourg*, *Gunsbourg*, *Hambourg* (Hamburg), *Habsbourg*
(Habsburg), *Luxembourg*, *Mecklembourg* (Mecklenburg), *Saint-
Pétersbourg* (Saint Petersburg), *Salzbourg* (Salzburg), *Strasbourg*,
Tiffenbourg, *Vaurabourg*

NOTE:
/g/ or silent *g* are both correct in the words *amygdales* (tonsils),
legs (bequest), and *joug* (yoke), where the pronunciation [ʒu] is
most common in a purely physical sense (i.e., non-metaphorical).

/k/

in the town of *Bourg* in Eastern France, *Bourg-en-Bresse*, and in the
word *tungstène* [tœ̃kstɛnə] (tungsten)

in *liaison*, in traditional pronunciation:
un joug insupportable (an unbearable yoke)

NOTES for *liaison*:
Liaison from *g* as /k/ is possible, but is often no longer practised;
silent *g* is the alternative.

NOTES for loanwords and foreign names:
/ʤ/ for English 'soft' *g* (often spelled *dg*):   *Bridge*, *gin* [ʤin].
/ʤ/ or /ʒ/ in Italian spellings before *e* or *i*:   *agitato*, *Geminiani*.
/ʤ/, /ʤj/, or /ʒj/ in the Italian spelling *gi* before another vowel:
giocoso, *Giordano*.
/g/ for English and Italian 'hard' *g*, and in German
vocabulary: *Carnegie Hall*, *Hagen*, *Gesler*, *largo*.
/lj/ is most common in the Italian spelling *-gli-*:   *Bentivoglio*,
imbroglio [ɛ̃brɔljo].
/gli/ is heard in a few Italian names with the spelling *-gli-*:   *Modigliani*.

ge | *see ea, eâ, eai, ean, eo, eô, -eoi-, -eon, -eons, eu, g*

NOTE:
In the *ge* spelling, 'softening' *e* does not alter the pronunciation of
the vowel(s) that follow(s).

FRENCH PRONUNCIATION A–Z | 173

-gg- **/gʒ/**
before a vowel:

Aggée (Haggai), *suggestion* (suggestion)
⚠ /g/ in a few words: *Honegger, toboggan* (slide/chute)

/g/
before a consonant:
agglutiner (to stick together), *aggravation* (worsening)

NOTES for Italian loanwords and names:
/dʒ/, /dʒj/, or /ʒj/ in the spelling -ggi- before another
vowel: *arpeggio.*

gh **/g/**
nearly always in names:
Diaghilev, D'Enghien, Ghéon, Ghislenghien, Herreweghe, Huyghe,
Levegh, Maghreb, Seghers, Singher, Van Gogh, Van Lerberghe
⚠ /ʒ/ in a few names: *Inghelbrecht, Mareugheol, Verneugheol*

NOTES for loanwords and foreign names:
/g/ in Italian words: *larghetto.*
English words with this spelling are usually approximated
(i.e., silent ~~gh~~, /f/, etc.).

gn **/ɲ/**
in most cases:
agneau (lamb), *De Brétigny, Champagne, digne* (worth), *Espagne*
(Spain), *fagne* (fen), *gagner* (to win/earn), *gnangnan* (soppy), *gnôle*
(hooch), *gnons* (bruises/knocks), *D'Hérigny, ignoré* (unknown/
undiscovered), *je joigne* (I combine), *Kervigné, Longny, montagne*
(mountain), *non-alignement* (political non-alignment), *orignal*
(moose), *peigne* (comb), *Quaregnon, régner* (to reign), *signature,*
Tassigny, uniligne (code: one-liner), *vigne* (vine), *Wattignies, Xertigny*

/gn/
in a few cases, especially words of scholarly origin:
agnostique (agnostic), *Boduognat* (Boduognatus), *cognitif* (cognitive),
diagnostic (diagnosis), *gnome, gnossienne, gnou* (gnu), *ignition,*
Magnence (Magnentius), *Magnus, Polygnote* (Polygnotus), *Progné*
(Procne), *pugnacité* (pugnacity), *récognition* (recognition), *stagnant,*
stagnation, stagner (to stagnate), *syngnathe* [sɛ̃gnatə] (pipefish)

NOTES for loanwords and foreign names:
/ɲ/ in Italian vocabulary: *dal segno.*
/gn/ in German vocabulary: *Wagner.*

-gnier   /ɲe/
in a few cases:
châtaignier [ʃatɛɲe] (chestnut tree), *guignier* [giɲe] (gean cherry tree), *Lugnier, peignier* [pɛɲe] (comb maker), *De Régnier, Viognier*

gu   /g/
in most cases before a vowel other than *a*:
Daguerre, distinguer (to distinguish), *guerre* (war), *gueule* (mouth/mug), *Guillaume* (William), *Guillot, guillotine, Guitry, Guy, Leguérinel, longue* (long), *Sauguet*

/gɥ/
in a few cases before *e, i, ï*, or *y* in the middle of a word:
aiguille (needle), *Aguillon, aiguïté* [ɛgɥite] (pointed/shrillness), *ambiguïté* (ambiguity), *arguer* (to deduce), *contiguïté* (contiguity), *exiguïté* [ɛgzigɥite] (shortness), *Guyanne* (Guyana), *Guyon, inguinal, linguiste* (linguist), *linguistique* (linguistic)

NOTES:
/g/ and /gɥ/ are both correct in a few cases: *aiguiser* (to sharpen), *consanguinité* (consanguinity), *De Guise.*
In most cases involving the *gu* spelling, 'hardening' *u* does not alter the pronunciation of the vowel(s) that follow(s).

-gu,   /gy/
-guë, -güe   in adjectives ending in *-gu* (masculine) and *-guë* or *-güe* (feminine). In these words, the *u* 'hardens' the *g*, and is also pronounced:
aigu/aiguë/aigüe (acute), *ambigu/ambiguë/ambigüe* (ambiguous), *besaigue/besaiguë/besaigüe* (mortise axe), *bégu/béguë/bégüe* (stuttering), *contigu/contiguë/contigüe* (adjoining), *exigu/exiguë/ exigüe* (cramped), and the noun *ciguë/cigüe* (hemlock)

NOTES:
Tréma ˝ (dieresis diacritic) is an indication that the spelling *-ue* is not simply silent 'hardening' *u* and mute *e*, but that this syllable should instead be pronounced with the vowel /y/. It is normally placed over the *ë* in older spellings, and over the *ü* in modern spellings.

FRENCH PRONUNCIATION A–Z | 175

gua	/**gwa**/ nearly always: *Alguazil, Antigua, guano, iguane* (iguana), *jaguar, lingual,* *Guadalquivir, Guadeloupe, Nicaragua* ⚠ silent ʉ in a few cases: /ga/ in *aiguail* [ɛgaj] (dew on foliage), *Guadet*. NOTE: *Couguar* (cougar) is pronounced [kugaːɾ] or [kugwaːɾ]; the latter is also spelled *cougouar*.
guai, guay	/**gɛ**/ in *camarguais* (from the Camargue), *guai/guais* (shotten), and in names with *-guay*: *Leguay, Guay, Duguay-Trouin*. NOTE: Names ending in *-guay* are often pronounced with /ge/; /gɛ/ is possible in very careful pronunciation.
-guë, -güe	*see -gu*
-gueil, *-gueill-*	/**gœj**/ always: *Bourgueil, Longueil, Montorgueil, orgueil* (pride), *orgueilleux* (arrogant)
gueu	/**gø**/ always as the final sound in a word, or before /z/: *agueusie* (loss of taste), *fougueux* (impetuous), *gueux* (pauper), *gueuser* (to beg for money), *Périgueux* /**gœ**/ always before a pronounced consonant other than /z/: *dragueur* (womanizer), *fugueur* (runaway), *gueule* [gœlə] (mouth/mug), *gueuler* (to shout), *harangueur* (orator), *ligueur* (agitator), *longueur* (length), *rigueurs* (rigours), *vigueur* (vigour), *zingueur* (zinc roofer)
-guï-, -güi-	/**gɥi**/ in a few nouns: *ambiguïté/ambigüité* (ambiguity), *contiguïté/contigüité* (contiguity), *exiguïté/exigüité* (exiguity) NOTE: Refer to the note under *-gu, -guë, -güe* for information on the placement of *tréma* ̈ .

176 | FRENCH LYRIC DICTION

— H ○ [aʃ] —

h

ħ

always silent:

abhorrer (to abhor), *Abraham*, *ahuri* (stupefied), *Cahen*, *dehors* (outside), *s'enrhumer* (to catch a cold), *euh…* (er…), *Hahn*, *haine* (hatred), *Halévy*, *hautbois* (oboe), *Hébé*, *Hector*, *hein?* (hey?), *Henri*, *herbe* (grass), *Heugel*, *heureux* (happy), *hibou* (owl), *hirondelle* (swallow), *Hoffmann*, *honte* (shame), *hôtel* (hotel), *Houat*, *Huguenots*, *huile* (oil), *humain* (human), *humble*, *Hyacinthies* (Hyacinthia), *hymne* (hymn), *hypothèque* (mortgage), *inhibé* (inhibited), *Ispahan* (Isfahan), *Jehan*, *Nohain*, *ohé!* (hey!), *pouah!* (yuck!), *peuh!* (phooey!), *Prudhomme*, *rehausser* (to raise), *Syrah*, *tahitien* (Tahitian), *théorie* (theory), *véhicule* (vehicle)

⚠ Occasionally /h/ is heard in exclamations and violent sentiments, at the discretion of the speaker: o_ho_!, a_ha_!, _halte_! (stop!), *je te _hais_!* (I hate you)

NOTES:

Intervocalic silent *ħ* often separates syllables in French. Vowels on either side of *h* are each pronounced normally, and form hiatus: *cahier* (notebook), *dehors* (outside), *envahir* (to invade), *Lahor*, *Méhul*, *trahi* (betrayed).

Linking to aspirated *h* may not occur: *la | harpe* (the harp), *Les | Halles.*

NOTES for *liaison*:

Proper names with initial mute *h* usually behave as if they had aspirated *h* when they follow *ces*, *des*, *les*, and *chez*. *Liaison* is not made: *d'Henri* (of Henry); *chez | Henri* (at Henry's place); *les | Henri* (the Henrys).

— I ○ [i] —

i, î

/i/

in most cases—usually before a consonant (other than a single *m* or *n* unless it is followed by another vowel), or as the last letter of a word:

abîme (abyss), *bizarre* (strange), *calice* (chalice), *Chaminade*, *cheminée* (chimney), *Couzinou*, *dîner* (dinner/to dine), *énigme* (mystery), *finir* (to finish), *vous fîtes* (you made/did), *Gallimard*, *Guînes*, *Ibert*, *Icare* (Icarus), *ici* (here), *Idas*, *if* (yew), *igloo* [iglu], *ignoble* (despicable), *Ikelmer*, *il* (he), *île* (island), *imagination* (imagination), *Imaüs*, *inhumer* (to bury), *inutile* (useless), *Iphigénie* (Iphigenia), *ipomée* (morning glory), *iris*, *Iseult* (Isolde), *italien* (Italian), *ivre* (intoxicated), *Ixelles*, *izard*,

Jéricho, kilo, Linossier, lit (bed), *Mérimée, mirage, Nîmes, Ninon, olive, Padmâvatî, primaire* (primary), *qui* (who), *Quinault, richesse* (wealth), *Simone, stimuler* (to urge on), *triste* (sad), *utile* (useful), *vîmes* (we saw), *Widal, ximénie* (mountain plum), *yttria, zigue* (guy)

/j/
before another vowel other than /ə/:
adieu (farewell), *bien* (well/good), *Coppélius, Diémer, émotion* (emotion), *fier* (proud), *galion* (galleon), *Hortensius, Iarbas, Iéna* (Jena), *ion, Kiev, loriot* (oriole), *miel* (honey), *Octavien, piano, quiétude* (tranquillity), *De Rieux, sociaux* (social), *tiers* (third), *unifié* (unified), *Viardot, Wiéner, Xénia, Yniold, zinnia*

⚠ /i/ after a consonant plus *l* or *r*: *Chabrier, crier* [kʁie] (to cry out), *Gabriel, oubliant* [ubliã] (forgetting). An alternative and accepted pronunciation of /ij/ also exists for this spelling: *crier* [kʁi.je] (to cry out), *oubliant* [u.bli.jã] (forgetting).

NOTE:
In the score, *i* before another vowel sound is often set as dieresis with /i/: *ri-ant* [ʁi.ã] (laughing).

NOTES for English loanwords:
Vowel sounds are usually approximated.
/i/: *clipper* [klipɛːʁ] or [klipœːʁ] (boat: clipper), *milady* [milɛdi], *milord* [milɔːʁ], *miss* [mis], *mistress* [mistʁɛs], *sandwich* [sãdwitʃ] or [sãdwiʃ], *spider* [spidɛːʁ].
/œ/ before *r* in a few words: *flirt* [flœʁt], *flirter* (to flirt), *girl* [gœʁl], *tee-shirt* [ti ʃœʁt].
/aj/: *design* [dizajn], *iceberg* [ajsbɛʁg], *Wilde*.
Silent *i* in the borrowed word *business* [biznɛs].

ï, ÿ
/i/
after most vowels, before a consonant:
Anaïs, Boïto, caraïbe (Caribbean), *celluloïd* (celluloid), *coït* (coitus), *Dancaïre, Faÿ, haïr* (to hate), *Héloïse, héroïque* (heroic), *introït* (introit), *Léïla, Louÿs, maïs* (corn), *Moïse* (Moses), *mosaïque* (mosaic), *Moÿse, naïf* (naive), *Thaïs, xiphoïde* (xiphoid), *Zaïre*

in some cases in the *-aï* spelling at the end of a name:
Altaï, Adonaï, Anaï

/j/
before another vowel, especially when intervocalic:
aïe ! [aj] (ouch!), *aïeul* (ancestor), *aïeux* (ancestors), *Dostoïevski, glaïeul* (gladiola), *ïambique* (iambic), *Naïade, païen* (pagan)

⚠ /i/ in *ouïe* (hearing)

in some cases before a consonant, especially in an unstressed
syllable, and in borrowed names with adopted French spellings:
Bahreïn (Bahrain), *Koweït* (Kuwait), *Tchaïkovsky, Thaïlande* (Thailand)

in most cases as the last letter of a word or name:
bonsaï, Bolchoï (Bolshoi), *Dubaï, Foleÿ, Hanoï, Shanghaï, shar-peï*
(shar pei), *toï, toï, toï !* [tɔj], *tokaï* (Hungarian Tokay), *Tolstoï*

NOTE:
/i/ and /j/ are both heard in some cases, especially in the *-aï*
spelling at the end of a word or name: *Hawaï, Hokusaï, Oudaï,
samouraï* (samurai).

ie

/i/
in the future and conditional verb tenses:
j'oublierai [ublire] (I will forget), *nous oublierions* [ublirjõ] (we would
forget)

always at the end of a syllable, especially when word-final:
Alexandrie (Alexandria), *amie* (friend), *Béotie, brie* (Brie cheese),
il crie (he cries out), *fantaisie* (vision/whim), *Ophélie* (Ophelia),
ralliement (rallying), *Sophie, vie* (life)

⚠ /je/ in the name *Siebel* and the word *diesel* [djezɛl]

NOTES:
In this spelling in French words, *e* is not /ə/ when a letter
follows it in the same syllable (other than in the *-es* and *-ent*
endings):   *ciel* [sjɛl] (sky), *Daniel, fief* (fiefdom), *fiel* (venom), *fierté*
(pride), *grief* [grief] (grievance), *hier* (yesterday), *Joliette, miel*
(honey), *la mienne* (mine), *relief, Riel, vierge* (virgin).
Often set as /iə/ when verse-final: *ma sœur, je confie* (my sister,
I entrust).

ien, ïen

/jɛ̃/
in conjugations of the verbs *venir* (to come) and *tenir* (to hold), and
all related verbs:
il contient [kõtjɛ̃] (it contains), *il convient* (it suits), *je maintiens*
(I keep), *elle tient* [tjɛ̃] (she holds), *je viens* [vjɛ̃] (I come)

at the end of a word, or before a different consonant (other than *t*),
which may be either silent or pronounced:

FRENCH PRONUNCIATION A–Z | 179

Les Acharniens (the Acharnians), *Amiens, ancien* (former),
aoûtien [ausjɛ̃] (August vacationer), *Appien* (Appian),
Athéniens (Athenians), *bien* (well/good), *bienfait* (kindness),
biscaïen (Biscayan), *bohémien* (Bohemian), *Les Boïens* (the Boii),
Carlovingien (Carolignian), *chien* (dog), *Damiens, Dioclétien*
(Diocletian), *Enghien, Fabien, indien* (Indian), *Julien, lien* (link),
Luquiens, Les Mandubiens (the Mandubii), *le mien* (mine), *païen*
(pagan), *Pharisiens* (Pharisees), *plébéien* [plebejɛ̃] (plebeian),
Quintilien, rien (nothing), *Sébastien, le tien* (yours), *Titien* (Titian)

⚠ /jɑ̃/ in the word *chienlit* (bedlam/carnival disguise)

NOTE:
/jɛnə/ in the -*ienne* and -*ïenne* endings: *Aléoutiennes* (Aleutians),
Bienne, biscaïenne (Biscayan), *Caspienne, Les Éoliennes*
(the Aeolians), *Estienne, Parisienne* (Parisian woman),
plébéienne (plebeian), *Sienne* (Siena), *Vienne* (Vienna), *Vivienne*.

⚠ /iɛ̃/ in the spelling -*ien* and /iɛnə/ in the spelling -*ienne* after
a consonant plus *l* or *r*:   *Adrien, Adrienne, Cyprien, Cyprienne,
Hadrien* (Hadrian), *zoroastrien* (Zoroastrian). Alternative and
accepted pronunciations of /ijɛ̃/ and /ijɛnə/ also exist in these
spellings: *Adrien* [a.dɾi.jɛ̃], *Adrienne* [a.dɾi.jɛ.nə].

NOTES for *liaison:*
⚠ Denasalization occurs in *liaison* as /jɛn/ from masculine adjectives
in the singular form ending in the spelling -*ien*:   *un ancien‿amant*
(a former lover).
Nasality is retained as /jɛ̃n/ in *liaison* from the words *bien*
(well/good), *rien* (nothing), and *combien* (how much/how
many):   *bien‿aimé* (beloved), *rien‿à faire* (nothing to do),
combien‿est-ce que ça coute ? (how much does that cost?).

-*ience*   /jɑ̃ːsə/
at the end of a word:
prescience (foresight), *science* (knowledge)

-*ient*   /jɑ̃/
nearly always when not a verb:
ambient (ambiant), *conscient* (conscious), *efficient, orient, patient*
NOTE:
/iɑ̃/ or the accepted alternative pronunciation of /ijɑ̃/ in the
word *client* and derivatives: *clientèle*

⚠ /jɛ̃/ in conjugations of the verbs *tenir* (to hold), *venir* (to come)
and related verbs—*see* **ien**

180 | FRENCH LYRIC DICTION

-ier

/je/
in most cases:
acier (steel), *atelier* (workshop), *Bacquier*, *Berthelier*, *bustier*, *cahier* (notebook), *Chapelier*, *dossier* (file), *écolier* (schoolboy), *Ferrier*, *gosier* (throat), *Gressier*, *Hallier*, *Hucquelier*, *Isolier*, *janvier* (January), *Jourfier*, *Letellier*, *Linossier*, *luthier* (instrument maker), *métier* (craft), *Montpellier*, *nier* (to deny), *Olivier*, *papier* (paper), *Perrier*, *pommier* (apple tree), *premier* (first), *quartier* (district), *rosier* (rose bush), *Roullier*, *Saulnier*, *Sennelier*, *sentier* (path), *terrifier* (to terrify), *Texier*, *Tézier*, *Tournier*, *usurier* (money lender), *Vasnier*, *Villequier*, *vivier* (breeding ground), *Xavier*

⚠ /ie/ after a consonant plus *l* or *r*:   *bouclier* [buklie] (shield), *Chabrier*, *crier* (to cry out), *février* (February), *ouvrier* (labourer), *peuplier* (poplar), *sanglier* (wild boar), *tablier* (apron), *trier* (to sort). An alternative and accepted pronunciation of /ije/ also exists for this spelling: *crier* [kri.je] (to cry out), *tablier* [ta.bli.je] (apron).

NOTES for *liaison*:
Liaison is made in singing with /r/ from verbs in the infinitive:
à prier‿au saint lieu (at prayer in the holy place).

⚠ *Liaison* from masculine adjectives in the singular form ending in /je/ shift to /jɛr/ in *liaison*, most notably from the words *premier* (first) and *dernier* (last):   *le premier‿acte* (the first act).

/jeːr/
in the following words:
avant-hier (the day before yesterday), *fier* (proud), *hier* (yesterday)

-iers

/je/
in names, in the plural form of words ending in /e/, and in the word *volontiers* (gladly):
ateliers (workshops), *Béziers*, *Carabiniers*, *Colomiers*, *Désaugiers*, *Deslauriers*, *Desrosiers*, *De Formoutiers*, *métiers* (crafts), *Moustiers*, *Pamiers*, *Pithiviers*, *Poitiers*, *quartiers* (districts), *sentiers* (paths), *Teniers*, *Villiers*, *Vouziers*

/jeːr/
in a few verb conjugations and names:
j'acquiers (I acquire), *je conquiers* (I conquer), *Quiers*, *je requiers* (I require/call for), *Thiers*, *tiers* (a third)

FRENCH PRONUNCIATION A–Z | 181

-ii- /ij/
in the first- and second-person plural imperfect and subjunctive
tenses of verbs whose infinitives end in -ier:
que vous confiiez [kõ.fi.je] (that you confide), nous étudiions
[e.tydi.jo] (we were studying)

-il /il/
in most cases in a word or name, when not preceded by a vowel:
Alguazil, avril (April), Brésil (Brazil), cil (eyelash), fil (string), gril
(grill), il (he), mil (millet), Miromesnil, péril (danger), Schlémil

/i/
in some words:
fournil (bakery), fraisil (coal cinders), fusil (gun), gentil (nice), outil
(tool), persil (parsley)

NOTES:
/i/ and /il/ are both correct in a few words: babil (warbling), baril
(cask), chenil (kennel), coutil (fabric: ticking), fenil (hay barn), grésil
(sleet), nombril (navel). In the Poulenc setting of Lune d'avril of
La courte paille with text by Carême, grésil is always sung with
/il/, in order to rhyme with avril.
/i/ in sourcil (eyebrow) is the norm, but /il/ is also correct.

⚠ /ij/ for the adjective gentil (nice) before a vowel or mute h:
gentilhomme [ʒãtijɔmə] (gentleman), gentil enfant [ʒãti jãfã] (nice child)

/j/
at the end of a word, after a vowel sound:
cercueil (coffin), détail (detail), Dubreuil, fenouil (fennel), orgueil
(pride), Raspail, Rueil, soleil (sun)

ilh /ij/
in French names, after a consonant or silent h̶:
Guilhem, Milhaud, Paladilhe

/j/
in French names, after a vowel sound:
Anouilh, Bouilhet, Meilhac, Pineuilh, Samazeuilh

⚠ /il/ in silhouette, and philharmonique (philharmonic)

ill- see ll

182 | FRENCH LYRIC DICTION

-ill-

/ij/
in most cases, after a consonant or silent ʜ:
anguille (eel), *Antilles*, *artillerie* (artillery), *babiller* (to chatter),
Bastille, *béquille* (crutch), *billard* (billiard), *bille* (billiard ball),
billet (ticket), *billot* (block), *Cadillac*, *Camille*, *carillon* (chimes),
Cendrillon (Cinderella), *Chantilly*, *chenille* (caterpillar), *cheviller* (to peg),
Cochenille, *coquillages* (shells), *corbillard* (hearse), *Dutilleux*,
échantillon (sample), *épillet* (small spike), *Escamillo*, *famille* (family),
fille (girl/daughter), *fillette* (little girl), *gaspiller* (to waste), *Gentilly*,
gorille (gorilla), *grillon* (cricket), *Guillaume Tell* (William Tell),
Guillot, *habiller* (to dress), *jonquille* (daffodil), *lentille* (lentil), *mantille*
(mantilla scarf), *Manzanilla*, *maquillage* (makeup), *mordiller*
(to nibble at), *myrtille* (blueberry), *outiller* (to equip), *pastille* (lozenge),
Pedrillo, *pétiller* (to sparkle), *papillon* (butterfly), *pupille* (pupil), *quilles*
(bowling pins), *Romilly*, *scintillant* (sparkling), *Séguedille*, *Séville*, *sillon*
(furrow), *tilleul* (lime tree) *vanille* (vanilla), *Villon*

/il/
in some cases, after a consonant or silent ʜ:
Achille (Achilles), *bacille* (bacillus), *De Banville*, *Belleville*, *codicille*
(codicil), *Cyrille*, *Delille*, *distiller* (to distill), *Fillastre*, *Gilles*, *Guillain*,
Hillemacher, *instiller* (to instill), *Lafillé*, *Lillas Pastia*, *Lucille*, *Millandy*,
mille (thousand), *Millerand*, *osciller* (to swing/rock), *papille* (papilla),
pénicilline (penicillin), *scille* (scilla), *titiller* (to titillate), *tranquille*
(peaceful), *verticille* (worm), *vaudeville*, *village*, *villanelle*, *ville* (city),
Villemain, *Villeneuve*
NOTE:
By far the most commonly encountered words on the above list
with /il/ are *mille* (thousand), *tranquille* (peaceful), and *ville* (city).

/j/
after a vowel sound:
abeille (bee), *je cueille* (I pluck), *feuille* (leaf/sheet), *Genouillac*,
grenouille (frog), *Marseille*, *Neuilly*, *orgueilleux* (arrogant), *Tailleferre*,
volaille (poultry)

-illi-

/j/
after a vowel sound, before another vowel:
bailliage [baja:ʒə] (bailiwick), *groseillier* [grozɛje] (currant bush),
joaillier/joaillière [ʒɔaje]/[ʒɔajɛ:rə] (jeweller), *médaillier* [medaje] (medal
chest), *quincaillier/quincaillière* [kɛ̃kaje]/[kɛ̃kajɛ:rə] (hardware dealer)

FRENCH PRONUNCIATION A–Z | 183

/jj/
in the spellings *-ailli-, -eilli-, -euilli-, -ouilli-, -ueilli-* of the first- and
second-person plural imperfect and subjunctive verb tenses:
que vous conseilliez [kõ.sɛj.je] (that you advise), *nous cueillions*
[kœj.jõ] (we were plucking), *nous effeuillions* [e.fœj.jõ] (we were
stripping the leaves off), *nous travaillions* [tra.vaj.jõ] (we were
working), *que vous verrouilliez* [vɛ.ruj.je] (that you lock)

/ɥjj/
after a consonant, or after u that is not silent, in the first- and
second-person plural imperfect and subjunctive verb tenses:
que vous aiguilliez [ɛ.gɥij.je] (that you direct), *vous gaspilliez*
[gas.pij.je] (you were wasting), *nous nous maquillions* [ma.kij.jõ]
(we were putting on makeup)

/ij/
in many cases after a consonant, before another vowel:
marguillier/marguillière [margije]/[margijɛːrə] (churchwarden/
churchwarden's wife), *Merguillier, serpillière* [sɛrpijɛːrə] (floor
mop), *vanillier* [vanije] (vanilla plant)

/ilj/
in a few cases after a consonant or u that is not silent, before
another vowel:
Aubervilliers, Baraguey-d'Hilliers, Beauvilliers, billion (trillion),
bougainvillier (bougainvillea), *De Brinvilliers, Cuvillier, L'Huillier,
Largillière,* milliard (billion), *millier* (about a thousand), *million* (million),
Rillieux, Thuillier, Tilliard, Tillier, Tillières, Villiers de l'Isle-Adam

/ili/
in a few cases after a consonant or silent ʉ, before a consonant
(notably in the *milli-* prefix), and occasionally when word-final:
capilliculture (hair care), *cyrillique* (Cyrillic), *imbécillité* (imbecility),
lapilli, Lilliput, milligramme (milligram), *millilitre, millimètre,
pénicilline* (penicillin), *schilling, tranquillisant* (soothing/
tranquilizer), *traquillité* (tranquility), *vaudevilliste* (Vaudevillian)
⚠ /iji/ in a few cases: *pointillisme* [pwɛ̃tijismə] (pointillism),
pointilliste (pointillist), *vermillis* (tracks of a rooting wild boar)

184 | FRENCH LYRIC DICTION

/ji/
after a vowel sound, either when word-final or followed by a
consonant:
accueilli (welcomed), *bouilli* (boiled), *bouillir* (to boil), *cueillir*
(to pluck), *faillite* (bankruptcy), *tressaillir* (to tremble),
vieilli (aged), *vieillir* (to grow old)

im /ɛ̃/
before a different pronounced consonant:
chimpanzé [ʃɛ̃pãze] (chimpanzee), *Édimbourg* (Edinburgh), *grimper*
(to climb), *imbécile* (imbecile), *imbu* (imbued), *impossible*, *impôt*
(tax), *limbe* (limb), *Mimbaste*, *nimbe* (halo), *pimpant* (elegant),
Quimper, *Rimbaud*, *simple*, *timbre* (stamp/tone)
NOTE:
The *im* spelling is not nasalized before a vowel.—*see **i***

/im/
at the end of a few scholarly words:
intérim (interim), *olim*, *passim*
⚠ /ɛ̃/ in the French pronunciation of the name *Joachim*

NOTES for nasalization of loanwords and foreign names:
/ɛ̃/ in some cases, especially in names with adopted French
spellings: *Édimbourg* (Edinburgh), *imbroglio* [ɛ̃brɔljo].
/im/ in most foreign names: *Himly, Kimbolth, Rimsky-Korsakov, Simca*.

ïm /im/
always at the end of a name, especially in ancient names:
Éphraïm, Haïm, Manahïm, Séboïm (Zeboim)

/ɛ̃/
before a consonant in a few names:
Coïmbatore, Coïmbre

imm- *see -**mm-***

in /ɛ̃/
at the end of a word, or before a different consonant, which may
be either silent or pronounced:
alpin (alpine), *badin* (light-hearted), *Clorinde* (Clorinda), *Desjardins*,
étincelle (sparkle), *fin* (end), *gingival* (gum), *hyacinthe* (hyacinth), *inclus*
(included), *indice* (clue), *informer* (to inform), *ingrat* (ungrateful),
injuste (unfair), *inlassablement* (tirelessly), *inquiet* (worried), *insecte*

FRENCH PRONUNCIATION A–Z | 185

(insect), *intolérable* (intolerable), *invisible, jardin* (garden), *Kœchlin,*
linteau (lintel), *matin* (morning), *nervin* (nervous system),
orphelin (orphan), *prince, Quintin, Rosalinde* (Rosalind), *sapin* (fir),
Tintin, utérin (uterine), *il vint* (he came), *Weckerlin, Yssingeaux, Zerbin*
NOTE:
The *in* spelling is not nasalized before a vowel or mute *h.—see* **i**

NOTES for *liaison:*

⚠ Denasalization occurs in *liaison* as /in/ from the masculine adjective
divin (divine) in the singular form: *le divin‿enfant* (the divine infant).
This denasalization does not apply to the adjective *malin* (evil),
where nasality is retained in *liaison:* *malin‿esprit* [malɛ̃ nɛspri]
(evil spirit).

NOTES for nasalization of loanwords and foreign names:
/ɛ̃/ in some vocabulary, especially in names with adopted French
spellings: *Berlin, brindisi, Dublin, Hindou* (Hindu), *intermezzo,*
interview [ɛ̃tɛrvju], *Kremlin, Pékin* (Peking), *Quintus, Singapour,*
Singer, Vercingétorix, De Vinci.
/in/ other vocabulary: *Gerschwin, hendiadyin* [ɛ̃djadin]
(hendiadys), *Hindemith, Lindorf, mackintosh* [makintɔʃ], *rinforzando,*
Rubinstein, sprint [sprint], *Windsor.*

în	**/ɛ̃/**

the verbs *tenir* (to hold) and *venir* (to come) in the *passé simple* and
imperfect subjunctive tenses:
nous tînmes [tɛ̃:mə], *vous tîntes* [tɛ̃:tə], *nous vînmes* [vɛ̃:mə],
vous vîntes [vɛ̃:tə] (we/you held/came), *qu'il tînt* [tɛ̃], *qu'il vînt* [vɛ̃]
(that he held/came)

ïn	**/ɛ̃/**

before a consonant, and at the end of most ancient names:
Caïn, coïncidence (coincidence), *Ébroïn, Tubalcaïn*

/in/
before a vowel:
cocaïne (cocaine), *égoïne* (handsaw), *héroïne* (heroine)

-ing	**/iŋ/**

in a few onomatopoeic interjections, and in many English nouns
assimilated into French:
building [bildiŋ], *camping* [kãpiŋ], *casting* [kastiŋ], *ding ! dring !*
(ring!), *jogging* [dʒɔgiŋ] (jog/tracksuit), *meeting* [mitiŋ] (meet),

186 | FRENCH LYRIC DICTION

parking [paʁkiŋ] (parking lot), *planning* [planiŋ] (schedule),
pressing [pʁɛsiŋ] (drycleaning), *shopping* [ʃɔpiŋ], *télémarketing*
[telemaʁketiŋ] (telemarketing), *rowing* [ʁɔwiŋ], *smoking* [smɔkiŋ]
(tuxedo), *swing* [swiŋ], *yearling* [ljœʁliŋ], *yachting* [ljɔtiŋ]

⚠ /ɛ̃/ in *shampooing* [ʃɑ̃pwɛ̃] (shampoo)

inn-   *see **nn***

irr-   *see -**rr***

-is, -ïs   *see -**s***

-it, ît   *see -**t***

— J ○ [ʒi] —

j   /ʒ/
               always:
               ajout (addition), *bijoux* (jewellery), *cajou* (cashew), *Dijon, éjecter*
               (to eject), *Fréjus, il galèje* (he teases), *goujon* (dowel), *hors-jeu*
               (offside), *injure* (insult), *Jacques, j'ai* (I have), *jais* (jet black),
               jamais (never/ever), *jaune* (yellow), *je* (I), *Jean, jeu* (game),
               à jeun (fasting), *jeune* (young), *Jitomir, Jolivet, jouer* (to play),
               jour (day), *juif* (Jewish), *jus* (juice), *j'y vais* (I'm going), *kinkajou,*
               Latarjet, majeur (main/major), *naja* (cobra), *objet* (object), *Pujol,*
               quadrijumeau (quadrigeminal), *rejeter* (to reject), *séjour* (sojourn),
               toujours (always/still), *unijambiste* (one-legged man), *Valjean*

               NOTES for loanwords and foreign names:
               /j/ and initial /lj/ from German, Scandinavian, and Slavic
               languages: *fjeld, fjord* [fjɔʁd] or [fjɔːʁ], *Janatchek,* (Janáček),
               Jankélévitch, Johann, junker, poljé (polje), *Von Karajan.*
               /dʒ/ in most English words: *jazz* [dʒaːz], *jogging* [dʒɔgiŋ] (jog/
               tracksuit), *John, Joyce.*
               /ʒ/ for some English words assimilated into French: *jockey* [ʒɔkɛ],
               jury [ʒyʁi].
               /x/ or more simply /h/ in Spanish words, some of which occur
               occasionally in the repertoire: *jota, marijuana, mojito, navaja.*
               Other approximations for Spanish *j* are devoiced uvular *r* /ʁ̥/ and
               /ʒ/. The latter is the norm for the names *Don Juan* and *Juan Gris.*

FRENCH PRONUNCIATION A–Z | 187

— K ○ [kɑ] —

k

/k/
always:
anorak, bikini, Charlesky, Dukas, Érik, Floreski, Godebska, houka
(hookah), Irak (Iraq), Janatchek (Janáček), Kahn, kaléidoscope
(kaleidoscope), kangourou (kangaroo), karité (shea), Kéléyi,
kermesse (fun fair), khan, kilomètre (kilometre), klaxon (horn),
Klee, Kleinzach, koala, Kœchlin, Kœnig, Kœstler, Kœtzingue, korê/
korè [kɔrɛ] (kore), Koubitzky, Kruysen, Kuentz, Kunc, Kypris,
Lakmé, mazurka, Nilakantha, okapi, De Patek, Quimper-Karadec,
Roussalka (Rusalka), saké, tokaï (Hungarian Tokay), Ukraine,
Vikings, whisky [|wiski], Xenakis, yak, Zakros

NOTES for loanwords and foreign names:
/n/ is most often heard for kn- spellings in a few English words
where the k is silent: knickers [nikœːɾ] or [nikœɾs].

— L ○ [ɛl] —

l

/l/
in most cases:
alarme (alarm), Balzac, cobalt, délicat (fragile), éléphant (elephant),
falot (bland), galant (gallant), holà! (hey!), Irlande (Ireland), jaloux
(jealous), kleptomane (kleptomaniac), là-bas (over there), laine
(wool), las (weary), Lautréamont, Leconte de Lisle, léger (light), lent
(slow), Lescaut, Leucade (Lefkada), leur (their/them), lin (flax), lion
(lion), lit (bed), loi (law), loin (far), Loire, longtemps (a long time),
lorsque (while), louange (praise), lourd (heavy), luire (to shine),
lundi (Monday), lutin (elf), moulin (mill), Nil (Nile), olive, palme
(palm), qualité (quality), rouler (to roll), salé (salty), tulipe (tulip),
ultime (final), véhicule (vehicle), wagon-lit (sleeping car), xylitol,
Yougoslavie (Yugoslavia), zèle (zeal)

in most cases as the last letter of a word or name:
amical (friendly), annuel (annual), bocal (jar), Bréval, cheval (horse),
ciel (sky), football [fut boːl] (football/soccer), idéal (ideal), légal
(legal), linceul (shroud), Marcel, Maréchal, music-hall [myzi koːl]
(music hall), Narbal, Ploërmel, pluriel (plural), poil (fur), rappel
(reminder) Ravel, Roussel, Tourel, Wartel

188 | French Lyric Diction

ł
sometimes silent as the last letter of a word:
cul (backside), *gentil* (nice), *outil* (tool), *saoul* [su] (drunk)

in names with the *-aul-* spelling before a consonant:
Aulnoye-Aymeries, Faulquemont, Gaultier, Paulmier, Paulmy, Saulcy, Saulnier, Saulteux, Saulxures
Note:
/l/ and silent *ł* are both heard in the names *Aulnay, Aulne, Aulnoy,* and the word *aulne* (alder).

lh /l/
always, except after *i*:
Carvalho, Delhi, Lhérie, Lhomond, malhabile (clumsy), *Malherbe, malheur* (misfortune), *malhonnête* (dishonest), *Mulhouse, Nolhac, Poulhan*

ll /l/
in most cases after a vowel:
aller (to go), *alliance, Arbell, belle* (beautiful), *Boëllmann, Bollinger, cellule* (cell), *collège* (college), *dalle* (slab), *Fallières, folle* (crazy), *Gallet, Hallier, idyllique* (idyllic), *intelligent, Jullien, Lasalle, Lerolle, Lully, malle* (car trunk), *mille* (thousand), *Montpellier, pelle* (shovel), *Pelletier, Pollion* (Pollio), *rébellion* (rebellion), *Sibylle, tellement* (so), *Thill, tranquille* (peaceful), *Vallès, ville* (city)
Note:
The spelling *-ill-* is usually pronounced /j/ after another vowel.—*see -**ill-***

/ll/
at the beginning of a word in the spelling *ill-*:
illégitime (illegitimate), *illisible* (illegible), *illumination, illusion* (illusion), *illustre* (illustrious)

Notes for Spanish loanwords with the *ll* spelling:
These words are usually realized with /j/ in French, particularly noteworthy in Bizet's **Carmen**: *banderilleros* (also *francisé* in Escamillo's aria as « *banderilles* » [bɑ̃dərijə]), *caballeros, Manzanilla.*

— M ○ [ɛm] —

m /m/
before a vowel:
amour (love), *bémol* (flat), *Camus, drame* (drama), *Émile, famille* (family), *gamin* (kid), *homard* (lobster), *imiter* (to imitate), *jumeau* (twin), *kilomètre* (kilometre), *larme* (tear), *main* (hand), *manger*

(to eat), *mardi* (Tuesday), *Le Masne, mauve, médaille* (medal), *menace, mère* (mother), *meuble* (furniture), *Meung, Meunier, miel* (honey), *mille* (thousand), *mioche* (kid), *molle* (soft), *Montmartre, moules* (mussels), *muet* (mute), *mur* (wall), *Mylio, numéro* (number), *orme* (elm), *Pomey, quasiment* (nearly), *Rameau, serment* (oath), *timide* (shy), *unanime* (unanimous), *volume, Wasmes, Ximénès, Yémen, Zamora*

in many cases after a vowel at the end of a syllable in borrowed words—*see specific spellings*

/˜/
causes nasalization of the preceding vowel in most cases where a consonant follows—*see each vowel for nasalized spellings with* **m**

-mb, -mbs	*see -b, -s*
-mm-	/m/ nearly always: *assommer* (to knock out), *comme* (like/as), *dilemme* (dilemma), *flamme* (flame), *gamme* (musical scale/range), *Gommecourt, grammaire* (grammar), *homme* (man), *Jammes, Lemmens, pomme* (apple), *nous sommes* (we are) /mm/ at the beginning of a word in the spelling *imm-*: *immense* (immense), *immédiat* (immediate), *imminence, immoler* (to sacrifice), *immortel* (immortal) ⚠ /ɛ̃m/ in a few words with the spelling *imm-*: *immangeable* (inedible), *immanquable* (inevitable), *immanquablement* (inevitably), *immariable* (unmarriable), *immettable* (unwearable)
mn	/mn/ in most words, especially where *m* ends a syllable and *n* begins the next, including some ancient names: *Agamemnon, automnal* (autumnal), *calomnie* (slander), *Clytemnestre* (Clytemnestra), *gymnase* (gymnasium), *hymne* (hymn/anthem), *indemne* (unscathed), *mnémonique* (mnemonic), *omnibus, omnipotent, Polymnie* (Polyhymnia), *Le Semnoz, somnoler* (to slumber), *Vertumne* (Vertumnus)

190 | FRENCH LYRIC DICTION

/n/

silent m in a few words:

automne (autumn), *condamner* (to condemn), *damner* (to damn),
recondamner (to resentence)

-mp, -mps,
-mpt, -mpts

see -p, -ps, -pt, -pts

— N o [ɛn] —

n

/n/

in most cases before a vowel or mute *h*, or after a consonant
other than *g*:

âne (donkey), *bonheur* (happiness), *canapé* (sofa), *dénoncer* (to denounce),
énorme (enormous), *fanal* (headlight), *gouvernement* (government),
Hanovre (Hanover), *inaperçu* (unnoticed), *journal* (newspaper), *kiné*
(physio), *Lamartine, Monique* (Monica), *nain* (dwarf), *De Nangis, net*
(clear/distinct), *neuf* (nine), *neutre* (neutral), *Nevers, nez* (nose),
nièce (niece), *Noémie, noix* (nut), *non* (no), *nos* (our), *Nourabad, nuit*
(night), *nul* (non-existent), *nylon, onyx, Panurge, quenelles* (fish
dumplings), *Renoir, La Seine, traîner* (to drag), *unité* (unit/unity),
vinaigre (vinegar), *Wiéner, xénon* (xenon), *Yvelines, zonal*

in many cases after a vowel at the end of a syllable in borrowed
words—*see specific spellings*

/˜/

causes nasalization of the preceding vowel in most cases where a
consonant follows, or as the last letter of a word—*see each vowel for
nasalized spellings with **n***

NOTES for *liaison*:
Where *liaison* is permitted in singing, it is made with /n/ from
word-final, nasalizing *-n.—see specific spellings*

ñ

NOTES:
The letter *ñ* is foreign to French, but sometimes encountered
in borrowed Spanish vocabulary, as in the name of the pianist
Ricardo Viñes. In the repertoire, *señor* and *señora* are found in Bizet's
Carmen, as well as in Ravel's ***L'heure espagnole***, in which *Doña Sol* is
also mentioned. In all these cases, and in general, the pronunciation
should be /ɲ/. In the same Ravel opera is the character *Don Inigo
Gomez*, which is sometimes spelled as « *Iñigo* », but this name is

always pronounced with /n/. It should also be noted that the dance form *habanera* does not have the letter ñ, despite numerous instances of this misspelling. It is pronounced [|abaneɾa] in French.

-nc, -nd /ˉ/
usually causes nasalization of the preceding vowel, with silent final *e, d*:
ajonc (gorse shrub), *allemand* (German), *on attend* (one waits), *banc* (bench), *blanc* (white), *on convainc* (one convinces), *on défend* (one defends), *Durand*, *Edmond*, *franc* (frank), *goéland* (gull), *Hélinand*, *infécond* (infertile), *jonc* (reed), *Leblanc*, *marchand* (merchant), *Morand*, *Normand* (Norman), *D'Osmond*, *profond* (deep), *quand* (when), *rond* (circle/round), *second* (second), *tronc* (trunk), *on vainc* [vɛ̃] (one conquers), *il vend* (he sells)

⚠ /ˉg/ nasality with final -g in *zinc* [zɛ̃:g]
/ˉk/ nasality with final -c in *onc* [õːk] (never)
NOTE:
Donc (well/so/then) is pronounced [dõk] or [dõ]. See Chapter 7: 'Words with Variable Pronunciations'.

NOTES for *liaison*:
Where *liaison* is permitted in singing, it is made with /t/ from word-final -nd: *il m'apprend à jouer* (he teaches me to play), *quand on veut se faire adorer* (when one wants to be adored), *la poule pond un œuf* (the chicken lays an egg).
Liaison is exceedingly rare from verbs ending in *-vainc*.
Liaison is made with /k/ from the word *franc* (frank) in several expressions: *franc et quitte* (free and clear), *franc arbitre* (free will).

NOTES for nasalization of loanwords and foreign names:
Nasalization and the pronunciation of final consonant can be quite unpredictable in names, and should be consulted on a case-by-case basis; notably unstable are those ending in *-land*, which can be [lɑ̃], [lɑ̃:d], or [land].

-ncs, -nct, *see -ct, -s, -ts*
-ncts, -nds,
-ngs

ng /ˉ/
causes nasalization of the preceding vowel in most cases at the end of a word:
basting [bastɛ̃] (joist timber), *Cambreling*, *Chassang*, *coing* (quince),

192 | French Lyric Diction

étang (pond), *hareng* [|aɾɑ̃] (herring), *Hornaing, long, Maing, Neung, Nostang, orang-outang* [ɔɾɑ̃ gutɑ̃] (orangutan), *poing* [pwɛ̃] (fist), *rang* (row), *sang* (blood), *shampooing* [ʃɑ̃pwɛ̃] (shampoo), *seing* (signature), *Seraing, Tourcoing*

causes nasalization of the preceding vowel in derivatives of the word *vingt* (twenty), and in a few cases where the root of a word ends in -*ng* and is followed by a consonant in the next syllable: *longtemps* (a long time), *sangsue* (leech), *vingtaine* (about twenty), *vingtième* (twentieth)

NOTE:
When *n* ends one syllable, and *g* begins the next, the *n* is usually silent and causes nasalization of the preceding vowel, and the *g* is pronounced normally: *anglais* [ɑ̃glɛ] (English), *danger* [dɑ̃ʒe], *Hongrie* (Hungary), *Langlois, songer* [sõʒe] (to think of).

NOTES for *liaison*:
Liaison from final -*ng* with /k/ is possible, but is often no longer practised; the nasal vowel followed by silent ~~ng~~ is the alternative: *un long̬ hiver* or *un long | hiver* (a long winter)

NOTES for nasalization of loanwords and foreign names:
/ŋ/ is very common in borrowed vocabulary, especially in English words with final -*ing*:   *camping* [kɑ̃piŋ], *Jungfrau, Kensington, Klingsor, Longfellow, Nan-King, parking* [paɾkiŋ] (parking lot), *planning* [planiŋ] (schedule), *pressing* [pɾɛsiŋ] (drycleaning), *smoking* [smɔkiŋ] (tuxedo), *swing* [swiŋ], *Washington, Wellington.*
/ŋg/ is often heard within a word or name before *l* or *r*, or before a vowel: *Buckingham, Furtwängler, Nottingham, zingara, zingaro, zingarello.* The same is true of the spelling -*nk*-, which is most often pronounced [ŋk]:   *Helsinki, Schenker.*
/˜g/ (nasality with final 'hard' *g*) is quite common at the end of a word after *a* or *o*:   *bang* [bɑ̃:g], *boomerang* [bumǝɾɑ̃:g], *gang* [gɑ̃:g], *gong* [gõ:g], *ping-pong* [piŋ põ:g], *rotang* [ɾɔtɑ̃:g] (rattan), *sarong* [saɾõ:g].
/˜/ (nasality with silent ~~ng~~) and /ŋ/ are sometimes both possible, especially in names: *Angkor, Bangkok.*

-ngt, -ngts   *see* **-t, -ts**

-nh-   /n/
nearly always:
anhéler (pant), *Bernhardt, Blavinhac, bonhomme* (man), *Copenhague, inhibé* (inhibited), *Ivanhoé, piranha.—see also* **en**

FRENCH PRONUNCIATION A–Z | 193

-nk- see **ng**

nn /n/
nearly always:
anniversaire (birthday), *Boëllmann*, *canne* (cane), *D'Haussmann*,
Loyonnet, *Nanny*, *ordonnance* (prescription), *panneau* (sign),
renne (reindeer), *Rozenn*, *la sienne* (his/hers/one's/its), *suranné*
(outdated), *Tannat*, *Yvonne*

/nn/
at the beginning of a word in the spelling *inn-*:
innombrable (innumerable), *innommable* (unspeakable), *innover*
(to innovate)

⚠ The word *innocent* and its derivatives are not subject to this
special doubling; articulation with /n/ is normal.

-ns, -nt, see **-s, -t, -ts**
-nts

— O o [o] —

o /ɔ/
in most cases—usually before a consonant (other than a single *m*
or *n* unless it is followed by another vowel):
aorte (aorta), *bol* (bowl), *bonheur* (happiness), *Chopin*, *corps* (body),
Doria, *éolien* (Aeolian), *folie* (madness), *Fromental*, *gothique* (Gothic),
hochet (rattle), *ironie* (irony), *Isolier*, *joli* (pretty), *Kolassi*, *local*, *mode*
(style), *note*, *oasis*, *obtenir* (to obtain), *occupé* (filled), *ode*, *offrir*
(to offer), *ogre*, *oïl* (northern French language), *okapi*, *olive*,
omission, *onyx*, *option*, *Oreste*, *osciller* (to swing/rock), *otage*
(hostage), *ovale* (oval), *oxygène* (oxygen), *Oyonnax*, *Ozanam*, *porter*
(to wear/carry), *quotidien* (daily), *Rodrigue*, *sort* (fate), *tort* (wrong),
utopie (utopia), *vol* (flight), *Wotan*, *Xhoris*, *yole* (skiff), *Zola*

/o/
when bearing an *accent circonflexe* ^ (circumflex)—*see* **ô**

when it is the final sound in a word—either as the last letter, or
before (a) silent letter(s), most notably in final *-os* and *-ot*:
alto, *Baillot*, *Cuénod*, *Diderot*, *écho* (echo), *flot* (surge), *galop*, *Girod*,
Gounod, *héros* (hero), *îlot* (islet), *jabot*, *kilo*, *Loriod*, *mot* (word), *nos* (our),
oh !, *les os* (the bones), *pot*, *Quito*, *rodéo* (rodeo), *sirop* (syrup), *sot*
(idiot), *trop* (too/too much), *Utrillo*, *Viardot*, *Warot*, *Yvetot*, *zéro* (zero)

before -ss- in derivatives of words where the spelling -os- is pronounced /o/, as well as words beginning in *foss*—*see* **-oss-**

before /z/:
arroser (to water), *Berlioz*, *chose* (thing), *Dalcroze*, *dose*, *gosier* (throat), *Don José*, *Joseph*, *Montrose*, *morose*, *narcose* (narcosis), *opposer* (to counter), *Poséidon*, *rose* (rose/pink), *rosée* (dew), *Rosette*, *Rozenn*, *Le Semnoz*, *supposer* (to assume), *Villecroze*, *viscose*

⚠ /ɔz/ in a few unstressed syllables: *cosaque* (Cossack), *losange* (diamond), *mosaïque* (mosaic), *Mozart*, *ozone*, *philosophe* (philosopher), *philosophie* (philosophy), *sosie* (spitting image)

in many cases in words ending in -*ome* and -*one*—*see* **-ome, -one**

in most cases, in careful pronunciation before /sj/, often in the suffix -*tion*:
commotion (shock), *dossier* (file), *dévotion* (devotion), *émotion* (emotion), *grossier* (uncouth), *locomotion*, *lotion*, *motion*, *notion*, *potion*, *promotion*

NOTES:
/ɔ/ is also heard in everyday speech in the words ending in -*otion*.
Os (bone/bones) is pronounced [ɔs] in the singular form, and [o] in the plural form. See Chapter 7: 'Words with Variable Pronunciations'.
Stressed closed /o/ tends to open to /ɔ/ in everyday speech in the following cases:
When stress is lost as the first part of an expression: *mot-à-mot* [mɔ ta mo]. (word for word), *croc-en-jambe* [krɔ kɑ̃ ʒɑ̃:bə] (stumble), *pot-au-lait* [pɔ to lɛ] (jug of milk).
In hyphenated or compound words were the first part ends in -*o*:
auto-immune [ɔtɔ imynə].
The word *trop* when followed by an adjective or adverb: *trop tard* [trɔ tar] (too late). See Chapter 7: 'Words with Variable Pronunciations'.
These modifications are often avoided in careful pronunciation, including vocal music.

ô

/o/
nearly always:
aumônier (chaplain), *côte* (rib/shore), *drôle* (funny), *Drôme*, *hôte* (host/guest), *impôt* (tax), *Jérôme*, *Lancôme*, *nô* (noh), *Pentecôte* (Pentecost), *Rhône*, *tôt* (early/sooner), *Vendôme*
NOTE:
Closed /o/ sometimes opens to /ɔ/ in everyday speech in the unstressed syllables of a few words: *côtelé* (ribbed), *côtelette* (cutlet),

FRENCH PRONUNCIATION A–Z· | 195

hôtel (hotel), *hôtelier* (hotelier), *hôtellerie* (hotel industry), *hôtesse* (hostess), and especially in *hôpital* (hospital) and *rôti* (roasted). Both pronunciations are correct, even in careful pronunciation.

oa

/ɔa/
in words where the vowels belong to different syllables, notably in the prefix *co-*:
boa, coaguler (to coagulate), *Croatie* (Croatia), *Joachim, koala, oasis*
NOTE:
The vowel of the prefix *co-* may close somewhat.

NOTES for English loanwords and names:
/oː/ in most vocabulary: *goal* [goːl], *toast* [toːst].

œ

/e/
in some vocabulary of Latin origin:
Comœdia, fœtus (fetus), *œsophage* (esophagus), *Œdipe* (Oedipus), *Phœbé* (Phoebus)

⚠ /ɛ/ before /s/:   *œstrus* (animal: in heat), *œstrogène* (estrogen)

oe, oê

/wa/
in a few words:
moelle (marrow), *poêle* (stove/frying pan) and derivatives: *moelleux* (soft/moist), *poêlon* (saucepan)

/ɔɛ/
in words where the vowels belong to different syllables, notably in the prefix *co-*:
coexister (to coexist), *coercition* (coercion)
NOTE:
The vowel of the prefix *co-* may close somewhat.

NOTES for loanwords and foreign names:
/ø/ in German vocabulary, opening to /œ/ for some speakers: *foehn* (mountain wind), *Goethe, lœss* (loess).
The spellings *œ* and *oe* are inconsistent in borrowed words, and are often used interchangeably.

oë

/ɔɛ/
in most cases:
Joëlle (Joelle), *Noël* (Christmas), *poëme* (poem), *poëte* (poet)
NOTE:
Poëme and *poëte* are now spelled *poème* and *poète*.

196 | FRENCH LYRIC DICTION

/ɔe/
in a few words, especially in older spellings where *ë* is in a free
syllable (i.e., ending in *ë*, not a consonant), now spelled *oé*:
canoë (canoe), *Féroë* (Faroe), *goéland* (gull), *goélette* (schooner),
goëmon (seaweed), *Noëmie* (Naomi)

/wɛ/
in a few cases:
boësse (wire brush), *boëtte* (bait), *foëne* (pronged harpoon)
NOTE:
These words are often encountered with variations in spelling
(i.e., *boëte, bouette, fouëne, fouène*).

œil, œill-   **/œj/**
always:
œil (eye), *œillade* (wink), *œillère* (visor), *œillet* (carnation),
œilletonner (to deadhead)

-oët, -ouët   **/wɛt/**
always in French names:
Carnoët, Le Faouët, Moët, Perrier-Jouët, Plancoët, Porhoët
NOTE:
/ɔɛt/ is possible as a secondary, careful pronunciation for names
ending in *-oët*.

œu   **/ø/**
when it is the final sound in a word—either as the last letter, or
before (a) silent letter(s):
bœufs (bulls), *Desbœufs, nœud* (knot), *nœuds* (knots), *Rœulx, vœu*
(wish), *vœux* (wishes)

/œ/
before a pronounced consonant:
bœuf (bull), *chœur* (choir/chorus), *cœur* (heart), *écœurer*
(to sicken), *Francœur, hors-d'œuvres* (appetizers), *Lebœuf,*
manœuvre (manoeuvre), *œuf* (egg), *œuvre* (work/opus),
Sacré-Cœur (Sacred Heart), *sœur* (sister)

NOTE:
Bœuf(s) and *œuf(s)* (bull/bulls) and (egg/eggs) are pronounced
[bœf], [œf] in the singular form, [bø] and [ø] in the plural form.
See Chapter 7: 'Words with Variable Pronunciations'.

FRENCH PRONUNCIATION A–Z | 197

-œuil, -œuill-	/œj/ in a few names: *Escœuilles, Vœuil*
-œux	/ø/ in the word *vœux* (wishes), and in names: *Nœux, Quœux, Rœux, Saint-Denœux*
oi, oî, oie	/wa/ in most cases, when not before a nasalizing *n*: *ils aboient* (they bark), *Antoine, avoine* (oats), *Badoit, Benoît, boîte* (box), *cloître* (cloister), *Croiza, déploiement* (deployment), *doigt* (finger), *espoir* (hope), *foi* (faith), *foie* (liver), *fois* (time), *joie* (joy), *Moinaux, je noie* (I drown), *oie* (goose), *patrimoine* (heritage), *Poitiers, soie* (silk), *quoi* (what), *roi* (king), *Roissy, Savoie* (Savoy), *Troie* (Troy), *voie* (lane), *ils voient* (they see), *Yvoire*

/wɑ/
in many cases in traditional pronunciation, when not followed by a nasalizing *n*, especially after a consonant plus *r*:
adroit (adept), *croire* (to believe), *croît* (the young of animals), *droit* (right/straight), *effroi* (fear), *endroit* (place), *étroit* (narrow), *froid* (cold), *Homfroi, Mainfroid, maladroit* (awkward), *proie* (pray), *La Rive Droite* (the Right Bank), *La Soufroide*

⚠ /wɑː/ is the norm in -*roir* endings: *apparoir* (to appear), *bourroir* (tamping rod), *comparoir* (to appear before), *gaufroir* (embossing press), *miroir* (mirror), *ouvroir* (workroom), *saupoudroir* (sprinkler/shaker), *terroir* (soil/land), *tiroir* (drawer)

NOTES:
Occasionally, -*oie* is set as /waə/ when verse-final: *complice de ma joie* (accomplice of my joy).
The spellings *oi, oî*, and *oie* are often pronounced with 'bright' *a*, as /wa/. This is more modern, and is generally the norm; 'dark' /ɑ/ is also suitable for vocal music.

oï	*see* ï
-oign-	/waɲ/ nearly always: *De Boigne, De Coigny, éloigner* (to distance), *vous joignez* (you connect), *poignard* (dagger), *poignée* (handle), *poignet* (wrist),

soigner (to tend), *Ségur-Lamoignon*, *témoignage* (testimony),
témoigner (to testify)

⚠ /ɔɲ/ in *oignon* [ɔɲõ] (onion)
NOTE:
Sometimes /waɲ/, but usually /ɔɲ/ in *encoignure* [ãkɔɲyːrə] (corner).

oin, -oing, /wɛ̃/
-ouin at the end of a word, or before a consonant, which may be either
silent or pronounced:
Ardoin, *babouin* (baboon), *baragouin* (gibberish), *Beaudouin*, *bédouin*
(fellow), *besoin* (need), *Les Camoins*, *chafouin* (wily), *coin* (corner),
coing (quince), *Cointreau*, *Cysoing*, *foin* (hay), *goinfre* (glutton),
Hardouin, *Hoin*, *Loing*, *lointain* (distant), *maringouin* (mosquito),
marsouin (porpoise), *moins* (less/minus), *pingouin* (penguin),
Poincaré, *poing* (fist), *sagouin* (slob), *shampooing* [ʃãpwɛ̃] (shampoo),
témoin (witness), *Tourcoing*
NOTE:
The *oin* and *ouin* spellings are not nasalized before a vowel.—*see oi, ou*

-ois, -oix /wa/
always:
je bois (I drink), *choix* (choice), *fois* (time), *poix* (peas)

/wɑ/
in many cases in traditional pronunciation, especially after a
consonant plus *r*:
bavarois (Bavarian), *bois* (wood), *je crois* (I believe), *croix*
(cross), *Delacroix*, *Dubois*, *hautbois* (oboe), *hongrois* (Hungarian),
Montmartrois (inhabitant of Montmartre), *mois* (month), *noix*
(nuts), *pois* (pea), *Quincampoix*, *trois* (three), *voix* (voice)

NOTE:
The spellings *-ois* and *-oix* are often pronounced with 'bright' *a*, as
/wa/. This is more modern, and is generally the norm; 'dark' /ɑ/
is also suitable for vocal music.

NOTES for *liaison*:
Where *liaison* is permitted, it is regularly made in singing with /z/:
je crois͜ entendre encore (I believe I still hear), *on entend des
voix͜ éperdues* (one hears distraught voices).

om /õ/
before a different consonant, which may be either silent or
pronounced:

FRENCH PRONUNCIATION A–Z | 199

bombe (bomb), *Bompard, Christoph Colomb* (Christopher Columbus), *compact, Compiègne, De Compostelle, complet* (complete/full), *comte* (count), *comté* (Comté cheese), *dompter* (to tame), *Domrémy, Fombeure, Gombert, Hautecombe, Lombard, nombreux* (numerous), *plomb* (metal: lead), *pomper* (to pump), *ombre* (shade), *Omphale, Palombie, Pompadour, Rombas, rompu* (broken off), *Sombreuil, somptueux* (sumptuous), *Sompuits, Vieux-Colombier, wombat* [|wõba]

in the word *nom* (name) and derivatives:
prénom (given name), *pronom* (pronoun)

in the title *Dom*, and at the end of a few names:
Absalom, Billom, Condom, Dom Pérignon, Drom, Riom

NOTES for nasalization of loanwords and foreign names:
/õ/ in some cases, especially in names with adopted French spellings: *Colombie* (Columbia), *compost* [kõpɔst], *Hombourg, Pompée* (Pompey).
/ɔm/ is common, especially at the end of a name: *Cromwell, Édom, Epsom.*

-ome   /oːmə/
at the end of several words:
arome/arôme (aroma), *atome* (atom), *axiome* (axiom), *brome* (bromine), *chrome* (chrome), *fibrome* (fibroma), *gnome, idiome* (idiom), *lipome* (lipoma), *monochrome* (monochromatic), *polychrome* (polychromatic), *rhizome, sarcome* (sarcoma), *staphylome* (staphyloma)

/ɔmə/
at the end of most other words:
cardamome (cardamom), *majordome* (major-domo/steward)

NOTE:
/oːmə/ and /ɔmə/ are both correct in some words: *carcinome* (carcinoma), *hippodrome* (racetrack), *tome, vélodrome* (velodrome).

omm   /ɔm/
always:
assommé (knocked out), *Belhomme, comment* (how), *Comminges, dommage* (pity), *Dommange, Franchomme, gomme* (eraser), *Gommecourt, homme* (man), *nommer* (to name), *ommatidia* (ommatidium), *pomme* (apple), *Pommery, sommaire* (summary), *tomme* (Tomme cheese)

on	**/õ/**

at the end of a word, or before a different consonant, which may be either silent or pronounced:
Avignon, bon (good), *contre* (against), *don* (gift), *échelon* (rung), *fondre* (to melt), *Goncourt, Hongrie* (Hungary), *ils iront* (they will go), *jongler* (to juggle), *long, Manon, non* (no), *oncle* (uncle), *pondre* (to lay/produce), *nous quittons* (we leave), *rond* (round), *ils sont* (they are), *De Tréfontaine, unisson* (unison), *ils vont* (they go), *wagon* (car/carriage), *Yverdon-les-Bains, zircon*

at the end of some familiar names, and most ancient and biblical names:
Aaron, Didon, Jason, Odéon, Panthéon, Samson

⚠ *Monsieur* (mister) is pronounced [məsjø]

NOTE:
The *on* spelling is not nasalized before a vowel or mute *h.—see **o***

NOTES for *liaison*:
Where *liaison* is permitted in singing, it can be made after the nasal vowel with /n/: *mon‿enfant* (my child), *on‿est très heureux* (we're very happy).

⚠ Denasalization occurs in *liaison* as /ɔn/ from the masculine adjective *bon* (good) in the singular form, and in words where *bon-* is followed by a vowel or mute *h*: *un bon‿ami* (a good friend), *bonhomme* (man), *bonheur* (happiness), *bonifier* (to enhance).

/ɔn/
in most cases in the negation *non-* before a vowel:
non-activité (inactivity), *non-intervention* (hands-off)

in the Spanish title *Don* before a vowel:
Don Inigo Gomez

NOTES for nasalization of loanwords and foreign names:
/õ/ in some cases, especially in names with adopted French spellings: *concerto, électron, Gonzalve, ion, Japon* (Japan), *Londres* (London), *micron, Monte-Carlo, nylon, rondo, Toronto.*
/ɔn/ is also common, especially at the end of a name: *Byron, eleison, Houston, Washington.*
/õ/ and /ɔn/ are sometimes both possible: *klaxon* [klaksõ] or [klaksɔn] (horn), *Klondike, Yukon.*

FRENCH PRONUNCIATION A–Z | 201

-one   /oːnə/
in a few cases:
cyclone (cyclone), *icone/icône* (icon), *zone* (zone)

/ɔnə/
in most cases:
Antigone, *Babylone* (Babylon), *carbone* (carbon), *Énone*, *Hermione*,
Madone (Madonna), *D'Ollone*, *pentagone* (pentagon), *trombone*
(trombone/paperclip), *Vérone* (Verona)

NOTE:
/oːnə/ and /ɔnə/ are both correct in *Amazone* (Amazon) and *ozone*.

onn   /ɔn/
always:
abandonner (to abandon), *bonne* (good), *connu* (known), *donner*
(to give), *Essonne*, *fredonner* (to hum), *Gandonnière*, *Heilbronn*,
illusionniste (conjurer), *jargonner* (to speak jargon), *klaxonner*
(to honk), *Lemonnier*, *Monnier*, *nonne* (nun), *ordonné* (organized),
personne (person), *questionner* (to question), *résonner* (to resonate),
Sorbonne, *tonnerre* (thunder), *unidirectionnel* (unidirectional),
visionner (to view), *Yonne*

-ons, -ont   see **on**, **-s**, **-t**

oo   /ɔə/
in words with *coo-* and *zoo-*:
coopérer (to cooperate), *zoologie* (zoology)
NOTE:
The vowel of the prefix *co-* may close somewhat.

⚠   /ɔ/ in *alcool* and derivatives: *alcoolique* (alcoholic), *alcoolisme* (alcoholism)

⚠   /o/ in *zoo*

NOTES for English loanwords:
/u/ is the norm: *bootlegger* [butlɛgœːɾ], *cool* [kul], *foot-ball*
[fut boːl] (football/soccer), *groom* [gɾum] (bellboy), *igloo* [iglu].

os   see **o**

-os   /o/
in the following words:
chaos, *clos* (closed), *dispos* (fresh/fit), *dos* (dos), *éclos* (hatched/
bloomed), *enclos* (enclosure), *forclos* (foreclosed), *gros* (large/fat),

héros (hero), *huis-clos* (behind closed doors), *los* (praise), *propos* (remarks), *repos* (rest)

at the end of a few names:
Cros, Duclos, Ducos, De Laclos

/ɔs/
in all other cases, mostly in words of scholarly origin:
albatros, cosmos, pathos, rhinocéros (rhinoceros)

in most names:
Bernanos, Carlos, Desnos, Éros

NOTE:
A secondary, somewhat less elevated pronunciation of /oːs/ exists for nearly all words and names that end in -os where word-final -s is pronounced.

-oss-   /os/
in derivatives of words where the spelling *os* is pronounced /o/, as well as words beginning in *foss-*:
Défossé, dossier (folder), *fosse* (pit), *fossette* (dimple), *grosse* (large/fat)
NOTE:
/ɔs/ is also correct in *fossile* (fossil), *fossoyeur* (grave/ditch digger), and *fossoyer* (to dig a grave/ditch).

/ɔs/
in all other cases:
bosse (hump/bump), *brosse* (brush), *carrosse* (carriage), *Écosse* (Scotland), *gosse* (kid), *Gossec, Linossier, Mossoul* (Mosul), *Ossian, possible, rosse* (nasty), *rossignol* (nightingale), *Saragosse* (Zaragoza)

-ot, -ôt   /o/
nearly always:
argot (slang), *aussitôt* (immediately), *Baillot, bientôt* (soon), *caillot* (clot), *dépôt* (delivery/yard), *Diderot, Drouot, Egrot, entrepôt* (warehouse), *flot* (surge), *gigot* (leg of lamb), *Henriot, îlot* (islet), *impôt* (tax), *jabot, lot* (prize), *maillot* (undershirt), *mot* (word), *nabot* (shorty), *ocelot, plutôt* (rather), *pot, prévôt* (provost), *rôt* (roast), *sabot* (hoof), *sitôt* (as soon as), *sot* (idiot), *Talbot, tantôt* (shortly/ earlier/sometimes), *tôt* (early/sooner), *Viardot, Warot, Yvetot*

⚠   /ɔt/ in *dot* (dowry) and *Lot*

FRENCH PRONUNCIATION A–Z | 203

ou, où, /u/
oû   in most cases:
Aznavour, bout (end/piece), *coût* (cost), *croûte* (crust), *douce* (soft/gentle), *Éourres, four* (oven), *gouffre* (chasm), *goûter* (to taste), *Hindoue* (Hindu), *Issoudun, jour* (day), *Koukouli, lourd* (heavy), *moûts* (grape must), *nous* (we), *ou* (or), *où* (where), *pour* (for), *ragoût* (stew), *Roussel, sous* (under), *tout* (all/everything), *voûte* (vault), *Wouwerman, Yourcenar, zazou*

/w/
before another vowel other than /ə/:
avoué (lawyer), *Boué, couard* (coward), *couiner* (to squeak), *douane* (customs), *Édouard, fouailler* (to whip), *fouiner* (to nose about), *gouache, inouï* (unheard), *jouer* (to play), *Louis, mouette* (gull), *nouer* (to tie), *ouailles* (flock), *ouananiche* (freshwater salmon), *ouaouaron* (bullfrog), *ouest* (west), *oui* (yes) *ouï-dire* (hearsay), *ouïe* (hearing), *ouïes* (gills), *ouïr* (to hear), *ouistiti* (marmoset), *pingouin* (penguin), *rouer* (to beat), *secouer* (to shake), *Thouars, voué* (destined for), *zouave* (fool)

⚠ /u/ after a consonant plus *l* or *r*: *brouette* (wheelbarrow), *éblouir* (to dazzle), *prouesse* (feat)

NOTE:
In the score, *ou* before another vowel sound is often set as dieresis with /u/: *lou-an-ge* [lu.ã:.ʒə] (praise).

NOTES for *liaison*:
Liaison is not possible to a few words beginning in *ou-* as /|w/:
oui (yes), *ouistiti* (marmoset).
Liaison may be made or not to the word *ouate* (cotton wool) and derivates: *ouaté* (quilted).

NOTES for English loanwords:
/u/ in some words: *scout* [skut].
/aw/ in other words, approximating the diphthong: *black-out* [blakaut].

oue /u/
in the future and conditional verb tenses:
je jouerai [ʒuʀe] (I will play), *nous jouerions* [ʒuʀjõ] (we would play)

always at the end of a syllable, especially when word-final:
j'avoue (I admit), *boue* (mud), *dénouement* (outcome), *dévouement* (dedication), *Padoue* (Padua), *roue* (wheel), *rouerie* (astuteness)

NOTES:
In this spelling in French words, *e* is not /ə/ when a letter follows it in the same syllable (other than in the *-es* and *-ent* endings): *fouet* [fwɛ] (whip), *jouet* (toy), *pirouette*, *Rouen*. Often set as /uə/ when verse-final: *qui vient caresser sa joue* (which caresses her cheek).

-ouët	*see -oët*

-ouil, -ouill-   /uj/
always:
agenouilloir [aʒənujwaːɾ] (kneeler), *bouillabaisse*, *bouillir* (to boil), *bouilloire* [bujwaːɾə] (kettle), *Bouilly*, *chatouillement* (tickling), *épouiller* (to delouse), *fenouil* (fennel), *Genouillac*, *grenouille* (frog), *grouiller* (to mill about), *mouiller* (to get wet), *nouilles* (noodles), *Rambouillet*, *Rouillard*, *rouiller* (to rust), *Souillot*, *touiller* (to toss), *De La Trémouille*, *Trouillefou*

-ouin   *see oin*

-oum, -oun   /um/, /un/
in a few words, notably:
atchoum! (achoo!), *boum!* (boom!), *Cameroun* (Cameroon), *Haroun*, *Khartoum*, *pantoum*, *simoun* (simoon), *vroum!* (vroom!)

-out, -oût   *see -t*

-oux   /u/
always:
Arnoux, *bijoux* (jewellery), *cailloux* (pebbles), *choux* (cabbages), *doux* (gentle/soft), *époux* (spouse), *Falloux*, *genoux* (knees), *hiboux* (owls), *jaloux* (jealous), *Ledoux*, *Mantoux*, *Nectoux*, *poux* (lice), *roux* (red-head), *saindoux* (lard), *Troispoux*, *Ventoux*

ow   /o/
in some borrowed English vocabulary:
bungalow [bœ̃galo], *chow-chow* [ʃo ʃo], *cow-boy* [kobɔj] (cowboy), *Longfellow*, *show* [ʃo]

/aw/
in other borrowed English vocabulary, approximating the diphthong:
Brown, *Cape Town*

FRENCH PRONUNCIATION A–Z | 205

/ɔv/
in Slavic ames:
Landowska, Minkowski
NOTE:
For some speakers, Slavic names with *ow* are pronounced
/ɔf/ before an unvoiced consonant.

⚠ /u/ in the word *clown* [klun]

oy /waj/
in most cases before another vowel:
Boyer, Desnoyers, Doyen, joyeux (happy), *Noyon, Pont-en-Royans,
Royan, Royer, Soyer, Les Troyens* (The Trojans), *vous voyez* (you see)
NOTE:
/wajj/ in verb tenses with the *-oyi-* spelling, distinguishing them from
tenses pronounced /waj/ with the spelling *-oy-*: *nous croyions* [kʁwaj.jõ]
(we were believing), *que vous croyiez* [kʁwaj.je] (that you believe).

/ɔj/
before another vowel in a few cases:
boyard (boyar), *caloyer* (caloyer monk), *coyau* (sprocket),
coyote [kɔjɔtə], *Goya, goyave* (guava), *Hirigoyen, Loyola, Loyonnet,
Mazoyères-Chambertin, oyat* (beachgrass), *Oyonnax, Les Samoyèdes*
(the Samoyedic people), *Serkoyan*

in conjugations of the archaic verb *ouïr* (to hear):
nous oyons (we hear), *vous oyez* (you hear), *oyant* (hearing), and
especially in the imperative *oyez !* (hear ye!)
NOTE:
/ɔjj/ in verb tenses of *ouïr* that have the *-oyi-* spelling, distinguishing
them from tenses pronounced /ɔj/ with the spelling *-oy-*: *nous
oyions* [ɔj.jõ] (we were hearing), *que vous oyiez* [ɔj.je] (that you hear).

/wa/
in a few names before a consonant:
Boylesves, Coypel, Coysevox

-oy, -oye, -oyes /wa/
always in names:
*D'Aulnoy, Bonnefoy, Chesnoy, Cloyes, Delvoye, Duvernoy, Essoyes,
Fourcoy, Geoffroy* (Geoffrey), *Herleroy, Jouffroy, Lavoy, Lavoye,
Millevoye, Ormoy, Quesnoy, Rouvroy, Roye, Savoy, Troy, Troyes, Vernoy*

oz *see o*

206 | FRENCH LYRIC DICTION

— P ○ [pe] —

p

/p/

in most cases:

après (after), *Bonaparte, Cyclope* (Cyclops), *départ* (departure), *expression, Fallope, groupe* (group), *hysope* (hyssop), *impact, jupe* (skirt), *képi, Lapissida, mépris* (scorn), *Napoléon, option, pain* (bread), *Pan, Paris, Pasdeloup, pauvre* (poor), *pelouse* (lawn), *pénible* (troublesome), *peste* (plague), *peu* (little) *peur* (fear), *pied* (foot), *pire* (worse), *pluie* (rain), *pneu* (tire), *poilu* (hairy), *Pollux, Pons, pour* (for), *preuve* (proof), *puis* (then), *pur* (pure), *Quimperlé, râpé* (grated), *sape* (sap), *tapis* (carpet), *usurper* (to steal), *vapeur* (steam), *Winnipeg, xérocopier* (to xerox copy), *youpi !* (yippee!), *Zampa*

-p

~~p~~

usually silent as the last letter of a word or name, including after a nasalizing *m*:

beaucoup (much/a lot), *camp, cantaloup* (cantaloupe), *champ* (field), *coup* (blow/stroke), *drap* (sheet), *galop, loup* (wolf), *Pasdeloup, Saint-Loup, sparadrap* (surgical tape), *sirop* (syrup), *trop* (too/too much)

NOTE:

Silent final ~~p~~ remains silent at the end of the first part of a compound word before another consonant: *Champmeslé, Champsaur*.

/p/

as the last letter of a few words, especially interjections:

cap (mark/course), *cep* (vine stock), *hep !* (hey!) *hip !, hop !, houp !* (hup!), *julep, stop !, top !*

in *liaison* from *beaucoup* (much/a lot) and *trop* (too/too much) only:

beaucoup‿aimé (much loved), *trop‿heureuse* (too happy)

NOTE:

Trop (too/too much) is pronounced [tro] or [trɔp], depending on the context. See Chapter 7: 'Words with Variable Pronunciations'.

NOTES for loanwords and foreign names:

/p/ is the norm in vocabulary of other languages, including the end of many English words: *clip* [klip], *handicap* [|ãdikap], *leadership* [lidœrʃip].

pf

/pf/

in most cases, especially for borrowed German vocabulary:

Pfeffel, pfennig [pfɛnig], *pfft !* (pshaw!), *Les Schtroumpfs* (The Smurfs)

FRENCH PRONUNCIATION A–Z | 207

NOTE:
/p/ may be articulated very lightly, or disappear altogether; /f/ could therefore be considered a secondary pronunciation for this spelling.

⚠ /f/ in French compound words, where the two letters belong to separate syllables, with the first ending in silent *p*: *Champfleury*.

ph /f/
always:
aleph, alphabet, blasphème (blasphemy), *Cléophas* (Cleopas), *Daphné, éléphant* (elephant), *francophone, graphie* (spelling), *homophone, Iphigénie* (Iphigenia), *Joseph, kymographe* (kymograph), *lexicographe* (lexicographer), *Méphistophélès, nénuphar* (lily pad), *Ophélie, phare* (lighthouse), *phase, phénomène* (phenomenon), *Phidylé, phlox, Phœnix, photo, phrasé* (phrasing), *Phthie* (Phthia), *sphère* (sphere), *trophée* (trophy), *vibraphone, Westphalie* (Westphalia), *xylophone, zéphyr* (zephyr)

pn- /pn/
at the beginning of a word:
pneu (tire), *pneumatique* (pneumatic)

pp /p/
always:
appétit (appetite), *Coppélius, Dieppe, grippe* (flu), *Hepp, Hippolyte* (Hippolytus), *hippopotame* (hippopotamus), *nappe* (tablecloth), *Philippe, Poppée* (Poppaea), *rappel* (reminder), *trappe* (trap), *Xanthippe, zipper* (to zip)

NOTES for Italian loanwords and names:
/p(p)/ consonant lengthening may or may not be made in musical terms and names: *Beppo, troppo.*

ps- /ps/
at the beginning of a word or name:
psaume (psalm), *pseudonyme* (pseudonym), *psoriasis, Psyché* (Psyche), *psychologie* (psychology)

-ps /ps/
in a few cases:
Aups, biceps, Cécrops, Chéops, chips [ʃips] (potato chips), *laps* (period), *Lesseps, oups !* (oops!), *Pélops, reps* (rep: ribbed fabric), *schnaps* (Schnapps), *triceps*

208 | FRENCH LYRIC DICTION

~~ps~~

in all other cases, especially after a nasalizing *m*, and in the plural
form of words ending in silent *~~p~~*:
D'Aulps, Bontemps, corps (body), *je corromps* (I corrupt/bribe),
Descamps, galops, Le Horps, j'/tu interromps (I/you interrupt), *longtemps*
(a long time), *tu romps* (you break), *temps* (time), *Vieuxtemps*

NOTES for *liaison*:
Liaison is possible from word-final *-ps*, but is rare from verbs ending
in *-omps* (i.e., only in a very elevated tone); where *liaison* is permitted
in singing, it can be made with /z/: *les champs̮ et les prés* (the fields
and the meadows), *longtemps̮ encore* (still a long time), *je romps̮ à
jamais les liens fraternels!* (I break the fraternal bonds forever!).

pt-

/pt/
at the beginning of a word or name:
Ptah, ptérodactyle (pterodactyl), *Ptolémée* (Ptolemy), *ptose* (ptosis)

-pt-

/t/
in the following words, and most of their derivatives, unless
listed below:
baptême (baptism), *baptiste* (Baptist), *compter* (to count), *comptine*
(nursery rhyme), *dompter* (to tame), *exempter* (to make exempt),
promptitude (swiftness), *sculpture* (sculpture), *septième* (seventh)

/pt/
in the following words, and most of their derivatives, unless
listed above:
adapter (to adapt), *adopter* (to adopt), *aptitude* (aptitude), *captif*
(captive), *consomptif* (wasting away), *contemptible* (contemptible),
Égypte (Egypt), *excepter* (to except), *Néoptolème* (Neoptolemus),
Neptune, prescripteur (prescriber), *présomptueux* (presumptuous),
rédempteur (redeemer), *septembre* (September), *Septème, septique*
(septic), *septuor* (septet), *somptueux* (sumptuous), *symptomatique*
(symptomatic), *Triptolème* (Triptolemus)

⚠ /ps/ in the word *ineptie* (ineptness)

/ps/
in *-ption* endings:
L'Assomption (Assumption), *conception, consomption* (consumption),
corruption, exemption, prescription (dictate), *rédemption* (redemption)

FRENCH PRONUNCIATION A–Z | 209

-pt, -pts /pt/
in a few cases:
abrupt, abrupts (steep/abrupt), *Apt, concept, concepts, rapt*
(kidnapping), *rapts* (kidnappings), *transept, transepts*

⚠ /t/ in *sept* (seven). See Chapter 7: 'Numbers'.

NOTE:
In the line « *Vraiment cet homme a des biceps qui dépassent tous mes
concepts...* » from Ravel's ***L'heure espagnole***, it is customary for
Concepcion to sing an intentional mispronunciation of the plural
concepts as [kõsɛps], in order to create a comical rhyme with *biceps*
[bisɛps].

~~pt, pts~~
silent in some cases, especially after a nasalizing *m*:
Belrupt, Blancherupt, Chalupt, exempt, exempts (exempt), *Grandrupt,
prompt, prompts* (ready), *il corrompt* (he corrupts/bribes), *elle
interrompt* (she interrupts), *on rompt* (one breaks), *Villerupt*

NOTES for *liaison*:
Where *liaison* is permitted in singing, it is made with /t/ and /z/,
but is rare from verbs ending in *-ompt* (i.e., only in a very elevated
tone):   *qui rompt‿avec la tradition* (which breaks with tradition),
Dieux, si prompts‿autrefois à les réduire en poudre (gods, once so quick
to reduce them to dust).

— Q ∘ [ky] —

q /k/
always:
cinq (five), *coq* (rooster), *Iraq, Lecoq, Montuq, qat* (khat),
Qatar, Rivenq

⚠ silent *q* in *cinq* (five) as an adjective before a pronounced
consonant: *cinq garçons* (five boys). See Chapter 7: 'Numbers'.

qu /k/
in most cases before a vowel:
Alquif, bouquet, coquille (shell), *disque* (disc), *équipe* (team), *Frasquita,
Guadalquivir, Hennequin, inquiet* (worried), *jusque* (till), *kiosque*
(kiosk), *Lalique, musique* (music), *nuque* (neck), *oblique* (slanted),
panique (panic), *quadrille, quai* (wharf), *qualité* (quality), *quand*
(when), *que* (that/which), *quel* (which), *queue* (tail),

qui (who/which), *quinze* (fifteen), *quoi* (what), *quotidien* (daily),
reliquat (remainder), *squelette* (skeleton), *tragique* (tragic), *unique*,
vainqueur (conqueror), *Wasquehal*, *xanthique* (xanthic), *yttrique*
(yttric), *zoologique* (zoological)

⚠ /ky:/ in *piqûre* (injection/shot)

/kw/

in many words with the spelling *qua*:
adéquat (appropriate), *aquarelles* (watercolours), *aquarium*
[akwaʁjɔm] (aquarium), *desquamer* [dɛskwame] (to peel off),
équateur (equator), *Équateur* (Ecuador), *équation* (equation),
quadruple, *quatuor* [kwatɥɔːʁ] (quartet: piece of music), *squameux*
(scaly), *square* [skwaːʁə] (park/square), *squatine* (angelfish)

NOTES:
/kw/ and /k/ are both correct in a few words: *Quadragésime*
(Quadragesima), *quadratique* (quadratic), *Quadrifrons, quadrilatéral*
(quadrilateral), *quadrisyllabique* (four-syllable), *quantique*
(adjective: quantum), *quantum* (noun: quantum), *quartette*
(quartet of players), *quorum, quota.*
The word *quasi* is pronounced [kazi] *à la française.* In the poem *Clair
de lune* by Verlaine, it would not be wrong to sing « *quasi triste* »
(quasi sad) with the Latin pronunciation [kwazi], which creates
a lovely rhyme with « *paysage choisi* » (chosen landscape) [ʃwazi].
This rather esoteric delivery could very likely have been the
original intention of the poet, although it must be noted that this
is not the norm for the well-known settings of this poem.

/kɥ/

in several cases, usually with the spelling -*qui*-:
aquifère (aquifer), *équidistant* (equidistant), *équilatéral* (equilateral),
obliquité (obliqueness), *Quirinal, Quirinus, réquiem* [ʁekɥiɛm]
(requiem), *sesquicentenaire* (sesquicentennial), *ubiquité* (ubiquity)

⚠ /k/ in some common words beginning in *équi*-: *équilibre* (balance),
équinoxe (equinox), *équipe* (team), *équitable* (equitable), *équité* (equity),
équivalent (equivalent), *équivoque* (equivocal), and their derivatives

NOTE:
/kɥ/ and /k/ are both correct in some cases: *équestre*
(equestrian), *équidé* (member of the horse family), *questeur*
(quaestor), *questure* (quaestorship), *quiescent, quiétisme* (quietism),
quiétude (quiet), *quinquagénaire* (person in his/her fifties),
quinquennat (five-year term), *Quinctilius, Quintilien, Quintus.*

Notes for loanwords and foreign names:
/kw/ in English and Italian vocabulary: *Queensland, tranquillo.*
/kv/ in German vocabulary: *Quantz.*

qua, que, qué	see *qu*

queu, queue	/kø/

at the end of a word, or before a silent letter:
aqueux (watery), *belliqueux* (aggressive), *queue* (tail), *queues* (tails), *visqueux* (slimy)

in a stressed syllable, before /z/:
moqueuse (slimy), *muqueuse* (mucous membrane), *traqueuse* (nervous woman)

in an unstressed syllable:
équeuter (to remove the stems from), *queuter* (to screw up)

/kœ/
in a stressed syllable before a pronounced consonant other than /z/:
chroniqueur (columnist), *diagnostiqueur* (diagnostician), *liqueur* (liquor), *moqueur* (teasing), *plaqueur* (plater), *Queuille, remorqueur* (tug boat).

qui, quo	see *qu*

— R o [ɛːR] —

r

/ɾ/
in most cases, including before a consonant which may be either silent or pronounced:
art, Berlioz, carte (card), *dire* (to say), *érable* (maple), *Fauré, Grétry, héron* (heron), *Istres, jurer* (to swear), *Klingsor, lire* (to read), *mordre* (to bite), *nerf* (nerve), *D'Orléans, porte* (door), *Quarton, rang* (row), *rare, rat, réel* (real), *repas* (meal), *rêve* (dream), *rier* (to laugh), *rincer* (to rinse), *riz* (rice), *robe* (dress), *rond* (round), *rose* (rose/pink), *roué* (sly), *rouge* (red), *rue* (road), *ruines* (ruins), *Sartre, trésor* (treasure), *Urbain, vrai* (true), *Warin, xérès* (sherry), *ypréau* (white poplar), *zèbre* (zebra)

NOTE:
Uvular *r* often replaces apical *r* in modern singing practice, and always replaces it in speech. See Chapter 3 for an explanation of these variants.

212 | FRENCH LYRIC DICTION

-r
silent after the letter *e* in the stressed syllable of a large number
of words and names—*see -er, -ers, -ier, -iers*

-rc   *see c*

-rd, -rds   /ɾ/
always:
d'abord (at first/for a start), *bavard* (chatty), *bords* (banks),
canard (duck), *dard* (stinger), *Édouard, Fragonard, gourd* (numb),
homard (lobster), *Isnard, jobard* (gullible), *Lesgards, lourd* (heavy),
Montagnards, il mord (it bites), *je mords* (I bite), *nord* (north),
oreillard (lop-eared), *je perds* (I lose), *poignard* (dagger), *Quittard,*
remords (remorse), *Richard, sourd* (deaf), *il tord* (it twists), *tu tords*
(you twist), *vieillard* (old man), *zonard* (dropout)

NOTES for *liaison:*
Liaison is generally not permitted from the word-final *-rd* spelling.
⚠ *Liaison* with /t/ is permitted in singing from word-final *-rd* in
inversion of the verb only, which is very rarely encountered:
mord‿il? (Does it bite?).
Liaison is made in singing with /z/ from word-final *-rds* in the
plural form, but is rare from verbs with this ending (i.e., only in a
very elevated tone): *regards‿impénitents* (incorrigible stares),
je perds‿encore (I lose again).

remm-   /ɾãm/
at the beginning of a word:
remmailler (to darn), *remmailloter* (to swaddle again), *remmancher*
(to put a new handle on), *remmener* (to bring back)

ress-   *see e*

-rf, -rg   *see f, g*

rh, rrh   /ɾ/
always:
cirrhose (cirrhosis), *enrhumé* (with a cold), *Gomorrhe* (Gomorrah),
Jourdan-Morhange, myrrhe (myrrh), *Rhadamiste* (Rhadamistus),
Rhené-Baton, Rhin (Rhine), *rhinocéros* (rhinoceros), *Rhodes, Rhône,*
rhum [ɾɔm] (rum)

FRENCH PRONUNCIATION A–Z | 213

-rr-

/rr/
at the beginning of a word in the spelling *irr-*:
irrationnel (irrational), *irréconciliable* (irreconcilable), *irrésistible*
(irresistible), *irriter* (to irritate)

in the future and conditional tenses of a few *-ir* verbs, most
notably *courir* (to run) and *mourir* (to die):
je courrai, tu courras, il/elle/on courra, nous courrons, vous courrez,
ils/elles courront (I/you/he/she/one/it/we/you/they will run)
je courrais, tu courrais, il/elle/on courrait, nous courrions, vous courriez,
ils/elles courraient (I/you/he/she/one/it/we/you/they would run)
je mourrai, tu mourras, il/elle/on mourra, nous mourrons, vous mourrez,
ils/elles mourront (I/you/he/she/one/it/we/you/they will die)
je mourrais, tu mourrais, il/elle/on mourrait, nous mourrions, vous
mourriez, ils/elles mourraient (I/you/he/she/one/it/we/you/they
would die)
NOTES:
The pronunciation of the spelling *-rr-* with rolled /rr/ helps to
distinguish these verb tenses from other very similar ones spelled
with single *-r-* as flipped /ɾ/.
Other intervocalic spellings of *-rr-* can also be rolled, where
heightened expressivity is desired: *horrible, marronner* (to gripe),
terreur (terror).

-rs

/ɾ/
in most cases:
j'acquiers (I acquire), *ailleurs* (elsewhere/besides), *alors* (so/then),
Audemars Piguet, Bongars, Cahors, Cendrars, Cinq-Mars, concours
(competition), *je conquiers* (I conquer), *convers* (layperson),
cours (course), *débours* (expenses), *dehors* (outside), *discours*
(pronunciation), *divers* (varied), *je dors* (I sleep), *envers* (towards),
D'Escars, fors (except), *Gauthier-Villars, Gers, hors* (out of/apart from),
Lastours, Loève-Veimars, je meurs (I die), *Montbars, mors* (bit for horses),
Naours, parcours (route/course), *pervers* (perverse), *Plessis-lès-Tours,*
plusieurs (several), *rebours* (backward), *recours* (recourse), *tu requiers*
(you require/call for), *revers* (back side), *secours* (help), *je sers* (I serve),
Thouars, tiers (a third), *Tours, à travers* (through/across), *univers*
(universe), *Vaucouleurs, Vaurs, velours, Vercors, vers* (toward/around)

/ɾs/
in a few cases:
Ars, cers (Cers wind), *mars* (March), *ours* (bear)

NOTE:
/ɾ/ or /ɾs/ in a few cases: *Anvers, mœurs* (manners/morals), *Salers.*

⚠ silent ~~rs~~ in *gars* [gɑ] (guy/guys), *volontiers* (gladly), some names
ending in *-ers*, and almost all names ending in *-iers—see* **-ers, -iers**

NOTES for *liaison:*
Liaison is generally not permitted from the word-final *-rs* spelling.

⚠ *Liaison* with /z/ is permitted in singing from plural *-rs* only:
chers‿instants (dear moments), *divers‿attractions* (varied attractions),
leurs‿amours (their loves), *plusieurs‿amis* (several friends).
Liaison is also made from *tiers* (third) only in the expressions
le Tiers‿État (the Third Estate), and *tiers‿ordre* (third order), as
well as from the word *toujours* (always/still) in some cases.
See Chapter 5: 'The Use of *Liaison* in Common Vocabulary' and
Chapter 7: 'Words with Variable Pronunciations'.

-rt, -rts

/ɾ/
always:
Albert, art, beaux-arts (fine arts), *Brasparts, concert, court* (short),
départs (departures), *écart* (distance), *Favart, Flaubert, effort, export,
fort* (strong/strongly/very), *Goncourt, Hébert, Ibert, Jacmart, Jobert,
Lambert, mort* (death), *on meurt* (one dies), *mort* (death), *Niort, offert*
(free/given), *ouvert* (open), *part* (portion), *Prévert, Questembert,
Robert, Rouart, Salabert, on sort* (one goes out), *sports, support*
(support/shelf), *tort* (wrong), *vert* (green), *Walcourt*

NOTES for *liaison:*
Liaison is generally not permitted from the word-final *-rt* spelling.

⚠ *Liaison* with /t/ is permitted in singing from word-final *-rt* in
inversion of the verb only: *sort‿on*? (is one going out?).

⚠ *Liaison* with /t/ is permitted in singing from the adverb *fort*
(strongly/very):   *fort‿aimable* (very friendly).
Liaison is permitted in singing with /z/ from word-final plural *-rts*:
arts‿et métiers (arts and crafts), *mes yeux verts‿et dorés* (my green
and golden eyes).

NOTES for loanwords and foreign names:
/ɾ/ in familiar names: *Marie-Stuart* (Mary, Queen of Scots),
Mozart, Ruckert, Schubert.
/ɾt/ is also quite common: *Lord Elfort, flirt* [flœɾt], *Rupert, Misia Sert,
shorts* [ʃɔɾt], *Stuttgart, tee-shirt* [ti ʃœɾt], *yaourt* [ljauɾt] (yoghurt).
/ɾ/ or /ɾt/ in a few cases: *fart* (ski wax), *Gevaert, yogourt* (yoghurt).

FRENCH PRONUNCIATION A–Z | 215

— S o [ɛs] —

s-

/s/
at the beginning of a word or name:
sable (sand), *Saint-Michel* (Saint Michael), *Samuel, sans* (without),
Sauguet, sbire (henchman), *Scribe, secours* (help), *La Seine, sérénade*
(serenade), *si* (if), *Siebel, skier* (to ski), *slave* (Slavic), *smoking*
[smɔkiŋ] (tuxedo), *sœur* (sister), *Solange, sont* (are), *souahéli*
(Swahili), *soupe* (soup), *sport, Strasbourg, suite, sur* (on), *svelte*
(slender), *swing* [swiŋ], *Syrinx*

NOTES for loanwords and foreign names:
Word-initial *s-* is typically unvoiced /s/, even in German
vocabulary: *Semperoper, senza.*
/ʃ/ and /s/ are usually both heard in German names with initial
sp- and *st-* spellings: *Spohr, Stein, Stoltz, Strauss, Stuttgart.*
/ʃ/ in *glockenspiel, Singspiel.*

-s-

/s/
before or after another consonant, including after a nasalizing *m* or *n*:
ainsi (like that), *bonsoir* (good evening), *chanson* (song), *danseuse*
(dancer), *Escudier, fastidieux* (tedious), *Gainsbourg, hispanique*
(Hispanic), *inconstant, jasmin* (jasmine), *kinesthésique* (kinesthetic),
Lescaut, masque (mask), *ostensoir* (monstrance), *pastèque*
(watermelon), *question, romantisme* (romanticism), *Samson, test,*
Ursule, version, Walewska, xyste (xystus), *zeste* (zest)

⚠ /z/ in *Alsace, Arsace, Belsunce, Elsa,* and *Strasbourg,* as well as
subsistance [sybzistɑ̃:sə] (subsistence/keeping), *subsistant*
(remaining), *subsister* (to live on), *balsamique* (balsamic) and
derivatives: *alsacien* (Alsatian), *balsamier* (balsam tree)
NOTE:
/s/ or /z/ in *subside* (grant/allowance) and derivatives: *subsidiaire*
(subsidiary).

after most prefixes of a scholarly origin, especially (among many
others) *a-, aéro-, anti-, auto-, co-, homo-, octo-, para-, photo-, poly-,*
re-, su-, uni-:
aérosol (aerosol), *antiseptique* (antiseptic), *asymétrie* (asymmetry),
autosuffisant (self-sufficient), *cosignataire* (co-signer), *homosexuel*
(homosexual), *octosyllabe* (eight-syllable), *parasol, photosynthèse*
(photosynthesis), *polysyllabe* (polysyllabic), *resurgir* (to surface),
susurrer (to whisper), *unisexe* (unisex)

⚠ /z/ in a few cases after prefixes of a scholarly origin: *chromosome,*
dinosaure (dinosaur), *parasite*

216 | FRENCH LYRIC DICTION

in most compound words, including names beginning in *De-, Du-, Le-, La-*:
Beauséjour, Dessay, Duseigneur, Lasalle, Lesueur, tournesol
(sunflower), *vraisemblable* (credible), *vraisemblablement* (in all
probability), *vraisemblance* (credibility)

/z/

in most cases when intervocalic, and not a compound word:
abasourdir (to deafen), *Basile, chemise* (shirt), *nous disons*
(we say), *Ésope* (Aesop), *fusée* (rocket), *Giselle, hasard* (chance),
isolé (secluded), *jaseur* (chattering), *Késie, lisible* (legible), *mesure*
(measure), *nasal, oser* (to dare), *peser* (to weigh), *quasi* (almost),
raisin (grape), *saison* (season), *Tunisie* (Tunisia), *usine* (factory),
vision, Wisigoths (Visigoths), *xylose, Ysaÿe, Zélise*

after the prefixes *bi-, dé-, dy-, mé-, pré-, ré-*, and in the prefix
trans-, before a vowel or mute *h*:
bisannuel (biennial), *désagréable (wish), déshonneur* (dishonour),
dysorthographie (difficulty in spelling), *mésaventure* (misfortune),
résultat (result), *préserver* (to protect), *transaction, transhumer*
(to move to summer pastures), *transition, transit, transiter*
(to pass through)

⚠ A few such words have unvoiced /s/, especially when the main
part of the word after the prefix contains a root that can stand
alone with initial *s-*:   *désacraliser* (deconsecrate), *désatelliser*
(to remove from orbit), *désensibilisation* (desensitization), *désodé*
(salt-free), *désulfurer* (desulphurize), *dysenterie* (dysentery),
préséance (precedence), *présélectionner* (to shortlist), *présénile*
(presenile), *présérie* (preproduction), *présupposition* (presupposition),
réséquer (to excise), *résipiscence* (remorse), *transept, Transylvanie*
(Transylvania)
NOTE:
/z/ and /s/ are both correct in *désuet* (old-fashioned).

NOTES:
The pronunciation of French family and place names is very
irregular. The letter *s* before a consonant in names is sometimes
silent *s* (e.g., *Aubespine, Vosges, Leconte de Lisle*), sometimes /s/
(e.g., *Monestier*). In the case of French surnames, those beginning
in *Des-* usually have silent *s* (e.g., *Deschamps*), while a few have
/s/ (e.g., *Desnos*); the opposite is true for those beginning in *Les-*,
which usually have /s/ (e.g., *Lescaut*), but a few have silent *s* (e.g.,
Lesgards). There are even some surnames that are pronounced

FRENCH PRONUNCIATION A–Z | 217

either with or without *s*, according to the individual in question.
Refer to Part Three of this book for a case-by-case account.

NOTES for loanwords and foreign names:
Intervocalic -*s*- is normally voiced /z/: *Eisenach, risoluto.*
In Italian and German vocabulary, the voicing of *s* next to another
consonant is quite unpredictable.
Voiced/unvoiced *s* from English follows the original, with some
anomalies, such as *base-ball* [bɛz boːl].

-*s*   -*s*

silent as the last letter of a word, as an indication of the plural form:
aimés (loved), *amis* (friends), *contents* (happy), *les* (the)

silent in the spelling -*es* as mute *e* in the plural form, in verb
endings, and in names—*see e, -es*

usually silent as the last letter after a vowel in monosyllables:
tu as (you have), *bas* (bottom/low), *bois* (wood), *bras* (arm), *bris*
(breakage), *buis* (boxwood), *cas* (case), *ces* (these), *des* (of the),
dès (from/starting at), *dos* (back), *tu es* (you are), *je fis* (I made/did),
fois (time), *tu fus* (you were), *gras* (fat/greasy), *gris* (grey),
gros (large/fat), *jus* (juice), *las* (weary), *les* (the), *lès/lez* (near),
mais (but), *mes* (my), *mis* (clothed), *mois* (month), *nous* (we), *pas*
(not/step), *pis* (worse), *pois* (pea), *puis* (then), *pus, ras* (cropped),
ris (laughter), *ses* (his/her/one's), *sis* (situated), *tas* (pile),
tes (your), *toi* (you), *trois* (three), *tu vas* (you go), *vous* (you)
NOTE:
Silent final *s* remains silent at the end of the first part of a
compound word before another consonant: *desquels* (which),
Desrochers, Grosville, Lesgards, lesquels (which), *mesdames* (ladies).

silent in many polysyllabic words and names as the last letter
after a vowel:
abus (misuse), *Alexis, anglais* (English), *appas* (charms), *je m'assieds*
(I sit), *Baldous, brebis* (ewe), *Carpentras, Chablis, chaos, je choisis*
(I choose), *colis* (package), *compas* (compass), *confus* (distressed),
Cros, coulis, coutelas (large knife), *damas* (damask), *Degas, Denis,*
débris (fragments), *dessous* (below), *dessus* (above), *dispos* (fresh/
fit), *Dubois, Dumas, éclos* (hatched/bloomed), *enclos* (foreclosed),
épais (thick), *vous êtes* (you are), *exclus* (excluded), *fracas* (racket),
François, héros (hero), *hormis* (except for), *inclus* (included), *jamais*
(never), *Jésus, Judas, lilas* (lilac), *Lucas, marquis, matelas* (mattress),
mépris (scorn), *Nicolas, obtus* (obtuse), *obus* (shell), *Oubradous,*

paradis (paradise), *Paris, parvis* (forecourt), *Pays-Bas* (Netherlands), *permis* (permit/licence), *propos* (remarks), *remous* (eddy), *repas* (meal), *repos* (rest), *je résous* (I resolve), *soumis* (submissive), *souris* (mouse), *sournois* (sneaky), *taffetas* (taffeta), *tamis* (sieve), *tapis* (carpet), *Thomas, treillis* (trellis), *trépas* (death), *verglas* (icy patch), *vernis* (varnish)

silent at the end of a word or name after *r*, or after one or more silent consonants, including nearly all cases after a nasalizing *m* or *n*: *Aix-les-Bains, Auvers, Bongars, Cahors, champs* (fields), *Cinq-Mars, je convaincs* (I convince), *daims* (bucks), *dans* (in), *Desjardins, encens* (incense), *essaims* (swarms), *étangs* (ponds), *faims* (hungry), *fonds* (funds/collection), *nous gagnons* (we win), *lods* (land tax), *Loève-Veimars, tu mets* (you put), *Moislains, Naours, oblong, nous partons* (we are leaving), *nous partions* (we were leaving), *Philistins* (Philistines), *plombs* (sinkers), *poids* (weight), *pouls* [pu] (pulse), *je prends* (I take), *quatre-vingts personnes* (80 people), *rangs* (rows), *Reims, tu réponds* (you answer), *rets* (snare), *je sens* (I feel/smell), *temps* (time), *Tours, tréfonds* (depths), *je vaincs* (I conquer), *tu vends* (you sell), *Vézins, Villers, volontiers* (gladly)

/z/
in *liaison*

NOTES for *liaison*:
Where *liaison* is permitted, it is regularly made in singing with /z/: *les adieux* (farewells), *nous avons* (we have), *je te fais un promet* (I'm making you a promise), *tu es à moi!* (you are mine!), *si tu as un ami à sauver* (if you have a friend to save), *tu m'aimes et tu me suivras* (you love me and you'll follow me), *nous sommes à genoux* (we are on our knees), *vous êtes un vrai paladin* (you are a true paladin), *et les belles écouteuses* (and the beautiful listeners), *des feuilles et des branches* (leaves and branches), *aux gros yeux* (big-eyed), *je m'assieds à vos pieds* (I sit at your feet), *pas un mot* (not a word), *puis il revient* (then it returns), *sous un ciel étoilé* (under a starry sky), *j'obéis à nos dieux* (I obey our gods), *confus et troublé* (distressed and upset), *soumis à ton pouvoir* (submitted to your power), *dans un bois solitaire* (in a solitary wood), *prends un cheval de bonne race* (take a horse of fine pedigree), *réponds à ma tendresse* (respond to my tenderness), *voyons un peu* (let's just see), *les champs et les prés* (the fields and the meadows), *Dieux, si*

prompts autrefois à les réduire en poudre (gods, once so quick to
reduce them to dust), *regards impénitents* (incorrigible stares),
masques et bergamasques (masks and Bergamo masks), *de longues et
très tendres plaintes* (in long and very tender moans).
Liaison is quite rare from verbs ending in -*ous*, -*ouds*, and -*rds*
(i.e., only in a very elevated tone): *je résous un problème* (I'm
resolving a problem), *tu couds une jolie robe* (you sew a lovely dress),
je perds encore (I lose again).
Liaison is exceedingly rare from verbs ending in -*vaincs*.

/s/
as the last letter of a word after a vowel in a large group of
monosyllabic and polysyllabic words:
albatros, aloès (aloe), *amaryllis, angélus* (angelus), *as* (ace), *atlas,
autobus* (bus), *bis* (encore/repeat), *bus, cactus, chorus, cosmos,
couscous, crocus, ès* (degree in letters), *le(s) fils* [fis] (the son/sons),
fœtus (fetus), *gratis* (free of charge), *gus* (guy), *hélas* (alas), *hiatus,
ibis, iris* (iris), *jadis* (in times past), *lis/lys* (lily), *logos* (logo), *maïs*
(corn), *mas* (Provençal guesthouse), *métis* (mixed-race), *omnibus*
(local train), *opus, pathos, pénis* (penis), *prospectus* (leaflet), *radius,
rébus* (rebus), *rhinocéros* (rhinoceros), *sinus, tamaris* (tamarisk),
tennis, utérus (uterus), *virus, vis* (screw), *xérès* (sherry)

in most names ending in -*as* /aːs/, -*ès* /ɛs/, -*is* or -*ïs* /is/, -*os* /ɔs/ or
/oːs/, -*us* or -*üs* /ys/, -*ys* or -*ÿs* /is/:
*Adonis, Agnès, Anaïs, Antinoüs, Arcalaüs, Argus, Atlas, Atys, Bacchus,
Bilitis, Carlos, Chloris, Coppélius, Desnos, Devriès, Éros, Francis, Loïs,
Louÿs, Mendès, Mercédès, Moralès, Moréas, Pelléas, Polonius, Thaïs,
Tircis, Tirésias, Vénus, Ys*

⚠ silent in a few names: *Alexis, Arcis, Carabas, Carpentras, Chablis,
Cros, Decrès, Degas, Denis, Dubas, Ducros, Dumas, Duplessis, Jésus,
Judas, Lucas, Nicolas, Paris, Thomas*

NOTES:
Final -*s* in few words is either /s/ or silent *s*:   *ananas* (pineapple),
détritus (rubbish), *sus* (down with/in addition).
Las is pronounced [laːs] as a short form of *hélas* (alas) and [lɑ]
when it means 'weary'.
Plus (more/in addition/plus) is pronounced [ply], [plys], or [plyz].
Tous (all/everybody) is pronounced [tu], [tus], or [tuz]. See
Chapter 7: 'Words with Variable Pronunciations'.

The noun *sens* (sense/senses) is always pronounced [sã:s], in the singular and the plural forms, including before a vowel: *un sens* (a sense), *les cinq sens* (the five senses), *nos sens extasiés* (our enraptured senses).

⚠ Nouns ending in -*s* /s/ can link as /sz/ in the plural form, as a special, optional *liaison*; this is possible in singing, but is rarely heard: *nos sens̲ extasiés* [sãs zɛkstazje] (our enraptured senses), *les fils̲ aimés* [fis zɛme] (beloved sons).

NOTES for loanwords:
In English and Spanish borrowed vocabulary, the plural form shown with word-final -*s* is somewhat problematic because, unlike French, plural -*s* is not silent in these languages. Decisions are often required, particularly in a piece such as Bizet's **Carmen**, where several such loanwords are encountered:
/s/ is the norm, but silent -*s* is possible in *banderilleros* [bãdəɾijəɾo] or [bandeɾijeɾɔs], *caballeros* [kabajeɾo] or [kabajeɾɔs], *chulos* [ʃylo] or [tʃulɔs], *sombreros* [sõbɾeɾo] or [sɔmbɾeɾɔs] (in which a mixture of pronunciation elements from the variations shown above is possible in each case).
Silent -*s* is required in *toréros* [tɔɾeɾo], *señors* [seɲɔːɾ], and *picadors* [pikadɔːɾ], which have all been *francisés*. Correct Spanish grammar and spelling would be: *toɾeros, señoɾes,* and *picadoɾes*. (Also note that *toréador* is an invented French word.)
/s/ is the norm in *à deux cuartos* [kwaɾtɔs] (which is often changed to *a dos cuartos*).
Silent -*s*, or /s/, or *liaison* with /z/ are all possible in the line « *señoras̲ et caballeros* ».

sc   /sk/
before *a, o, ô,* or *u*:
Ascagne, biscôme (Swiss gingerbread), *biscuit* (cookie), *cascade, discuter* (to discuss), *escargot* (snail), *Fieramosca, Gascon, Huascar, Ionesco, Judas-Iscariote* (Judas Iscariot), *kaléidoscope* (kaleidoscope), *lascar* (shady character), *Muscat, Nelusco, Oscar, Pascale, quiscale* (grackle), *Roscanvel, scandale* (scandal), *scolaire* (school-related), *sculpture* (sculpture), *Toscane* (Tuscany), *uranoscope* (stargazer), *vasculaire* (vascular), *Wisconsin*

/s/

before *e, é, è, i,* or *y*:

ascenseur (elevator), *bioluminescence, convalescent, descendre*
(to go down), *efflorescent, fascinant* (fascinating), *géoscience*
(geoscience), *hyoscine, iridescent, lascif* (lustful), *multidisciplinaire*
(multidisciplinary), *nitescence* [nitɛsã:sə] (lustre), *obscène*
(obscene), *piscine* (pool), *quiescent* (calm), *réminiscence*
(recollection), *sceau* (seal), *scène* (scene), *scénique* (scenic), *science*
(science), *scintille* (sparkle), *scissure* (fissure), *scythe* (Scythian),
transcendant (transcendent), *viscéral* (visceral)

NOTES for Italian loanwords and names:
/ʃ/ in most vocabulary: *crescendo.*
/ʃ/ or /s/ in a few words, the latter often in more traditional
pronunciation: *fasciste, fascisme* (fascist, fascism).
/ʃj/ and less frequently /sj/ in the spelling *sci* before another
vowel: *Brescia, Scio.*

sch

/ʃ/

in most vocabulary, usually borrowed into French:
Beuscher, Delunsch, Deschamps, escher (bait), *Eschig, Fursch-Madi,*
Gerschwin, Guéberschwihr, Hirsch, Leschenault, Peschard, pschitt!
(hiss!), *Rothschild, scheik* [ʃɛk] (sheikh), *Schéhérazade, schéma*
(outline), *schème* (framework), *schisme* (schism), *schiste* (shale),
Schlémil, Schneider, Schœnewerk, Schubert, Schultheis, Schumann,
Les Schtroumpfs (The Smurfs), *Schwerlein, Taschereau, Wisches*

/sk/

in a few cases, especially borrowed vocabulary and words of a
scholarly origin:
Escholier, Schiaparelli, schizophrénie (schizophrenia), *Schola Cantorum*

NOTES for loanwords and foreign names:
/ʃ/ in German vocabulary: *Fischer, Schiller.*
/sk/ in Italian vocabulary: *Ischia, scherzo.*

sh

/z/

in French words, where the two letters belong to separate
syllables, notably in the spelling *désh-*:
déshériter (to disinherit), *déshonneur* (dishonour), *Deshoulières,*
Malesherbes

NOTES:

⚠ Silent *sh* in names where silent *s* ends one part of the name, and
aspirated *h* begins the next part: *Deshayes.*

222 | FRENCH LYRIC DICTION

/s/ is the norm, and /sh/ is also possible in the French border villages ending in -sheim: *Éguisheim, Molsheim*.

NOTES for loanwords and foreign names:
/ʃ/ is common, especially in English vocabulary: *crash* [kraʃ], *Hiroshima, Lakshmi, Marshall, shako* [ʃako], *shampooing* [ʃɑ̃pwɛ̃] (shampoo), *Shéhérazade, Shylock, smash* [smaʃ], *Usher, Washington*.

squ	*see* **qu**

ss

/s/
always:
assassin (assassin), *bassin* (pond), *boss, De Croissy, Debussy, essor* (flight), *express* (express train/espresso), *frisson* (shiver), *glisser* (to slip), *D'Haussmann, issue* (way out), *Jusseaume, kermesse* (fun fair), *lisse* (smooth), *lœss* (loess), *messe* (mass), *Narcisse* (Narcissus), *Ousset, passer* (to pass), *Quessoy, russe* (Russian), *suisse* (Swiss), *tasse* (cup), *unisson* (unison), *vitesse* (speed), *Wyss, Xhendelesse, Yssingeaux*

-st

~~st~~
silent in the word *est* (is)

silent in many names:
Béhoust, Benoist, Beynost, Chambost, Champlost, Charest, Crémarest, Forest, Le Gast, Genest, Laforest, Leforest, Marest, Martinvast, Prévost, Prouvost, Pruvost, Saint-Clost, Saint-Genest, Saint-Jean-de-Niost, Le Wast

/st/
in some cases:
Alost, ballast, Barlest, Béost, Beust, Brest, Bucarest (Bucharest), *Budapest, Chiboust, compost, Diest, Ernest, l'est* (east), *Faust, Furst, Fust, Haust, Le Lagast, lest* (ballast), *Marrast, l'ouest* (west), *Orist, Plouguenast, Proust, Quost, Saint-Igest, test, toast* [toːst], *whist* [|wist], *zest!* (fiddlesticks!)

NOTES:
/st/ or /s/ in a few names: *Chârost, Crest, Dubost, Saint-Just, Saint-Priest*.
Christ is pronounced [krist] or [kri], depending on the context. See Chapter 7: 'Words with Variable Pronunciations'.

-stion	*see* **ti**

— T ○ [te] —

t

/t/

in most cases:

Autriche (Austria), *bateau* (boat), *citron* (lemon), *doute* (doubt),
entre (between), *fatigué* (tired), *Gautier, Hector, italien* (Italian),
juteux (juicy), *Koltès, Latone* (Latona), *matin* (morning), *nature,*
opéra (opera), *pâte* (pastry), *quatre* (four), *révolte* (revolt),
Silvestre, table (table), *taire* (to keep quiet), *tas* (pile), *taux* (rate),
tenir (to hold), *ténor* (tenor), *teuton* (Teutonic), *tiare* (tiara),
Tinville, titre (title), *ton* (tone/your), *Torlogne, Touareg* (Tuareg),
tournée (tour), *très* (very), *tu* (you), *tuile* (tile), *tungstène* (tungsten),
ustensile (utensil), *vite* (fast), *Witikind, Xaintrailles, Yalta,*
zélateur (zealot)

-t

~~t~~

usually silent as the last letter of a word or name after a vowel:

achat (shopping), *alphabet, apprêt* (preparation/primer), *artichaut*
(artichoke), *attribut* (trait), *il aurait* (he would have), *aussitôt*
(immediately), *Badoit, benêt* (simple), *Benoît, Bidaut, bientôt* (soon),
bouquet, Bourget, Caplet, elles chantaient (they were singing), *il*
chantait (he was singing), *ci-gît* (here lies), *Clicquot, Costallat, crédit*
(credit), *elle croit* (she believes), *coût* (cost), *debout* (standing), *début*
(start), *défaut* (flaw), *dégoût* (disgust), *distrait* (distracted), *doigt*
[dwa] (finger), *effet* (effect), *endroit* (place), *qu'on eût* (that one had
to), *il fait* (he makes/does), *filet* (net) *forêt* (forest), *fût* (cask), *goût*
(taste), *guichet* (box office), *hoquet* (hiccup), *immédiat* (instant),
inédit (unpublished), *inquiet* (worried), *institut* (institute), *Jolivet,*
jouet (toy), *lait* (milk), *Lescaut, livret* (booklet), *lot* (prize), *Manet,*
ils marchent (they walk), *on marcherait* (one would walk), *Massenet,*
mât (mast), *maudit* (damned), *menuet* (minuet), *Monet, mont*
(mount), *motet, muet* (mute), *mulet* (mule), *navet* (turnip), *Nicolet,*
objet (object), *Odet, Pannetrat, Paquet, parfait* (perfect), *partout*
(everywhere), *Passerat, petit* (small), *plutôt* (rather), *poignet* (wrist/
cuff), *pont* (bridge), *pot* (pot), *prêt* (ready), *profit, projet* (project),
ragoût (stew), *regret, reliquat* (remainder), *sabbat* (Sabbath), *salut*
(hail/greetings), *sanscrit* (Sanskrit), *souhait* (wish), *subit* (sudden),
sujet (subject), *surtout* (especially), *tantôt* (shortly/earlier/
sometimes), *on veut* (one wants), *violet* (purple), *vivat !* (hurrah!),
Vuarnet, Watelet, ysopet

silent at the end of a word or name after *r*, or after one or more
silent consonants, including after a nasalizing *m* or *n*:
amant (lover), *Archambault*, *art*, *Beaumont*, *Belcourt*, *Chalupt*,
Chaumont, *court* (short), *croyant* (believing), *défunt* (deceased),
Dupont, *empreint* (imbued), *emprunt* (loan), *est* (is), *exempt* (exempt),
fort (strong/strongly/very), *Grandrupt*, *Fromont*, *gant* (glove),
Hellespont, *insolent*, *instinct* (instinct), *elle joint* (she combines),
Laurent, *mont* (mountain), *Nogent*, *ils ont* (they have), *il peint*
(he paints), *port*, *prompt* (ready), *quart* (quarter), *Quinault*, *quint*
(fifth), *respect* (respect), *Richemont*, *Robert*, *Schubert*, *ils sont*
(they are), *sort* (fate), *teint* (complexion), *Thibault*, *urgent*,
vert (green), *vingt* (twenty), *on vint* (one came), *Warnant*,
Yves Saint-Laurent, *zézayant* (lisping)

NOTE:
In most cases, a silent final *t* remains silent at the end of the first
part of a compound word before another consonant: *hautbois*
(oboe), *Montblanc*, *Petitpas*.

⚠ /t/ in some compound names beginning in *Mont-* before *r*:
Montreuil, *Montrichard*.

/t/
in *liaison*

NOTES for *liaison*:
Where *liaison* is permitted, it is regularly made in singing with /t/:
l'on m'avait averti (I was warned), *les étoffes flottaient au vent*
(the material floated in the wind), *cent hommes marchent à sa suite*
(a hundred men walk in his wake), *que veut-on ?* (what does one
want?), *faut-il qu'en un jour* (must it be that in one day),
il absout à jamais (he absolves for ever), *croyant être un beau*
personnage (believing to be a handsome character), *empreint au*
cœur (imprinted on my heart), *que sont-ils devenus ?* (what have
they become?), *vingt hommes* (twenty men), *elles se moquent un*
peu de lui (they make fun of him a bit), *ils voguent à pleines voiles*
(they sail at full speed).
Liaison is quite rare from verbs ending in -ompt (i.e., only in a
very elevated tone):   *qui rompt avec la tradition* (which breaks
with tradition).

as the last letter of several words and a few names:
abrupt (steep/abrupt), *accessit* (certificate of merit), *aconit*
(monkshood), *affidavit*, *ballast*, *Béost*, *Brest*, *brut* (crude/raw),

Calicut, Chiboust, chut! [ʃt] (sh!), *cobalt, coït* (coitus), *compost, concept, déficit* (deficit), *Diest, dot* (dowry), *Ernest, l'est* (east), *exit* (theatre exit), *fait* (fact), *Faust, flirt* [flœrt], *granit* (granite), *Hamlet, huit* (eight), *Inghelbrecht, internet, introït* (introit), *Japhet* (Japheth), *Josaphat, Labrit, Le Lagast, Lilliput, Lot, lut* (joining cement), *malt, Marrast, mat* (matte/olive coloured), *mazout* (fuel oil), *net* (clear/distinct), *l'ouest* (west), *pat* (stalemate), *pickpocket, prétérit* (preterite tense), *prurit* (itchiness), *Quérigut, rapt* (kidnapping), *rit* (rite), *rut* (rutting), *sept* (seven), *soit!* (so be it!), *Soult, Tanit, Tilsit, toast* [toːst], *transept, transit, ut* (the note C), *vermout* (vermouth), *volt, water-closet* [|watɛr klozɛt] (toilets), *yacht* [|jɔt], *zut!* (drat!)

⚠   silent *t* in *huit* as an adjective before a pronounced consonant: *huit femmes* (eight women). See Chapter 7: 'Numbers'.

NOTES:
The word *août* (August) is pronounced [u] or [ut].
The pronunciations [au] and [aut] are outdated; however either one of these two-syllable versions is required in Poulenc's **Dialogues des Carmélites** in the line of the *2ᵉ Commissaire*, as the word is set to two notes: « A-oût ».
The word *fait* as a noun (fact) can be pronounced [fɛ], but is usually pronounced [fɛt].
The word *rot* pronounced as [ro] means 'burp'; pronounced as [rɔt] it means 'vine rot'.
The word *fat* (smug) is pronounced either [fat] or [fa]; in the plural form, *fats* is pronounced [fa] only.
The word *but* (goal) is usually pronounced [byt], but can also be pronounced [by]. In Ravel's *Chanson à boire* from **Don Quichotte à Dulcinée**, with text by Morand, [byt] is often sung; however, [by] is possible, creating a homophone and play on words with the line « *lorsque j'ai <u>bu</u>* » (when I am drunk).
Soit (so be it/very well/be) is pronounced [swa] or [swat]. See Chapter 7: 'Words with Variable Pronunciations'.

tch, tsch   /tʃ/
as one word element, often in borrowed vocabulary:
atchoum! (achoo!), *Batcheff, caoutchouc* (rubber), *Chostakovitch, Etcheverry, Gretchen, Janatchek* (Janáček), *Jankélévitch, kitsch, match* (game), *Meerovitch, putsch* [putʃ], *Rogatchewsky, scotcher* [skɔtʃe] (to tape together), *Souvtchinsky, Tchaïkovsky, Tchèque* (Czech), *tchin!* (cheers!), *tchou-tchou!* (choo choo!)

226 | FRENCH LYRIC DICTION

NOTE:
/ʃ/ or /k/ when silent *t* belongs to the end of one part of a word,
and *ch* begins the next: *De Montchrestien, Pontchartrain, Pontchâteau.*

th

/t/
nearly always:
aneth (dill), *Bathori, cithare* (zither), *Dorothée, éther* (ether),
Gauthier, Hyacinthies (Hyacinthia), *Judith, luth* (lute), *Mathieu*
(Matthew), *Nathanaël* (Nathaniel), *Panthéon, rythme* (rhythm),
Scythes (Scythians), *spath* (spar), *thalamus, Thèbes* (Thebes),
théorie (theory), *Theuriet, Thibault, Thierry, thon* (tuna), *Thulé*
(Thule), *vermouth, Werther, Xanthe* (Xanthus), *zénith* (zenith)

⚠ silent *th* in the words *asthme* [asmə] (asthma), *bizuth* [bizy]
(newbie), *isthme* [ismə] (land bridge), and *goth* [go] (Gothic) and
derivatives: *asthmatique* (asthmatic), *isthmique* (Isthmian),
Wisigoths (Visigoths)

ti

/ti/
in most cases—usually before a consonant (other than a single *m* or
n unless it is followed by another vowel), or at the end of a word:
actif (active), *averti* (informed), *bâti* (built), *butiner* (to gather
pollen), *cantique* (canticle), *détirer* (to stretch out), *églantine* (wild
rose), *englouti* (submerged), *furtif* (furtive), *gentil* (nice), *hostile,*
intime (intimate), *justice, Lamartine, il a menti* (he lied), *natif*
(native), *optique* (optical), *politique* (political), *quotidien* (daily),
retirer (to pull back), *sentir* (to feel/smell), *timide* (shy), *ultime*
(ultimate), *votif* (votive), *yéti* (yeti)

/sj/
in the suffixes *-tier* as a verb infinitive, *-tié* as a past participle,
and *-tions* and *-tiez* as first- and second-person plural verb endings
in the present tense of the verbs *argutier* (to quibble), *balbutier*
(to stammer), *différentier* (to differentiate), *initier* (to initiate),
and *transsubstantier* (to transubstantiate) only:
nous argutions (we quibble), *vous différentiez* (you differentiate),
transsubstantié (transubstantiated)

in a few isolated words and their derivatives:
propitiation, rational (rationale), *rationnel* (rational), *spartiate* (Spartan)

when not preceded by the letter *s* in the suffixes *-tiable,*
-tial(e)/-tiaux, -tiaire, -tiel(le), -tience, -tien(ne), -tient(e),
-tieux/tieuse, -tion, -tionnaire, -tium and their derivatives:

Aléoutiennes (Aleutians), *ambitieux/ambitieuse* (ambitious), *aoûtien* [ausjɛ̃] (August vacationer), *consortium* [kɔ̃sɔrsjɔm], *dictionnaire* (dictionary), *Dioclétien* (Diocletian), *égyptien(ne)* (Egyptian), *essentiel(le)* (essential), *Gatien, Gratien* (Gratian), *initiative, insatiabilité* (insatiability), *insatiable* (insatiable), *initial(e)* (first), *nation, nuptiaux* (nuptial), *patience, patient(e)* (patient), *ration, tertiaire* (tertiary), *vénitien(ne)* (Venetian)

⚠ /tj/ in a few words: *antienne* (antiphony/refrain), *chrétien,* *chrétienne,* (Christian), *entretien* (upkeep), *maintien* (maintenance), *soutien* (support)

/tj/
when the suffixes normally pronounced /sj/ (as shown above) are preceded by the letter *s,* which may be silent in names: *bestial(e)/bestiaux* (bestial), *bestiaire* (bestiary), *Estienne,* *De Montchrestien, question, suggestions, vestiaire* (cloakroom)

in the endings *-tiens* and *-tient* of the verb *tenir* (to hold) and derivatives:
je/tu tiens [tjɛ̃] (I/you hold), *il/elle/on contient* [kɔ̃tjɛ̃] (he/she/one/ it contains)

in the noun and adjective suffixes *-tié, -tième,* and *-tier/-tière*: *amitié* (friendship), *centième* (hundredth), *héritière* (heiress), *inimitié* (enmity), *matière* (subject), *moitié* (half), *pénultième* (penultimate), *pitié* (pity), *quartier* (district), *septième* (seventh), *vingtième* (twentieth)

in a few words:
châtier (to punish), *étiage* (low water level), *étiologie* (etiology), *galimatias* [galimatjɑ] (gibberish), *volontiers* (gladly)

in the first- and second-person plural *-tions* and *-tiez* verb endings in the past tense, (other than the small list of verbs shown above): *nous étions* (we were), *vous étiez* (you were), *nous chantions* (we were singing), *vous partiez* (you were leaving)

NOTES:
In several cases, the ending *-tions* can exist both as the first-person plural verb ending, as well as a plural noun ending, each with a different pronunciation and meaning: *les adoptions* [adɔpsjɔ̃] (the adoptions); *nous adoptions* [adɔptjɔ̃] (we were adopting). Sometimes /sj/, sometimes /tj/ in the suffixes *-tio* and *-tiole*: /sj/ in *gratiole* (hedgehyssop), *Horatio, pétiole* (leafstalk).

228 | FRENCH LYRIC DICTION

/tj/ in *il s'étiole* (it withers), *étiolement* (blanching).
In the word *patio*, /tj/ is preferable, but /sj/ is also correct.

-tie

/si/
in most cases after a vowel:
on argutie (one quibbles), *aristocratie* (aristocracy), *Croatie*
(Croatia), *Dalmatie* (Dalmatia), *facétie* (prank), *Galatie* (Galatia),
Helvétie (Helvetica), *j'initie* (I initiate), *minutie* (minutia), *suprématie*
(supremacy), *voyoucratie* (thuggery)

⚠ /ti/ in the first-person and third-person singular conjugations
of the verb *châtier* (to punish): *je châtie* (I punish), *on châtie*
(one punishes)

NOTE:
Often set as /siə/ when verse-final: *quand j'étais roi de Béotie*
(when I was king of Beotia).

/ti/
in feminine participles of word-final *-ti*:
garantie (guaranteed), *rôtie* (roasted), *elle est sortie* (she went out)

in a few names after a vowel:
Claretie, Clytie, Satie, Sarmatie

after a consonant including a nasalizing *n*, especially after *s*:
amnistie (amnesty), *apprentie* (apprentice), *Approntie, Christie,*
dynastie (dynasty), *garantie* (guarantee/warranty), *modestie*
(modesty), *ortie* (nettle), *sortie* (exit)

⚠ /si/ in *ineptie* (ineptness), and *inertie* (inertia)

NOTE:
Often set as /tiə/ when verse-final: *elle est partie* (she left).

-tion

/sjõ/
as a noun suffix, when not preceded by the letter *s*:
action, L'Assomption (The Assumption of Mary), *civilisation*
(civilization), *édition* (edition), *fonction* (function), *lotion, nation*
(country), *ration, sanction, vocation*

FRENCH PRONUNCIATION A–Z | 229

ts-   /ts/
            at the beginning of foreign words assimilated into French, and the
            onomatopoeic interjection *tsoin-tsoin !* (ba-da-boom!):
            tsar (czar), *tsarine* (czarina), *tsé-tsé* [tse tse] (tsetse fly), *Tsigane*
            (Gypsy), *tsunami*

-ts   ~~ts~~
            silent in most French names, at the end of a word in the plural
            form, and in verb endings, including after a nasalizing *n*:
            acquêts (acquests), *Desmarets*, *distincts* (distinct), *gants* (gloves),
            Les Gets, *insolents* (insolent), *instincts*, *Louchats*, *je mets* (I put),
            un mets (a dish), *nuits* (nights), *tu permets* (you permit), *ponts*
            (bridges), *prêts* (ready), *quatre-vingts presonnes* (eighty people),
            rets (snare), *saints*, *Sompuits*, *je vêts* (I dress)
       ⚠   /ts/ at the end of a few French names: *Bats, Beydts*

tsch   see **tch**

tt   /t/
            always:
            attacher (to attach), *butte* (hillock), *Charlotte*, *dette* (debt), *émietter*
            (to crumble), *flotter* (to float), *glotte* (glottis), *hutte* (hut), *inattendu*
            (unexpected), *Juliette*, *kilowatt*, *Lucette*, *Mistinguett*, *natte* (braid),
            opérette (operetta), *Poussette*, *Don Quichotte* (Don Quixote), *rattraper*
            (to recapture), *sottise* (nonsense), *Thierrette*, *Utter*, *Vuitton*, *Watteau*,
            Yvette, *zapette* (tv remote)

            NOTES for Italian loanwords and names:
            /t(t)/ consonant lengthening may or may not be made in musical
            terms and names: *allegretto, larghetto, Ninetta, Scarlatti, sotto voce.*

tz   /ts/
            in most cases in borrowed German words, often at the end of a name:
            Biarritz, Kœtzingue, Ropartz
            NOTE:
            /dz/ is heard in a few names: *Kreutzer, Metzervisse, Schweitzer.*
            /s/ in a few names: *Dujardin-Beaumetz, Metz.*
            silent ~~tz~~ in a few names: *Betz, Catz, Lametz.*

— U ○ [y] —

u, û

/y/

in most cases—usually before a consonant (other than a single *m* or *n* unless it is followed by another vowel), or as the last letter of a word:

ardu (arduous), *bûcher* (pyre), *curé* (vicar), *dû* (dues/owed), *écume* (foam), *flûte* (flute), *fumoir* (smoking room), *Gustave, humeur* (mood), *illusion, juge, Junon* (Juno), *Kurdistan, lu* (read), *lune* (moon), *mûr* (ripe), *nu* (naked), *opus, piqûre* (injection/shot), *plume* (feather), *ruche* (hive), *sûr* (sure), *tu* (you), *tumulte* (uproar), *ubiquité* (ubiquity), *Ucalégon, ufologie* (ufology), *Ugalde, Uhlans, Ukraine, ultra, unité* (unit/unity), *upsilon, urbain* (urban), *usé* (worn), *utopie* (utopia), *uvule* (uvula), *Uxelles, Uzès, vu* (seen), *Woluwe, xérus* (ground squirrel), *Zurich*

/ɥ/

before another vowel other than /ə/:

buisson (bush) *Cuénod, depuis* (since), *Éluard, fuir* (to flee), *gratuit* (free), *Huard, insinuer* (to imply), *juin* (June), *lui* (him), *muer* (to shed), *nuage* (cloud), *ossuaire* (ossuary), *puissance* (power), *Quirinus, ruelle* (lane), *sanctuaire* (sanctuary), *tuer* (to kill), *usuel* (usual), *Vuitton*

⚠ /y/ after a consonant plus *l* or *r*: *affluent* (tributary), *Bruant, Cruas, cruel* (cruel), *fluor* (fluorine), *gluant* (slimy), *gruau* (gruel), *Gruaz, obstruer* (to block), *truand* (crook); however, /ɥ/ is maintained in the progression of consonant plus *l* or *r* when followed by *i*: *affruiter* (to grow fruit), *bruit* (noise), *Bruix, détruire* (to destroy), *ébruiter* (to disclose), *fluide* (fluid), *fruit* (fruit), *parapluie* (umbrella), *pluie* (rain), *pruine* (bloom), *truite* (trout).

NOTE:

In the score, *u* before another vowel sound is often set as dieresis with /y/: *su-a-ve* [sy.a:.və] (smooth).

/w/

before another vowel in some words, especially in the spelling *qua*: *aquarelles* (watercolours), *aquarium* [akwaɾjɔm] (aquarium), *cacahuète* [kakawɛtə] (peanut), *chihuahua, équateur* (equator), *Guadalquivir, iguane* (iguana), *jaguar, lingual, quadruple, quatuor* [kwatɥɔ:r] (quartet: piece of music), *quetsche* [kwɛtʃə] (damson), *square* [skwa:rə] (park/square)

FRENCH PRONUNCIATION A–Z | 231

NOTE:
Cacahuète (peanut) may also be spelled *cacahouète*; a secondary
pronunciation for *cacahuète* is [kakaɥɛtə].

h

usually silent after *g* and *q*—*see specific spellings*

NOTES for loanwords and foreign names:
/u/ is common in much borrowed vocabulary, including words from
Italian, Spanish, German, and Latin, among other languages: *alléluia,
blues* [bluːz], *Bruckner, Buxtehude, Dubrovnik, Fuchs, Furtwängler, haïku,
risoluto, rubato, Schubert, Schumann, tutti, Zurga.*
/u/ or /y/ in a few cases: *Banyuls, Bruch, Cherubini, chulos* [ʃylo] or
[ʧuləs], *subito, tsunami, Zuniga.*
/w/ is common before another vowel, especially in Spanish
vocabulary: *cuartos, Manuelita, Vanuatu, zarzuela* [saɾswela].
/ɥ/ in some words: *affettuoso, diminuendo.*
/w/ or /ɥ/ in a few cases: *De Casa Fuerte, huerta, Inuits, marijuana,
Ruodi, La Zuecca.*
Vowel sounds are usually approximated from English.
/œ/ in *Buckingham, club* [klœb], *hamburger* [|ãbœrgœːɾ], *puzzle*
[pœzl], *surf* [sœrf] (surfing).
/ju/ in *Hume*, /u/ in *pudding.*
/y/ is normal in some very common adopted words: *budget*
[bydʒɛ], *tunnel* [tynɛl].
/œ/ and /y/ are both heard in some words: as *pull-over* [pylɔvɛːɾ]
or [pulɔvœːɾ] (sweater), *Purcell.*
/i/ in the word *business* [biznɛs].
Lunch is pronounced [lœnʧ] or [lœ̃ːʃ].
jodhpurs is pronounced [ʒɔdpuːɾ] or [ʒɔdpyːɾ].
Punch (as a fist punch) is pronounced [pœnʧ], *punch* (as the drink)
is pronounced [põːʃ].
The borrowed English word *pub* is pronounced [pœb], while the
French word *pub* (ad) is pronounced [pyb].

ue   **/y/**
in the future and conditional verb tenses:
je tuerai [tyɾe] (I will kill), *nous tuerions* [tyɾjõ] (we would kill)

always at the end of a syllable, especially when word-final:
avenue, charrue (plough), *cohue* (crowd/scramble), *dénuement*
(deprivation), *statue*

NOTES:

In this spelling in French words, *e* is not /ə/ when a letter follows it in the same syllable (other than in the *-es* and *-ent* endings):   *actuel* [aktɥɛl] (current), *bluet* (cornflower), *duel, Emmanuel, muet* (mute), *ruelle* (lane), *tuer* [tɥe] (to kill).

Often set as /yə/ when verse-final: *l'inconnue̱* (the unknown woman).

/ə/

after *g* or *q*, either as the last letter of a word, or before *-s* or *-ent*: *tu attaques* (you attack), *ils attaquent* (they attack), *Hugues* (Hugh), *longue, longues* (long), *que* (that/which), *tu vogues* (you sail), *ils voguent* (they sail)

NOTES for *liaison*:

Liaison is made in singing with /z/ from *-ues* and with /t/ from *-uent*:   *masques͜ et bergamasques* (masks and Bergamo masks), *de longues͜ et très tendres plaintes* (in long and very tender moans), *elles se moquent͜ un peu de lui* (they make fun of him a bit), *ils voguent͜ à pleines voiles* (they sail at full speed).

-ueil, -ueill-   /œj/

always after *c* and *g*—*see* **cueil, cueill, -gueil, -gueill-**

-uill-   /ɥij/

in a few cases: *aiguille* (needle) [ɛgɥijə], *aiguillette* [ɛgɥijɛtə] (military shoulder braid), *aiguillon* [ɛgɥijõ] (insect sting), *cuiller* [kɥijɛːɾ] (spoon), *juillet* [ʒɥijɛ] (July), *Juillan, Vuillard, Vuillermoz*

/ij/

in most cases after *g* or *q* and silent **u**: *anguille* [ãgijə] (eel), *Anguilla, coquille* (shell), *Coquillère, guillemets* (quotation marks), *guilleret* (perky), *Guillaume* (William), *Guillot, Piquillo, quilles* (bowling pins)

um   /œ̃/

before a consonant, which may be either silent or pronounced: *Humbert, humble, Umpeau*

NOTE:

The spelling *um* is not nasalized before a vowel.—*see* **u**

/ɔm/
at the end of a word:
album (album), *aquarium*, *décorum* (decorum), *harmonium*,
minimum, *opium*, *rhum* (rum), *vacuum* [vakɥɔm]

⚠ /œ̃/ in *parfum* (perfume)
NOTE:
The interjection *hum...* (hmm...) is pronounced [|œm]

NOTES for nasalization of loanwords and foreign names:
/ɔ̃/ followed by *b* in a few names and scholarly
words: *col<u>um</u>barium* [kɔlɔ̃baɾjɔm], *Columbia*, *Columbus*, *rhumb*
[ɾɔ̃:b] (navigation by compass).
/um/ in German names: *Blum*, *Humperdinck*.
/ɔm/ at the end of some Latin words and many names: *Actium*, *ad
libitum*, *Herculanum* (Herculaneum), *Latium*, *Nahum*, *Schola Cantorum*.
/œm/ in a few English words and names: *dumping* [dœmpiŋ],
Humphrey, *Trump*.
/œ̃/ or /ɔ̃/ in a few cases: *Humboldt*, *Humfroy*, *lumbago*.

un /œ̃/
at the end of a word, or before a consonant, which may be either
silent or pronounced:
aucun (none/not one/any), *brun* (brown), *Bunsen*, *chacun* (each
one), *défunt* (dead), *Dunkerque*, *emprunt* (loan), *falun* (shelly sand),
Gunsbourg, *Huntziger*, *Issoudun*, *junte* (junta), *Kunq*, *lundi* (Monday),
Melun, *Nuncq*, *Ossun*, *Les Pétuns* (the Petun), *quelqu'un* (someone),
Rungis, *shunt* [ʃœ̃:t], *Ténébrun*, *un* (one/a), *Verdun*
NOTE:
The spelling *un* is not nasalized before a vowel.—*see* **u**

NOTES for *liaison*:
Where *liaison* is permitted in singing, it can be made after the
nasal vowel with /n/: *aucun‿homme en ce lieu* (no man in this
place), *plus d'un‿ami fidèle* (more than a faithful friend).

/ɔ̃/
in a few cases, mostly in scholarly words:
acupuncture (acupuncture), *avunculaire* (avuncular), *De profundis*
[de pɾɔfɔ̃dis] (from the depths), *infundibuliforme* (funnel-shaped),
unciforme (hook-shaped)

NOTE:
/ɔ̃:/ and /œ̃:/ are both correct in the word *jungle*.

234 | FRENCH LYRIC DICTION

Notes for nasalization of loanwords and foreign names:
/ɶ̃/ in a few cases: *bungalow* [bɶ̃galo], *Les Huns* (the Huns), *nunc* [nɶ̃:k].
/œn/ in several borrowed English words: *fun* [fœn], *Hunt*, *punch* [pœntʃ] (fist: punch).
/õ/ in a few cases: *Arundel*, *punch* [põ:ʃ] (drink: punch), *secundo*.
/un/ in other foreign names, especially German ones: *Duntalmo*, *Sundgau*, *Unterwald*.
The English word *lunch* is pronounced either [lɶ̃:ʃ] or [lœntʃ].

-us, -üs *see -s*

-ut, -ût *see -t*

uy /ɥij/
before another vowel:
appuyer (to press on), *bruyamment* (noisily), *bruyant* (noisy), *Châtelguyon*, *écuyer* (horseman), *ennuyeux* (boring), *fuyard* (fugitive), *vous fuyez* (you flee), *Guyana*, *Guyane* (French Guyana), *Guyau*, *Guyot*, *Le Hennuyer*, *Huyot*, *Juyol*, *tuyau* (pipe/hose), *tuyère* (nozzle), *De La Vauguyon*

⚠ /yj/ in the following names: *Berruyer*, *gruyère* (Gruyere cheese), *Gruyère*, *Truyère*
Notes:
/yj/ is the norm, but /ɥij/ is also correct in *bruyère* (heather), *De La Bruyère*, *Les Bruyères*.
/ɥijj/ in verb tenses with the -*uyi*- spelling, distinguishing them from tenses pronounced /ɥij/ with the spelling -*uy*-: *nous fuyions* [fɥij.jõ] (we were fleeing), *que vous fuyiez* [fɥij.je] (that you flee).

/ɥi/
at the end of a word, or before a consonant, often in names:
Chapuy, *Dupuy*, *Dupuytren*, *Huy*, *Huyghe*, *Huyghens*, *Huysmans*, *De Maud'huy*, *Pont de Chéruy*, *puy* (volcanic peak), *Le Puy*, *Puy de Dôme*, *Puyjoli*, *Puylaurens*, *Puys*, *Puységur*, *Ruy Blas*, *Ruysdaël*

⚠ /i/ in the names *Guy*, *Guys*, *Péguy*

— V ∘ [ve] —

v

/v/
always:
avaler (to swallow), *bavarder* (to chat), *chèvre* (goat), *devinette* (riddle), *éventail* (fan), *fauve* (wild cat), *gavotte, Halévy, ivrogne* (drunkard), *Javert, Kosovo, Lecouvreur, mouvement* (motion), *novice, Olivier, pavane, le qui-vive* (the alert), *Ravel, servir* (to serve), *trêve* (truce), *uvulaire* (uvular), *vain, val* (valley), *Vanzo, Vasnier, vautour* (vulture), *vélo* (bike), *venir* (to come), *Verlaine, on veut* (one wants), *veuve* (widow), *vide* (empty), *vieux* (old), *voir* (to see), *Voltaire, ils vont* (they go), *vous* (you), *vraiment* (really), *Vuillermoz, Vulcan, Woëvre, Xavier, Yves, Zavatta*

Notes for loanwords and foreign names:
/f/ in Slavic names, especially those with the spelling *ov*:   *Diaghilev, Kiev, Kirov, Rimsky-Korsakov.*
/v/ or /f/ in the German term *leitmotif* [lajtmɔtiːv] or [lajtmɔtif].

— W ∘ [dubləve] —

w

/v/
in most vocabulary, including initial *W-* in names of French and German origin:
Bouxwiller, Gewurztraminer, Hedwige, De Kostrowitski, Lefébure-Wély, Minkowski, Neuwiller, Paderewski, Rogatchewsky, Saint-Wandrille, Schweitzer, Unterwald, Wagner, wagon (car/carriage), *wagon-lit* (sleeping car), *wagonnet* (mining cart), *De Wailly, Waldeck, Waldor, Walhalla, Walkyrie* (Valkyrie), *Walpurgis, De Warens, Warot, wassingue* (floor cloth), *Watteau, Weber, Wèbre, Weckerlin, Wenceslas, Werther, Westphalie, Widal, Wilhelm Meister, Willette, Woëvre, Wotan, Wouwerman, Wrangel, De Wrède, Wurtemberg, Wyss*
Note:
Slavic names with the spelling *ow* are sometimes pronounced with /ɔf/ before an unvoiced consonant.

/w/
in many words, including initial *W-* in names of English and Belgian origin:
Cromwell, Delaware, Gerschwin, Hawaï, kiwi, Longwy, Malawi, Ottawa, Rwanda, Saskatchewan, swing [swiŋ], *tramway* [tʀamwɛ]

236 | FRENCH LYRIC DICTION

(streetcar line), *Tweed*, *walkman* [|wokman], *wallaby* [|walabi], *Wallonie*, *wapiti* (elk), *Wasquehal*, *water-closet* [|watɛr klozɛt] (toilets), *watt*, *web* [|wɛb] (world-wide-web), *webcam* [|wɛbkam], *webmaster* [|wɛbmastœːr], *week-end* [|wikɛnd], *Wellington*, *Wessex*, *western* [|wɛstɛrn] (western film), *Westminster*, *wi-fi* [|wifi], *wigwam*, *Wilde*, *Winnaretta*, *Woluwe*, *wombat* [|wõba], *Wyoming*, *Zimbabwe*

NOTE:
/w/ or /v/ in many Belgian names with initial *W-*: *Walcourt*, *Wandre*, *Wasme*.

wh-

/w/
always, at the beginning of borrowed English vocabulary:
wharf [|warf], *whippet* [|wipɛt], *whisky* [|wiski], *whist* [|wist], *Whistler*, *Whitehall*, *Whitman*.

NOTES for *liaison*:
Liaison is not made to borrowed English vocabulary with word-initial *w-* and *wh-*.

— X ○ [iks] —

x-

/gz/
at the beginning of most words, especially before *a*, and in many names:
xanthane (xanthan), *Xanthe* (Xanthus), *Xanthi*, *xanthie* (orange swallow), *xanthine* (xanthin), *Xanthippe*, *xanthome* (xanthoma), *xanthophylle* (xanthophyll), *Xavier*, *Xénocrate* (Xenocrates), *Xénophane* (Xenophanes), *Xénophon* (Xenophon), *Xerxès* (Xerxes), *Ximénès* (Jiménez)

/ks/
at the beginning of a few words and names:
xyste (xystus), *Xénia*, *Xertigny*, *Xuthos* (Xuthus)

/s/
at the beginning of a few names:
Xaintois, *De Xaintonge*, *Xaintrailles*

NOTES:
/gz/ and /ks/ are both correct in several scholarly words beginning in *xé-*, *xi-*, and *xyl-*, as well as in many names; the

voiced pronunciation tends to be more modern, and is the
norm: *Xenakis, xénarthres* (xenarthrans), *xénon* (xenon), *xénophile*
(xenophile), *xénophobe* (xenophobic), *xénophobie* (xenophobia),
xérès (*sherry*), *xérocopier* (to xerox copy), *xérodermie* (xeroderma),
xérophyte (xerophyte), *xérus* (ground squirrel), *ximénie* (mountain
plum), *xiphoïde* (xiphoid), *xiphophore* (swordtail), *xylème, xylène,
xylidine, xylocope* (carpenter bee), *xylographie* (xylography),
xylophage (wood-boring insect), *xylophone, xylose*.
/gz/ and /ks/ are also correct in *Xaintois*.
/k/ is occasionally heard in a few cases: *xérès* (shery), *Xérès*
(Jerez), *Ximénès* (Jiménez).

-*x*-

/ks/
in most cases:
Alexandre (Alexander), *boxe* (boxing), *complexité, dextérité*
(dexterity), *extraordinaire* (extraordinary), *fixer* (to attach to),
galaxie (galaxy), *Haxo, Ixion, juxtaposer* (to juxtapose), *klaxonner*
(to honk), *luxe* (luxury), *maximum, nixe* (nixie), *oxymore*
(oxymoron), *paradoxe* (paradox), *relaxer* (relax), *saxophone,
taxi, unisexe* (unisex), *vexer* (to offend), *zootaxie* (zootaxy)

/gz/
in the spellings *ex-* and *inex-* before a vowel or mute *h*:
exact (correct), *exagérer* (to exaggerate), *exalter* (to exalt),
examen (exam), *exaspérer, exaucer, Exékias, exemple* (example),
exercer (to exercise/practise), *exhaler* (to exhale), *exhausser*
(to raise up), *exhibition* (display), *exiger* (to require), *exil, exister*
(to exist), *exonérer* (to exonerate), *exorbitant, exotique* (exotic),
exubérant (exuberant), *exulter* (to exult), *Exupère, inexact*
(inaccurate), *inexhaustible, inexistant* (nonexistent), *inexorable,
Saint-Exupéry*
NOTE:
/ks/ is sometimes heard for emphasis in the words *exécrer*
(to loathe), *exécrable* (loathsome), and *exécration* (loathing).

in the prefixes *hexa-* and *sexa-:*
hexagonal, hexagone (hexagon), *Hexaméron, Hexaples* (Hexapla),
sexagénaire (person in his/her sixties), *Sexagésime* (Sexagesima)
NOTE:
/ks/ is less common, but also correct in the prefix *sexa-*.

238 | FRENCH LYRIC DICTION

/s/
in a few cases:
Bruxelles (Brussels), *soixante* (sixty), *Uxelles*, *Xerxès* (Xerxes)

/z/
in ordinal numbers:
sixième [sizjɛmə] (sixth), *dixième* [dizjɛmə] (tenth)

-x

✻
most often silent as the last letter of a word or name, after a vowel:
afflux, *aux* (to/at the), *Bernex*, *Bex*, *Bordeaux*, *Capponex*, *Chamonix*, *Champeix*, *Chastellux*, *choix* (choice), *cieux* (skies), *Conjux*, *courroux* (anger), *croix* (cross), *crucifix*, *deux* (two), *doux* (gentle/soft), *eaux* (waters), *eux* (they/them), *faux* (false), *flux* (flow/stream), *Fouleix*, *influx* (upsurge), *jaloux* (jealous), *neveux* (nephews), *noix* (nut), *Oyonnax*, *paix* (peace), *perdrix* (partridge), *je peux* (I can), *taux* (rate), *Verjux*, *vœux* (wishes)

/ks/
as the last letter in some cases, including after a nasalizing *n*:
Aix, *Ajax*, *anthrax*, *apex*, *Benelux*, *borax*, *box* (cubicle/stall), *Cadix*, *codex*, *Dupleix*, *Félix* (Felix), *Gex*, *hélix* (helix), *index*, *larynx*, *lux* (light), *onyx*, *phlox*, *Pollux*, *sphinx*, *Styx*, *Syphax*, *syrinx* (syrinx/pan flute), *thorax*, *Wessex*

/s/
as the last letter of a few words:
coccyx, *six* (six), *dix* (ten)

⚠ silent ✻ in *six* and *dix* as adjectives before a pronounced consonant: *six portes* (six doors), *dix livres* (ten books). See Chapter 7: 'Numbers'.

/z/
in *liaison*

NOTES for *liaison*:
Where *liaison* is permitted, it is regularly made in singing with /z/: *je rêve aux͜ amours défunts* (I dream of love lost), *deux͜ ans* (two years), *doux͜ et frêles* (sweet and frail), *je veux͜ encor demeurer* (I still want to stay).

FRENCH PRONUNCIATION A–Z | 239

-xc- /ksk/
in the spellings *exc-* and *inexc-* before *a, o, u,* or a consonant:
excavation, exclamation, excommunication, excursion, inexcusable

/ks/
in the spellings *exc-* and *inexc-* before *i* or *e*:
excellent [ɛksɛlɑ̃] (excellent), *Excenevex, exciter* [ɛksite] (to excite),
inexcitable [inɛksitablə]

-xs- /ks/
in the spelling *exs-*:
exsanguination [ɛksɑ̃ginasjõ], *exsuder* [ɛksyde] (to exude)
NOTE:
/ɛgz/ or /ɛks/ in *exsangue* (bloodless).

— Y ○ [igʀɛk] —

y /i/
in most cases—usually before a consonant (other than a single *m*
or *n* unless it is followed by another vowel), or as the last letter
of a word:
anonyme (anonymous), *byzantin* (Byzantine), *Clymène, dynastie*
(dynasty), *Endymion, ferry, gymnopédie, Hyménée* (Hymen),
idyllique (idyllic), *jury* [ʒyɾi], *kyrie* [kiɾje], *lys* (lily), *martyr*
(martyr), *nylon, Ory, pachyderme* (pachyderm), *Quessy, rythme*
(rhythm), *Sully, synode* (synod), *type* (guy/type), *Ulysse* (Ulysses),
Vichy, Wyns, xylène (xylene), *y* (there/about it), *Ygraine, Yniold,
Ypres, Ys, yttrium, Yvette, Yzeure, zymase*

/j/
before another vowel:
Astyanax, balayer (to sweep), *cyan, dyade* (dyad), *essuyer* (to wipe),
fayot (bean), *hyacinthe* (hyacinth), *ichtyologie* (ichthyology), *joyeux*
(joyful), *kayak, Lafayette, mayonnaise, noyé* (drowned), *oyez!* (hear
ye!), *Pleyel, royaume* (kingdom), *savoyard, Thyeste, uruguayen*
(Urugayan), *voyeur, yak, Yémaldin, Yèvres, yeux* (eyes), *Yoan, Youkali,
zyeuter* (to ogle)

⚠ /i/ after a consonant plus *l* or *r*: *Amphitryon, dryade* (dryad),
Hamadryade (Hamadryad). An alternative and accepted
pronunciation of /ij/ also exists for this spelling: *embryon*
[ɑ̃.bɾi.jõ] (embryo).

240 | FRENCH LYRIC DICTION

NOTE:
In the score, *y* before another vowel sound is often set as dieresis with /i/: *hy-a-cin-the* [i.a.sɛ̃:.tə] (hyacinth).

NOTES for *liaison*:
Liaison is normally not possible to words with the initial *y*-spelling as /|j/, except in the words *yeux* (eyes), *yeuse* (helm oak), and in some French names.

ÿ   *see* **ï**

-ye, -yes   /i/
after a consonant:
Barye, Érinnyes (Erinyes), *Libye* (Libya), *mye* (mya), *rallye* (rally), *Titye* (Tityos)

NOTE:
Although rarely encountered, this spelling could be set as /iə/ when verse-final: *tel que des meurtriers devant les Érinnyes* (like murderers before The Furies).

NOTES for English loanwords:
Vowel sounds are usually approximated.
/i/: *baby* [bɛbi], *dandy* [dãdi], *jury* [ʒyɾi], *milady* [milɛdi], *Salisbury, whisky* [|wiski].
/aj/: *bye-bye* [baj baj], *Bryon, Hyde-Park, Madame Butterfly, rye* [ɾaj] (drink: rye), *Shylock, Wyoming.*
/|j/ without *liaison*, at the beginning of a word: *yacht* [|jɔt], *yankee* [|jãki], *yearling* [|jœɾliŋ], *yeoman* [|jɔman].

-yen   /jɛ̃/
always:
D'Ayen, citoyen (citizen), *doyen* (oldest person/dean), *Doyen, mitoyen* (dividing), *moyen* (means/middle), *Payen, Troyen* (Trojan)
NOTE:
/jɛnə/ in the *-yenne* ending: *Cayenne, Cheyennes, citoyenne* (citizen), *Guyenne, Mayenne.*

NOTES for *liaison*:
⚠   Denasalization occurs in *liaison* as /jɛn/ from masculine adjectives in the singular form, most notably from the word *moyen* (middle): *moyen âge* (Middle Ages).

FRENCH PRONUNCIATION A–Z | 241

-ylle   /ilə/
always:
Bathylle, chlorophylle (chlorophyll), *idylle* (idyll/romance), *Sibylle*

ym, yn   /ɛ̃/
at the end of a word, or before a different consonant:
asymptomatique (asymptomatic), *cymbale* (cymbal), *Cynthie, Gédoyn, Jocelyn, larynx, lymphe* (lymph), *nymphe, Olympe, Olympia, Olympie, ornithorynque* (platypus), *sympathique* (nice), *syncopé* (syncopated), *thym* (thyme), *tympan* (eardrum), *Tyndaris*
NOTE:
The spelling *ym* and *yn* is not nasalized before a vowel.—*see* **y**

-ys, -ÿs   *see* **-s**

— Z ○ [zɛd] —

z   /z/
in most cases:
azure, Balzac, Cazalis, douze (twelve), *Éléazar, falzar* (trousers), *gazouiller* (to twitter), *Hazard, Izeaux, Jézabel* (Jezebel), *Kazakhstan, lézard* (lizard), *De Mézières, Nazareth, onze* (eleven), *Panzéra, quatorze* (fourteen), *rizière* (paddy field), *sizain* (sestet), *treize* (thirteen), *Uzès, Vezolot, zabre* (zabrus beetle), *Zachée, Zampa, Zanzibar, zéro* (zero), *zeugme* (zeugma), *zinc, zizanie* (discord), *zone, zoo* [zo], *Zosime, zouave* (fool), *Zoulou* (Zulu), *zozo* (nitwit), *La Zuecca, Zurich, zygote*

-z   z̶
always silent in second-person plural *-ez* verb endings:
vous chantez (you sing), *vous dansiez* (you were dancing), *vous marcherez* (you will walk), *vous parleriez* (you would talk)

usually silent as the last letter of a word, after a vowel, especially in names:
Agassiz, assez (enough), *Auguez, Bruz, Les Carroz d'Arâches, Chanaz, Chavanoz, Chevroz, chez* (at the home/place of), *Chooz, La Clusaz, Condroz, Contrevoz, Cormoz, Deprez, Dumouriez, Duprez, La Forclaz, Grez, Grovlez, Gruaz, Jaquet-Droz, Laisnez, lez* (near), *Marboz, Marclaz, Minjoz, Morez, nez* (nose), *Praz, Ramuz, raz* (strait), *rez-de-chaussée* (ground floor), *riz* (rice), *Saint-Geniez-d'Olt, Saint-Jorioz, Saint-Tropez, Sciez, La Vernaz*

/z/
in *liaison*

NOTES for *liaison*:
Liaison is regularly made in singing with /z/, notably from second-person plural -*ez* verb endings: *assez heureux* (quite happy), *chez elle* (at her place), *chantez à Dieu* (sing to God), *vous irez au théâtre* (you will go to the theatre).

as the last letter of a few words and several names:
Alliot-Lugaz, Berlioz, Booz, Boulez, Cloëz, Culoz, Deldevez, Depraz, Descombaz, Echenoz, fez, Firouz, gaz [gɑːz] (gas), *Hafiz, lapiaz* (lapies), *Legoëz, Luz, merguez, Ormuz, Potez, rémiz* (remiz tit bird), *Saint-Jean-de-Luz, Le Semnoz, Suez, Thorez, Vuillermoz, Wallez*
NOTE:
/ɛːz/ or /ɛs/ in many names from the south of France and Spain: *Fernandez, Rodriguez, Senez.*

NOTES for loanwords and foreign names:
/ts/ in most Italian and German vocabulary: *Graz, grazioso, Kreuzberg, Maelzel.*
/dz/ is also sometimes heard in Italian and German vocabulary, as well as in a few initial *z-* words: *Menzel, scherzo, sforza, Zeus, zingara, zingaro, zingarello.*
/s/ in a few borrowed words, especially in Spanish vocabulary: *Aztèques* (Aztecs), *Joachaz, zarzuela* [sarswela].

zz   **/dz/**
in borrowed Italian words:
mezzanine, mezzo-soprano, mozzarelle/mozzarella, paparazzi, pizza, pizzeria [pidzerja], *pizzicato, pupazzo*

/z/
in borrowed English words:
blizzard [blizaːr], *gin-fizz* [dʒin fiːz] (gin fizz cocktail), *grizzli* [grizli] (grizzly bear), *jazz* [dʒaːz], *puzzle* [pœzl]

NOTE:
/dz/ and /z/ are both correct in *Brazzaville, lazzi* (taunt), and *razzia* (raid).

PART THREE

Pronunciation Dictionaries

Preamble to Part Three

Two French pronunciation dictionaries follow. The first is an alphabetical list of the names of people, places, and things, shown with phonetic transcription in IPA. Entries are predominantly names encountered in, or directly associated with, French vocal repertoire, and the arts and culture of France and French-speaking regions. They include the titles of operas and literary works, the names of well-known fictional and mythological characters, operatic roles, *patronymes* (surnames) of composers, singers, instrumentalists, visual artists, conductors, authors, poets, librettists, and historical figures, *prénoms* (given names) commonly used in French, the countries of the world, *toponymes* (names of current and historical regions, cities, and settlements), with particular focus on the pronunciation of challenging French place names, as well as the designated *gentilés* (labels for the inhabitants of those places).

The second dictionary is a much shorter alphabetical list of the standard French pronunciation for borrowed Italian musical terms. Musicians all over the world regularly use these Italian loanwords. Vocabulary such as *crescendo* and *legato* is routinely anglicized in everyday use in English, and is just as readily *francisé* in French. Transcription is provided for the most common Italian musical terms as they are normally used in a modern French setting.

About the System of Transcription

Transcriptions reflect pronunciation in an elevated tone. Where multiple pronunciations are included, one is generally a more authentic version of a foreign name, whereas other option(s) is/are *francisé* to a greater degree. The first pronunciation shown is the one more commonly used and/or respected. Names with lengthened vowels are indicated with the /:/ symbol; half-lengthening is not shown. Vocalic harmonization is avoided. Mute *e* is shown as /ə/ in all possible positions, including word-final (with the exception of /waə/). Mute *e* should be dropped as normal in speech, especially when word-final. Syneresis is shown wherever possible with /j/, /w/, or/ɥ/. Such words are often encountered in the score as dieresis, set in their own syllables containing /i/, /u/, or /y/ respectively. These topics are all explained in Chapter 2. As in Part Two, flipped /ɾ/ is shown, but rolled /r/ and uvular *r* are also possible variants, as explained in Chapter 3. Thus, a name such

246 | FRENCH LYRIC DICTION

as *Ariane*, shown as [aʀjanə], could be [aʀian], or a combination of those variable phonemes. Affricates are shown in their 'uncompressed' notation when they occur over a syllabic barrier in a name, (e.g., /tʃ/, as in *Puccini* [putʃini]), while affricates that occur in a single syllable are given in their 'compressed' notation, (e.g., /ʧ/, as in *Tchaïkovsky* [ʧajkɔfski]). In the progression of consonant + *li* or *ri* + vowel, interpolated /j/ before the main vowel sound is not indicated, but is of course possible: that is, *Chabrier* may be realized as [ʃabʀie] or [ʃabʀije]. Names with prefixes (*De*, *Des*, *Du*, *Le*, *La*, etc.) are alphabetized under the main part of the name. Transcriptions beginning in vowels or aspirated *h* into which *liaison* is not permitted are marked with | . A single character between parentheses ( ) indicates either a variation in the spelling of a word, or a phoneme that can be pronounced or dropped.

Pronunciation Dictionary of Proper Nouns

— A —

Aaron aarõ
Abadie abadiə
Abaris abaʀis
Abauzit abozit
Abbad abad
Abbadides abadidə
Abbadie abadiə
Abbans-Dessous abã dəsu
Abbans-Dessus abã dəsy
Abbas aba:s
Abbassides abasidə
    or abasidə
Abbé abe
Abbéville abevilə
Abbeville abəvilə
Abdérame abdeʀamə
Abdolonyme abdɔlɔnimə
Abel abɛl
Abélard abela:ʀ
Abelé abəle
Abénaquis abenaki
Abencérages (Les) lɛ zabẽseʀa:ʒə
Abidjan abidʒã
Abigaël abigaɛl
Abigaïl abigail
Abimélech abimelɛk
Abirounère abiʀunɛ:ʀə
Abner abnɛ:ʀ
Abou D(h)abi/Aboû-Dabî abu dabi
Aboulker abulkɛ:ʀ
About abu
Abraham abʀaam
Abrial abʀial
Abruzzes abʀy:zə
Absalom apsalõ
Absalon apsalõ
Absil apsil
Absyrte apsiʀtə
Abu Dhabi abu dabi
Abyssin(s) abisẽ
Abyssine(s) abisinə
Abyssinie abisiniə

Abyssinien(s) abisinjẽ
Abyssinienne(s) abisinjɛnə
Acadie akadiə
Acante akã:tə
Acapulco akapulko
Acaste akastə
Accurse akyʀsə
Achab akab
Achaïe akaiə
Achaïos/Achaios akajɔs *or* akajo:s
Achard aʃa:ʀ
Acharniens (Les) lɛ zakaʀnjẽ
Achate akatə
Achaz aka:z
Ache (D') daʃə
Achéron akeʀõ
Achille aʃilə
Achilléide akileidə
Achis akis
Acis asis
Ackermann akɛrman
Ackté akte
Açoka asɔka
Açores asɔ:ʀə
Acropole akʀɔpɔlə
Actéon akteõ
Actium aksjɔm
Adam adã
Adamas adama:s
Adamastor adamasto:ʀ
Adamos adamɔs *or* adamo:s
Adams adams
Adario adaʀjo
Addis-Abéba adi sabeba
Adélaïde adelaidə
Adèle adɛlə
Adélie adeliə
Adémar adema:ʀ
Adenis adəni
Ader adɛ:ʀ
Aderer adeʀɛ:ʀ
Adiny adini
Adiousias adjuzja:s

Admète admɛtə
Adolphe adɔlfə
Adonaï adɔnai
Adonis adɔnis
Adraste adʀastə
Adriatique adʀiatikə
Adriel adʀiɛl
Adrien adʀiẽ
Adrienne adʀiɛnə
Adza adza
Ægir eʒi:ʀ
Ælla ela
Æmilius emiljys
Ænoë enɔe
Æschylus eskilys
Afars afa:ʀ
Affre afʀə
Afghan(s) afgã
Afghane(s) afganə
Afghanistan afganistã
Africain(s) afʀikẽ
Africaine(s) afʀikɛnə
Afrique afʀikə
Agamemnon agamɛmnõ
Agar aga:ʀ
Agassiz agasi
Agathe agatə
Agathocle agatɔklə
Agathon agatõ
Agde agdə
Agen aʒẽ
Agésilas aʒezila:s
Aggée agʒe
Agis aʒis
Aglaé aglae
Aglante aglã:tə
Agnès aɲɛs
Agostini agostini
Agoult (D') dagu
Agrippine agʀipinə
Aguessac agɛsak *or* agesak
Aguesseau (D') dagɛso
    or dageso

PRONUNCIATION DICTIONARIES | 247

Aguillon aguijɔ̃
Ahmed amɛd
Aicard ɛka:ɾ
Aïda aida
Aignan ɛɲã
Aignay-le-Duc ɛɲɛ lə dyk
Aiguillon eguijɔ̃ *or* eguijɔ̃
Aillant ajã
Aimé ɛme *or* eme
Aimée ɛmeə *or* emeə
Aimon ɛmɔ̃
Ain ɛ̃
Ainois ɛnwa
Ainoise(s) ɛnwa:zə
Airvault ɛrvo
Aisne ɛnə
Aïtoff ajtɔf
Aix ɛks
Aix-en-Provence ɛk sã prɔvã:sə
Aix-les-Bains ɛks lɛ bɛ̃
Aixonnais ɛksɔnɛ
Aixonnaise(s) ɛkɔnɛ:zə
Ajaccio aʒaksjo
Ajax aʒaks
Akhtamar aktama:ɾ
Alabama alabama
Aladin aladɛ̃
Alagna alaɲa
Alain alɛ̃
Alain-Fournier alɛ̃ furnje
Alamir alami:ɾ
Alaouddin alaudɛ̃
Alard ala:ɾ
Alari alaɾi
Alarie alaɾiə
Alaska alaska
Alava alava
Alba alba
Albanais albanɛ
Albanaise(s) albanɛ:zə
Albane (L') lalbanə
Albani albani
Albanie albaniə
Albans albã
Albaÿdé albaide
Albéniz albenis
Albens albɛ̃:s
Albers albɛrs
Albert albɛ:ɾ
Alberta albɛrta
Albert-Birot albɛr biro
Alberti albɛrti
Albertine albɛrtinə
Albertville albɛrvilə
Albi albi
Albine albinə
Albinoni albinɔni
Alboni albɔni
Albret albrɛ
Albuquerque albykɛrkə
Alcade alkadə
Alcala alkala
Alcarazas (D') dalkaɾaza:s
Alcard alka:ɾ
Alcazar alkaza:ɾ
Alcée alseə
Alceste alsɛstə

Alcibiade alsibjadə
Alcide alsidə
Alcindor alsɛ̃dɔ:ɾ
Alcine alsinə
Alcman alkmã
Alcmène alkmɛnə
Alcyon alsjɔ̃
Alcyone alsjɔnə
Aleatico/Aléatico aleatiko
Alecton alɛktɔ̃
Alemar alema:ɾ
Alençon alãsɔ̃
Aléoutiennes aleusjɛnə
Alès alɛs
Alexandra alɛksãdɾa
Alexandre alɛksã:dɾə
Alexandrie alɛksãdɾiə
Alexandrin(s) alɛksãdɾɛ̃
Alexandrine(s) alɛksãdɾinə
Alexis alɛksi
Alfaroubeira (D') dalfaɾubɛɾa
Alfred alfrɛd
Alger alʒe
Algérie alʒeɾi
Algérien(s) alʒeɾjɛ̃
Algérienne(s) alʒeɾjɛnə
Algonquins algɔ̃kɛ̃
Alguazil algwazil
Alhambra alãbɾa
Alheim al(h)ajm
Ali ali
Alicante alikã:tə
Alice alisə
Aligoté aligɔte
Alim alim
Aline alinə
Alissa alisa
Alix aliks
Alizard aliza:ɾ
Alkan alkã
Alkandre alkã:dɾə
Alkor alkɔ:ɾ
Alladine aladinə
Allah ala
Allais alɛ
Allard ala:ɾ
Allauch alo
Alleghanys alegani
Allégret alegɾɛ
Allemagne aləmaɲə
Allemand(s) aləmã
Allemande(s) aləmã:də
Allier alje
Alliot-Lugaz aljo lyga:z
Allorge alɔrʒə
Allouard alwa:ɾ
Almaïde almaidə
Almansor/Almanzor almãzɔ:ɾ
Almaviva almaviva
Almirante almiɾã:tə
Almire almi:ɾə
Aloès/Aloës alɔɛs
Alonse alɔ̃:sə
Alost alɔst
Alpes alpə
Alphand alfã
Alphée alfeə

Alphise alfi:zə
Alphonse alfɔ̃:sə
Alquié alkje
Alquif alkif
Alsace alzasə
Alsacien(s) alzasjɛ̃
Alsacienne(s) alzasjɛnə
Altaï altai
Altamor altamɔ:ɾ
Altamoras altamɔɾa:s
Altdorf altdɔrf
Altéry alteɾi
Altès altɛs
Altinoglu altinɔgly
Altkirch altkirʃ
Alvar alva:ɾ
Alvarès alvaɾɛs
Alvarez alvaɾɛ:z *or* alvaɾɛs
Alvaro alvaɾo
Amable amablə
Amade amadə
Amadis amadis
Amadou amadu
Amahelli/Amahelly amaɛli
Amalasonte amalazɔ̃:tə
Amalec amalɛk
Amalécites amalesitə
Amalou amalu
Amalthée amalteə
Aman amã
Amathée amateə
Amaury amoɾi
Amazily amazili
Amazone(s) amazo:nə *or* amazonə
Amazonie amazɔniə
Ambert ãbɛ:ɾ
Ambès ãbɛs
Ambez ãbɛ:z *or* ãbɛs
Amboise ãbwa:ze
Amédée amedeə
Ameilhon amejɔ̃
Amélie ameliə
Amellér amɛlɛ:ɾ
Aménophis amenɔfis
Américain(s) ameɾikɛ̃
Américaine(s) ameɾikɛnə
Améric-Vespuce ameɾik vɛspysə
Amérique ameɾikə
Amiens amjɛ̃
Amint(h)e amɛ̃:tə
Amiot amjo
Ammien amjɛ̃
Amnhès amnɛs
Amor (D') damɔ:ɾ
Amorgos amɔɾgos *or* amɔɾgo:s
Amoroso amoɾozo
Amos amos *or* amo:s
Amour amu:ɾ
Ampère ãpɛ:ɾə
Amphimédon ãfimedɔ̃
Amphion ãfjɔ̃
Amphitryon ãfitɾiɔ̃
Amrou amɾu
Amsterdam amstɛrdam
Amurat amyɾa *or* amyɾat
Amy ami
Anacharsis anakaɾsis

Anacréon anakreõ
Anada anada
Anaël anaɛl
Anahita anaita
Anaï anai
Anaïde anaidə
Anaïs anais
Anasazis anasazi
Anastase anastɑ:zə
Anastasie anastaziə
Anatole anatɔlə
Anaxagore anaksagɔ:rə
Anaximandre anaksimã:drə
Anaximène anaksimɛnə
Ancelot ãsəlo
Ancenis ãsəni
Ancessy ãsɛsi *or* ãsesi
Anchise ãʃi:zə
Andalouse ãdalu:zə
Andelys (Les) lɛ zãdəli
Andéros ãderos *or* ãdero:s
Andocide ãdɔsidə
Andorran(s) ãdɔrã
Andorrane(s) ãdɔranə
Andorre ãdɔ:rə
André ãdre
Andrée ãdreə
Andreloux ãdrəlu
Andrès ãdrɛs
Andres (Don) dɔ nãdrɛs
Andrew ãdru
Andrieux ãdriø
Andromaque ãdrɔmakə
Andromède ãdrɔmɛdə
Andronique ãdrɔnikə
Andros ãdros *or* ãdro:s
Anet (*person*) anɛ
Anet (*place*) anɛt
Angèle ãʒɛlə
Angelici ãʒelisi
Angelina ãʒelina
Angélique ãʒelikə
Angellier ãʒəlje
Ange-Pitou ãʒə pitu
Angers ãʒe
Angevin(s) ãʒəvɛ̃
Angevine(s) ãʒəvinə
Angkor aŋkɔ:r *or* ãkɔ:r
Anglebert (D') dãgləbɛ:r
Anglesches ãglɛʃə
Angleterre ãglətɛ:rə
Anglo-Saxons ãglo saksõ
Angludet (D') dãglydɛ
Angola ãgɔla
Angolais ãgɔlɛ
Angolaise(s) ãgɔlɛ:zə
Angot ãgo
Angoulême ãgulɛmə
Angoumois ãgumwa
Angoumoisain(s) ãgumwazɛ̃
Angoumoisaine(s) ãgumwazɛnə
Angsoka ãsɔka
Anguilla ãgija
Anguillai(s) ãgijɛ
Anguillaise(s) ãgijɛ:zə
Anita anita
Anjou ãʒu

Ankara ãkara
Anna ana
An(n)aëlle anaɛlə
Anne ɑ:nə *or* anə
Annecy anəsi
Annette anɛtə
Annick anik
Annœullin anœlɛ̃ *or* anœjɛ̃
Annot anɔt
Anouilh anuj
Anouk anuk
Anquetil ãkətil
Ans ã:s
Ansaldy ãsaldi
Anseaume ãso:mə
Anselme ãsɛlmə
Anselmus ãsɛlmys
Ansembourg ãsãbu:r
Ansermet ãsɛrmɛ
Ansseau ãso
Antarctique ãtarktikə
Antéchrist ãtekrist
Antée ãteə
Anténor ãtenɔ:r
Antibes ãtibə
Antifer ãtifɛ:r
Antigny (D') dãtiɲi
Antigone ãtigɔnə
Antigua ãtigwa
Antiguais ãtigwɛ
Antiguaise(s) ãtigwɛ:zə
Antillais ãtijɛ
Antillaise(s) ãtijɛ:zə
Antilles ãtijə
Antimaque ãtimakə
Antinoé/Antinoë ãtinoe
Antinoüs ãtinɔys
Antioche ãtjɔʃə
Antipater ãtipatɛ:r
Antisthène ãtistɛnə
Antium ãsjɔm
Antoine ãtwanə
Antoinette ãtwanɛtə
Antommarchi ãtɔmarki
Anton ãtɔn *or* antɔn *or* ãtõ
Antonia ãtɔnja *or* antɔnja
Antonin ãtɔnɛ̃
Antonio ãtɔnjo
Antony ãtɔni
Antraigues (D') dãtrɛgə
Anubis anybis
Anvers ãvɛ:r *or* ãvɛrs
Aod aɔd
Aoste ɔstə *or* aɔstə
Aoustin utɛ̃
Apaches apaʃə
Apennins apenɛ̃
Aphrodita afrɔdita
Aphrodite afrɔditə
Apis apis
Apollidon apɔlidõ
Apollinaire apɔlinɛ:rə
Apollodore apɔlɔdɔ:rə
Apollon apɔlõ
Apollonios apɔlɔnjos *or* apɔlɔnjo:s
Apollonius apɔlɔnjys
Appalaches apalaʃə

Appel apɛl
Appenzell apɛ̃zɛl
Appia apja
Appien apjɛ̃
Approntie aprõtiə
Aprahamian apraamjã
Apt apt
Apulée apyleə
Aquin akɛ̃
Aquitain(s) akitɛ̃
Aquitaine(s) akitɛnə
Arabe arabə
Arabelle arabɛlə
Arabie arabiə
Arabie Saoudite arabi sauditə
Arabie Séoudite arabi seuditə
Aracynthe arasɛ̃:tə
Arago arago
Aragon aragõ
Aragonais aragonɛ
Aragonaise(s) aragonɛ:zə
Arakel arakel
Aral aral
Aramits aramits
Arapian arapjã
Araquil arakil
Ararat arara
Aratos aratos *or* arato:s
Arban arbã
Arbas arba:s
Arbell arbɛl
Arbresle (L') larbrɛlə
Arcabonne arkabɔnə
Arcachon arkaʃõ
Arcadie arkadiə
Arcalaüs arkalays
Arcas arka:s
Arcésilas arsezila:s
Archainbaud arʃɛ̃bo
Archambault arʃãbo
Archambaut arʃãbo
Archard arʃa:r
Archas arka:s
Archélaos arkelaos *or* arkelao:s
Archémore arʃemɔ:rə
Archidamos arkidamos *or* arkidamo:s
Archiloque arʃilɔkə
Archimède arʃimɛdə
Arcins arsɛ̃
Arcis arsi
Arcourt (D') darku:r
Arctique arktikə
Arcueil arkœj
Arcueil-Cachan arkœj kaʃã
Ardan-Canile ardã kanilə
Ardèche ardɛʃə
Ardéchois ardeʃwa
Ardéchoise(s) ardeʃwa:zə
Ardennais ardənɛ *or* ardenɛ
Ardennaise(s) ardənɛ:zə *or* ardenɛ:zə
Ardennes ardɛnə
Ardentes ardã:tə
Ardoin ardwɛ̃
Ardouin ardwɛ̃

Aremberg (D')/Arenberg (D') daʀɛ̃bɛːʀ

Arembourg (D') daʀɑ̃buːʀ

Aren aʀɛn

Arenc aʀɛ̃ːk

Aréthuse aʀetyːzə

Argant aʀgɑ̃

Argante aʀgɑ̃ːtə

Argelès-Gazost aʀʒəlɛs gazɔst

Argens *(place)* aʀʒɛ̃ːs

Argens (D') daʀʒɑ̃ːs

Argenson (D') daʀʒɑ̃sɔ̃

Argentan aʀʒɑ̃tɑ̃

Argenteuil aʀʒɑ̃tœj

Argentin(s) aʀʒɑ̃tɛ̃

Argentine(s) aʀʒɑ̃tinə

Argien(s) aʀʒjɛ̃

Argienne(s) aʀʒjɛnə

Argonautes aʀgonoːtə

Argos aʀgɔs *or* aʀgoːs

Argus aʀgys

Ariane aʀjanə

Arias (Don) dɔ naʀjaːs

Aricie aʀisiə

Ariège aʀjɛːʒə

Ariégois aʀjeʒwa

Ariégoise(s) aʀjeʒwaːzə

Ariel aʀjɛl

Arinthod aʀɛ̃to

Ariodant aʀjɔdɑ̃

Arioste (L') laʀjɔstə

Arioviste aʀjovistə

Aristarque aʀistaʀkə

Aristée aʀisteə

Aristide aʀistidə

Aristippe aʀistipə

Aristobule aʀistɔbylə

Aristodème aʀistɔdɛmə

Aristogiton aʀistɔʒitɔ̃

Aristophane aʀistɔfanə

Aristote aʀistɔtə

Arius aʀjys

Arizona aʀizɔna

Arkansas aʀkɑ̃saːs *or* aʀkanzaːs

Arkel/Arkël aʀkɛl

Arkor (D') daʀkɔːʀ

Arlange (D') daʀlɑ̃ːʒə

Arlanc aʀlɑ̃

Arlequin aʀləkɛ̃

Arles aʀlə

Arletty aʀlɛti *or* aʀleti

Armagnac aʀmaɲak

Armand aʀmɑ̃

Armandie aʀmɑ̃diə

Armel aʀmɛl

Arménie aʀmeniə

Arménien(s) aʀmenjɛ̃

Arménienne(s) aʀmenjɛnə

Armide aʀmidə

Arminius aʀminjys

Armor aʀmɔːʀ

Armorique aʀmɔʀikə

Arnaud aʀno

Arnaude aʀnoːdə

Arnauld aʀno

Arnavaux (Les) lɛ zaʀnavo

Arne aʀnə

Arnes aʀnə

Arnobe aʀnɔbə

Arnoldson aʀnɔldsɔn

Arnould aʀnu

Arnoult aʀnu

Arnoux aʀnu

Aron aʀɔ̃

Arondelle aʀɔ̃dɛlə

Aronte aʀɔ̃ːtə

Arral aʀal

Arras aʀɑːs

Arrau aʀaw

Arrauzau aʀozo

Arrens aʀɛ̃ːs

Arrien aʀjɛ̃

Arrieu aʀjø

Arromanches-les-Bains
aʀɔmɑ̃ʃə lɛ bɛ̃

Ars aʀs

Arsace aʀzasə

Arsandaux aʀsɑ̃do

Arsène aʀsɛnə

Arsène Lupin aʀsɛnə lypɛ̃

Artaban aʀtabɑ̃

Artabaze aʀtabɑːzə

Artassens aʀtasɛ̃ːs

Artaud aʀto

Artaxerxes aʀtagzɛʀsɛs

Artémidore aʀtemidɔːʀə

Artémise aʀtemiːzə

Arthébuze aʀtebyːzə

Arthur aʀtyːʀ

Arthus aʀtys

Artois aʀtwa

Artôt aʀto

Artus aʀtys

Aruba aʀyba

Arundel aʀɔ̃dɛl

Arveiller aʀvejə

Arvers aʀvɛːʀ

Asaël azaɛl

Ascagne askaɲə

Ascanio askanjo

Asclépiade asklepjadə

Asdrubal asdʀybal

Aseaume azoːmə

Aser azɛːʀ

Asfeld asfɛld

Asie aziə

Asmodée asmodeə

Asnelles anɛlə *or* anɛlə

Asnières anjɛːʀə

Asoka asɔka

Aspasie aspaziə

Asphodèle asfɔdɛlə

Assens asɛ̃ːs

Assise (D') dasiːzə

Asso aso

Assomption (L') lasɔ̃psjɔ̃

Assuérus/Assuërus asɥerys

Assur asyːʀ

Assurbanipal asyʀbanipal

Assyrie asiʀiə

Astaroth astaʀɔt

Astarté astaʀte

Asti asti

Astolfo astɔlfo

Astolphe astɔlfə

Astrée astreə

Astrid astʀid

Astruc astʀyk

Asturias astyʀjaːs

Asturies astyʀiə

Astyage astjaːʒə

Astyanax astjanaks

Atalante atalɑ̃ːtə

Atalide atalidə

Atar ataːʀ

Ataturk atatyʀk

Athalie ataliə

Athanaël atanaɛl

Athanaïs atanais

Athanase atanɑːzə

Athelstan atɛlstɑ̃ *or* atɛlstan

Athènes atɛnə

Athénien(s) atenjɛ̃

Athénienne(s) atenjɛnə

Athos atɔs *or* atoːs

Atlan atlɑ̃

Atlanta atlanta

Atlantide atlɑ̃tidə

Atlantique atlɑ̃tikə

Atlas atlɑːs

Atrée atreə

Atride atʀidə

Attaignant (L') latɛɲɑ̃

Attale atalə

Atticamègue atikamɛgə

Atticus atikys

Attila atila

Atys atis

Aubanel obanɛl

Aube oːbə

Aubel (D') dobɛl

Aubenas obəna

Aubépine obepinə

Auber obɛːʀ

Aubert obɛːʀ

Aubertin obɛʀtɛ̃

Aubervilliers obɛʀvilje

Aubéry obeʀi

Aubespine (L') lobepinə

Aubigné obiɲe

Aubigny (D') dobiɲi

Aubin obɛ̃

Aubois obwa

Auboise(s) obwaːzə

Aubrac obʀak

Aubriet obʀiɛ

Aubry obʀi

Aubusson obysɔ̃

Aucassin et Nicolette okasɛ̃
e nikɔletə

Auch oːʃ

Auchan oʃɑ̃

Auclert oklɛːʀ

Audaux odo

Aude oːdə

Audel odɛl

Audemars Piguet odəmaʀ pigɛ

Audenge odɑ̃ːʒə

Audiberti odibɛʀti

Audois odwa

Audoise(s) odwaːzə

250 | FRENCH LYRIC DICTION

Audran odrɑ̃
Audrey odrɛ
Auer oɛːr
Aufide ofidə
Auge oːʒə
Auger oʒe
Augereau oʒəro
Augias oʒjaːs
Augier oʒje
Auguez oge
Auguin ogɛ̃
Auguste ogystə or ɔgystə
Augustin ogystɛ̃ or ɔgystɛ̃
Augustule ogystylə or ɔgystylə
Aulide olidə
Aulnay onɛ or olnɛ
Aulne oːnə or olnə
Aulnoy (D') donwa or dolnwa
Aulnoye-Aymeries onwa ɛmərjə
Aulps (D') do
Ault oːlt
Aulu-Gelle oly ʒɛlə
Aumale omalə
Aumont omɔ̃
Aunis onis
Aups oːps
Aurèle ɔrɛlə
Aurélie oreliə
Aurélien oreljɛ̃
Auriacombe ɔrjakɔ̃ːbə
Auric ɔrik
Aurillac ɔrijak
Auriol ɔrjol
Aurispa awrispa
Aurora ɔrɔra
Aurore ɔrɔːrə
Auros ɔrɔs or ɔrɔːs
Auryale ɔrjalə
Auschwitz awʃvits or oʃvits
Ausone ozonə
Ausonie ozoniə
Aussourd osuːr
Austerlitz ostɛrlits or ostɛrlits
Australasie ostralaziə or ɔstralaziə
Australie ostraliə or ɔstraliə
Australien(s) ostraljɛ̃ or ɔstraljɛ̃
Australienne(s) ostraljɛnə
    or ɔstraljɛnə
Austro-Hongrois ostro ɔ̃grwa
    or ɔstro ɔ̃grwa
Austro-Hongroise(s) ostro ɔ̃grwaːzə
    or ɔstro ɔ̃grwaːzə
Autant-Lara otɑ̃ lara
Autran otrɑ̃
Autrans otrɑ̃
Autriche otriʃə
Autriche-Hongrie otri ʃɔ̃griə
Autrichien(s) otriʃjɛ̃
Autrichienne(s) otriʃjɛnə
Autun otœ̃
Auvergne ovɛrɲə
Auvers ovɛːr
Auvity oviti
Auvray ovrɛ
Auxerre osɛːrə or ɔsɛːrə
Auxerrois osɛrwa or ɔsɛrwa
Auxerroise(s) osɛrwaːzə or ɔsɛrwaːzə

Auxi-le-Château oksi lə ʃato
Auxois oswa
Auxon osɔ̃
Auxonne osɔnə
Avallon avalɔ̃
Avaugour (D') davoguːr
Avenel (D') davənɛl
Avent avɑ̃
Aventin avɑ̃tɛ̃
Averdoingt avɛrdwɛ̃
Avesnes avɛnə
Aveyron avɛrɔ̃
Aveyronnais avɛronɛ
Aveyronnaise(s) avɛronɛːzə
Avignon aviɲɔ̃
Avon avɔ̃
Avoriaz avɔrja or avɔrjaːz
Avranches avrɑ̃ːʃə
Avray avrɛ
Avril avril
Axat aksat or aksa
Aÿ/Ay ai
Ayala ajala
Ayen (D') dajɛ̃
Ayio Costanndino ajo kɔstandino
Ayio Sidero/Ayio Sidéro ajo sidero
Aymé ɛme
Aywaille ɛwaːjə or ɛwajə
Azaël azaɛl
Azay-le-Rideau azɛ lə rido
Azelma azɛlma
Azerbaïdjan azɛrbajdʒɑ̃
Azerbaïdjanais azɛrbajdʒanɛ
Azerbaïdjanaise(s) azɛrbajdʒanɛːzə
Aznavour aznavuːr
Azof azof
Azor azoːr
Aztèques astɛkə

— B —

Baal baal
Babaïan babajan
Babel babɛl
Babet babɛ
Babylas babilaːs
Babylone babilonə
Babylonien(s) babilɔnjɛ̃
Babylonienne(s) babilɔnjɛnə
Baccarat bakara
Bacchante bakɑ̃ːtə
Bacchis bakis
Bacchus bakys
Bacchylide bakilidə
Bacco bak(k)o
Bach bak
Bachanales bakanalə
Baché baʃe
Bachelet baʃəlɛ
Bacilly (De) də basiji
Backhuysen bakœjzɛn
Bacquier bakje
Bactria baktria
Badal badal
Bade badə
Baden badɛn
Baden-Baden badɛn badɛn

Badiali badjali
Badoglio badɔljo
Badoit badwa
Badonviller badɔ̃vile
Bagdad bagdad
Bagès baʒɛs
Bagnères-de-Bigorre baɲɛrə də
    bigɔːrə
Bagnolet baɲɔlɛ
Bagota bagɔta
Baguer bageːr
Bahamas baamɑːs
Bahamien(s) baamjɛ̃
Bahamienne(s) baamjɛnə
Bahorel baɔrɛl
Bahrayn barajn
Bahreïn barɛjn
Bahreïnien(s) barɛjnjɛ̃
Bahreïnienne(s) barɛjnjɛnə
Baïf baif
Baïkal baikal
Baillargues bajargə
Baille baːjə or bajə
Bailleul bajœl
Bailli baji
Baillot bajo
Bailly baji
Baïse baiːzə
Bajazet baʒazɛ
Baker bekeːr
Bakkhos bakɔs or bakoːs
Balanchine balɑ̃ʃinə
Balandard balɑ̃daːr
Balanqué balɑ̃ke
Balavoine balavwanə
Balbon balbɔ̃
Baldo baldo
Baldous baldu
Balducci baldutʃi or baldytʃi
Baldwin baldwin
Bâle bɑːlə
Balguerie balgəriə
Bali bali
Balkans balkɑ̃
Ballard balaːr
Ballot balo
Ballu baly
Bally bali or baji
Balmain balmɛ̃
Baltard baltaːr
Balt(h)azar baltazaːr
Balthy balti
Baltique baltikə
Balzac balzak
Bamako bamako
Bamatabois bamatabwa
    or bamatabwa
Bancelin bɑ̃səlɛ̃
Baneins banɛ̃
Banès banɛs
Bangkok baŋkɔk or bɑ̃kɔk
Bangladais bɑ̃gladɛ
Bangladaise(s) bɑ̃gladɛːzə
Bangladesh bɑ̃gladɛʃ
Bangols-sur-Cèze baɲɔl syr sɛːzə
Banier banje
Banville (De) də bɑ̃vilə

PRONUNCIATION DICTIONARIES | 251

Banyuls banjuls *or* baɲyls
Baptiste batistə
Baptistin batistɛ̃
Baptistine batistinə
Bar baːr
Barabas baraba:s
Barac barak
Baraguey-d'Hilliers baragɛ dilje
Barail (Du) dy baraj
Barbade barbadə
Barbadien(s) barbadjɛ̃
Barbadienne(s) barbadjɛnə
Barbaroux barbaru
Barbavano barbavano
Barbe barbə
Barbe-Bleue barbə blø
Barber barbɛːr
Barbereau barbəro
Barberousse barbərusə
Barbès barbɛs
Barbey d'Aurevilly barbɛ dɔrəviji
  or barbɛ dɔrəvili
Barbeyrac (De) də barbɛrak
Barbier barbje
Barbot barbo
Barboteu barbotø
Barboude barbudə
Barbuda barbyda *or* barbuda
Barbudien(s) barbydjɛ̃
  or barbudjɛ̃
Barbudienne(s) barbydjɛnə
  or barbudjɛnə
Barbusse barbysə
Barcelone barsələnə
Barcelonnette barsələnɛtə
Bardac bardak
Bardesane bardəzanə
Bardon bardɔ̃
Bardot bardo
Barelli barɛli
Barenboïm barɛnbɔim
Barentin barɑ̃tɛ̃
Barents barɛ̃ːs
Bargue bargə
Barielle barjɛlə
Barillier (Le) lə barilje
Barils bari
Barjols barʒɔl
Barkouf barkuf
Bar-le-Duc bar lə dyk
Barlest barlɛst
Barnabé barnabe
Barneveldt barnəvɛlt
Barney barnɛ
Barnolt barnɔlt
Baroilbet barwalbɛ
Baron barɔ̃
Baroux baru
Barr baːr
Barraine barɛnə
Barral baral
Barras bara:s
Barraud baro
Barrault baro
Barré barе
Barre (De La) də la baːrə
  or də la baːrə

Barrès barɛs
Barrias barja:s
Barrière barjɛːrə
Barroilhet barwajɛ
Barry (Du) dy bari
Bar-sur-Aube bar sy roːbə
Bart baːr
Bartas (Du) dy barta:s
Bartet bartɛ
Barthes bartə
Barthès bartɛs
Barthez bartɛːz *or* bartɛs
Bartholdi bartɔldi
Bartholdy bartɔldi
Bartholomé bartɔlome
Bartok bartɔk
Baruch baryk
Barye barjə
Basile bazilə
Basilide bazilídə
Basnage bana:ʒə
Basoche bazɔʃə
Basques baskə
Basquiat baskja
Basse-Navarre basə navaːrə
Bassens (E France) basɑ̃
Bassens (W France) basɛ̃:s
Basset basɛ
Basse-Terre (La) la basə tɛːrə
Bassi basi
Bastia bastja
Bastide bastidə
Bastié bastje
Bastille (La) la bastijə
Bastin bastɛ̃
Ba-ta-clan bataklɑ̃
Bataille bata:jə
Bataves bata:və
Batcheff batʃɛf
Bathilde batildə
Bathille/Bathylle batilə
Bathori batɔri
Batignolles (Les) lɛ batiɲɔlə
Baton Rouge batɔ̃ ruːʒə
Batrachomyomachie
  batrakɔmjɔmaʃiə
Bats bats
Battu baty
Batz (De) də ba
Bauby bobi
Bauche boːʃə
Baucheron de Boissoudy
  boʃərɔ̃ də bwasudi
Baucis bosis
Baudelaire bodəlɛːrə
Baudelocque bodəlɔkə
Baudo bodo
Baudouin bodwɛ̃
Baudoux bodu
Baudrillart bodrija:r
Bauduen bodyɛn
Baugé boʒe
Baugé-Chambalud boʒe ʃɑ̃baly
Bauges boːʒə
Baugnies boɲiə
Baume boːmə
Baurans borɑ̃

Baux bo
Bavarois bavarwa *or* bavarwa
Bavaroise(s) bavarwa:zə *or*
  bavarwa:zə
Bavière bavjɛːrə
Bawr (De) də boːr
Bayard baja:r
Bayeux bajø
Bayle bɛlə
Bayonne bajɔnə
Bayreuth bajrœːt
Bazaine bazɛnə
Bazan bazɑ̃
Bazas baza:s
Bazille bazijə
Bazin bazɛ̃
Béancourt beɑ̃kuːr
Béarn bearn
Béarnaise (La) la bearnɛːzə
Béatrice beatrisə
Béatrice et Bénédict beatri se
  benedikt
Béatrix beatriks
Beaubourg bobuːr
Beaucaire bokɛːrə
Beaucamp bokɑ̃
Beauce boːsə
Beauchamp boʃɑ̃
Beauchesne boʃɛnə
Beaudin bodɛ̃
Beaudo(u)in bodwɛ̃
Beaufays bofai
Beauharnais (De) də boarnɛ
Beaujeu boʒø
Beaujolais boʒɔlɛ
Beaumanoir (De) də bomanwaːr
Beaumarchais bomarʃɛ
Beaumavielle bomavjɛlə
Beaumesnil bomenil *or* bomɛnil
Beaumette bomɛtə
Beaumetz-lès-Loges bomɛts lɛ lɔːʒə
  or bome lɛ lɔːʒə
Beaumont bomɔ̃
Beaune boːnə
Beauneveu bonəvø
Beauplain boplɛ̃
Beaupréau bopreo *or* bopro
Beauquier bokje
Beauregard borəga:r
Beaurepaire (De) də borəpɛːrə
Beauséjour boseʒuːr
Beausoleil bosɔlɛj
Beausset (Le) lə bosɛ
Beauvais bovɛ
Beauvau bovo
Beauvilliers bovilje
Beauvoir (De) də bovwaːr
Beauvois bovwa
Beauzée bozeə
Bébert bebɛːr
Bécassine bekasinə
Bécaud beko
Becket bɛkɛt
Beckmans bɛkmɑ̃ːs
Béclard beklaːr
Becque bɛkə
Bède bɛdə

252 | FRENCH LYRIC DICTION

Bedeau bədo
Bedford bɛtford or bɛtfɔːr
Béduer bedɥe
Beethov betɔːv
Beethoven betɔvɛn
Beez be
Bégearss beʒaʀs
Béhoust beu
Beijing bɛjʒiŋ
Beissier bɛsje
Beistegui (De) də bɛstəgi
Béjart beʒaːr
Belaïef belajɛf
Bélanger belãʒe
Bélarusse(s) belarysə
Belaud bəlo
Belazor belazɔːr
Belcourt bɛlkuːr
Belfort bɛlfɔːr or befɔːr
Belge(s) bɛlʒə
Belgique bɛlʒikə
Belgrade bɛlgradə
Belgrand bɛlgrã
Belhomme bɛlɔmə
Bélisaire belizɛːrə
Bélise beliːzə
Belize/Bélize beliːzə
Bélizéen(s) belizeẽ
Bélizéenne(s) belizeɛnə
Bélizien(s) belizjẽ
Bélizienne(s) belizjɛnə
Bellac bɛlak or belak
Bellaigue bɛlɛgə or belɛgə
Bellanger bɛlãʒe or belãʒe
Bellangère bɛlãʒɛːrə or belãʒɛːrə
Bellaribi-Le Moal belaribi lə mɔal
    or belaribi lə mɔal
Bellay bɛlɛ or belɛ
Bellay (Du) dy bɛlɛ or dy belɛ
Belleau bɛlo or belo
Bellecour bɛləkuːr
Belle-Isle bɛ lilə
Bellême bɛlɛmə or belɛmə
Bellencombre bɛlãkɔ̃ːbrə
    or belãkɔ̃ːbrə
Bellenot bɛlano
Bellérophon belerɔfɔ̃ or belerɔfɔ̃
Bellesme bɛlɛmə or belɛmə
Bellessort bɛlɛsɔːr or belɛsɔːr
Bellevaux bɛlavo
Belleville bɛləvilə
Belley bɛlɛ or belɛ
Belleysans bɛlɛsã or belɛsã
Bellini belini or belini
Belloc bɛlɔk or belɔk
Bellon bɛlɔ̃ or belɔ̃
Bellone bɛlɔnə or belɔnə
Bellovèse bɛlɔvɛːzə or belɔvɛːzə
Bellune bɛlynə or belynə
Belmondo bɛlmɔ̃do
Belphégor bɛlfegɔːr
Belrupt bɛlry
Belsunce de Castelmoron bɛlzṏːsə
    də kastɛlmɔrɔ̃
Bélus belys
Belvès bɛlvɛs
Belzébuth bɛlzebyt

Bemberg bɛmbɛrg
Bembo bɛmbo or bɛ̃bo
Bême bɛmə
Benaïm/Bénaïm benaim
Bénard benaːr
Bénarès benaʀɛs
Benda (French person) bɛ̃da
Benda (German/Czech person) bɛnda
    or bɛ̃da
Bender bɛ̃dɛːr
Bénédict benedikt
Benelux benelyks
Bénévent benevã
Bengalais bɛ̃gale
Bengalaise(s) bɛ̃galɛːzə
Bengale bɛ̃galə
Bengali(s) bɛ̃gali
Bénin benẽ
Béninois beninwa
Béninoise(s) beninwaːzə
Benjamin bɛ̃ʒamẽ
Benoist bənwa
Benoît bənwa
Benoîte bənwatə
Benserade (De) də bɛ̃səradə
Bentivoglio bɛ̃tivɔljo
Bentson bɛntsɔn
Benvenuto Cellini bɛnvenuto
    tʃelini or bɛ̃venyto selini
    or bɛ̃venyto selini
Benvolio bɛnvɔljo
Benzi bɛnzi
Béost beost
Béotie beɔsiə
Beowulf beowulf
Beppo bɛp(p)o
Bérain berẽ
Béranger berãʒe
Béranger (De) də berãʒe
Bérard beraːr
Béraud bero
Berbié bɛrbje
Bercioux bɛrsju
Bercy bɛrsi
Bérenger berãʒe
Bérénice berenisə
Berg bɛrg
Bergame bɛrgamə
Berger bɛrʒe
Bergerac bɛrʒərak
Bergerat bɛrʒəra
Bergerette bɛrʒərɛtə
Bergheim bɛrg(h)ajm
Berginella bɛrʒinɛla
Bergson bɛrksɔn
Berio berjo
Bériot berjo
Berkenfield bɛrkɛnfild or bɛrkənfild
Berl bɛrl
Berlin bɛrlẽ
Berlinois bɛrlinwa
Berlinoise(s) bɛrlinwaːzə
Berlioz bɛrljoːz
Bernac bɛrnak
Bernadet bɛrnadɛ
Bernadets bɛrnadɛ
Bernadette bɛrnadɛtə

Bernadotte bɛrnadɔtə
Bernanos bɛrnanɔs or bɛrnanoːs
Bernard bɛrnaːr
Bernardin bɛrnardẽ
Bernardino bɛrnardino
Bernay bɛrnɛ
Berne bɛrnə
Berne-Bellecour bɛrnə bɛləkuːr
Bernède bɛrnɛdə
Bernex bɛrnɛ
Bernhardt bɛrnaːr
Bernicat bɛrnika
Bernier bɛrnje
Bernis bɛrnis
Bernou(i)lli bɛrnuji
Bernstamm bɛrnstam
Bernstein bɛrnʃtajn
    or bɛrnstajn
Berquier bɛrkje
Berr beːr
Berri bɛri
Berriau bɛrjo
Berruyer bɛryje
Berry bɛri
Bersi bɛrsi
Berstel bɛrstɛl
Bertal bɛrtal
Bertelin bɛrtəlẽ
Berthauld bɛrto
Berthe bɛrtə
Berthelier bɛrtəlje
Berthelot bɛrtəlo
Bertheroy bɛrtərwa
Berthet bɛrtɛ
Berthier bɛrtje
Berthold bɛrtold
Bertillon bɛrtijɔ̃
Bertin bɛrtẽ
Berton bɛrtɔ̃
Bertram bɛrtram
Bertrand bɛrtrã
Berven bɛrvẽ
Berzelius/Berzélius bɛrzeljys
Besançon bəzãsɔ̃
Besbre bɛbrə
Bescherelle beʃərɛlə or beʃɛrɛlə
Besenval bəzãval
Beslay bɛlɛ or belɛ
Beslier belje or bɛlje
Besme bɛmə
Besnard benaːr or bɛnaːr
Besnehard bɛsneaːr
Besnier benje or bɛnje
Besnoit bɛnwa or bɛnwa
Besozzi bezɔdzi
Bessand-Massenet bɛsã masənə
    or bɛsã masənə
Bessans bɛsã or besã
Bessemer bɛsəmeːr
Bessens bɛsẽːs or besẽːs
Bessières bɛsjɛːrə or besjɛːrə
Besson bɛsɔ̃ or besɔ̃
Bestiaire bɛstjɛːrə
Béthencourt betãkuːr
Bethléem/Bethlehem bɛtleɛm
Bethsabée bɛtsabeə
Béthulie betyliə

Béthune betynə
Bétout betu
Betti bɛti *or* beti
Bettly bɛtli
Betz bɛ
Beuchot bøʃo
Beudant bødɑ̃
Beugnot bøɲo
Beurette bœrɛtə
Beurnonville (De) də bœrnõvilə
Beuron bøɾõ
Beuscher bøʃɛːɾ
Beust bœst *or* bøːst
Beveren bevərɛn
Bex bɛ
Beydts bɛjts
Beyle bɛlə
Beylié (De) də bɛlje
Beynac bɛnak
Beyne-Heusay bɛ nøzɛ
Beynost bɛno
Beyrand bɛɾɑ̃
Beyrouth bɛɾut
Bèze bɛːzə
Béziers bezje
Bezons bəzõ
Bezzina bɛdzina
Bhoutan butɑ̃
Bhoutanais butanɛ
Bhoutanaise(s) butanɛːzə
Bia bja
Bianco bjɑ̃ko
Biarritz bjaɾits
Biau bjo
Bible (La) la biblə
Bic bik
Bichat biʃa
Bidault bido
Bidaut bido
Biélorusse(s) bjelɔɾysə
Biélorussie bjelɔɾysiə
Biélorussien(s) bjelɔɾysjɛ̃
Biélorussienne(s) bjelɔɾysjɛnə
Bienaimé bjɛ̃nɛme *or* bjɛ̃neme
Bienne bjɛnə
Bienvenüe bjɛ̃vənyə
Bierset bjɛɾsɛ *or* bjɛɾzɛ
Biesme bjɛmə
Biéval bjeval
Bigorre bigɔːɾə
Bigot bigo
Bigouden bigudɛ̃
Biju biʒy
Bilbaut-Vauchelet bilbo voʃəlɛ
Bilhaud bijo
Bilitis bilitis
Billac/Bilhac bijak
Billaud bijo
Billaudot bijodo
Billault bijo
Billom bijõ
Billot bijo
Billy (De) də biji
Binchois bɛ̃ʃwa
Binet binɛ
Binger bɛ̃ʒe
Binoche binɔʃə

Bir-Hakeim bi ɾakɛm
Birkenfeld biɾkənfɛld
Birman(s) biɾmɑ̃
Birmane(s) biɾmanə
Birmanie biɾmaniə
Birmingham biɾmiŋgam *or* biɾmɛ̃gam
Bis bis
Bisance bizɑ̃ːsə
Biscaye biskajə
Biscotin biskɔtɛ̃
Bissau-Guinéen(s) bisaw gineɛ̃
Bissau-Guinéenne(s) bisaw gineɛnə
Bisson bisõ
Bixio biksjo
Bizet bizɛ
Blaise blɛːzə
Blake blɛk
Blanc blɑ̃
Blancard blɑ̃kaːɾ
Blancarde (La) la blɑ̃kaɾdə
Blanchard blɑ̃ʃaːɾ
Blanche blɑ̃ːʃə
Blanchecotte blɑ̃ʃəkɔtə
Blancherupt blɑ̃ʃəɾy
Blanchot blɑ̃ʃo
Blanc-Mesnil blɑ̃ menil *or* blɑ̃ mɛnil
Blancpain blɑ̃pɛ̃
Blankenberge blɑ̃kɛnbɛɾgə
Blanqui blɑ̃ki
Blau blo
Blaudeix blodɛ
Blavet blavɛ
Blavinhac blavinak
Blaye blajə
Blazé blɑːzə
Blaze de Bury blɑzə də byɾi
Blehen bləhɛ̃
Blendecques blɑ̃dɛkə
Blenheim blɛnɛm
Blès blɛs
Blesle blɛlə
Bletterans blɛtəɾɑ̃ *or* bletəɾɑ̃
Bleuse bløːzə
Bleuzé bløze
Bloch blɔk
Blois blwa
Blondeau blõdo
Blondel blõdɛl
Blondin blõdɛ̃
Blondinette blõdinɛtə
Blot blo
Bloy blwa
Blucher/Blücher blyʃɛːɾ
Blum blum
Boabdil bɔabdil
Bobêche/Bobèche bɔbɛʃə
Bobigny bɔbiɲi
Bobillot bɔbijo
Bobinet bɔbinɛ
Boccace bɔkasə
Boccherini bɔk(k)eɾini
Bochsa bɔksa
Bodard bɔdaːɾ
Bodin bɔdɛ̃

Boduognat bɔdɥɔgna
Boèce bɔɛsə
Boëge bɔɛːʒə
Bœgner bøgnɛːɾ *or* bœgnɛːɾ
Boëllmann bɔɛlman
Boëly bɔeli
Boën bɔɛ̃
Boers buːɾ
Bœrsch bœɾʃ
Boësset/Boesset bɔɛsɛ
Boétie/Boëtie (La) la bɔesiə
Bohême/Bohème bɔɛmə
Bohémien(s) bɔemjɛ̃
Bohémienne(s) bɔemjɛnə
Boieldieu/Boïeldieu bwaldjø *or* bɔjɛldjø *or* bwaɛldjø
Boïens bɔjɛ̃
Boigne (De) də bwaɲə
Boigny bwaɲi
Boileau-Despréaux bwalo dɛpɾeo *or* bwalo depɾeo
Boillot bwalo
Boilly bwaji
Boisard bwazaːɾ
Boischaud bwaʃo
Bois-d'Oingt (Le) lə bwa dwɛ̃
Boisdeffre (De) də bwadɛfɾə
Boisgelin bwaʒəlɛ̃
Boisgobey bwagɔbɛ
Boisguillebert bwagiləbɛːɾ
Boisjolin (De) də bwajɔlɛ̃
Boislisle bwalilə
Boismont bwamõ
Boismortier bwamɔɾtje
Boispréau (De) də bwapɾeo
Boisrobert bwaɾɔbɛːɾ
Bois-Rosé bwa ɾoze
Boisseaux bwaso
Boisselot bwasəlo
Boissole bwasɔlə
Boissonnet bwasɔnɛ
Boissy d'Anglas bwasi dɑ̃glɑːs *or* bwasi dɑ̃glɑ
Boiste bwastə
Boitel bwatɛl
Boïto bɔito
Boitteau bwato
Boizel bwazɛl
Bolchoï bɔlʃɔj
Boleslas bɔlɛslɑːs
Boleyn bɔlɛn
Bolingbroke bɔliŋbɾɔk
Bolivar bɔlivaːɾ
Bolivie bɔliviə
Bolivien(s) bɔlivjɛ̃
Bolivienne(s) bɔlivjɛnə
Bollinger bɔlɛ̃ʒe
Bolonais bɔlɔnɛ
Bombardier bõbaɾdje
Bombay bõbɛ
Bompard bõpaːɾ
Bonaguil bɔnagil
Bonald bɔnald
Bonaparte bɔnapaɾtə
Bonardi bɔnaɾdi
Bonaventure bɔnavɑ̃tyːɾə
Bondeville bõdəvilə

Bongars bõgaːr	Bosnienne(s) bɔsnjɛnə	Bourdet burdɛ
Bonheur bɔnœːr	Bosphore bɔsfɔːrə	Bourdieu burdjø
Boniface bɔnifasə	Bosquet bɔskɛ	Bourdin burdɛ̃
Bonis bɔnis	Bosquier-Gavaudan bɔskje gavodã	Bourdon burdõ
Bonn bɔn	Bosquin bɔskɛ̃	Bourg (E France) buːr
Bonnard bɔnaːr	Bosredon bɔrədõ	Bourg (W France) burk
Bonnassieux bɔnasjø	Bossuet bɔsɥe	Bourg d'Oisans (Le) lə bur dwazã
Bonne bɔnə	Bossy bɔsi	Bourgault-Ducoudray burgo
Bonneau bɔno	Bost bɔst	dykudrɛ
Bonnechose bɔnəʃoːzə	Boston bɔstɔn or bɔstõ	Bourg-en-Bresse bur kã bresə
Bonne-Espérance bɔ nsɛperãːsə	Bosvieil bovjɛj	Bourgeois burʒwa
Bonnefoy bɔnəfwa	Botiaux bɔtjo	Bourgeoise(s) burʒwaːzə
Bonnélie bɔnelia	Botrel bɔtrɛl	Bourges burʒə
Bonnemains bɔnəmɛ̃	Botswana bɔtswana	Bourget burʒɛ
Bonnemère bɔnəmɛːr	Botswanais bɔtswanɛ	Bourgneuf-en-Retz burnœ fã rɛ
Bonnenveine bɔnəvɛnə	Botswanaise(s) bɔtswanɛːzə	or burnœ fã rɛs
Bonnerot bɔnəro	Bottin bɔtɛ̃	Bourgogne burgɔɲə
Bonnet bɔnɛ	Boubonnaise(s) burbɔnɛːzə	Bourgtheroulde burtərudə
Bonneval bɔnəval	Bouché buʃe	or burteruldə
Bonneveaux bɔnəvo	Boucher buʃe	Bourgue burgə
Bonneville bɔnəvilə	Boucheron buʃərõ	Bourguébus burgeby
Bonnières (De) də bɔnjeːrə	Bouches-du-Rhône buʃə dy roːnə	Bourgueil burgœj
Bonniot bɔnjo	Bouchet (Le) lə buʃɛ	Bourguignat burgiɲa
Bonnivet bɔnivɛ	Bouchety/Bouchéty buʃeti	Bourmauck burmoːk
Bons-en-Chablais bõ ã ʃablɛ	Bouchoir buʃwaːr	Bourrillon burijõ
Bontemps bõtã	Bouchor buʃɔːr	Boursault burso
Bontoux bõtu	Bouclon (De) də buklõ	Bourvil burvil
Bonvalot bõvalo	Boucot buko	Bousbecque busbɛkə
Boos boːs	Bouddha buda	Bousquet buskɛ
Booz bɔoːz	Boudin budɛ̃	Boussac busak
Bordeaux bɔrdo	Boudouresque budurɛskə	Boussenot busəno
Bordelais bɔrdəlɛ	Boué bwe	Boussens busɛ̃ːs
Bordes bɔrdə	Bouëxière (La) la bwɛsjeːrə	Boutet de Monvel butɛ də mõvɛl
Bordèse bɔrdɛːzə	Bouffar bufaːr	Boutry butri
Bordier bɔrdje	Boufflers (De) də buflɛːr	Bouts bawts or buts
Bordurie bɔrdyria	Bougarber bugarbe	Bouval buval
Boréades bɔreadə	Bougival buʒival	Bouvet buvɛ
Boréas bɔreaːs	Bouguereau bugəro	Bouvier buvje
Borée bɔrea	Bouhélier (De) də buelje	Bouxières busjeːrə
Borel bɔrɛl	Bouhy bui	Bouxwiller buksvileːr
Borel-Clerc bɔrɛl klɛːr	Bouilhet bujɛ	Bouyer buje
Borella bɔrɛla	Bouillon buʒõ	Bovary bɔvari
Borelli bɔrɛli	Bouilly buji	Bovet bɔvɛ
Borels (Les) lɛ bɔrɛl	Boukay bukɛ	Bovy bɔvi
Borély bɔreli	Boulanger bulãʒe	Boyard bɔjaːr
Borgel bɔrʒɛl	Boulay-Moselle bulɛ mozɛlə	Boyardville bɔjarvilə
Borghèse bɔrgeːzə	or bulɛ mɔzɛlə	Boyer bwaje
Borghi-Mamo bɔrgi mamo	Boulez bulɛːz	Boylesves bwalɛːvə
Borgia bɔrʒja	Boulle bula	Bozouls bozul
Borgo bɔrgo	Boullo(n)gne (De) də bulɔɲə	Brabançonne brabãsɔnə
Borilée bɔrilea	Boulogne bolɔɲə	Brabant brabã
Borne (Le) lə bɔrnə	Boulogne-Billancourt bulɔɲə	Braconnier brakɔnje
Bornemann bɔrnəman	bijãkuːr	Bracquemond brakəmõ
Bornier bɔrnje	Boulogne-sur-Mer bulɔɲə syr meːr	Bradamante bradamãːtə
Borodine bɔrodinə	Boulonnais bulɔnɛ	Brahim-Djelloul braim dʒelul
Bororos bɔrɔro	Boulonnais(e) bulɔnɛːzə	Brahma brama or brama
Borthayre bɔrteːrə	Boulotte bulɔtə	Brahman(s) bramã or bramã
Boscain bɔskɛ̃	Bour buːr	Brahmane(s) bramanə or bramanə
Boschot bɔʃo	Bourbon burbõ	Brahme(s) braːmə or bramə
Boscq bɔsk	Bourbon-l'Archambault burbõ	Brahmine(s) braminə or braminə
Bosdedore bodədɔːrə	larʃãbo	Brahms brams
Bosdeveix bodəvɛ	Bourbon-Montpensier burbõ	Braille braːjə or brajə
Bosguérard bogeraːr	mõpãsje	Brambilla brãbija
Bosnie bɔsnia	Bourbonnais burbɔnɛ	Branchu brãʃy
Bosnie-Herzégovine bɔsni	Bourbonnais burbɔnə	Brancour brãkuːr
ɛrzegovinə	Bourdais-Massenet burdɛ	Brandebourg brãdəbuːr
Bosnien(s) bɔsnjɛ̃	masənɛ	Brander brãdeːr
	Bourdelle budrɛlə	

PRONUNCIATION DICTIONARIES | 255

Brandus brɑ̃dys
Branly brɑ̃li
Braque brakə
Brare braːrə
Bras (Le) lə brɑ
Brasparts braspaːr
Brassaï brasaj
Brassens brasɛ̃ːs
Brasseur .brasœːr
Bratislava bratislava
Braudel brodɛl
Brauner bronɛːr
Brax braks
Brayer (De) də brɛje or də brɛje
Braz (Le) lə brɑːz
Brazzaville bradzavilə or brazavilə
Brecht brɛʃt or brɛkt
Bredau brədo
Breguet brɛgɛ
Bréjean brəʒɑ̃
Bréjean-Silver brəʒɑ̃ silvɛːr
Brel brɛl
Brélia brelja
Brême brɛmə
Bremond brəmɔ̃
Bren brɛn
Brendel brɛndɛl
Brenner brɛnɛːr
Brennus brɛnys or brenys
Brens (E France) brɑ̃
Brens (W France) brɛ̃ːs
Brescia brɛʃja or brɛsja
Bresdin brɛde or brɛdɛ̃
Brésil brezil
Brésilien(s) breziljɛ̃
Brésilienne(s) breziljɛnə
Breslau brɛslo
Bresle brɛlə
Bresles brɛlə
Bresse brɛsə
Bressuire brɛsɥiːrə or brɛsɥiːrə
Brest brɛst
Bretagne brətaɲə
Breteuil brətœj
Bréthencourt brɛtɑ̃kuːr
Brethous-Lafargue brətu lafargə
Brétigny (De) də bretiɲi
Bretillien(s) brɛtiljɛ̃
Bretillienne(s) brɛtiljɛnə
Breton brətɔ̃
Bretonne brətɔnə
Brette brɛtə
Bréval breval
Brevet brəvɛ
Bréville (De) də brevilə
Briançon briɑ̃sɔ̃
Briarée briareə
Bricourt brikuːr
Brideau brido
Bridge bridʒ
Brid'oison bridwazɔ̃
Brie briə
Brienon brienɔ̃
Brieux briø
Briey briɛ
Brigitte briʒitə
Brignac (De) də briɲak

Brignoles briɲɔlə
Brillat-Savarin brija savarɛ̃
Brimont (De) də brimɔ̃
Bringuier brɛ̃gje
Brinvilliers (De) də brɛ̃vilje
Briolanie briɔlaniə
Briot brio
Brioude briudə
Bris (Le) lə bri
Brisbane brisbanə
Briséis/Briséïs brizeis
Brissaud briso
Brisson brisɔ̃
Brissot briso
Britannicus britanikys
Britten britɛn
Brivadois brivadwa
Brive-la-Gaillarde brivə la gajardə
Brix bri
Brizeux brizø
Brno bœrno
Broadway brɔdwɛ
Brocéliande brɔseljɑ̃ːdə
Broglie (De) də brɔj
Brogni brɔɲi
Brogniart brɔɲaːr
Brohly broli
Brongniart brɔɲaːr or brɔ̃ɲaːr
Brontë brɔ̃te or brɔnte
Brooklyn bruklin
Broons brɔ̃
Brosne broːnə
Brossolette brɔsɔlɛtə
Brothier brɔtje
Brouckère brukɛːrə
Broussaille brusaːjə
Brown brawn
Brown-Séquard brun sekwaːr
or brɔn sekaːr
Bruant bryɑ̃
Bruch bruk or bryk
Brucien(s) brysjɛ̃
Brucienne(s) brysjɛnə
Bruck bruk
Bruckner bruknɛːr
Brugel bryʒɛl
Bruges bry:ʒə
Brugnon bryɲɔ̃
Brühlmann brylman
Bruix brɥiks
Brujon bryʒɔ̃
Brumaire brymɛːrə
Brummel brymɛl
Brunco brœ̃ko
Brune brynə
Bruneau bryno
Brunehaut brynəo
Brunei brynɛj
Brunéien(s) brynejɛ̃
Brunéienne(s) brynejɛnə
Brunelleschi brynɛlɛski
Brunerie (De La) də la brynəriə
Brunet brynɛ
Brunet-Lafleur brynɛ laflœːr
Bruno bryno
Brunschvicg brœ̃ʃvik
Brunswick (German person) brunsvik

Brunswick (De) də brœ̃svik
or də brɔ̃svik
Bruslé bryle
Bruslon brylɔ̃
Brusvilly brysvili
Brutus brytys
Bruxelles brysɛlə
Bruxellois brysɛlwa
Bruxelloise(s) brysɛlwaːzə
Bruxières-les-Mines brysjɛrə
le minə
Bruyère (De La) də la bryjɛːrə
or də la brɥijɛːrə
Bruyères bryjɛːrə or brɥijɛːrə
Bruz bry
Bubaste bybastə
Bubastis bybastis
Bucarest bykarɛst
Bucéphale bysefalə
Buchez byʃe or byʃeːz
Buchillot byʃijo
Buckingham bœkiŋgam
Bucy bysi
Budapest bydapɛst
Budé byde
Buëch bɥɛʃ
Bueil bɥɛj
Buenos Aires bɥeno zɛːrə
Buet bɥɛ
Buffet byfɛ
Bugeaud de la Piconnerie byʒo də la
pikɔnəriə
Bugey byʒɛ
Bug-Jargal byg ʒargal
Buguet bygɛ
Buick bɥik
Bukovine/Bucovine bykɔvinə
Bukovinien(s)/
Bucovinien(s) bykɔvinjɛ̃
Bukovinienne(s)/
Bucovinienne(s) bykɔvinjɛnə
Bulgarie bylgariə
Bulgarien(s) bylgarjɛ̃
Bulgarienne(s) bylgarjɛnə
Bülow bylɔːv or bylo
Buloz byloːz
Bunsen bœ̃zɛn
Burani burani
Burdeau byrdo
Burdino byrdino
Burgos burgos or byrgoːs
Burkina Faso byrkina faso
Burkinais byrkinɛ
Burkinaise(s) byrkinɛːzə
Burles byrlə
Burrhus byrys
Burundais burundɛ
Burundaise(s) burundɛːzə
Burundi burundi
Busiris byziris
Busnach bysnak
Busoni buzɔni or byzɔni
Bussang bysɑ̃
Busser/Büsser bysɛːr
Bussine bysinə
Bussonnet bysɔnɛ
Butor bytɔːr

256 | FRENCH LYRIC DICTION

Butte bytə
Buttes-Chaumont bytə ʃomõ
Buxeuil byksœj
Buxtehude bukstə(h)udə
Buxy bysi *or* byksi
Buzenval byzɛ̃val
Byron bajɾɔn
Byrrh biːɾ
Byzance bizɑ̃ːsə

— C —

Caballé kabaje
Cabanel kabanɛl
Cabarrus kabaɾy
Cabassu kabasy
Cabel kabɛl
Cabo kabo
Cabot kabo
Cabriolo kabɾiɔlo
Cabucelle (La) la kabysɛlə
Caby kabi
Cacatois kakatwa
Caccini katʃini
Cachemire kaʃəmiːɾə
Cacique kasikə
Cadalen kadalɛ̃
Cadi kadi
Cadieu kadjø
Cadillac kadijak
Cadiou kadju
Cadix kadiks
Cadmée kadmeə
Cadmus kadmys
Cadol kadɔl
Cadou kadu
Cadoudal kadudal
Caen kɑ̃
Caestre kastɾə
Cage kɛdʒ
Cagliostro kaljɔstro
or kagliostro
Cagnard kaɲaːɾ
Cahen kaɛ̃ *or* kaɛn
Cahingt kaɛ̃
Cahors kaɔːɾ
Cahusac (De) də kayzak
Caïffa kaifa
Cailhau kajo
Cailhava de l'Estandoux kajava də
lɛstɑ̃du
Caillat kaja
Caillaux kajo
Caillavet (De) də kajavɛ
Caillebotte kajəbɔtə
Caillois kajwa
Caillols (Les) lɛ kajɔl
Caillot kajo
Caïmans kaimɑ̃
Caïn kaɛ̃
Cain kɛ̃
Caïnan kainɑ̃
Caïphe kaifə
Caire (Le) lə kɛːɾə
Cairote(s) kɛɾɔtə
Caïus/Caius kajys
Çakountala sakuntala

Calábre kalɑːbɾə *or* kalabɾə
Calabresi kalabɾezi
Calade (La) la kaladə
Calaïs kalais
Calais kalɛ *or* kalɛ
Calas kalɑːs
Calchas kalkɑːs
Calcutta kalkyta
Calédonie kaledɔniə
Calédonien(s) kaledɔnjɛ̃
Calédonienne(s) kaledɔnjɛnə
Calérien kaleɾjɛ̃
Calgary kalgaɾi
Calicut kalikyt
Californie kalifɔɾniə
Caligula kaligyla
Calisis kalizis
Calisto kalisto
Calix kali
Callaisien(s) kalɛzjɛ̃
Callaisienne(s) kalɛzjɛnə
Callas kalɑːs
Callelongue kaləlõːgə
Callicrate kalikɾatə
Callicratès kalikɾatɛs
Callières (De) də kaljɛːɾə
Callimaque kalimakə
Callinos kalinɔs *or* kalinoːs
Callirrhoé kaliɾɔe
Callisthène kalistɛnə
Calmann-Lévy kalman levi
Calvados kalvadoːs
Calvaire kalvɛːɾə
Calvé kalve
Calvi kalvi
Calvocoressi kalvɔkɔɾɛsi *or* kalvɔkɔɾesi
Camargo kamaɾgo
Camargue kamaɾgə
Cambacérès kɑ̃basɛɾɛs
Cambardi kɑ̃baɾdi
Cambay kɑ̃bɛ
Cambodge kɑ̃bɔdʒə
Cambodgien(s) kɑ̃bɔdʒjɛ̃
Cambodgienne(s) kɑ̃bɔdʒjɛnə
Cambon kɑ̃bõ
Cambrai kɑ̃bɾɛ
Cambreling kɑ̃bɾəlɛ̃
Cambremer kɑ̃bɾəmɛːɾ
Cambrézis kɑ̃bɾezi
Cambron kɑ̃bɾõ
Cambyse kɑ̃biːzə
Camerata kameɾata
Camerlo kamɛɾlo
Cameroun kaməɾun
Camerounais kaməɾunɛ
Camerounaise(s) kaməɾunɛːzə
Camille kamijə
Camoëns kamɔɛ̃ːs
Camoins (Les) lɛ kamwɛ̃
Camp (Du) dy kɑ̃
Campan kɑ̃pɑ̃
Campéador kɑ̃peadɔːɾ
Campeggio kampɛdʒ(j)o *or* kampɛʒjo
or kɑ̃pɛdʒ(j)o *or* kɑ̃pɛʒjo
Campistron kɑ̃pistɾõ
Campo-Tasso kɑ̃po taso
or kampo taso

Campouriez kɑ̃puɾjɛːz *or* kɑ̃puɾjɛs
Campra kɑ̃pɾa
Campredon kɑ̃pɾədõ
Camus kamy
Camus (Le) lə kamy
Cana kana
Canaan kanaɑ̃
Canada kanada
Canadien(s) kanadjɛ̃
Canadienne(s) kanadjɛnə
Canal kanal
Cananéen(s) kananeɛ̃
Cananéenne(s) kananeɛnə
Canaux kano
Candaule kɑ̃doːlə
Candi kɑ̃di
Candide kɑ̃didə
Canebière kanəbjɛːɾə
Canens kanɛ̃ːs
Canenx kanɛ̃ːs
Canet kanɛ
Cannes kanə
Canrobert kɑ̃ɾɔbɛːɾ
Cantabre kɑ̃taːbɾə *or* kɑ̃tabɾə
Cantacuzène kɑ̃takyzɛnə
Cantal kɑ̃tal
Canteloube kɑ̃təlubə
Cantor kɑ̃tɔːɾ
Cantorbéry kɑ̃tɔɾbeɾi
Canut kany *or* kanyt
Caoudal kaudal
Cap (Le) lə kap
Cap-Breton kap bɾətõ
Cap-d'Ail kap daj
Cape Town kɛp tawn
Capelette (La) la kapələtə
Capelier kapəlje
Capet kapɛ
Capharnaüm kafaɾnaɔm
Capitole kapitɔlə
Capitolin kapitɔlɛ̃
Caplet kaplɛ
Capoul kapul
Capri kapɾi
Capricorne kapɾikɔɾnə
Capucin(s) kapysɛ̃
Capucine(s) kapysinə
Capulet(s) kapylɛ
Capus kapy
Capuzzi kapudzi
**Cap-Verdien(s)/
Capverdien(s)** kapvɛɾdjɛ̃
**Cap-Verdienne(s)/
Capverdienne(s)** kapvɛɾdjɛnə
Cap-Vert kap vɛːɾ
Carabas (De) də kaɾaba
or də kaɾabɑːs
Carabiniers kaɾabinje
Carabosse kaɾabosə
Caracas kaɾakɑːs
Carafa kaɾafa
Caraïbes kaɾaibə
Caraman kaɾamɑ̃
Carbonne kaɾbɔnə
Carcasson kaɾkasõ
Carcassonne kaɾkasɔnə
Cardin kaɾdɛ̃

PRONUNCIATION DICTIONARIES | 257

Cardinal kaʁdinal
Carême kaʁɛmə
Carentan kaʁɑ̃tɑ̃
Caresmier kaʁemje *or* kaʁɛmje
Carhaix kaʁɛ
Caribéen(s) kaʁibeɛ̃
Caribéenne(s) kaʁibeɛnə
Carissimi kaʁisimi
Carladès kaʁladɛs
Carlier kaʁlje
Carling kaʁlɛ̃
Carlos kaʁlos *or* kaʁlo:s
Carlovingien kaʁlɔvɛ̃ʒjɛ̃
Carlu kaʁly
Carlux kaʁlyks *or* kaʁly
Carmagnola kaʁmaɲɔla
Carmanère kaʁmanɛːʁə
Carmel kaʁmɛl
Carmélite(s) kaʁmelitə
Carmen kaʁmɛn
Carmencita kaʁmɛnsita
Carmet kaʁmɛ
Carmouche kaʁmuʃə
Carnac kaʁnak
Carné kaʁne
Carnéade kaʁneadə
Carnegie Hall kaʁnɛgi oːl
Carnoët kaʁnwɛt *or* kaʁnɔɛt
Carnot kaʁno
Caroline kaʁɔlinə
Caroline du Nord kaʁɔlinə dy nɔːʁ
Caroline du Sud kaʁɔlinə dy syd
Caron kaʁõ
Carpates kaʁpatə
Carpeaux kaʁpo
Carpentier kaʁpɑ̃tje
Carpentras kaʁpɑ̃tɾɑ
Carpiagne kaʁpjaɲə
Carraud kaʁo
Carré kaʁe
Carrière kaʁjɛːʁə
Carriès kaʁjɛs
Carroz d'Arâches (Les) lɛ kaʁo daʁɑːʃə
Carsix kaʁsi
Cartailhac kaʁtajak
Cartellier kaʁtɛlje *or* kaʁtelje
Carthage kaʁtaːʒə
Carthaginois kaʁtaʒinwa
Carthaginoise(s) kaʁtaʒinwaːzə
Cartier kaʁtje
Cartieri kaʁtjeʁi
Cartigny kaʁtiɲi
Carvaille kaʁvaːjə *or* kaʁvajə
Carvalho kaʁvalo
Caryll kaʁil
Caryste kaʁistə
Casa Fuerte (De) də kaza fwɛʁtə *or* də kaza fɥɛʁtə
Casablanca kazablɑ̃ka
Casadesus kazadəsy
Casals kazals
Casanova de Seingalt kazanova də sɛ̃galt *or* kazanova də sẽgal
Cascadetto kaskadɛt(t)o
Casella kazɛla
Casimir kazimiːʁ

Caspari kaspaʁi
Caspienne kaspjɛnə
Cassandre kasɑ̃ːdʁə
Cassandro kasɑ̃dʁo *or* kasandʁo
Cassard kasaːʁ
Cassel kasɛl
Cassin kasɛ̃
Cassiope kasjɔpə
Cassiopée kasjɔpeə
Cassis (*drink*) kasis
Cassis (*place*) kasi
Cassius kasjys
Cassou kasu
Castaing kastɛ̃
Casteau kasto
Castellane kastɛlanə *or* kastelanə
Castellanne kastɛlanə *or* kastelanə
Castellet (Le) lə kastɛlə *or* lə kastele
Castelli kastɛli
Castelnau kastɛlno
Castelnaud kastɛlno
Castelsarrasin kastɛlsaʁazẽ
Castets kastɛ *or* kastɛts
Castiglione kastiljɔne *or* kastigliɔnə
Castilhon kastijõ
Castillan(s) kastijɑ̃
Castillane(s) kastijanə
Castille kastijə
Castillet (Le) lə kastije
Castillon (De) də kastijõ
Castor kastoːʁ
Castres (*place*) kastʁə
Castries (De) (*person*) də kastʁə
Catalan(s) katalɑ̃
Catalane(s) katalanə
Catalogne katalɔɲə
Catarina kataʁina
Catay katɛ
Catel katɛl
Catelet (Le)/Câtelet (Le) lə katələ
Catelin katəlẽ
Cathelat katəla
Catherine katəʁinə
Catilina katilina
Catinat katina
Caton katõ
Cattenom katənɔm
Cattier katje
Catulle katylə
Catus katys
Catz kɑ
Caucase kokɑːzə
Caucasie kokaziə
Caulnes koːnə
Caurroy (Du) dy kɔʁwa
Caus (De) də ko
Causses koːsə
Cauterets kotəʁɛ
Caux ko
Cavaignac kavɛɲak
Cavaillé-Coll kavaje kɔl
Cavaillon kavajõ
Cavalli kavali
Cavelti kavɛlti
Cayenne kajɛnə
Caylus kɛlys

Cayolle kajɔlə
Cayrol kɛʁɔl
Cayugas kajuga
Cayx kɛ
Cazalès kazalɛs
Cazalis kazalis
Cazals kazals *or* kazal
Cazaux kazo
Cazeneuve kazənœːvə
Cazes kɑːzə
Cazette kazɛtə
Cazotte kazɔtə
Cé se
Cécil sesil
Cécile sesilə
Cécrops sekʁops
Cédric sedʁik
Celcius sɛlsjys
Célénus selenys
Célestin selɛstẽ
Célestine selɛstinə
Célie seliə
Célimène selimɛnə
Céline selinə
Cellier sɛlje *or* selje
Cellini tʃelini *or* sɛlini *or* selini
Celse sɛlsə
Cenci tʃɛnsi *or* sẽsi
Cendrars sɑ̃dʁaːʁ
Cendrille sɑ̃dʁijə
Cendrillon sɑ̃dʁijõ
Cenis səni
Centrès sɑ̃tʁɛs
Céos seɔs *or* seo:s
Céphale et Procris sefa le prɔkris
Céphée sefeə
Céphise sefiːzə
Cépion sepjõ
Cerbère sɛʁbɛːʁə
Cérès seʁɛs
Céret seʁɛ
Cernay sɛʁne
Cernuschi tsɛʁnuski *or* sɛʁnyski
Cers sɛʁs
Cervantès sɛʁvɑ̃tɛs
Cervin sɛʁvẽ
Césaire sezɛːʁə
César sezaːʁ
Cesbron-Viseur sesbʁõ vizœːʁ
Cesne sɛnə
Cévennes sevɛnə
Ceylan sɛlɑ̃
Ceylanais sɛlanɛ
Ceylanaise(s) sɛlanɛːzə
Cézanne sezanə
Cézens sezẽːs
Chaalis ʃali
Chabaleyret (De) də ʃabalɛʁe
Chabaneix (De) də ʃabane
Chabaud ʃabo
Chablis ʃabli *or* ʃabli
Chabot ʃabo
Chabrias kabʁiaːs
Chabrier ʃabʁie *or* ʃabʁie
Chabroux ʃabʁu
Chabrun ʃabʁœ̃
Chadeigne ʃadɛɲə

258 | FRENCH LYRIC DICTION

Chadourne ʃaduɾnə
Chagall ʃagal
Chagnon ʃaɲõ
Chaignaud ʃɛɲo
Chailley ʃaje
Chaillot ʃajo
Chaix ʃɛks or ʃɛ
Chalanda ʃalãda
Chalcédoine kalsedwanə
Chalcidique kalsidikə
Chalcis kalsis
Chalcocondyle kalkɔkõdilə
Chalcondyle kalkõdilə
Chaldée kaldeə
Chaldéen(s) kaldeẽ
Chaldéenne(s) kaldeɛnə
Chaleins ʃalẽ
Chaliapine ʃaljapinə
Challans ʃalã
Challet ʃalɛ
Chalmin ʃalmẽ
Châlons ʃalõ
Châlons-en-Champagne ʃalõ ã
ʃãpaɲə
Chalon-sur-Saône ʃalõ syɾ so:nə
Chalupt ʃaly
Châlus ʃaly
Cham kam
Chambellan ʃãbɛlã or ʃãbelã
Chambertin (Le) lə ʃãbɛɾtẽ
Chambéry ʃãberi
Chambonnières ʃãbɔnjɛ:ɾə
Chambord ʃãbɔ:ɾ
Chambost ʃãbo
Chamerot ʃamɛɾo
Chamfort ʃãfɔ:ɾ
Chaminade ʃaminadə
Chamonix ʃamɔni
Champagne ʃãpaɲə
Champagnole ʃãpaɲɔlə
Champagnolles ʃãpaɲɔlə
Champaigne (De) də ʃãpaɲə
Champcenetz (De) də ʃãsanə
or də ʃãsanə
Champdeniers ʃãdənje
Champdivers ʃãdivɛ:ɾ
Champeix ʃãpɛ
Champfleury ʃãflœɾi
Champion ʃãpjõ
Champlain (De) də ʃãplẽ
Champlatreux ʃãplatrø
Champlitte ʃãlitə
Champlost ʃãlo
Champmeslé ʃamele or ʃãmele
Champmol (De) də ʃãmɔl
Champollion ʃãpɔljõ
Champsaur ʃãsɔ:ɾ
Champs-Élysées ʃã zelizeə
Champtoceaux ʃãtɔso
Chamrousse ʃãrusə
Chanaan kanaã
Chananéen(s) kananeẽ
Chananéenne(s) kananeɛnə
Chanaz ʃana
Chancel ʃãsɛl
Chandeleur ʃãdəlœ:ɾ
Chandon ʃãdõ

Chandos ʃãdɔs or ʃãdo:s
Chaneins ʃanẽ
Chanel ʃanɛl
Chanlaire ʃãlɛ:ɾə
Chansarel ʃãsaɾɛl
Chantal ʃãtal
Chantavoine ʃãtavwanə
Chantecler ʃãtɛklɛ:ɾ
Chantepie ʃãtəpiə
Chantilly ʃãtiji
Chantrier ʃãtrie
Chao ʃao
Chaon kaõ
Chaource ʃaursə
Chapaillou(x) ʃapaju
Chapelier ʃapəlje
Chapelle ʃapɛlə
Chapelle-d'Angillon ʃapɛlə dãʒilõ
Chaplain ʃaplẽ
Chappe ʃapə
Chap(p)elou ʃapəlu
Chapuy ʃapɥi
Char ʃa:ɾ
Charasson ʃaɾasõ
Charbonnier ʃaɾbɔnje
Chardin ʃaɾdẽ
Chardonnay ʃaɾdone
Charens ʃaɾẽ:s
Charentais ʃaɾãtɛ
Charentaise(s) ʃaɾãtɛ:zə
Charente ʃaɾã:tə
Charenton ʃaɾãtõ
Charès kaɾɛs
Charest ʃaɾɛ
Charité (La) la ʃaɾite
Charites/Karites kaɾitə
Charix ʃaɾi
Charlemagne ʃaɾləmaɲə
Charles ʃaɾlə
Charlesky ʃaɾlɛski
Charles-Paul ʃaɾlə pɔl
Charles-Quint ʃaɾlə kẽ
Charleville ʃaɾləvilə
Charleville-Mézières ʃaɾləvilə
mezjɛ:ɾə
Charlot ʃaɾlo
Charlotte ʃaɾlɔtə
Charmion kaɾmjõ
Charolais ʃaɾɔlɛ
Charolaise(s) ʃaɾɔlɛ:zə
Charolles ʃaɾɔlə
Charon kaɾõ or kaɾõ
Charonne ʃaɾɔnə
Chârost (person) ʃaɾo or ʃaɾɔst
Chârost (place) ʃaɾo
Charpentier ʃaɾpãtje
Charpini ʃaɾpini
Charron ʃaɾõ or ʃaɾõ
Charroux ʃaɾu
Charton-Demeur ʃaɾtõ dəmœ:ɾ
Chartran ʃaɾtrã
Chartres ʃaɾtrə
Chartreuse ʃaɾtrø:zə
Chartreux ʃaɾtrø
Charybde kaɾibdə
Chasles ʃa:lə
Chaslin ʃaslẽ

Chasnay ʃasnɛ
Chassang ʃasã
Chastel ʃatɛl or ʃastɛl
Chastelard ʃatəla:ɾ or ʃastəla:ɾ
Chastellain ʃatɛlẽ or ʃastəlẽ
Chastellux ʃatəly
Chastres ʃastrə
Châtaignerie (La) la ʃatɛɲəɾiə
Château-Arnoux ʃato aɾnu
Châteaubourg ʃatobu:ɾ
Châteaubriand ʃatobriã
Châteaubriant ʃatobriã
Château-Chinon ʃato ʃinõ
Château-d'Œx ʃato dɛ
Château-du-Loir ʃato dy lwa:ɾ
Châteaudun ʃatodœ̃
Château-d'Yquem ʃato dikɛm
Château-Gaillard ʃato gaja:ɾ
Châteaugiron ʃatoʒiɾõ
Château-Gontier ʃato gõtje
Châteauguay ʃatoge or ʃatoge
Château-Haut-Brion ʃato o briõ
Château-Lafite ʃato lafita
Château-Lagrange ʃato lagrã:ʒə
Château-Landon ʃato lãdõ
Château-la-Pompe ʃato la põ:pə
Château-Latour ʃato latu:ɾ
Château-la-Vallière ʃato la valjɛ:ɾə
Châteaulin ʃatolẽ
Château-Margaux ʃato margo
Châteaumeillant ʃatomejã
Châteauneuf ʃatonœf
Châteauneuf-du-Faou ʃatonœf dy fu
Châteauneuf-du-Pape ʃatonœf
dy papə
Châteauponsac ʃatopõsak
Château-Porcien ʃato pɔrsjẽ
Châteaurenard ʃatorəna:ɾ
Château-Renault ʃato rəno
Châteauroux ʃatoru
Château-Salins ʃato salẽ
Château-Thierry ʃato tjɛɾi
Châteauvillain ʃatovilẽ
Châteillon ʃatɛjõ
Châtel ʃatɛl
Châtelaillon ʃatelajõ
Châtelard (Le) lə ʃatəla:ɾ
Châtelaudren ʃatelodrẽ
Châteldon ʃatɛldõ
Châtelet (Le) lə ʃatɛlɛ
Châtelguyon ʃatɛlgɥijõ
Châtelineau ʃatəlino
Châtellerault ʃatɛləɾo
Châtelperron ʃatɛlpɛɾõ
Châtelus-Malvaleix ʃatəly malvalɛ
Châtenay-Malabry ʃatɛnɛ malabri
Châtenois ʃatɛnwa
Châtillon ʃatijõ
Châtre (La) la ʃa:trə
Chaucer ʃosɛ:ɾ
Chaude-Aigues ʃodə zɛgə
Chaudfontaine ʃofõtɛnə
Chaudron ʃodrõ
Chaulnes ʃo:nə
Chaume ʃo:mə
Chaumet ʃomɛ
Chaumette ʃomɛtə

PRONUNCIATION DICTIONARIES | 259

Chaumont ʃomõ
Chaussée ʃoseə
Chaussée-d'Antin ʃoseə dãtɛ̃
Chaussier ʃosje
Chausson ʃosõ
Chauvelot ʃovəlo
Chauvet ʃove
Chauvigny ʃoviɲi
Chaux-de-Fonds (La) la ʃo də fõ
Chavannes ʃavanə
Chavanoz ʃavano
Chazal ʃazal or ʃazal
Chazot (De) də ʃazo or də ʃazo
Chélard ʃela:r
Chelles ʃɛlə
Chenal ʃənal
Chênex ʃɛnɛ
Chénier ʃenje
Chenonceau ʃənõso
Chenonceaux ʃənõso
Chéops keɔps
Cher ʃɛːr
Cherbourg ʃɛrbuːr
Cherbuliez ʃɛrbylje
Chéreau ʃero
Chéret ʃerɛ
Cherokees ʃeroki
Chéronée keronea
Chersonèse kɛrsɔnɛːzə
Chérubin ʃerybɛ̃
Cherubini kerubini or ʃerybini
Cherveix ʃɛrve
Chesnais ʃenɛ or ʃene
Chesnard ʃenaːr or ʃenaːr
Chesnay (Le) lə ʃenɛ or lə ʃene
Chesné ʃene or ʃene
Chesne (Le) lə ʃenə
Chesnelong ʃenəlõ or ʃenəlõ
Chesnet ʃenɛ or ʃene
Chesnoit ʃenwa or ʃenwa
Chesnot ʃeno or ʃeno
Chesnoy ʃenwa or ʃenwa
Chester tʃestœːr or ʃesteːr
Cheurlin ʃœrlɛ̃
Chevalet ʃəvalɛ
Cheval(l)ier ʃəvalje
Cheverny ʃəvɛrni
Chevillard ʃəvijaːr
Chevroz ʃəvro
Cheyennes ʃejenə
Chézy ʃezi
Chianti kjãti or kjanti
Chiboust ʃibust
Chicago ʃikago
Childéric ʃilderik
Chilhac ʃijak
Chili ʃili
Chilien(s) ʃiljɛ̃
Chilienne(s) ʃiljɛnə
Chillon ʃijõ
Chilpéric ʃilperik
Chimène ʃimɛnə
Chimère ʃimɛːrə
Chine ʃinə
Chinois ʃinwa
Chinoise(s) ʃinwaːzə
Chinon ʃinõ

Chios kjɔs or kjoːs
Chirac ʃirak
Chivot ʃivo
Chloé/Chloë kloe
Chlopicki klɔpitski
Chloris klɔris
Choaspès kɔaspɛs
Chobillon ʃobijõ
Choéphores kɔefɔːrə
Choiseul-Francières (De) də ʃwazœl
    frãsjeːrə
Choisnel ʃwanɛl
Choisy ʃwazi
Cholet ʃolɛ
Chollet ʃole
Chooz ʃo
Chopin ʃopɛ̃
Chorèbe kɔrɛːbə
Chorégies d'Orange kɔreʒi dɔrãːʒə
Choron ʃorõ
Chosroès kɔsrɔɛs
Chostakovitch ʃɔstakɔvitʃ
Choudens ʃudɛ̃ːs
Choufleuri ʃuflœri
Chouquet ʃuke
Chrestien kretjɛ̃
Chrétien kretjɛ̃
Chrétien-Vaguet kretjɛ̃ vage
Chrisante krizãːtə
Christ krist
Christ, Jésus ʒezy kri
Christelle kristɛlə
Christian kristjã
Christiane kristjanə
Christie kristi
Christiné kristine
Christine kristinə
Christophe kristɔfə
Christophe Colomb kristɔfə kɔlõ
Chromis krɔmis
Chrysaline krizalinə
Chrysaor krizaɔːr
Chryséis krizeis
Chrysippe krizipə
Chrysler krislɛːr
Chrysodule krizɔdylə
Chrysostome krizɔstoːmə
Churchill tʃœrtʃil or ʃœrtʃil
Chymène ʃimenə
Chypre ʃiprə
Chypriote(s) ʃipriotə
Ciboulette sibulɛtə
Cicéron siserõ
Cicérone siserɔnə
Cico siko
Cid (Le) lə sid
Cidalyse sidaliːzə
Cieszyn tʃjeʃin
Cieutat sjøta
Cigna tʃiɲa
Cilea tʃilea
Cimarosa tʃimaroza or ʃimaroza
Cincinnati sinsinati or sɛ̃sinati
Cinéas sineaːs
Cinna sina
Cinq-Mars sɛ̃ maːr
Cint(h)i-Damoreau sɛ̃ti damɔro

Cinto tʃinto
Cioran tʃɔran
Cipaye sipajə
Cipriani tʃipriani or sipriani
Circé sirse
Ciry siri
Cithéron siterõ
Citroën sitrɔɛn
Clair klɛːr
Claire klɛːrə
Clairette klɛrɛtə
Clairin klɛrɛ̃
Clairval klɛrval
Clairville klɛrvilə
Clamecy klaməsi
Claon (Le) lə klaõ
Clapisson klapisõ
Clara klara
Clarchies klarʃiə
Clarence klarɛns or klarãːsə
Clarens (France) klarɛ̃ːs
Clarens (Switzerland) klarã
Claretie klarətiə
Clarine klarinə
Claris de Florian klaris də flɔrjã
Clarisse klarisə
Clarke klark
Claude kloːdə
Claudel klodɛl
Claudien klodjɛ̃
Claudine klodinə
Claudio klawdjo or klodjo
Claudius klodjys
Clauzel klozɛl
Clavé klave
Claverie klavəriə
Claye klɛ
Claye-Souilly klɛ suji
Clayette (La) la klɛtə
Cléante kleãːtə
Cléarque klearkə
Clefmont klemõ
Clélie kleliə
Clémence klemãːsə
Clemenceau klemãso
Clément klemã
Clementi klemɛnti
Clémentine klemãtinə
Cléobule kleobylə
Cléomène kleomenə
Cléomer kleomeːr
Cléon kleõ
Cléone kleonə
Cléopâtre kleopaːtrə
Cléophas kleofaːs
Clérambault klerãbo
Clerc klɛːr
Clercq klɛːr
Clergue klɛrgə
Clermont klɛrmõ
Clermont-Ferrand klɛrmõ fɛrã
Clerval (De) də klɛrval
Clésinger klezɛ̃ʒe
Cleveland klevlãːd
Clichy kliʃi
Clicqout kliko
Clignancourt kliɲaku:r

260 | FRENCH LYRIC DICTION

Climène klimɛnə
Cliquet klikɛ
Cliquet-Pleyel klikɛ plɛjɛl
Clisson klisõ
Clitandre klitɑ̃:drə
Cloërec klɔerɛk
Cloëz klɔɛ:z
Cloots klo:ts
Clopin klɔpɛ̃
Clorinde klɔrɛ̃:də
Closel (Du) dy klozɛl
Clotaire klɔtɛ:rə
Clot(h)ilde klɔtildə
Clotho klɔto
Cloud klu
Clouzot kluzo
Clovis klɔvis
Cloyes klwa
Cloÿs klɔi
Clusaz (La) la klyza
Cluytens klɥitɛ̃:s or klœjtɛ̃:s
Clymène klimɛnə
Clytemnestre klitemnɛstrə
Clytie klitiə
Coadou kɔadu
Cobalet kɔbalɛ
Cobourg kɔbu:r
Cocardes kɔkardə
Cochenille kɔʃənijə
Cochereau kɔʃəro
Cochin kɔʃɛ̃
Cockburn kɔburn or kɔkbœrn
Cocteau kɔkto
Cocyte kɔsitə
Codet kɔdɛ
Codinas kɔdinɑ:s
Cœdès sedɛs
Cœslin køslin
Coëtlogon kɔetlɔgõ
Coëtquidan kɔetkidɑ̃
Cœuroy kœrwa
Coëvrons (Les) lɛ kwɛvrõ
Cohen kɔɛn
Cohl ko:l or kɔl
Coiffier kwafje
Coigny (De) də kwaɲi
Coïmbatore kɔɛ̃batɔ:rə
Coïmbre/Coimbre kɔɛ̃:brə
Coin kwɛ̃
Cointreau kwɛ̃tro
Coislin kwalɛ̃
Colas kɔla
Colbert kɔlbɛ:r
Colchide kɔlʃidə
Colchos kɔlkos or kɔlko:s
Colette kɔlɛtə
Coligny kɔliɲi
Coligny-Châtillon (De) də kɔliɲi
  ʃɑtijõ
Colin kɔlɛ̃
Colin Muset kɔlɛ̃ myzɛ
Colisée kɔlizeə
Collaer kɔlɛ:r
Collard kɔla:r
Collasse kɔla:sə
Collatin kɔlatɛ̃
Collé kɔle

Colle kɔlə
Collet kɔlɛ
Colleuille kɔlœjə
Collin kɔlɛ̃
Colline kɔlinə
Collinet kɔlinɛ
Colmar kɔlma:r
Cologne kɔlɔɲə
Colomb, Cristophe kristɔfə kɔlõ
Colombe kɔlõ:bə
Colombie kɔlõbiə
Colombie-Britannique kɔlõbi
  britanikə
Colombien(s) kɔlõbjɛ̃
Colombienne(s) kɔlõbjɛnə
Colombine kɔlõbinə
Colomiers kɔlɔmje
Colone kɔlɔnə
Colonna-Walewski kɔlɔna valɛvski
Colonne kɔlɔnə
Colophon kɔlɔfõ
Colorado kɔlɔrado
Colossien(s) kɔlɔsjɛ̃
Colossienne(s) kɔlɔsjɛnə
Coluche kɔlyʃə
Columbia kɔlõbja
Columbus kɔlõbys
Columelle kɔlymɛlə
Colville kɔlvilə
Comanches kɔmɑ̃:ʃə
Combarieu kõbarjø
Combeferre kõbəfɛ:rə
Combloux kõblu
Combraille(s) kõbra:jə
Combre kõ:brə
Côme ko:mə
Command kɔmɑ̃
Commercy kɔmɛrsi
Comminges kɔmɛ̃:ʒə
Commode kɔmɔdə
Comnène kɔmnɛnə
Comœdia kɔmedja
Comores kɔmɔ:rə
Comorien(s) kɔmɔrjɛ̃
Comorienne(s) kɔmɔrjɛnə
Compain kõpɛ̃
Compains kõpɛ̃
Compeix kõpɛ
Compère kõpɛ:rə
Compiègne kõpjɛɲə
Compostelle (De) də kõpɔstɛlə
Comps kõ:ps
Comtat Venaissin kõta vənɛsɛ̃
Comte kõ:tə
Comté de Foix kõte də fwa
Comtet kõtɛ
Comus kɔmys
Concepcion kõsɛpsjõ or kõsɛpsjɔn
Concorde kõkɔrdə
Condé kõde
Condette kõdɛtə
Condillac kõdijak
Condom kõdõ
Condroz kõdro
Conflans kõflɑ̃
Confolens kõfɔlɑ̃
Confucius kõfysjys

Congo kõgo
Congolais kõgɔlɛ
Congolaise(s) kõgɔlɛ:zə
Conjux kõʒy
Conneau kɔno
Connecticut kɔnɛktikyt
Conrad kõrad
Conradin kõradɛ̃
Constance kõstɑ̃:sə
Constans kõstɑ̃
Constant kõstɑ̃
Constantin kõstɑ̃tɛ̃
Constantine kõstɑ̃tinə
Constantinople kõsɑ̃tinɔplə
Conte (Le) lə kõ:tə
Contescourt kõtesku:r
Conti kõti
Contrevoz kõtrəvo
Coolidge kulidʒ
Cools ko:ls
Copeau kɔpo
Copenhague kɔpɛnagə
Copernic kɔpɛrnik
Copland kɔplɑ̃:d
Coppée kɔpeə
Coppélia kɔpelja
Coppélius kɔpeljys
Coppens kɔpɑ̃
Copponex kɔpɔnɛ
Coquard kɔka:r
Coquatrix kɔkatriks
Coquelin kɔkəlɛ̃
Coquenard kɔkəna:r
Coquillère kɔkijɛ:rə
Coran (Le) lə kɔrɑ̃
Corazza kɔradza
Corbière kɔrbjɛ:rə
Corboz kɔrbo:z
Corbulon kɔrbylõ
Corbusier (Le) lə kɔrbyzje
Corcy (De) də kɔrsi
Corcyre kɔrsi:rə
Corday kɔrdɛ
Cordier kɔrdje
Cordoue (De) də kɔrduə
Coré kɔre
Corée kɔreə
Coréen(s) kɔreɛ̃
Coréenne(s) kɔreɛnə
Corelli kɔreli
Corentin kɔrɑ̃tɛ̃
Corinne kɔrinə
Corinthe kɔrɛ̃:tə
Corinthien(s) kɔrɛ̃tjɛ̃
Corinthienne(s) kɔrɛ̃tjɛnə
Coriolan kɔriɔlɑ̃
Coriolis kɔrjɔlis
Corisande kɔrizɑ̃:də
Corite kɔritə
Cormon kɔrmõ
Cormoz kɔrmo
Cornarino Cornarini
  kɔrnarino kɔrnarini
Corneau kɔrno
Corneille kɔrnɛjə
Cornélie kɔrnelia
Cornélius kɔrneljys

PRONUNCIATION DICTIONARIES | 261

Cornière kɔrnjɛːrə
Cornilla (La) la kɔrnija
Cornouaille kɔrnwaːjə
Cornouailles kɔrnwaːjə
Cornubert kɔrnybɛːr
Cornus kɔrnys
Cornut kɔrny
Corogne (La) la kɔrɔɲə
Coront kɔrõ
Corot kɔro
Corps kɔːr
Correas kɔreaːs
Corrège (Le) lə kɔrɛːʒə
Corrégidor kɔreʒidɔːr
Correns kɔrɛ̃ːs
Corrèze kɔrɛːzə
Corrézien(s) kɔrezjɛ̃
Corrézienne(s) kɔrezjɛnə
Corse kɔrsə
Corte kɔrte
Cortez kɔrtɛːz *or* kɔrtɛs
Corti kɔrti
Corton kɔrtõ
Cortot kɔrto
Corybantes kɔribãːtə
Coryphée kɔrifea
Coscoletto kɔskɔlɛt(t)o
Cosette kɔzetə *or* kɔzɛtə
Cosma kɔsma
Cosme koːmə
Cosme de Médicis kɔsmə də medisis
Cosnac konak
Cosne koːnə
Cosne-Cours-sur-Loire konə kur syr lwaːrə
Cosnefroy konəfrwa *or* konəfrwa
Cosquer kɔske
Cosqueville kɔskəvilə
Cossé (De) də kɔse
Cossira kɔsira
Costa Rica kɔsta rika
Costallat kɔstala
Costanndino kɔstandino
Costaricain(s) kɔstarikɛ̃
Costaricaine(s) kɔstarikɛnə
Costaricien(s) kɔstarisjɛ̃
Costaricienne(s) kɔstarisjɛnə
Costarmoricain(s) kɔstarmɔrikɛ̃
Costarmoricaine(s) kɔstarmɔrikɛnə
Coste kɔstə
Coste (De La) də la kɔstə
Costeley kɔstəle *or* kotəle
Cot kɔt
Côt ko
Côte d'Azur kotə dazyːr
Côte d'Émeraude kotə dɛməroːdə *or* kotə demaroːdə
Côte d'Ivoire kotə divwaːrə
Côte d'Or kotə dɔːr
Côte-de-l'Or kotə də lɔːr
Cotentin kɔtãtɛ̃
Côte-Rôtie kotə rotiə *or* kotə rotiə
Côtes koːtə
Côte-Saint-André (La) la kotə sɛ̃ tãdre
Côte-Saint-Luc kotə sɛ̃ lyk
Côtes-du-Nord kotə dy nɔːr

Côtes-du-Rhône kotə dy roːnə
Cotignac kɔtiɲak
Cotonou kɔtɔnu
Cotta kɔta
Cottret kɔtrɛ
Coty kɔti
Coubertin (De) də kubɛrtɛ̃
Couderc kudɛːr
Coué kwe
Couëron kwerõ
Couesnon kwenõ *or* kwɛnõ
Couffoulens kufulɛ̃ːs
Coulogne (De) də kulɔɲə
Coulounieix kulunje
Couperin kupərɛ̃
Couptrain kutrɛ̃
Courajod kuraʒo
Couraud kuro
Courbet kurbɛ
Courcelles (De) də kursɛlə
Courfeyrac kurfɛrak
Courgains kurgɛ̃
Courjal kurʒal
Courrières kurjɛːrə
Cours-la-Reine kur la rɛnə
Courteline kurtəlinə
Courtils kurti
Courtomer kurtɔmɛːr
Courvoisier kurvwazje
Couserans kuzərã
Cousin kuzɛ̃
Coussens kusɛ̃ːs
Cousteau kusto
Coutances kutãːsə
Coutens kutɛ̃ːs
Coutras kutra
Couture kutyːrə
Couve de Murville kuvə də myrvilə
Couzeix kuzɛ
Couzinou kuzinu
Covent-Garden kɔvɛnt gardən
Cowl, Darry dari ko:l
Coypel kwapɛl
Coysevox kwazəvɔks *or* kwazəvo
Cracovie krakoviə
Crakentorp krakentɔrp
Cranmer kranmœːr *or* krãmɛːr
Crans-sur-Sierre krã syr sjɛːrə
Craon krã *or* kraõ
Craonnais(s) kranɛ
Craonnaise(s) kranɛːzə
Craonne kranə
Crapet krapɛ
Craponne (De) də krapɔnə
Cras kraːz
Cratinos kratinɔs *or* kratinoːs
Crau kro
Crebassa krebasa
Crébillon krebijõ
Crécy-Crécy (De) də kresi kresi
Creil krɛj
Crémarest kremarɛ
Crémieux kremjø
Crémont kremõ
Créon kreõ
Crépin krepɛ̃
Crespel krɛspɛl

Crespin *(person)* krɛspɛ̃
Crespin *(place)* krɛspɛ̃ *or* krepɛ̃
Crespy *(person)* krɛspi *or* krepi
Crespy *(place)* krepi
Cressida krɛsida *or* kresida
Crest krɛst *or* krɛ
Crésus krezys
Crète krɛtə
Créteil kretɛj
Creuse krøːzə
Créüse/Créuse krey:zə
Creusois krøzwa
Creusoise(s) krøzwaːzə
Crevel krəvɛl
Crillon krijõ
Crimée krimeə
Criméen(s) krimeɛ̃
Criméenne(s) krimeɛnə
Criots krio
Cris kri
Crisnée krisneə
Croate(s) krɔatə
Croatie krɔasiə
Crobyle krɔbilə
Croche krɔʃə
Crochet krɔʃɛ
Croisette krwazetə
Croisne krwanə
Croisset (De) də krwasɛ
Croissy (De) də krwasi
Croix-Rouge (La) la krwa ru:ʒə *or* la krwa ru:ʒə
Croiza krwaza
Crommelynck krɔməlɛ̃:k
Cromwell krɔmwɛl
Croquefer krɔkəfɛːr
Cros kro
Crosne kroːnə
Crosnier kronje
Crosti krɔsti
Crottes (Les) lɛ krɔtə
Crould/Croult (Le) lə kru
Croulebarbe kruləbarbə
Crouslé krule
Croÿ/Croy/Crouy krui
Croze kroːzə
Crozet krɔzɛ
Cruas kryaːs
Cruppi krypi
Crusoé/Crusoë kryzoe
Cruveilhier kryvɛje
Ctésippe ktezipə
Cuba kyba
Cubain(s) kybɛ̃
Cubaine(s) kybɛnə
Cuénod kɥeno
Cuers kɥɛrs
Cuesmes kɥemə
Cuevas (De) də kɥevaːs
Cui kɥi
Cujas kyʒaːs *or* kyʒa
Culloden kœlɔdən *or* kylodən
Culoz kyloːz
Cumes kymə
Cumia kymja
Cunégonde kynegõ:də
Cuniot kynjo

262 | FRENCH LYRIC DICTION

Cunlhat kœ̃ja
Cuperly kypɛrli
Cupidon kypidõ
Cuq kyk
Cuq-Toulza kyk tulza
Curaçao kyraso
Curiaces (Les) lɛ kyrjasə
Curie kyriə
Curiel kyrjɛl
Cusset kysɛ
Custine (De) də kystinə
Cuvier kyvje
Cuvillier kyvilje
Cyaxare sjaksa:rə
Cybèle sibɛlə
Cyclades sikladə
Cydalise sidali:zə
Cydnus sidnys
Cynire sini:rə
Cynthie sɛ̃tiə
Cypriani sipriani
Cyprien siprjɛ̃
Cyprienne siprjɛnə
Cypriote(s) sipriotə
Cypris sipris
Cyrano sirano
Cyrène sirɛnə
Cyrille sirilə
Cyrus sirys
Cysoing sizwɛ̃
Cythère sitɛ:rə
Cythérée sitereə
Czerny tʃɛrni or gzɛrni or ksɛrni

— D —

Dabadie dabadiə
Dac dak
Dacca daka
Dachau daʃo
Dagon dagõ
Daguerre dagɛ:rə
Daignaud dɛɲo
Dakar daka:r
Dakota du Nord dakota dy nɔ:r
Dakota du Sud dakota dy syd
Daladier daladje
Dalayrac dalɛrak
Dalcroze dalkro:zə
Dalesme dalɛmə
Dali dali
Dalida dalida
Dalila dalila
Dalinde dalɛ̃:də
Dallapiccola dalapi(k)ola
Dallas dala:s
Dallier dalje
Dalloz dalo:z
Dalmatie dalmasiə
Dalmatien(s) dalmasjɛ̃
Dalmatienne(s) dalmasjɛnə
Dalmont dalmõ
Dalmorès dalmɔrɛs
Dalou dalu
Dam (Van) vã dam
Damaris damaris
Damas damɑ:s

Damascène damasɛnə
Damase damɑ:zə
Dambach dambak
Damia damja
Damien damjɛ̃
Damiens damjɛ̃
Damis damis
Damoclès damɔklɛs
Damon damõ
Dampierre (De) də dɑ̃pjɛ:rə
Danaé danae
Danaïdes danaidə
Danbé dɑ̃be
Dancaïre dɑ̃kai:rə
Danchet dɑ̃ʃɛ
Dancla dɑ̃kla
Danco dɑ̃ko
Dandelot dɑ̃dəlo
Dandolo dɑ̃dɔlo
Dandrieu dɑ̃driø
Danemark danəmark
Daniderff danidɛrf
Daniel danjɛl
Danièle danjɛlə
Danieli danjeli
Danielle danjɛlə
Daniel-Lesur danjɛl ləsy:r
Danois danwa
Danoise(s) danwa:zə
Dante dɑ̃:tə
Danton dɑ̃tõ
Dantzig dɑ̃tsig
Danube danybə
Dapertutto dapɛrtut(t)o
Daphénéo dafeneo
Daphné dafne
Daphnis dafnis
Daquin dakɛ̃
Daragnès daraɲɛs
Darbans darbɑ̃
Darbel darbɛl
Darboy darbwa
Darcey darsɛ
Darcieux darsjø
Darck dark
Darclée darkleə
Dardanelles dardanɛlə
Dardanus dardanys
Darius darjys
Darlay darlɛ
Darnault darno
Darracq darak
Dartaux darto
Dartois dartwa
Darty darti
Darval(l)o darvalo
Dassy dasi
Daubenton dobɑ̃tõ
Daudet dodɛ
Daumesnil domenil or domenil
Daumier domje
Daunais donɛ
Dauphin dofɛ̃
Dauphiné dofine
Dauphine dofinə
Daurat dɔra
Dautremer dotrəmɛ:r

Daussoulx dosu
Dauvergne dovɛrɲə
Davenescourt davənɛsku:r
Davesne davenə
David david
Davioud davju
Davos davos or davo:s
Davoust davu
Davout davu
Dax daks
Dearly derli
Debladis dəbladis
Déborah debɔra
Debret dəbrɛ
Debreu dəbrø
Deburau dəbyro
Debussy dəbysi
Decaisne dəkenə
Décaméron dekamerõ
Dèce dɛsə
Dechevaux-Dumesnil dəʃəvo dymenil
  or dəʃəvo dymenil
Declomesnil dəklɔmenil
  or dəklɔmɛnil
Decourcelle dəkursɛlə
Decrès dəkrɛ
Dédale dedalə
Dédé dede
Deffayet dɛfaje or defaje
Deffès dɛfɛs or defɛs
Défossé(s) defose or defose
Degas dəga
Déhodenc deodɛ̃:k
Deinze dɛ̃:zə
Déjanire deʒani:rə
Delaborde dəlabɔrdə
Delacôte dəlako:tə
Delacour dəlaku:r
Delacroix dəlakrwa or dəlakrwa
Delafosse dəlafo:sə
Delage dəla:ʒə
Delahante dəlaɑ̃:tə
Delahaye dəlae
Delalande dəlalɑ̃:də
Delambre dəlɑ̃:brə
Delamorinière dəlamɔrinjɛ:rə
Delamotte dəlamɔtə
Delannoy dəlanwa
Delanoë dəlanoe
Delaporte dəlapɔrtə
Delaquerrière dəlakɛrjɛ:rə
Delaseurie dəlazœriə
Delâtre dəla:trə
Delaunay dəlonɛ
Delaunay-Riquier dəlonɛ rikje
Delaunois dəlonwa
Delavesne dəlavenə
Delavigne dəlaviɲə
Delaware dəlawa:rə
Delbos dɛlbo:s
Delcassé dɛlkase
Deldevez dɛldəvɛ:z
Delescluze dəlɛkly:zə or dəlekly:zə
Delessert dəlɛsɛ:r or dəlesɛ:r
Delestre-Poirson dəlɛtrə pwarsõ
Delesvaux dəlɛvo or dəlevo
Deletré dəletre

PRONUNCIATION DICTIONARIES | 263

Deleuze dələø:zə
Delhi dɛli
Delibes dəlibə
Délie deliə
Delille dəlilə
Delisle dəlilə
Dell'Acqua dɛlakwa
Della Volta dɛla vɔlta
Delle dɛlə
Delmarès dɛlmarɛs
Delmas dɛlma:s
Delmet dɛlmɛ
Delna dɛlna
Deloffre dəlɔfrə
Delon dəlõ
Delorme dəlɔrmə
Delormel dəlɔrmɛl
Delorn dəlɔrn
Delpech dɛlpɛʃ
Delphes dɛlfə
Delpit dɛlpi
Delpouget dɛlpuʒɛ
Delrieu dɛlrjø
Delunsch dəlœ:ʃ
Del Vala dɛl vala
Delvaux dɛlvo
Delvincourt dɛlvɛ̃ku:r
Delvoye dɛlvwa
Démade demadə
Démarate demaratə
Démêloir demɛlwa:r
Demers dəmɛrs
Déméter demetɛ:r
Démétrios demetrios or demetrio:s
Demets dəmɛ
Demigny demiɲi
Démocrite demokritə
Démogoron demɔgɔrõ
Démosthène demostɛnə
Demoulin dəmulɛ̃
Demoustier dəmutje or dəmustje
Demugeot dəmyʒo
Demy dəmi
Deneuve dənœ:və
Denève dənɛ:və
Denfert-Rochereau dãfɛr rɔʃəro
Denis dəni
Denise dəni:zə
Denize dəni:zə
Dennery dɛnəri
Denon dənõ
Denonville (De) də dənõvilə
Dens dɛ̃:s
Denver dɛnvɛ:r
Denya dɛnja
Denys dəni
Déodat deoda
Dépaquit depaki
Depardieu dəpardjø
Deperthes dəpɛrtə
Depraz dəpra:z
Deprez dəpre
Dequesne dəkɛnə
Der dɛ:r
Derain dərɛ̃
Dercourt-Plaut dɛrkur plo
Derème dərɛmə

Derenne dərɛnə
Dérivis derivis
Déroulède derulɛdə
Derrida dɛrida
Dervaux dɛrvo
Des Grieux dɛ griø
Desains dəsɛ̃
Desaix dəsɛ
Desandre dezãdrə
Desanti dəsãti
Desargues dezargə or dezargə
Désaugiers dezoʒje
Desault dəso or dəzo
Desbains dɛbɛ̃ or debɛ̃
Desbancs dɛbã or debã
Desbarbieux dɛbarbjø or debarbjø
Desbarreaux dɛbaro or debaro
Desbats dɛba or deba
Desbazeilles dɛbazɛjə or debazɛjə
Desbeaux dɛbo or debo
Desbenoit dɛbənwa or debənwa
Desbisson(s) dɛbisõ or debisõ
Desblaches dɛblaʃə or deblaʃə
Desbœuf dɛsbœf
Desbœufs dɛbø or debø
Desbois dɛbwa or debwa or dɛbwa
  or debwa
Desbonnet(s) dɛbɔnɛ or debɔnɛ
Desbordes dɛbɔrdə or debɔrdə
Desbordes-Valmore dɛbɔrdə
  valmɔ:rə or debɔrdə valmɔ:rə
Desboutin dɛbutɛ̃ or debutɛ̃
Descamps dɛkã or dekã
Descargues dɛkargə or dekargə
Descartes dɛkartə or dekartə
Descaves dɛka:və or deka:və
Descazeaux dɛkazo or dekazo
Deschamps dɛʃã or deʃã
Deschamps-Jéhin dɛʃã ʒeɛ̃ or deʃã ʒeɛ̃
Deschanel dɛʃanɛl or deʃanɛl
Desclais dɛklɛ or deklɛ
Desclosages dɛkloza:ʒə or dekloza:ʒə
Desclosures dɛklozy:rə or deklozy:rə
Descombaz dɛkõba:z or dekõba:z
Descombes dɛkõ:bə or dekõ:bə
Descos dɛskɔs or desko:s
Descostes dɛkɔstə or dekɔstə
Descout dɛsku
Descoutures dɛkuty:rə or dekuty:rə
Descroizilles dɛkrwazijə
  or dekrwazijə
Descuves dɛky:və or deky:və
Desdémone dɛsdemonə
Desèze dəsɛ:zə
Desflaches dɛflaʃə or deflaʃə
Desfontaine(s) dɛfõtɛnə or defõtɛnə
Desforges dɛfɔrʒə or defɔrʒə
Desfossé(s) dɛfose or defose or dɛfose
  or defose
Desgenettes dɛʒənɛtə or deʒənɛtə
Desgoutte(s) dɛgutə or degutə
Deshayes dɛɛ or dee
Deshoulières dɛzulje:rə or dezulje:rə
Désirade deziradə
Désiré dezire
Désirée dezireə
Desjardins dɛʒardɛ̃ or deʒardɛ̃

Desjobert deʒɔbɛ:r or deʒɔbe:r
Deslandes dɛlã:də or delã:də
Deslandres dɛlã:drə or delã:drə
Deslauriers dɛlɔrje or delɔrje
Desloges dɛlɔ:ʒə or delɔ:ʒə
Deslys dɛlis or delis
Desmahis dɛmai or demai
Desmarais dɛmarɛ or demarɛ
Desmarets dɛmarɛ or demarɛ
Desmasures dɛmazy:rə or demazy:rə
Desmichels dɛmiʃɛl or demiʃɛl
Desmoulin(s) dɛmulɛ̃ or demulɛ̃
Desnoiresterres dɛnwarɛtɛ:rə
  or denwarɛtɛ:rə
Desnos dɛsnos
Desnouveaux dɛnuvo or denuvo
Desnoyers dɛnwaje or denwaje
Desormière dɛzɔrmje:rə
  or dezɔrmje:rə
Desparmet dɛsparmɛ
Despautère depotɛ:rə or depote:rə
Despaux dɛspo
Despert dɛspe:r
Despiau dɛspjo
Desplanques dɛplã:kə or deplã:kə
Desplat dɛspla
Despois dɛpwa or depwa or dɛpwa
  or depwa
Desportes dɛpɔrtə or depɔrtə
Despréaux dɛpreo or depreo
Despretz dɛpre or depre
Desprez/Despres/Després/Des Prez
  dɛ pre or de pre
Desproges dɛprɔ:ʒə or deprɔ:ʒə
Despujols dɛpyʒɔl or depyʒɔl
Desqueyroux dɛskɛru
Desrieux dɛrjø or derjø
Desrochers dɛrɔʃe or derɔʃe
Desroches dɛrɔʃə or derɔʃə
Desrosiers dɛrozje or derozje
Desrousseaux dɛruso or deruso
Desruelles dɛryɛlə or deryɛlə
Dessalines dɛsalinə or desalinə
Dessay dəsɛ
Dessens dɛsɛ̃:s or desɛ̃:s
Destal dɛstal
Destel dɛstɛl
Destouche(s) dɛtuʃə or detuʃə
Destour dɛstu:r
Destrée dɛstreə
Destrem(e)au dɛstremo
Destutt de Tracy dɛstyt de trasi
Desvallières dɛvalje:rə or devalje:rə
Desvaux dɛvo
Desvergne devɛrɲə or devɛrɲə
Desvignes deviɲə or deviɲə
Desvoivres dɛvwa:vrə or devwa:vrə
Desvres dɛ:vrə
Detaille dəta:jə
Detroit detrwa or ditrœjt
Détroyat detrwaja
Deucalion døkaljõ
Deûle (La) la dø:lə
Deutz dø:ts
Deux-Sèvres dø sɛ:vrə
Devellereau dəvɛləro
Devéria dəverja

264 | FRENCH LYRIC DICTION

Devieilhe dəvjɛjə or dəvjɛlə
Devismes dəvimə
Devivier dəvivje
Devos dəvɔs or dəvo:s
Devriès dəvriɛs
Dezeuze dəzø:zə
Dezobry dəzɔbri
Dhaka daka
Dheune dø:nə
Diaforus djafɔrys
Diaghilev djagilɛf
Diakonova djakɔnɔva
Diane djanə
Diaz dja:z or djas
Diaz de la Pena djaz də la peɲa
Dicéphile disefilə
Dickens dikɛns or dikɛ̃:s
Diderot didəro
Didier didje
Didon didõ
Die diə
Diégo djego
Diègue (Don) dõ djɛgə
Diémer djeme:r
Dieppe djɛpə
Dierx djɛrks
Diesel djezɛl or dizɛl
Diest dist
Dietrich ditriʃ
Dietsch ditʃ
Dieu djø
Dieudonné djødɔne
Dieulafoy djølafwa
Digne diɲə
Digne-les-Bains diɲə lɛ bɛ̃
Dignimont diɲimõ
Dijon diʒõ
Dikson diksõ or diksɔn
Dilbeek dilbek or dilbɛk
Dinan dinã
Dinard dina:r
Dinarque dinarkə
Dindyme dɛ̃dimə
Dinochau dinɔʃo
Dinorah dinɔra
Dioclétien djɔklesjɛ̃
Diodore djɔdɔ:rə
Diogène djɔʒɛnə
Diomède djɔmɛdə
Dionée djɔneə
Dionysos djɔnizos or djɔnizo:s
Diophante djɔfɑ̃:tə
Dior djɔ:r
Diphile difilə
Dircé dirse
Disraeli disraeli
Distel distɛl
Divoire divwa:rə
Divonne divɔnə
Dixmont dimõ
Djakarta dʒakarta
Djamileh dʒamilɛ
Django dʒaŋgo or dʒãgo
Djella dʒela
Djibouti dʒibuti
Djiboutien(s) dʒibutjɛ̃
Djiboutienne(s) dʒibutjɛnə

Djinns dʒin
Doche dɔʃə
Docquois dɔkwa
Doètte dɔɛtə
Doha dɔa
Dole dɔlə
Dom Pérignon dõ periɲõ
Dombasle dõbɑ:lə
Dombrowski dombrɔvski
    or dõbrɔvski or dombrɔfski
    or dõbrɔfski
Domerc dɔmɛ:r
Dominicain(s) dɔminikɛ̃
Dominicaine(s) dɔminikɛnə
Dominiquais dɔminikɛ
Dominiquaise(s) dɔminikɛ:zə
Dominique dɔminikə
Domino dɔmino
Domitien dɔmisjɛ̃
Dommange dɔmã:ʒə
Domrémy/Domremy dõremi
Don Carlos dõ karlo:s
Don José dõ ʒoze
Don Juan dõ ʒɥã
Don Sanche dõ sã:ʃə
Doña Sol dɔɲa sɔl
Donat dɔna
Dondeyne dõdɛnə
Doniau-Blanc dɔnjo blã
Donizetti dɔnizet(t)i
Donnay dɔnɛ
Dorchain dɔrʃɛ̃
Dordognais dɔrdɔɲɛ
Dordognaise(s) dɔrdɔɲɛ:zə
Dordogne dɔrdɔɲə
Dordrecht dɔrdrɛk or dɔrdrɛkt
Doré dɔre
Dorélac dɔrelak
Dorgelès dɔrʒəlɛs
Doria dɔrja
Dorien(s) dɔrjɛ̃
Dorienne(s) dɔrjɛnə
Dorine dɔrinə
Dorion dɔrjõ
Doris dɔris
Dormans dɔrmã
Dorny dɔrni
Dorothée dɔroteə
Dortzal dɔrtsal
Dorus dɔrys
Dorval dɔrval
Dorville dɔrvilə
Dosdane dodanə
Dosia dozja or dɔzja
Dosne do:nə
Dostoïevski dɔstɔjefski
Douai dwe
Douains dwɛ̃
Douarnenez dwarnəne
Douatte dwatə
Doubaï dubaj
Doublemar dubləma:r
Doubs du
Doucet dusɛ
Douglas dugla:s
Doullens dulã
Doumenc dumɛ̃:k

Doumer dume:r
Doumergue dumɛrgə
Dourga durga
Dourian durjã
Dourlinski durlinski
Dousset dusɛ
Douvres du:vrə
Doux du
Douzens duzɛ̃:s
Dowland dawland
Doyen dwajɛ̃
Drach drak
Draco drako
Dracon drakõ
Draguignan draginã
Dran drã
Dranem dranɛm
Drappier drapje
Dresde drɛsdə
Dreuilh drœj
Dreux drø
Dreyfus drɛfys
Dreyfus-Barney drɛfys barnɛ
Drigo drigo
Drom drõ
Drôme dro:mə
Drômois dromwa
Drômoise(s) dromwa:zə
Drouet druɛ
Drouin druɛ̃
Drouot druo
Drouyn de Lhuys druɛ̃ də lɥis
Droz dro or dro:z
Drucker dryke:r
Druet drɥɛ
Druides dryidə
Druze dry:zə
Dubaï/Dubay dubaj
Dubas dybɑ
Dubel dybɛl
Dubeslay dybelɛ or dybɛlɛ
Dublin dyblɛ̃
Dubocq dybɔk
Dubois dybwa or dybwɑ
Dubos/Bos (Du) dybo or dybɔs
Dubosc dybɔsk
Dubose dybo:zə
Dubost dybo or bybɔst
Dubreuil dybrœj
Dubrovnik dubrɔvnik
Dubuffet dybyfɛ
Dubuis dybɥi
Duc dyk
Ducasble dyka:blə
Ducasse dykasə
Duchambge dyʃɑ̃:ʒə
Duchamp dyʃã
Duchamp-Villon dyʃã vijõ
Duchêne dyʃɛnə
Duchesne dyʃɛnə
Duchesnois dyʃɛnwa or dyʃɛnwa
Ducis dysis or dysi
Duclos dyklo
Ducor dykɔ:r
Ducos duko
Ducquois dykwa
Ducroquet dykrɔkɛ

PRONUNCIATION DICTIONARIES | 265

Ducuing dykɥɛ̃
Duez dɥɛːz *or* dɥe
Dufau dyfo
Dufault dyfo
Dufaure dyfoːrə
Dufaut dyfo
Dufay dyfɛ
Dufour dyfuːr
Dufourcq dyfurk
Dufourny dyfurni
Dufranne dyfranə
Dufresne dyfrɛnə
Dufresnois dyfrɛnwa *or* dyfrɛnwa
Dufriche dyfriʃə
Dufy dyfi
Dugardin dygardɛ̃
Dugazon dygazɔ̃ *or* dygazɔ̃
Duglé dygle
Duguay-Trouin dyge trɥɛ̃ *or*
    dyge trɥɛ̃
Duhesme dyɛmə
Duingt dwɛ̃
Dujardin dyʒardɛ̃
Dujardin-Beaumetz dyʒardɛ̃ bomɛs
Dukas dykaːs
Dulac dylak
Dulaurens dylɔrɑ̃ːs
Dulcinée dylsineə
Dullin dylɛ̃
Dumanoir dymanwaːr
Dumas dyma
Dumaux dymo
Dumay dymɛ
Dumesnil dymenil *or* dymɛnil
Dumesny/Dumény dymeni
Dumont dymɔ̃
Dumont d'Urville dymɔ̃ dyrvilə
Dumouriez dymurje
Duncan dœŋkan *or* dœ̃kɑ̃
Duni dyni
Dunkerque dœ̃kɛrkə
Dunstan dœnstan *or* dœ̃stɑ̃
Duntalmo duntalmo
Dupanloup dypɑ̃lu
Duparc dypark
Duparquet dyparkɛ
Dupas dypa
Dupérier dyperje
Duperré dypɛre
Dupetit-Thouars dypəti twaːr
Dupeuty dypøti
Dupeyron dypɛrɔ̃
Dupin dypɛ̃
Dupleix dyplɛks
Duplessis dyplesi *or* dyplesi
Dupond dypɔ̃
Dupont dypɔ̃
Duprato dyprato
Dupré dypre
Duprez dypre
Dupuis dypɥi
Dupuy dypɥi
Dupuytren dypɥitrɛ̃
Duquesne dykɛnə
Duquesnel dykɛnɛl *or* dykɛnɛl
Duquesnoy dykɛnwa *or* dykɛnwa
Durance dyrɑ̃ːsə

Durancy dyrɑ̃si
Durand dyrɑ̃
Duras dyraːs
Durdilly dyrdiji
Durendal dyrɑ̃dal
Durenne dyrɛnə
Durer/Dürer dyrɛːr
Duresnel dyrenɛl *or* dyrɛnɛl
Durey dyrɛ
Durkheim dyrkɛm
Duroc dyrɔk
Durozeau dyrozo
Duru dyry
Duruflé dyryfle
Dusart dysaːr
Duseigneur dysɛɲœːr
Dussault dyso
Dussaulx dyso
Dussek dysɛk
Dusseldorf/Düsseldorf dysɛldɔrf
Dutilleux dytijø
Dutoit dytwa
Dutronc dytrɔ̃
Duval dyval
Duvernoy dyvɛrnwa
Duveyrier dyvɛrje
Duvivier dyvivje
Dvorak/Dvorjak dvɔrʒak
Dyck (Van) vɑ̃ dik

— E —

Éantide eɑ̃tidə
Éaque eakə
Eauze/Éauze eoːzə
Ebersmünster/
    Ébersmunster ebɛrsmynstɛːr
Éblé eble
Eboli ebɔli
Ébroïn ebrɔɛ̃
Ecclésiaste eklezjastə *or* ɛklezjastə
Echenoz (author) ɛkənoːz
Échezeaux eʃezo
Échézeaux eʃezo
Échion ekjɔ̃
Écos eko
Écossais ekosɛ
Écossaise(s) ekosɛːzə
Écosse ekɔsə
Écouen ekwɑ̃
Eda-Pierre eda pjɛːrə
Éden edɛn
Edgar ɛdgaːr
Edgard ɛdgaːr
Édimbourg edɛ̃buːr
Édith edit
Edme ɛdmə
Edmond ɛdmɔ̃
Edmonde ɛdmɔ̃ːdə
Edmont ɛdmɔ̃
Edmonton ɛdmɔntɔn
Édom edɔm
Édouard edwaːr
Éduens edɥɛ̃
Edwige/Edvige ɛdviːʒə
Eeklo eklo

Égée eʒeə
Égérie eʒeriə
Egger ɛgʒɛːr
Égilone eʒilɔnə
Éginhard eʒinaːr
Égisthe eʒistə
Églantine (D') deglɑ̃tinə
Égletons eglətɔ̃
Églé egle
Egrot ɛgro
Ègrot ɛgro
Éguisheim egis(h)ajm
Égypte eʒiptə
Égyptien(s) eʒipsjɛ̃
Égyptienne(s) eʒipsjɛnə
Eichendorff ajʃɛndɔrf
Eiffel ɛfɛl
Einstein ajnʃtajn *or* ɛnʃtajn
Einvaux ɛ̃vo
Eisenach ajzənak
Eix ɛks
Ékhô eko
El Salvador ɛl salvadɔːr
Elbe ɛlbə
Elbeuf (D') dɛlbœf
Eldorado ɛldorado
Éléazar eleazaːr
Électre elɛktrə
Élégyne eleʒinə
Éléonore eleɔnɔːrə
Éleusis eløzis
Elfe ɛlfə
Elfort ɛlfort
Elgar ɛlgaːr
Éliacin eljasɛ̃
Élias eljaːs
Élie eliə
Éliette eljɛtə
Éliézer eljezɛːr
Élisabeth elizabɛt
Élise eliːzə
Élisée elizeə
Elisène elizɛnə
Elizondo elisondo *or* elizɔ̃do
Elle ɛlə
Ellébeuse (D') delebøːzə *or* dɛlebøːzə
Ellen ɛlɛn *or* elɛn
Elleviou eləvju
Elliot ɛljot *or* ɛljot
Elodie elɔdiə
Élon elɔ̃
Elorn/Élorn elɔrn
Elsa ɛlza
Elseneur ɛlsənœːr
Elssler ɛlslɛːr
El-Tour ɛl tuːr
Éluard elɥaːr
Elven ɛlvɛ̃
Elvire ɛlviːrə
Elzire ɛlziːrə
Emer emɛːr
Émeri/Émery eməri *or* ɛməri
Emerson emərson
Émile emilə
Émilie emiliə
Émilien emiljɛ̃
Émirats Arabes Unis emira ara byni

266 | FRENCH LYRIC DICTION

Émirien(s) emiɾjɛ̃
Émirienne(s) emiɾjɛnə
Emma ɛma *or* ema
Emmanuel ɛmanɥɛl
   or emanɥɛl
Emmanuelle ɛmanɥɛlə
   or emanɥɛlə
Emmaüs ɛmays *or* emays
Emmental ɛmɛntal *or* emɛntal
   or ɛmɛ̃tal *or* emɛ̃tal
Empis ɑ̃pi
Enco-de-Botte ɛ̃ko də bɔtə
Endor ɑ̃dɔːɾ
Endoume ɑ̃dumə
Endrèze ɑ̃dɾɛːzə
Endymion ɑ̃dimjɔ̃
Énéas eneas
Énée eneə
Énéide (L') leneidə
Enesco enɛsko
Enescu enɛsku
Engayresque ɑ̃gɛɾɛskə
Enghien (*place*) ɑ̃gjɛ̃ *or* ɑ̃gɛ̃
Enghien (D') (*person*) dɑ̃gɛ̃
Enjolras ɑ̃ʒɔlɾɑːs
Ennéades (Les) lɛ zɛneadə *or* lɛ
   zeneadə
Ennery (D') dɛnəɾi
Ennius ɛnjys *or* enjys
Ennodius ɛnɔdjys *or* enɔdjys
Enoch enɔk
Énone enonə
Ensisheim ɛnsis(h)ajm
Ensoleillad (L') lɑ̃sɔlejad
Entragues (D') dɑ̃tɾagə
Entrains ɑ̃tɾɛ̃
Entremont ɑ̃tɾəmɔ̃
Entzheim ɛnts(h)ajm
Éole eɔlə
Éoliennes (Les) lɛ zeɔljɛnə
Éourres euːɾə
Épaphos epafɔs *or* epafɔːs
Épaphus epafys
Épernay epɛɾnɛ
Epfig ɛpfig
Éphèse efɛːzə
Éphésien(s) efezjɛ̃
Éphésienne(s) efezjɛnə
Éphore efɔːɾə
Éphraïm efraim
Épicaste epikastə
Épicharme epikaɾmə
Épictète epiktɛtə
Épicure epikyːɾə
Épidaure epidɔːɾə
Épigones (Les) lɛ zepigɔnə
Épinal epinal
Épine (L') lepinə
Épiphane epifanə
Épiphanie epifaniə
Éponine epɔninə
Éprémesnil (D') depɾemenil
   or depɾemɛnil
Epsom ɛpsɔm
Équateur ekwatœːɾ
Équatorien(s) ekwatɔɾjɛ̃

Équatorienne(s) ekwatɔɾjɛnə
Érard eɾaːɾ
Érasme eɾasmə
Éraste eɾastə
Ératosthène eɾatɔstɛnə
Erckmann-Chatrian ɛɾkman ʃatɾiɑ̃
Érèbe eɾɛbə
Érétrie eɾetɾiə
Érévan eɾevɑ̃
Éric eɾik
Érié eɾje
Érik eɾik
Érin eɾin
Érin(n)yes eɾiniə
Ériphyle eɾifilə
Erlanger ɛɾlɑ̃ʒe
Erlo ɛɾlo
Erlon ɛɾlɔ̃
Ermerance ɛɾməɾɑːsə
Ernelinde ɛɾnəlɛ̃ːdə
Ernest ɛɾnest
Ernst ɛɾnst
Éros/Érôs eɾos *or* eɾoːs
Érostrate eɾostɾatə
Erstein ɛɾʃtajn
Érynnis eɾini
Érythrée eɾitɾeə
Érythréen(s) eɾitɾeɛ̃
Érythréenne(s) eɾitɾeɛnə
Ésaïe ezaiə
Ésaü ezay
Escalaïs ɛskalais
Escalaïs-Lureau ɛskalais lyɾo
Escalier ɛskalje
Escalquens ɛskalkɛ̃ːs
Escamillo ɛskamijo
Escande ɛskɑ̃ːdə
Escandorgue (L') lɛskɑ̃dɔɾgə
Escarène (L') lɛskaɾɛnə
Escarmain ɛskaɾmɛ̃
Escars (D') dekaːɾ
Escartefigue ɛskaɾtəfigə
Escaut ɛsko
Eschenbach ɛʃɛnbak
Eschig ɛʃig
Eschine ɛʃinə
Escholier ɛskɔlje
Eschyle ɛʃilə
Esclarmonde ɛsklaɾmɔ̃ːdə
Esclavonie ɛsklavɔniə
Escœuilles ɛskœjə
Escoffier ɛskɔfje
Escorpain ɛskɔɾpɛ̃
Escotais (L') lekɔtɛ
Escoublac ɛskublak
Escousse ɛskusə
Escudier ɛskydje
Escurial ɛskyɾjal
Esdras ɛsdɾɑːs
Esmain ɛsmɛ̃
Esménard ɛsmenaːɾ
Esméralda ɛsmeralda
Esnault-Pelterie ɛsno pɛltəɾi
   or eno pɛltəɾi
Esneux ɛsnø
Esneval (L') lenəval *or* lɛnəval

Éson ezɔ̃
Ésope ezopə
Espagne ɛspaɲə
Espagnol(s) ɛspaɲɔl
Espagnole(s) ɛspaɲɔlə
Espérandieu ɛspeɾɑ̃djø
Esperey (D') depeɾɛ
Esperney epɛɾnɛ
Espernil epɛɾnil
Espinasse ɛspinasə
Espinel ɛspinɛl
Espirac ɛspiɾak
Esposito ɛspozito
Esque ɛskə
Esquelbecq ɛskɛlbɛk
Esquerdes ɛskɛɾdə
Esquibien ɛskibjɛ̃
Esquilar ɛskilaːɾ
Esquirol ɛskiɾɔl
Esquiros ɛskiɾos *or* ɛskiɾoːs
Essling ɛsliŋ
Essonne ɛsɔnə *or* esɔnə
Essoyes eswa *or* ɛswa
Estaing ɛstɛ̃
Estaque (L') lɛstakə
Estaunié ɛstonje
Este (D') dɛstə
Estelle ɛstɛlə
Esterhazy ɛsteɾazi
Esternay ɛstɛɾnɛ
Estève ɛstɛːvə
Esther ɛstɛːɾ
Estienne etjɛnə *or* ɛstjɛnə
Estieu ɛstjø
Estissac ɛstisak
Estoile (L') letwalə
Estonie ɛstɔniə
Estonien(s) ɛstɔnjɛ̃
Estonienne(s) ɛstɔnjɛnə
Estourmel ɛstuɾmɛl
Estrablin ɛstrablɛ̃
Estramadure ɛstramadyːɾə
Estrebay ɛstrəbɛ
Estrées (D') detreə
Estrella ɛstrɛla
Est-Timorais ɛst timoɾɛ
Est-Timoraise(s) ɛst timoɾɛːzə
Esty ɛsti
Esvre (L') lɛːvrə
Étampes etɑ̃ːpə
États-Unis eta zyni
Etchalar etʃalaːɾ
Etcheverry etʃəvɛɾi
Étéocle eteoklə
Étex etɛks
Éthan etan
Éthiopie etjɔpiə
Éthiopien(s) etjɔpjɛ̃
Éthiopienne(s) etjɔpjɛnə
Ethuin etɥɛ̃
Étienne etjɛnə
Etna ɛtna
Étoges etɔːʒə
Etremont (D') dɛtrəmɔ̃
Étrœungt etɾœ̃
Étrurie etɾyɾiə

PRONUNCIATION DICTIONARIES | 267

Étrusque etryskə
Eu ø
Euclide øklidə
Eude ø:də
Eudes ø:də
Eudoxie ødɔksiə
Eugène øʒɛnə
Eugénie øʒeniə
Eulalie ølaliə
Euler ølɛ:r
Eumée ømeə
Eumène ømɛnə
Euménides ømenidə
Euménidies ømenidiə
Eunice ønisə
Eunoé ønɔe
Eupen øpɛn
Euphrate øfratə
Eupolis øpolis
Eurasie øraziə
Eure œ:rə
Eurélien(s) øreljẽ
Eurélienne(s) øreljɛnə
Euripide øripidə
Europe ørɔpə
Euryale ørjalə
Eurybathès øribatɛs
Euryclée ørikleə
Eurydice øridisə
Eurymache ørimakə
Eurysthée øristeə
Eusèbe øzɛbə
Eusebio øzebjo
Eustache østaʃə
Eustis østis
Euthychès øtikɛs
Eut(h)yclès øtiklɛs
Eutrope øtrɔpə
Euzet øzɛ
Évandre evã:drə
Evans evans or evã:s
Évans evã
Évariste evaristə
Ève ɛ:və
Evellin/Évellin evəlẽ
Evere evɛ:rə
Evergem evərgɛm
Évian evjã
Éviradnus eviradnys
Évreux evrø
Évry evri
Exbrayat eksbraja
Excenevex eksɛnəvɛ
Exékias ɛgzekja:s
Exelmans ɛksɛlmã:s or egzɛlmã:s
Exmes ɛmə
Expert ɛkspɛ:r
Expilly ɛkspiji
Extrême-Orient ɛkstrɛ mɔrjã
Exupère ɛgzypɛ:rə
Eybens ɛbẽ
Eyguières ɛgjɛ:rə
Eylau ɛlo
Eyreams ɛrɛams
Ézéchias ezekja:s
Ézéchiel ezekjɛl
Ezraël ɛzraɛl

— F —

Fabert fabɛ:r
Fabien fabjẽ
Fabio fabjo
Fabius fabjys
Fabre fa:brə or fabrə
Fabrice fabrisə
Fabricius fabrisjys
Fabvier favje
Fagianelli fa(d)ʒjanɛli
Fahrenheit farɛnajt
Fail (Du) dy faj
Faillot fajo
Falbaire de Quingey falbɛ:r də kẽʒe
Falcon falkõ
Falconi falkɔni
Falguière falgjɛ:rə
Falkland folklã:d
Fall fal
Falla (De) dɛ faja
Fallet falɛ
Fallières faljɛ:rə
Fallon falõ
Fallope falɔpə
Falloux falu
Falsacappa falsakap(p)a
Fanchette fãʃɛtə
Fanella fanɛla
Fanély faneli
Fanny fani
Fanon fanõ
Fantapié fãtapje
Fantasio fãtazjo
Fantin-Latour fãtẽ latu:r
Fantosme fãto:mə
Faou (Le) lə fu
Faouët (Le) lə fawɛt
Faramond faramõ
Farandole farãdɔlə
Farfouilla farfuja
Fargue fargə
Farina farina
Farnie farni
Farrenc farẽ:k
Fatima fatima
Fatmé fatme
Faubourg fobu:r
Faubourg Saint-Germain fobur sẽ ʒɛrmẽ
Faubourg-du-Roule fobur dy rulə
Faubourg-Montmartre fobur mõmartrə
Fauchois foʃwa
Fauchon foʃõ
Fauconnet fokɔnɛ
Faullin folẽ
Faulquemont fokəmõ
Faune fo:nə
Faure fo:rə
Fauré fore
Faust fo:st
Fausta fosta or fɔsta
Faustine fostinə
Fauvette fovɛtə
Favart fava:r

Favel favɛl
Favre fa:vrə or fa:vrə
Faÿ fai
Fayçal fɛsal
Fayence fajã:sə
Fayet (Le) lə faje
Fayette (La) la fajɛtə
Fayl-Billot fɛl bijo or fɛj bijo
Faÿ-lès-Nemours fai lɛ nəmu:r
Fayol fajɔl
Fayolle fajɔlə
Fé-an-nich-ton feãniʃtõ
Féart fea:r
Febvre fɛ:vrə
Fécamp fekã
Fechner feʃnɛ:r
Fédor fedo:r
Feillet fɛje
Feix fɛks
Fel fɛl
Féletz felɛs
Félia felja
Félicien felisjẽ
Félicité felisite
Félix feliks
Feltre fɛltrə
Fenella/Fénella fenɛla
Fénelon fenəlõ or fenəlõ
Fenestre fənɛtrə
Fé-ni-han feniã
Fenice (La) la fenitʃe
Fenouillet fənuje
Féraldy feraldi
Férat fera
Ferdinand ferdinã
Féréol fereɔl
Féria/Feria (De) də ferja
Fermat (De) də fɛrma
Fernand fɛrnã
Fernand Cortez fɛrnã kɔrte:z or fɛrnã kɔrtes
Fernandel fɛrnãdɛl
Fernandez fɛrnãdɛ:z or fɛrnandes
Fernay fɛrne
Fernier fɛrnje
Féroé/Féroë ferɔe
Ferrand ferã
Ferrare fera:rə
Ferrari ferari
Ferrat fera
Ferré fere
Ferréol fereɔl
Ferrier fɛrje
Ferro fero
Ferroud feru
Ferry fɛri
Ferté-Alais (La) la fɛrte ale
Fervaal ferva:l
Fès fɛs
Fête-Dieu (La) la fɛtə djø
Fétis fetis
Feuchère føʃɛ:rə
Feuillantines fœjãtinə
Feuillate fœjatə
Feuillet fœje
Feuilly fœji
Feuquières føkjɛ:rə

268 | FRENCH LYRIC DICTION

Feure (De) də fœːrə
Feurs fœːr
Février fevrie
Fexhe fɛksə
Feydeau fɛdo
Fezensac/Fézensac fezãsak
Fiamina fjamina
Fichini fiʃini
Fidelin fidəlɛ̃
Fidès fidɛs
Fidji fidʒi
Fidjien(s) fidʒjɛ̃
Fidjienne(s) fidʒjɛnə
Field fild
Fieramosca fjɛramɔska
Fieschi fjɛski
Fiesole fjɛzɔlə
Fiesque fjɛskə
Figaro figaro
Filhol fijɔl
Fillastre fila:trə
Fingal fɛ̃gal
Finistère finiste:rə
Finistérien(s) finisterjɛ̃
Finistérienne(s) finisterjɛnə
Finlandais fɛ̃lãdɛ
Finlandaise(s) fɛ̃lãde:zə
Finlande fɛ̃lã:də
Finnois finwa
Finnoise(s) finwa:zə
Finzi finzi
Fiorella fjɔrɛla
Firouz firu:z
Fischer-Dieskau fiʃɛr diskaw
Fismes fimə
Fistoulari fistulari
Fizdale fizdɛl
Flaccus flakys
Flahaut flao
Flamand(s) flamã
Flamande(s) flamã:də
Flambeau flãbo
Flameng flamɛ̃:g
Flament flamã
Flammarion flamarjõ
Flandre(s) flã:drə
Flassens flasɛ̃:s
Flaubert flobe:r
Flavien flavjɛ̃
Flavy flavi
Flaxland flakslã:d or flaksland
Flèche (La) la flɛʃə
Flécheux fleʃø
Fleix flɛks
Flem (Le) lə flɛm
Flers flɛːr
Flers (in Normandy) flɛrs
Flers (De) də flɛːr
Fleurant flœrã
Fleurette flœrɛtə
Fleurigny flœriɲi
Fleurus floerys or flørys
Fleury floeri or fløri
Fléville flevilə
Floh flo
Florac flɔrak
Flore flɔːrə

Florence flɔrã:sə
Florent flɔrã
Florentin flɔrãtɛ̃
Florentin(s) flɔrãtɛ̃
Florentine flɔrãtinə
Florentine(s) flɔrãtinə
Floreski/Floresky flɔrɛski
Florestan flɔrɛstã
Florestine flɔrɛstinə
Florian (De) də flɔrjã
Floride flɔridə
Florise flɔri:zə
Florival flɔrival
Flotow flɔtɔ:v or flɔto
Flourens flurɛ̃:s
Flüe (De) də flyə
Foch fɔʃ
Fock fɔk
Fodor fɔdɔ:r
Foix fwa
Fokine fɔkinə
Foleÿ fɔlɛj
Folie-Méricourt (La) la fɔli meriku:r
Folies-Bergères (Les) lɛ fɔli berʒe:rə
Folle-Verdure (De) də fɔlə vɛrdy:rə
Fombeure fõbœ:rə
Fondary fõdari
Fontainas fõtɛna:s
Fontaine (De La) də la fõtɛnə
Fontainebleau fõtɛnəblo
Fontenay-le-Comte fõtɛnə lə kõ:tə
Fontenelle fõtənɛlə
Fontenoy fõtənwa
Fontnouvelle fõnuvɛlə
Fontrailles fõtra:jə
Forbach fɔrbak
Forcalquier fɔrkalkje
Force (De La) də la fɔrsə
Forclaz (La) la fɔrkla
Forens fɔrã
Forest fɔrɛ
Forêt-Fouesnant (La) la fɔrɛ fwɛnã or
   la fɔrɛ fwɛnã
Forey fɔrɛ
Forez fɔrɛ or fɔrɛ:z
Forget fɔrʒɛ
Forgues fɔrgə
Formoutiers (De) də fɔrmutje
Fornarina fɔrnarina
Forqueray fɔrkərɛ
Fort fɔ:r
Fort-de-France fɔr də frã:sə
Fortunat fɔrtyna
Fortune fɔrtynə
Fortunio fɔrtynjo
Fos fos
Fossey fosɛ
Foucauld fuko
Foucault fuko
Fouché fuʃe
Fouchécourt fuʃeku:r
Foucher fuʃe
Fougères fuʒɛ:rə
Fouleix fulɛ
Foulques fulkə
Fouquié fukje
Fouquier-Tinville fukje tɛ̃vilə

Fourcade furkadə
Fourcaud furko
Fourcoy furkwa
Fourdain furdɛ̃
Fourestier furɛstje
Fouret furɛ
Fourier furje
Fourneau furno
Fournet furnɛ
Fournier furnje
Fournillier furnije
Fourques furkə
Fourragère (La) la furaʒe:rə
Fours fu:r
Foy fwa
Fra Diavolo fra djavolo
Fragoletto fragɔlet(t)o
Fragny (De) də fraɲi
Fragonard fragɔna:r
Fraigneau frɛɲo
Français frãsɛ
Française(s) frãse:zə
Françaix frãsɛ
France frã:sə
Francell frãsɛl
Francesco frãtʃesko
Francfort frãkfɔ:r
Franche-Comté frãʃə kõte
Franchet d'Esperey/Franchet
   d'Espèrey frãʃe dɛspɛrɛ
Franchomme frãkɔmə
Francine (De) də frãsinə
Francis frãsis
Francisque frãsiskə
Franck frã:k
Francmesnil frãmenil
   or frãmɛnil
Franc-Nohain frã nɔɛ̃
Francœur frãkœ:r
François frãswa
François (Le) lə frãswa
Françoise frãswa:zə
Frandin frãdɛ̃
Frank frã:k
Franklin frãklɛ̃
Frantz frants or frans
Franz (French person) frã:s
Franz (German person) frants or frans
Frascata (De) də fraskata
Frasne fra:nə
Frasnes fra:nə
Frasquinella fraskinɛla
Frasquita fraskita
Fratellini fratelini or fratelini
Fratin fratɛ̃
Frayssinous fresinus
   or fresinu
Frébault frebo
Frédégonde fredegõ:də
Frédéric(k) frederik
Fredericq frederik
Frédérique frederikə
Fréhel freɛl
Freiberg frajbɛrg
Freischutz/Freischütz frajʃyts
Fréjus freʒys
Frémaux fremo

PRONUNCIATION DICTIONARIES | 269

Fremiet/Frémiet fremje
Frénaud freno
Frescobaldi freskobaldi
Fresnay frenɛ or frene
Fresnaye (De La) də la frene
    or də la frenɛ
Fresne frɛnə
Fresneau freno or frɛno
Fresnel frɛnɛl or frenɛl
Fresnes frɛnə
Fresnet frɛnɛ or frene
Fresnoy frɛnwa or frenwa
Fresny frɛni or freni
Freud frøːd
Freund frœjnd
Fréval freval
Freÿr freiːr
Friant friɑ̃
Fribourg fribuːr
Frick frik
Fridolin fridɔlɛ̃
Friedrich fridriʃ
Friesz friɛːz or fries
Frijsh friʃ
Frimouskino/Frimousquino
    frimuskino
Friquet frikɛ
Frise friːzə
Fritelli (De) də friteli
Fritz frits
Fritzchen fritʃən or fritʃen
Frollo frɔlo
Froment (De) də frɔmɑ̃
Fromental frɔmɑ̃tal
Fromentin frɔmɑ̃tɛ̃
Fromont frɔmɔ̃
Frontenac (De) də frɔ̃tənak
Frontignac (De) də frɔ̃tiɲak
Frontin frɔ̃tɛ̃
Frosch frɔʃ
Frozier-Marrot frozje maro
Fructidor fryktidɔːr
Frugy fryʒi
Fuchs fuks
Fugère fyʒɛːrə
Fuji fuʒi
Fulgence fylʒɑ̃ːsə
Fuller fylɛːr
Fulvie fylvia
Fumet fymɛ
Funès (de) də fynɛs
Furens fyrɑ̃
Fursch-Madi fyrʃ madi
Furst/Fürst fyrst
Furstemberg fyrstɛ̃bɛːr
Furtwängler furtvɛŋglɛːr
Fust fust
Fux fuks
Fuzelier fyzəlje

— G —

Gabeaud abo
Gabin gabɛ̃
Gabon gabɔ̃
Gabonais gabonɛ
Gabonaise(s) gabonɛːzə

Gabriel gabriɛl
Gabrieli gabrieli
Gabrielle gabriɛlə
Gabroche gabroʃə
Gaël gael
Gaëlle gaɛlə
Gaëls gael
Gaétan/Gaëtan gaetɑ̃
Gaetana/Gaétana/Gaëtana gaetana
Gaïa gaja
Gaigneron (De) də gɛɲərɔ̃
Gail gaj
Gailhard gajaːr
Gaillard gajaːr
Gaillon gajɔ̃
Gainsborough gɛ̃zbɔru or gɛnsbɔru
    or gɛnzbərø
Gainsbourg gɛ̃zbuːr or gɛ̃sbuːr
Galaad galaad
Galabert galabɛːr
Galanis galanis
Galaor galaɔːr
Galapagos galapagos or galapagoːs
Galatée galateə
Galates galatə
Galatie galasiə
Galavis galavis
Galère galɛːrə
Galerne galɛrnə
Galiane galjanə
Galice galisə
Galicie galisiə
Galicien(s) galisjɛ̃
Galicienne(s) galisjɛnə
Galien galjɛ
Galilée galileə
Galiléen(s) galileɛ̃
Galiléenne(s) galileɛnə
Galissonnière (De La) də la
    galisɔnjɛːrə
Gall gal
Galland galɑ̃
Gallas (people) gala
Gallas (surname) galaːs
Galles galə
Gallet galɛ
Gallien galjɛ̃
Gallieni galjeni
Galliera galjera
Gallimard galimaːr
Galli-Marié gali marje
Gallois galwa
Gallois-Montbrun galwa mɔ̃brœ̃
Gallon galɔ̃
Gallus galys
Galois galwa
Gamaliel gamaljɛl
Gamay gamɛ
Gambetta gɑ̃bɛta or gɑ̃beta
Gambie gɑ̃biə
Gambien(s) gɑ̃bjɛ̃
Gambienne(s) gɑ̃bjɛnə
Gambrinus gɑ̃brinys
Gance gaːsə
Gand gɑ̃
Gandara (De La) də la gɑ̃dara
Ganderax gɑ̃dəraks

Gandonnière gɑ̃dɔnjɛːrə
Gandubert gɑ̃dybɛːr
Ganeça ganəsa
Gange gɑ̃ːʒə
Ganne ganə
Gantéri gɑ̃teri
Gaouri gauri
Gap gap
Garat gara
Garches garʃə
Garcia garsja
Garcia-Lorca garsja lɔrka
Garcias garsjaːs
Garcin garsɛ̃
Gard gaːr
Garde-Adhémar (La) la gar dademaːr
Gardefeu gardəfø
Garden gardɛn
Gardes gardə
Gardet gardɛ
Gardois gardwa
Gardoise(s) gardwaːzə
Gardoute gardutə
Gare de l'Est garə də lɛst
Gare du Nord garə dy nɔːr
Garéoult gareul
Garetti garɛti or gareti
Gargaillou gargaju
Gargantua gargɑ̃tya
Garigliano gariljano or garigljano
Garin de Monglane garɛ̃ də mɔ̃glanə
Garner garnɛːr
Garnier garnje
Garnier-Pagès garnje paʒɛs
Garonnais garonɛ
Garonnais(e) garonɛːzə
Garonne garonə
Garoute garutə
Garvarentz garvarɛns
Gary gɛri
Gascogne gaskɔɲə
Gascon gaskɔ̃
Gaskell gaskɛl
Gasnier gasnje or ganje
Gaspar gaspaːr
Gaspard gaspaːr
Gassendi gasɛ̃di
Gassier gasje
Gast (Le) lə ga
Gastebois gatəbwa or gatəbwa
Gaston gastɔ̃
Gateaux gato
Gatien gasjɛ̃
Gâtinais gatinɛ
Gâtine gatinə
Gâtineau gatino
Gaubert gobɛːr
Gauchet goʃɛ
Gaudin godɛ̃
Gaudineau godino
Gaule goːlə
Gaulle (De) də goːlə
Gaulois golwa
Gaultier gotje
Gaureaut (De) də gɔro
Gaussin gosɛ̃
Gauthier gotje

270 | FRENCH LYRIC DICTION

Gauthier-Villars gotje vila:r
Gautier gotje
Gauville govilə
Gava gava
Gavaudan gavodã
Gavaudan-Ducamel gavodã dykamɛl
Gaveau gavo
Gavel gavɛl
Gaveston gavɛstõ or gavɛstɔn
Gavoty gavɔti
Gavroche gavrɔʃə
Gay ge or gɛ
Gay-Lussac ge lysak or gɛ lysak
Gaza gaza
Gédalge ʒedalʒə
Gédéon ʒedeõ
Gédoyn ʒedwɛ̃ or ʒedoɛ̃
Geel gel or gɛl
Geibel gajbɛl
Gelboé ʒɛlbɔe
Gellée ʒəlea
Gélon ʒelõ
Gembloux ʒ̃ablu
Geminiani dʒeminjani or ʒeminjani
Gendron ʒ̃adrõ
Gênes ʒɛnə
Génésareth ʒenezarɛt
Genest ʒənɛ
Genet ʒənɛ
Genève ʒ̃ənɛ:və
Geneviève ʒənəvjɛ:və
Genevois ʒənəvwa or ʒɛnəvwa
Genevoise(s) ʒənəvwa:zə
    or ʒɛnəvwa:zə
Gengis Khan dʒɛndʒis ka:n or ʒɛ̃ʒis kã
Genièvre ʒənjɛ:vrə
Génio ʒenjo
Genk gɛŋk
Genlis ʒ̃alis
Gennevilliers ʒenɔlak
Génois ʒenwa
Génoise(s) ʒenwa:zə
Génolhac ʒenɔlak
Genouilhac (De) də ʒənujak
Genouillac ʒənujak
Gens ʒ̃a:s
Genséric ʒ̃aserik
Gensonné ʒ̃ɛsɔne
Gentilly ʒ̃atiji
Genty ʒ̃ati
Gentz gɛnts
Genval ʒɛnval
Geoffroi/Geoffroy ʒɔfrwa
Geôlier ʒolje
Georges ʒɔ:rʒə
Georgette ʒɔrʒɛtə
Géorgie ʒeɔrʒiə
Géorgien(s) ʒeɔrʒjɛ̃
Géorgienne(s) ʒeɔrʒjɛnə
Georgina ʒɔrʒina
Georgine ʒɔrʒinə
Géori ʒeɔri
Gépides ʒepidə
Gérald ʒerald
Gerar ʒera:r
Gérard ʒera:r
Gérardmer ʒerarme

Gerbéviller ʒɛrbevile
Géricault ʒeriko
Germain ʒɛrmɛ̃
Germains ʒɛrmɛ̃
Germaine ʒɛrmɛnə
Germanie ʒɛrmaniə
Gernand gɛrnã
Gérolstein/Gerolstein ʒerɔlʃtajn
    or ʒerɔlstajn or ʒerɔlstɛn
    or gerɔlʃtajn
Gérôme ʒero:mə
Géronte ʒerõ:tə
Gers ʒɛ:r
Gerschwin gərʃwin
Gersois ʒɛrswa
Gersoise(s) ʒɛrswa:zə
Gertrude ʒɛrtrydə
Gervais ʒɛrvɛ
Gervaise ʒɛrvɛ:zə
Gerveaux-Sabatier ʒɛrvo sabatje
Gervex ʒɛrvɛks
Gerville-Réache ʒɛrvilə reaʃə
Gervinus ʒɛrvinys
Gespunsart ʒɛspœ̃sa:r
Gessen gɛsɛn
Ges(s)ler gɛslɛ:r
Gestapo gɛstapo
Gestel ʒɛstɛl
Gesves ʒɛ:və
Gethsémani ʒɛtsemani
Gets (Les) lɛ ʒɛ
Gétules ʒetylə
Geüs ʒeys
Gevaert/Gevaërt gevart or geva:r
Gévaudan gevodã
Gewurztraminer gevyrʃtraminɛ:r
Gex ʒɛks
Ghaisne de Bourmont (De) də gɛnə
    də burmõ
Ghana gana
Ghanéen(s) ganeɛ̃
Ghanéenne(s) ganeɛnə
Ghazel gazɛl
Ghéon geõ
Ghestem gɛstɛm
Gheusi gøzi
Ghil gil
Ghiselle gizɛlə
Ghislain gilɛ̃ or ʒislɛ̃
Ghislaine gilɛnə or ʒislɛnə
Ghislenghien gilãgjɛ̃
Ghisoni gizoni
Ghÿs ʒis
Giacomelli dʒ(j)akɔmɛli
    or ʒ(j)akɔmɛli
Giacomo dʒ(j)akɔmo or ʒ(j)akɔmo
Gibault dʒibo
Gibbons gibɔns
Gibraltar ʒibralta:r
Gide ʒidə
Gien ʒjɛ̃
Giens ʒjɛ̃
Gigolette ʒigɔlɛtə
Gigondas ʒigõda:s
Gigout ʒigu
Gil Blas ʒil bla:s
Gilbert ʒilbɛ:r

Gilibert ʒilibɛ:r
Gill ʒil
Gille ʒilə
Gillenormand ʒilənɔrmã
Gilles ʒilə
Gillet ʒilɛ
Gillouin ʒilwɛ̃
Gilly ʒili
Gilot ʒilo
Ginastera ʒinastera
Gindraux ʒɛ̃dro
Giono ʒjono
Giordano dʒ(j)ɔrdano or ʒjɔrdano
Giovannetti dʒ(j)ɔvanɛt(t)i
    or ʒjɔvanɛt(t)i
Giovanni dʒ(j)ɔvani or ʒjɔvani
Giraffier ʒirafje
Girard ʒira:r
Girard-Duverne ʒirar dyvɛrnə
Girardot ʒirardo
Girard-Perregaux ʒirar pɛrəgo
Giraud ʒiro
Giraudeau ʒirodo
Giraudoux ʒirodu
Girault ʒiro
Giren ʒirɛ̃
Girette ʒirɛtə
Girod ʒiro
Giroflé-Girofla ʒirofle ʒirofla
Gironde ʒirõ:də
Girondin(s) ʒirõdɛ̃
Girondine(s) ʒirõdinə
Giroud ʒiru
Giroussens ʒirusɛ̃:s
Giscard d'Estaing ʒiska:r dɛstɛ̃
Giselle ʒizɛlə
Gisors ʒizɔ:r
Giulietta dʒuljɛt(t)a or ʒyljɛt(t)a
Givenchy ʒivãʃi
Giverny ʒivɛrni
Givet ʒivɛ
Glainans glɛnã
Glasgow glasgo
Glass glas
Glazounov glazunɔf
Glière gliɛ:rə
Glinka gliŋka or glinka
Gloria-Cassis (De) də glɔrja kasis
Glover glɔvɛ:r
Gluck glyk
Glycère glisɛ:rə
Gnafron ɲafrõ
Gnossienne gnɔsjɛnə
Gobbi gɔbi
Gobelins gɔbəlɛ̃
Gobi gɔbi
Godard gɔda:r
Godebska gɔdɛpska
Godebski gɔdɛpski
Godefrois gɔdəfrwa or gɔdəfrwa
Godefroy gɔdəfrwa or gɔdəfrwa
Godet gɔdɛ
Godin gɔdɛ̃
Godowski gɔdɔvski or gɔdɔfski
Goethe gø:tə or gœtə
Goff (Le) lə gɔf
Gogh (Van) vã gɔg or van gɔg

PRONUNCIATION DICTIONARIES | 271

Golaud gɔlo
Golgotha gɔlgota
Goliath gɔljat
Goll gɔl
Golo gɔlo
Golschmann gɔlʃman
Gombert gõbɛːr
Gomès gɔmɛs
Gomez gɔmɛːz or gɔmɛs
Gomiécourt gɔmjekuːr
Gommecourt gɔmǝkuːr
Gomorrhe gɔmɔːrǝ
Goncourt gõkuːr
Gondebaud gõdǝbo
Gondinet gõdinɛ
Gondremarck gõdrǝmark
Gontran gõtrã
Gonzague gõzagǝ
Gonzalve gõzalvǝ
Gora gɔra
Gordien gɔrdjẽ
Gordini gɔrdini
Gorecki gɔrɛtski
Gorgias gɔrʒjaːs
Gorgon gɔrgõ
Gorgones gɔrgɔnǝ
Gorki gɔrki
Gormas gɔrmaːs
Gorr gɔːr
Gossec gɔsɛk
Gosselin gɔsǝlẽ
Gosset gɔsɛ
Got go
Got(h)s go
Gotha gɔta
Gouais gwɛ
Goublier gublie
Goudard gudaːr
Goudeau gudo
Goudes (Les) lɛ gudǝ
Goueffon gwɛfõ
Gouges (De) dǝ guːʒǝ
Gouin/Goüin gwẽ
Goulden guldɛn
Goult gu
Goulue (La) la gulyǝ
Gounod guno
Gourdon gurdõ
Gourmont (De) dǝ gurmõ
Goustranville gustrãvilǝ
Goutte-d'Or gutǝ dɔːr
Gouverné guvɛrne
Gouvion-Saint-Cyr (De) dǝ guvjõ
  sẽ siːr
Gouvix guvi
Gouvy guvi
Gouy d'Arcy (De) dǝ gwi darsi
Gouzien guzjẽ
Goya gɔja
Goyau gɔjo
Grâal/Graal graːl
Grabasson grabasõ
Gracchus grakys
Gracq grak
Gracques grakǝ
Graguge gragyːʒǝ
Graham graam

Grainger grɛndʒeːr
Gramet gramɛ
Gramme gramǝ
Grammont gramõ
Gramont gramõ
Grancher grãʃe
Grande-Bretagne grãdǝ brǝtaɲǝ
Grandet grãdɛ
Grandgagnage grãgaɲaːʒǝ
Grangé grãʒe
Grand-Guignol (Le) lǝ grã giɲɔl
Grandjany grãʒani
Grandjean grãʒã
Grand-Lemps (Le) lǝ grã lẽːs
Grand-Meaulnes grã moːnǝ
Grandmesnil grãmɛnil or grãmǝnil
Grandmougin grãmuʒẽ
Grandpré grãpre
Grandrupt grãry
Grandval (De) dǝ grãval
Grandville grãvilǝ
Grandvilliers grãvilje
Grange (La) la grãːʒǝ
Grange-Batelière grãʒǝ batǝljeːrǝ
Granier granje
Grantaire grãtɛːrǝ
Granville grãvilǝ
Grappelli grapeli or grapeli
Gras gra
Grasse graːsǝ
Grasset grasɛ
Grassi grasi
Gratien grasjẽ
Grau gro
Graulhet groje
Gravelotte gravǝlɔtǝ
Gravesande gravǝzãːdǝ
Gravollet gravɔlɛ
Graz grats
Grec(s) grɛk
Grèce grɛsǝ
Greco (Le) lǝ greko
Grecque(s) grɛkǝ
Green grin
Greenaway grinawɛ
Greenwich grinwitʃ
Greffuhle grɛfylǝ or grɛfylǝ
Gregh grɛg
Grégoire gregwaːrǝ
Gregorio/Grégorio gregɔrjo
Gréhon greõ
Grémont gremõ
Grenade grǝnadǝ
Grenadien(s) grǝnadjẽ
Grenadienne(s) grǝnadjɛnǝ
Grenadin(s) grǝnadẽ
Grenadine(s) grǝnadinǝ
Grenelle grǝnɛlǝ
Grenier grǝnje
Grenoble grǝnɔblǝ
Grenoullière (La) la grǝnujeːrǝ
Grenville grɛnvilǝ
Gresle (La) la grɛlǝ
Gresly grɛli or grɛli
Gresse grɛsǝ
Gresset grɛsɛ or grɛsɛ
Gressier grɛsje or grɛsje

Gressy (De) dǝ grɛsi or dǝ grɛsi
Gretchen grɛtʃɛn
Gretel grɛtɛl
Grétry gretri
Greuze grøːzǝ
Grévin grevẽ
Grevisse grevisǝ
Grévy grevi
Grey grɛ
Grez grɛ
Grieg grig
Grieumard griømaːr
Grieux (Des) dɛ griø
Griffoni grifoni
Grignon griɲõ
Grigny griɲi
Grillet grijɛ
Grimaud grimo
Grimbert grẽbɛːr
Grimod De La Reynière grimo dǝ la
  rɛnjeːrǝ
Grindel grẽdɛl
Gringoire grẽgwaːrǝ
Griolet griɔlɛ
Griotte griɔtǝ
Gris, Juan ʒɥã gris or hwan gris
Grisar grizaːr
Grisélidis grizelidis
Griset grizɛ
Grisey grizɛ
Grisi grizi
Grisier-Montbazon grizje mõbazõ
Grison grizõ
Grittly gritli
Grivot grivo
Groënland/Groenland grɔɛnlãːd
Groënlandais/
  Groenlandais grɔɛnlãdɛ
Groënlandaise(s)/
  Groenlandaise(s) grɔɛnlãdɛːzǝ
Groland grɔlã
Gros gro
Grosbois grobwa or grobwa
Gros-Caillou (Le) lǝ gro kaju
Grosclaude grokloːdǝ
Groscolas grokɔla
Grosdidier grodidje
Grosjean groʒã
Groslay grolɛ
Grosley grolɛ
Groslier grolje
Grosmaire gromɛːrǝ
Grosne groːnǝ
Grosnier gronje
Grosperrin gropɛrẽ
Grospierre gropjeːrǝ
Grospiron gropirõ
Grosrichard groriʃaːr
Grostenquin grotãkẽ
Grosville grovilǝ
Grotius grosjys
Grouchy (De) dǝ gruʃi
Grousset grusɛ
Grovlez grovle
Gruaz grya
Grues gryǝ
Grus grys

272 | FRENCH LYRIC DICTION

Gruyère gryjɛːrə
Gruyères gryjɛːrə
Guadalajara guadalaara
   or guadalahara
Guadalena gwadalena
Guadalquivir gwadalkiviːr
Guadeloupe gwadəlupə
Guadeloupéen(s) gwadəlupeɛ̃
Guadeloupéenne(s) gwadəlupeɛnə
Guam gwam
Guardona gwardɔna
Guatémala gwatemala
Guatémaltèque(s) gwatemaltɛkə
Guay ge *or* gɛ
Gubisch gubiʃ
Guéberschwihr gebərʃviːr
Guébriant (De) də gebriɑ̃
Guebwiller gebvileːr
Guelfes (Les) lɛ gɛlfə
Guéneau geno
Guénégaud (De) də genego
Guenièvre gənjɛːvrə
Guépratte gepratə
Guer gɛːr
Guéranger (Dom) dõ gerɑ̃ʒe
Guérard geraːr
Guerche (La) la gɛrʃə
Guerchin (Le) lə gɛrʃɛ̃
Guéret gerɛ
Guérin gerɛ̃
Guéritte geritə
Guernesey gɛrnəzɛ
Guesclin (Du) dy geklɛ̃ *or* dy gɛklɛ̃
Guesde gɛdə
Guesdon gedõ *or* gɛdõ
Guesne (La) la gɛnə
Gueymard/Guéymard gemaːr
Guez ge
Guez de Balzac ge də balzak
Guèze gɛːzə
Guggenheim gugənajm
   or gygənajm
Guichard giʃaːr
Guichardin (Le) lə giʃardɛ̃
Guiche (De) də giʃə
Guichen giʃɛ̃
Guide (Le) lə gidə
Guidel gidɛl
Guilamat gilama
Guilbert gilbɛːr
Guildhall gildoːl
Guiers gje
Guilhem gijɛm
Guillain gilɛ̃
Guillard gijaːr
Guillaud gijo
Guillaumat gijoma
Guillaume gijoːmə
Guillaume Tell gijomə tɛl
Guille gijə
Guillemain gijəmɛ̃
Guillemat-Szarvas gijəma sarvaːs
Guillemet gijəmɛ
Guillemette gijəmɛtə
Guillemin gijəmɛ̃
Guillemot gijəmo
Guillery gijəri

Guillet gijɛ
Guillon gijõ
Guillot gijo
Guillotin gijɔtɛ̃
Guillou giju
Guilmant gilmɑ̃
Guimet gimɛ
Guimond gimõ
Guinand ginɑ̃
Guinard ginaːr
Guinée gineə
Guinée-Bissau gine bisaw
Guinéen(s) gineɛ̃
Guinéenne(s) gineɛnə
Guînes ginə
Guingamp gɛ̃gɑ̃
Guinon ginõ
Guionie gijoniə
Guiot gijo
Guiraud giro
Guiraudon girodõ
Guiscard giskaːr
Guiscriff giskrif
Guise (*place*) gɥiːzə
Guise (De) də gɥiːzə *or* də giːzə
Guitry gitri
Guizot gizo
Gunsbourg gœzbuːr *or* gœsbuːr
Gustave gysta:və
Gustavia gystavja
Gutenberg gytɛ̃bɛːr
Guttinguer gytɛ̃gɛːr
Guy gi
Guyana gɥijana
Guyanais gɥijanɛ
Guyanaise(s) gɥijanɛːzə
Guyane gɥijanə
Guyanien(s) gɥijanjɛ̃
Guyanienne(s) gɥijanjɛnə
Guyau gɥijo
Guyenne gɥijɛnə
Guylain gilɛ̃
Guylaine gilɛnə
Guynemer ginəmɛːr
Guyon gɥijõ
Guyot gɥijo
Guys gis
Guzman gusman *or* guzman
   or gyzmɑ̃
Gwendoline gwɛndolinə
Gygès ʒiʒɛs
Gylippe ʒilipə
Gymnopédie ʒimnopediə

— H —

Haas | as *or* | ɑːs
Habacuc abakyk
Habeneck abənɛk
Habsbourg | apsbuːr *or* apsbuːr
Hachette | aʃɛtə
Hackaert | akaːr
Hadès | adɛs
Hadji adʒi
Hadramaout (Le) lə | adramaut
Hadrien adriɛ̃
Hafiz | afiːz

Hagen | agən *or* agɛn
Hagondange | agõdɑ̃ːʒə
Hague (La) la | agə
Haguenau | agəno
Hahn | ɑːn *or* | an
Haidan ɛdɑ̃
Haillan (Le) lə | ajɑ̃
Haillicourt ajikuːr
Haïm | aim
Hainaut (Le) lə | ɛno
Haine | ɛnə
Hainl | ajnəl
Haisière (La) la | ɛzjɛːrə
Haïti aiti
Haïtien(s) aisjɛ̃
Haïtienne(s) aisjɛnə
Halanzier alɑ̃zje
Halanzier-Dufrénoy/Halanzier-
   Dufresnoy alɑ̃zje dyfrenwa
   or alɑ̃zje dyfrɛnwa
Haldat alda
Halévy alevi
Halicarnasse alikarnasə
Hall | al
Hallays | alɛ
Halle (La) la | alə
Hallencourt alɑ̃kuːr
Haller | aleːr
Halles (Les) lɛ | alə
Hallier | alje
Hallier (Le) lə | alje
Hallot (Le) lə | alo
Hallue (L') lalyə
Hallyday alidɛ
Halmont (D') dalmõ
Halou | alu
Haltière (De La) də la | altjɛːrə
Ham | am
Hamadryade amadriadə
Hamardière (La) la | amardjɛːrə
Hambourg | ɑ̃buːr
Hambourgeois | ɑ̃burʒwa
Hambourgeoise(s) | ɑ̃burʒwaːzə
Hameaux (Les) lɛ | amo
Hamel | amɛl
Hamelet (Le) lə | amələ
Hamelin amələ̃
Hamelle | amɛlə
Hamet (Le) lə | amɛ
Hamlet amlɛt
Hamoir | amwaːr
Hamon amõ
Handel/Hændel | ɛndɛl *or* ɛndɛl
Hangard | ɑ̃gaːr
Hannibal anibal
Hanniset anizɛ
Hannon anõ
Hannut | any
Hanoï/Hanoi | anɔj *or* anɔj
Hanotaux anɔto
Hanouard (Le) lə | anwaːr
Hanovre | anɔːvrə
Hanriot ɑ̃rjo
Hans | ɑ̃(n)s *or* | ans
Hanse | ɑ̃ːsə
Hanséatiques | ɑ̃seatikə
Hantaï ɑ̃taj

PRONUNCIATION DICTIONARIES | 273

Hantes (La) la | ɑ̃:tə
Harald | arald
Harang | arɑ̃
Harare | ara:rə
Haraucourt aroku:r
Harazée (La) la | arazeə
Harbaville | arbavilə
Harburg | arburg
Hardalle (La) la | adalə
Hardouin ardwɛ̃
Hardouinaie (La) la | ardwinɛ
Hardoye (La) la | ardwa
Hardy-Thé ardi te
Harfleur arflœ:r
Harismendy | arismɛ̃di
Harispe | arispə
Harlay | arlɛ
Harlem | arlɛm
Harlowe arlo or arlɔ:və
Harmande (La) la | armɑ̃:də
Harmoye (La) la | armwa
Harnes arnə
Haroué arwe
Haroun arun or arun
Harpe (La) la | arpə
Harpière (La) la | arpjɛ:rə
Harpignies arpiɲiə
Harpocrate arpokratə
Harris | aris
Harsault | arso
Hartemann | artəman or artaman
Hartmann | artman or artman
Harvard arva:r
Harvey | arvɛ
Harwell arwɛl
Haskil | askil
Hasparren asparɛn
Haspres aspra
Hasse | asə
Hasselmans | asɛlmɑ̃:s
Hasselt | asɛlt
Hassler | aslɛ:r
Hastière astjɛ:rə
Hathor atɔ:r
Hatier atje
Hatteras | atərɑ:s
Hatto | ato
Haubais (Le) lə | obɛ
Haubette (La) la | obɛtə
Haubourdin oburdɛ̃
Haucourt (Le) lə | oku:r
Haudriettes odriɛtə
Haug o:g
Haumont omõ
Hauranne (De) də | ɔranə
Haussmann (D') dɔsman
Haussonville osõvilə
Haussy osi
Haust | o:st
Haut-Brion | o briõ
Haut-de-Seine | o də sɛnə
Hauteclocque (De) də | otəklɔkə
Hautecombe | otəkõ:bə
Hautefort (De) də | otəfɔ:r
Hauteluce otəlysə
Hauterive otəri:və
Hauteville otəvilə

Haute-Volta | otə vɔlta
Haute-Voltaïque(s) | otə vɔltaikə
Haut-Karabakh | o karabak
Haut-Kœnigsbourg | o kønigsbu:r
Hautpoul opul
Hautpoul (D') dopul
Hauts-de-Seine | o də sɛnə
Haüy aɥi or aɥi
Havanais | avanɛ
Havanaise(s) | avanɛ:zə
Havane (La) la | avanə
Havas ava:s
Havel | afɛl
Havet avɛ
Havre (Le) lə | a:vrə
Hawaï/Hawaii awai or awaj
Haxo akso
Hayange ajɑ̃:ʒə
Haydée aideə
Haydn | ajdn or ajdn
Haye | ɛ
Haye (La) la | ɛ
Haye-Descartes (La) la | ɛ dɛkartə
   or la | ɛ dekartə
Haye-du-Puits (La) la | ɛ dy pɥi
Haye-Pesnel (La) la | ɛ penɛl
   or la | ɛ penɛl
Haÿ-les-Roses (L') lai lɛ ro:zə
Haynin (De) də | ɛnɛ̃
Hazan azɑ̃
Hazard aza:r
Hazebrouck azəbruk
Heath | it
Heaulme (Le) lə | o:mə
Heautontimoroumenos
   eotɔntimɔrumenɔs
   or eotɔntimɔrumeno:s
Hébé ebe
Hébert ebɛ:r
Hébertot ebɛrto
Hébraïque(s) ebraikə
Hébreu ebrø
Hébreux ebrø
Hébrides ebridə
Hébron ebrõ
Hécate ekatə
Hécatée ekateə
Hector ɛktɔ:r
Hécube ekybə
Hédé ede
Hédouville eduvilə
Hedwige ɛdvi:ʒə
Héglon eglõ
Heidelberg ajdɛlbɛrg or | ajdəlbɛrg
Heidsieck ajdsik or ɛdsik
Heifetz | ajfɛts or ɛfɛts
Heilbron(n) | ajlbrɔn
Heiltz-le-Maurupt ɛlts lə mɔry
   or ɛl lə mɔry
Heine | ajnə or | ɛnə
Heinsius ɛ̃sjys
Heldy | ɛldi
Héléna elena
Hélène elɛnə
Helenos elenos or eleno:s
Helenus/Hélénus elenys
Helffer | ɛlfɛ:r

Héliades eljadə
Hélicon elikõ
Hélie eliə
Hélinand elinɑ̃
Héliodore eljodɔ:rə
Héliograbale eljɔgrabalə
Héliopolis eljɔpolis
Hélios eljɔs or eljo:s
Hell | ɛl
Hellade (L') lɛladə or leladə
Helle (La) la | ɛlə
Hellemmes ɛlɛmə or elɛmə
Hellen ɛlɛn or elɛn
Hellène(s) ɛlɛnə or elɛnə
Hellert (Le) lə | elɛ:r or lə | elɛ:r
Hellespont ɛlɛspõ or elɛspõ
Helmond ɛlmɔnd
Helmont (Van) va nɛlmont
Héloïse elɔi:zə
Helpe (L') lɛlpə
Helsinki ɛlsiŋki
Helvétie ɛlvesiə
Helvétius ɛlvesjys
Hem (Le) lə | ɛm
Hemingway emiŋwe or emiŋwe
Hémon emõ
Hémonstoir emõstwa:r
Hénault eno
Hendaye ɑ̃dajə
Hénin-Liétard enɛ̃ ljeta:r
Hennebert ɛnəbɛ:r
Hennebont ɛnəbõ
Henne-Morte ɛnə mɔrtə
Hennequin ɛnəkɛ̃
Hennessy | ɛnasi
Hennevé ɛnave
Hennuyer (Le) lə | ɛnɥije
   or lə | enɥije
Hénoch enɔk
Henri ɑ̃ri
Henriade (La) la | ɑ̃rjadə
Henrietta ɑ̃rjɛta or ɑ̃rjeta
Henriette ɑ̃rjɛtə
Henriot ɑ̃rjo
(H)enrique (Don) dɔ nɛnrika
Henriquel ɑ̃rikɛl
Henry ɑ̃ri
Héphaïstos efaistos or efaisto:s
Hepp ɛp
Héra era
Héraclée erakleə
Héraclès/Héraklès eraklɛs
Héraclide eraklidə
Héraclides eraklidə
Héraclite eraklitə
Hérault ero
Herbart ɛrba:r
Herbault ɛrbo
Herbé ɛrbe
Herbert ɛrbɛ:r
Herbignac ɛrbiɲak
Herbillon ɛrbijõ
Herbin ɛrbɛ̃
Herculanum ɛrkylanɔm
Hercule ɛrkylə
Herder | ɛrdɛ:r
Héré ere

274 | FRENCH LYRIC DICTION

Heredia | eʁedja
Hérelle eʁɛlə
Hérelle (La) la | eʁɛlə
Herent | eʁɛnt
Hérent eʁɑ̃
Herentals | eʁɛntals
Hergé ɛʁʒe
Hériat eʁja
Héricault (D') deʁiko
Héricourt (*place*) eʁikuːʁ
Héricourt (De) (*person*) də | eʁikuːʁ
Hérie (La) la | eʁia
Hérigny (D') deʁiɲi
Hérisson (*in Chabrier's L'Étoile; place*) | eʁisɔ̃
Hérisson (D') (*person*) deʁisɔ̃
Herleroy ɛʁləʁwa
Herlière (La) la | ɛʁljɛːʁə
Herlys (D') deʁlis
Herman ɛʁman or | ɛʁman
Hermann ɛʁman or | ɛʁman
Hermant ɛʁmɑ̃
Herment ɛʁmɑ̃
Hermès ɛʁmɛs
Hermia ɛʁmja
Herminie ɛʁminiə
Hermione ɛʁmjɔnə
Hermitage (L') lɛʁmitaːʒə
Hermite ɛʁmitə
Hermocrate | ɛʁmɔkʁatə or ɛʁmɔkʁatə
Hermodore | ɛʁmɔdɔːʁə or ɛʁmɔdɔːʁə
Hermosa ɛʁmoza
Hernani | ɛʁnani or ɛʁnani
Héro eʁo
Hérode eʁɔdə
Hérodiade eʁɔdjadə
Hérodote eʁɔdɔtə
Hérold eʁɔld
Héroult eʁu
Herpin ɛʁpɛ̃
Herpinière (La) la | ɛʁpinjɛːʁə
Herrand ɛʁɑ̃
Herreweghe | ɛʁəvɛg
Herriot ɛʁjo
Hers ɛʁs
Herseaux ɛʁso
Hersent ɛʁsɑ̃
Herstal | ɛʁstal or ɛʁstal
Hers-Vif ɛʁ vif
Hérules eʁylə
Herve | ɛʁvə
Hervé ɛʁve
Hervelois (D') dɛʁvəlwa
Hervière (La) la | ɛʁvjɛːʁə
Hervieu ɛʁvjø
Héry (De) də | eʁi
Herzégovine ɛʁzegovinə
Herzog ɛʁzɔg
Hesbaye | ɛsbɛ
Hesdin edɛ̃
Hésiode ezjɔdə
Hésione ezjɔnə
Hespérides ɛspeʁidə
Hesse | ɛsa
Hettange ɛtɑ̃ːʒə or etɑ̃ːʒə
Hettich | etiʃ or | etiʃ
Hétu | ety

Hetzel ɛtsɛl or | ɛtsɛl
Heu (De) də | ø
Heuchin øʃɛ̃
Heugel øʒɛl
Heule (La) la | œlə
Heurtebise øʁtəbiːzə
Hève (La) la | ɛːvə
Héxaméron egzameʁɔ̃
Hexaples ɛgzaplə
Heyrieux ɛʁjø
Hézo (Le) lə | ezo
Hibernie ibɛʁniə
Hidraot idʁao
Hiérax jeʁaks
Hiéroclès jeʁɔklɛs
Hiéron jeʁɔ̃
Hiéronyme jeʁɔnimə
Hiersac jɛʁsak
Hilaire ilɛːʁə
Hildegarde ildəgaʁdə
Hildebrand ildəbʁɑ̃ːd or | ildəbʁɑ̃ːd
or ildəbʁɑ̃d or | ildəbʁɑ̃d
Hillemacher iləmaʃe
Hillier ilje
Himilcon imilkɔ̃
Himly imli
Hindemith indəmit or | indəmit
Hindou(s)/Indou(s) ɛ̃du
Hindoue(s)/Indoue(s) ɛ̃duə
Hinglé (Le) lə | ɛglə
Hingrie (La) la | ɛ̃gʁiə
Hinoyosa (De) də | inɔjoza
Hipparque ipaʁkə
Hippias ipjɑːs
Hippocrate ipɔkʁatə
Hippolyte ipɔlitə
Hippomène ipɔmɛnə
Hipponax ipɔnaks
Hir (Le) lə | iːʁ
Hiram iʁam
Hire (La) la | iːʁə
Hirigoyen iʁigɔjen
Hirn iʁn
Hiroshima iʁɔʃima or | iʁɔʃima
Hirsch | iʁʃ
Hirschmann | iʁʃman
Hirsingue iʁsɛ̃ːgə
Hirson iʁsɔ̃
Hitler | itlɛːʁ
Hittorff itɔʁf
Hivert ivɛːʁ
Hoche | ɔʃə
Hochfelden ɔkfɛldɛn or ɔxfɛldɛn
Hocquart ɔkaːʁ
Hocquet | ɔkɛ
Hocquincourt ɔkɛ̃kuːʁ
Hodler ɔdlɛːʁ
Hoël | ɔɛl
Hoëne ɔɛnə or wɛnə
Hœrdt | œʁt
Hoffman ɔfman
Hoffmann ɔfman
Hogneau (L') lɔɲo
Hogue (La) la | ɔgə
Hoguette (La) la | ɔgɛtə
Hoin | wɛ̃
Hokusaï ɔkusai or ɔkysai

Holbach (D') dɔlbak
Holbein ɔlbajn or ɔlbɛn
Hollandais | ɔlɑ̃dɛ
Hollandaise(s) | ɔlɑ̃dɛːzə
Hollande | ɔlɑ̃ːdə
Hollard ɔlaːʁ
Hollogne ɔlɔɲə
Hollywood | ɔliwud or ɔliwud
Holmès ɔlmɛs
Holst | ɔlst
Homais | ɔmɛ
Hombourg | ɔbuːʁ
Homécourt ɔmekuːʁ
Homère ɔmɛːʁə
Homfroi ɔ̃fʁwa or ɔ̃fʁwa
Hondschoote | ɔ̃tskɔtə or ɔ̃tskɔtə
Honduras | ɔ̃dyʁɑːs
Hondurien(s) | ɔ̃dyʁjɛ̃
Hondurienne(s) | ɔ̃dyʁjɛnə
Honegger ɔnegeʁ
Honfleur | ɔ̃flœːʁ or ɔ̃flœːʁ
Hong Kong ɔŋ kɔŋ or ɔ̃(ŋ) kɔ̃ːg
Hongrie | ɔ̃gʁiə
Hongrois | ɔ̃gʁwa or | ɔ̃gʁwa
Hongroise(s) | ɔ̃gʁwaːzə
or | ɔ̃gʁwaːzə
Honolyly ɔnɔlyly
Honorat ɔnɔʁa
Honoré ɔnɔʁe
Honorine ɔnɔʁinə
Hontan (La) la | ɔ̃tɑ̃
Hôpital-Saint-Louis ɔpital sɛ̃ lwi
or ɔpital sɛ̃ lwi
Hoppenot | ɔpəno
Horace ɔʁasə
Horaces (Les) lɛ zɔʁasə
Horatio ɔʁasjo
Horeb ɔʁɛb
Horgne (La) laʁ | ɔʁɲə
Hormisdas ɔʁmisdaːs
Horn | ɔʁn
Hornaing ɔʁnɛ̃
Hornes (De) də | ɔʁnə
Hornu ɔʁny
Horowitz | ɔʁɔvits
Horps (Le) lə | ɔːʁ
Horre (La) la | ɔːʁə
Hortense ɔʁtɑ̃ːsə
Hortensius ɔʁtɑ̃sjys
Horus ɔʁys
Hospital (De L') də lɔpital
or də lɔpital
Hostein ɔstɛ̃
Hostiaz/Hostias ɔstja
Hôtel-de-Ville ɔtel də vilə
or ɔtel də vilə
Hottento(t)s ɔtɑ̃to
Houat | wat
Hoube (La) la | ubə
Houchard | uʃaːʁ
Houches (Les) lɛ zuʃə
Houdain | udɛ̃
Houdan | udɑ̃
Houdar De La Motte udaʁ də la mɔtə
Houdeng-Aimeries | udɛ̃ emaʁiə
Houdeng-Gœgnies | udɛ̃ gøɲiə
or | udɛ̃ goɲiə

PRONUNCIATION DICTIONARIES | 275

Houdon | udõ
Houga (Le) lə | uga
Hougue (La) la | ugə
Houhou | uu
Houlgate | ulgatə
Houlme (Le) lə | ulmə
Hourdel (Le) lə | urdɛl
Hourtin urtɛ̃
Houssay | usaj
Houssaye | usɛ
Houston | justɔn
Houtmann | utman
Houville (D') duvilə
Houx (Le) lə | u
Houzée (La) la | uzeə
Hozier ozje
Huard | ɥaːr
Huascar | ɥaska:r
Huberdeau ybɛrdo
Hubert ybɛːr
Huc | yk
Hucheloup yʃəlu
Huchet yʃɛ
Hucqueliers ykəlje
Hudson ytsɔn
Hüe y
Huelgoat | ɥɛlgwat
Huet ɥɛ
Hugo | ygo or ygo
Huguenet | ygənɛ
Huguenot(s) | ygəno
Huguenote(s) | ygənɔtə
Hugues ygə
Huguet | ygɛ
Huguette | ygɛtə
Huillier (L') lɥilje
Huisne ɥinə
Hull | œl or | yl
Hulpe (La) la | ylpə
Humbert œ̃bɛːr
Humboldt (*bodies of water*) œ̃bɔlt or | õbɔlt
Humboldt (*German person*) | umbɔlt
Hume | jumə
Humfroy œ̃frwa or õfrwa
Humières ymjɛːrə
Hummel | umɛl
Humperdinck | umpɛrdiŋk
Humphrey | œmfrɛ
Hunald ynald
Hunawihr | ynaviːr
Hunéric ynerik
Huningue | ynɛ̃ːgə or ynɛ̃ːgə
Huns | œ̃
Hunt | œnt
Huntziger œ̃tsiʒɛːr
Huon | ɥõ
Huon de Bordeaux ɥõ də bɔrdo
Huppert ypɛːr
Huré yre
Hurepoix (Le) lə | yrəpwa or lə | yrəpwa
Huriel yrjɛl
Hurons | yrõ
Hurtaut (Le) lə | yrto
Hus | ys or ys
Husnot ysno

Hus(s), Jean ʒɑ̃ | ys
Hussigny ysiɲi
Hussites | ysitə
Hutin ytɛ̃
Huveaune yvoːnə
Huy | ɥi
Huyghe | ɥigə
Huyg(h)ens | ɥigɛ̃:s or ɥigɛ̃:s or | ɥiʒɛ̃:s or ɥiʒɛ̃:s
Huyot | ɥijo
Huysmans ɥismɑ̃:s
Hyacinthe jasɛ̃:tə
Hyacinthies jasɛ̃:tiə
Hyades jadə
Hyale jalə
Hydala idala
Hydaspe idaspə
Hyde-Park | ajd park
Hydra idra
Hyères jɛːrə
Hygie iʒiə
Hygin iʒɛ̃
Hylas ilaːs
Hymen imen
Hyménée imeneə
Hymette imɛtə
Hypathie ipatiə
Hypéride iperidə
Hypérion iperjõ
Hypermnestre ipɛrmnɛstrə
Hyrcanie irkaniə
Hyspa ispa
Hystaspe istaspə

— I —

Iarbas | jarbaːs
Iarbe | jarbə
Ibérie iberiə
Ibert ibɛːr
Ibos iboːs
Ibrahim ibraim
Ibsen ipsen
Ibycos ibikɔs or ibikoːs
Icare ikaːrə
Icaunais ikonɛ
Icaunaise(s) ikonɛ:zə
Ida ida
Idaho idao or ajdao
Idas idaːs
Idoménée idomeneə
Idumée idymeə
Iéna jena
Ifs if
Ignace iɲasə
Ignatiev/Ignatief ignatjef
Igny iɲi
Ikelmer ikɛlmɛːr
Île-de-France ilə də frɑ̃:sə
Île-de-la-Cité ilə də la site
Île-du-Prince-Édouard ilə dy prɛ̃ sedwaːr
Iliade iljadə
Ilion iljõ
Illiers ilje
Illinois ilinwa
Illione iljɔnə

Illyrie iliriə
Imaüs imays
Imbault ɛ̃bo
Imbert ɛ̃bɛːr
Ina ina
Incas ɛ̃ka
Inde ɛ̃:də
Indiana (*novel*) ɛ̃djana
Indiana (*state*) indjana
Indianapolis indjanapolis
Indien(s) ɛ̃djɛ̃
Indienne(s) ɛ̃djɛnə
Indochine ɛ̃dɔʃinə
Indochinois ɛ̃dɔʃinwa
Indochinoise(s) ɛ̃dɔʃinwa:zə
Indonésie ɛ̃doneziə
Indonésien(s) ɛ̃donezjɛ̃
Indonésienne(s) ɛ̃donezjɛnə
Indou(s)/Hindou(s) ɛ̃du
Indoue(s)/Hindoue(s) ɛ̃duə
Indoustan ɛ̃dustɑ̃
Indra ɛ̃dra
Indre ɛ̃:drɛ
Indus ɛ̃dys
Indy (D') dɛ̃di
Inès inɛs
Inésille inezijə
Inghelbrecht ɛ̃ʒɛlbrɛʃt or ɛ̃gɛlbrɛʃt
Ingres ɛ̃:grə
Inigo Gomez (Don)/Iñigo Gomez (Don) do ninigo gomɛ:z or do ninigo gomɛs
Innsbruck insbruk or insbryk
Innus inu
Insulinde ɛ̃sylɛ̃:də
Interpol ɛ̃tɛrpol
Inuits inɥit or inwit
Invalides (Les) lɛ zɛ̃validə
Io jo
Iolcos jolkɔs or jolko:s
Iolé jole
Ion jõ
Ionesco | jonesko or jonesko
Iopas jɔpaːs
Iowa ajowa
Iphicrate ifikratə
Iphigénie ifiʒeniə
Iphise ifiːzə
Irak/Iraq irak
Irakien(s)/Iraquien(s) irakjɛ̃
Irakienne(s)/Iraquienne(s) irakjɛnə
Iran irɑ̃
Iranien(s) iranjɛ̃
Iranienne(s) iranjɛnə
Irène irɛnə
Iris iris
Irlandais irlɑ̃dɛ
Irlandais(e) irlɑ̃dɛ:zə
Irlande irlɑ̃:də
Irma irma
Iroquois irokwa
Irroy irwa
Is is
Isaac izaak or izak or iza:k
Isabeau izabo
Isabelle izabɛlə
Isabey izabɛ

276 | FRENCH LYRIC DICTION

Isaïe izaiə
Isambert izɑ̃bɛːr
Isaoun izaun
Isaure izoːrə
Isbergues isbɛrgə
Iscariote iskarjɔtə
Ischia iskja
Isée izeə
Isère izɛːrə
Isérois izerwa
Iséroise(s) izɛrwaːzə
Iseu(l)t izø
Isidore izidɔːrə
Isis izis
Islamabad islamabad
Islandais islɑ̃dɛ
Islandaise(s) islɑ̃dɛːzə
Islande islɑ̃ːdə
Isly isli
Ismaël/Ismael ismaɛl
Ismaël-Garcin ismaɛl garsɛ̃
Ismène ismɛnə
Isnard isnaːr
Isnardon isnardɔ̃
Isocrate izɔkratə
Isola izɔla
Isolier izɔlje
Isoline izɔlinə
Ispahan ispaɑ̃
Isques iskə
Israël israɛl
Israélien(s) israeljɛ̃
Israélienne(s) israeljɛnə
Issalim isalim
Issoire iswaːrə
Issoudun isudœ̃
Issy-les-Moulineaux isi lɛ mulino
Istanbul istɑ̃bul
Istres istrə
Isturbide istyrbidə
Italie italiə
Italien(s) italjɛ̃
Italienne(s) italjɛnə
Ithaque itakə
Ivaldi ivaldi
Ivanhoé/Ivanhoë ivanɔe
Ivanowna ivanɔvna
Ives | ajvz or ajvz
Ivoirien(s) ivwarjɛ̃
Ivoirienne(s) ivwarjɛnə
Ixelles iksɛlə
Ixion iksjɔ̃
Izeaux izo

—J—

Jaboune ʒabunə
Jacinthe ʒasɛ̃ːtə
Jacmart ʒakmaːr
Jacob ʒakɔb or ʒakob
Jacobé ʒakɔbe
Jacobins ʒakɔbɛ̃
Jacobites ʒakɔbitə
Jacobs | jakɔbz
Jacquard ʒakaːr
Jacquart ʒakaːr
Jacqueline ʒakəlinə or ʒakəlinə

Jacquemaire ʒakəmɛːrə
Jacquemin ʒakəmɛ̃
Jacques ʒaːkə
Jacquesson ʒakəsɔ̃
Jacquet ʒakɛ
Jacquette ʒakɛtə
Jacquillat ʒakija
Jacquin ʒakɛ̃
Jacquinot ʒakino
Jacquot ʒako
Jade | jadə
Jadin ʒadɛ̃
Jaeger-LeCoultre ʒɛʒɛr ləkultrə
Jaëll ʒaɛl
Jagellon ʒaʒɛlɔ̃ or ʒaʒɛlɔ̃
Jahel ʒaɛl
Jaime ʒɛmə
Jakarta dʒakarta
Jallais ʒalɛ
Jamaïcain(s)/Jamaïquain(s)
    ʒamaikɛ̃
Jamaïcaine(s)/
    Jamaïquaine(s) ʒamaikɛnə
Jamaïque ʒamaikə
Jamblique ʒɑ̃blikə
Jamin ʒamɛ̃
Jamioulx ʒamju
Jammes ʒamə
Jamoigne ʒamwaɲə
Jamyn ʒamɛ̃
Jan | jan
Janacopoulos janakɔpuloːs
Janatchek | janatʃɛk
Jancey ʒɑ̃sɛ
Jane ʒanə
Janequin ʒanəkɛ̃
Janet ʒanɛ
Janicule ʒanikylə
Janine ʒaninə
Janisson ʒanisɔ̃
Jankélévitch | jɑ̃kelevitʃ
Janne ʒanə
Jannet ʒanɛ
Jansen | jansən or ʒɑ̃sɛn
Jansénius ʒɑ̃senjys
Janus ʒanys
Japhet ʒafɛt
Japon ʒapɔ̃
Japonais ʒapɔnɛ
Japonaise(s) ʒapɔnɛːzə
Jaques-Dalcroze ʒakə dalkroːzə
Jaquet-Droz ʒakɛ dro
Jarnac ʒarnak
Jarno ʒarno
Jaroussky ʒaruski
Jarre ʒaːrə
Jarrot ʒaro
Jarry ʒari
Jason ʒazɔ̃
Jaubert ʒobɛːr
Jauffret ʒofrɛ
Jaufré-Rudel ʒofre rydɛl
Jaumillot ʒomijo
Jauréguiberry ʒɔregibɛri
Jaurès ʒɔrɛs
Java ʒava
Javel ʒavɛl

Javelinot ʒavəlino
Javert ʒavɛːr
Javotte ʒavɔtə
Jean ʒɑ̃
Jean-Antoine ʒɑ̃ ɑ̃twanə
Jean-Philippe ʒɑ̃ filipə
Jean-Aubry ʒɑ̃ obri
Jean-Baptiste ʒɑ̃ batistə
Jeanmaire ʒɑ̃mɛːrə
Jeanne ʒaːnə or ʒanə
Jeanne d'Arc ʒanə dark
    or ʒanə dark
Jeanneret ʒanərɛ
Jeanneton ʒanətɔ̃
Jeannette ʒanɛtə
Jeannine ʒaninə
Jeannotte ʒanɔtə
Jéchonias ʒekɔnjaːs
Jeeper dʒipœːr
Jehan ʒəɑ̃
Jehin/Jéhin ʒeɛ̃
Jéhova ʒeɔva
Jéhu ʒey
Jéliotte/Jélyotte ʒeljɔtə
Jemmy ʒɛmi
Jenny dʒɛni or ʒɛni
Jénoc ʒenɔk
Jephté ʒɛfte
Jérémie ʒeremiə
Jéricho ʒeriko
Jérôme ʒeroːmə
Jersey ʒɛrzɛ
Jérusalem ʒeryzalɛm
Jésus ʒezy
Jésus-Christ ʒezy kri
Jeynevald ʒɛjnevald
Jeypore ʒepoːrə
Jézabel ʒezabɛl
Jezraël ʒɛzrael
Jim-Cocks dʒim kɔks
Jitomir ʒitɔmiːr
Joab ʒɔab
Joabel ʒɔabɛl
Joachaz ʒɔakaːs
Joachim (foreign person) ʒɔakim
    or | jɔakim
Joachim (French person) ʒɔaʃɛ̃
Joad ʒɔad
Joaquin ʒɔakin
Joas ʒɔaːs
Job ʒɔb
Jobert ʒɔbɛːr
Jobin ʒɔbɛ̃
Jocaste ʒɔkastə
Jocelyn ʒɔsəlɛ̃
Joconde (La) la ʒɔkɔ̃ːdə
Jodoigne ʒɔdɔɲə
Joël ʒɔɛl
Joëlle ʒɔɛlə
Joffre ʒɔfrə
Johann | jɔan
Johannesburg | joanəsburg
    or ʒɔanəsbyrg
John dʒɔn
Joliette ʒɔljɛtə
Joliveau ʒɔlivo
Jolivet ʒɔlivɛ

PRONUNCIATION DICTIONARIES | 277

Joly ʒɔli
Jonas ʒɔnɑːs
Jonathan ʒɔnatã
Jonathas ʒɔnatɑːs
Joncières ʒõsjɛːrə
Joncs ʒõ
Jongen jõgɛn
Jonquière (De La) də la ʒõkjɛːrə
Jonzac ʒõzak
Joplin ʒɔplẽ
Jordaens ʒɔrdãːs
Jordan ʒɔrdã
Jordanie ʒɔrdaniə
Jordanien(s) ʒɔrdanjẽ
Jordanienne(s) ʒɔrdanjɛnə
Josabeth ʒɔzabɛt
Josaphat ʒɔzafat
Josas ʒɔzɑːs
Joseph ʒɔzɛf
Josèphe ʒɔzɛfə
Joséphine ʒɔzefinə
Joset ʒɔzɛ
Josette ʒɔzɛtə
Josias ʒɔzjɑːs
Josquin ʒɔskẽ
Josselin ʒɔsəlẽ
Josué ʒɔzɥe
Jouatte ʒwatə
Joubert ʒubɛːr
Jouberti ʒubɛrti
Jouffroy ʒufrwa
Jouffroy d'Abbans ʒufrwa dabãːs
  or ʒufrwa dabã
Jouhandeau ʒuãdo
Jouhaux ʒuo
Jounet ʒunɛ
Jourdain ʒurdẽ
Jourdan-Morhange ʒurdã mɔrãːʒə
Jourfier ʒurfje
Journe ʒurnə
Journet ʒurnɛ
Jouslin de la Salle ʒulẽ də la salə
Jouteux ʒutø
Jouve ʒuːvə
Jouvenel (De) də ʒuvənɛl
Jouvet ʒuvɛ
Jouy (De) də ʒwi
Jovien ʒɔvjẽ
Joyce dʒɔjs
Juan ʒɥã or xwan or hwan
Juana xwana or hwana
Juba ʒyba
Jubilés ʒybile
Juda ʒyda
Judaïsme ʒydaismə
Judas ʒyda
Judas Iscariote ʒyda iskarjɔtə
Jude ʒydə
Judée ʒydeə
Judéen(s) ʒydeẽ
Judéenne(s) ʒydeɛnə
Judic ʒydik
Judicaël ʒydikaɛl
Judith ʒydit
Juif(s) ʒɥif
Juillan ʒɥijã
Juilly ʒɥiji or ʒyji

Juin ʒɥẽ
Juive(s) ʒɥiːvə
Jules ʒylə
Julia ʒylja
Juliano ʒyljano
Julie ʒyliə
Julien ʒyljẽ
Juliette ʒyljɛtə
Jullien ʒyljẽ
Jumilhac ʒymijak
Jungfrau | juŋfraw
Junius ʒynjys
Junon ʒynõ
Jupin ʒypẽ
Jupiter ʒypitɛːr
Jupiter Stator ʒypitɛr statɔːr
Jura ʒyra
Jurassien(s) ʒyrasjẽ
Jurassienne(s) ʒyrasjɛnə
Jusseaume ʒysoːmə
Juste ʒystə
Justin ʒystẽ
Justine ʒystinə
Jutra ʒytra
Jutras ʒytrɑ
Juturne ʒytyrnə
Juvénal ʒyvenal
Juyol ʒɥijɔl
Juzeau ʒyzo

— K —

Kabalevski kabalɛfski
Kaboul kabul
Kabylie kabiliə
Kaddisch kadiʃ
Kadidja kadidʒa
Kadoor kaduːr
Kahn kaːn
Kaiser kajzɛːr
Kaisin kɛzẽ
Kalahari kalaari
Kali kali
Kalman kalman
Kamir kamiːr
Kandinsky kãdinski or kãdẽski
Kansas kanzɑːs or kãsɑːs
Kansas City kanzas siti or kãsas siti
Kant kãːt
Karachi karaʃi
Karadec karadɛk
Karajan (Von) von karajan
Karénine, Anna ana kareninə
Karites/Charites karitə
Karl karl
Karnac karnak
Karoui karwi
Kätchen kɛtʃɛn
Katmandou katmãdu
Katz kats
Katzenthal katsəntal
Kaysersberg kajzərsbɛrg
Kazak(h)(s) kazak
Kazak(h)stan kazakstã
Keats kits
Keck kɛk
Ké-ki-ka-ko kekikako

Kéléyi keleji
Kellermann kelɛrman
Kelm kɛlm
Kensington kensiŋton
Kentucky kɛntyki
Kenya kenja
Kényan(s) kenjã
Kényane(s) kenjanə
Kerguélen/Kerguelen kɛrgelɛn
Kéroul kerul
Kerrieu kɛrjø
Kervigné kɛrviɲe
Késie keziə
Kessel kɛsɛl
Kharkov karkof
Khartoum kartum
Khatchat(o)urian katʃaturjã
  or katʃaturjan
Khéops keops
Kientzheim kintshajm or kintzajm
Kiev kjɛf or kjɛːv
Kiki kiki
Kilimandjaro kilimãdʒaro
Kimbolth kimbolt
Kinémacolor kinemakɔlɔːr
Kinshasa kinʃasa
Kintzheim kintshajm or kintzajm
Kirghistan kirgistã
Kirghize(s) kirgiːzə
Kirghizie kirgiziə
Kirghizistan kirgizistã
Kirov kirof
Kléber klebɛːr
Klee kle
Klein (French person) klẽ
Klein (German person) klajn
Kleinzach klajnzak
Klincksieck kliŋsik
Klingenthal kliŋəntal
Klingsor kliŋsɔːr
Klondike klõdikə or klɔndajk
Klopstock klɔpʃtɔk or klɔpstɔk
Knoks, Fort fɔr knɔks
Koch kɔk
Kochanska kɔʃãska
Kodaly kɔdaj
Kœchlin keklẽ or kɛklẽ
Koehl køːl
Kœnig køniɡ or kœniɡ
Kœrner kœrnɛːr
Kœstler kœstlɛːr
Kœtzingue køtsẽːgə or kœtsẽːgə
Koffel kɔfel
Ko-ko-ri-ko kokoriko or kɔkɔriko
Kolassi kɔlasi
Kolb kɔlb
Koltès kɔltɛs
Korngold kɔrngold
Kosma kɔsma
Kosovar(s) kɔsɔvaːr
Kosovare(s) kɔsɔvaːrə
Kosovo kɔsɔvo
Kossovien(s) kɔsɔvjẽ
Kossovienne(s) kɔsɔvjɛnə
Kostrowitsky (De) də kɔstrɔvitski
Koubitzky kubitski
Koukouli kukuli

278 | FRENCH LYRIC DICTION

Koukouma kukuma
Koweït kowɛjt
Koweïtien(s) kowɛjtjɛ̃
Koweïtienne(s) kowɛjtjɛnə
Krackenthorp krakentɔrp
Kratos kratɔs or kratɔ:s
Krauze kro:zə or krawzə
Kremlin krɛmlɛ̃
Kreubé krøbe
Kreutzer krødzɛ:r
Kreuzberg krœjtsbɛrg
Kribine kribinə
Kriff krif
Krishna/Krichna kriʃna
Kroïsos/Kroisos krɔizɔs or krɔizɔ:s
Krug krug
Kruysen krœjsɛn
Kuala-Lumpur kwala lumpu:r
Kuentz kynts
Kufferath kyfɛrat or kyfərat
    or kufɛrat or kufarat
Kunc/Kunq kœ̃:k
Kurde(s) kyrdə
Kurdistan kyrdistã
Kusnach(t) kysnak or kysnakt
Kypris kipris

— L —

Laban labã
Labarre laba:rə or laba:rə
Lablanche lablã:ʃə
Laborde labɔrdə
Laboul(l)aye (De) də labulɛ
Labre lɑ:brə or labrə
Labrit labrit
Labroca labrɔka
Lacan lakã
Lacassagne lakasaɲə .
Laclos (De) də laklo
Lacombe lakõ:bə
Lacoste lakɔstə
Lacouf lakuf
Lacroix lakrwa or lakrwa
Ladislas ladislɑ:s
Ladmirault lamiro
Ladurie ladyria
Ladvocat lavɔka
Laënnec laenɛk or laenek
Laërce laɛrsə
Laërte laɛrtə
Laethem-Saint-Martin latɛm
    sɛ̃ martɛ̃
Lætitia letisja
Lafaix-Gontié lafɛ gõtje
Lafarge lafarʒə
Lafargue lafargə
Lafayette lafajɛtə
Lafenestre lafənɛtrə
Lafeuillade/La Feuillade la fœjadə
Laffage lafa:ʒə
Laffillé lafile
Laffin lafɛ̃
Laffitte lafitə
Lafitte lafitə
Lafont lafõ
Lafont (De) də lafõ

Laforest lafɔrɛ
Laforêt lafɔrɛ
Laforgue lafɔrgə
Lagast (Le) lə lagast
Laget laʒɛ
Lagos lagɔs or lagɔ:s
Lagrange lagrã:ʒə
Laguingeole lagɛ̃ʒɔlə
Laguiole lagjɔl or lajɔl
Lagut lagy
Lahor lao:r
Lahore lao:rə
Lahoussaye lausɛ
Laigle lɛglə
Laïs lais
Laisné lene or lɛne
Laisnez lene or lɛne
Laïus/Laius lajys
Lajarte (De) də laʒartə
Lakmé lakme
Lakshmi lakʃmi
Lalande lalã:də
Lalanne lalanə
Lalbenque lalbɛ̃:kə
Lalé lale
Lalène-Laprade lalɛnə
    lapradə
Lalique lalikə
Lallier lalje
Lally-Tollendal lali tɔlãdal
    or lali tɔlɛ̃dal
Lalo lalo
Laloy lalwa
Lamartine lamartinə
Lambert lãbɛ:r
Lambiotte lãbjɔtə
Lambray lãbrɛ
Lamech lamɛk
Lamennais lamɛnə
Lametz lame
Lamoureux lamurø
Lampsaque lãpsakə
Lamy lami
Lana lana
Lancastre lãkastrə
Lance lã:sə
Lancelot lãsəlo
Lancien lãsjɛ̃
Lancôme lãko:mə
Lancret lãkrɛ
Landais lãdɛ
Landaise(s) lãdɛ:zə
Landau landaw or lãdo
Landerneau lãdɛrno
Landes lã:də
Landi lãdi
Landouzy lãduzi
Landowska landɔvska or lãdɔvska
    or landɔfska or lãdɔfska
Lanester lanɛstɛ:r
Lange lã:ʒə
Langé lãʒe
Langeais lãʒɛ
Langle de Cary lãglə də kari
Langlois lãglwa
Langon lãgõ
Langrée lãgrea

Langres lã:grə
Languedoc lãgədɔk
Languidic lãgidik
Lanmeur lãmœ:r
Lannes lanə
Lannilis lanilis
Lannion lanjõ
Lanrezac lãrəzak
Lans lã:s
Lanson lãsõ
Lanternick lãtɛrnik
Lanvin lãvɛ̃
Lany lani
Laocoon laɔkɔõ
Laodice laɔdisə
Laon lã
Laonnais lanɛ
Laonnaise(s) lanɛ:zə
Laonnois lanwa
Laonnoise(s) lanwa:zə
Laos laɔs or laɔ:s
Laotien(s) laɔsjɛ̃
Laotienne(s) laɔsjɛnə
Laoula laula
Lapalud lapaly
Laparra lapara
Lapeyrère lapɛrɛ:rə
Lapeyrette lapɛrɛtə
Lapissida lapisida
Lapithes lapitə
Lapointe lapwɛ̃:tə
Lapommeraye (De) də lapɔmərɛ
Laponie laponiə
Laporte lapɔrtə
Laprade lapradə
Lapresle laprɛlə
Laquedives lakədi:və
Larbaud larbo
Lardé larde
Larfaillou larfaju
Largentière larʒãtjɛ:rə
Largillière larʒiljɛ:rə
Lariboisière laribwazjɛ:rə
Larivaudière larivodjɛ:rə
Larnazou larnazu
Laromiguière laromigɛ:rə
Larousse larusə
Larrey larɛ
Larrieu larjø
Larrivée larivea
Laruette larɥɛtə
Laruns larœ̃:s
Larzac larzak
Lasalle lasalə
Lascaris laskaris
Lascaux lasko
Las Cases (De) də las kɑ:zə
Lascoux lasku
Lasègue lasɛgə
Lasne lanə
Lasnier lanje
Lassailly lasaji
Lassalle lasalə
Lassus (De) də lasys
Lasteyrie (De) də lastɛria
Lastours latu:r
Latarjet latarʒɛ

PRONUNCIATION DICTIONARIES | 279

Latil latil
Latium lasjɔm
Latone latɔnə
Latour (De) də latu:r
Latricières latrisjɛ:rə
Lattes latə
Lattès latɛs
Lattre de Tassigny (De) də latrə
    də tasiɲi
Laubespin lobepɛ̃
Launay (De) də lonɛ
Launer lonɛ:r
Laura lɔra
Laure lɔ:rə
Laurecisque lɔrəsiskə
Laurence lɔrɑ̃:sə
Laurencin lɔrɑ̃sɛ̃
Laurens (person) lɔrɑ̃:s
Laurens (place) lɔrɛ̃:s
Laurent lɔrɑ̃
Laurent-Perrier lɔrɑ̃ pɛrje
Laurette lɔrɛtə
Lauriston lɔristɔ̃
Lausanne lozanə
Laussel losɛl
Lautréamont lotreamɔ̃
Lauweryns lovɛrɛ̃:s
Lauxière losjɛ:rə
Lauzières lozjɛ:rə
Lauzon (De) də lozɔ̃
Laval laval
Lavallière lavaljɛ:rə
Lavastre lavastrə
Lavater lavatɛ:r
Laveaux lavo
Laveran lavərɑ̃
Lavery lavəri
Lavignac laviɲak
Lavinie laviniə
Lavoisier lavwazje
Lavoy lavwa
Lavoye lavwa
Law lo
Laxou laksu
Layolle lajɔlə
Layraud lɛro
Lazare laza:rə
Lazuli lazyli
Lazzari ladzari
Léa lea
Léandre leɑ̃:drə
Léaut leo
Lebeau ləbo
Lebedeff lɛbɛdɛf
Lebey ləbɛ
Leblanc ləblɑ̃
Lebœuf ləbœf
Leboucher ləbuʃe
Lebrun ləbrœ̃
Lecesne ləsɛnə
Lechesne ləʃɛnə
Leclair ləklɛ:r
Leclerc ləklɛ:r
Leclercq ləklɛ:r
Lecocq ləkɔk
Lecœur ləkœ:r
Lecomte ləkɔ̃:tə

Leconte ləkɔ̃:tə
Leconte de Lisle ləkɔ̃:tə də lilə
Lecouvreur ləkuvrœ:r
Lecques (Les) lɛ lɛkə
Leczinska/Leszczynska lɛgzɛ̃ska
    or lɛksɛ̃ska
Leczinski/Leszczynski lɛgzɛ̃ski
    or lɛksɛ̃ski
Léda/Leda leda
Ledoux lədu
Ledru-Rollin lədry rɔlɛ̃
Leeds lids
Leers lɛrs
Lefébure-Wély ləfebyrə veli
Lefebvre ləfɛ:vrə
Lefeul ləfœl
Lefèvre ləfɛ:vrə
Leforest ləfɔrɛ
Lefort ləfɔ:r
Lefortier ləfɔrtje
Legay ləge or ləgɛ
Léger leʒe
Légo lego
Legoëz ləgɔɛ:z
Legouvé ləguve
Legrand ləgrɑ̃
Legrenzi legrɛntsi or legrɛ̃zi
Legros ləgro
Leguay ləge or ləgɛ
Leguérinel ləgerinɛl
Leguerney ləgɛrnɛ
Lehar lea:r
Lehmann leman
Leibnitz lajbnits or lɛbnits
Leibovitz/Leibowitz lɛbɔvits
Leigh-Hunt li | œnt
Léïla/Leïla leila
Leipzig lajptsig or lɛpsig
Lejeune ləʒœnə
Lekeu ləkø
Lellaing ləlɛ̃
Leloire ləlwa:rə
Lelong ləlɔ̃
Lémaïde lemaidə
Lemaigre ləmɛgrə
Lemaire ləmɛ:rə
Lemaistre ləmɛtrə
Lemaître ləmɛtrə
Léman lemɑ̃
Lemberg lembɛrg
Lembeye lɑ̃bɛjə
Lemerre ləmɛ:rə
Lemesle ləmɛlə
Lemmens lemɛns or lemɛ̃s
Lemoine ləmwanə
Lemonnier ləmɔnje
Lempdes lɑ̃:də
Léna lena
Lenclos lɑ̃klo
Lénéka leneka
Lenepveu lənəvø
Lénine leninə
Léningrad leningrad
Lenoble lənɔblə
Lenoir lənwa:r
Lens lɑ̃:s
Lentulus lɛ̃tylys

Léo leo
Léocadia leɔkadja
Lecœna leena
Léon leɔ̃
Léona leɔna
Léonard leɔna:r
Léonato/Leonato leɔnato
Léonce leɔ̃:sə
Léon-Duval leɔ̃ dyval
Léonidas leɔnida:s
Léonie leɔniə
Léonin leɔnɛ̃
Léonor leɔnɔ:r
Léonore leɔnɔ:rə
Léopold leɔpold
Léopoldville leɔpɔlvilə
Léotard leɔta:r
Leprestre ləprɛtrə
Leproux ləpru
Lequesne ləkɛnə
Lequien ləkjɛ̃
Lerberghe (Van) vɑ̃ lɛrbɛrgə
    or van lɛrbɛrgə
Léreins lerɛ̃:s
Lérins lerɛ̃:s
Lerme (De) də lɛrmə
Lerolle lərɔlə
Leroux ləru
Leroy lərwa or lərwa
Lesage ləsa:ʒə
Lesaint ləsɛ̃
Lesbazeilles lebazɛjə or lebazɛjə
Lesbie lɛsbiə
Lesbos lɛsbos or lɛsbo:s
Lesbre lɛbrə
Lesbroussart lɛbrusa:r or lebrusa:r
Lescar lɛska:r
Lescaut lɛsko
Leschenault leʃəno or leʃəno
Leschesne leʃɛnə or leʃɛnə
Lesclide lɛsklidə
Lesconil lɛskɔnil
Lescot lɛsko
Lescun lɛskœ̃
Lescure lɛsky:rə
Lescurel lɛskyrɛl
Lesdiguières (De) də lɛ(s)digjɛ:rə
    or də ledigjɛ:rə
Lesgards lega:r or lega:r
Lésigny leziɲi
Leslie lɛsliə
Lesne lɛnə
Lesneven lɛsnəvɛ̃
Lesnier lenje or lɛnje
Lesothan(s) lesɔtɑ̃
Lesothane(s) lesɔtanə
Lesotho lesɔto
Lesparre-Médoc lɛsparə medɔk
Lespérou lɛsperu
Lespès lɛspɛs
Lespesses lɛspɛsə
Lespinasse lɛspinasə
Lespugue lɛspygə
Lesseps lɛsɛps or leseps
Lessing lesiɲ or lesiŋ
Lestocq lɛstɔk
Lestrange (De) də lɛstrɑ̃:ʒə

280 | FRENCH LYRIC DICTION

Lestrygons lɛstrigɔ̃
Lesueur ləsɥœ:r
Lesurques ləsyrkə
Leszczynska/Leczinska lɛgzɛ̃ska
   or lɛksɛ̃ska
Leszczynski/Leczinski lɛgzɛ̃ski
   or lɛksɛ̃ski
Letellier lətɛlje or lətelje
Leterrier lətɛrje
Lettonie letɔniə or letɔniə
Letton(n)e(s) lɛtɔnə or letɔnə
Letton(s) lɛtɔ̃ or letɔ̃
Leucade løkadə
Leucippe løsipə
Leuctres lø:ktrə
Leuthold løtɔld
Leuven (De) də løvɛn
Levadé ləvade
Levant ləvɑ̃
Levantin(s) ləvɑ̃tɛ̃
Levantine(s) ləvɑ̃tinə
Levasseur ləvasœ:r
Levegh ləvɛg
Léveillé leveje
Levens ləvɛ̃:s
Lévesque levɛkə
Lévézou levezu
Lévi levi
Levielli ləvjɛli
Levier ləvje
Lévis (De) də levis or də levi
Lévi-Strauss levi strɔ:s
Lévites levitə
Lévy/Levy levi
Lévy-Dhurmer levi dyrmɛ:r
Lewis luis
Leybardie (De) də lɛbardiə
Leyde (De) də lɛdə
Leygues lɛgə
Leymen lɛmɛn
Lhérie leriə
Lhéry leri
Lhomond lɔmɔ̃
Lhote lɔtə
Lia lja
Liamine ljaminə
Liamone ljamɔnə
Liancourt ljɑ̃ku:r
Liban libɑ̃
Libanais libanɛ
Libanaise(s) libanɛ:zə
Libère libɛ:rə
Libéria/Liberia liberja
Libérien(s) liberjɛ̃
Libérienne(s) liberjɛnə
Libon libɔ̃
Libourne liburnə
Libye libiə
Libyen(s) libjɛ̃
Libyenne(s) libjɛnə
Lichtenberg liʃtənbɛrg
Licinius lisinjys
Lido lido
Lidoine lidwanə
Liebermann libɛrman or libɑrman
Liebig (brand) ljebig
Liebig (person) libig

Liechtenstein liʃtənʃtajn
Liechtensteinois liʃtənʃtajnwa
Liechtensteinoise(s) liʃtənʃtajnwa:zə
Liège ljɛ:ʒə
Liénard ljenar
Liepvre ljɛ:vrə
Liers ljɛrs
Lifar lifa:r
Ligérien(s) liʒerjɛ̃
Ligérienne(s) liʒerjɛnə
Ligeti ligeti
Ligny liɲi
Ligures ligy:rə
Ligurie ligyriə
Lili lili
Lillas Pastia lilɑs pastja
Lille lilə
Lillers lile:r
Lilliput lilipyt
Lima lima
Limagne limaɲə
Limoges limɔ:ʒə
Limonest limɔnɛ
Limours limu:r
Limousin(s) limuzɛ̃
Limousine(s) limuzinə
Limoux limu
Linas linɑ:s
Lincée lɛ̃seə
Lindorf lindɔrf
Linguet lɛ̃gɛ
Linné line
Linossier linɔsje
Lin(t)z lints or lins
Liorat ljɔra
Lipari lipari
Lipchitz lipʃits
Lisbé lisbe
Lisbonne lisbɔnə
Lischen li(s)ʃən or li(s)ʃɛn
Lise li:zə
Lisette lizɛtə
Lisfranc lisfrɑ̃
Lisieux lizjø
Lisle (De) də lilə
Lison lizɔ̃
Liszt list
Lit(h)uanie lityaniə
Lit(h)uanien(s) lityanjɛ̃
Lit(h)uanienne(s) lityanjɛnə
Littré litre
Litvinne litivinə
Liverpool liverpul or livɑrpul
Livet livɛ
Livie liviə
Livourne livurnə
Livradois livradwa
Livry livri
Lizarda lizardə
Lizarabengoa lizarabengoa
Ljubljana ljubliana
Lobau lɔbo
Loches lɔʃə
Locle (Du) dy lɔklə
Locmariaquer lɔkmarjakɛ:r
Locoé/Locoë lɔkoe
Locuste lɔkystə

Lodéon lɔdeɔ̃
Lodève lɔdɛ:və
Lodi lɔdi
Lodoïska/Lodoiska lɔdɔiska
Loeb lœb
Loèche lɔɛʃə or lwɛʃə
Lœna lena
Loève-Veimars lɔɛvə vɛma:r
Logan lɔgan
Logistelle lɔʒistɛlə
Lohengrin lɔɛngrin
Loïc lɔik
Loing lwɛ̃
Loir lwa:r
Loire lwa:rə
Loiret lwarɛ
Loirétain(s) lwaretɛ̃
Loirétaine(s) lwaretɛnə
Loïs lɔis
Loïsa lɔiza
Loisne lwanə
Lombard lɔ̃ba:r
Lombarde lɔ̃bardə
Lombardie lɔ̃bardiə
Lombez lɔ̃bɛ:z or lɔ̃bɛs
Londeix lɔ̃dɛks
Londres lɔ̃:drə
Long lɔ̃
Longchamp lɔ̃ʃɑ̃
Longeault lɔ̃ʒo
Longfellow lɔ̃felo
Longin lɔ̃ʒɛ̃
Longines lɔ̃ʒinə
Longny lɔ̃ɲi
Longueil lɔ̃gœj
Longueville lɔ̃gəvilə
Longuyon lɔ̃gɥijɔ̃ or lɔ̃gjɔ̃
Longvic lɔ̃vi
Longwy lɔ̃wi
Lons lɔ̃:s or lɔ̃
Lons-le-Saunier lɔ̃s lə sonje
   or lɔ̃ lə sonje
Lopez lɔpɛ:z or lɔpɛs
Lorca lɔrka
Lorédan lɔredɑ̃
Lorenzaccio lɔrɛnzatʃʃo or lɔrɛ̃zatʃʃo
   or lɔrɛ̃zaksjo
Lorenzo lɔrɛnʣo
Loret lɔrɛ
Lorget lɔrʒɛ
Lorient lɔrjɑ̃
Lorillard lɔrija:r
Loriod lɔrjo
Lormier lɔrmje
Lormon lɔrmɔ̃
Lormoy (De) də lɔrmwa
Lorrain(s) lɔrɛ̃
Lorraine lɔrɛnə
Lorraine(s) lɔrɛnə
Lorrez lɔre
Lorris lɔris
Lortat lɔrta
Los Angeles lɔ sɑ̃ʒələs
   or lɔ sɑ̃(n)ʤələs
Lot lɔt
Loth lɔt
Lothaire lɔtɛ:rə

PRONUNCIATION DICTIONARIES | 281

Loti lɔti
Lotois lɔtwa
Lotoise(s) lɔtwaːzə
Loubens lubɛ̃ːs
Loubet lubɛ
Louboutin lubutɛ̃
Louchard luʃaːr
Louchats luʃa
Loucheur luʃœːr
Louhans luɑ̃
Louis lwi
Louise lwiːzə
Louisiane lwizjanə
Louison lwizõ
Loustot lusto
Louvain luvɛ̃
Louveigné luvəɲe
Louvet luvɛ
Louvet de
    Couvray/Couvrai luvɛ də kuvrɛ
Louviers luvje
Louvois luvwa
Louvre luːvrə
Louÿs lwis
Lovano lovano
Loyola lɔjɔla
Loyonnet lɔjɔnɛ
Loÿs lɔis
Loysel lwazɛl
Lozère lozɛːrə
Luart lɥaːr
Lubbert lybɛːr
Luberon lybərõ or lyberõ
Lubéron lyberõ
Lubin lybɛ̃
Lublin lyblɛ̃
Luc lyk
Lucain lykɛ̃
Lucas lykɑ
Lucayes lykajə
Lucazeau lykazo
Luccioni lytʃɔni
Luce lysə
Lucerne lysɛrnə
Lucette lysɛtə
Lucie lysiə
Lucie de Lamermoor lysi də lamɛrmɔːr
Lucien lysjɛ̃
Lucifer lysifɛːr
Lucille lysilə
Lucinde lysɛ̃ːdə
Lucine lysinə
Lucius lysjys
Luçon lysõ
Lucques lykə
Lucrèce lykrɛsə
Lucullus lykylys
Lude (Le) lə lydə
Ludovic lydɔvik
Lugano lugano or lygano
Lugné-Poë lyɲe po
Lugnier lyɲe
Luigini lɥi(d)ʒini or lui(d)ʒini
Lully lyli
Lumière lymjɛːrə
Luminy lymini
Lunel lynɛl

Lunéville lynevilə
Lupin lypɛ̃
Luquiens lykjɛ̃
Lurcain lyrkɛ̃
Lurçat lyrsa
Lurette lyrɛtə
Lusace lyzasə
Lusiades lyzjadə
Lusitania lyzitanja
Lusitanie lyzitaniə
Luther lytɛːr
Lutoslawski lutoslavski
Luxembourg lyksãbuːr
Luxembourgeois lyksãburʒwa
Luxembourgeoise(s) lyksãburʒwaːzə
Luz lyːz
Lyautey ljotɛ
Lycaon likaõ
Lyc(h)as likaːs
Lycomède likɔmedə
Lycophron likɔfrõ
Lycurgue likyrgə
Lyda lida
Lydia lidja
Lydie lidiə
Lydien(s) lidjɛ̃
Lydienne(s) lidjɛnə
Lyncée lɛ̃seə
Lyon ljõ or liõ
Lyonel ljɔnɛl
Lyonnais ljɔnɛ
Lyonnaise(s) ljɔnɛːzə
Lyotard ljotaːr
Lysandre lizã:drə
Lysias lizjaːs
Lysimaque lizimakə
Lysinska lizinska
Lysippe lizipə

— M —

Maar maːr or mɑːr
Maaseik mazɛjk
Maasmechelen masmɛkələn
Maastricht maastriʃt or mastrik(t)
    or mastriʃt or mastrik(t)
Mab mab
Mabeuf mabœf
Mabilleau mabijo
Macaire makɛːrə
Macbeth makbɛt
Macédoine masedwanə
Macédonie masedɔniə
Macédonien(s) masedɔnjɛ̃
Macédonienne(s) masedɔnjɛnə
Mac(c)habées makabeə
Machaon makaõ
Machart maʃaːr
Machault maʃo
Machaut maʃo
Machiavel makjavɛl
Mac-Irton ma kirtõ or ma kirtɔn
Mackenzie makenzi or makɛ̃zi
Mac-Mahon mak maõ
Mâcon makõ
Macrin makrɛ̃
Macrobe makrɔbə

Macron makrõ
Madagascar madagaskaːr
Madame Butterfly madamə bœtərflaj
Madécasses madekasə
Madelaine madəlɛnə
Madeleine madəlɛnə
Madelon madəlõ
Madère madɛːrə
Madiane madjanə
Madianite madjanitə
Madone madɔnə
Madras madrɑːs
Madrid madrid
Madrilène madrilɛnə
Mady madi
Maël-Carhaix maɛl karɛ or mɛl karɛ
Maelzel mɛltsɛl
Maës/Maes mɑːs
Maësen (De) də mɛsen
Maëstricht mastriʃt or mastrik(t)
    or mastriʃt or mastrik(t)
Maeterlinck metɛrlɛ̃ːk
Magali magali
Magdala magdala
Magellan maʒɛlã or maʒelã
Magen magɛ̃
Magendie maʒɛ̃diə
Magenta maʒɛta
Maghreb magrɛb
Maginot maʒino
Magloire maglwaːrə
Magnan maɲã
Magnard maɲaːr
Magnence maɲãːsə
Magnus magnys
Magny (De) də maɲi
Magon magõ
Magre magrə
Magritte magritə
Maguelonne magəlɔnə
Mahler malɛːr
Mahmoud mamud
Maho mao
Mahomed maomɛd
Mahomet maomɛ
Mahouda mauda
Maïa/Maia maja
Maîche mɛʃə
Maignan mɛɲã
Maigret mɛgrɛ
Maillard majaːr
Maillart majaːr
Maille maːjə
Maine mɛnə
Mainfroi mɛ̃frwa or mɛ̃frwa
Mainfroid mɛ̃frwa or mɛ̃frwa
Maing mɛ̃
Maintenon (De) də mɛ̃tənõ
Maison-Blanche mɛzõ blãːʃə
Maistre mɛstrə
Maistre (De) də mɛstrə
Maistre (Le) lə mɛstrə
Maixandeau mɛksãdo
Majorien maʒɔrjɛ̃
Majorque maʒɔrkə
Malachie malakiə or malaʃiə
Malais malɛ

282 | FRENCH LYRIC DICTION

Malaise(s) malɛːzə
Malaisie malɛziə
Malaisien(s)/Malaysien(s) malɛzjɛ̃
Malaisienne(s)/
  Malaysienne(s) malɛzjɛnə
Malakoff malakɔf
Malatromba malatrõba or malatrɔmba
Malaunay malonɛ
Malawi malawi
Malawite(s) malawitə
Malaysia malɛzja
Maldives maldiːvə
Maldivien(s) maldivjɛ̃
Maldivienne(s) maldivjɛnə
Malec malɛk
Malécites malesitə
Malesherbes maləzɛrbə
Malet malɛ
Malgache(s) malgaʃə
Malgoire malgwaːrə
Malherbe malɛrbə
Mali mali
Malibran malibrã
Malien(s) maljɛ̃
Malienne(s) maljɛnə
Maligny maliɲi
Malipiero malipjero
Malkine malkinə
Mallabrera malabrera
Mallarmé malarme
Mallet malɛ
Malleterre malətɛːrə
Mallika malika
Malmasson malmasõ
Malmedy/Malmédy malmədi
  or malmedi
Malmesbury malməsbyri
Malmousque malmuskə
Malot malo
Malouin(s) malwɛ̃
Malouine(s) malwinə
Malpassé malpasе or malpase
Malraux malro
Maltais maltɛ
Maltaise(s) maltɛːzə
Malte maltə
Malvasio malvazjo
Malvine malvinə
Mamers mamɛrs
Man Ray man rɛ
Manahïm manaim
Manassé manase
Mançanarès/Mançanarez mãsanarɛs
  or mãsanarɛːz
Manceaux mãso
Manche (La) la mã:ʃə
Manchester mantʃɛstеːr or mãʃɛstеːr
Manchois mãʃwa
Manchoise(s) mãʃwaːzə
Manchot(s) mãʃo
Manchote(s) mãʃɔtə
Mandchourie mãtʃuriə
Mandubiens mãdybjɛ̃
Manet manɛ
Manéthon manetõ
Manfredi manfredi
Mangin mãʒɛ̃

Manière manjeːrə
Manille manijə
Maniquet manikɛ
Manitoba manitɔba
Mannheim man(h)ajm
Manoah manɔa
Manoëla mãsar wela
Manola manɔla
Manon manõ
Manon Lescaut manõ lɛsko
Manouri manuri
Mans (Le) lə mã
Mansard Baillet mãsar baje
Mansart mãsaːr
Manseng mãsɛ̃
Mansle mã:lə
Mante-Rostand mãtə rɔstã
Mantes-la-Jolie mãtə la ʒoliə
Mantoue mãtuə
Mantoux mãtu
Mantovani mãtɔvani
Manuel manɥɛl
Manuelita manwelita
Manuguerra manygera
Manzanilla manzanija or mãzanija
  or mansanija
Manziarly (De) də mãzjarli
Maquet makɛ
Marais marɛ
Marancour (De) də marãkuːr
Marans marã
Maraschino maraskino
Marasquin maraskɛ̃
Marathon maratõ
Marboz marbo
Marc mark
Marcachu markaʃy
Marc-Antoine mar kãtwanə
Marc-Aurèle mar kɔrɛlə
Marceau mɔrso
Marcel marsɛl
Marcelle marsɛlə
Marcel(l)in marsəlɛ̃
Marcel(l)ine marsəlinə
Marcellus marsɛlys or marselys
Marchal marʃal
Marchand marʃã
Marche marʃə
Marchesi markezi
Marchoisne marʃwanə
Marchot marʃo
Marcien marsjɛ̃
Marclaz markla
Marcotte markɔtə
Marcoussis markusi
Marcouville markuvilə
Mardochée mardɔʃеa
Maréchal mareʃal
Maresquel marɛskɛl
Marest marɛ
Maresville marɛsvilə
Mareugheol marøʒɔl
Margaine margɛnə
Margared margared
Margaux margo
Margot margo
Margraves margraːvə

Marguerite margəritə
Mariani marjani
Marianne marjanə
Marie mariə
Marié marje
Marié de L'Isle marje də lilə
Marie-Antoinette mari ãtwanɛtə
Marie-Blanche mari blãːʃə
Marie-Laure mari lɔːrə
Marie-Madeleine mari madələnə
Marienbad marjenbad
Marienbourg marjãbuːr
Marie-Stuart mari stɥaːr
Mariéton marjetõ
Mariette marjɛtə
Marignan mariɲã
Marigny mariɲi
Marilhat marija
Marillac marijak
Marimon marimõ
Marin (Le) lə marɛ̃
Marine marinə
Mariotte marjɔtə
Maritain maritɛ̃
Maritana maritana
Marius marjys
Marivaux marivo
Markevitch markevitʃ
Marlborough (De) (person)
  də malburu or də malbru
Marlois marlwa
Marmande marmãːdə
Marmont marmõ
Marmontel marmõtɛl
Marmoutier marmutje
Marnais marnɛ
Marnaise(s) marnɛːzə
Marnat marna
Marne marnə
Marny marni
Maroc marɔk
Marocain(s) marɔkɛ̃
Marocaine(s) marɔkɛnə
Marot maro
Mârouf maruf
Marquerie markəriə
Marqueste markɛstə
Marquet markɛ
Marrakech marakɛʃ
Marrast marast
Mars mars
Marsala marsala
Marsan marsã
Marseillaise marsɛjeːzə
Marseille marsɛjə
Marshall marʃal
Marshallais marʃalɛ
Marshallaise(s) marʃalɛːzə
Marsias marsja:s
Martel martɛl
Martell martɛl
Martens martɛ̃:s
Marthe martə
Marthold (De) də martold
Marti marti
Martial marsjal
Martin martɛ̃

Martine martinə
Martinelli martineli *or* martineli
Martinet martine
Martinez martine:z *or* martines
Martiniquais martinikɛ
Martiniquaise(s) martinikɛ:zə
Martinique martinikə
Martinon martinõ
Martinot martino
Martinu martinu
Martinvast martẽva
Marty marti
Martyl martil
Marville marvilə
Marx marks
Mary mɛri
Marycinthe marisẽ:tə
Maryland mɛriland *or* marilã
Maryse mari:zə
Marzens marzẽ:s
Masaniello mazanjelo
Mascagni maskaɲi
Mascarille maskarijə
Masne (Le) lə ma:nə
Masqué maske
Massachusetts masatʃusɛts
or masaʃysɛts
Massard masa:r
Massarena (De) də masarena
Massart masa:r
Massat masa *or* masat
Massé mase
Massée maseə
Masséna masena
Massenet masənɛ
Massepain masəpẽ
Massillon masijõ
Massine masinə
Massis masis
Massol masɔl
Masson masõ
Massy masi
Mastaing mastẽ
Mastio mastjo
Mastrilla mastrija
Mat(t)hias matja:s
Matamore matamo:rə
Mataquin matakẽ
Mathan matã
Mathé mate
Mathéo mateo
Mathias matja:s
Mathieu matjø
Mathilde matildə
Mathisen matisen
Mathot mato
Mathurin matyrẽ
Mathusalem matyzalɛm
Matignon matiɲõ
Matisse matisə
Matrat matra
Matthieu matjø
Maubeuge mobø:ʒə
Maubourg mobu:r
Mauclair moklɛ:r
Mauclerc moklɛ:r
Maud'huy (De) də modɥi

Maude mo:də
Mauduit modɥi
Maugiron moʒirõ
Mauillon mojõ
Maunoury monuri
Maupas mopa
Maupassant (De) də mopasã
or də mopasã
Maupeou (De) də mopu
Maupertuis mopɛrtɥi
Maupin (De) də mopẽ
Mauprey moprɛ
Mauran morã
Maurane moranə
Maure (Le) lə mo:rə
Maurel morɛl
Maurepas morəpa
Maures mo:rə
Maurétanie moretaniə
Maurevert morəvɛ:r
Mauriac morjak
Mauriat morja
Maurice morisə
Mauricien(s) morisjẽ
Mauriecienne(s) morisjɛnə
Mauritanie moritaniə
Mauritanien(s) moritanjẽ
Mauritanienne(s) moritanjɛnə
Maurras mora:s
Maurs mo:r *or* mors
Mausole mozolə
Mauvens movẽ:s
Mauvernay movɛrnɛ
Mauzens mozẽ:s
Max maks
Maxence maksã:sə
Maxime maksimə
Maximien maksimjẽ
Maximilien maksimiljẽ
Maya maja
Mayas maja
Mayaud majo
Mayence majã:sə
Mayennais majɛnɛ
Mayennaise(s) majɛnɛ:zə
Mayenne majɛnə
Mayer majɛ:r
Mayeux majø
Maynard mɛna:r
Mayol majol
Mayotte majɔtə
Mazalbert mazalbɛ:r
Mazargues mazargə
Mazarin mazarẽ
Mazarine mazarinə
Mazas maza:s
Mazeppa mazɛpa
Mazis-Chambertain mazi ʃãbɛrtẽ
Mazoyères-Chambertain mazojɛrə
ʃãbɛrtẽ
Mazzoni madzoni
Meaux mo
Mécène mesɛnə
Meck (Von) vɔn mɛk
Mecklembourg mɛklẽbu:r
or mɛklãbu:r
Mecque (La) la mɛkə

Médée medeə
Médicis (De) də medisis
Médine medinə
Méditerranée mediterraneə
Méditerranéen(s) mediterraneẽ
Méditerranéenne(s) mediterraneɛnə
Medjé medje
Médor medo:r
Médrano medrano
Médus medys
Méduse medy:zə
Meerovitch/Méerovitch mejerovitʃ
Mégathyme megatimə
Mégère meʒɛ:rə
Méhul meyl
Mehun məœ̃
Meije mɛ:ʒə
Meilhac mejak
Meillet mejɛ
Meissonnier mɛsɔnje
Meister majstɛ:r
Meix (Le) lə mɛ
Mélanchthon melãktõ *or* melãktɔn
Mélantho melãto
Melazzo meladzo
Melba mɛlba
Melbourne mɛlburnə
Melchior mɛlkjɔ:r
Melchissédec mɛlkisedɛk
Melcthal mɛlktal
Méléagre meleagrə
Mélen/Melen melẽ
Mélesville melɛsvilə
Méliès meljɛs
Mélisande melizã:də
Mélisse melisə
Mellon mɛlõ *or* melõ
Mellos (De) də melɔs *or* də melo:s
or də melɔs *or* də melo:s
Mellot-Joubert melo ʒubɛ:r
or melo ʒubɛ:r
Melon məlõ
Melpomène mɛlpomɛnə
Melun məlœ̃
Membrée mãbreə
Memphis (*in Egypt*) mẽfis
Memphis (*in the U.S.*) mɛmfis
Ménades menadə
Ménandre menã:drə
Ménard mena:r
Mencius mẽsjys
Mende mã:də
Mendelssohn mendɛlson
or mẽdɛlson
Mendès mẽdɛs
Ménélas menela:s
Ménestrel menɛstrɛl
Menier mənje
Ménilmontant menilmõtã
Ménippe menipə
Menjaud mãʒo
Menneville (De) də mənəvilə
Menotti menot(t)i
Mens mẽ:s
Menton mãtõ
Mentor mẽto:r
Menu məny

284 | FRENCH LYRIC DICTION

Menuhin menyin
Menzel mɛntsɛl or mɛndzɛl or mɛzɛl
Méphisto mefisto
Méphistophélès mefistɔfɛlɛs
Mer mɛːr
Méran merã
Mercadante mɛrkadãːtə
　or mɛrkadante
Mercédès mɛrsedɛs
Mercié mɛrsje
Mercier mɛrsje
Mercure mɛrkyːrə
Mercutio mɛrkysjo
Mère l'Oye mɛrə lwa or mɛrə lwa
Mérentié merãtje
Mérey merɛ
Merguillier mɛrgije
Mérilhou meriju
Mérimée merimea
Merle mɛrlə
Merleau-Ponty mɛrlo põti
Merlin mɛrlɛ̃
Mermet mɛrmɛ
Mérode merɔdə
Mérope merɔpə
Merri mɛri
Merrill mɛril
Merson mɛrsõ
Mertzen mɛrtsen
Méru (De) də mery
Méry meri
Méryem de Magdala merjɛm də
　magdala
Meslay melɛ or mɛlɛ
Meslier melje or mɛlje
Meslin melɛ̃ or mɛlɛ̃
Mesmaecker mɛsmekeːr
Mesmer mɛsmɛːr
Mesmes (De) də mɛmə
Mesnage menaːʒə or menaːʒə
Mesnager menaʒe or mɛnaːʒe
Mesnières menjɛːrə or mɛnjɛːrə
Mesnil menil or mɛnil
Mesnildrey menildrɛ or mɛnildrɛ
Mésopotamie mezɔpɔtamiə
Mésopotamien(s) mezɔpɔtamjɛ̃
Mésopotamienne(s) mezɔpɔtamjɛnə
Mespaul mɛspɔl
Mesplé mɛsple
Mespoulet mɛspulɛ
Mesquer mɛskɛːr
Messager mɛsaʒe or mɛsaʒe
Messaline mɛsalina or mesalinə
Messiaen mɛsjã or mesjã
Messie mɛsiə or mesiə
Messier mɛsje or mesje
Messine mesinə or mesinə
Messonier mesɔnje or mesɔnje
Messour məsuːr
Mestadier mɛstadje
Mestépès mɛstepɛs
Mestro mɛstro
Mesvres mɛːvrə
Mesvrin mevrɛ̃ or mɛvrɛ̃
Méta meta
Métabief metabjɛf or metabje
Métastase metastɑːzə

Métaure metɔːrə
Météhen meteã
Métella metɛla or metela
Méténier metenje
Métra metra
Metternich metɛrnik or metɛrnik
Metz mɛs
Metz-Campagne mɛs kãpaɲə
Metzervisse mɛdzɛrvisə
Metzinger mɛtsɛ̃ʒe
Metzler metsleːr
Metz-Ville mɛs vilə
Meudon mødõ
Meulan mølã
Meung mœ̃
Meunier mønje
Meuniers mønje
Meurchin mœrʃɛ̃
Meurice mørisə
Meuriot mørjo
Meursac mœrsak
Meursault mœrso
Meurthe mœrtə
Meuse møːzə
Meusien(s) møzjɛ̃
Meusienne(s) møzjɛnə
Meusnier mønje
Mexicain(s) mɛksikɛ̃
Mexicaine(s) mɛksikɛnə
Mexico mɛksiko
Mexique mɛksikə
Meyer mejeːr
Meyerbeer mejɛrbeːr
Mézenc mezɛ̃ːk
Mézeray mezarɛ or mezarɛ
Mézières (De) də mezjɛːrə
Mézy (De) də mezi
Miami mjami
Miarka mjarka
Micaëla mikaela or mikaela
Michaël/Mickaël mikaɛl
Michaëlle mikaɛlə
Michaud miʃo
Michaux miʃo
Micheau miʃo
Michée miʃea
Michel miʃɛl
Michel-Ange mikɛ lãːʒə
Michèle miʃɛlə
Michelet miʃəlɛ
Micheletti mikelɛti or mikeleti
Michelin miʃəlɛ̃
Micheline miʃəlinə
Michelle miʃɛlə
Michigan miʃigã
Michot miʃo
Michu miʃy
Miclos miklo
Micmacs mikmak
Micronésie mikrɔneziə
Micronésien(s) mikrɔnezjɛ̃
Micronésienne(s) mikrɔnezjɛnə
Midas midɑːs
Midi midi
Migeot miʒo
Mignon miɲõ
Mignonne miɲɔnə

Migot migo
Miguel migɛl
Mikéli/Mikeli mikeli
Mikhaël mikaɛl
Milady milɛdi
Milan milã
Milde mildə
Milhau (De) də mijo
Milhaud mijo
Milhavet mijavɛ
Millandy milãdi
Millardet mijardɛ
Millau mijo
Millerand milərã
Millet milɛ or mijɛ
Millevoye milavwa
Milliaud miljo
Millière (La) la miljɛːrə
Milliet miljɛ
Millot mijo
Milon milõ
Milord milɔːr
Miltiade milsjadə
Mily-Meyer mili mejeːr
Mimbaste mɛ̃bastə
Mimi mimi
Mimnerme mimnɛrmə
Minerve minɛrvə
Minjoz mɛ̃ʒo
Minka miɲka or minka
Minkowski miɲkɔvski or miɲkɔfski or
　minkɔvski or minkɔfski
Minneapolis mineapolis
Minnesota minezɔta or minesɔta
Minorque minɔrkə
Minos minɔs or minoːs
Minotaure minɔtɔːrə
Minsk minsk
Minturnes mɛ̃tyrnə
Miolan-Carvalho mjɔlã karvalo
Miot mjo
Mira mira
Mirabelle mirabɛlə
Miranda miranda or mirãda
Mirande mirãːdə
Mirbeau mirbo
Mireille mirɛjə
Mirette mirɛtə
Mirmont (De) də mirmõ
Miro, Joan ʒɔan miro
Miroir mirwaːr
Miromesnil miromenil
　or miromɛnil
Misraki misraki
Mississippi misisipi
Missouri misuri
Mistinguett mistɛ̃gɛt
Mistral mistral
Mithridate mitridatə
Mitouflard mituflaːr
Mitry mitri
Mitterrand mitɛrã
Moab moab
Mockel mɔkɛl
Mocker mɔkeːr
Modène mɔdɛnə
Modigliani mɔdigliani

Modrakowska mɔdrakɔvska
or mɔdrakɔfska
Moët mwɛt or mɔɛt
Moët et Chandon mwɛ te ʃãdõ
or mɔɛ te ʃãdõ
Mogadiscio mɔgadiʃo or mɔgadiʃʃo
Mogol mɔgɔl
Mohaves mɔa:və
Mohawks mɔo:k or mo(h)a:k
Mohicans mɔikã
Moinaux mwano
Moineaux mwano
Moirans mwarã
Moisdon mwadõ
Moïse mɔi:zə
Moislains mwalɛ̃
Moisson mwasõ
Moldave(s) mɔlda:və
Moldavie mɔldaviə
Moldavien(s) mɔldavjɛ̃
Moldavienne(s) mɔldavjɛnə
Molé mɔle
Molé-Truffier mɔle tryfje
Molière mɔljɛ:rə
Molina mɔlina
Molinari mɔlinari
Molitor mɔlitɔ:r
Mollet mɔlɛ
Molliens mɔljɛ̃
Moloch mɔlɔk
Molsheim mɔls(h)ajm
Moluques (Les) lɛ mɔlykə
Molyneux mɔlinø
Momus mɔmys
Monaco mɔnako
Moncey mõsɛ
Monchablon mõʃablõ
Monclar mõkla:r
Moncontour mõkõtu:r
Moncton mɔŋktɔn
Mondonville mõdõvilə
Mondutaigny mõdytɛɲi or mõdytɛɲi
Monégasque(s) mɔnegaskə
Monestier mɔnɛstje
Monet mɔnɛ
Monfort (De) də mõfɔ:r
Monge mõ:ʒə
Mongeot mõʒo
Mongin mõʒɛ̃
Mongol(s) mõgɔl
Mongole(s) mõgɔlə
Mongolie mõgɔliə
Monime mɔnimə
Monique mɔnikə
Monjauze mõʒo:zə
Monluc mõlyk
Monmart mõma:r
Mon(n)a Lisa mɔna liza
Monnaie (La) la mɔnɛ
Monnet mɔnɛ
Monnier mɔnje
Monréal mõreal
Monrose mõro:zə
Monrousseau mõruso
Mons mõ:s
Monsigny mõsiɲi
Monsols mõsɔl

Mont mõ
Mont Afrique mõ afrikə or mõ tafrikə
Montagnac (De) də mõtaɲak
Montagnards mõtaɲa:r
Montagne (La) la mõtaɲə
Montagu mõtagy
Montaigne mõtɛɲə
Mont Aigoual mõ tɛgwal or mõ ɛgwal
Montaigu(s) mõtɛgy or mõtegy
Montaigut mõtɛgy or mõtegy
Montalambert mõtalãbe:r
Montaland mõtalã
Montalant mõtalã
Montalieu-Vercieu mõtaljø vɛrsjø
Montalivet (De) də mõtalivɛ
Montalte (De) də mõtaltə
Montan Berton mõtã bɛrtõ
Montana mõtana or mɔntana
Montand mõtã
Montaner mõtanɛ:r
Montargis mõtarʒi
Montastruc mõtastryk
Montataire mõtate:rə
Mont Athos mõ atɔs or mõ tatɔs
or mõ ato:s or mõ tato:s
Montauban mõtobã
Montaubry mõtobri
Montausier mõtozje
Montbars mõba:r
Montbazens mõbazɛ̃:s or mõbazɛ̃
Montbazon mõbazõ
Montbéliard mõbelja:r
Montbenoît mõbənwa
Mont Blanc mõ blã
Montbrison mõbrizõ
Montbron mõbrõ
Montbrun mõbrœ̃
Montcalm mõkalm
Montceau mõso
Montchrestien (De) də mõkretjɛ̃
Montcornet mõkɔrnɛ
Montcuq mõkyk
Mont Dauphin mõ dofɛ̃
Mont-de-Marsan mõ də marsã
Montdidier mõdidje
Monte-Carle mõte karlə
Monte-Carlo mõte karlo
Montéclair mõteklɛ:r
Monte-Cristo mõte kristo
Monteil mõtɛj
Monténégrin(s) mõtenegrɛ̃
Monténégrine(s) mõtenegrinə
Monténégro mõtenegro
Montépin mõtepɛ̃
Montes (in Bizet's Carmen) mõntɛs
or mõtɛs
Montespan mõtɛspã
Montesquieu (De) də mõtɛskjø
Montesquiou (De) də mõtɛskju
Mont Etna mõ ɛtna or mõ tɛtnà
Monteux mõtø
Monteverde mõtevɛrdə
Monteverdi mõntevɛrdi or mõtevɛrdi
Montevideo mõtevideo
Montez mõtɛ:z or mõtɛs
Montézuma/Montezuma mõtezyma
Montfaucon mõfokõ

Montferrand mõfɛrã
Montfleury mõflœri
Montfort mõfɔ:r
Montfortain (De) də mõfortɛ̃
Montgelas mõʒəla
Montgeron mõʒərõ
Mont Gibel mõ ʒibɛl
Montgiscard mõʒiska:r
Montglas (De) də mõgla
Montgolfier mõgɔlfje
Monthabor mõtabɔ:r
Mont Hécla mõ ekla or mõ tekla
Montherland (De) də mõtɛrlã
Montholon (De) də mõtɔlõ
Mont Ida mõ ida or mõ tida
Montigny mõtiɲi
Montils (Les) lɛ mõti
Montjau (De) də mõʒo
Montlhérie mõleriə
Montlosier mõlozje
Montlouis mõlwi
Montluc mõlyk
Montluçon mõlysõ
Montmagny mõmaɲi
Montmajour mõmaʒu:r
Montmarault mõmaro
Montmart mõma:r
Montmartin mõmartɛ̃
Montmartre mõmartrə
Montmartrois mõmartrwa
or mõmartrwa
Montmartroise(s) mõmartrwa:zə
or mõmartrwa:zə
Montmaur mõmɔ:r
Montmédy mõmedi
Montmoreau mõmɔro
Montmorency mõmɔrãsi
Montmorillon mõmɔrijõ
Montmort mõmɔ:r
Montmorin-Saint-Hérem (De)
də mõmɔrɛ̃ sɛ̃ terɛm
Mont Œta mõ eta or mõ teta
Montoire mõtwa:rə
Montolieu mõtɔljø
Montolivet mõtɔlivɛ
Mont Olympe mõ ɔlɛ̃:pə or mõ tɔlɛ̃:pə
Montorgueil mõtɔrgœj
Montpaon mõpaõ
Montparnasse mõparna:sə
or mõparnasə
Montpellier mõpəlje or mõpɛlje
Montpensier (De) də mõpãsje
Montrachet mõraʃɛ
Montréal mõreal
Montredon mõrədõ
Montréjeau mõtreʒo or mõreʒo
Montrésor mõtrezo:r
Montret mõtrɛ
Montreuil mõtrœj
Montreux mõtrø
Montrevault mõtrəvo
Montrevel mõrəvɛl
Montrichard mõtriʃa:r
Montriond mõtriõ or mõrjõ
Montrond mõrõ
Montrose (person) mõro:zə
Montrose (place) mõtro:zə

286 | FRENCH LYRIC DICTION

Montrouge mõɾu:ʒə
Mont-Royal mõ ɾwajal
Mont Saint-Michel mõ sɛ̃ miʃɛl
Montserrat mõsɛɾa
Montsouris mõsuɾi
Monvel mõvɛl
Monza (De) də mõza or də mondza
Monzie (De) də mõziə
Moore mu:ɾ or mɔ:ɾ
Moralès mɔɾalɛs
Moralez mɔɾale:z or mɔɾalɛs
Morand mɔɾã
Morave(s) mɔɾa:və
Moravie mɔɾaviə
Morax mɔɾaks
Morbihan mɔɾbiã
Morbihannais mɔɾibanɛ
Morbihannaise(s) mɔɾibanɛ:zə
Morcenx mɔɾsɛ̃:s
Morcerf (De) də mɔɾse:ɾ
Moréas mɔɾea:s
Moreau mɔɾo
Moreau-Febvre mɔɾo fɛ:vɾə
Moreau-Sainti mɔɾo sɛ̃ti
Morel mɔɾɛl
Morel-Retz mɔɾɛl ɾɛ or mɔɾɛl ɾɛs
Morellet mɔɾɛle or mɔɾele
Moreno mɔɾeno
Morère mɔɾɛ:ɾə
Mores mɔ:ɾə
Moret mɔɾɛ
Moretti mɔɾɛt(t)i
Morez mɔɾe
Morfontaine mɔɾfõtɛnə
Morgane mɔɾganə
Morgat mɔɾga
Moriah mɔɾja
Morice mɔɾisə
Morin mɔɾɛ̃
Morini mɔɾini
Morisot mɔɾizo
Morlaas mɔɾla:s
Morlaix mɔɾlɛ
Morlanwelz mɔɾlãwe
Morlier mɔɾlje
Morlot mɔɾlo
Mornal mɔɾnal
Morny (De) də mɔɾni
Morosaglia mɔɾosalja
Morphée mɔɾfeə
Mortagne-au-Perche mɔɾta ɲo peɾʃə
Mortier mɔɾtje
Morus mɔɾys
Morvan mɔɾvã
Morvins mɔɾvɛ̃
Moryn mɔɾɛ̃
Moscou mɔsku
Moscovite(s) mɔskovitə
Mosellan mozɛlã or mɔzɛlã
Mosellane(s) mozɛlanə or mɔzɛlanə
Moselle mozɛlə or mɔzɛlə
Mosnac monak
Mossoul mɔsul
Mothe-Houdancour (La) la mɔ tudãku:ɾ
Mothe Le Vayer (La) la mɔtə lə vaje

Motte (De La) də la mɔtə
Motte-Servolex (La) la mɔtə sɛɾvɔlɛks
Motteville mɔtəvilə
Moucheron muʃəɾõ
Mouchez muʃe or muʃe:z
Moulié mulje
Mouliérat muljeɾa
Moulin mulɛ̃
Moulinié mulinje
Moulins mulɛ̃
Mouloudji muludʒi
Mounet-Sully munɛ syli
Mourenx muɾɛ̃:s
Mouret muɾɛ
Mouric muɾik
Mourzouk muɾzuk
Mousmé musme
Mousnereau munəɾo
Moussol musɔl
Moussorgsky musɔrski
Moussoulens musulɛ̃:s
Moustier mustje or mutje
Moustiers mustje or mutje
Moustoir mustwa:ɾ
Moÿ mɔi
Moyen-Orient mwaje nɔɾjã
Moÿse mɔi:zə
Mozambicain(s) mozãbikɛ̃ or mɔzãbikɛ̃
Mozambicaine(s) mozãbikenə or mɔzãbikenə
Mozambique mozãbikə or mɔzãbikə
Mozart mɔza:ɾ
Mule mylə
Mulhouse mylu:zə
Muller mylɛ:ɾ
Mumm mum or mœm
Munch/Münch mynʃ
Munich mynik
Münster/Munster mynstɛ:ɾ
Munt (De) də mynt
Murail myɾaj
Murano myɾano
Murat myɾa
Muratore myɾato:ɾə
Murbach muɾbak
Murcie myɾsiə
Mur-de-Barrez myɾ də baɾɛ:z or myɾ də baɾɛs
Muret myɾɛ
Murger myɾʒe:ɾ
Murillo myɾijo
Musard myza:ɾ
Muscadelle myskadɛlə
Muscat myska
Musigny myziɲi
Musin myzɛ̃
Musnier mynje
Musset (De) də mysɛ
Musulman(s) myzylmã
Musulmane(s) myzylmanə
Musy myzi
Mutzig mutsig
Myanmar mjanma:ɾ

Myanmarais mjanmaɾɛ
Myanmaraise(s) mjanmaɾɛ:zə
Mycènes misɛnə
Mylio miljo
Myriel miɾjɛl
Myrmidon miɾmidõ
Myrtale miɾtalə
Myrtil miɾtil
Mysène mizɛnə
Mytis mitis

— N —

Nabis nabis
Nabuchodonosor nabykɔdɔnɔzɔ:ɾ
Nadar nada:ɾ
Nadia nadja
Nadir nadi:ɾ
Nagasaki nagazaki
Nagoya nagɔja
Nahandove nahandɔ:və
Nahum naɔm
Naïade najadə
Nailloux naju
Nairobi najɾɔbi or neɾɔbi
Naïs nais
Najac naʒak
Nâkamtî nakamti
Namibie namibiə
Namibien(s) namibjɛ̃
Namibienne(s) namibjɛnə
Nancy nãsi
Nangis (De) də nãʒi
Nankin nãkɛ̃
Nan-King nan kiŋ
Nan(n)ette nanɛtə
Nanny nani
Nanphie nãfiə
Nansouty nãsuti or nãzuti
Nanterre nãtɛ:ɾə
Nantes nã:tə
Nantier nãtje
Nantier-Didiée nãtje didjeə
Nantua nãtɥa
Naouri nauɾi
Naours nau:ɾ
Naples naplə
Napoléon napɔleõ
Napolitain(s) napɔlitɛ̃
Napolitaine(s) napɔlitɛnə
Narbal naɾbal
Narbonne naɾbɔnə
Narcisse naɾsisə
Narçon naɾsõ
Nardin naɾdɛ̃
Narval naɾval
Naskapis naskapi
Natchez (Les) lɛ natʃe:z
Nat(h)alie nataliə
Nathan natã
Nathanaël natanaɛl
Nault no
Nauplie nopliə
Navajos/Navahos nava(h)o or navaʒo
Navarrais navaɾɛ

PRONUNCIATION DICTIONARIES | 287

Navarraise(s) navaʁɛ:zə
Navarre navaːʁə
Navarrenx navaʁɛ̃:s
Naya naja
Nazaréen(s) nazaʁeɛ̃
Nazaréenne(s) nazaʁeɛnə
Nazareth nazaʁɛt
Néarque neaʁkə
Nebraska nebʁaska
Necker nɛkɛːʁ
Nectoux nɛktu
Néère neɛːʁə
Néerlandais neɛʁlɑ̃dɛ
Néerlandaise(s) neɛʁlɑ̃dɛ:zə
Négrette negʁɛtə
Négrier negʁie
Néhémie neemiə
Nell nɛl
Nélusko/Nelusco nelysko
Néméa nemea
Némésis nemezis
Némirovsky nemiʁofski
Nemours nəmuːʁ
Nemrod nɛmʁod
Néoptolème neoptɔlɛmə
Néo-Zélandais neo zelɑ̃dɛ
   or neo zelɑ̃dɛ
Néo-Zélandaise(s) neo zelɑ̃dɛ:zə
   or neo zelɑ̃dɛ:zə
Népal nepal
Népalais nepalɛ
Népalaise(s) nepalɛ:zə
Neptune nɛptynə
Néqueçaur nekəsɔːʁ
Nérac neʁak
Nérée neʁeə
Néréides neʁeidə
Nérine neʁinə
Néris neʁis
Néron neʁõ
Nerval (De) də nɛʁval
Nervil nɛʁvil
Nescafé nɛskafe
Nesle nɛlə
Nesmond nemõ or nɛmõ
Nesmy nemi or nɛmi
Nespoulous nɛspulus
Ness, Loch lɔk nɛs
Nessir nesiːʁ or nesiːʁ
Nestor nɛstɔːʁ
Neufbourg (Le) lə nøbuːʁ
Neuf-Brisach nøbʁizak
Neufchâteau nøʃato
Neufchâtel nøʃatɛl
Neufvilles nøvilə
Neuilly nœji
Neuilly-sur-Seine nœji syʁ sɛnə
Neumann nœjman or nøman
Neunkirchen nœjnkiʁʃən
   or nønkiʁʃən
Neustadt nœjʃtat or nøstat
Neustrie nøstʁiə
Neuville nøvilə
Neuwiller nœjviːʁ or nøviːʁ
Néva neva
Nevada nevada
Nevers nəvɛːʁ

Neveu nəvø
Neveux nəvø
New Delhi nju dɛli
New Hampshire nju | ɑ̃pʃœːʁ
   or nju | ampʃœːʁ
New Jersey nju ʒɛʁzɛ
New York nu jɔʁk
Newcastle njukas(t)oel
Newton njutɔn
Ney nɛ
Nézet-Séguin nezɛ segɛ̃
Niagara njagaʁa
Nibelle nibɛlə
Nicandre nikɑ̃:dʁə
Nicaragua nikaʁagwa
Nicaraguayen(s) nikaʁagwajɛ̃
   or nikaʁagwɛjɛ̃
Nicaraguayenne(s) nikaʁagwajɛnə
   or nikaʁagwɛjɛnə
Nice nisə
Nicéphore nisefɔːʁə
Nicias nisjaːs
Nicklausse niklo:sə or niklaws
Nicodème nikodɛmə
Nicolas nikɔla
Nicole nikɔlə
Nicolet nikɔlɛ
Nicolette nikɔlɛtə
Nicolini nikolini
Nicomède nikomɛdə
Nicopolis nikopolis
Nicot niko
Nicou niku
Niédermeyer njedɛʁmɛjeːʁ
Niedermorschwihr nidɛʁmɔʁʃviːʁ
Niedermorschwiller nidɛʁmɔʁʃvileːʁ
Niel njɛl
Nietzsche nitʃə
Nièvre njɛ:vʁə
Niger niʒɛːʁ
Nigérgiane(s) niʒeʁjanə
Nigeria/Nigéria niʒeʁja
Nigérian(s) niʒeʁjɑ̃
Nigérien(s) niʒeʁjɛ̃
Nigérienne(s) niʒeʁjɛnə
Nijinsky niʒinski
Nil nil
Nilakantha nilakɑ̃ta
Nilsson nilson
Nîmes nimə
Nimidoff nimidof
Nin nin
Nina nina
Ninetta ninɛt(t)a
Ninette ninɛtə
Ninon ninõ
Niobé njobe
Niort njɔːʁ
Nippon nipõ
Niquet nikɛ
Niquette nikɛtə
Nisita nizita
Nitocris nitɔkʁis
Nivard nivaːʁ
Nivelle nivɛlə
Nivernais nivɛʁnɛ
Nivernaise(s) nivɛʁnɛ:zə

Nivette nivɛtə
Nivillers nivileːʁ or nivile
Nixe niksə
Noailles (De) də nwa:jə
Nodier nodje
Noé noe
Noël noɛl
Noémi/Noëmi noemi
Noémie/Noëmie noemiə
Nœux nø
Nogent noʒɑ̃
Nogent-le-Rotrou noʒɑ̃ lə ʁotʁu
Nogent-sur-Marne noʒɑ̃ syʁ maʁnə
Nogent-sur-Seine noʒɑ̃ syʁ sɛnə
Noguera/Noguéra nogeʁa
Nohain noɛ̃
Noilhan nwajɑ̃
Noir nwaːʁ
Noiret nwaʁɛ
Nolhac nolak
Nontron nõtʁõ
Noraïme noʁaimə
Nord noːʁ
Nord-Africain(s) no ʁafʁikɛ̃
Nord-Africaine(s) no ʁafʁikɛnə
Nord-Américain no ʁameʁikɛ̃
Nord-Américaine(s) no ʁameʁikɛnə
Nordau noʁdo
Nordausques noʁdo:skə
Nord-Coréen(s) noʁ koʁeɛ̃
Nord-Coréenne(s) noʁ koʁeɛnə
Nordique noʁdikə
Nordiste(s) noʁdistə
Noré noʁe
Norfolk noʁfolk
Noriac noʁjak
Normand noʁmɑ̃
Normandie noʁmɑ̃diə
Norrent noʁɑ̃
Northumberland noʁtœmbɛʁlɑ̃:d
   or noʁtõbɛʁlɑ̃
Norvège noʁvɛːʒə
Norvégien(s) noʁvezjɛ̃
Norvégienne(s) noʁvezjɛnə
Norvins noʁvɛ̃
Nostang nostɑ̃
Nostre (Le) lə noːtʁə
Nota nota
Noté note
Notre-Dame notʁə damə
Nottingham notiŋgam
Notti-Pagès noti paʒɛs
Nouakchott nwakʃot
Nougaro nugaʁo
Nouguès nugɛs
Nouméa numea
Nourabad nuʁabad
Nouradin nuʁadɛ̃
Nour-Eddin nu ʁedin
Noureïev nuʁejef
Nourrit nuʁi
Nouveau-Brunswick nuvo bʁonzwik
   or nuvo bʁœnswik
Nouveau-Mexique nuvo mɛksikə
Nouvelle-Angleterre nuvɛ lɑ̃glɛtɛ:ʁə
Nouvelle-Calédonie nuvɛlə kaledoniə
Nouvelle-Écosse nuvɛ lekosə

288 | FRENCH LYRIC DICTION

Nouvelle-Galle du Sud nuvɛlə galə dy syd
Nouvelle-Guinée nuvɛlə ginɛə
Nouvelle-Orléans nuvɛ lɔrleã
Nouvelle-Zélande nuvɛlə zelã:də
Noverre nɔvɛ:rə
Noyers (C France) nwajɛ:r
Noyers (S France) nwaje
Noyon nwajõ
Nubie nybiə
Nubien(s) nybjɛ̃
Nubienne(s) nybjɛnə
Nucingen nysɛ̃ʒɛn or nysiŋgɛn
Nueil nɥɛj
Nuits nɥi
Nuits-Saint-Georges nɥi sɛ̃ ʒɔrʒə
Nuitter nɥitɛ:r
Numa nyma
Numérien nymerjɛ̃
Numide nymidə
Numidie nymidiə
Nuncq nœ̃:k
Nuremberg nyrɛ̃bɛ:r
Nussy nysi
Nyons njõ:s

— O —

Oasis ɔazis
Obernai ɔbɛrnɛ
Obéron ɔberõ
Oberth (D') dɔbɛrt
Oberthal ɔbɛrtal or ɔbɛrtal
Obin ɔbɛ̃
Oc ɔk
Ocatvie ɔktaviə
Occident ɔksidã
Occitane (L') lɔksitanə
Occitanie ɔksitaniə
Océan ɔseã
Océane ɔseanə
Océanides ɔseanidə
Ochozias ɔkozja:s
Ochsé ɔkse
Octaïr ɔktai:r
Octave ɔkta:və
Octavie ɔktaviə
Octavien ɔktavjɛ̃
Odéon ɔdeõ
Oderen ɔdərɛn
Odessa ɔdɛsa or ɔdesa
Odet ɔde
Odette ɔdɛtə
Odile ɔdilə
Odin ɔdɛ̃
Odoacre ɔdɔakrə
Œdipe edipə
Œnone enɔnə
Œser øzɛ:r
Oex/Oëx ɔɛ
Offenbach ɔfɛnbak
Ogéas ɔʒea:s
Ogier ɔʒje
Ohio ɔajo
Ohnet ɔnɛ
Oïl ɔil or ɔjl or ɔj
Oise wa:zə

Ojibwés/Ojiboués ɔʒibwe
Oklahoma ɔklaɔma
Ol(l)ivier ɔlivje
Olargues ɔlargə
Olenina-d'Alheim olenina dal(h)ajm
Olibrius ɔlibriys
Olivarès (D') dɔlivarɛs
Olivie ɔliviə
Ollone (D') dɔlɔnə
Oloron-Sainte-Marie ɔlɔrõ sɛ̃tə mariə
Olympe ɔlɛ̃:pə
Olympia ɔlɛ̃pja
Olympie ɔlɛ̃piə
Olynthe ɔlɛ̃:tə
Omahas ɔmaa
Oman ɔmã
Omanai(s) ɔmanɛ
Omanaise(s) ɔmanɛ:zə
Omani(s) ɔmani
Omanie(s) ɔmaniə
Ombrie ɔbriə
Ombrien(s) õbriɛ̃
Ombrienne(s) õbriɛnə
Omphale ɔfalə
Ondenc õdɛ̃:k
Ondin õdɛ̃
Ondine õdinə
Onéguine oneginə
Onésime onezimə
Onex onɛ
Onnaing onɛ̃
Onnéiouts onejut
Onondagas onondaga or onõdaga
Ontario õtarjo
Opéra-Comique opera kɔmikə
Ophel ɔfel
Ophélia ɔfelja
Ophélie ɔfeliə
Ophir ɔfi:r
Oppenheim ɔpɛn(h)ajm
Oppien ɔpjɛ̃
Ops ɔps
Oran ɔrã
Oray ɔrɛ
Orberthal ɔrbɛrtal
Ordonneau ɔrdɔno
Oréal (L') lɔreal
Oregon/Orégon ɔregõ
Orenbourg ɔrɛ̃bu:r
Oreste ɔrɛstə
Orff ɔrf
Orfila ɔrfila
Oriane ɔrjanə
Orient ɔrjã
Origène ɔriʒɛnə
Orion ɔrjõ
Orist ɔrist
Orithyie ɔritiiə
Orkenise ɔrkəni:zə
Orlamonde ɔrlamõ:də
Orlando ɔrlãdo
Orléanais ɔrleanɛ
Orléanaise(s) ɔrleanɛ:zə
Orléans (D') dɔrleã
Ormoy ɔrmwa
Ormus ɔrmys

Ormuz ɔrmy:z
Ornans ɔrnã
Orne ɔrnə
Oroès ɔrɔɛs
Oronte orõ:tə
Orose oro:zə
Orphée ɔrfeə
Orphéon(s) ɔrfeõ
Orsay ɔrsɛ
Orthès ɔrtɛs
Orthez ɔrtɛs or ɔrtɛ:z
Orvault ɔrvo
Orvieto ɔrvjeto
Ory ɔri
Osaka ɔsaka
Oscar ɔska:r
Osée ozeə
Osiride ɔziridə
Osiris ɔziris
Oslo ɔslo
Osmanville ɔsmãvilə
Osmond (D') dɔsmõ
Osne o:nə
Ossian ɔsjã
Ossun ɔsœ̃
Ostel ɔstɛl
Ostrava ɔstrava
Ostricourt ɔstriku:r
Ostrogoths ɔstrɔgo
Otéro ɔtero
Othello ɔtelo
Othon ɔtõ
Ottawa ɔtawa
Ottevaere ɔtəva:rə
Otto ɔto
Ot(t)omis ɔtɔmi
Oubradous ubradu
Oudaï udai or udaj
Oudart uda:r
Oudinot udino
Oudot udo
Ouen wã
Ouf uf
Ouganda ugãda
Ougandais ugɑ̃dɛ
Ougandaise(s) ugɑ̃dɛ:zə
Oulchy-le-Château uʃi lə ʃato
Oulmont ulmõ
Ouma uma
Ouranos uranɔs or urano:s
Ourdine urdinə
Ourrias urja:s
Oury uri
Ousset usɛ
Oust (place) ust
Oust (river) u
Oustrac (D') dustrak
Outaouais utawɛ
Ouvrard uvra:r
Ouzbek(s) uzbɛk
Ouzbèke(s)/Ouzbèque(s) uzbɛkə
Ouzbékistan uzbekistã
Ovide ɔvidə
Ox ɔks
Oxford ɔksfɔrd
Oyonnax ɔjona
Ozanam ɔzanam

— P —

Pachelbel pakəlbɛl
Pachymère paʃimɛːrə
Pacifique pasifikə
Pacini patʃini
Pacory pakɔri
Paderewski padɛrɛvski
Padilla padija
Padma padma
Padmâvatî padmavati
Padoue paduə
Pæan peã
Paganini paganini
Page (Le) lə paːʒə
Pagès paʒɛs
Pagnol paɲɔl
Paillard pajaːr
Pailleron pajərõ
Paimpol pɛ̃pɔl
Painlevé pɛ̃ləve
Païsiello/Paisiello pajzjɛlo
Paixhans pɛksã or pɛksãːs
Pakistan pakistã
Pakistanais pakistanɛ
Pakistanaise(s) pakistanɛːzə
Paladilhe paladijə
Palais-Bourbon palɛ burbõ
Palaiseau palɛzo
Palais-Royal palɛ rwajal
Palama palama
Palamède palamɛdə
Palatin palatɛ̃
Palémon palemõ
Paléologue paleɔlɔgə
Palerme palɛrmə
Palès palɛs
Palestine palɛstinə
Palestinien(s) palɛstinjɛ̃
Palestinienne(s) palɛstinjɛnə
Palestrina palɛstrinə
Paley palɛ
Palffy palfi
Palicot paliko
Palières paljɛːrə
Palinure palinyːrə
Palladium paladjɔm
Pallas palaːs
Palluau palɥo
Palma palma
Palmerston palmɛrstõ
    or palmɛrston
Palombie palõbiə
Paméla pamela
Pamiers pamje
Pampelune pãpəlynə
Pampon pãpõ
Pan pã
Panama panama
Paname panamə
Panaméen(s) panameɛ̃
Panaméenne(s) panameɛnə
Panard panaːr
Panatellas panatɛlaːs or panatelaːs
Pança pãsa
Pancrace pãkrasə
Pandion/Pandiôn pãdjõ

Pandolfe pãdɔlfə
Pandolphe pãdɔlfə
Pandore pãdoːrə
Pangée pãʒeə
Pangloss pãglɔs
Panhard pãaːr
Pannetrat panətra
Panouse (La) la panuːzə
Panseron pãsərõ
Pantagruel pãtagryɛl
Panthée pãteə
Panthéon pãteõ
Panurge panyrʒə
Panzéra pãzera
Paola pawla
Paphos pafɔs or pafoːs
Papineau papino
Papineau-Couture papino kutyːrə
Papinien papinjɛ̃
Papouasie papwaziə
Papouasien(s) papwazjɛ̃
Papouasienne(s) papwazjɛnə
Papouasie-Nouvelle-Guinée papwazi
    nuvɛlə ginеə
Pâques paːkə
Paquet pakɛ
Paquette pakɛtə
Paquita pakita
Paracelse parasɛlsə
Paraguay paragwɛ or paragɥɛ
Paraguayen(s) paragwɛjɛ̃
    or paragɥɛjɛ̃ or paragwajɛ̃
Paraguayenne(s) paragwɛjɛnə
    or paragɥɛjɛnə or paragwajɛnə
Paray parɛ
Parentis parãtis
Parès parɛs
Paris (city) pari
Paris (surname) paris
Pâris (person) paris
Parisien(s) parizjɛ̃
Parisienne(s) parizjɛnə
Parisis parizi
Parme parmə
Parménide parmenidə
Parménion parmenjõ
Parmentier parmãtje
Parnasse parnaːsə or parnasə
Parnassiens parnasjɛ̃ or parnasjɛ̃
Parny (De) də parni
Parques (Les) lɛ parkə
Parséïs parseis
Parseval-Deschenes parsəval deʃɛnə
    or parsəval deʃɛnə
Parseval-Grandmaison parsəval
    grãmezõ
Parsifal parsifal
Parthenay partənɛ
Parthénis/Parthœnis partenis
Parthénon partenõ
Parux pary
Parvati parvati
Parvy parvi
Parys (Van) vã paris
Parysatis parizatis
Pascal paskal
Pascale paskalə

Pascoul paskul
Pas-de-Calais pa də kalɛ
    or pa də kalɛ
Pasdeloup padəlu
Pasdevant padəvã
Pasdoc pasdɔk
Pas-en-Artois pa ã nartwa
Pasgrimaud pagrimo
Pasiphaë/Pasiphaé pazifae
Pasquale (Don) dõ paskwale
Pasquarello pask(w)arɛlo
    or pask(w)arelo
Pasquier paskje or pakje
Pasquin paskɛ̃
Passerat pasəra or pasəra
Passereau pasəro or pasəro
Passy pasi
Pasteur pastœːr
Pastia pastja
Pastor pastɔːr
Pastré pastre
Patacha pataʃa
Patachon pataʃõ
Patata patata
Paté pate
Patek (De) də patɛk
Pathé pate
Patorni patɔrni
Patrice patrisə
Patricia patrisja
Patrick patrik
Patrocle patrɔklə
Patti pati
Paturelle patyrɛlə
Patusset patysɛ
Pau po
Pauillac/Pauilhac/Paulhac pojak
Paul pɔl
Paule poːlə
Paulette polɛtə
Paulhan polã or pojã
Paulhenc polɛ̃ːk
Paulin polɛ̃
Pauline polinə
Paulmier pomje
Paulmy pomi
Paulus (French/Latin person) polys
Paulus (German person) pawlus
    or polys
Pausanias pozanjaːs
Pausole pozolə
Pavilly paviji
Pavlov pavlof
Payan pajã
Payen pajɛ̃
Payenne pajɛnə
Payet pajɛ or pajɛt
Pays-Bas pei ba or pei ba
Paz (La) la paːz or la pas
Pearly perli
Pécoud peku
Pécour pekuːr
Pedrillo pedrijo
Pédro pedro
Pedro (Don) dõ pedro
Peer Gynt pɛr gynt
Pégase pegaːzə

Pégoud pegu
Péguy pegi
Peignot pɛɲo
Péjaudie (De La) də la peʒodiə
Pékin pekɛ̃
Péladan peladã
Pélage pela:ʒə
Pélée peleə
Péléon peleõ
Peletier (Le) lə pɛlətje
Pélias pelja:s
Pélie/Pelie peliə
Pélissier pelisje
Pelléas pɛlleaːs or pelleaːs
Pellegrin pɛləgrɛ̃
Pellerat pɛlərə
Pelletan pɛlətã
Pelletier pɛlətje
Pélopidas pelopidaːs
Pélopide(s) pelopidə
Péloponnèse peloponɛːzə
Pélops pelops
Pelouze pəluːzə
Péluse pelyːzə
Pembroke pɛmbrokə
Pénau peno
Pendjab pɛndʒab
Pénélope penelopə
Penmarch (De) də pɛ̃maːr
Pennsylvanie pɛnsilvaniə
Pentagone pɛ̃tagonə
Pentateuque pɛ̃tatøːkə
Pentecôte pãtəkoːtə
Penthée pɛ̃teə or pãteə
Penthésilée pɛ̃tezileə or pãtezileə
Penthièvre pɛ̃tjɛːvrə
Pépin pepɛ̃
Pépinière (De La) də la pepinjɛːrə
Pepita/Pépita pepita
Pépito pepito
Pepo Illo pepo ijo
Perche pɛrʃə
Perchuque pɛrʃykə
Percier pɛrsje
Perdix pɛrdiks
Perec pɛrɛk
Pérégally peregali
Pérégrina/Peregrina (La)
  la peregrina
Péreire pɛrɛːrə
Père-Lachaise pɛrə laʃɛːzə
Perez pɛrɛːz or pɛrɛs
Pergame pɛrgamə
Pergolèse pɛrgolɛːzə
Pergolesi pɛrgolezi
Périandre perjãːdrə
Péricaud periko
Périchole (La) la perikolə
Périclès periklɛs
Périer perje
Pérignon periɲõ
Périgord perigoːr
Périgueux perigø
Périlhou periju
Périne perinə
Périnette perinɛtə
Périon perjõ

Périsson perisõ
Perlemuter pɛrləmytɛːr
Pernet pɛrnɛ
Pernette pɛrnɛtə
Pernod pɛrno
Pernot pɛrno
Perny pɛrni
Pernyn/Pernin pɛrnɛ̃
Péronilla peronija
Péronne peronə
Pérotin perotɛ̃
Pérou peru
Pérouse peruːzə
Perpignac pɛrpiɲak
Perpignan pɛrpiɲã
Perraud pɛro
Perrault pɛro
Perrégaux pɛrego
Perregaux pɛrəgo
Perret pɛrɛ
Perrette pɛrɛtə
Perrier pɛrje
Perrier-Jouët pɛrje jwɛt
Perrin pɛrɛ̃
Perrold pɛrold
Perronnet pɛronɛ
Perros-Guirec pɛros girɛk
Perrot pɛro
Persan(s) pɛrsã
Persane(s) pɛrsanə
Perse pɛrsə
Persée perseə
Perséphone persefonə
Persique pɛrsikə
Persuis persɥi
Perth pɛrt
Pertinax pɛrtinaks
Pérugin peryʒɛ̃
Péruvien(s) peryvjɛ̃
Péruvienne(s) peryvjɛnə
Péruwelz perywe or pɛrwe
Peschard peʃaːr
Pesmes pɛmə
Pesne pɛnə
Pesquidoux (De) də peskidu
Pessac pɛsak or pesak
Pessard pesaːr or pesaːr
Pessart pesaːr or pesaːr
Pétain petɛ̃
Petermann petɛrman
Péterpip petɛrpip
Petibon pətibõ
Pétion de Villeneuve petjõ də
  vilnœːvə
Petit pəti
Petitgirard pətiʒiraːr
Petipa pətipa
Petitpas pətipa
Pétrarque petrarkə
Petrograd/Pétrograde petrograd
Pétrone petronə
Petronilla petronila
Petrouchka petruʃka
Petrucciani petrutʃjani
Pétuns petœ̃
Peugeot pøʒo
Peutinger pøtɛ̃ʒɛːr

Peyre pɛːrə
Peyrefitte pɛrəfitə
Peyrègne perɛɲə
Peyrens pɛrɛ̃ːs
Peyrolles pɛrolə
Peyrottes pɛrotə
Pézenas pezənaːs or pezənaːs
Pfeffel (p)fɛfɛl or (p)fefɛl
Phaestos/Phaëstos faestos
  or faestoːs
Phaéton/Phaëton faetõ
Phaïstos faistos or faistoːs
Phalaris falaris
Phalempin falãpɛ̃
Phanar fanaːr
Phanariote(s) fanarjotə
Phani fani
Phantase fãtaːzə
Phanuel fanɥɛl
Phaon faõ
Pharamond faramõ
Pharaon faraõ
Pharès farɛs
Pharisiens farizjɛ̃
Pharnace farnasə
Pharo (Le) lə faro
Pharos faros or faroːs
Pharsale farsalə
Phase faːzə
Phéaciens feasjɛ̃
Phébé febe
Phébus febys
Phédon fedõ
Phèdre fɛdrə
Phélip(p)eaux/Phélyp(p)eaux felipo
Phémios femjos or femjoːs
Phénice fenisə
Phénicie fenisiə
Phénicien(s) fenisjɛ̃
Phénicienne(s) fenisjɛnə
Phénix feniks
Phérécrate ferekratə
Phérécyde feresidə
Phéréklos fereklos or ferekloːs
Phérès ferɛs
Phidias fidja:s
Phidylé fidile
Philadelphie filadɛlfiə
Philæ file
Philaminte filamɛ̃ːtə
Philarète filarɛtə
Philèbe filebə
Philelphe filɛlfə
Philémon filemõ
Philènes filɛnə
Philétas filetaːs
Philibert Vaillant filibɛːr vajã
Philidor filidoːr
Philine filinə
Philinte filɛ̃ːtə
Philip(p)on filipõ
Philipot filipo
Philippe filipə
Philippe Égalité fili pegalite
Philippes filipə
Philippien(s) filipjɛ̃
Philippienne(s) filipjɛnə

PRONUNCIATION DICTIONARIES | 291

Philippin(s) filipɛ̃
Philippines filipinə
Philippiques filipikə
Philipponnat filipɔna
Philippoteaux filipɔto
Philis filis
Philiscos filiskɔs or filisko:s
Philistins filistɛ̃
Philistos filistɔs or filisto:s
Phillipsbourg filipsbu:r
Philocôme filɔko:mə
Philocrète filɔkrɛtə
Philoctète filɔktɛtə
Philodème filɔdɛmə
Philolaos filɔlaɔs or filɔlao:s
Philolaüs filɔlays
Philomèle filɔmɛlə
Philomène filɔmɛnə
Philon filɔ̃
Philopœmen filɔpemɛn
Philostrate filɔstratə
Philotas filɔta:s
Philoxène filɔksɛnə
Phinée fineə
Phlégéton fleʒetɔ̃
Phlégréen(s) flegreɛ̃
Phlégréenne(s) flegreenə
Phobétor fɔbeto:r
Phobos fɔbɔs or fɔbo:s
Phocas fɔka:s
Phocée fɔseə
Phocéen(s) fɔseɛ̃
Phocéenne(s) fɔseɛnə
Phocide fɔsidə
Phocion fɔsjɔ̃
Phocylide fɔsilidə
Phœbé febe
Phœnix feniks
Pholien fɔljɛ̃
Phorbas fɔrba:s
Phorcas fɔrka:s
Phormion fɔrmjɔ̃
Phosphore fɔsfɔ:rə
Photin fɔtɛ̃
Photios fɔtjɔs or fɔtjo:s
Phraatès fraatɛs
Phraortès fraɔrtɛs
Phrixos friksɔs or frikso:s
Phronime frɔnimə
Phrygie friʒiə
Phrygien(s) friʒjɛ̃
Phrygienne(s) friʒjɛnə
Phryné frine
Phrynichos frinikɔs or friniko:s
Pht(h)iotide ftjɔtidə
Phthie ftiə
Phyllis filis
Phylo filo
Piaf pjaf
Piaget pjaʒɛ
Pialat pjala
Piau pjo
Pibrac pibrak
Picabia pikabja
Picard pika:r
Picardes pikardə
Picardie pikardiə

Picasso, Pablo pablo pikaso
Piccadilly pikadili
Piccinni pitʃini
Pichegru piʃəgry
Picheran piʃərã
Pichon piʃɔ̃
Picon pikɔ̃
Picot piko
Picpus pikpys
Picquet du Boisguy pikɛ də
    bwagi
Pie piə
Piedcourt pjeku:r
Piémont pjemɔ̃
Piemontoise pjemɔ̃twa:zə
Pierné pjɛrne
Pierre pjɛ:rə
Pierrette pjɛrɛtə
Pierrot pjɛro
Pierrot Lunaire pjɛro lynɛ:rə
Pietro/Piétro pjetro
Piféar pifea:r
Pigalle pigalə
Pigeon piʒɔ̃
Pigeonneau piʒono
Pilate pila:tə or pilatə
Pils pils
Pilsen pilsɛn or pilzən
Pilsenois pilzənwa
Pilsenoise(s) pilzənwa:zə
Pinchard pɛ̃ʃa:r
Pinchon pɛ̃ʃɔ̃
Pindare pɛ̃da:rə
Pineau pino
Pineuilh pinœj
Pingault pɛ̃go
Pingot pɛ̃go
Pingré pɛ̃gre
Piper-Heidsieck pipœ rajdsik
    or pipœ redsik
Pipertrunck pipɛrtrœŋk
Piquepaille pikəpa:jə
Piquillo pikijo
Piquion pikjɔ̃
Pirée pireə
Piriou pirju
Pirithoüs piritɔys
Pisandre pizã:drə
Pise pi:zə
Pisistrate pizistratə
Pison pizɔ̃
Pissarro pisaro
Pitchounette pitʃunɛtə
Pithiviers pitivje
Pitichinaccio pitikinatʃjo
Pitoëff pitɔɛf
Piton pitɔ̃
Pitou pitu
Pittsburgh pitsbœrg or pitsbyrg
Pixérécourt piksereku:r
Pizan/Pisan pizã
Place-Vendôme plasə vãdo:mə
Placidie plasidiə
Planard plana:r
Plancoët plãkwɛt or plãkɔɛt
Plançon plãsɔ̃
Planel planɛl

Plantagenêt plãtaʒɛnɛ
Plantard plãta:r
Plantey plãte
Plasson plasɔ̃
Platard plata:r
Platée plateə
Platon platɔ̃
Plaute plo:tə
Pléiades plejadə
Plescop pleskop
Plessis-lèz-Tours/Plessis-lès-
    Tours plesi lɛ tu:r or plesi lɛ tu:r
Plestin plestɛ̃
Pleurtuit plœrtyi
Pleuven pløvɛ̃
Pléven plevɛn
Pleyben plɛbɛ̃
Pleyel plɛjɛl
Pline plinə
Ploërmel plɔɛrmel
Plœ(u)c plœk
Plouagat pluagat or pluaga
Plouaret pluarɛt or pluarɛ
Plouer plue:r
Plougastel-Daoulas plugastɛl daula:s
Plougrescant plugrɛskã
Plouguenast plugənast
Plouhinec pluinɛk
Ploumanac'h plumanak
Ploumoguer plumɔge
Plouvier pluvje
Plusquellec plyskɛlɛk
Plutarque plytarkə
Pluton plytɔ̃
Pluvigner plyviɲe
Podesta pɔdesta
Poe po
Poher pɔe:r
Poincaré pwɛ̃kare
Pointe-à-Pitre pwɛ̃ ta pitrə
Poiret pwarɛ
Poirier pwarje
Poirson pwarsɔ̃
Poise pwa:zə
Poissy pwasi
Poisvert pwavɛ:r
Poitiers pwatje
Poitou pwatu
Poix (De) də pwa
Pol pɔl
Pol Roger pɔl rɔʒe
Polaire pɔlɛ:rə
Polignac pɔliɲak
Polin pɔlɛ̃
Poliphème pɔlifɛmə
Politien pɔlisjɛ̃
Pollet pɔlɛ
Pollion pɔljɔ̃
Pollux pɔlyks
Pologne pɔlɔɲə
Polonais pɔlɔnɛ
Polonaise(s) pɔlɔnɛ:zə
Polonius pɔlɔnjys
Polybe pɔlibə
Polycarpe pɔlikarpə
Polyclète pɔliklɛtə
Polycrate pɔlikratə

292 | FRENCH LYRIC DICTION

Polydore polidɔːrə
Polydorus polidɔrys
Polyeucte pɔljøːktə
Polygnote polignɔtə
Polymnie polimniə
Polynésie polineziə
Polynésien(s) polinezjɛ̃
Polynésienne(s) polinezjɛnə
Polynice polinisə
Polyphème polifɛmə
Polyxène poliksɛnə
Poméranie pɔmeraniə
Poméranien(s) pɔmeranjɛ̃
Poméranienne(s) pɔmeranjɛnə
Pomerol pɔmərɔl
Pomey pɔmɛ
Pommery pɔmɛri
Pommier pɔmje
Pomone pɔmɔnə
Pompadour põpaduːr
Pompée põpeə
Pompéi põpei
Pompéo/Pompeo põpeo
Pompidou põpidu
Pomponnet põpɔnɛ
Ponce Pilate põsə pilaːtə
   or põsə pilatə
Poncet põsɛ
Ponchard põʃaːr
Poncin põsɛ̃
Pondjiclis põdʒiklis
Ponge põːʒə
Poniatowski pɔnjatɔvski
   or pɔnjatɔfski
Ponnelle pɔnɛlə
Pons (person) põːs
Pons (place) põ
Ponsard põsaːr
Ponsardin põsardɛ̃
Ponscarme põskarmə
Pont-à-Marcq põ ta mark
Pont-à-Celles põ ta sɛlə
Pontacq põtak
Pont-à-Mousson põ ta musõ
Pontailler põtaje
Pontarlier põtarlje
Pont-Audemer põ todəmɛːr
Pontault-Combault põto kõbo
Pont-aux-Dames põ to damə
Pont-aux-Moines põ to mwanə
Pont-à-Vandin põ ta vãdɛ̃
Pont-Aven põ tavɛn
Pontchartrain põʃartrɛ̃
Pontchâteau põʃato
Pont d'Ain põ dɛ̃
Pont-de-Bir-Hakeim põ də bi rakɛm
Pont-de-Chéruy põ də ʃerɥi
Pont-de-Flandre põ də flãːdrə
Pont-de-l'Arche põ də larʃə
Pont-de-Roide põ də rwadə
Pont-de-Veyle põ də vɛlə
Pont-de-Vivaux põ də vivo
Pont-du-Château põ dy ʃato
Pontécoulant põtekulã
Pont-en-Royans põ tã rwajã
Pont-Euxin põ tøksɛ̃
Pont-Évêque põ tevɛkə

Pontevès põtəvɛs
Pontgibaud põʒibo
Ponthieu põtjø
Pontius põsjys
Pontivy põtivi
Pontmercy põmɛrsi
Pontoise põtwaːzə
Pontsablé (De) də põsable
Ponts-de-Cé (Les) lɛ põ də se
Ponzio põzjo
Popesco popɛsko
Pophos pofɔs or pofoːs
Popincourt popɛ̃kuːr
Popolani popolani
Popp pɔp
Poppée popeə
Poquelin pokəlɛ̃
Porc-Épic pɔr kepik
Porcus pɔrkys
Porel pɔrɛl
Porhoët pɔrwet or pɔrɔet
Port-Arthur pɔ rartyːr
Port-au-Prince pɔ ro prɛ̃ːsə
Port-aux-Français pɔ ro frãsɛ
Porte pɔrtə
Porte d'Aix pɔrtə dɛks
Porte-Dauphine pɔrtə dofinə
Port-en-Bessin pɔ rã bɛsɛ̃
   or po rã besɛ̃
Porte-Saint-Denis pɔrtə sɛ̃ dəni
Porte-Saint-Martin pɔrtə sɛ̃ martɛ̃
Portici pɔrtitʃi
Portland pɔrtlãːd or pɔrtland
Porto Rico pɔrto riko
Portugais pɔrtyge
Portugaise(s) pɔrtygeːzə
Portugal pɔrtygal
Port-Vendres pɔr vãːdrə
Posa poza
Posa (De) də poza
Poséidon pozeidõ
Post(h)umia pɔstymja
Potel pɔtɛl
Potez pɔtɛːz
Potsdam pɔtsdam
Pottier pɔtje
Potvin pɔtvɛ̃
Pouchkine puʃkinə
Poudenx pudɛ̃ːs
Pougens puʒɛ̃ːs
Pouget puʒɛ
Pougin puʒɛ̃
Pouilly-Fuissé puji fɥise
Poujade puʒadə
Poul pul
Poulain (Le) lə pulɛ̃
Poulbot pulbo
Poulenard pulənaːr
Poulenc pulɛ̃ːk
Poulet pulɛ
Poulhan pulã
Poulig(u)en (Le) lə puligɛ̃
Poultier pultje
Poumayrac pumɛrak
Poupon pupõ
Poupette pupɛtə
Pouquet pukɛ

Pouqueville pukəvilə
Pourceaugnac (De) də pursɔɲak
Pourna purna
Pourtalès (De) də purtalɛs
Pourville purvilə
Pouspourikas puspurikaːs
Poussette pusɛtə
Poussin pusɛ̃
Pouyastruc pujastryk
Pozzi pɔdzi
Pradel pradɛl
Prado prado
Praetorius pretɔrjys
Prague pragə
Praguois pragwa
Praguoise(s) pragwaːzə
Prascovia praskɔvja
Praslin pralɛ̃ or pralɛ̃
Praslon (De) də pralõ or də pralõ
Prats-de-Mollo pra də mɔlo
   or prats də mɔjo
Praxitèle praksitɛlə
Pray (De) də prɛ
Praz pra
Préault preo
Pré-aux-Clercs pre o klɛːr
Prédour (Le) lə preduːr
Pré-en-Pail pre ã paj
Préger/Preger preʒe
Presle (De La) də la prɛlə
Presles prɛlə
Presley prɛlɛ
Presme prɛmə
Presto prɛsto
Prestre (Le) lə prɛtrə
Pretoria pretɔrja
Prêtre prɛtrə
Prével prevɛl
Prévert prevɛːr
Prévost prevo
Prévôt prevo
Priam priam
Priape priapə
Prim prim
Prin prɛ̃
Princet prɛ̃sɛ
Printemps prɛ̃tã
Priscille prisilə
Priscillien prisiljɛ̃
Prithivi pritivi
Privas priva
Proche-Orient prɔ ʃɔrjã
Procida prɔsida
Procope prɔkɔpə
Progné prɔgne
Prokesch-Osten prɔkɛ ʃɔsten
Prokofiev prɔkɔfjɛf
Prométhée prɔmeteə
Properce prɔpɛrsə
Proserpine prɔzɛrpinə
Prosper prɔspɛːr
Protée prɔteə
Proténor prɔtenɔːr
Protésilas prɔtezilaːs
Protopopov/Protopopoff prɔtɔpɔpɔf
Proudhon prudõ
Proust prust

Prouvaire pʁuvɛːʁə
Prouvost pʁuvo
Provence pʁɔvãːsə
Provins pʁɔvɛ̃
Provost pʁɔvo
Prudence pʁydãːsə
Prudhomme/Prud'homme pʁydɔmə
Prudhon/Prud'hon pʁydõ
Prunet pʁynɛ
Prunier pʁynje
Prunières pʁynjɛːʁə
Prusse (La) la pʁysə
Prussien(s) pʁysjɛ̃
Prussienne(s) pʁysjɛnə
Pruvost pʁyvo
Psammétique psametikə
Psyché psiʃe
Psylles psilə
Ptah ptɑ or pta
Ptolémée ptɔlemeə
Puccini putʃini
Pueblos pɥeblo or pweblo
Puech (Le) lə pɥeʃ
Puerto Rico pwɛʁto ʁiko
Puget pyʒɛ
Pugno pyɲo
Puisaye pɥizɛ
Pujol pyʒɔl
Pulchérie pylkeʁiə or pylʃeʁiə
Pulcinella pultʃinɛla or pultʃinela
Puligny pyliɲi
Pullman pulman or pylman
Purcell pœʁsɛl or pyʁsɛl
Putiphar pytifaːʁ
Putz pyts
Puvis de Chavannes pyvi də ʃavanə
Puy (Le) lə pɥi
Puy de Dôme pɥi də doːmə
Puy-en-Velay (Le) lə pɥi ã vəlɛ
Puyjoli pɥiʒɔli
Puylaurens (De)/Puilaurens (De) də pɥilɔʁãːs
Puylaurens (place) pɥilɔʁɛ̃ːs or pɥilɔʁã
Puymorens pɥimɔʁɛ̃ːs
Puys pɥi
Puységur pɥisegyːʁ
Py pi
Pygmalion pigmaljõ
Pylade piladə
Pyongyang pjɔɲjaŋ or pjõgjãːg or pjõɲjãːŋ
Pyrame piʁamə
Pyrénéen(s) piʁeneẽ
Pyrénéenne(s) piʁeneɛnə
Pyrénées piʁeneə
Pyrex piʁɛks
Pyrrhus piʁys
Pythagore pitagoːʁə
Pythéas piteaːs
Pythée piteə

— Q —
Qatar kataːʁ
Qatari(s) kataʁi
Qatarie(s) kataʁiə
Qatarien(s) kataʁjẽ

Qatarienne(s) kataʁjɛnə
Quadragésime kadʁaʒezimə or kwadʁaʒezimə
Quadrifrons kwadʁifʁõːs
Quai d'Orsay ke dɔʁsɛ
Quaix kɛ
Quantz kvãts
Quaregnon kaʁəɲõ
Quarré kaʁe
Quarton kaʁtõ
Quasimodo kazimodo
Quatrefages katʁəfaːʒə
Quatremère katʁəmɛːʁə
Québec kebɛk
Québecois kebɛkwa
Québecoise(s) kebɛkwaːzə
Queensland kwinslãːd
Quelaines kəlɛnə
Quélen (De) də kelẽ
Quémoy kemɔj
Quend kã
Queneau kəno
Quentin kãtẽ
Quérard keʁaːʁ
Quercy kɛʁsi
Quérigut keʁigyt
Quervain (De) də kɛʁvẽ
Quesnault keno or kɛno
Quesnay kenɛ or kɛnɛ
Quesnel kenɛl or kɛnɛl
Quesnoit kenwa or kɛnwa
Quesnot keno or kɛno
Quesnoy kenwa or kɛnwa
Quesnoy (Le) lə kenwa or lə kɛnwa
Quessoy keswa or kɛswa
Quessy kesi or kɛsi
Questembert kɛstãbɛːʁ
Quettehou kɛtəu or kɛtu
Queuille kœjə
Quéval keval
Quéven kevɛn
Quiberon kibəʁõ
Quicherat kiʃəʁa
Quichotte (Don) dõ kiʃɔtə
Quiers kjeːʁ
Quiévrain kjevʁẽ
Quiévrechain kjevʁəʃẽ
Quiévy kjevi
Quilico kwiliko
Quillan kijã
Quillet kijɛ
Quimerch kimɛʁʃ
Quimper kẽpeːʁ
Quimper-Karadec kẽpeʁ karadɛk
Quimperlé kẽpeʁle
Quin(c)tilius kẽtiljys or kɥẽtiljys
Quinault kino
Quincampoix kẽkãpwa or kẽkãpwa
Quincey kwinsɛ
Quincy (De) də kẽsi
Quinet kinɛ
Quinquagésime kẽkaʒezimə or kɥẽkwaʒezimə
Quinsac kẽsak
Quinte-Curce kẽtə kyʁsə or kɥẽtə kyʁsə

Quintilien kẽtiljẽ or kɥẽtiljẽ
Quintin kẽtẽ
Quintinie (De La) də la kɥẽtiniə
Quinton kẽtõ ·
Quintus kẽtys or kɥẽtys
Quinzard kẽzaːʁ
Quiquengrogne kikãgʁɔɲə
Quirin kiʁẽ
Quirinal kɥiʁinal
Quirinus kɥiʁinys
Quirot kiʁo
Quissac kisak
Quistinic kistinik
Quito kito
Quittard kitaːʁ
Quœux kø
Quost kɔst

— R —
Râ ʁa
Rabanne ʁabanə
Rabastens ʁabastẽːs
Rabat ʁaba
Rabaud ʁabo
Rabelais ʁabəlɛ
Rachel ʁaʃel
Rachet ʁaʃɛ
Rachmaninov/
Rakhmaninov ʁakmaninɔf
Racine ʁasinə
Radamante ʁadamãːtə
Radegonde ʁadəgõːdə
Radetzky ʁadɛtski
Radiguet ʁadigɛ
Raffet ʁafɛ
Rafrina ʁafʁina
Ragonde ʁagõːdə
Raguse (De) də ʁagyːzə
Rahon ʁaõ
Raimbaud ʁẽbo
Raimbaut ʁẽbo
Raimu ʁɛmy or ʁẽmy
Raincy (Le) lə ʁẽsi
Raiponce ʁɛpõːsə
Rais (De)/Retz (De), Gilles ʒilə də ʁɛ
Raismes ʁɛmə
Rakhmaninov/
Rachmaninov ʁakmaninɔf
Rallier ʁalje
Ralph ʁalf
Ramavacon ʁamavakõ
Rambaud ʁãbo
Rambervillers ʁãbɛʁvile
Rambouillet ʁãbujɛ
Rameau ʁamo
Ramée ʁameə
Ramerupt ʁaməʁy
Ramillies ʁamijiə or ʁamiliə
Ramiro ʁamiro
Ramon ʁamõ
Ramouzens ʁamuzẽːs
Rampal ʁãpal
Ramsès ʁamsɛs
Ramus ʁamys
Ramuz ʁamy
Ranc ʁãːk

Randolphe rãdɔlfə
Randon rãdõ
Raon-l'Étape raõ letapə
Raoul raul
Raoult raul
Raoux rau
Raphaël/Raphael rafaɛl
Raphaëlle rafaɛlə
Raquet-Delmée rakɛ dɛlmeə
Raspail raspaj
Raspoutine rasputinə
Rassa rasa
Ratan-Sen 'ratan sɛn
Ratti rati
Raunay ronɛ
Raveau ravo
Ravel ravɛl
Ravenne ravɛnə
Ravina ravina
Ravizé ravize
Ray, Man man rɛ
Rayet rajɛ
Raymond rɛmõ
Raymonde rɛmõ:də
Raynal rɛnal
Raynard rɛna:r
Raynaud rɛno
Raz ra
Rê rɛ
Réage rea:ʒə
Réaumur reomy:r
Réaup reo:p
Rebais rəbɛ
Rébecca rebɛka
Rebel rəbɛl
Reber rebe:r
Reboul rəbul
Reboux rəbu
Récamier rekamje
Rédélé redele
Redon rədõ
Redouté rədute
Regelly/Régelly reʒɛli or reʒeli
Régina reʒina
Régine reʒinə
Regnal rəɲal
Regnard rəɲa:r
Regnaud rəɲo or rɛɲo
Regnault rəɲo or rɛɲo
Régnier (De) də rɛɲe
Reichshoffen rajʃ(s)ɔfɛn
    or rajʃ(s)ofɛn
Reichstadt rajʃtat
Reid (La) la rɛd or la rɛ
Reille rɛjə
Reims rɛ̃:s
Reinach rɛnak
Reiner rajnœ:r
Reinhardt rɛnart
Reiset (De) də rɛzɛ
Réjane reʒanə
Réju reʒy
Rektah rɛkta
Relin rəlɛ̃
Remacle rəmaklə
Rembrandt rãbrã
Remendado remɛndado

Rémi rɛmi
Remi rɛmi or rɛmi
Rémois rɛmwa
Rémoise(s) rɛmwa:zə
Rémond rɛmõ
Remoulins rəmulɛ̃
Rémus/Remus rɛmys
Rémusat remyza
Rémuzat remyza
Rémy rɛmi
Renaissance rənɛsã:sə
Renaix rənɛ
Renan rənã
Renard rəna:r
Renaud rəno
Renaudot rənodo
Renauld rəno
Renault rəno
Renaux rəno
René rəne
Renée rəneə
Renens rənã
Renescure rənɛsky:rə
Renié rənje
Rennes rɛnə
Renoir rənwa:r
Renwez rãve or rãwe
Réole (La) la reolə
Repos rəpo
Resnais rɛnɛ
Resnel (Du) dy rɛnɛl or dy rɛnɛl
Respighi rɛspigi
Rességuier (De) də rəsegje
Restany rɛstani
Restaut rɛsto
Restif De La Bretonne rɛtif də la
    brətɔnə
Restigné rɛstiɲe
Restout rɛtu or rɛstu
Reszke (De) də rɛʃke
Rethel rətɛl
Réty reti
Retz (De) də rɛ or də rɛs
Retz (De)/Rais (De), Gilles ʒilə də rɛ
Reuchsel røksɛl
Reuilly rœji
Réunion reynjõ
Reverdy rəvɛrdi
Révial revjal
Révoil revwal
Rey rɛ
Reyer rɛje:r
Reynaldo rɛnaldo
Reynaud rɛno
Reynauld rɛno
Reyne rɛnə
Rhadamante radamã:tə
Rhadamiste radamistə
Rhénanie renaniə
Rhené-Baton rəne batõ
Rhin rɛ̃
Rhodanien(s) rodanjɛ̃
Rhodanienne(s) rodanjɛnə
Rhode Island ro dajlã:d
Rhodes rodə
Rhodes (Greek island) rodə
Rhodes (person) rods or rodə

Rhodésie rodeziə
Rhodésien(s) rodezjɛ̃
Rhodésienne(s) rodezjɛnə
Rhône ro:nə
Rhône-Alpes ro nalpə
Rhorer rore
Rialland rjalã
Rians rjã:s or rjã
Riaux (Les) lɛ rjo
Ribaud ribo
Ribeauvillé ribovile
Ribeira ribɛra
Riboutté ribute
Ricardo rikardo
Richard riʃa:r
Richault riʃo
Richelieu riʃəljø
Richemont riʃəmõ
Richepin riʃəpɛ̃
Richmond ritʃmond or riʃmõ
Richter riʃte:r
Rico riko
Ricordi rikɔrdi
Ricou riku
Ricquier rikje
Riel rjɛl
Riesling risliŋ
Rieu (De) də rjø
Rieux rjø
Riez rjɛs
Riga riga
Rigaud rigo
Rigault rigo
Rigaut rigo
Rilhac rijak
Rilke rilkə
Rillieux riljø
Rimailho rimajo
Rimbaud rɛ̃bo
Rime rimə
Rimsky-Korsakov rimski kɔrsakɔf
Rio de Janeiro rjo də ʒanɛro
Rio-Janeire rjo ʒanɛ:rə
Riom rjõ
Rioton rjɔtõ
Rioz rjo
Rioux rju
Ripardos ripardos or ripardo:s
Riquewihr rikəvi:r
Risler rislɛ:r
Ristori ristɔri
Ritt rit
Ritta rita
Ritter-Ciampi ritɛr tʃãpi
Ritz ritz
Rive Droite (La) la rivə drwatə
    or la rivə drwa:tə
Rive Gauche (La) la rivə go:ʃə
Rive-de-Gier rivə də ʒje
Rivenq rivɛ̃:k
Rivier rivje
Riviera (La) la rivjera
Rivière rivjɛ:rə
Rivières (De) də rivjɛ:rə
Rivoire rivwa:rə
Roanne roanə
Robbe-Grillet robə grije

PRONUNCIATION DICTIONARIES | 295

Robert ɾobɛːɾ
Robespierre ɾobɛspjɛːɾə
Robillard ɾobijaːɾ
Robin ɾobɛ̃
Robin des Bois ɾobɛ̃ dɛ bwa
   or ɾobɛ̃ dɛ bwa
Robin-Luron ɾobɛ̃ lyɾõ
Robinson ɾobɛ̃sõ
Robiquet ɾobikɛ
Roblès ɾoblɛs
Roboam ɾoboam
Rocambole ɾokãbɔlə
Rocard ɾokaːɾ
Roch ɾɔk
Roché ɾɔʃe
Roche ɾɔʃə
Roche-au-Moine (La) la ɾɔ ʃo
   mwanə
Roche-Bernard (La) la ɾɔʃə bɛɾnaːɾ
Roche-Blanche ɾɔʃə blã:ʃə
Rocheblave ɾɔʃabla:və
Rochechouart ɾɔʃəʃwaːɾ
Roche-Derrien (La) la ɾɔʃə dɛɾjɛ̃
Rochefort ɾɔʃəfɔːɾ
Rochefort-en-Terre ɾɔʃəfɔ ɾã tɛːɾə
Rochefoucauld (La) la ɾɔʃəfuko
Rochelle (La) la ɾɔʃɛlə
Roche-Posay (La) la ɾɔʃə pozɛ
Rochereuil (De) də ɾɔʃəɾœj
Rocheron ɾɔʃəɾõ
Roche-sur-Yon (La) la ɾɔʃə sy ɾjõ
Rocheuses (Les) lɛ ɾɔʃø:zə
Rochois (Le) lə ɾɔʃwa
Rod ɾod
Rodenbach ɾodɛnbak
Rodez ɾodɛːz or ɾodɛs
Rodier ɾodje
Rodin ɾodɛ̃
Rodolphe ɾodɔlfə
Rodrigo ɾodɾigo
Rodrigue ɾodɾigə
Rodriguez ɾodɾigɛːz or ɾodɾigɛs
Rœderer ɾedəɾɛːɾ or ɾedəɾɛːɾ
Rœsgen-Champion ɾoesgɛn
   ʃãpjõ
Rœulx ɾø
Rœux ɾø
Rogatchewsky ɾogatʃɛvski
Roger ɾɔʒe
Roger-Ducasse ɾɔʒe dykasə
Roger-Fernay ɾɔʒe fɛɾnɛ
Rohmer ɾomɛːɾ or ɾomeːɾ
Roissy ɾwasi
Roland ɾɔlã
Roland-Garros ɾɔlã gaɾoːs
Roland-Manuel ɾɔlã manɥɛl
Rolland ɾɔlã
Rolle ɾɔlə
Rollin ɾɔlɛ̃
Rollinat ɾolina
Rolls Royce ɾols ɾœjs
Romain ɾomɛ̃
Romains ɾomɛ̃
Romanée-Conti ɾomane kõti
Romanov/Romanoff ɾomanɔf
Romans ɾomã
Rombas ɾõba

Romberg ɾõbɛɾg
Romboïdal ɾõbɔidal
Rome ɾɔmə
Roméo ɾomeo
Romilly ɾomiji
Romorantin-Lanthenay ɾomoɾãtɛ̃
   lãtənɛ
Romuald ɾomɥald
Romulus ɾomylys
Ronarc'h ɾonaɾk
Ronis ɾonis
Ronsard (De) də ɾõsaːɾ
Ronsin ɾõsɛ̃
Roosevelt ɾuzəvɛlt or ɾozəvɛlt
Ropartz ɾopaɾts
Rophé ɾofe
Roqueblave ɾokəbla:və
Roquefort ɾokəfɔːɾ
Roquemaure ɾokəmo:ɾə
Roqueplan ɾokəplã
Roques ɾokə
Roquette ɾokɛtə
Rorem ɾoɾɛm
Rosalès (De) də ɾozalɛs
Rosalie ɾozaliə
Rosalinde ɾozalɛ̃:də
Rosaline ɾozalinə
Rosay ɾozɛ
Roscanvel ɾoskãvɛl
Roscoff ɾoskɔf
Rose ɾo:zə
Rosemonde ɾozəmõ:də
Rosenberg ɾozɛnbɛɾg
Rosendaël ɾozɛndal
Rosenthal ɾozɛ̃tal or ɾozɛntal
Rosette ɾozɛtə
Rosheim ɾoz(h)ajm or ɾos(h)ajm
Rosine ɾozinə
Rosita ɾozita
Rosmala ɾosmala
Rosmor ɾosmo:ɾ
Rosnes ɾosnə
Rosnoën ɾosnoɛn
Rosny ɾoni
Rosolio ɾozɔljo
Rosporden ɾospɔɾdɛ̃
Rossi ɾosi
Rossif ɾosif
Rossignol ɾosiɲol
Rossinante ɾosinã:tə
Rossini ɾosini
Rostand ɾostã
Rostrenen ɾostɾənɛ̃
Rostropovitch ɾostɾopovitʃ
Roth ɾot
Rothenberger ɾotənbɛɾgeːɾ
Rothier ɾotje
Rothsay (De) də ɾotsɛ
Rot(h)schild ɾotʃild
Rots ɾo
Rotterdam ɾotɛɾdam
Rouart ɾwaːɾ
Roubaix ɾubɛ
Roubert ɾubɛːɾ
Roubion ɾubjõ
Rouché ɾuʃe
Rouchefoucauld (La) la ɾuʃəfuko

Roucher ɾuʃe
Roucoux ɾuku
Roucy (De) də ɾusi
Rouen ɾwã
Rouennais ɾwanɛ
Rouennaise(s) ɾwanɛ:zɛ
Rouergue ɾwɛɾgə
Rouërie (De La) də la ɾuɛɾiə
   or də la ɾuɛɾiə or də la ɾwaɾiə
Rouffach ɾufak
Rouget ɾuʒɛ
Rouget de Lisle ɾuʒɛ də lilə
Rougier ɾuʒje
Rougon-Macquart ɾugõ makaːɾ
Rouhier ɾuje
Rouillard ɾujaːɾ
Rouits ɾwits
Roujon ɾuʒõ
Roulans ɾulã
Rouleau ɾulo
Roulers ɾulɛɾs
Roullens ɾulɛ̃:s
Roullet (Du) dy ɾulɛ
Roullier ɾulje
Roumain(s) ɾumɛ̃
Roumaine(s) ɾumɛnə
Roumanie ɾumaniə
Roumanille ɾumanijə
Roumens ɾumɛ̃:s
Roussalka/Rusalka ɾusalka
Rousseau ɾuso
Rousseau-Lagrave ɾuso lagɾa:və
Roussel ɾusɛl
Rousselière ɾusəljeːɾə
Rousset ɾusɛ
Roussillon ɾusijõ
Roussy ɾusi
Routot ɾuto
Rouvier ɾuvje
Rouville ɾuvilə
Rouvroy ɾuvɾwa or ɾuvɾwa
Roux ɾu
Roux (Le) lə ɾu
Roxane ɾɔksanə
Roy (Le) lə ɾwa or lə ɾwa
Roya ɾwaja
Royan ɾwajã
Royat ɾwaja
Royaume-Uni ɾwajo myni
Roye ɾwa
Royer ɾwaje
Royère ɾwajeːɾə
Roze ɾo:zə
Rôze ɾo:zə
Rozenn ɾozɛn
Roziès ɾozjɛs
Rubé ɾybe
Rubel ɾybɛl
Ruben ɾybɛn or ɾybɛ̃
Rubens ɾybɛ̃:s
Rubicon ɾybikõ
Rubinstein ɾubinʃtajn or ɾybinʃtajn
   or ɾubinstajn or ɾybinstajn
   or ɾybinʃtɛn or ɾybinstɛn
Ruchottes ɾyʃɔtə
Ruckert ɾykeːɾ
Rude ɾydə

296 | FRENCH LYRIC DICTION

Rueil ʁɥɛj
Ruelle ʁɥɛlə
Ruffey ʁyfɛ
Rufin ʁyfɛ̃
Rufisque ʁyfiskə
Ruggiero ʁudʒ(j)eʁo or ʁuʒjeʁo
or ʁydʒ(j)eʁo or ʁyʒjeʁo
Ruhlmann ʁulman
Ruhr ʁuːʁ
Ruinart ʁɥinaːʁ
Ruitz ʁɥi
Rungis ʁœ̃ʒis
Ruodi ʁwɔdi or ʁɥɔdi
Rupert ʁypɛʁt
Rupt ʁy
Rurik ʁyʁik
Rusalka/Roussalka ʁusalka
Russe(s) ʁysə
Russie ʁysiə
Rutebeuf ʁytəbœf
Ruth ʁyt
Rutli/Rütli ʁytli
Rutules ʁytylə
Ruy Blas ʁɥi blaːs
Ruysdaël ʁɥisdaːl or ʁɥisdal
or ʁœjsdal
Rwanda/Ruanda/Rouanda ʁwãda
or ʁwanda
**Rwandais/Ruandais/
Rouandais** ʁwãdɛ
**Rwandaise(s)/Ruandaise(s)/
Rouandaise(s)** ʁwãdɛːzə
Ryes ʁi
Rzeszow ʒɛʃɔːv

— S —

Saas Fee saas fe or sas fe
Sabaoth sabaɔt
Sabin sabɛ̃
Sabine sabinə
Sabines (Les) lɛ sabinə
Sabins sabɛ̃
Sables-d'Olonne (Les) lɛ sablə dɔlɔnə
or lɛ sablə dɔlɔnə
Sablière (La) la sabliɛːʁə
or la sabliɛːʁə
Sablon sablɔ̃
Sacher za(h)ɛːʁ
Sachs saks
Sacramento sakʁamento
Sacré-Cœur sakʁe kœːʁ
Sacy (De) də sasi
Sad(d)ucéen(s) sadyseɛ̃
Sade sadə
Sahara saaʁa
Saïgon/Saigon saigɔ̃ or sajgɔ̃
or sɛgɔ̃
Saillagouse sajaguːzə
Saillans sajã
Sailly saji
Sainbris (De) də sɛ̃bʁi
Saineville sɛnəvilə
Sain-Laon sɛ̃ lɔ̃
Sains-en-Gohelle sɛ̃ ã gɔɛlə
Saint-Albin sɛ̃ talbɛ̃
Saint-Amant sɛ̃ tamã

Saint-Ambroise sɛ̃ tãbʁwaːzə
or sɛ̃ tãbʁwaːzə
Saint-André sɛ̃ tãdʁe
Saint-Angénor sɛ̃ tãʒenɔːʁ
Saint-Antoine sɛ̃ tãtwanə
Saint-Arnaud sɛ̃ taʁno
Saint-Aubin sɛ̃ tobɛ̃
Saint-Augustin sɛ̃ togystɛ̃
or sɛ̃ tɔgystɛ̃
Saint-Avold sɛ̃ tavɔld or sɛ̃ tavɔl
or sɛ̃ tavo
Saint-Barnabé sɛ̃ baʁnabe
Saint-Barthélemy sɛ̃ baʁtelami
or sɛ̃ baʁtelami
Saint-Bénézet sɛ̃ benezɛ
Saint-Benoît sɛ̃ bənwa
Saint-Brieuc sɛ̃ bʁiø
Saint-Bris sɛ̃ bʁi
Saint-Chamas sɛ̃ ʃama
Saint-Charles sɛ̃ ʃaʁlə
Saint-Chély sɛ̃ ʃeli
Saint-Christophe sɛ̃ kʁistɔfə
Saint-Christophe-et-Niévès sɛ̃ kʁistɔ
fe njeves
Saint-Claude sɛ̃ kloːdə
Saint-Clost sɛ̃ klo
Saint-Cloud sɛ̃ klu
Saint-Corentin sɛ̃ kɔʁãtɛ̃
Saint-Cosme/Saint-Côme sɛ̃
koːmə
Saint-Cyr sɛ̃ siːʁ
Saint-Daniel sɛ̃ danjɛl
Saint-Denis sɛ̃ dəni
Saint-Denœux sɛ̃ dənø
Saint-Dier sɛ̃ dje
Saint-Dizier sɛ̃ dizje
Saint-Domingue sɛ̃ dɔmɛ̃ːgə
Sainte-Agnès sɛ̃ taɲɛs
Sainte-Amaranthe sɛ̃ tamaʁãːtə
Sainte-Anne sɛ̃ taːnə or sɛ̃ tanə
Sainte-Avoye sɛ̃ tavwa
Sainte-Beuve sɛ̃tə bœːvə
Sainte-Blaise sɛ̃tə blɛːzə
Sainte-Catherine sɛ̃tə kataʁinə
Sainte-Chapelle sɛ̃tə ʃapɛlə
Sainte-Clotilde sɛ̃tə klɔtildə
Sainte-Foy sɛ̃tə fwa
Sainte-Gelais sɛ̃tə ʒəlɛ
Sainte-Hélène sɛ̃ telɛnə
Sainte-Lucie sɛ̃tə lysiə
Sainte-Lucien(s) sɛ̃tə lysjɛ̃
Sainte-Lucienne(s) sɛ̃tə lysjɛnə
Sainte-Marguerite sɛ̃tə
maʁɡəʁitə
Sainte-Marthe sɛ̃tə maʁtə
**Sainte-Menehould/Sainte-
Ménehould** (in Poulenc's
Tirésias) sɛ̃tə meneuld
**Sainte-Menehould/Sainte-
Ménehould** (place) sɛ̃tə mənu
Sainte-Mesme sɛ̃tə mɛmə
Saint-Émilion sɛ̃ temiljɔ̃
Sainte-Palaye sɛ̃tə palɛ
Sainte-Rosalie sɛ̃tə ʁozaliə
Saintes sɛ̃ːtə
Saint-Escure sɛ̃ tɛskyːʁə
Sainte-Sophie sɛ̃tə sɔfiə

Saint-Esprit sɛ̃ tɛspri
Saint-Étienne sɛ̃ tetjɛnə
Sainte-Trinité sɛ̃tə trinite
Saint-Eustache sɛ̃ tøstaʃə
Saint-Exupéry sɛ̃ tɛgzypeʁi
Saint-Fargeau sɛ̃ faʁʒo
Saint-Flour sɛ̃ fluːʁ
Saint-Fons sɛ̃ fɔ̃
Saint-François sɛ̃ fʁãswa
Saint-François d'Assise sɛ̃ fʁãswa
dasiːzə
Saint-Fulgent sɛ̃ fylʒã
Saint-Gaudens sɛ̃ godɛ̃ːs
Saint-Gelais sɛ̃ ʒəlɛ
Saint-Genais sɛ̃ ʒənɛ
Saint-Genest sɛ̃ ʒənɛ
Saint-Geniez-d'Olt sɛ̃ ʒənje dɔlt
Saint-Genis sɛ̃ ʒəni
Saint-Genix sɛ̃ ʒəni
Saint-Georges (De) də sɛ̃ ʒɔʁʒə
Saint-Germain sɛ̃ ʒɛʁmɛ̃
Saint-Germain-des-Prés sɛ̃
ʒɛʁmɛ̃ de pʁe
Saint-Germain-en-Laye sɛ̃ ʒɛʁmɛ̃ ã lɛ
Saint-Germain-l'Auxerrois sɛ̃ ʒɛʁmɛ̃
lɔksɛʁwa or sɛ̃ ʒɛʁmɛ̃ lɔksɛʁwa
Saint-Gervais sɛ̃ ʒɛʁvɛ
Saint-Gille sɛ̃ ʒilə
Saint-Girons sɛ̃ ʒiʁɔ̃
Saint-Guilhem-le-Désert sɛ̃ gijɛm lə
dezeːʁ or sɛ̃ gilɛm lə dezeːʁ
Saint-Guy sɛ̃ gi
Saint-Haon-le-Châtel sɛ̃ tã lə ʃatɛl
or sɛ̃ tã lə ʃatɛl
Saint-Héand sɛ̃ teã
Saint-Henri sɛ̃ tãʁi
Saint-Hilaire sɛ̃ tilɛːʁə
Saint-Hildebrand sɛ̃ tildəbʁã
Saint-Honoré sɛ̃ tɔnɔʁe
Saint-Iconostase sɛ̃ tikɔnɔstaːzə
Saint-Igest sɛ̃ tiʒɛst
Saint-Jacques de Compostelle
sɛ̃ ʒakə də kɔ̃pɔstɛlə
Saint-Jean sɛ̃ ʒã
Saint-Jean-d'Angély sɛ̃ ʒã dãʒeli
Saint-Jean-d'Aulps sɛ̃ ʒã do
Saint-Jean-de-Losne sɛ̃ ʒã də loːnə
Saint-Jean-de-Luz sɛ̃ ʒã də lyːz
Saint-Jean-de-Maurienne sɛ̃ ʒã də
mɔʁjɛnə
Saint-Jean-de-Niost sɛ̃ ʒã də njost
Saint-Jérôme sɛ̃ ʒeʁoːmə
Saint-Jorioz sɛ̃ ʒɔʁjo
Saint-Joseph sɛ̃ ʒɔzɛf
Saint-Julien sɛ̃ ʒyljɛ̃
Saint-Julien-d'Arpaon sɛ̃ ʒyljɛ̃
daʁpaɔ̃
Saint-Julien-en-Genevois sɛ̃ ʒyljɛ̃ ã
ʒənəvwa
Saint-Junien sɛ̃ ʒynjɛ̃
Saint-Just (De) də sɛ̃ ʒyst
Saint-Just (place) sɛ̃ ʒyst or sɛ̃ ʒy
Saint-Lambert sɛ̃ lãbɛːʁ
Saint-Laurent sɛ̃ lɔʁã
Saint-Laurent-du-Maroni sɛ̃ lɔʁã
dy maʁoni
Saint-Lazare sɛ̃ lazaːʁə

PRONUNCIATION DICTIONARIES | 297

Saint-Lévitique sɛ̃tə levitikə
Saint-Lizier sɛ̃ lizje
Saint-Lô sɛ̃ lo
Saint-Louis sɛ̃ lwi
Saint-Loup sɛ̃ lu
Saint-Maixent sɛ̃ mɛksã
Saint-Malo sɛ̃ malo
Saint-Mandé sɛ̃ mãde
Saint-Marc sɛ̃ maːr
Saint-Marc (Evangelist) sɛ̃ mark
Saint-Marc Girardin sɛ̃ mar ʒirardɛ̃
 or sɛ̃ mark ʒirardɛ̃
Saint-Marceaux (De) də sɛ̃ marso
Saint-Marcel sɛ̃ marsɛl
Saint-Marin sɛ̃ marɛ̃
Saint-Marinais sɛ̃ marinɛ
Saint-Marinaise(s) sɛ̃ marinɛːzə
Saint-Martin sɛ̃ martɛ̃
Saint-Martin-de-Valamas sɛ̃ martɛ̃
 də valamaːs
Saint-Maur sɛ̃ moːr
Saint-Mauront sɛ̃ morõ
Saint-Menet sɛ̃ mənɛ
Saint-Mère-Église sɛ̃ mɛ regliːzə
Saint-Merri sɛ̃ mɛri
Saint-Michel sɛ̃ miʃɛl
Saint-Mihiel sɛ̃ mijɛl or sɛ̃ mjɛl
Saint-Mitre sɛ̃ mitrə
Saint-Nazaire sɛ̃ nazɛːrə
Saint-Nicolas sɛ̃ nikola
Saint-Omer sɛ̃ tɔmɛːr
Saintonge sɛ̃tõːʒə
Saint-Ouen (N France) sɛ̃ twã
Saint-Ouen (near Paris) sɛ̃ twɛ̃
Saint-Ouf sɛ̃ tuf
Saint-Paër sɛ̃ paɛːr
Saint-Patrick sɛ̃ patrik
Saint-Paul sɛ̃ pol
Saint-Pé-de-Léren sɛ̃ pe də lerɛn
Saint-Père sɛ̃ pɛːrə
Saint-Père-en-Retz sɛ̃ pɛ rã re
 or sɛ̃ pɛ rã rɛs
Saint-Pétersbourg sɛ̃ petɛrsbuːr
Saint-Phar sɛ̃ faːr
Saint-Pierre sɛ̃ pjɛːrə
Saint-Pierre-et-Miquelon sɛ̃ pjɛ re
 mikəlõ
Saint-Pol-Roux sɛ̃ pol ru
Saint-Preux sɛ̃ prø
Saint-Priest sɛ̃ pri or sɛ̃ priɛst
Saint-Rémy (De) də sɛ̃ remi
Saint-Quentin sɛ̃ kãtɛ̃
Saint-Quirin sɛ̃ kirɛ̃
Saint-Raphaël sɛ̃ rafaɛl
Saint-Saëns sɛ̃ sãːs
Saint-Saulge sɛ̃ soːʒə
Saint-Sever (N France) sɛ̃ səvɛːr
Saint-Sever (S France) sɛ̃ səve
Saint-Séverin sɛ̃ sevarɛ̃
Saint-Siège sɛ̃ sjɛːʒə
Saint-Sulpice sɛ̃ sylpisə
Saint-Sylvestre sɛ̃ silvɛstrə
Saint-Thomas sɛ̃ toma
Saint-Tronc sɛ̃ trõ
Saint-Tropez sɛ̃ trɔpe
Saint-Vaast sɛ̃ va
Saint-Valentin sɛ̃ valãtɛ̃

Saint-Varent sɛ̃ varã
Saint-Viateur sɛ̃ vjatœːr
Saint-Victor sɛ̃ viktɔːr
Saint-Vincent sɛ̃ vɛ̃sã
Saint-Vincent-de-Paul sɛ̃ vɛ̃sã də pol
Saint-Wandrille sɛ̃ vãdrijə
Saint-Witz sɛ̃ vis or sɛ̃ vits
Saint-Wladimir sɛ̃ vladimiːr
Saint-Ybard sɛ̃ tibaːr
Saint-Yon sɛ̃ tjõ
Saint-Yorre sɛ̃ tjɔːrə
Saint-Yrieix-la-Perche sɛ̃ tirjɛ
 la pɛrʃə
Saïs sais
Saix (De) də sɛ
Salabert salabɛːr
Salacrou salakru
Saladin saladɛ̃
Salamanque salamãːkə
Salbris salbri
Salers salɛːr or salɛrs
Saléza saleza
Salgar salgaːr
Salieri saljeri
Salins salɛ̃
Salis salis
Salisbury salisbyri
Salles salə
Salluste salystə
Salmon salmõ
Salomé salome
Salomon salɔmõ
Salomonais salɔmɔnɛ
Salomonaise(s) salɔmɔnɛːzə
Salpêtrière salpetrieːrə
Salses salsə
Salt Lake City solt lɛk siti
Saltarello saltarɛlo
Saluces salysə
Saluste du Bartas salystə dy bartaːs
Salvador salvadɔːr
Salvadorien(s) salvadɔrjɛ̃
Salvadorienne(s) salvadɔrjɛnə
Salvayre salvɛːrə
Salvien salvjɛ̃
Salzbourg salzbuːr or salsbuːr
Sam sam
Samain samɛ̃
Samarien(s) samarjɛ̃
Samarienne(s) samarjɛnə
Samaritain(s) samaritɛ̃
Samaritaine(s) samaritɛnə
Samazeuilh samazœj
Samer same
Samoa samoa
Samoan(s) samɔã
Samoane(s) samɔanə
Samoëns samwɛ̃ or samɔɛ̃ːs
Samothrace samɔtrasə
Samoyède(s)/Samoïède(s) samɔjedə
Samson sãsõ
Samuel samɥɛl
San Antonio sa nantɔnjo or sa nãtɔnjo
San Diego san djego or sã djego
San Fransisco sã frãsisko
San Juan san xwan or san hwan
 or sã ʒɥã

Sancerre sãsɛːrə
Sanche sãːʃə
Sanchez (French person) sãʃɛːz
Sanchez (Spanish person) santʃes
 or sã(t)ʃes
Sancho sãʃo
Sancho Pança sãʃo pãsa
Sanchoniaton sãkɔnjatõ
Sand, George ʒɔrʒə sãːd
Sandeau sãdo
Sander sandeːr
Sanderson sandɛrson or sãdɛrson
Sangar sãgaːr
Sangaride sãgaridə
Sangnier sãɲe or saɲe
Sangrado sãgrado or sangrado
Sanniassy sanjasi
Sanson sãsõ
Santa Fé sãta fe or santa fe
Santarem sãtarɛm
Santerre sãtɛːrə
Santiago sãtjago or santjago
Santillane sãtijanə
Santoméen(s) sãtɔmeɛ̃
Santoméenne(s) sãtɔmeenə
Sao Paulo sao polo
Sao Tomé-et-Principe sao tome e
 prɛ̃sipe
Saône soːnə
Saoudien(s) saudjɛ̃
Saoudienne(s) saudjɛnə
Saphir safiːr
Sapin sapɛ̃
Sap(p)ho safo
Saqui saki
Sara sara
Saragosse saragosə
Saraïevo/Sarajevo sarajevo
Sarapo sarapo
Sarasate sarazatə
Sarasin sarazɛ̃
Sarcelles sarsɛlə
Sarcos sarkos or sarkoːs
Sardaigne sardɛɲə
Sardanapale sardanapalə
Sardes sardə
Sardou sardu
Sargasses sargasə
Sarkozy sarkozi
Sarlat-la-Canéda sarla la kaneda
Sarmatie sarmatiə
Saron sarõ
Sarpourenx sarpurɛ̃ːs
Sarrail saraj
Sarrasin sarazɛ̃
Sarrasine sarazinə
Sarrasins/Sarrazins sarazɛ̃
Sarraute saroːtə
Sarre saːrə
Sarrebourg sarəbuːr
Sarreguemines sarəgəminə
Sarroca saroka
Sartène sartɛnə
Sarthe sartə
Sarthois sartwa
Sarthoise(s) sartwaːzə
Sartre sartrə

298 | FRENCH LYRIC DICTION

Sarwégur/Sarvégur sarvegy:r
Saskatchewan saskatʃawan
Satan satɑ̃
Satarem (De) də satarɛm
Satie satiə
Saturne satyrnə
Saturnin satyrnɛ̃
Saubens sobɛ̃:s
Saugues so:gə
Sauguet sogɛ
Saul sɔl
Saül sayl
Saulcis/Saulcy sosi
Saulnier sonje
Sault so
Saulteux sotø
Saulx so
Saulx-le-Duc so lə dyk
Saulx-les-Chartreux so lɛ ʃartrø
Saulxures sosy:rə
Saulzsais sozɛ
Saumaise some:zə
Saumur somy:r
Saussaies sosɛ
Saussens sosɛ̃:s
Saussine (De) də sosinə
Sautereau sotəro
Sauternes sotɛrnə
Sautet sotɛ
Sautreuil sotrœj
Sauvage sova:ʒə
Sauvageot sovaʒo
Sauvaget sovagɛ
Sauxillanges soksilɑ̃:ʒə
Savagnin savaɲɛ̃
Savari savari
Saverne savɛrnə
Savignol saviɲɔl
Savoie savwa
Savoisien(s) savwazjɛ̃
Savoisienne(s) savwazjɛnə
Savoy savwa
Savoyard(s) savwaja:r
Savoyarde(s) savwajardə
Sax saks
Saxe saksə
Saxonnex saksɔnɛ
Say sɛ
Scaër skɛ:r
Scala (La) la skala
Scaliger skaliʒɛ:r
Scamandre skamɑ̃:drə
Scandinave(s) skɑ̃dina:və
Scandinavie skɑ̃dinaviə
Scaramouche skaramuʃə
Scaremberg/Scaramberg skarɑ̃bɛrg
Scarlatti skarlat(t)i
Scarron skarɔ̃ or skarɔ̃
Sceaux so
Scée seə
Scey sɛ
Scey-Montbéliard (De) də sɛ mɔ̃bɛlja:r
Schaeffer ʃefɛ:r
Schaeffner ʃefnɛ:r
Schaerbeek skarbɛk or skarbek
Scharley ʃarlɛ

Scheffer ʃefɛ:r or ʃefe:r
Schéhérazade ʃeerazadə
Scheler ʃele:r
Schenker ʃeŋkɛ:r
Schenneberg ʃenəbɛrg
Schiaparelli skjaparɛli or skjapareli
Schiller ʃile:r
Schlegel ʃlegɛl
Schlémil ʃlemil
Schlesinger ʃlezɛ̃ʒɛ:r
Schlosser ʃlose:r
Schmidt ʃmit
Schmitt ʃmit
Schneider (French person) ʃnede:r
Schneider (German person) ʃnajde:ɾ
Schnitzler ʃnitsle:r
Schœffer ʃefɛ:r or ʃefe:r
Schœlcher ʃelʃe:r or ʃœlʃe:r
Schenker ʃeŋkɛ:r
Schoenberg ʃønbɛrg or ʃœnbɛrg
Schœneck ʃønɛk or ʃœnɛk
Schœnewerk ʃønəvɛrk or ʃœnəvɛrk
Schœnnbrunn ʃønbryn or ʃœnbryn
Schola Cantorum skɔla kɑ̃tɔrɔm
Schopenhauer ʃɔpenawɛ:r
Schtroumpf ʃtrum(p)f
Schubert ʃube:r
Schultheis ʃultɛs
Schumann ʃuman
Schütz ʃyts
Schweitzer ʃvajtze:r or ʃvedze:r
Schwer(d)tlein ʃvɛrtlajn
Schwerlein ʃvɛrlajn
Schwitz ʃvits
Schwyz ʃvits
Sciez sje
Scindia sɛ̃dja
Scio ʃʃo or sjo
Scipion sipjɔ̃
Sclayn sklaɛ̃
Scolastica skɔlastika
Scot(t) skɔt
Scotto skɔt(t)o
Scriabine skriabinə
Scribe skribə
Scylla sila
Scyros sirɔs or siro:s
Scythes sitə
Seattle siatœl or seatœl
Sébastian sebastjɑ̃
Sébastiani sebastjani
Sébastien sebastjɛ̃
Sébasto sebasto
Sébastopol sebastɔpɔl
Séboïm seboim
Séchan seʃɑ̃
Sedaine sədɛnə
Sedan sədɑ̃
Sédécias sedesjɑ:s
Sédillot sedijo
Sédir sedi:r
Sedlinsky sɛdlinski
Séez/Sées se
Ségala segala
Segalen segalɛn or segalɛ̃
Seghers segɛrs
Segond səgɔ̃

Segré səgre
Séguedille segədijə
Séguier segje
Séguin segɛ̃
Seguin (island) səgɛ̃
Seguin (person) səgɛ̃ or segɛ̃
Ségur segy:r
Ségur-Lamoignon segy:r lamwaɲɔ̃
Seine sɛnə
Seingalt (De) də sɛ̃galt or də sɛ̃gal
Seinomarin(s) senɔmarɛ̃
Seinomarine(s) senɔmarinə
Séjan seʒɑ̃
Séléné selene
Sélestat selɛsta
Selika/Sélika selika
Sellenick selənik
Sellers selɛrs
Seltz sɛls
Selva sɛlva
Sélysette selizɛtə
Sem sɛm
Sémillon semijɔ̃
Séminoles seminɔlə
Sémiramis semiramis
Sémire semi:rə
Semnoz (Le) lə semno:z
Sémonide semɔnidə
Sémos semɔs or semo:s
Semperoper sɛmperope:r
Sempey sɑ̃pe
Sempronius sɛ̃prɔnjys
Sénarens senarɛ̃:s
Senart sena:r
Sénart sena:r
Sénécas seneka
Senecé sɛnəse
Sénéchal seneʃal
Sénégal senegal
Sénégalais senegalɛ
Sénégalaise(s) senegalɛ:zə
Sénèque senɛkə
Senez sənɛ:z or sɛnɛs
Senghor sɛ̃gɔ:r or sɑ̃gɔ:r
Senlis sɑ̃lis
Sennachérib sɛnakerib or senakerib
Sennelier sɛnəlje
Sens sɑ̃:s
Séoudien(s) seudjɛ̃
Séoudienne(s) seudjɛnə
Séoul seul
Séphora sefɔra
Septante sɛptɑ̃:tə
Septème sɛptɛmə
Septmoncel sɛmɔ̃sɛl
Septmonts (De) də sɛmɔ̃
Septuagésime sɛptɥaʒezimə
Seraing sərɛ̃
Séraphin serafɛ̃
Sérapis serapis
Serbe(s) sɛrbə
Serbie sɛrbiə
Séré sere
Serengeti/Sérengéti serɛ̃geti
Serge sɛrʒə
Sérieys serjɛs
Seringe sərɛ̃:ʒə

PRONUNCIATION DICTIONARIES | 299

Serkoyan sɛrkɔjã
Sermet sɛrmɛ
Serpette sɛrpɛtə
Serrault sɛro
Serres (De) də sɛːrə
Sert, Misia miʃa sɛrt
Sertorius sɛrtɔrjys
Sérurier seryrje
Servières sɛrvjɛːrə
Sesmaisons semezõ
Sésostris sezɔstris
Seth sɛt
Sétubal setybal
Seurat sœra
Sévérac severak
Séverac (De) də sevərak or də sevərak
Sévère sevɛːrə
Séverin sevarɛ̃
Sévérus severys
Séveste sevɛstə
Sévigné (De) də seviɲe
Séville sevijə
Sèvres sɛːvrə
Sexagésime sɛgzaʒezimə
    or sɛksaʒezimə
Seychelles seʃɛlə
Seychellois seʃɛlwa
Seychelloise(s) seʃɛlwaːzə
Seyne (La) la sɛnə
Seyrig sɛrig
Seznec sɛznɛk
Sganarelle sganarɛlə
Shakespeare ʃɛkspiːr
Shanghaï ʃaŋgaj or ʃãgaj
Shéhérazade ʃeerazadə
Shepherd ʃepœrd
Shiva ʃiva
Shylock ʃajlɔk
Siam sjam
Siamois sjamwa
Siamoise(s) sjamwaːzə
Sibelius sibeljys
Sibérie siberiə
Sibérien(s) siberjɛ̃
Sibérienne(s) siberjɛnə
Sibert sibɛːr
Sibille sibijə
Sibylle sibilə
Sichée siʃeə
Sichem siʃɛm
Sicile sisilə
Sicilien(s) sisiljɛ̃
Sicilienne(s) sisiljɛnə
Sidaner (Le) lə sidanɛːr
Sidéro/Sidero sidero
Sidon sidõ
Sidonie sidɔniə
Siebel/Siébel sjebɛl
Sieg sig
Siégen sjegɛn
Siegfried sigfrid
Sienkiewics sjɛnkevitʃ
Sienne sjɛnə
Sierra (La) la sjɛra
Sierra Leone sjɛra leɔnə
Sierra-Léonais sjɛra leɔnɛ
Sierra-Léonaise(s) sjɛra leɔnɛːzə

Sieyès sjejɛs
Sifroid/Sifroy sifrwa
Sigalens sigalɛ̃ːs
Sigée siʒeə
Sigismond siʒismõ
Signac siɲak
Signoret siɲɔrɛ
Sigoulès sigulɛs
Sigurd sigyrd
Silène silenə
Silenus silenys
Silésie sileziə
Silésien(s) silezjɛ̃
Silésienne(s) silezjɛnə
Siloé silɔe
Silvain silvɛ̃
Silvanire silvaniːrə
Silvestre silvɛstrə
Silvio silvjo
Silvy silvi
Simca simka
Siméon simeõ
Simon simõ
Simone simɔnə
Simoneau simono
Simon-Girard simõ ʒiraːr
Simonide simɔnidə
Simon-Max simõ maks
Simonnet simɔnɛ
Simons simõːs
Sinaïde sinaidə
Sinclair sɛ̃klɛːr
Sindbad sindbad
Singapour sɛ̃gapuːr
Singapourien(s) sɛ̃gapurjɛ̃
Singapourienne(s) sɛ̃gapurjɛnə
Singer sɛ̃ʒɛːr or sɛ̃ʒe or siŋgœːr
Singer-Polignac sɛ̃ʒɛr pɔliɲak
Singhal singal
Singher sɛ̃gɛːr
Sinon sinõ
Siohan sjɔã
Sion sjõ
Sioux sju
Siraudin sirodɛ̃
Sirius sirjys
Siroco sirɔko
Sirven sirvɛ̃
Sisley sislɛ
Sisyphe sizifə
Sita/Sitâ sita
Siva siva or ʃiva
Sivry (De) də sivri
Sixtine sikstinə
Sizes siːzə
Skira skira
Slaves slaːvə
Slovaque(s) slɔvakə
Slovaquie slɔvakiə
Slovène(s) slɔvenə
Slovénie slɔveniə
Smetana smetana
Sminthée smɛ̃teə
Smith smit
Smyrne smirnə
Snédèr (La) la snedɛːr
Soboul sɔbul

Socrate sɔkratə
Sodome sɔdɔmə
Sofia sɔfja
Soiron swarð
Soissons swasõ
Solange sɔlã:ʒə
Solenière (De) sɔlənjɛːrə
Soler (Le) lə sole
Soles sɔlə
Solesmes sɔlɛmə
Solférino sɔlferino
Solié sɔlje
Sologne sɔlɔɲə
Solre-le-Château sɔr lə ʃato
Solti ʃɔlti
Solvay sɔlvɛ
Somalie sɔmaliə
Somalien(s) sɔmaljɛ̃
Somalienne(s) sɔmaljɛnə
Somarone sɔmarɔnə
Sombreuil sõbrœj
Somma sɔma
Somme sɔmə
Sompuis sõpɥi
Sompuits sõpɥi
Sonde (La) la sõːdə
Sophie sofiə
Sophocle sɔfɔklə
Sophonie sɔfɔniə
Sophonisbe sɔfɔnisbə
Sor sɔːr
Sorbonne sɔrbɔnə
Sore(c)k sɔrɛk
Sorel sɔrɛl
Sorlingues sɔrlɛ̃ːgə
Sormiou sɔrmju
Sosiphane sozifanə or sozifanə
Sosithée soziteə or soziteə
Sosthène sɔstenə
Sotchi sɔtʃi
Sothys sɔtis
Sottens sɔtã
Souabe swabə
Souberbielle subɛrbjɛlə
Soubies subiə
Soudan sudã
Soudanais sudanɛ
Soudanaise(s) sudanɛːzə
Souillac sujak
Souillot sujo
Soulacroix sulakrwa or sulakrwa
Soulé sule
Soulié sulje
Soult sult
Soultz sults
Soultzbach sultsbak
Soultzmatt sultsmat
Soumet sumɛ
Soupault supo
Souric surik
Sousceyrac suserak
Sousfroide (La) la sufrwaːdə
    or la sufrwadə
Soustrot sustro
Soutine, Chaïm ʃaim sutinə
Soutiran sutirã
Souvtchinsky suftʃinski

300 | FRENCH LYRIC DICTION

Soviétique(s) sɔvjetikə
Soyer swaje
Spakos spakɔs or spako:s
Spalanzani spalanzani or spalãzani
Spartacus spartakys
Sparte spartə
Spartiate sparsjatə
Spencer spɛnsɛ:r
Sperata sperata
Spiers spirs
Spinelly spinɛli or spineli
Spleen splin
Splendiano splãdjano
Spohr ʃpo:r or spo:r
Spontini spɔntini or spõtini
Spuller spylɛ:r
Sri Lanka sri lãka
Srilankais srilãkɛ
Srilankaise(s) srilãkɛ:zə
Staal sta:l or stal
Staal de Launay sta:l də lonɛ
   or stal də lonɛ
Stace stasə
Staël (De) də sta:l or də stal
Stains stɛ̃
Staline stalinə
Stamaty stamati
Stanislas stanisla:s
Stavisky staviski
Steenvorde stɛ̃vordə
Stein ʃtajn or stajn
Steiner ʃtajnɛ:r or stajnɛ:r or stɛnɛ:r
Steinkerque/Steenkerque stɛ̃kɛrkə
Steinlen stɛnlɛn or stɛ̃lɛn
Steinway stajnwɛ or stɛnwɛ
Stekel stɛkɛl
Stella stɛla or stela
Stendhal stɛ̃dal
Sténone stenɔnə
Stéphane stefanə
Stéphanie stefaniə
Stéphano stefano
Stésichore steziko:rə
Stilicon stilikõ
Stobée stɔbea
Stockhausen ʃtokawzən or stɔkozɛn
Stockholm stɔkɔlm
Stoléru stɔlery
Stoltz stɔlts or ʃtɔlts
Strabon strabõ
Stradivarius stradivarjys
Strasbourg strazbu:r
Strasbourg-Campagne strazbur kãpaɲə
Strasbourg-Ville strazbur vilə
Straton stratõ
Stratonice stratɔnisə
Straus(s) ʃtraws or straws or ʃtro:s
   or stro:s
Stravinski stravinski
Strozzi strɔdzi
Stuart stɥa:r
Stuttgart stytgart or ʃtutgart
Stutzmann stytsman
Styx stiks
Suarès sɥarɛs
Suchet syʃɛ
Sud-Africain(s) sy dafrikɛ̃

Sud-Africaine(s) sy dafrikɛnə
Sud-Américain(s) sy damerikɛ̃
Sud-Américaine(s) sy damerikɛnə
Sud-Coréen(s) syd korɛɛ̃
Sud-Coréenne(s) syd korɛɛnə
Suède sɥɛdə
Suédois sɥedwa
Suédoise(s) sɥedwa:zə
Suénon sɥenõ
Suétone sɥetɔnə
Sueur (Le) lə sɥœ:r
Suez sɥɛ:z
Suffren (street) syfrɛn
Suffren (all other cases) syfrɛ̃
Suger syʒe
Suisse sɥisə
Suissesse(s) sɥisɛsə
Sujol syʒɔl
Sully syli
Sully Prudhomme syli prydɔmə
Sulpice sylpisə
Sultane syltanə
Sumatra symatra
Sundgau sundgo or syndgo
Supervielle sypɛrvjɛlə
Suppé sype
Suriname syrinamə
Surinamien(s) syrinamjɛ̃
Surinamienne(s) syrinamjɛnə
Surrey syrɛ or sœrɛ
Suse sy:zə
Sussex sysɛks
Sutherland sytɛrlã:d or sœdərland
Suzanne syzanə
Suzon syzõ
Swazi(s) swazi
Swazie(s) swaziə
Swaziland swazilã:d or swaziland
Sydney sidnɛ
Sylla sila
Sylphe silfə
Sylphie silfiə
Sylva silva
Sylvain silvɛ̃
Sylvandre silvã:drə
Sylvane silvanə
Sylvaner silvanɛ:r
Sylvanire silvani:rə
Sylvestre silvɛstrə
Sylviano silvjano
Sylvie silviə
Symmaque simakə
Syphax sifaks
Syracuse siraky:zə
Syrah sira
Syrie siriə
Syrien(s) sirjɛ̃
Syrienne(s) sirjɛnə
Syrinx sirɛ̃:ks
Szulc sylk or ʃylts
Szymanowski simanɔvski
   or simanɔfski

— T —

Tabarly tabarli
Taché taʃe

Tacite tasitə
Tacmas takmɑ:s
Tadjik(s) tadʒik
Tadjike(s) tadʒikə
Tadjikistan tadʒikistã
Tadolini tadɔlini
Taffanel tafanɛl
Tage ta:ʒə
Taglioni taljɔni
Tahiti taiti
Tahitien(s) taisjɛ̃
Tahitienne(s) taisjɛnə
Tailhade tajadə
Taillandier tajãdje
Tailleferre tajəfɛ:r
Taipei/Taïpei/Taïpeh tajpɛ or tajpɛj
Taitbout tɛtbu
Taittinger tɛtɛ̃ʒe
Taiwan/Taïwan tajwan
Taiwanais/Taïwannais tajwanɛ
Taiwanaise(s)/
   Taïwannaise(s) tajwanɛ:zə
Taix tɛ
Taj Mahal taʒ maal
Talazac talazak
Talbot talbo
Talépulca talepylka
Tallemand des Réaux taləmã dɛ reo
Talleyrand talrã or talɛrã
Tallien taljɛ̃
Tallis talis
Talma talma
Talmud talmyd
Talon talõ
Talpain talpɛ̃
Talthybios taltibjɔs or taltibjo:s
Tamagno tamaɲo
Tamerlan tamɛrlã
Tamise tami:zə
Tamoyo tamɔjo
Tampa tampa or tãpa
Tananarive tananari:və
Tancrède tãkrɛdə
Tanit tanit
Tannat tana
Tannhäuser tanozɛ:r
Tantale tãtalə
Tantalos tãtalɔs or tãtalo:s
Tanzanie tãzaniə
Tanzanien(s) tãzanjɛ̃
Tanzanienne(s) tãzanjɛnə
Tapioca tapjɔka
Tarapote tarapɔtə
Tarascon taraskõ
Tarbé tarbe
Tarbes tarbə
Tardieu tardjø
Tarente (De) də tarã:tə
Tarifa tarifa
Tarn tarn
Tarnais tarnɛ
Tarnaise(s) tarnɛ:zə
Tart (De) də ta:r
Tartare tartɑ:rə
Tartas tartɑ:s
Taschereau taʃəro

PRONUNCIATION DICTIONARIES | 301

Taskin taskɛ̃
Tasmanie tasmaniə
Tasmanien(s) tasmanjɛ̃
Tasmanienne(s) tasmanjɛnə
Tasse (Le) lə tasə
Tassigny tasiɲi
Tastu tasty
Tati tati
Tatius tasjys
Taunus tonys
Taupier topje
Tauride toridə
Tautin totɛ̃
Tavannes (De) də tavanə
Taven tavɛn
Tazieff tazjɛf
Tchad tʃad
Tchadien(s) tʃadjɛ̃
Tchadienne(s) tʃadjɛnə
Tchaïkovsky tʃajkɔfski
Tchécoslovaque(s) tʃekɔslɔvakə
Tchécoslovaquie tʃekɔslɔvakiə
Tchèque(s) tʃɛkə
Tchernobyl tʃɛrnɔbil
Tchitor tʃitɔːr
Tebaldi tebaldi
Téhéran teerɑ̃
Teilhard De Chardin tɛjar də ʃardɛ̃
Teisserenc de Bort tɛsərɛ̃k də bɔːr
Teissié tɛsje
Teitgen tɛtʒɛn
Télaïre telaiːrə
Télamon telamɔ̃
Télasco/Telasco telasko
Tel-Aviv tɛ laviːv
Telemann teləman
Télémaque telemakə
Télème telɛmə
Télèphe telɛfə
Tell tɛl
Tellier tɛlje or telje
Ténare tenaːrə
Tence tɑ̃ːsə
Ténébrun tenebrœ̃
Ténédos tenedos or tenedoːs
Ténériffe/Tenerife tenerifə
Teniers tenje
Tennessee tenesi
Terana terana
Térée tereə
Térence terɑ̃ːsə
Teresa tereza
Ternes tɛrnə
Terpandre tɛrpɑ̃ːdrə
Terpsichore tɛrpsikɔːrə
Terracine terasinə
Terrail tɛraj
Terrasse tɛrasə
Terrasson tɛrasɔ̃
Terre-Neuve tɛrə nœːvə
Terrier tɛrje
Tersandre tɛrsɑ̃ːdrə
Tertullien tɛrtyljɛ̃
Tesnier tenje or tɛnje
Tesnière tɛnjeːrə or tɛnjɛːrə
Tessier tɛsje or tesje
Têt tɛt

Tétrarque tetrarkə
Tétu tety
Teucer tøseːr
Teugels tøʒɛls
Teulet tølɛ
Teutons tøtɔ̃
Texas tɛksɑːs
Texier tɛksje
Teyte tɛtə
Tézier tezje
Thaïlandais tajlɑ̃dɛ
Thaïlandaise(s) tajlɑ̃dɛːzə
Thaïlande tajlɑ̃ːdə
Thaïs tais
Thalès talɛs
Thalie taliə
Thanatos tanatos or tanatoːs
Thann tan
Thaon tɑ̃ or taɔ̃
Thébaïde tebaidə
Thébain(s) tebɛ̃
Thébaine(s) tebɛnə
Thèbes tɛbə
Thémire temiːrə
Thémistocle temistɔklə
Thénardier tenardje
Théocrite teokritə
Théodat teoda
Théodora teodɔra
Théodore teodɔːrə
Théodoret teodɔrɛ
Théodoric teodɔrik
Théodorine teodɔrinə
Théodose teodoːzə
Théodosie teodoziə
Théon teɔ̃
Théone teonə
Théonis teonis
Théophane teofanə
Théophile teofilə
Théophilus teofilys
Théophraste teofrastə
Théopompe teopɔ̃ːpə
Théramène teramɛnə
Thérésa tereza
Thérèse terɛːzə
Thersite tɛrsitə
Thésée tezeə
Thespis tɛspis
Thessalie tesaliə or tesaliə
Thessalien(s) tesaljɛ̃ or tesaljɛ̃
Thessalienne(s) tesaljɛnə
  or tesaljenə
Thessalonicien(s) tesalɔnisjɛ̃
  or tesalɔnisjɛ̃
Thessalonicienne(s) tesalɔnisjɛnə
  or tesalɔnisjenə
Thessalonique tesalɔnikə
  or tesalɔnikə
Thétis tetis
Theuriet tørje
Théus (De) də teys
Thévenard tevənaːr or tevənaːr
Thévenet tevɛnə or tevɛnə
Theys tɛ
Thibaud tibo
Thibault tibo

Thibaut tibo
T(h)ible tiblə
Thibet tibɛ
Thiboust tibu or tibust
Thierret tjɛrɛ
Thierrette tjɛrɛtə
Thierry tjɛri
Thiers tjeːr
Thiéry tjeri
Thill til
Thillot (Le) lə tijo
Thionville-Est tjɔ̃vi lɛst
Thionville-Ouest tjɔ̃vi lwɛst
Thoas tɔɑːs
Thomas tɔma
Thomas d'Aquin tɔma dakɛ̃
Thomé tɔme
Thomson tɔmsɔn
Thônes toːnə
Thonon-les-Bains tɔnɔ̃ lɛ bɛ̃
Thony tɔni
Thoré (De) də tɔre
Thorel tɔrɛl
Thoreau tɔro
Thorenc tɔrɑ̃
Thorens tɔrɑ̃ or tɔrɛ̃ːs
Thorez tɔrɛːz
Thorrenc tɔrɛ̃ːk
Thou tu
Thouars twaːr
Thrasybule trazibylə
Thucydide tysididə
Thueyts tɥɛj
Thuillier-Leloir tɥilje ləlwaːr
Thulé tyle
Thuret (De) də tyrɛ
Thurgovie tyrgɔviə
Thuringe tyrɛ̃ːʒə
Thyeste tjɛstə
Tibère tibɛːr
Tiberge tibɛrʒə
Tibre tibrə
Tibulle tibylə
Tiefenbach tifənbak or tifɛnbak
Tiffauges tifoːʒə
Tiffenbourg tifənbuːr or tifɛnbuːr
Tigny (De) də tiɲi
Tigrane tigranə
Tilleur tijœːr or tilœːr
Tilliard tiljaːr
Tillier tilje
Tillières tiljeːrə
Tilly tiji
Tilmant tilmɑ̃
Tilsit tilsit
Timagène timaʒɛnə
Timée timeə
Timoléon timɔleɔ̃
Timone (La) la timɔnə
Timor Oriental timo rɔrjɑ̃tal
Timothée timɔteə
Timour timuːr
Tinan (De) də tinɑ̃
Tinée tineə
Tintin tɛ̃tɛ̃
Tintoret (Le) lə tɛ̃tɔrɛ
Tinville tɛ̃vilə

302 | French Lyric Diction

Tiphaine tifɛnə
Tiquetonne tikətɔnə
Tirard tiraːr
Tircis tirsis
Tirésias tirezjaːs
Tirmont tirmõ
Tirso tirso
Tirynthe tirɛ̃ːtə
Tisiphone tizifɔnə
Tissot tiso
Titan titã
Titania titanja
Titanide titanidə
Tite titə
Tite-Live titə liːvə
Tithon titõ
Titien tisjɛ̃
Titine titinə
Titus titys
Titye titiə
Titzikan titsikan
Tiviane tivjanə
Tlaxcaltèques tlakskaltɛkə
Tobago tobago
Tobie tobiə
Toby tɔbi
Toché tɔʃe
Togo tɔgo
Togolais tɔgɔlɛ
Togolaise(s) tɔgɔlɛːzə
Tokyo tɔkjo
Tolède tɔlɛdə
Tolstoï tɔlstoj
Toltèques tɔltɛkə
Tolu tɔly
Tom tɔm
Tomasi tɔmazi
Tombouctou tõbuktu
Tonga tõga or tɔnga
Tong(u)ien(s) tõgjɛ̃ or tɔngjɛ̃
Tong(u)ienne(s) tõgjɛnə
  or tɔngjɛnə
Tonio tɔnjo
Tonneins tɔnɛ̃ːs
Topor tɔpoːr
Tora(h) (La) la tɔra
Torcy tɔrsi
Torlogne tɔrlɔɲə
Toronto tɔrõto
Torquemada tɔrkemada
Tortelier tɔrtəlje
Toscane tɔskanə
Touareg twarɛg
Touchatout tuʃatu
Toudouze tuduːzə
Toul tul
Toulet tulɛ
Toulon tulõ
Toulouse tuluːzə
Toulouse-Lautrec tuluzə lotrɛk
Touraine turɛnə
Tourangeau turãʒo
Tourangeau(x) turãʒo
Tourangelle(s) turãʒɛlə
Tourcoing turkwɛ̃
Tour-du-Pin (La) la tur dy pɛ̃
Tourel turɛl

Touret turɛ
Tourgueniev/Tourguéniev turgenjɛf
Tourière (La) la turjɛːrə
Tournemire turnəmiːrə
Tourneur turnœːr
Tourneux turnø
Tourniaire turnjɛːrə
Tournier turnje
Tournon-sur-Rhône turnõ syr roːnə
Tournus turny
Tours tuːr
Tourte turtə
Toussaint tusɛ̃
Toussus tusy
Toutânkhamon tutãkamõ
Touzet tuzɛ
Trachiniennes (Les) lɛ trakinjɛnə
Trafalgar trafalgaːr
Tragin traʒɛ̃
Tramayes tramajə
Tranchant trãʃã
Transylvain(s) trãsilvɛ̃
Transylvaine(s) trãsilvɛnə
Transylvanie trãsilvaniə
Transylvanienne(s) trãsilvanjɛnə
Tranyslvanien(s) trãsilvanjɛ̃
Trebelli-Bettini trebɛli bɛtini
  or trebɛli bɛtini
Trébizonde trebizõːdə
Trécourt trekuːr
Tréfeu trefø
Tréfontaine (De) də trefõtɛnə
Tréfort trefoːr
Tréfouël trefwɛl
Trégastel tregastɛl
Trégor tregoːr
Tréguier tregje
Treilhard trɛjaːr
Treille (La) la trɛjə
Trélat trela
Trémois tremwa
Trémolini tremɔlini
Trémo(u)ille/(De La) də la tremujə
Trempont trãpõ
Trenet trɛnɛ
Trestraou trɛstrau
Trets trɛ or trɛts
Trèves trɛːvə
Trévi trevi
Trévise treviːzə
Trézelle trezɛlə
Trézène trezɛnə
Trial trial
Trianon trianõ
Tribonien tribɔnjɛ̃
Tricasse (Van) vã trikaːsə
Triel triɛl
Trinidadien(s) trinidadjɛ̃
Trinidadienne(s) trinidadjɛnə
Trinité (La) la trinite
Trinité-et-Tobago trinite e tobago
Trintignant trɛ̃tiɲã
Triolet triɔlɛ
Tripoli tripoli
Triptolème triptɔlɛmə
Trissin (Le) lə trisɛ̃
Tristan tristã

Tristan L'Hermite tristã lɛrmitə
Tristapatte tristapatə
Triton tritõ
Troade troadə
Troarn trɔarn
Trocadéro trokadero
Trochu trɔʃy
Troësne/Troesne (La) la trɔɛnə
Trogue-Pompée trɔgə põpeə
Troie trwa
Troillet trwajɛ
Trois-Évêchés trwa zevɛʃe or trwa zevɛʃe
Troisgras trwagra or trwagra
Troismonts trwamõ or trwamõ
Troispoux trwapu or trwapu
Troisvaux trwavo or trwavo
Trollope trɔlɔpə
Trotski trɔtski
Trouard-Riolle truar rjɔlə
Trouillefou trujəfu
Troupenas trupəna
Troy trwa
Troyat trwaja
Troyen(s) trwajɛ̃
Troyenne(s) trwajɛnə
Troyes trwa
Troyon trwajõ
Truc tryk
Truck tryk
Truffaut tryfo
Truffier tryfje
Truffot tryfo
Truillet-Soyer trujiɛ swaje
Trump trœmp
Trutat tryta
Truyère tryjɛːrə
Tsarskoïé-Sélo tsarskɔje selo
Tsigane tsiganə
Tual tɥal
Tubalcaïn tybalkaɛ̃
Tubiana tybjana
Tuileries tɥilariə
Tulasne tylaːnə
Tuléar tyleaːr
Tulipatan tylipatã
Tulle tylə
Tullie tyliə
Tullins tylɛ̃
Tullius tyljys
Tunis tynis
Tunisie tyniziə
Tunisien(s) tynizjɛ̃
Tunisienne(s) tynizjɛnə
Turba-Rabier tyrba rabje
Turbigo tyrbigo
Turc(s) tyrk
Türckheim tyrk(h)ajm
Turenne tyrɛnə
Turin tyrɛ̃
Turkestan tyrkɛstã
Turkmène(s) tyrkmɛnə
Turkménie tyrkmeniə
Turkménistan tyrkmenistã
Turp tyrp
Turque(s) tyrkə
Turquie tyrkiə
Tweed twid

PRONUNCIATION DICTIONARIES | 303

Tybalt tibalt
Tycho Brahé tiko brae
Tyndare tɛ̃daːɾə
Tyndaris tɛ̃daris
Typhée tifeə
Typhon tifõ
Tyr tiːɾ
Tyrcis tirsis
Tyre tiːɾə
Tyrien tiɾjɛ̃
Tyrolien(s) tiɾɔljɛ̃
Tyrolienne(s) tiɾɔljɛnə
Tyrrhénie tiɾeniə
Tyrrhénien(s) tiɾenjɛ̃
Tyrrhénienne(s) tiɾenjɛnə
Tyrtée tiɾteə
Tzara tsaɾa
Tzipine tsipinə

— U —

Ubaje ybajə
Ubalde ybaldə
Ubaye ybajə
Ubu yby
Ucalégon ykalegõ
Ugalde ygaldə
Uhlans | ylɑ̃
Ukraine ykɾɛnə
Ukrainien(s) ykɾɛnjɛ̃
Ukrainienne(s) ykɾenjɛnə
Ulpien ylpjɛ̃
Ulric(h) ylɾik
Ulrique ylɾikə
Ulster ylstɛːɾ
Ulysse ylisə
Umfroy œ̃fɾwa or õfɾwa
Umpeau œ̃po
Undine œ̃dinə
Unterwald untɛrvald
Uranie yraniə
Uranus yranys
Urbain yɾbɛ̃
Urbal (D') dyɾbal
Urdens yɾdɛ̃ːs
Urgande yɾgɑ̃ːdə
Urgel yɾʒɛl
Urgèle yɾʒɛlə
Uri uɾi or yɾi
Uria-Monzon yɾja mɔnzɔn
   or uɾja mɔnzɔn
Urien yɾjɛ̃
Urraque yrakə
Ursins (Des) dɛ zyrsɛ̃
Ursule yrsylə
Uruguay yɾygwɛ or yɾygɥɛ
Uruguayen(s) yɾygwɛjɛ̃ or yɾygɥɛjɛ̃
   or yɾygwajɛ̃
Uruguayenne(s) yɾygwejɛnə
   or yɾygɥɛjɛnə or yɾygwajɛnə
Usher yʃɛːɾ
Ussé yse
Ussel ysɛl
Utah yta
Uthal ytal
Utrecht ytɾɛk or ytɾɛkt
Utrillo ytɾijo

Utter ytɛːɾ
Uxelles ysɛlə
Uxellodunum ykselɔdynɔm
   or ykselɔdynɔm
Uzès yzɛs

— V —

Vacaresco vakaɾesko
Vacher vaʃe
Vacheron Constantin vaʃɾõ kõstãtɛ̃
Vachot vaʃo
Vacquerie vakəɾiə
Vadé vade
Vaduz vaduts or vady:z
Vaëz vaɛːz or vaɛs
Vaguet vagɛ
Vaillant vajɑ̃
Vaillant-Couturier vajɑ̃ kutyɾje
Vaillard vajaːɾ
Vailly-sur-Aisne vɛli sy ɾɛnə
   or veli sy ɾɛnə
Vailly-sur-Sauldre vaji syɾ soːdrə
Val d'Oise val dwaːzə
Valabrègue valabɾɛːgə
Valachie/Valaquie valakiə
Valadon valadõ
Valaincourt (De) də valɛ̃kuːɾ
Valangoujar valɑ̃guʒaːɾ
Valayre valɛːɾə
Valbarelle (La) la valbaɾɛlə
Valbon valbõ
Val-de-Grâce val də gɾɑːsə
Val-de-Marne val də maɾnə
Val-Démoné val demone
Valdès valdɛs
Valdiguier/Valdiguié valdigje
Valée valeə
Valençay valɑ̃sɛ
Valence valɑ̃ːsə
Valencien(s) valɑ̃sjɛ̃
Valencienne(s) valɑ̃sjɛnə
Valengin valɑ̃ʒɛ̃
Valens valɛ̃ːs
Valentin valɑ̃tɛ̃
Valentine valɑ̃tinə
Valentinien valɑ̃tinjɛ̃
Valentiniens valɑ̃tinjɛ̃
Valentino valɑ̃tino
Valentinois valɑ̃tinwa
Valère valɛːɾə
Valérie valeɾiə
Valérien valeɾjɛ̃
Valerius/Valérius valeɾjys
Valéry valeɾi
Valjean valʒɑ̃
Valkyrie valkiɾiə
Valladolid valadolid
Vallauris valoɾis
Vallès valɛs
Vallet (person; E France) valɛ
Vallet (W France) valɛt
Vallier valje
Vallin valɛ̃
Valmy valmi
Valmy-Baysse/
   Valmy-Baisse valmi bɛsə

Valois (De) də valwa
Valois-Saint-Rémy (De) də valwa
   sɛ̃ ɾemi
Valréas valɾeaːs
Vals vals
Valsien valsjɛ̃
Van Cleef & Arpels vɑ̃ klɛ fe aɾpɛl(s)
   or van klɛ fe aɾpəls
Van Dam vɑ̃ dam
Van Der Elst/Van Der Helst
   vɑ̃ dɛ ɾelst or van də ɾelst
Vanderprout vɑ̃dɛɾpɾut
Van Dyck vɑ̃ dik
Van Gelder vɑ̃ gɛldɛːɾ
Van Gennep vɑ̃ ʒɛnɛp
Van Gogh vɑ̃ gɔg or van gɔg
Van Goyen vɑ̃ gɔjen or van gɔjen
Van Helmont va nɛlmõ
Van Lerberghe vɑ̃ lɛɾbɛɾgə
   or van lɛɾbɛɾgə
Van Zandt vɑ̃ zɑ̃ːt
Vancouver vɑ̃kuvɛːɾ
Vancy (De) də vɑ̃si
Vanderbilt vɑ̃dɛɾbilt
   or vandɛɾbilt
Vanglor vɑ̃glɔːɾ
Vanier vanje
Vanina vanina
Vanloo/Van Loo vɑ̃lo
Vannes vanə
Vanni-Marcoux vani maɾku
Vans (Les) lɛ vɑ̃ːs or lɛ vɑ̃
Vanuatu vanwatu
Vanxains vɑ̃sɛ̃
Vanzo vɑ̃zo
Vaour vauːɾ
Var vaːɾ
Varbel vaɾbɛl
Varedha/Varédha vaɾeda
Varèse vaɾɛːzə
Vargues vaɾgə
Varney vaɾnɛ
Varois vaɾwa
Varoise(s) vaɾwaːzə
Varron vaɾõ
Varsovie varsoviə
Vartan vaɾtɑ̃
Vasco de Gama vasko də gama
Vascons vaskõ
Vasnier vanje or vanje
Vasseur vasœːɾ
Vassiliki vasiliki
Vasteville vastəvilə
Vasto (Del) dɛl vasto
Vathiménil vatimenil
Vati(s)mesnil (De) də vatimenil
   or də vatimenil
Vatican vatikɑ̃
Vau (Le) lə vo
Vauban vobɑ̃
Vaucluse vokly:zə
Vauclusien(s) voklyzjɛ̃
Vauclusienne(s) voklyzjɛnə
Vaucorbeil vokoɾbɛj
Vaucouleurs vokulœːɾ
Vaud vo
Vaudemont vodəmõ

304 | FRENCH LYRIC DICTION

Vaudoyer vodwaje
Vaudreuil (De) də vodrœj
Vaufrèges vofrɛːʒə
Vaugelas voʒəla
Vaughan Williams von wiljams
  or vogan wiljams
Vaugirard voʒiraːr
Vauguyon (De La) də la voɡɥijõ
Vaulx vo
Vaulx (La) la vo
Vaulx-en-Velin vo ã vəlɛ̃
Vaurabourg vorabuːr
Vaurs voːr
Vauthrin votrɛ̃
Vauvert vovɛːr
Vauvillers vovilɛːr
Vauxcelles vosɛla
Vaux-le-Vicomte vo lə vikõːtə
Veber vebɛːr
Veigy-Foncenex vɛʒi fõsənɛ
Veil vɛj
Vélabre (Le) lə velaːbrə or lə velabrə
Vélasquez/Vélazquez velaskɛːz
  or velaskɛs
Velay vəlɛ
Vellescot vɛlɛsko
Vellones vɛlonə or velonə
Venceslas/Wenceslas vɛ̃sɛslaːs
Vendée vãdeə
Vendéen(s) vãdeɛ̃
Vendéenne(s) vãdeɛnə
Vendôme vãdoːmə
Vénétie venesiə
Venezuela venezɥela
Vénézuélien(s) venezɥeljɛ̃
Vénézuélienne(s) venezɥeljɛnə
Venise vəniːzə
Vénitien(s) venisjɛ̃
Vénitienne(s) venisjɛnə
Venoge (De) də vənɔːʒə
Ventadour vãtaduːr
Ventoux vãtu
Vénus venys
Ver vɛːr
Vercingétorix vɛrsɛ̃ʒetoriks
Vercors vɛrkɔːr
Verdi vɛrdi
Verdier vɛrdje
Verdière vɛrdjɛːrə
Verdot vɛrdo
Verdun vɛrdœ̃
Verduron vɛrdyrõ
Verget vɛrʒɛ
Vergin vɛrʒɛ̃
Vergnes vɛrɲə
Vergnet vɛrɲe
Vergniaud vɛrɲo
Vergt vɛːr
Verhaeren vɛrarɛn
Verjux vɛrʒy
Verlain vɛrlɛ̃
Verlaine vɛrlɛnə
Verlet vɛrlɛ
Vermand vɛrmã
Vermandois vɛrmãdwa
Vermandoise(s) vɛrmãdwaːzə

Vermenton vɛrmãtõ
Vermont vɛrmõ
Vernaz (La) la vɛrna
Verne vɛrnə
Verneix vɛrnɛ
Vernet vɛrnɛ
Verneugheol vɛrnøʒol
Verneuil vɛrnœj
Vernon vɛrnõ
Vernoy vɛrnwa
Vérone veronə
Véronèse veronɛːzə
Véronique veronikə
Verreau vɛro
Verrier (Le) lə vɛrje
Verrocchio (Le) lə vɛrok(k)jo
Verrot vɛro
Versailles vɛrsaːjə
Verseuil vɛrsœj
Vertumne vɛrtymnə
Vertus vɛrty
Vervins vɛrvɛ̃
Vesgre vɛgrə
Vesle vɛlə
Vesoul vəzul or vəzu
Vespasien vɛspazjɛ̃
Vesta vɛsta
Vestris vɛstris
Vestvali (Von) fon vɛstvali
Vésubie vezybiə
Vésuve vezyːvə
Véturie vetyriə
Veuillot vœjo
Veuve Clicquot vœvə kliko
Vexin vɛksɛ̃
Veyron-Lacroix vɛrõ lakrwa
  or vɛrõ lakrwa
Veys vɛ
Vézelay vezəlɛ or vezəlɛ
Vézins vezɛ̃
Vezolot vezɔlo
Vezzani vɛdzani
Vhita vita
Viadène vjadɛnə
Viallet vjalɛ
Vian vjã
Viardot vjardo
Viardot-Garcia vjardo garsja
Viau (De) də vjo
Vibraye vibrɛ
Vicdessos vikdɛsoːs or vikdesoːs
Vichnevskaïa viʃnɛfskaja
Vichy viʃi
Victoire viktwaːrə
Victor viktɔːr
Victorien viktɔrjɛ̃
Victor-Perrin viktor pɛrɛ̃
Vidal de la Blache vidal də la blaʃə
Videix vidɛ
Vieille vjɛjə
Vienne vjɛnə
Viennois vjɛnwa
Viennoise(s) vjɛnwaːzə
Vierne vjɛrnə
Vierzon vjɛrzõ
Viêt-Nam vjɛt nam

Vietnamien(s) vjɛtnamjɛ̃
Vietnamienne(s) vjɛtnamjɛnə
Vieu vjø
Vieuille vjœjə
Vieux-Colombier vjø kɔlõbje
Vieuxtemps vjøtã
Vigan (Le) lə vigã
Vigneau viɲo
Vigneron viɲərõ
Vigny (De) də viɲi
Vikings vikiŋ
Vilard vilaːr
Vilbac (De) də vilbak
Vildrac vildrak
Villabella vilabɛla
Villa-Lobos vila lobos et vila loboːs
Villandry vilãdri
Villard vilaːr
Villard-de-Lans vilar də lãːs
  or vilar də lã
Villaret vilarɛ
Villars vilaːr
Villaume vijoːmə
Villebichot viləbiʃo
Villebougin viləbuʒɛ̃
Villecresnes viləkrɛnə
Villecroze viləkroːzə
Villefranche-de-Rouergue viləfrãʃə
  də rwɛrgə
Villefranche-sur-Saône viləfrãʃə
  syr soːnə
Villelume (De) də viləlymə
Villemain viləmɛ̃
Villenauxe vilano:ksə
Villeneuve vilanœːvə
Villeneuve-sur-Lot vilanœvə syr lot
Villequier viləkje
Villers vilɛːr
Villers-Bocage vilɛr bɔkaːʒə
Villersexel vilɛrsɛksɛl
Villerupt vilary
Villette (La) la vilɛtə
Villiers vilje
Villiers de l'Isle-Adam vilje də li ladã
Villon vijõ
Vilmorin (De) də vilmorɛ̃
Vimeu vimø
Vimeux vimø
Vimy vimi
Vincenette vɛ̃sənɛta
Vincennes vɛ̃sɛna
Vincent vɛ̃sã
Vincentais vɛ̃sãtɛ
Vincentaise(s) vɛ̃sãtɛːzə
Vinci (De) də vɛ̃si
Viñes viɲes
Vingtrie (De La) də la vɛ̃triə
Viognier vjoɲe
Viomesnil (De) də vjomenil
  or də vjomenil
Viosne vjoːnə
Vire viːrə
Virgile virʒilə
Virginie virʒiniə
Virginie-Occidentale virʒini
  oksidãtalə

PRONUNCIATION DICTIONARIES | 305

Viriathe virjatə
Viroflay virɔflɛ
Viroubova virubɔva
Visapour vizapuːr
Visconti viskõti
Vismes vimə
Visse visə
Viste (La) la vistə
Vistule vistylə
Vitellius viteljys or viteljys
Vitruve vitryːvə
Vitry-le-François vitri lə frãswa
Vittel vitɛl
Vivaldi vivaldi
Vivarais vivarɛ
Viverols vivərɔl
Vivien vivjẽ
Vivienne vivjɛnə
Vix viks
Vizentini vizɛntini
Vlaminck (De) də vlamɛ̃ːk
Vœuil vœj
Vogüé vɔgɥe
Voïvodine vɔjvɔdinə
Volga vɔlga
Volhynie vɔliniə
Volsques vɔlskə
Voltaire vɔltɛːrə
Von Meck fɔn mɛk
Von Vestvali fɔn vɛstvali
Vosges voːʒə
Vosgien(s) vɔʒjẽ
Vosgienne(s) vɔʒjɛnə
Vosne-Romanée vonə rɔmanea
Vougeot vuʒo
Voulte (La) la vultə
Vouvray vuvrɛ
Vouziers vuzje
Vranken vrãkɛn
Vresme vrɛmə
Vrillière (La) la vriljɛːrə or la vrijɛːrə
Vritz vri
Vuarnet vɥarnɛ
Vuillard vɥijaːr
Vuillaume vɥijoːmə
Vuillemin vɥijəmẽ
Vuillermoz vɥijɛrmoːz
Vuitton vɥitõ
Vulcain vylkẽ
Vulcan vylkã

— W —

Waas/Waes | was
Wace vasə or | wasə
Wafflard vafklaːr
Wagner vagnɛːr
Wagnière vaɲɛːrə
Wagram vagram
Wailly (De) də vaji
Wal-Berg val bɛrg
Walcourt | walkuːr or valkuːr
Waldeck valdɛk
Waldeck-Rousseau valdɛk ruso
Waldor valdɔːr
Walewska valɛvska

Walewski valɛvski
Walhalla valala
Walkyrie valkiriə
Wallez valɛːz
Wallis-et-Futuna | wali se futuna
Wallon (person) valõ
Wallonie | waloniə
Wallonnes(s) | walɔnə or valɔnə
Wallon(s) | walõ or valõ
Walpurgis valpyrʒis
Waltzing valsẽ
Walter valtɛːr
Walter Furst/Fürst valtɛr fyrst
Walton | waltɔn
Wandre | wãːdrə or vãːdrə
Wanfercée | wãfɛrsea or vãfɛrsea
Wantzenau (La) la vãtsəno
Warche (La) la | warʃə or la varʃə
Waregem | warəgɛm
Waremme | warɛmə or varɛmə
Warens (De) də varã or də varɛ̃ːs
Warin varɛ̃
Warnant | warnã or varnã
Waroquier (De) də varɔkje
Warot varo
Wartel vartɛl
Washington | waʃiŋtɔn
Wasmes | wamə or vamə
Wasquehal | waskal
Wasselonne vasəlɔnə
Wassigny | wasiɲi or vasiɲi
Wassy vasi
Wast (Le) lə va
Watelet vatəlɛ
Waterloo | watɛrlo
Watteau vato
Wattignies | watiɲiə or vatiɲiə
Wavre | waːvrə or vaːvrə
Weber vebɛːr
Webern vebɛrn
Wèbre vɛːbrə
Weckerlin vekɛrlẽ
Weil vɛjl
Weill vajl or vɛjl
Weiller vɛlɛːr
Weimar vajmaːr
Weisweiller vajsvɛlɛːr
Welles | wɛls
Wellington | weliŋtɔn
Wenceslas/Venceslas vɛ̃sɛslaːs
Wendats | wɛndat
Wendel (De) də vẽdɛl
Wendes vãːdə
Werner vɛrnɛːr
Werther vɛrtɛːr
Wessex | wesɛks
Westermann vɛstɛrman
Westminster | wɛstminstɛːr
Westphalie vɛstfaliə
Wetzlar vɛtslaːr
Whistler | wistlɛːr
Whitehall | wajtoːl
Whitman | witman
Whittington | witiŋtɔn
Widal vidal
Widor vidɔːr

Wieck vik
Wiéner/Wiener vjenɛːr
Wilde | wajld
Wilder vildɛːr
Wilfird vilfrid
Wilhelm Meister vilɛlm
majstɛːr
Willaumez vijome or vijomɛːz
Willette vilɛtə
Williams | wiljams
Willis | wilis
Wilmotte vilmɔtə or | wilmɔtə
Wimille vimilə or | wimilə
Windsor | windzɔːr or | wintsɔːr
Winnaretta | winarɛta
Winnipeg | winipɛg
Wisches viʃə
Wischnou viʃnu
Wisconsin | wiskɔnsin
Wisigoths vizigo
Wissembourg visãbuːr or visɛbuːr
Witikind vitikẽ or vitikɛ̃ːd
Witkowski vitkovski or vitkofski
Woëvre | waːvrə or vwaːvrə
Wohanka vɔðka
Wolf vɔlf
Wolff vɔlf
Woluwé/Woluwe | wɔlywe
or | wɔlye
Woolf | wulf or ulf
Wormhoudt | wɔrmut or vɔrmut
Worth vɔrt
Wotan vɔtã
Wotan (in Wagner) vɔtan
Wouwerman vuverman
Wrangel vrãgel or vrãʒel
Wrède vrɛdə
Wroclaw vrɔklaːv or vrɔtslaːv
or vrɔtslaf
Wurtemberg vyrtɛbeːr
Wyns vinz or vins
Wyoming | wajomiŋ
Wyss vis

— X —

Xaintois sɛ̃twa or gzɛ̃twa or ksɛ̃twa
Xaintonge (De) də sɛ̃tõːʒə
Xaintrailles sɛ̃trɑːjə
Xant(h)ippe gzãtipə
Xant(h)e gzãːtə
Xant(h)i gzãːti
Xavier gzavje
Xenakis gzenakis or ksenakis
Xénia ksenja
Xénocrate gzenɔkratə
Xénophane gzenofanə
Xénophon gzenofõ
Xérès gzerɛs or kserɛs or kerɛs
Xertigny ksɛrtiɲi
Xerxès gzɛrsɛs
Xhendelesse | ãdələsə or hãdələsə
Xhoffraix | ɔfrɛ or hofrɛ
Xhoris | ɔris or horis
Ximénès gzimenɛs or kimenɛs
Xuthos ksytɔs or ksytoːs

— Y —

Yadwigha |jadwiga
Yakar |jakaːr
Yale |jɛl
Yalta |jalta
Yaoundé |jaunde
Yeats |jits
Yémaldin jemaldin *or* |jemaldin
Yémen |jemɛn
Yéménite(s) |jemenitə
Yen |jɛn
Yerres jɛːrə
Yeu jø
Ygène iʒɛnə
Ygraine igrɛnə
Yniold injɔld
Yoan(n)/Yohan(n) |jɔan
Yolcos jɔlkɔs *or* jɔlkoːs
Yonne jɔnə
York |jɔrk *or* jɔrk
Youca |juka
Yougoslave(s) |jugoslaːvə
Yougoslavie |jugoslaviə
Youkali |jukali
Young juŋ *or* |juŋ
Yourcenar |jursənaːr
Youville (D') djuvilə
Ypres iprə
Ys is
Ysaÿe/Ysaye izai
Yseult izø
Yssingeaux isɛ̃ʒo
Yukon |jukɔ̃ *or* |jukɔn *or* |jykɔ̃
Yvain ivɛ̃
Yveline ivəlinə
Yvelines ivəlinə
Yvelinois ivəlinwa
Yvelinoise(s) ivəlinwaːzə
Yverdon-les-Bains ivɛrdɔ̃ lɛ bɛ̃
Yves iːvə
Yves Saint-Laurent ivə sɛ̃ lɔrɑ̃
Yvetot ivəto
Yvette ivɛtə

Yvoire ivwaːrə
Yvonne ivɔnə
Yzeure izœːrə

— Z —

Zaboulistan zabulistɑ̃
Zacchée zakeə
Zacharie zakariə
Zachée zaʃeə *or* zakeə
Zadig zadig
Zafari zafari
Zagreb zagrɛb
Zagros zagroːs
Zaïde zaidə
Zaïre zaiːrə
Zaïrois zairwa
Zaïroise(s) zairwaːzə
Zaïs zais
Zakros zakrɔs *or* zakroːs
Zambie zɑ̃biə
Zambien(s) zɑ̃bjɛ̃
Zambienne(s) zɑ̃bjɛnə
Zamora zamɔra
Zampa (*opera*) zampa *or* zɑ̃pa
Zampieri ʣampjeri *or* tsampjeri
Zanetta ʣanɛt(t)a *or* tsanɛt(t)a
Zanetti zanɛti *or* zaneti
Zanzibar zɑ̃zibaːr
Zarlino ʣarlino *or* tsarlino
Zavatta zavata
Zazie zaziə
Zébaoth zebaɔt
Zedda ʣɛda
Zégris zegri
Zelensky zelɛnski
Zélide zelidə
Zélise zeliːzə
Zellenberg tsɛlənbɛrg *or* zelɛnbɛrg
Zémire zemiːrə
Zénobie zenɔbiə
Zénon zenɔ̃
Zéphire zefiːrə
Zéphirine zefirinə

Zéphoris zefɔris
Zéphyr zefiːr
Zerbin zɛrbɛ̃
Zerline zɛrlinə
Zétulbé zetylbe
Zeus ʣøːs
Zeuxis zøksis
Ziegler ziglɛːr *or* ziglœːr
Ziem zjɛm
Ziliante ziljɑ̃ːtə
Zima zima
Zimbabwe zimbabwe
Zimbabwéen(s) zimbabweɛ̃
Zimbabwéenne(s) zimbabweɛnə
Zimmermann zimɛrman
   or tsimərman
Zingara(s) ʣiŋgara *or* tsiŋgara
Zingaro(s) ʣiŋgaro *or* tsiŋgaro
Zinnia zinja
Ziriphile zirifilə
Zizel zizɛl
Zoé zoe
Zoïle zoilə
Zola zɔla
Zopyre zopiːrə
Zoraïde zoraidə
Zorastra zorastra
Zorastre zorastrə
Zoroastre zoroastrə
Zorobabel zorɔbabɛl
Zorro zoro
Zosime zozimə
Zoulou(s) zulu
Zouloue(s) zuluə
Zucchi ʣuk(k)i *or* tsuk(k)i
Zuecca (La) la zɥɛk(k)a
   or la zwɛk(k)a
Zuléïma zyleima
Zuniga zyniga *or* zuniga
Zurga zurga
Zurich zyrik
Zurichois zyrikwa
Zurichoise(s) zyrikwaːzə
Zwickau tsvikaw

Pronunciation Dictionary of Borrowed Italian Musical Terms

About the System of Transcription for the Pronunciation Dictionary of Borrowed Italian Musical Terms

The loanwords on the following list are more likely to be spoken than sung. Uvular *r* is therefore shown, as /ʀ/. Where multiple pronunciations are often used in French, options are given. Word stress—usually on the penultimate syllable in Italian—is shifted by most speakers to the final syllable in French. Consonant lengthening is made by some speakers, especially for the unvoiced plosives /tt/, /kk/, and /pp/.

accelerando atʃeleʀando *or* atʃeleʀã(n)do
ad libitum ad libitɔm
adagio adadʒ(j)o *or* adaʒjo
affettuoso afet(t)ɥozo
agitato a(d)ʒitato
allargando alaʀgando *or* alaʀgã(n)do
allegretto/allégretto alegʀɛt(t)o
allegro/allégro alegʀo
andante andante *or* ã(n)dã(n)te
andantino andantino *or* ã(n)dã(n)tino
animato animato
appoggiatura apɔdʒ(j)atyʀa *or* apɔʒjatyʀa
   sometimes as: **appog(g)iature**
   apɔdʒ(j)aty:ʀə *or* apɔʒjaty:ʀə
arioso aʀjozo
arpeggio aʀpedʒ(j)o *or* aʀpeʒjo
   often as: **arpège** aʀpɛ:ʒə
bel canto bɛl kanto *or* bɛl kã(n)to
brioso bʀiozo
cadenza kadɛntsa *or* kadɛndza *or* kadẽ(n)tsa
   or kadẽ(n)dza
cantabile kãtabile
capriccio kapʀitʃjo
coloratura kɔlɔʀatyʀa *often as:* **colorature** kɔlɔʀaty:ʀə
con grazia kon gʀatsja
con moto kon mɔto
concerto kõsɛʀto
crescendo kʀeʃendo
da capo da kapo
dal segno dal seɲo
decrescendo/décrescendo dekʀeʃendo
diminuendo diminɥendo
dolce dɔltʃe
dolcissimo dɔltʃisimo
dolente dɔlɛnte
espressivo ɛspʀɛsivo
fine fine
forte fɔʀte
fortepiano fɔʀtepjano
rinforzando ʀinfɔʀtsando *or* ʀinfɔʀdzando
   or ʀinfɔʀtsã(n)do *or* ʀinfɔʀdzã(n)do
fortissimo fɔʀtisimo
giocoso dʒ(j)ɔkozo *or* ʒjɔkozo
grave gʀa:və
grazioso gʀatsjozo
intermezzo ĩtɛʀmɛdzo
largamente laʀgamɛnte
larghetto laʀgɛt(t)o
largo laʀgo
legato/légato legato
leggiero ledʒ(j)eʀo *or* leʒjeʀo

lento lɛnto
maestoso maɛstozo
marcato maʀkato
meno mosso meno mɔso
mesto mɛsto
mezzo forte mɛdzo fɔʀte
mezzo piano mɛdzo pjano
mezza voce mɛdza vɔtʃe
moderato/modérato mɔdeʀato
molto mɔlto
morendo mɔʀendo
pianissimo pjanisimo
piano pjano
più mosso pju mɔso
pizzicato pidzikato
poco pɔko
prestissimo pʀestisimo
presto pʀesto
primo pʀimo
rallentando ʀalɛntando *or* ʀalẽ(n)tã(n)do
ripieno ʀipjeno
risoluto ʀizoluto
ritardando ʀitaʀdando *or* ʀitaʀdã(n)do
ritenuto/riténuto ʀitenuto
rondo (rondeau) ʀõdo
rubato ʀubato
scherzando skɛʀtsando *or* skɛʀdzando *or* skɛʀtsã(n)do
   or skɛʀdzã(n)do
scherzo skɛʀdzo
semplice sɛmplitʃe
sempre sɛmpʀe
secundo səkõdo
senza sɛntsa *or* sɛndza *or* sẽ(n)tsa *or* sẽ(n)dza
sforza sfɔʀdza
sforzando sfɔʀtsando *or* sfɔʀdzando *or* sfɔʀtsã(n)do
   or sfɔʀdzã(n)do
simile simile
smorzando smɔʀtsando *or* smɔʀdzando *or* smɔʀtsã(n)do
   or smɔʀdzã(n)do
sostentuo/sosténuto sɔstenuto
sotto voce sɔt(t)o vɔtʃe
staccato stak(k)ato
stringendo stʀindʒendo
subito sybito *or* subito
tempo tɛmpo
tenuto/ténuto tenuto
tranquillo tʀãkwilo
tremolo tʀemolo
troppo tʀɔp(p)o
tutti tut(t)i
vivace vivatʃe

Bibliography

Académie française. 'Les rectifications de l'orthographe.' *Journal officiel de la République Française*, № 100 (1990): 2–18.

ADAMS, DAVID. *A Handbook of Diction for Singers: Italian, German, French*. 3rd ed. New York: Oxford University Press, 2002.

ADLER, KURT. *Phonetics and Diction in Singing; Italian, French, Spanish and German*. Minneapolis: University of Minnesota Press, 1965.

ALVERGNAT, VICTOR. *The Modern Class Book of French Pronunciation: Containing All the Rules, with Their Exceptions, Which Govern the Pronunciation of the French Language*. Boston: Schoenhof and Moeller, 1872.

Association Française des Professeurs de Chant pour L'Étude et la Recherche. *La mélodie française : Actes du Colloque (1995)*. Paris: Conservatoire National Supérieur de Musique et de Danse de Paris, 1996.

BANVILLE, THÉODORE DE. *Petit traité de la poésie française*. Paris: Le Clerc, 1872.

BARBEAU, ALFRED, and GUSTAF EMIL RODHE. *Dictionnaire phonétique de la langue française*. Stockholm: P. A. Norstedt, 1930.

BAUDOT, MARCEL. 'Remarques sur la prononciation des noms de lieux de la France.' *Revue internationale d'onomastique* 14, № 2 (1962): 93–106.

BERNAC, PIERRE. *Francis Poulenc et ses mélodies*. Paris: Éditions Buchet-Chastel, 1977.

BERNAC, PIERRE. *The Interpretation of French Song*. London: Cassel, 1970.

Bescherelle. *Le nouveau Bescherelle : l'art de conjuguer : dictionnaire de douze mille verbes*. Paris: Hatier, 1980.

BOOTH, TRUDIE MARIA. *French Phonetics: A Guide to Correct Pronunciation of French*. Lanham, MD: University Press of America, 1997.

CASTEL, NICO, et al. *French Opera Libretti: With International Phonetic Alphabet Transcriptions, Word for Word Translations, Including a Guide to the IPA and Notes on the French Transcriptions, Volume I*. Geneseo, NY: Leyerle, 1999.

CASTEL, NICO, et al. *French Opera Libretti: With International Phonetic Alphabet Transcriptions, Word for Word Translations, Including a Guide to the IPA and Notes on the French Transcriptions, Volume II*. Geneseo, NY: Leyerle, 2000.

CASTEL, NICO, et al. *French Opera Libretti: With International Phonetic Alphabet Transcriptions, Word for Word Translations, Including a Guide to the IPA and Notes on the French Transcriptions, Volume III*. Geneseo, NY: Leyerle, 2005.

CASTEL, NICO, et al. *Gluck and Monteverdi Opera Libretti: With International Phonetic Alphabet Transcriptions, Word for Word Translations, Notes on the French and Italian Transcriptions*. Geneseo, NY: Leyerle, 2008.

CASTEL, NICO, et al. *Italian/French Bel Canto Opera Libretti. Volume III*. Geneseo, NY: Leyerle, 2002.

Le Centre National de la Recherche Scientifique. 'Le TLFi : Trésor de la Langue Française informatisé.' ATILF/CNRS—Université de Lorraine. http://atilf.atilf.fr/tlf.htm.

COBB, MARGARET G. *The Poetic Debussy*. Rochester, NY: University of Rochester Press, 1994.

COLLOT, ALEXANDER G. *A New and Improved Standard French and English and English and French Dictionary*. Philadelphia: C. G. Henderson & Co., 1852.

DELATTRE, PIERRE. 'La liaison en Français, tendances et classification.' *French Review* 21, № 2 (1947): 148–157.

DEMERS, JEANNE. *Phonétique théorique et pratique (français moderne)*. Montréal: Centre de Psychologie et de Pédagogie, 1962.

DIBBERN, MARY. *Carmen: A Performance Guide*. Hillside, NY: Pendragon Press, 2000.

DIBBERN, MARY. *Faust, Roméo et Juliette: A Performance Guide*. Hillside, NY: Pendragon Press, 2006.

DIBBERN, MARY. *The Tales of Hoffmann: Performance Guide*. Hillside, NY: Pendragon Press, 2002.

DONNAN, THOMAS M. *French Lyric Diction*. Lanham, MD: University Press of America, 1994.

EUREN, SIGURD FREDRIK. *Étude sur l'R Français: Vol. I. Prononciation et changements de l'R*. Uppsala: Almqvist & Wiksell, 1896.

FOUCHÉ, PIERRE. *Traité de prononciation française*. 2nd ed. Paris: Klincksieck, 1959.

GARTSIDE, ROBERT. *Interpreting the Songs of Gabriel Fauré*. Geneseo, NY: Leyerle, 1996.

GARTSIDE, ROBERT. *Interpreting the Songs of Maurice Ravel*. Geneseo, NY: Leyerle, 1992.

GAUDIN, LOIS. 'La prononciation des noms de personnes.' *French Review* 11, № 1 and № 2 (1937): 44–49, 138–146.

GEDDES, JAMES. *French Pronunciation: Principles and Practice and a Summary of Usage in Writing and Printing*. New York: Oxford University Press, 1913.

GERMAIN, FRANÇOIS, and ELLEN RISSINGER. *Chantez!: An Interactive Handbook of French Diction for Singers*. Mac OS. V. 41.0.2272.76. Singing Diction, LLC., 2020.

GRAMMONT, MAURICE. *Traité pratique de prononciation française*. Paris: Delagrave, 1914.

GRAMMONT, MAURICE. *Traité pratique de prononciation française*. 9th ed. Paris: Delagrave, 1938.

GREVISSE, MAURICE. *Le bon usage: grammaire française*. Paris-Gembloux: Duculot, 1936.

GREVISSE, MAURICE, and ANDRÉ GOOSSE. *Le bon usage: grammaire française*. 16th ed. Brussels: De Boeck, 2016.

GRUBB, THOMAS. *Singing in French: A Manual of French Diction and French Repertoire*. New York: Schirmer, 1979.

HAHN, REYNALDO. *Du chant*. Paris: P. Lafitte, 1920.

HAHN, REYNALDO. *On Singers and Singing*. Translated by Léopold Simoneau. Portland, OR: Amadeus Press, 1990.

HAHN, REYNALDO. *Thèmes variés*. Paris: Janin, 1946.

HALLARD, MARIE-PAULE. *Le français chanté: Phonétique et aspects de la langue en chant classique*. Lyon: Symétrie, 2020.

HALLARD, MARIE-PAULE. 'Réflexions sur la liaison, l'enchaînement consonantique et l'hiatus en chant classique.' *Le journal de l'Association Française des Professeurs de Chant*, № 19 (2012): supplement.

Handbook of the International Phonetic Association: A Guide to the Use of the International Phonetic Alphabet. New York: Cambridge University Press, 1999.

HENNEBERT, FRÉDÉRIC. *Cours élémentaire de prononciation de lecture à haute voix et de récitation*. 9th ed. Tournai: H. Casterman, 1856.

HUNTER, DAVID. *Understanding French Verse: A Guide for Singers*. New York: Oxford University Press, 2005.

JACK, JAMES WILLIAM. *Manual of French Pronunciation and Diction Based on the Notation of the Association Phonétique Internationale*. London: Harrap, 1922.

JOHNSON, GRAHAM, and JEREMY SAMS. *Poulenc: The Life in the Songs*. New York: Liveright, 2020.

JOHNSON, GRAHAM, and RICHARD STOKES. *A French Song Companion*. Oxford: Oxford University Press, 2000.

JOHNSON, GRAHAM, and RICHARD STOKES. *Gabriel Fauré: The Songs and Their Poets*. Farnam, Surrey: Ashgate Publishing, 2009.

KAMMANS, LOUIS-PHILIPPE. *La prononciation française d'aujourd'hui : manuel à l'usage des étudiants, des comédiens, des speakers*. 3rd ed. Amiens: Les éditions scientifiques et littéraires, 1964.

Éditions Larousse. *Larousse Advanced French-English/English-French Dictionary*. Paris: Larousse, 2007.

Éditions Larousse. *Le Larousse des noms propres*. Paris: Larousse, 2008.

BIBLIOGRAPHY | 311

LE ROUX, FRANÇOIS, and ROMAIN RAYNALDY. *Le chant intime: de l'interprétation de la mélodie française.* Paris: Fayard, 2004.

LE ROUX, FRANÇOIS, and ROMAIN RAYNALDY. *Le chant intime: The Interpretation of French Mélodie.* New York: Oxford University Press, 2021.

LE ROUX, FRANÇOIS, and ROMAIN RAYNALDY. *L'opéra français: une question de style: de l'interprétation lyrique.* Paris: Hermann, 2019.

LE ROY, GEORGES. *Grammaire de diction française.* Paris: Éditions de la Pensée Moderne, 1967.

LESAINT, M.-A. *Traité complet de la prononciation française dans la seconde moitié du XIXe siècle contenant les règles de prononciation de tous les mots de la langue française, de tous les termes propres aux arts, aux sciences et à l'industrie, et de tous les noms propres historiques, géographiques et mythologiques français et étrangers.* Hamburg: Mauke, 1871.

LEVAN, TIMOTHY. *Masters of the French Art Song: Translations of the Complete Songs of Chausson, Debussy, Duparc, Fauré & Ravel.* 1991. Lanham, MD: Scarecrow Press, 2001.

LITTRÉ, ÉMILE. Electronic version by François Gannaz. 'Le Littré (XMLittré v2). Dictionnaire Littré—Dictionnaire de la langue française.' https://www.littre.org/.

MARTINON, PHILIPPE. *Comment on prononce le français: traité complet de prononciation pratique avec les noms propres et les mots étrangers.* Paris: Larousse, 1913.

MESSIAEN, OLIVIER. Text by composer. *Chants de terre et de ciel.* Paris: Durand, 1939.

MILHAUD, DARIUS. Text by RENÉ CHALUPT. *Les soirées de Pétrograde.* Paris: Durand, 1920.

MOLIÈRE. Edited by GEORGES FORESTIER et al. *Œuvres complètes, vol. 2. Le bourgeois gentilhomme.* Paris: Gallimard, 2010.

MORIARTY, JOHN. *Diction: Italian, Latin, French, German: The Sounds and 81 Exercises for Singing Them.* Boston: E. C. Schirmer Music, 1975.

NÉRON, MARTIN. 'Language and Diction: To Bə or Not to Bə: Notes on the Muted E.' *Journal of Singing* 68, № 4 (2012): 431–441, № 5 (2012): 547–560.

NICHOLS, ROGER. *The Art of French song: 19th and 20th Century Repertoire: Complete with Translations and Guidance on Pronunciation.* London: Peters, 1999.

PANZÉRA, CHARLES. *50 Mélodies françaises: leçons de style et d'interprétation.* Brussels: Schott, 1964.

PASSY, PAUL. *Abrégé de prononciation française, phonétique et orthoépie, avec un glossaire des mots contenus dans le français parlé.* 4th ed. Leipzig: Reisland, 1914.

PASSY, PAUL. *Le français parlé: Morceaux choisis à l'usage des étrangers avec la prononciation figurée.* 8th ed. Leipzig: Reisland, 1930.

PASSY, PAUL. *Sounds of the French Language: Their Formation, Combination and Representation.* Translated by D. L. Savory and Daniel Jones. Oxford: Clarendon Press, 1907.

PASSY, PAUL, and HERMANN MICHAELIS. *Dictionnaire phonétique de la langue française: complément nécessaire de tout dictionnaire français.* 2nd ed. Hannover-Berlin: C. Meyer, 1914.

PIERRET, JEAN-MARIE. *Phonétique historique du français et notions de phonétique générale.* Nouv. éd. Louvain-La-Neuve: Peeters, 1994.

POULENC, FRANCIS. Text by GEORGES BERNANOS. *Dialogues des Carmélites.* Paris: Ricordi, 1957.

POULENC, FRANCIS. Text by various authors. *Intégrale des mélodies et chansons.* Paris: Durand, 2013.

POULENC, FRANCIS. *Journal de mes mélodies.* Paris: Grasset, 1964.

POULENC, FRANCIS. text by GUILLAUME APOLLINAIRE. *Les mamelles de Tirésias.* Paris: Heugel, 1947.

POULENC, FRANCIS. Text by JEAN COCTEAU. *La voix humaine.* Paris: Ricordi, 1958.

RAVEL, MAURICE. Text by ÉVARISTE DE PARNY. *Chansons madécasses.* Paris: Durand, 1926.

RAVEL, MAURICE. Text by PAUL MORAND. *Don Quichotte à Dulcinée.* Paris: Durand, 1934.

REMACLE, LOUIS. *Orthoépie: essai de contrôle de trois dictionnaires de prononciation française.* Liège: Faculté de philosophie et lettres de l'Université de Liège, 1994.

Le Robert. *Le Grand Robert des noms propres: Dictionnaire universel alphabétique et analogique des noms propres.* Paris: Le Robert, 1994.

Robert & Collins. *Le Grand Robert & Collins: Dictionnaire Anglais-Français/Français-Anglais.* Paris: Dictionnaires Le Robert, 2008.

ROUSSEL, ALBERT. Text by HENRI-PIERRE ROCHÉ. *Deux poèmes chinois.* Paris: Durand, 1934.

THOMAS, ADOLPHE V., and MIGUEL de TORO. *Dictionnaire des difficultés de la langue française.* Paris: Larousse, 2006.

THURWANGER, CAMILLE. *Musical Diction: An Orthologic Method for Acquiring a Perfect Pronunciation in the Speaking and Especially in the Singing of the French Language.* London: Novello, 1910.

WARNANT, LÉON. *Dictionnaire de la prononciation française dans sa norme actuelle.* Paris-Gembloux: Duculot, 1987.

WARNANT, LÉON, and LOUIS CHALON. *Orthographe et prononciation en français: les 12000 mots qui ne se prononcent pas comme ils s'écrivent.* 2nd ed. Brussels: Duculot, 2006.

Index

Listed below are the topics treated in this book, as well as the composers, poets, librettists, and titles for all musical examples. Page numbers in *italics* refer to musical examples; those in parentheses ( ) refer to pronunciation recommendations for surnames, characters or roles, and titles. References to footnotes are indicated with 'n'; references to works cited in the Bibliography are indicated with 'b'.

a, à, â, æ: pronunciation of, (alone, or as the first of two or more letters), 4, 5, 12, 13, 14, 19, 22, 109–110, 128–141, (246–250)
accent aigu. See acute accent
accent circonflexe. See circumflex accent
accent d'insistance. See stress
accent d'intensité. See stress
accent grave. See grave accent
accent tonique. See stress
acute accent ´ (*accent aigu*), 52, 149, 152
affricates. *See* consonants
alexandrine (*alexandrin*), 94
anonymous author, 76
Apollinaire, Guillaume, *50, 62, 67, 99, 102,* 108n, *111, 119,* (248), 311b
Auber, Daniel-François-Esprit, (162), (249)
    Le domino noir, 74

b: pronunciation of, 6, 30–31, 41, 141–142, (250–256)
Banville, Théodore de, 94, (141), (182), (250)
    Petit traité de poésie française, 94, 309b
Barbier, Jules, *40, 44, 53, 59, 60, 66, 67, 69, 94, 95, 98, 109, 117,* (251)
Baton, René-Emmanuel. *See* Rhené-Baton
Baudelaire, Charles, *37, 65, 99,* (132), (251)
Bayard, Jean-François, *59,* (251)
Berlioz, Hector, 53, (194), (211), (242), (252)
    La damnation de Faust, 76, 118, (139), (222), (225), (267)
    L'enfance du Christ, 67
    Les nuits d'été, 19
    Les Troyens, 112

Bernac, Pierre, 46, 111n, (142), (252), 309b
    The Interpretation of French Song, 46, 111n, 309b
Bizet, George, 97, 100, (141), (253)
    'Absence', *68*
    Carmen, 17, 19, 39, 62, 66, 70, 74, 96, 100, 100, 116, 117, 118, 119, (129), (159), 188, 190, 220, (257), (285), 310b
    'Chanson d'avril', *100*
    Les pêcheurs de perles, 76
Blau, Édouard, *75, 97, 98, 99,* (253)
Blès, Numa, 157, (253)
Bonneau, Dominique, 157, (254)
Bouchor, Maurice, *57,* (254)
Bouilhet, Louis, *100,* (181), (254)
Boulanger, Nadia, (161), (254)
    'Versailles', *17*

c: pronunciation of, (alone, or as the first of two or more letters), 6, 30–31, 41, 42, 63n, 142–146, (256–262)
c with cedilla ç (*c cédille*), 143
cabaret and *chanson* (popular song), 4, 35, 71
Cain, Henri, *96,* (142), (256)
Calvocoressi, Michel–Dimitri, *113,* (256)
Caplet, André, (165), (223), (256)
    Trois fables de Jean de la Fontaine, 17
Carême, Maurice, 181, (257)
Carré, Michel, *40, 44, 53, 59, 60, 66, 67, 76, 94, 95, 98, 109, 117,* (257)
Cazalis, Henri. *See* Lahor, Jean
cesura (*césure*), 94

314 | INDEX

Chabrier, Emmanuel, (130), (144), (177), (180), (246), (257)
    L'Étoile, (274)
    'Villanelle des petits canards', *62*
Chalupt, René, *102*, (209), (224), (258), 311b
Chaminade, Cécile, (176), (258)
    'Colette', *69*, (260)
chanson (popular song). *See cabaret*
Charpentier, Gustave, (258)
    Louise, *120*, (281)
Chausson, Ernest, 97n, (259), 311b
    'La caravane', *52*
    'Le charme', *59*
    'Le colibri', *114*
    'Les papillons', *113*
    Poème de l'amour et de la mer, *57*
Cherubini, Luigi, (231), (259)
    Médée, *114*, (154), (283)
circumflex accent ^ (*accent circonflexe*), 129, 193
Cocteau, Jean, *103*, *118*, (154), (260), 311b
Colette, (Sidonie-Gabrielle), *115*, (260)
Comédie-Française, 4, 4n, 56, 72
consonants
    affricates, 7, 40, 40n, 128, 246
    alveolar articulation, 30, 31, 33, 36, 40
    bilabial articulation, 30, 32
    consonant release (*la détente de la consonne*), 8, 37, 44, 101
    dental articulation, 8, 29, 30–31, 32–33
    devoicing, 4, 4n, 8, 33, 36, 36n, 186
    fricatives, 4n, 6, 31–32, 33, 36, 36n, 37, 40
    'hard' variants, 41–42, 52n, 142, 144–145, 171, 172, 174, 192
    inaudible release, 8, 44
    inflecting. *See inflecting consonants*
    intervocalic/between vowels, 29, 37, 41, 47, 52, 93, 176, 177, 213, 216, 217
    labialization, 8, 32, 35
    labio-dental articulation, 30, 31
    lateral articulation. *See l*
    lengthening of (*la gémination consonantique*), in unvoiced plosives of Italian loanwords, 144, 207, 229, 307; in prefixes, 111–112, 188, 189, 193, 213; of *r* (rolled), 37, 113, 213; phrasally, 113–114; traditional lengthening, 114
    nasal consonants, 32
    palatal articulation, 4n, 30, 32
    palatalization, 8, 31
    plosives, 4n, 6, 8, 23–24, 25, 29, 30–31, 36, 40, 44, 108, 111n, 307; aspirated articulation of, 8, 30, 31
    post-alveolar articulation, 30, 31, 35, 40
    retracted articulation, 8, 35
    silent. *See also individual letters*, as word-final, 43; in older French texts, 42n

'soft' variants, 41–42, 142–143, 144, 153, 161, 167, 171, 172
tap, trilled/rolled articulation. *See r*
uvular articulation. *See r*
velar articulation, 30, 32
velarization. *See l*
voiced vs. unvoiced, 29–33, 36, 40–42
consonant linking (*enchaînement consonantique*), 4, 9, 20, 38, 49–51, 55, 59, 64, 65n, 103, 310b
consonant-vowel flow, 3, 4, 45–54, 55, 108
consonnes flexionnelles. *See* inflecting consonants
Cormon, Eugène, 76, (260)

d: pronunciation of, 6, 30–31, 40, 41, 43, 63, 146–148, (262–265)
'dark' *a*/'bright' *a*. *See a, à, â, æ*
Debladis, Georgette, *61*, (262)
Debussy, Claude, 27, 42n, (46), 53, 96, 97, 100, (141), (146), (222), (262), 310b, 311b
    'Apparition', *77*, 98
    Ariettes oubliées, *101*, 118
    Chansons de Bilitis, *68*, 99, (219), (253)
    'En sourdine', *28*
    L'enfant prodigue, *115*
    Fêtes galantes, série I, *28*, 60
    'Mandoline', *front cover*, 96
    'Noël des enfants qui n'ont plus de maisons', *116*
    Pelléas et Mélisande, *58*, 93, 114, (114), 117, 119, (129), (151), (219), (283), (290)
    Trois ballades de François Villon, *65*
    Trois chansons de France, *75*
Delafosse, Léon, (262)
    Quintette de fleurs, *102*
Delibes, Léo, (163), (263)
    'Les filles de Cadix', *63*
    Lakmé, 97, 99, (187), (278)
denasalization. *See liaison*
Deschamps, Émile, *64*, (216), (221), (263)
détente de la consonne, la. *See* consonants: consonant release
diacritics. *See* phonetic transcription
dialogue, 4, 24, 35, 48n, 109
diction, description of, 3
dieresis (*diérèse*), 26–28, 52, 128, 177, 203, 230, 240, 245
dieresis diacritic ¨ (*tréma*), 52, 52n, 174, 175
digraphs, 41–42, 47
diphthong, 3, 5, 6, 11, 12, 14, 25n, 45, 130, 133, 139, 141, 155, 167, 203, 204
Donizetti, Gaetano, (264)
    La fille du régiment, *59*
doubled consonants. *See* consonant lengthening
Duparc, Henri, (142), (265), 311b
    'Chanson triste', *20*, 71, *71*

'L'invitation au voyage', *65*, *99*
'Phidylé', *16*, (207), (290)

e, é, è, ë: pronunciation of, (alone, or as the first of two or more letters), 3, 4, 5, 6, 12–22, 43–44, 93–104, 109–111, 148–170, (265–267)
e muet. See mute *e*
editions. *See* French musical editions
élision vocalique. See vocalic elision
Éluard, Paul, *44*, *50*, *63*, *103*, *112*, *115*, (230), (265)
emphatic stress. *See* stress
enchaînement consonantique. See consonant linking
euphonic *t* (*t euphonique*), 52
Euren, Sigurd Fredrik, 34–35, 36
   Étude sur l'R français, 34–35, 310b
everyday speech (*parler courant*), 4, 4n, 16, 16n, 21, 33, 44, 55, 93, 100, 101, 109, 110, 123, 150, 157, 159, 160, 163, 165, 194, 245

f: pronunciation of, 6, 31, 41, 42, 170–171, (267–269)
Fauré, Gabriel, (13), 97n, (139), (170), (211), (267), 310b, 311b
   'Au bord de l'eau', *120*
   'Les berceaux', *51*
   La bonne chanson, *96*
   'C'est la paix !', *61*
   'Chanson d'amour', *37*
   'La chanson du pêcheur', *77*
   'Clair de lune', *50*
   Cinq mélodies de Venise, *18*, *70*
   'Dans les ruines d'une abbaye', *95*
   'Ici-bas', *119*
   'Mai', *16*, *19*
   'Nell', *74*, (287)
   'Le papillon et la fleur', *27*
   Poème d'un jour, *39*, *112*
   'La rançon', *37*
Fontaine, Jean de la, *17*, (268)
Fouché, Pierre, 110, (268)
   Traité de prononciation française, 110, 310b
Franc-Nohain, *65*, (135), (268)
French, general characteristics of the language, 3–4, 15–16, 21, 29, 45–46, 48–49, 55, 93, 107–111; evolving pronunciation of, 4, 33–34, 42, 55; musical editions, 104–105
fricatives. *See* consonants

g: pronunciation of, (alone, or as the first of two or more letters), 6, 18–19, 30–32, 41, 42, 63–64, 171–175, (269–272)
Gandonnière, Almire, *76*, *118*, (201), (269)
Gautier, Théophile, *19*, *52*, *68*, *77*, *113*, (223), (270)
gémination consonantique, la. See consonants: lengthening of

Gérard, Rosemonde, *62*, (270)
Gille, Philippe, *73*, *97*, *98*, *99*, *109*, (270)
glides. *See* semiconsonants
glottal stop, 4, 8, 51, 108
Gluck, Christoph Willibald, 53, (145), (171), (270), 309b
   Iphigénie en Tauride, *76*, (176), (207), (275)
Gondinet, Edmond, *97*, *99*, (271)
Gounod, Charles, (14), 53, (147), (193), (271)
   Faust, *40*, *66*, *67*, *94*, *95*, *98*, (139), (222), (225), (267), 310b
   Roméo et Juliette, *44*, 53, *59*, *60*, *66*, *95*, *117*, (229), (277), (295), 310b
Grammont, Maurice, 127, (136), (271)
   Traité pratique de prononciation française, 127, 310b
Grandmougin, Charles, *39*, *112*, (271)
grave accent ` (*accent grave*), 52
Grémont, Henri. *See also* Hartmann, Georges, *76*, (271)
Grindel, Eugène. *See* Éluard, Paul
groupe phonétique, le. See phonetic group, the
Guillard, Nicolas-François, *76*, (272)

h: pronunciation of, 37–40, 41, 43, 52n, 176, (272–275); articulation in rare instances, 9, 39–40, 176; aspirated *h* (*h aspiré*), 37–40, 52n, 58, 83–84, 120–122, 156, 176, 221, 246; aspirated *h* words listed, 38; mute *h* (*h muet*), 37–39, 50, 66, 83, 136, 151, 158, 176, 181, 185, 190, 200, 216, 237; special cases with initial *h*, 39
Hahn, Reynaldo, 3, 35, (38), *97*, (130), (132), (176), (272), 310b
   'À Chloris', *98*, (144), (219), (259)
   Chansons grises, *101*
   Du chant, 3, 310b
   Études latines, *18*
   Les feuilles blessées, *116*
   'Paysage', *73*
   'Si mes vers avaient des ailes', *63*
   'Sur l'eau', *103*
   Thèmes variés, 35, 310b
Halévy, Fromental, (176), (235), (272)
   La juive, *75*
Halévy, Ludovic, *17*, *19*, *39*, *58*, *62*, *66*, *70*, *74*, *96*, *100*, *116*, *117*, *118*, *119*, (176), (235), (272)
Hartmann, Georges. *See also* Grémont, Henri, *75*, *98*, *99*, (273)
l'harmonisation vocalique. See vocalic harmonization
hiatus, 49, 51–52, 52n, 56, 73, 77, 149, 154, 161, 164, 176, 310b
Hoffman, François-Benoît, *114*, (274)
Houdar de la Motte, Antoine, *75*, (274)
Hugo, Victor, *16*, *19*, *27*, *59*, *63*, *95*, (171), (275)

316 | INDEX

hyphen/hyphenation, 17, 27, 45–46, 47, 50, 86, 95, 96, 101, 102, 194
Hyspa, Vincent, *58*, (275)

i, î, ï: pronunciation of, (alone, or as the first of two or more letters), 5, 12, 22, 25–27, 176–186, (275–276)
indirect *liaison* (*liaison indirecte*). See *liaison*
inflecting consonants (*consonnes flexionnelles*), 56
International Phonetic Alphabet (IPA): transcription in. See phonetic transcription

j: pronunciation of, 6, 31–32, 41, 186, (276–277)
Jacob, Max, *51*, *71*, *115*, *116*, (130), (141), (276)
Jones, Daniel, 11, 311b

k: pronunciation of, 41, 187, (277–278)

l: pronunciation of, (alone, or after *i*), 7, 26, 32–33, 41, 42, 111–112, 181–183, 187–188, (278–281);
    lateral consonant articulation, 7, 32–33;
    devoicing of, 4, 4n, 33; velarized *l*, 9, 33
Lahor, Jean, *20*, *71*, (132), (176), (278)
Lalo, Édouard, (278)
    Le roi d'Ys, 97
Leconte de Lisle, Charles Marie René, *16*, *18*, *74*, *114*, (148), (187), (216), (279)
Legrand, Maurice Étienne. See Franc-Nohain
Lemaire, Ferdinand, *73*, (279)
Le Roy, Georges, 72, (295)
    Grammaire de diction française, 72, 311b
liaison. *Refer also to final consonants throughout Part II*
    alteration of vowel in, 65
    denasalization in, 23, 65–69, 80, 86, 89, 135, 156, 179, 185, 200, 240
    differences of opinion on, 56, 72
    forbidden *liaison* (*liaison interdite*), 57–62;
        exceptions to forbidden *liaison*, 59, 60, 72–77
    historical use of, 55, 56, 89, 90
    indirect *liaison* (*liaison indirecte*), 108n
    list of use in common vocabulary, 78–92
    making decisions about, (considering syntax, affect on meaning, proper nouns, tone of text and speaker, musical setting), 69–71
    optional *liaison* (*liaison facultative*), 56–57
    rare examples and special cases of, 77
    required *liaison* (*liaison obligatoire*), 56
    special *liaison* from final /s/, 220
    spelling and pronunciation of, 63–64
Louÿs, Pierre, *68*, *99*, (177), (219), (281)
Lully, Jean-Baptiste, 53, (188), (281)
    Amadis, *73*, (247)

m: pronunciation of, (alone, as a nasalizing letter, or as the first of two or more letters), 7, 22–24, 32, 41, 43, 111–112, 135–136, 156–157, 184, 188–190, 198–199, 232–233, 241, (281–286)
Maeterlinck, Maurice, *58*, *93*, *114*, *117*, *119*, (146), (281)
Mallarmé, Stéphane, 77, *77*, *98*, (282)
Marot, Clément, 42n, (282)
Martinon, Philippe, 77, 110, (283)
    Comment on prononce le français, 77, 110, 311b
Massenet, Jules, 53, 97, 109, (165), (223), (283)
    'Ce que disent les cloches', 67
    Cendrillon, *96*, (142), (182), (257)
    Hérodiade, *76*, (274)
    Manon, (13), *73*, *97*, *98*, *109*, (129), (200), (282)
    Poème du souvenir, 64
    'Rien ne passe !', 69
    Werther, *75*, *98*, *99*, (162), (226), (235), (305)
Meilhac, Henri, *17*, *19*, *39*, *58*, *62*, *66*, *70*, *73*, *74*, *96*, *97*, *98*, *100*, *109*, *116*, *117*, *118*, *119*, (181), (283)
Messiaen, Olivier, (132), (284)
    Chants de terre et de ciel, *61* 311b
Meyerbeer, Giacomo, (154), (162), (284)
    Les Huguenots, (38), *64*, (176), (275)
Milhaud, Darius, (139), (181), (284)
    Les soirées de Pétrograde, 102, 311b
Milliet, Paul, *75*, *76*, *98*, *99*, (284)
Molière, 34, (152), (285)
    Le bourgeois gentilhomme, 34, 311b
monophthong, 3, 22, 26–27, 45, 52, 111
monosyllabic words, 51, 56, 78, 107–108, 110–111, 131, 163, 164, 217, 219
Monrousseau, Lucien, 69, (285)
Montesquiou, Robert de, *102*, (285)
Morand, Paul, *17*, *112*, (191), 225, (286), 311b
Moréas, Jean, *116*, (129), (219), (286)
Mozart, Wolfgang Amadeus, (194), (214), (286)
    'Dans un bois solitaire', 75
Musset, Alfred de, *63*, (286)
mute *e* (*e muet*). *See also* rhyme
    alternative names for, 15–16
    description of, 3, 4, 6, 12, 15, 93
    dropped/elided, 19–20, 49–51, 95, 103
    musical notation in poetry and lyric settings, 94–101
    musical notation in post-Romantic settings, 101–103
    pronunciation of consonant before word-final mute *e*, 43–44
    tasteful singing of, 103–104
    spellings of, 16–19, 45–46, 133, 148–151, 160–161, 163–164
    tied mute *e*, 96–97, 101–103
mute *h*. See *h*

INDEX | 317

n: pronunciation of, (alone, as a nasalizing letter, or as the first of two or more letters), 7, 22–24, 32, 41, 42, 43, 63, 65–68, 111–112, 132, 135–138, 153, 155, 156–161, 168, 178–179, 184–186, 190–193, 198, 200, 233–234, 240–241, (286–288)

ñ, borrowed in French, 190–191

nasal consonants. *See* consonants

nasal vowels; nasality; nasalization. *See* vowels

Nerval, Gérard de, *76*, *118*, (287)

numbers, French pronunciation of, 120–123; in dates, 123

o, ô, œ: pronunciation of, (alone, or as the first of two or more letters), 6, 13–15, 21, 22, 26, 193–205, (288)

Offenbach, Jacques, (145), (159), (171), (288)
  La belle Hélène, 138, (273)
  Les contes d'Hoffmann, 59, (137), 143, (176), (274), 310b
  La vie parisienne, 58

operetta and/or oratorio, xi, 4, 35, 52

Orléans, Charles d', 42n, *75*, (137), (211), (288)

p: pronunciation of, (alone, or as the first of two or more letters), 6, 30–31, 41, 42, 43, 63n, 206–209, (289–293)

Parny, Évariste de, *60*, 132, (289), 311b

Papadiamantopoulos, Ioannis. *See* Moréas, Jean

parler courant. See everyday speech

Passy, Paul, 34, 35, (289), 311b
  Sounds of the French Language, 34, 35, 311b

Pellegrin, Joseph, *39*, (290)

phonetic group, the (*le groupe phonétique*), 48–49, 52–53, 62, 69, 77, 83, 87, 91, 107–108

phonetic transcription, 5–15, 20–21, 22–23, 25–26, 30–33, 36, 40, 41–42; delimiters, 7, 7n; diacritics, 7–8, 21, 22; narrow transcription, 7, 12–15, 30–33, 35, 44, 111; broad transcription, 7; methods of, 53–54

phrasal stress. *See* stress

Piaf, Édith, 33, (170), (291)

plosives. *See* consonants

poetic metre, 93–94

polysyllabic words, 15n, 40, 48, 57, 109–110, 150–151, 217, 219

portamento (port de voix), 104n

Poulenc, Francis, 53, 97, 101, (142), (159), (292), 309b, 310b, 311b
  Banalités, *62*, 108n
  Le bestiaire, 119
  'Bleuet', *50*
  Calligrammes, 111
  Chansons gaillardes, *76*, 97

Cinq poèmes de Max Jacob, 71, *115*
Cinq poèmes de Paul Éluard, 103
La courte paille, 181
Dialogues des Carmélites, 123, 225, (257), 311b
'Main dominée par le cœur', 44
Les mamelles de Tirésias, 67, *99*, (129), (219), (296), (302), 311b
Métamorphoses, 110
Miroirs brûlants, 63
Parisiana, 51
Poèmes de Ronsard, 117
Quatre poèmes d'Apollinaire, 102
Quatre poèmes de Max Jacob, 116
Le travail du peintre, *50*, 112, 115
La voix humaine, 103, *118*, 311b

Prudhomme, René Armand François. *See* Sully Prudhomme

publishing houses. *See* French musical editions

q(u): pronunciation of, (alone, or as the first two of several letters), 18–19, 30–31, 41, 209–211, (293)

Quinault, Philippe, *73*, (177), (224), (293)

r: pronunciation of, (alone, or as the first of two or more letters), 4, 6–7, 31–32, 33–37, 41, 42, 43, 63, 65, 111–113, 211–214, (293–296); apical articulation of (flipped/rolled), 7, 33, 36–37, 41, 65n, 113, 128, 211, 245; burred *r*, 9, 33; devoicing of, 4n, 36, 186; historical pronunciation of, 33–35; retracted and labialized articulation of, 35; table of pronunciation variants, 36; uvular articulation of (*r grasseyé*), 4, 4n, 7, 8, 16n, 31–32, 33–36, 36n, 41, 65n, 113n, 128, 186, 245, 307; which variant to sing, 34–37

Rameau, Jean-Philippe, 53, (129), (154), (189), (293)
  Hippolyte et Aricie, *39*, (207), (249), (274)

Ravel, Maurice, 101, (150), (187), (235), (294), 310b, 311b
  Chansons madécasses, *60*, 132, 311b
  Cinq mélodies populaires grecques, 113
  Deux épigrammes de Clément Marot, 42n
  Don Quichotte à Dulcinée, 17, *112*, (151), (154), 225, (229), (265), (293), 311b
  L'enfant et les sortilèges, 115
  L'heure espagnole, 65, 190, 207
  Histoires naturelles, 102

recitative, 24, 52–53

Régnier, Henri de, *60*, (174), (294)

Renard, Jules, *102*, (294)

Rhené-Baton, (212), (294)
  Dans un coin de violettes, 68

318 | INDEX

rhyme (*rime*), 93–94, 138, 143, 181, 209;
    rhyme scheme, 94; masculine/feminine
    rhyme, 94–97; 'special slur' in feminine
    rhyme, 97–99, 104
Roché, Henri-Pierre, *18*, (295), 312b
Ronsard, Pierre de, *68*, *117*, (295)
Roussel, Albert, (187), (203), (295)
    Deux poèmes chinois, *18*, 312b
    Quatre poèmes, *60*
Roux, Paul-Pierre. *See* Saint-Pol-Roux

s: pronunciation of, (alone, or as the first of two
    or more letters), 6, 31–32, 41, 42, 43, 63,
    215–222, (296–300)
Saint-Georges, Henri de, *59*, (296)
Sainte-Beuve, Charles-Augustin, *95*, (296)
Saint-Pol-Roux, *120*, (297)
Saint-Saëns, Camille, 53, 97n, (132), (297)
    Cinq poèmes de Ronsard, *68*
    'La cloche', *59*
    'Dans les coins bleus', *95*
    Samson et Dalila, *73*, (135), (136), (200), (215),
    (262), (297)
Samain, Albert, *17*, (297)
Satie, Érik, (228), (298)
    'Omnibus automobile', *58*
    'La Diva de l'Empire', 157
schwa. *See* vowels: mute *e*
Scribe, Eugène, *64*, *74*, *75*, (215), (298)
semiconsonants, (glides, semivowels), 3, 6, 16n,
    25–26, 27
Shakespeare, William, *109*, (130), (153), (299)
silent consonants. *See* consonants: silent
    consonants
Silvestre, Armand, *37*, *59*, *64*, (223), (299)
spelling, older vs. modern, 42, 42n, 128–129, 131,
    152, 174, 195–196
stress
    emphatic stress (*accent d'insistance*), 48n, 107–
        109, 111
    primary phrasal stress (*accent tonique*), 3, 48–49,
        53, 93–94, 97, 100, 107
    word stress (*accent d'intensité*), 3, 8n, 21, 24,
        48–49, 107, 307
style soutenu, le, 4, 57, 64
Sully Prudhomme, *51*, *103*, *119*, *120*, (300)
syllabic stress and break indications, 8
syllabification, 28, 40, 45–51
syllables, checked and free, 45, 46, 95, 109, 131,
    151, 152, 196
syneresis (*synérèse*), 25, 27–28, 128, 245

t: pronunciation of, (alone, or as the first of two
    or more letters), 6, 30–31, 40, 42, 43, 63, 223–
    229, (300–303)

Tarn, Pauline Mary. *See* Vivien, Renée
Theuriet, André, *73*, (226), (301)
Thomas, Ambroise, (129), (218), (219), (301)
    Hamlet, *109*, (136), (166), (225), (272)
    Mignon, *59*, (284)
tone, level of, 4, 49, 71, 109, 110, 111n, 123, 127,
    147, 208, 209, 212, 219, 224, 245
tongue position/articulation, 11, 13, 14–15, 24,
    26, 30–35
transcription (IPA). *See* phonetic
    transcription
tréma. *See* dieresis diacritic

u, û: pronunciation of, (alone, or as the first of
    two or more letters), 6, 14, 18–19, 23, 26, 52n,
    230–234, (303)
uvular *r*. *See r*

v: pronunciation of, 6, 31, 42, 235, (303–305)
Verlaine, Paul, *front cover*, *18*, *28*, *50*, *60*, *70*, *96*, *96*,
    101, *118*, (132), 210, (235), (304)
Viau, Théophile de, *98*, (304)
Villon, François, 42n, *65*, (182), (304)
Vingtrie, Jean de la, *67*, (304)
Vivien, Renée, *68*, (305)
vocal tract, 30
vocalic aperture, 11–15, 20–21, 109–110;
    'in-between' apertures, 21–22
vocalic elision (*élision vocalique*). *See also* mute *e*:
    dropped/elided, 4, 38, 49, 51, 55
vocalic harmonization (*l'harmonisation
    vocalique*), 21, 109–111, 133, 140, 141, 153,
    155, 163, 167, 169, 245; in polysyllabic
    words, 109–110; of monosyllabic words,
    110–111
vocalic length, 7, 15n, 24–25, 25n, 48, 128,
    245; half-lengthening, 8, 25, 25n, 49n,
    128, 245
vowel diagram, 12
vowels
    aperture of. *See* vocalic aperture
    devoicing of, 4n
    denasalization of. *See* liaison
    diacritics in transcription of, (indications for
        raised, lowered, more rounded, devoiced
        vowels), 8
    front/back vowel spellings, 11–14, 31
    elision of. *See* vocalic elision
    harmonization of. *See* vocalic harmonization
    mixed vowel spellings, 14–15
    mute *e*. *See* mute *e*
    nasal vowels. *See also* liaison, 3, 4, 6, 11, 22–24;
        possible mispronunciations of, 23–24;
        spellings of, 22–23; when to
        nasalize, 23

open/closed. *See* vocalic aperture
primary cardinal vowel, 3, 5–6, 11,
    12–14
schwa. *See* mute *e*
lip-rounding of, (rounded/unrounded), 3,
    11–16, 22–23, 32

w: pronunciation of, 42, 235–236, (305)
Włodzimierz, Wilhelm Albert. *See* Apollinaire,
    Guillaume
word stress. *See* stress

words with variable pronunciations, 114–120

x: pronunciation of, 40n, 42, 43, 47, 63,
    236–239, (305)

y, ÿ: pronunciation of, (alone, or as the first of two
    or more letters), 12, 22, 26, 47, 52n, 239–241,
    (306)

z: pronunciation of, 6, 31–32, 40, 42, 43, 63,
    241–242, (306)